HISTORY OF ISRAELITE RELIGION

HISTORY
OF
ISRAELITE RELIGION

GEORG FOHRER

Translated by
David E. Green

Nashville • Abingdon Press • New York

Library of Congress Cataloging in Publication Data

FOHRER, GEORG. History of Israelite religion. Translation
of Geschichte der israelitischen Religion. Bibliography:
p.   1. Judaism—History—Ancient period. 2. Bible.
O. T.—Theology. I. Title.
      BM165.F6413   296'.09   72-2010

ISBN 0-687-17225-X

MANUFACTURED BY THE PARTHENON PRESS AT
NASHVILLE, TENNESSEE, UNITED STATES OF AMERICA

FOREWORD

Gustav Hölscher's *Geschichte der israelitischen und jüdischen Religion,* published as part of the "Sammlung Töpelmann" series in 1922, has long been out of print. Friedrich Horst had expressed his willingness to undertake a revision of Hölscher's work, but he died before he was able to set about the task. Johannes Hempel, who began the revision, was able to complete only a small portion of the planned work before his death. Finally, despite many other plans and obligations, I undertook the job, so that a new presentation of the history of Israelite religion, which has long been needed, could be published in the "de Gruyter Lehrbuch" series without further delay. I have limited myself, however, to bringing the presentation down to the period portrayed by the latest books of the Old Testament. Its continuation, in the form of a history of the Jewish religion, has been taken over by J. Maier. I do hope, however, that I shall be able to publish a theology of the Old Testament within a few years of this history of Israelite religion.

In order to keep the size of this book within reasonable limits, I have had to treat many questions quite briefly. The reader will find further material in the literature cited, including lexicon and encyclopedia articles; the bibliographies have been made as extensive as possible. In addition, the discussion in §§ 14, 15, and 17 in particular holds true generally for the late period of Israelite religion, too. Since the topics are dealt with in toto in these paragraphs, references from the exilic and post-exilic periods are frequently given.

I should like to express my gratitude first of all to Frau Hildegard Hiersemann for her indefatigable patience in producing the manuscript. I am also grateful to my assistants for their willing help, especially to Vicar Hans Werner Hoffman, who reviewed the manuscript in detail, helped correct the galleys, and planned and supervised the indexing, and to Dr. Gunther Wanke, who helped read the page proofs and furnished much other valuable assistance, and finally to Ulrike Engert, stud. theol., who produced the indexes. They all contributed significantly to the prompt and accurate publication of this book.

Erlangen, December 1967.   GEORG FOHRER

73034

CONTENTS

Part Two

The Religion of the Monarchy

CHAPTER ONE: KINGSHIP, THE SECOND INFLUENCE

CHAPTER TWO: YAHWISM IN THE PERIOD OF THE MONARCHY

CHAPTER THREE: PROPHECY, THE THIRD INFLUENCE

gious attitudes (286). 5. The place of the great prophetical figures in the history of religions (289).

CHAPTER FOUR: DEUTERONOMIC THEOLOGY, CONSEQUENCE AND FOURTH INFLUENCE

§ 21 Religious Developments 292
1. Background and early history (292). 2. Josiah's reformation (295).

§ 22 Theology and Life According to Deuteronomic Principles 296
1. Deuteronomic theology (297). 2. Life under the Deuteronomic law (300).
3. The pre-exilic Deuteronomistic school (303).

Part Three

The Religion of the Exilic Period

§ 23 The Religious Situation 307
1. The situation and the evidence (307). 2. Palestine (309). 3. Exile and Diaspora (311).

§ 24 Exilic Prophecy and Incipient Eschatology, the Fifth Influence   316
1. Ezekiel (316). 2. Other prophets (321). 3. Deutero-Isaiah (322).
4. Beginnings of eschatology (327).

Part Four

The Religion of the Post-Exilic Period

CHAPTER ONE: EARLY POST-EXILIC PERIOD

§ 25 Events and Figures 330
1. Return, rebuilding of the Temple, and religious attitude (330). 2. Early post-exilic prophecy (334). 3. Outcome (336).

§ 26 Development of Eschatology 337
1. Eschatological events (337). 2. The structure of eschatology (340).
3. Messianic expectation (347). 4. Outcome (352).

CHAPTER TWO: LATE POST-EXILIC PERIOD

§ 27 Events, Figures, and Religious Attitudes 354
1. The crisis of the Jerusalem community and Malachi (354). 2. The Priestly Document (355). 3. Nehemiah and Ezra (357). 4. The period after Ezra's reform (359). 5. The Samaritan community (368). 6. The Maccabean period and apocalypticism (369).

§ 28 Objects and Contents of Faith 372
1. Yahweh and angels, Satan and demons (372). 2. Yahweh, the world, and man (375). 3. The law (377). 4. Temple cult and synagogue worship (379). 5. Man's fate after death (385).

Indexes 391
1. Index of Passages (391). 2. Index of Hebrew Words (409). 3. General Index (410).

BIBLIOGRAPHIC INFORMATION
AND LIST OF ABBREVIATIONS

The bibliographies at the beginning of the individual paragraphs list the relevant literature alphabetically according to author; different works by the same author are listed in order of publication. Special studies of particular problems are cited in the footnotes. When an author's name followed by * is mentioned in the course of the presentation, it refers either to the general works listed below or to the bibliography immediately preceding.

It is impossible to give more than a representative selection from the scholarly literature, which has increased enormously. Those who seek additional bibliographical information on specific points have numerous resources at their disposal, particularly the bibliographical articles in ThR, the "Zeitschriftenschau" and "Bücherschau" in ZAW, the "Elenchus bibliographicus" in Bibl (published separately starting in 1968), as well as the *Internationale Zeitschriftenschau für Bibelwissenschaft und Grenzgebiete.*

1. General Works and Histories of Israelite Religion
(An author's name followed by * refers to these works.)

W. F. Albright, *From the Stone Age to Christianity,* 1940; 2nd ed., 1946; with a new introduction, 1957.
———, *Archaeology and the Religion of Israel,* 1942; 4th ed., 1956.
G. W. Anderson, *The History and Religion of Israel,* 1966.
F. Baumgärtel, *Die Eigenart der alttestamentlichen Frömmigkeit,* 1932.
A. Bertholet, *Kulturgeschichte Israels,* 1920 (English: *A History of Hebrew Civilization,* 1926).
K. Budde, *The Religion of Israel to the Exile,* 1899.
———, *Die altisraelitische Religion,* 1905 (= 2nd ed. of the above); 2nd ed., 1912.
B. D. Eerdmans, *De godsdienst van Israël,* 1930; 2nd ed. published as *The Religion of Israel,* 1947.
E. L. Ehrlich, *Kultsymbolik im Alten Testament und im nachbiblischen Judentum,* 1959.
W. Eichrodt, *Religionsgeschichte Israels,* 1969.
O. Eissfeldt, "Die israelitisch-jüdische Religion," in *Saeculum-Weltgeschichte,* Bd. II (1966), pp. 217-60.
J. Finegan, *Light from the Ancient Past,* 1946; 2nd ed., 1959.
G. Fohrer, *Glaube und Welt im Alten Testament,* 1948.

11

W. C. Graham and H. G. May, *Culture and Conscience: An Archaeological Study of the New Religious Past in Ancient Palestine,* 1936.

F. Giesebrecht, *Die Grundzüge der israelitischen Religionsgeschichte,* 1904.

J. Gray, *Archaeology and the Old Testament,* 1962.

J. Hänel, *Die Religion der Heiligkeit,* 1931.

J. Hempel, *Das Ethos des Alten Testaments,* 1938; 2nd ed., 1964.

————, "Die alttestamentliche Religion," in *HdO,* I.8.1 (1964), pp. 122-46.

G. Hölscher, *Geschichte der israelitischen und jüdischen Religion,* 1922.

P. Humbert, "Le génie d'Israël," *RHPhR,* VII (1927), 493-515.

Y. Kaufmann, *The Religion of Israel,* translated and abridged by M. Greenberg, 1960.

R. Kittel, *Die Religion des Volkes Israel,* 1921; 2nd ed., 1929 (English: *The Religion of the People of Israel,* 1925).

E. König, *Geschichte der alttestamentlichen Religion,* 1912.

A. Kuenen, *De godsdienst van Israël tot den ondergang van den Joodschen staat,* 1869-70 (English: *The Religion of Israel to the Fall of the Jewish State,* 1882-83).

A. Lods, *La religion d'Israël,* 1939.

M. Löhr, *Israelitische Religionsgeschichte,* 1906 (English: *A History of Religion in the Old Testament,* 1936).

K. Marti, *Geschichte der israelitischen Religion,* 1897; 3rd ed., 1907.

————, *Die Religion des Alten Testaments unter den Religionen des vorderen Orients,* 1906 (English: *The Religion of the Old Testament; Its Place Among the Religions and the Near East,* 1907).

I. G. Matthews, *The Religious Pilgrimage of Israel,* 1947.

P. Montet, *L'Égypte et la Bible,* 1959 (English: *Egypt and the Bible,* 1968).

S. Mowinckel, *Religion und Kultus,* 1953.

J. Muilenburg, "The History of the Religion of Israel," in *The Interpreter's Bible,* I (1962), 292-348.

————, *The Way of Israel: Biblical Faith and Ethics,* 1961.

W. O. E. Oesterley and T. H. Robinson, *Hebrew Religion,* 1930; 2nd ed., 1937.

H. van Oyen, *Ethik des Alten Testaments,* 1967.

A. Parrot, *Babylone et l'Ancien Testament,* 1956 (English: *Babylon and the Old Testament,* 1958).

A. Penna, *La Religione di Israele,* 1958.

R. H. Pfeiffer, *Religion in the Old Testament,* 1961.

H. Renckens, *De godsdienst van Israël,* 1963.

H. Ringgren, *Israelitische Religion,* 1963 (English: *Israelite Religion,* 1966).

E. Sellin, *Beiträge zur israelitisch-jüdischen Religionsgeschichte,* I & II, 1897-99.

————, *Die alttestamentliche Religion im Rahmen der andern altorientalischen,* 1907.

————, *Israelitisch-jüdische Religionsgeschichte,* 1933.

R. Smend, *Lehrbuch der alttestamentlichen Religionsgeschichte,* 1893; 2nd ed., 1899.

B. Stade, *Biblische Theologie des Alten Testaments,* I, 1905.

A. R. Stedman, *The Growth of Hebrew Religion,* 1949.

R. de Vaux, *Les institutions de l'Ancien Testament*, I, 1958; 2nd ed., 1961; II, 1960 (English: *Ancient Israel; Its Life and Institutions*, 1961).

A. Vincent, "La religion d'Israël," in M. Brillant and R. Aigrain, *Histoire des religions*, t. IV (n.d.), pp. 309-73.

T. C. Vriezen, *De godsdienst van Israël*, 1963 (English: *The Religion of Ancient Israel*, 1967).

W. L. Wardle, *The History and Religion of Israel*, 1935.

J. Wellhausen, "Israelitisch-jüdische Religion," in H. Pinneberg, *Die Kulturen der Gegenwart*, 1/4 (1905), 1-38 (reprinted in his *Grundrisse zum Alten Testament*, 1965, pp. 65-109).

A. Wendel, *Säkularisierung in Israels Kultur*, 1934.

2. Bibliographic Abbreviations

AcOr .... Acta Orientalia
AfO .... Archiv für Orientforschung
AIPh .... Annuaire de l'Institut de Philologie et d'Histoire Orientales et Slaves
AJA .... American Journal of Archaeology
AJSL .... American Journal of Semitic Languages and Literatures
ALBO .... Analecta Lovaniensia Biblica et Orientalia
ANEP .... J. B. Pritchard (ed.), The Ancient Near East in Pictures Relating to the Old Testament, 1954
ANET .... J. B. Pritchard (ed.), Ancient Near Eastern Texts Relating to the Old Testament, 1950; 2nd ed., 1955
AnSt .... Anatolian Studies
AOT .... H. Gressmann (ed.), Altorientalische Texte zum Alten Testament, 2nd ed., 1926
ARM .... Archives Royales de Mari
ArOr .... Archiv Orientální
ARW .... Archiv für Religionswissenschaft
ASTI .... Annual of the Swedish Theological Institute in Jerusalem
AThR .... Anglican Theological Review
BA .... The Biblical Archaeologist
BASOR .... Bulletin of the American Schools of Oriental Research
BEThL .... Bibliotheca Ephemeridum Theologicarum Lovaniensium
BHH .... Biblisch-Historisches Handwörterbuch
Bibl .... Biblica
BiLe .... Bibel und Leben
BiOr .... Bibliotheca Orientalis
BJRL .... Bulletin of the John Rylands Library
BRL .... K. Galling, Biblisches Reallexikon, 1937
BZ .... Biblische Zeitschrift
BZAW .... Beiheft zur Zeitschrift für die alttestamentliche Wissenschaft
CBL .... Calwer Bibellexikon

CBQ . . . . Catholic Biblical Quarterly
ChQR . . . . Church Quarterly Review
ChuW . . . . Christentum und Wissenschaft
CRAI . . . . Comptes Rendus de l'Académie des Inscriptions et Belles-Lettres
DTT . . . . Dansk Teologisk Tidsskrift
ET . . . . Expository Times
EvTh . . . . Evangelische Theologie
FF . . . . Forschungen und Fortschritte
GThT . . . . Gereformeerd Theologisch Tijdschrift
HdO . . . . B. Spuler (ed.) , Handbuch der Orientalistik
HThR . . . . Harvard Theological Review
HUCA . . . . Hebrew Union College Annual
IDB . . . . The Interpreter's Dictionary of the Bible
IEJ . . . . Israel Exploration Journal
Interpr . . . . Interpretation
JAOS . . . . Journal of the American Oriental Society
Jb . . . . Jahrbuch
JBL . . . . Journal of Biblical Literature
JBR . . . . Journal of Bible and Religion
JCSt . . . . Journal of Cuneiform Studies
JEOL . . . . Jaarbericht van het Vooraziatisch-Egyptisch Genootschap Ex Oriente Lux
JJS . . . . Journal of Jewish Studies
JMEOS . . . . Journal of the Manchester University Egyptian and Oriental Society
JNES . . . . Journal of Near Eastern Studies
JPOS . . . . Journal of the Palestine Oriental Society
JR . . . . Journal of Religion
JSS . . . . Journal of Semitic Studies
JThSt . . . . Journal of Theological Studies
KAI . . . . H. Donner and W. Röllig, Kanaanäische und aramäische Inschriften, 1962-64
KuD . . . . Kerygma und Dogma
LA . . . . Studii Biblici Franciscani Liber Annuus
MGWJ . . . . Monatsschrift für Geschichte und Wissenschaft des Judentums
MUB . . . . Mélanges de l'Université Saint-Joseph
NC . . . . La Nouvelle Clio
NkZ . . . . Neue kirchliche Zeitschrift
NRTh . . . . Nouvelle Revue Théologique
NT . . . . Novum Testamentum
NThS . . . . Nieuwe Theologische Studiën
NThT . . . . Nieuw Theologisch Tijdschrift
NTT . . . . Norsk Teologisk Tidsskrift
OLZ . . . . Orientalistische Literaturzeitung
Or . . . . Orientalia
OTS . . . . Oudtestamentische Studiën

OuTWP ....Die Ou Testamentiese Werkgemeenskap in Suid-
Afrika
PEFQSt ....Palestine Exploration Fund, Quarterly Statement
PEQ ....Palestine Exploration Quarterly
PJB ....Palästinajahrbuch
QDAP ....Quarterly of the Department of Antiquities in
Palestine
RA ....Revue d'Assyriologie et d'Archéologie Orientale
RB ....Revue Biblique
REJ ....Revue des Études Juives
RES ....Revue des Études Sémitiques
RGG ....Die Religion in Geschichte und Gegenwart, 3rd ed.
RGG ² ....Die Religion in Geschichte und Gegenwart, 2nd ed.
RHPhR ....Revue d'Histoire et de Philosophie Religieuses
RHR ....Revue de l'Histoire des Religions
RSO ....Rivista degli Studi Orientali
RThPh ....Revue de Théologie et de Philosophie
SEÅ ....Svensk Exegetisk-Årsbok
S-F ....E. Sellin and G. Fohrer, Einleitung in das Alte Testa-
ment, 10th ed., 1965 (English: Introduction to the
Old Testament, 1968)
SJTh ....Scottish Journal of Theology
StC ....Studia Catholica
StTh ....Studia Theologica
ThBl ....Theologische Blätter
ThLZ ....Theologische Literaturzeitung
ThQ ....Theologische Quartalschrift
ThR ....Theologische Rundschau
ThStKr ....Theologische Studien und Kritiken
ThW ....Theologisches Wörterbuch zum Neuen Testament
(English: Theological Dictionary of the New Testa-
ment)
ThZ ....Theologische Zeitschrift
UT ....C. H. Gordon, Ugaritic Textbook, 1965
VT ....Vetus Testamentum
VTSuppl ....Supplements to Vetus Testamentum
WdO ....Die Welt des Orients
WuD ....Wort und Dienst
WZ ....Wissenschaftliche Zeitschrift
WZKM ....Wiener Zeitschrift für die Kunde des Morgenlandes
ZA ....Zeitschrift für Assyriologie
ZAW ....Zeitschrift für die alttestamentliche Wissenschaft
ZDMG ....Zeitschrift der Deutschen Morgenländischen Gesell-
schaft
ZDPV ....Zeitschrift des Deutschen Palästina-Vereins
ZEE ....Zeitschrift für evangelische Ethik
ZMR ....Zeitschrift für Missionskunde und Religionswissen-
schaft

§ 1 Introduction

W. F. ALBRIGHT, "The Ancient Near East and the Religion of Israel," *JBL*, LIX (1940), 85-112; G. W. ANDERSON, "Hebrew Religion," in H. H. Rowley (ed.), *The Old Testament and Modern Study*, 1951, pp. 283-310; S. A. COOK, "Salient Problems in Old Testament History," *JBL*, LI (1932), 273-99; *idem*, "The Development of the Religion of Israel," *AIPH*, IV (1936), 539-50; O. EISSFELDT, "Israelitisch-jüdische Religionsgeschichte und alttestamentliche Theologie," *ZAW*, XLIV (1926), 1-12 (= his *Kleine Schriften*, I [1962], 105-14); *idem*, "Werden, Wesen, und Wert geschichtlicher Betrachtung der israelitisch-jüdisch-christlichen Religion," *ZMR*, XLVI (1931), 1-24 (= *ibid.*, pp. 247-65); W. A. L. ELMSLIE, "Ethics," in *Record and Revelation*, 1938, pp. 275-302; C. HARTLICH and W. SACHS, *Der Ursprung des Mythosbegriffes in der modernen Bibelwissenschaft*, 1952; J. HEMPEL, "Altes Testament und Religionsgeschichte," *ThLZ*, LXXXI (1956). 259-80; W. A. IRWIN, "The Study of Israel's Religion," *VT*, VII (1957), 113-26; A. JEPSEN, "Anmerkungen zur Phänomenologie der Religion," in *Bertholet-Festschrift*, 1950, pp. 267-80; A. S. KAPELRUD, "The Role of the Cult in Old Israel," in *The Bible and the Ancient Near East* (Albright Festschrift), 1965, pp. 44-56; Y. KAUFMANN, "Probleme der israelitisch-jüdischen Religionsgeschichte," *ZAW*, XLVIII (1930), 23-43; LI (1933), 35-47; E. KÖNIG, "Die legitime Religion Israels und ihre hermeneutische Bedeutung," *ibid.*, XLIX (1931), 40-45; A. LODS, "Origins," in *Record and Revelation*, 1938, pp. 187-215; C. C. MCCOWN, "Climate and Religion in Palestine," *JR*, VII (1927), 520-39; R. F. MERKEL, "Zur Religionsforschung der Aufklärungszeit," in *Bertholet-Festschrift*, 1950, pp. 351-64; R. RENDTORFF, "Kult, Mythos und Geschichte im alten Issrael," in *Rendtorff-Festgabe*, 1958, pp. 121-29; *idem*, "Die Entstehung der israelitischen Religion als religionsgeschichtliches und theologisches Problem," *ThLZ*, LXXXVIII (1963), 735-46; C. STEUERNAGEL, "Alttestamentliche Theologie und alttestamentliche Religionsgeschichte," in *Marti-Festschrift*, 1925, pp. 266-73; C. WESTERMANN, "Das Verhältnis des Jahweglaubens zu den ausserisraelitischen Religionen," in *Forschung am Alten Testament*, 1964, pp. 189-218; *idem*, "Sinn und Grenze religionsgeschichtlicher Parallelen," *ThLZ*, XC (1965), 489-96; F. F. WOOD, "The Contribution of the Bible to the History of Religion," *JBL*, XLVII (1928), 1-19; G. E. WRIGHT, "Archaeology and Old Testament Studies," *JBL*, LXXVII (1958), 39-51; *idem*, "Cult and History," *Interpr*, XVI (1962), 3-20.

1. *The study of Israelite religion.*[1] a) Historical study of Israelite religion began in the age of the Enlightenment and rationalism. It was then common practice to contrast reason and revelation, eternal truths of reason and chance truths of history, and to seek to demon-

---

[1] This section follows Eissfeldt's presentation in *ZMR;* cf. also *RGG*, I, 1256-57.

strate that Christianity was the ideal of a rational religion and high morality. This raised the problem of what criterion to use in distinguishing and delimiting the biblical material itself; it also made it necessary to explain the resultant features of biblical religion that clashed with this ideal. The criterion employed was comparison with other religions, in which the reason of the "Persian sage" might well anticipate revelation (Lessing), and which were discovered to have myth as their common starting point. Discordant features were explained as necessary accommodations to the limited concepts of the surrounding world (J. S. Semler, *Abhandlung von freier Untersuchung des Canon,* 1771-75) or as due to the influence of neighboring religions, which represented a lower stage of development (G. L. Bauer, *Hebräische Mythologie des Alten und Neuen Testaments,* 1802; G. P. C. Kaiser, *Biblische Theologie,* 1813-14).

Of course the goal of recovering from the Bible the pure religion of reason was based as completely on dogmatic considerations as was the equation of ecclesiastical doctrine with biblical theology on the part of the supranaturalism against which rationalism was contending. But it paved the way for a historical understanding of biblical religion by calling attention to the differences within the religion of the Bible, with its diverse religious conceptions and manifestations, as well as the differences between this religion and the dominant teaching and practice of Christianity. This produced a demand that the historical approach to the Bible be separated from the approach of dogmatic theology, as voiced in 1787 by J. P. Gabler in his address on the "real difference between biblical and dogmatic theology and the correct determination of the limits of these two disciplines." It also produced a demand that the religion of the Bible be seen within the framework of the total development of the religion of mankind. These demands resulted in many observations concerning the gradual development of biblical religion as well as the influences exerted on it by neighboring religions.

b) The next step was taken by J. G. Herder.[2] He applied his concept of a national spirit lying behind all literary creativity to Hebrew poetry, thus comprehending its nature better than anyone had before. He also could appreciate the specific manifestations of religion, instead of glossing over them or spiritualizing them. Above all, he sought to represent the development of universal history, thus doing justice to its individual stages (*Ideen zur Philosophie der*

---

[2] M. Doerne, *Die Religion in Herders Geschichtsphilosophie,* 1927.

Geschichte der Menschheit, 1784-91). The growth of religion also had to be studied in this context.

The notion of development, which had long been discussed, was lent added profundity by G. F. W. Hegel, and came to affect the study of biblical religion. This approach, however, ran the danger of being forced into the mold of a speculative philosophy of history and the schema of a logical course of development. These strictures apply particularly to W. Vatke's interpretation of how Israel's religion developed *(Die Religion des Alten Testaments,* 1835).[3] According to Vatke, this development was essentially a process of immanent growth; he paid much less attention to the influence of neighboring religions. Vatke's work also marked the first time the religion of the Bible was divided into two periods: the Old Testament period, or the period of Israelite religion and Judaism; and the New Testament period, or the period of the Christian religion. Practical reasons apparently underlay this division: "the attempt to base the presentation completely in the sources, and the impossibility of fulfilling this requirement for both epochs" (Eissfeldt).

c) The following decades were marked by the achievements of historical-critical studies, operating primarily in the field of literary criticism. This approach—notwithstanding the pioneering contributions of Kuenen* [4] and K. H. Graf—is associated with the name of Wellhausen,* who was followed by F. Bleek, Stade,* W. Robertson Smith, Smend,* C. Steuernagel, and others. This circle produced presentations of the history of Israelite religion characterized by the application of discoveries made by literary criticism to the history of religion, as well as the employment of all the methods used by secular historical scholarship. As a consequence, scholars began to speak of a history of Israelite religion (a term first used by Smend* in 1893). The influence of neighboring religions was not taken sufficiently into account; it was considered only in terms of the original relationship of the Israelites to other Semitic peoples, or the development of an Israelite-Canaanite syncretism following the Israelite occupation of Palestine. This is the more remarkable because there was no lack of studies of neighboring religions, some of them even written by representatives of the historical-critical school.

For the history of Israelite religion, studies of two other religions were especially significant: pre-Islamic Arabian religion, which was

---

[3] L. Perlitt, *Vatke und Wellhausen,* 1965.

[4] O. Eissfeldt, "Zwei Leidener Darstellungen der israelitischen Religionsgeschichte (A. Kuenen und B. D. Eerdmans)," *ZDMG,* LXXXV (1931), 172-95.

thought very near to the religion of the ancient Semites, and therefore to the pre-Mosaic religion of Israel (Wellhausen and, on a
broader basis, Robertson Smith) ; and Canaanite-Phoenician religion,
which the Israelites came upon when they occupied Palestine and
which influenced their religion (W. W. Graf Baudissin[5]).

  d) Toward the end of the 1880s, the religio-historical school came
into being;[6] it was of immense significance for further study of
Israelite religion. Its most important representatives in the Old
Testament field were H. Gunkel and H. Gressmann; for the later
period, the name of W. Bousset also deserves mention. This school
was not directly associated with rationalism and romanticism, but
there was a parallelism in the problems they studied, occasioned by
the historical inquiry that was being carried on everywhere. The
school was, however, influenced by Herder's philosophy of history
and his appreciation for the spiritual and intellectual life of nations
and individuals, visible in their myths and literature. In like fashion,
not only Wellhausen but also B. Duhm and A. Harnack, and to an
extent P. de Lagarde also, popularized the efforts of the religio-
historical scholars who preceded them. Finally, the religio-historical
school flourished in a period when there was a general increase in
religio-historical investigation.

  The religio-historical school drew a clear distinction between the
perspective of history and that of dogma, attacking the confusion
between them on the part of A. Ritschl. Its purpose was to subject
Israelite religion, Judaism, and Christianity to strictly historical
study, carried out not for theological reasons (e.g., in order to arrive
at a "rational religion") , but purely for its own sake, with a historical synthesis as the goal. The religion of Israel was seen in its relationship to the religions of the surrounding world, particularly
Mesopotamia and Egypt; Israelite religion itself was understood as
a piece of "history," a process taking place according to the "laws"
of intellectual, spiritual, and social life, within which its transform-
ing power was appreciated despite all dependence on pre-existing
forms.

  The achievement of these goals was aided by an expanded method-
ology. The religio-historical school took for granted the accepted
results of literary criticism around 1880. But it distinguished the
age of an idea sharply from its first appearance in writing: the latter

[5] O. Eissfeldt, "Vom Lebenswerk eines Religionshistorikers," *ZDMG*, LXXX
(1926), 89-130 (= his *Kleine Schriften*, I [1962], 115-42) .
  [6] *RGG*, V, 991-94.

can be preceded by a long oral tradition or even by a literary pre-history within another religion. In addition, the analysis produced by literary criticism was supplemented by the study of rhetorical and literary types *(Gattungen)*, especially of fairy tale, saga, and legend in prose tradition and of the psalm types.

e) At the same time, religio-historical study of the OT was also being carried on by others outside the religio-historical school, as one can see particularly in the works of Budde* and Kittel,* and in A. Bertholet's utilization of the results of comparative religion, espe-cially among primitive peoples.

The parallels to the OT found in Mesopotamian texts led to "Pan-Babylonism" [7] and the "Babel—Bible" theme (H. Winckler, A. Jeremias), especially since little was known at that time of Canaan-ite religion. The Sumero-Babylonian view of the world, with its astral religion and its concept of macrocosm and microcosm, with the order implied in the latter, appeared so singular "that this astral world view set its stamp on all the cultures and religions of the world; the biblical world view in particular owes its symbolic ex-pression to this world view." [8] Notwithstanding this extreme exag-geration and one-sidedness, Pan-Babylonism drew attention to sev-eral religious phenomena that were not fully appreciated until later: the connection between myth and cult, the rôle of the Babylonian king at the New Year's festival, and the cultic representation of reli-gious teaching.

f) Dialectical theology by and large brought religio-historical studies of biblical religion to a temporary halt. Although it did not actually oppose the religio-historical school, with which it was in fact connected in many ways, there came to be a sharp contrast between the two. To dialectical theology, the religio-historical approach was incidental, peripheral, and above all untheological. According to dialectical theology, Christianity cannot be lumped together with other religions under the common heading of "reli-gion" for purposes of comparison. On the contrary, the unique revelation of God in the Bible stands in contrast to other religions; this revelation speaks directly to the present, just as it spoke to the age in which it was given. It is therefore both unnecessary and super-fluous to study the prehistory and history of Christianity.

This theology did indeed address itself to the task of defining more closely the unique nature of Christianity and its God, a prob-

[7] *RGG, V*, 35-36.
[8] A. Jeremias in *RGG* [2], IV, 879.

lem that had not been solved by religio-historical theology; at the
same time, though, it did OT studies great harm through its renunciation of any religio-historical perspective, its disregard for an appropriate understanding of the uniqueness of Israelite religion, and its
revival of allegorical and typological interpretation of the OT. It
supplemented and corrected the theology that preceded it, but no
postulate of dogmatic theology can explain away the religio-historical
data pointed out by the earlier theology.

g) Since the advent of dialectical theology, numerous archaeological discoveries, the finding of new texts (like those recovered at
Ugarit), and the penetrating scholarship of Near Eastern studies
have made religio-historical investigations even more necessary. They
show how the territory of Palestine and the nation of Israel fit into
the world of the Near East and the eastern Mediterranean basin. It
is an indisputable fact that the OT came to incorporate various
notions belonging to other religions found among Israel's predecessors and neighbors. This applies not only to the primal history in
Genesis, the Psalms, and wisdom literature, but to the whole OT, to
the extent that none of its larger units is completely free of traces
or elements of non-Israelite religions. As a consequence, the OT
canon cannot be singled out for special treatment in the history of
religions as a unique entity. The study of Israelite religion within
the framework of the ancient Near Eastern religious world is therefore an indispensable part of OT studies; it is essential for a proper
understanding of the OT. Neither the exegesis nor the theology of
the OT can do without it.

Thus new religio-historical schools or parties have gradually come
into existence. New discoveries have made it possible for these
increasingly to take Canaanite religion into account. A cult-historical
school arose independently in both England and Scandinavia. It
emphatically rejects the notion of development as it applies to religion, finds a close relationship between the history of religions and
anthropology, and supports the hypothesis of a myth and ritual
pattern found throughout the Near East. In addition, the Scan-
dinavian school applied to the OT the cultic interpretation that was
originally developed for the history of Germanic religions, and
sought to demonstrate that a "royal ideology" was the basis of the
cultic pattern (A. S. Kapelrud, Mowinckel,* Ringgren*).[9] In con-

[9] K.-H. Bernhardt, *Das Problem der altorientalischen Königsideologie im Alten
Testament*, 1961; J. de Fraine, "Les implications du 'patternisme,'" *Bibl*, XXXVI
(1955), 59-73; R. Rendtorff, "Der Kultus im alten Israel," *Jb für Liturgik und
Hymnologie*, II (1956), 1-21.

trast to the cultic school, there is a school that focuses on individual piety, seeking to derive the uniqueness of Israelite religion from the structure of the spiritual experience for which it serves as a vehicle; this uniqueness can be observed, for example, in the tension between a feeling of dependency and intimacy on the one hand, and, on the other, a grandeur that compels obedience and service (Hempel*). Finally, an American school based on archaeology has come into being; it raises fundamental objections to the methods of both form-criticism and traditio-historical criticism, which take their criteria solely from the OT itself, as well as to the cult-historical method, which makes the cult determine the authoritative historical traditions. Instead, the American school demands the application of external criteria, especially those furnished by archaeology (Albright,* Wright).

In the meantime, we must not forget that others carry on religio-historical scholarship in the field of Israelite religion without belonging to or being associated with any of these schools. In many cases they try to plot a course between one-sided interpretations and extreme positions; they contribute to a synthesis of the various methods.

2. *Purpose and sources. a*) The purpose of presenting a history of Israelite religion is to depict the course of this religion's development as the history of one normal religion among many others, without undertaking theological value judgments or giving weight to apologetical considerations. It is also important to exhibit the changes and tensions that affected Israelite religion during its history of more than a thousand years. For this religion was neither homogeneous nor static. It underwent a process of historical evolution, exhibiting significant changes and developments occasioned by both internal and external influences. Furthermore, different movements and tendencies often existed side by side in the same period, in a state of tension or opposition. Any presentation of Israel's religious history must therefore bring this evolution and variety to light. At the same time, it must answer the question of what the various periods and movements have in common that outweighs their differences and makes it possible to speak of Israelite religion as a single entity. This way of stating the purpose of a history of Israelite religion distinguishes it from a theology of the OT, which—however conceived—must present the essential theological structures of a message, structures that, despite the variety of their historical mani-

festations, permeate the entire OT and remain important even beyond the OT period.

We can often observe how Israelite religion changes and evolves. For example, the Yahwistic image of God changes: first he is a God of refuge, then a God of war, and finally a God of universal peace, whose dominion is the entire world. The God of a special group becomes the God of a nation, and then the only God of all nations; he intervenes sporadically in battle, then acts repeatedly in the lives and fates of men and nations, and finally works continuously throughout the whole realm of nature. In the course of development, Yahweh is first worshiped anywhere, then in numerous local sanctuaries, and finally in a single sanctuary. Simple tribal cults give way to complex cultic ceremonies and finally to worship in spirit and in truth. Precautions for the protection of the tribe become numerous cultic, ethical, and legal regulations, which are in turn summarized in a single comprehensive commandment.

The tensions and contrasts are especially noticeable in the multitude of religious movements during the monarchy—the various approaches to life: conservative, magical, cultic, nationalist, wisdom, and prophetical—and in the conflict between eschatological prophecy and priestly theology during the post-exilic period.

But the common features can also be seen: the personal structure of faith, which is found even in the early tribal religion of Israel; the notion of a correlation between the acts and decisions of God and man, together with the notion of God's acting in the present in the lives of men and nations; the requirement that man's life and conduct be according to the rules that express God's will; and—the focal point of Israelite religion—belief in the dominion of God and in communion between man and God, both to be realized in the life of the believer, the nation, or the human world.

b) The most important source for our knowlege of Israelite religion is the OT. It is a well-known fact that the OT is not a single homogeneous book, but a collection of writings dating from quite different periods; often these writings are themselves not of a piece, and came into being over a considerable period of time. If they are to be used for a presentation of the history of Israelite religion, the dates of the individual writings or their component parts must first be determined as precisely as possible; traditio-historical criticism must also determine the age of the traditions and conceptions that have achieved fixed and final form in these writings. This is the task of exegesis and introduction. The present account of the history of

Israelite religion presupposes the conclusions of E. Sellin and G. Fohrer, *Einleitung in das Alte Testament,* 10th ed., 1965 (English: *Introduction to the Old Testament,* 1968).

A further source is furnished by the results of Palestinian archaeology. These results are particularly helpful in illuminating the external circumstances of Israelite religion, and contribute to our understanding of the primary source, the OT. They seldom have anything to say about the content of religious belief.

An indirect source for our understanding of religious concepts and phenomena within Israel is the textual and archaeological evidence of the neighboring religions. Striking similarities may lead to a more precise explanation of Israelite concepts and phenomena; they can often help fill out the fragmentary picture of Israelite religion, together with the concepts and phenomena that are sometimes only hinted at in the OT. When using this comparative material, we must of course be careful to observe and maintain the unique features of Israelite religion. Something that sounds like a feature of another religion need not have the same meaning it has in the other religion. Religious concepts or customs can have different meanings and purposes in two different religions, even when these religions are close neighbors geographically and historically. The ancient Near Eastern material must therefore always be employed with caution.

PART ONE

The Religion of the Early Period

CHAPTER ONE: THE RELIGIOUS BACKGROUND

§ 2 THE RELIGIOUS SUBSTRATUM AND THE RELIGION OF THE NOMADIC TRIBES

A. ALT, *Der Gott der Väter*, 1929 (= his *Kleine Schriften zur Geschichte des Volkes Israel*, I [1953], 1-78); T. BAUER, *Die Ostkanaanäer*, 1926; F. M. T. BÖHL, *Das Zeitalter Abrahams*, 1931; A. CAUSSE, *Du groupe éthnique à la communauté religieuse*, 1937; A. DUPONT-SOMMER, *Les Araméens*, 1949; R. DUSSAUD, *Les découvertes de Ras Shamra (Ugarit) et l'Ancien Testament*, 2nd ed., 1941; D. O. EDZARD, "Mari und Aramäer?" *ZA*, LVI (NF XXII [1964]), 142-49; G. GEMSER, *Vragen rondom de Patriarchenreligie*, 1958; H. GRESSMANN, "Sage und Geschichte in den Patriarchenerzählungen," *ZAW*, XXX (1910), 1-34; *idem, Mose und seine Zeit*, 1913; J. M. GRINTZ, "On the Original Home of the Semites," *JNES*, XXI (1962), 186-206; M. HARAN, "The Religion of the Patriarchs: An Attempt at a Synthesis," *ASTI*, IV (1965), 30-55; J. HOFTIJZER, *Die Verheissungen an die drei Erzväter*, 1956; J. M. HOLT, *The Patriarchs of Israel*, 1964; K. M. KENYON, *Amorites and Canaanites*, 1966; J.-R. KUPPER, "Northern Mesopotamia and Syria," in *The Cambridge Ancient History*, II:1, 1963; V. MAAG, "Der Hirte Israels," *Schweiz. Theol. Umschau*, XXVIII (1958), 2-28; *idem,* "Malkût Jhwh," *VTSuppl*, VII (1960), 129-53; J. MORGENSTERN, *Rites of Birth, Marriage, Death and Kindred Occasions Among the Semites*, 1966; S. MOSCATI, *The Semites in Ancient History*, 1959; M. NOTH, *Die Ursprünge des alten Israel im Lichte neuer Quellen*, 1961; S. NYSTRÖM, *Beduinentum und Jahwismus*, 1946; R. T. O'CALLAGHAN, *Aram-Naharaim*, 1948; A. PARROT, *Abraham et son temps*, 1946 (English: *Abraham and His Times*, 1968); L. ROST, "Die Gottesverehrung der Patriarchen im Lichte der Pentateuchquellen," *VTSuppl*, VII (1960), 346-59; H. H. ROWLEY, "Recent Discovery and the Patriarchal Age," *BJRL*, XXXII (1949/50), 3-38; H. SCHMÖKEL, *Geschichte des alten Vorderasien*, 1957; H. SEEBASS, *Der Erzvater Israel und die Einführung der Jahweverehrung in Kanaan*, 1966; C. STEUERNAGEL, "Jahwe und die Vätergötter," in *Beer-Festschrift*, 1935, pp. 62-71; R. DE VAUX, "La Palestine et la Transjordanie au II⁰ millénaire et les origines israélites," *ZAW*, LVI (1938), 225-38; *idem, Die hebräischen Patriarchen und die modernen Entdeckungen*, 1959 (originally published in *RB* between 1946 and 1949 as "Les patriarches hébreux et les découvertes modernes"); *idem,* "Les patriarches hébreux et l'histoire," *Studii Biblici Franciscani Liber annuus*, XIII

27

(1962/63), 287-97 (= his *Bible et Orient*, 1967, pp. 175-85); G. E. WRIGHT, "History and the Patriarchs," *ET*, LXXI (1959/60), 292-96; S. YEIVIN, "The Age of the Patriarchs," *RSO*, XXXVIII (1963), 277-302.

1. *Historical background.* The early history of the Israelites took place for the most part within the framework of one of the waves of Semitic migrations that emerged from the desert of Syria and Arabia with the goal of penetrating into the Fertile Crescent, a long belt of settled territory extending from the Persian Gulf through Mesopotamia to Syria and Palestine. There were several major waves of migration in the pre-Christian era, between which there were also infiltrations of smaller groups. The most important of these were: [1] (*a*) the Akkadian-Egyptian wave, which brought the Semites to Babylonia and Egypt shortly after 3000 B.C.; whether they also came into Syria is not known; (*b*) the Early Amorite wave, not universally recognized, around 2500-2300, which laid the foundations for the empire of Akkad; its significance for Syria is likewise not known; (*c*) the Canaanite wave,[2] around 2100-1700, which bore fruit in the west through the establishment of states (Alalakh, Carchemish, Aleppo, Qatna, Ugarit, etc.) as well as through the development of an independent civilization (alphabetic writing) and religion; (*d*) the Aramean wave, around 1400-900. Other migratory movements also affected the western part of the ancient Near East, especially the Hyksos,[3] probably of mixed racial origin, from 1700 on; the "Sea Peoples," including the Philistines,[4] around 1200 and afterward; and, at about the same time, straggling remnants of the Hittites following the fall of their empire in Asia Minor.[5]

[1] *BHH*, I, 237; *RGG*, III, 1690-93; *IDB*, IV, 269. See also the survey by A. Bea, "La Palestina Preisraelitica: Storia, popoli, cultura," *Bibl*, XXIV (1943), 231-60. In place of separate waves, other scholars assume a continuous process of penetration with certain peaks (Moscati).

[2] Many scholars designate the people making up this wave "Amorites"; others speak of "East Canaanites" (Bauer) or "Proto-Arameans" (Noth). See also: A. Alt, "Die älteste Schilderung Palästinas im Lichte neuer Funde," *PJB*, XXXVII (1941), 19-49; M. Noth, "Die syrisch-palästinische Bevölkerung des zweiten Jahrtausends v. Chr. im Lichte neuer Quellen," *ZDPV*, LXV (1942), 9-67. According to Noth, this wave came in as a new ruling class during the 19th and 18th centuries; their form of organization was still nomadic, and they were closely related to the contemporary ruling class in Mesopotamia. For arguments against this view, see D. O. Edzard in *ZA*, LVI (NF XXII [1964]), 142-49.

[3] *BHH*, I, 237-38; *RGG*, III, 498-99; *IDB*, II, 667.

[4] *BHH*, I, 238; *RGG*, V, 339-41; *IDB*, III, 791-95.

[5] *BHH*, I, 238; *RGG*, III, 299-303; *IDB*, II, 612-15; E. Forrer, "The Hittites in Palestine," *PEQ*, LXIX (1937), 100-115. According to Forrer, Hittites had come from Asia Minor to Jerusalem, Bethlehem, and Hebron as early as 1350.

The fourth or Aramean wave accounts for at least a large portion of the Israelites, who around this time penetrated from the desert and steppe into the settled territory east and west of the Jordan. They came with other related Aramean tribes such as the Ammonites, Moabites, and Edomites, the first two of which are characterized as pure-blooded by Gen. 19:30-38, a story which strikes us today as offensive. Ethnically, therefore, these Israelites should be called Arameans.[6] There are traces in Hebrew suggesting that they originally spoke Aramaic and did not adopt Hebrew, a Canaanite dialect of West Semitic, until they were in Palestine. There is an unmistakable Aramaic stratum in the personal names of the Israelites. Ancient and reliable traditions also associate Israel with the Arameans: Israel claims to be descended from a perishing Aramean (Deut. 26:5), and throughout Genesis refers to its kindred to the east as Arameans.

The Israelites nevertheless did not constitute a homogeneous ethnic group. The Aramean origin of the groups associated with the names of the patriarchs is dubious. According to Old Testament tradition, they came to Palestine from Mesopotamia; Gen. 24:10 refers to their homeland as Aram-naharaim (translated generally in the English Bible as "Mesopotamia," the term means "the land of the Arameans along the two rivers," referring to the Euphrates and one of its tributaries, perhaps the Balîkh). Had they been Arameans, they would have to have penetrated into Mesopotamia after 1400 and then migrated immediately to Palestine. Since contacts with earlier Mesopotamian traditions argue against such an origin, an earlier wave of migration is more likely.[7] Furthermore, tradition associates Israelites with numerous Arabic tribes, including Midian (Gen. 25:1-5, 12-18). The band that fled from Egypt under the leadership of Moses may have been of non-Aramean origin; in any case, it came to incorporate other elements (cf. Exod. 12:38).

At the beginning of Israel's history, therefore, we do not find a unified group of ethnically homogeneous tribes. We are instead dealing with families, groups, and tribes of very different origin, albeit predominantly Aramean. Within the territory of Palestine other elements, not least some Canaanites, were absorbed, and the Israelite people came into being. The outward situation of these

---

[6] *BHH*, I, 119-20; *RGG*, I, 531-32; *IDB*, I, 190-93.

[7] On the basis of certain intellectual parallels between Sumerian literature and the Bible, S. N. Kramer suggests Sumerian origin for some of Abraham's ancestors, who he claims lived for several generations in Ur or other Sumerian cities ("Sumerian Literature and the Bible," in Pontificio Istituto Biblico, *Studia Biblica et Orientalia*, III [1959], 185-204).

early Israelites is suggested by the term "'Apiru," which was first discovered in the Amarna Letters, correspondence between the Pharaos and kings of certain Palestinian city-states, and has since been attested throughout the entire ancient Near East from the 19th to the 12th century.[8] It originally referred to "persons without family affiliation" in the sociological sense, foreign mercenaries, captives, and slaves, and consequently foreigners of inferior legal status within a kingdom. The Hebrew expression " *'ibrî,*" which is connected with this term, characterizes the early Israelites as alien groups of inferior legal status. The reason is that before they settled in Palestine they were wandering nomads, staying only temporarily in the territory of one state or another.

2. *The Israelites as nomads.* The early Israelites were neither camel bedouin[9] (although they are depicted as owning camels), nor caravan drivers in the Negeb,[10] nor settled farmers, but small livestock nomads[11]—or, with reference to the animal they used for

---

[8] *BHH*, I, 296; *RGG*, III, 105-6; M. Astour, "Les étrangers à Ugarit et le statut juridique des Ḫabiru," *RA*, LIII (1959), 70-76; L. Baeck, "Der Ibri," *MGWJ*, LXXXIII (1939), published 1963), 66-80; R. Borger, "Das Problem der *'apiru* ('Ḫabiru')," *ZDPV*, LXXIV (1958), 121-32; J. Bottéro, *Le problème des Ḫabiru à la 4ème rencontre assyriologique internationale*, 1954; M. Greenberg, *The Ḫab/piru*, 1955; E. Chiera, "Ḫabiru and Hebrews," *AJSL*, XLIX (1932/33), 115-24; P. Dhorme, "Les Ḫabiru et les Hébreux," *JPOS*, IV (1924), 162-68; A. Jepsen, "Die Hebräer und ihr Recht," *AfO*, XV (1945/51), 54-68; B. Landsberger, "Über die Völker Vorderasiens im 3. Jahrtausend," *ZA*, XXXV (1924), 213-38; N. A. van Uchelen, *Abraham de Hebreër*, 1964. There is a great variety of opinion concerning the meaning of the expression and its relationship to " *'ibrî.*"

[9] B. Brentjes, "Das Kamel im Alten Orient," *Klio*, XXXVIII (1960), 23-52; W. Dostal, "The Evolution of Bedouin Life," in *L'antica società beduina*, 1959, pp. 11-34; J. P. Free, "Abraham's Camels," *JNES*, III (1944), 187-93; H. Klengel, "Zu einigen Problemen des altvorderasiatischen Nomadentums," *ArOr*, XXX (1962), 585-96; W. G. Lambert, "The Domesticated Camel in the Second Millennium, Evidence from Alalakh and Ugarit," *BASOR*, CLX (1960), 42-43; A. Pohl, "Das Kamel in Mesopotamien," *Or*, XIX (1950), 251-53; *idem*, "Nochmals das Kamel in Mesopotamien," *ibid.*, XXI (1952), 373-74; *idem*, "Zur Zähmung des Kamels, *ibid.*, XXIII (1954), 453-54; R. Walz, "Zum Problem der Domestikation der altweltlichen Cameliden," *ZDMG*, CI (1951), 29-51; *idem*, "Neue Untersuchungen zum Domestikationsproblem der altweltlichen Cameliden," *ibid.*, CIV (1954), 48-87; *idem*, "Beiträge zur ältesten Geschichte der altweltlichen Cameliden unter besonderer Berücksichtigung des Problems des Domestikationszeitpunktes," in *Actes IVe Congrès Anthropologique*, III (1956), 190-204.

[10] W. F. Albright, "Abram the Hebrew: A New Archaeological Interpretation," *BASOR*, CLXIII (1961), 36-54; *idem*, "Some Remarks on the Meaning of the Word *SḤR* in Genesis," *ibid.*, CLXIV (1961), 28; E. A. Speiser, "The Word *SḤR* in Genesis and Early Hebrew Movements," *ibid.*, pp. 23-28. For yet another view, see L. R. Fisher, "Abraham and his Priest-King," *JBL*, LXXXI (1962), 264-70; C. H. Gordon, "Abraham and the Merchants of Ura," *JNES*, XVII (1958), 28-31.

[11] *BHH*, II, 1319; *RGG*, IV, 1504-5; *IDB*, III, 558-60.

transport, ass nomads.[12] Such nomads live primarily in semi-desert and steppe with four to twelve inches of rainfall annually; they are restricted to areas and routes where water holes are close together and there is adequate pasturage. They repeatedly alternate between the steppe and settled territory, with which they have active relationships.[13] This is also the usual way the patriarchs are depicted: they are constantly on the move with their sheep and goats, interested in well rights (the song of the well in Num. 21:17-18, which resembles an incantation, may have been sung at the digging of such wells). They occasionally even secure the possession of land and combine a kind of farming with their keeping of flocks. Influenced by the civilization of the settled regions, they are already semi-nomads well on their way to settling in a single location—though this does not prevent them from robbing the inhabitants of the settled areas when opportunity presents itself (cf. Exod. 12:35-36).

Contrary to earlier assumptions, the patriarchs are not legendary figures, eponymous ancestors of families, or debased gods. They are historical persons, albeit of a different sort and significance from those assumed in the narratives of Genesis.[14] In the patriarchal traditions we find ancient Near Eastern names from the first half of the second millennium, the language and customs of the nomadic shepherds in the territory of Mari during the 20th through the 18th centuries, a parallelism between the names of Abraham's alleged relatives and place names in northern Mesopotamia, as well as legal

[12] Cf. R. Walz, "Gab es ein Esel-Nomadentum im Alten Orient?" in International Congress of Orientalists, *Akten des Vierundzwanzigsten Internationalen Orientalisten-Kongresses,* 1959, pp. 150-52; Walz cites evidence from the 19th century on.

[13] The information contained in the Mari texts concerning the nomads of Mesopotamia in the first half of the second millennium can be used to provide analogies to the Genesis traditions. See J.-R. Kupper, *Les nomades en Mésopotamie au temps des rois de Mari,* 1957; A. Parrot, "Mari et l'Ancien Testament," *RhPhR,* XXXV (1955), 117-20; see also the interpretation of the Safatenic inscriptions by O. Eissfeldt, "Das Alte Testament im Lichte der safatenischen Inschriften," *ZDMG,* CIV (1954), 88-118 (= his *Kleine Schriften,* III [1966], 289-317).

[14] In addition to the bibliography preceding § 2, see H. Gressmann, "Sage und Geschichte in den Patriarchenerzählungen," *ZAW,* XXX (1910), 1-34; A. Jepsen, "Zur Überlieferung der Vätergestalten," *WZ Leipzig,* III (1953/54), 265-81; E. Meyer, "Der Stamm Jakob und die Entstehung der israelitischen Stämme," *ZAW,* VI (1886), 1-16; B. Stade, "Lea und Rahel," *ibid.,* I (1881), 112-16; *idem,* "Wo entstanden die genealogischen Sagen über den Ursprung der Hebräer?" *ibid.,* 347-50.

practices of Hurrian origin from the period around 1500. In fact, these occur within the Old Testament only in narratives that purport to give an account of this period.[15] This is probably because individual reminiscences of conditions in Mesopotamia and of specific figures were kept alive in Palestine, in a tradition that continued to grow and receive elaboration.

The tradition contains specific details[16] concerning Abraham,[17] Isaac,[18] and Jacob;[19] the Joseph novella[20] can hardly contain a historical nucleus, representing instead an Israelite revision of an Egyptian wisdom narrative. Israel, on the other hand, who is equated with Jacob in Gen. 32:29; 35:10 (cf. 49:24), must be considered a separate patriarch. We may assume that in the 15th and 14th centuries there were more figures of this nature; the traditions concerning them did not become the common property of all Israel, and were therefore forgotten. Concerning the nomadic life of the later Israelite tribes before they settled in Palestine we know almost nothing. Only the tribal sayings[21] with their animal metaphors may derive in part from the nomadic period and allow us to draw certain conclusions.[22]

This nomadic existence, although not the fundamental element of Israelite religion, as Nyström suggests, is most likely a constitutive element of its history. For nomadic life leads to certain forms of society, and exhibits characteristic modes of conduct and religious peculiarities. Two fundamental rules of life are far-reaching hospitality, with the implicit obligation of the host to protect his guest,[23] who counts temporarily as a member of the clan with all the rights of such a member, and the pursuance of justice by private means, above all blood vengeance (cf. the Song of Lamech in Gen. 4:23-

[15] S-F, § 19.1. The patriarchs are accordingly to be dated sometime after 1500. —Cf. also J. H. Chamberlayne, "Kinship Relations Among the Early Hebrews," *Numen*, X (1963), 153-64; J. C. L. Gibson, "Light from Mari on the Patriarchs," *JSS*, VII (1962), 44-62; A. Malamat, "Mari and the Bible: Some Patterns of Tribal Organization and Institutions," *JAOS*, LXXXII (1962), 143-50. For certain restrictions, see M. Greenberg, "Another Look at Rachel's Theft of the Teraphim," *JBL*, LXXXI (1962), 239-48.

[16] S-F, § 19.1.
[17] *BHH*, I, 15-16; *RGG*, I, 68-71; *IDB*, I, 14-21.
[18] *BHH*, II, 775-76; *RGG*, III, 902-3; *IDB*, II, 728-31.
[19] *BHH*, II, 797-98; *RGG*, III, 517-20; *IDB*, II, 782-87.
[20] *BHH*, II, 886-88; *RGG*, III, 859-60; *IDB*, III, 981-86.
[21] A. H. J. Gunneweg, "Über den Sitz im Leben der sog. Stammessprüche," *ZAW*, LXXVI (1964), 245-55; H.-J. Kittel, *Die Stammessprüche Israels*, Dissertation, Berlin, 1959; H.-J. Zobel, *Stammesspruch und Geschichte*, 1965.
[22] S-F, § 8.1.   [23] *BHH*, I, 514, *RGG*, II, 1205; *IDB*, II, 654.

24) ,[24] through which the diminished vital force of a clan due to the death or injury of one of its members is compensated by an analogous injury to the guilty clan.

3. *The religious substratum.* Like other human societies, and partially in common with them, the early Israelites had certain conceptions, practices, and attitudes that retained their vitality in later times, while such material in other areas of life usually vanished after the change from nomadic to settled life. The religious substratum was preserved by being integrated into the faith and worship of the later period or by surviving separately as superstition, often attacked by the official religion.

a) Primitive material surrounds the crucial events in human life. These include circumcision, the surgical removal of the foreskin.[25] The practice is found among the Ammonites, Moabites, and Edomites, peoples related to Israel by origin, and in Egypt, albeit only as a requirement for priests. It is not found among the Assyrians, Babylonians, or Philistines, nor apparently among the Canaanites or Phoenicians (Gen. 34:14 ff.: Ezek. 32:30) .[26] Originally it may have been a rite of manhood or even an initiation for marriage (cf. Gen. 34:14 ff.). The short narrative of the circumcision of Moses' son by his mother Zipporah (Exod. 4:24-26) confirms or legitimizes the change to circumcision of infants. It must remain an open question whether the narrative views circumcision as protection against demons.

Some mourning customs[27] are also primitive, although it is no longer possible to determine which of the customs that appear in the OT (§ 17.3) were already practiced by the early Israelites. The purpose of these customs was originally twofold: to provide new vital force for the dead, for example by means of tears, which furnish creative, life-giving moisture;[28] or to avert the harm threatened by

[24] *BHH,* I, 261; *RGG,* I, 1331-32; IV, 216-17; *IDB,* I, 321.

[25] *BHH,* I, 223-25; *RGG,* I, 1090-91; *IDB,* I, 629-31.

[26] Herodotus appears to testify to the existence of the practice among the Phoenicians (cf. E. Meyer in *ZAW,* XXIX [1909], 152) ; this may represent a late borrowing. The pictorial representation from Megiddo *(ANEP,* p. 332) shows two prisoners, probably non-Canaanites, who are circumcised. For further discussion, see J. M. Sasson, "Circumcision in the Ancient Near East," *JBL,* LXXXV (1966) , 473-76; J. Schur, *Wesen und Bedeutung der Beschneidung im Licht der alttestamentlichen Quellen und der Völkerkunde,* 1937. H. Zeydner, "Kainszeichen, Keniter und Beschneidung," *ZAW,* XVIII (1898) , 120-35, suggests that circumcision is the "sign of Cain"; this theory is unlikely.

[27] *BHH,* III, 2021-22; *RGG,* IV, 998-1001; *IDB,* III, 452-54.

[28] M. Canney, "The Magic of Tears," *JMEOS,* 1926, pp. 47-54.

the departed spirit, for example by changing clothes as a means of disguise. A lament can have either purpose: to restore the dead to life or to banish the departed spirit.

b) Another primitive feature is the religiously motivated prohibition referred to by the term "taboo." Transgression of such taboos results in specific sanctions. Even the sacred can be taboo when the profane is not allowed to come in contact with it.[29] There was an ancient meat taboo that prohibited the eating not only of unclean animals (e.g., the pig[30]) or certain parts of clean animals (blood, fat), but also the flesh of animals not hunted or slaughtered by man (Lev. 17:15; 22:8; Ezek. 44:31). Linked to this is the blood taboo,[31] since life is "in the blood" (Lev. 17:14), so that an animal is not considered "dead" until its blood has been drained; only then can it be released for food (Gen. 9:4). The sexual sphere is full of taboos: copulation, emission, menstrual discharge, and abnormal discharges (of pus) in the genital region render the person concerned taboo, usually until the evening of the same day (Lev. 15:1 ff.). In addition, the "*ḥērem*," the utter destruction of all the spoils of battle, which is more likely associated with nomadic life than with permanent civilization, is best explained as a consequence of the taboo attaching to plunder taken from the domain of another deity.[32] The destruction of the booty actually serves to "purify" it, like the punishment of death by burning (e.g., Gen. 38:24). Usually, however, purification is accomplished through washing with water (e.g., Lev. 15:1 ff.).

c) A multiplicity of magical notions and practices were known to the Israelites, many of which they brought with them from their past when they settled in Palestine, where they were supplemented by Canaanite, Assyro-Babylonian, and Egyptian practices. For part of later Israel, one can even speak of a magical approach to life (§ 13.3). Once again, it is hard to determine what part of all this derives from the early period; likely possibilities include the magical

[29] *RGG*, VI, 598-600; A. C. James, *Taboo Among the Ancient Hebrews*, Dissertation, University of Pennsylvania, 1925; E. Pax, "Beobachtungen zum biblischen Sprachtabu," *LA*, XII (1961/62), 66-112.

[30] *BHH*, III, 1748-49; *IDB*, IV, 469; I. M. Price, "Swine in Old Testament Taboo," *JBL*, XLIV (1925), 154-57; R. de Vaux, "Les sacrifices de porcs en Palestine et dans l'Ancien Testament," in *Von Ugarit nach Qumran* (Eissfeldt Festschrift), 1958, pp. 250-65 (= his *Bible et Orient*, 1967, pp. 499-516).

[31] *BHH*, I, 259; *RGG*, I, 1327-28.

[32] *BHH*, I, 193; *RGG*, I, 860-61; *IDB*, I, 838-39.

use of clothing[33] or a staff (Moses, Elijah, Elisha), belief in the evil eye,[34] and the magical power of the hand (II Kings 5:11). Most important is the effectual magic word, whether spoken as blessing or curse[35] by the mouth of an ordinary man, especially at the hour of death (cf. Gen. 27:27 ff., 39-40; 48:15 ff., with the laying on of the "wrong" hand), or pronounced in rhythmic form, sometimes needing interpretation, by a leader filled with supernatural power (cf. Josh. 10:12). In the earliest period, such a leader might be the magician, seer, poet, and priest of the tribe all at once; Deborah is still reported to have sung a magical war song, paving the way for the defeat of the enemy (Judg. 5:12). It is reasonable to suppose that the concept of prophetism in I–II Kings, with its belief in the almost magical power of the "men of God" and prophetical leaders, is a remnant of that primitive culture, in which the various functions were still combined in a single person. The magical element of the early period continues on in the notion of the effectual power of prophetical words and actions (cf. even the late text Ecclus. 48:1 ff.).[36] This notion pervades all Israelite prophecy, where it is based on the will and the power of Yahweh. Since time immemorial amulets have served to ward off magical influences; they were familiar not only in Palestine, where excavations have uncovered many of them, but also in the nomadic realm.[37]

4. *The tribal religion of the early Israelites.* All recent studies of the religion of the early Israelites take as their point of departure the work of Alt, who viewed the terms "God of Abraham," "God of Isaac," "God of Jacob," "*paḥad yiṣḥāq*," and " *ʾăbîr yaʿăqōb*" as true divine names, which included the name of the founder of the cult. He maintained that worship of these "gods of the fathers" lasted until the adoption of Yahwism, while the *'ēlîm* mentioned in Genesis

[33] A. Jirku, "Zur magischen Bedeutung der Kleidung in Israel," *ZAW*, XXXVII (1917/18), 109-25.

[34] *BHH*, I, 257; *RGG*, I, 1321; A. Löwinger, "Der böse Blick," *Mitteilungen zur jüdischen Volkskunde*, XXIX (1926), 551-61.

[35] *RGG*, V. 1648-51; *IDB*, I, 446-48, 749-50; H. C. Brichto, *The Problem of "Curse" in the Hebrew Bible*, 1963; J. Hempel, "Die israelitischen Anschauungen von Segen und Fluch in Lichte altorientalischer Parallelen," *ZDMG*, LXXIX (1925), 20-110 (= his *Apoxysmata*, 1961, pp. 30-113); F. Horst, "Segen und Segenhandlungen in der Bibel," *EvTh*, VII (1947/48), 23-37 (= his *Gottes Recht*, 1961, pp. 188-202); S. Mowinckel, *Psalmenstudien V: Segen und Fluch in Israels Kult- und Psalmdichtung*, 1924.

[36] G. Fohrer, "Prophetie und Magie," in his *Studien zur alttestamentlichen Prophetie (1949-1965)*, 1967, pp. 242-64.

[37] *BHH*, I, 90-91; *RGG*, I, 345-47; *IDB*, I, 122-23.

with various epithets were local nature gods. This view has been modified or disputed at many points, so that our presentation must begin with a survey of the textual evidence.

Eissfeldt assumes that the gods of the fathers did not continue to be worshiped until the adoption of Yahwism; he thinks it likely that their worship was replaced first by the Canaanite religion of El, native to Palestine.[38] Gemser thinks in terms of a single god of the fathers; he understands the various designations as referring to the same deity appearing in different forms, and views the religion of El and the religion of the god of the fathers as two expressions of the same thing. Gressmann, Dussaud, and others find only a Hebrew El religion in the nomadic period. Still others, among them Anderson, Lewy, May, and Seebass, finding a parallel in Old Assyrian invocations, represent the view that in the gods of the patriarchs we are dealing with family gods or anonymous tribal gods.[39]

Wellhausen's description of the pagan Arab, that is, the camel bedouin, as being religiously indifferent certainly does not hold true for the early Israelites: "The man is an individual, his help is in his arm and his brother, no God assists him, no saint watches over his soul. His highest personal good in his honor, for the sake of which he forces his soul to venture what it dreads."[40] It has frequently been suggested that the religion of the early Israelites was a kind of animism, or more specifically a kind of polydaemonism (most recently by Matthews*). This view is no longer tenable; quite apart from other considerations, it is dubious whether such a religion existed anywhere in the ancient Near East in historical times. Neither is it possible to agree with Pedersen, according to whom the undifferentiated, unified culture of earliest Israel possessed no belief in a personal God, but concentrated all its faith on the will and abilities of magically endowed men.[41] The magical element certainly played some rôle in the primitive material, but belief in a personal God is also found, as we shall show.

Of course our knowledge concerning the religion of the early Israelites will always be limited; there are no extra-biblical sources, and the OT narratives or notes have been subjected to repeated revision and expansion. The two source strata J and N go so far as to assume that Yahweh was the God of the patriarchs—in contrast to E and P, which at least do not introduce the name of Yahweh until the Mosaic period, and to Gen. 35:1-7; Josh. 24:2, 14-15, where the ancestors of the Israelites are said to have worshiped other gods. The traditions are so difficult to interpret that there

---

[38] O. Eissfeldt, "El and Yahweh," JSS, I (1956), 25-37 (reprinted in German in his Kleine Schriften, III [1956], 386-97).

[39] K. T. Anderson, "Der Gott meines Vaters," StTh, XVI (1963), 170-88; J. Lewy, "Les Textes paléo-assyriens et l'Ancien Testament," RHR, CX (1934), 29-65; H. G. May, "The Patriarchal Idea of God," JBL, LX (1941), 113-28; idem, "The God of my Father—a Study of Patriarchal Religion," JBR, IX (1941), 155-58, 199-200; for the contrary view, see A. Alt, "Zum 'Gott der Väter,'" PJB, XXXVI (1940), 93-104.

[40] J. Wellhausen, Reste arabischen Heidentums, 2nd ed., 1897, p. 228.

[41] P. Pedersen, Israel, Its Life and Culture, I–IV, 1926-40.

is a great diversity of opinion as to how much of early Israelite religion we can recover. Maag, on the one hand, thinks that the patriarchal traditions are still well informed about the general characteristics of the nomadic religion.[42] Rost, on the other hand, arrives at the conclusion that none of the Pentateuchal sources furnishes a basis for any historically probable reconstruction; each provided an idealized picture for its own period. The truth probably lies somewhere between absolute confidence and absolute skepticism with regard to the sources.

a) The sources in fact usually do not speak of the "God of the fathers," but of the "God of my [your, his] father" (Gen. 31:5, 29; 43:23; 49:25; 50:17). The formula has Mesopotamian parallels, both in Old Assyrian texts—e.g., "I pray to Asshur, the god of your father"; "lifting up of hands for the well-being of PN before the god of her father"; "one golden goblet belonging to the gods of the father"—and in a Mari text—"through the god [or: the name of the god] of my father." Additional examples might be cited. The formulas found in Genesis therefore merely point to a clan god who is either anonymous or is not mentioned by name, worshiped by the members of the clan because of a decision made by one of their ancestors.

b) In other formulas the names of the fathers are mentioned, with or without the additional term "father": "the God of Abraham" (Gen. 31:53); "the God of Abraham your father" (Gen. 26:24; 28:13; 32:10); "the God of Isaac" (Gen. 28:13); "the God of my/his father Isaac" (Gen. 32:10 [Eng. 32:9]; 46:1); "The God of Nahor" (Gen. 31:53). In addition, there is the comprehensive formula "the God of Abraham, the God of Isaac, and the God of Jacob" (Exod. 3:6, 15), the only place where we hear of a "God of Jacob." In all these cases the situation is basically the same as in (*a*) above; the only difference is that the tribal gods are assigned to a specific group identified with the name of an ancestor.

c) We also find "El" as a term for God or as the name of the high god El. Here we must exclude the instances when El is mentioned in connection with Palestinian sanctuaries, where a second term is added to the name "El" (cf. § 4.2). It is also uncertain whether the name "Jacob-El" and "Joseph-El," which occur as place names in Egyptian lists of the 15th through 12th centuries (Thut-

[42] His argument is weak because he bases it on supposed parallels between early Israelite religion and the religion of contemporary herdsmen who go in search of new pasture ("transmigration"). The geographical and historical distance, however, is not easily spanned; neither can the wanderings of the patriarchal groups in Genesis 12:1 ff. be simply understood as transmigration.

mose III, Amen-hotep III [without historical value], Ramses II and III), are also to be taken as original patriarchal names.[43] In any case, it is certain that the name of the patriarch Israel, like that of Ishmael, contains the theophorous element "El." Gen. 33:20 speaks of "El the God of Israel," albeit in association with Shechem, which means that we are probably already dealing with a later stage. There is no single sure explanation for the occurrence of "El" in these names. We may be dealing with a mere term for "God," with a divine name that is an expression of a nomadic El religion, or with the name of the Canaanite high god El, taken over as the result of the early influence of the settled territory on the nomads, who already had dealings with it. We must note, however, that tradition without exception associates the patriarchs' encounters with El with Palestine, never with Mesopotamia or the Syro-Arabian desert.

d) The most primitive names are probably *paḥad yiṣḥāq* and *'ăbîr ya'ăqōb*, traditionally translated "Fear of Isaac" and "Mighty One of Jacob" (Gen. 31:42 [also in Gen. 31:53 as *"paḥad* of his father Isaac"]; 49:24). A more accurate translation would probably be "Kinsman of Isaac"[44] and "Champion, Defender of Jacob." In addition, we find *'eben yiṣrā'ēl*, "Rock of Israel" (Gen. 49:24). It has also been suggested on the basis of Gen. 15:1 that the God of Abraham was called *māgēn 'abrāhām*, "Shield of Abraham."[45] Thus each of the patriarchal clans has associated with it a term characterizing the particular deity in its relationship to the clan. These are not divine names, however.

e) We come finally to the proper names used in ancient Israel and among the Northwest Semites. These were frequently used in the Old Testament down to the tenth century, but rarely afterward, so that we are obviously dealing with an ancient type of name. These names include the elements *'am*, "clan, family"; *'āb*, "father"; and *'āḥ*, "brother." These elements designate the deity; many Semitic names have religious significance, and the elements mentioned are interchangeable with the name of a god (e.g., Abiezer—Eliezer, Abiram—Jehoram). Thus we find Abiram (Abraham)/Ahiram, "My (divine) father/brother is exalted"; Abiezer/Ahiezer, "My (divine) father/brother is (my) help"; Abimelek/Ahimelek, "My (divine)

---

[43] Cf. the survey in *ANET*, p. 242.

[44] Cf. W. F. Albright, *From the Stone Age to Christianity*, 2nd ed., 1946, pp. 188-89. An unlikely psychological explanation is given by N. Krieger, "Der Schrecken Isaaks," *Judaica*, XVII (1961), 193-95.

[45] E. A. Leslie, *Old Testament Religion in the Light of Its Canaanite Background*, 1936, p. 37.

father/brother is (my) king"; Eliab, "My God is (my) father"; Elişur, "My God is (my) rock"; Ammiel, "(The God) of my clan is (my) God." Apart from the fact that some of these names appear to use the word "El" as a designation of the deity rather than as a name, they are important because they cast light on the relationships that the early Israelites felt to exist between themselves and their tribal gods.

Our first conclusion, then, is that in the early period of Israel each clan (and probably also each tribe) worshiped its own particular god. This is the earliest discernible stage. There was a multiplicity of clan religions (and tribal religions), so that the tradition is correct in maintaining that the fathers worshiped other gods (Gen. 35:1-7; Josh. 24:2 14-15). All that is left, of course, is references to four of them. In these cases, at least, the personal relationship between the deity and the founder of the cult, who was probably also the founder or leader of the clan, plays an important rôle. Through the latter, the entire group together with its posterity became worshipers of the deity associated with their ancestor. The following features are characteristic:

a) According to the patriarchal traditions, there comes first a revelation of the deity to whom the attention of the founder or leader of the clan must somehow be drawn. There follows in response the choice of the deity on the part of the person concerned, since in practice it was the right of every independent man to choose his personal god. The choice includes the subsequent practice of a cult. The patriarchs are accordingly first of all recipients of revelation and cultic founders of Israel's early nomadic period; the personal relationships between them and their deities are specially emphasized, so that the names of the patriarchs appear in the term for their gods.

b) In Genesis 15, J tells (1bβ-2, 7-12, 17-18) how Abraham laments his childlessness; then, following Yahweh's command, he constructs a passage between animals that he has slaughtered and partially dismembered, through which pass a smoking fire pot and a flaming torch after dark. "On that day Yahweh made a covenant with Abram, saying, 'To your descendants I give this land, from the river of Egypt to the great river, the river Euphrates.'" This story is based on an ancient tradition, even if we are not dealing with the original words.[46] The deity makes a promise, promising land

---

[46] According to A. Caquot, "L'alliance avec Abram (Genèse 15)," *Semitica*, XII (1962), 51-66, we are dealing here with nothing more than a midrash after the fashion of Genesis 14, intended to glorify David and his dynasty by a

and descendants, and undertakes a permanent obligation to realize what has been promised.[47] This lays the foundation for a permanent association, which can also be prepared or established by a meal (Exod. 24:1-2, 9-11); this association is expressed in terms of kinship. The deity was considered the real head of the clan and could be termed "father" or "brother" by its earthly members, while they considered themselves "children," "brothers," or "kinsmen" of the deity.

c) The god of the clan is not a sky god; neither is he associated with a local sanctuary. He is a god who protects the wandering nomads as they travel. These nomads feel dependent on his leadership because they move among forces that are alien and often hostile. They seek his protection because he knows the routes and their dangers and will guide them safely. He causes the herds to increase, sees that the owners of the settled territories are benevolent during the annual transhumance, or gives to the weak nomad the cunning that will save him from the strong. He will finally help him gain land of his own and make his posterity abundant. The best expression of this whole complex of ideas is the idiom that the deity is or will be "with" the person concerned.

d) The cultic worship of early Israelite clan religion was probably very simple. There were probably animal sacrifices, usually offered by the heads of clans. The Passover sacrifice, for example, may originally have taken place at the beginning of the spring migration from the steppe to the settled territory.[48] It is hardly likely that altars were employed; they are not found among other Semitic nomads,

---

retrojection of the hereditary monarchy into the patriarchal period.—Cf. also J. Henninger, "Was bedeutet die rituelle Teilung eines Tieres in zwei Hälften?" *Bibl*, XXXIV (1953), 344-53; L. A. Snijders, "Genesis XV, the Covenant with Abram," *OTS*, XII (1958), 261-79.

[47] On the ritual itself, cf. Jer. 34:17 ff. and the Sfire stele I A 39-40. The expression "cut a *berit*" is attested as early as a fifteenth-century text from Qatna; cf. W. F. Albright in *BASOR*, CXXI (1951), 21-22.

[48] L. Rost, "Weidewechsel und altisraelitischer Festkalender," *ZDPV*, LXVI (1943), 205-16 (= his *Das kleine Credo und andere Studien zum Alten Testament*, 1965, pp. 101-12). It is unlikely, however, that the ceremony of the "scapegoat" on the Day of Atonement (Leviticus 16) originally inaugurated the return to the steppe in the fall. Equally unlikely is the theory of A. Brock-Utne, "Eine religionsgeschichtliche Studie zu dem ursprünglichen Passahopfer," *ARW*, XXXI (1934), 272-78, according to which the Passover was the sacrifice offered by the Palestinian population upon leaving winter quarters in village or town.— For a discussion of J. Pedersen, "Passahfest und Passahlegende," *ZAW*, LII (1934), 161-75, with its far-reaching consequences, see G. Fohrer, *Überlieferung und Geschichte des Exodus*, 1964, pp. 89-86; J. B. Segal, *The Hebrew Passover from the Earliest Times to A.D. 70*, 1963.

and are characteristic of the permanent sanctuaries in settled territory. It is possible, however, that the nomads had sacred stones and
trees, as in Palestine, which represented the deity. This assumption
is supported by the fact that the pre-Islamic bedouin of Arabia had
stones set up at their cultic sites, which they called "*nuṣb*," a word
derived from the same root as "massebah." They were also familiar
with sacred trees.

For the realm of ethics, Lev. 18:7 ff. can be cited. According to the
analysis of Elliger,[49] there was originally a decalogue comprising
apodictically formulated regulations; this decalogue is found in vss.
7-12, 14-16, with the addition of a commandment that originally
followed vs. 9. The original form of the commandments was: "You
shall not uncover the nakedness of [such and such a person]." The
circle of persons mentioned points to clan life such as existed in the
nomadic period. The clan was protected and hedged about by rules
of conduct referring to sexual activity in general, not to marriage.
We must therefore think in terms of a clan ethos that served to
preserve the way the clan lived, and therefore directed its regulations
personally to each member of the clan.

e) The personal element is characteristic of the structure of early
Israelite clan religion, as can be seen above all in the way this
religion came into being and was constituted, but also in its accompanying ethics. A second element is the mutual relationship between
the deity and man, which appears clearly in the sequence "revelation of the deity"—"decision and choice on the part of man"—
"promise and commitment by the deity"—"cultic response of man."
This structure also became fundamental to Yahwism.

5. *The position of the patriarchs*. In this presentation we have
depicted the patriarchs, the founders or leaders of the early Israelite
clans, as recipients of revelation. We may perhaps go a step further
and place them in the ranks of inspired leaders. In the undifferentiated, non-specialized civilization of nomads the functions of clan
leader, priest, seer, and even magician are not so sharply distinguished
as in the civilizations of settled peoples; they usually coalesce in a
single figure, who is considered inspired. This is the situation, for
example, in the case of the Arab *kāhin*. When a *kāhin* speaks as a
seer on the basis of dreams and presentiments, the dreams are

---

[49] K. Elliger, "Das Gesetz Leviticus 18," *ZAW*, LXVII (1955), 1-25 (= his
Kleine Schriften zum Alten Testament, 1966, pp. 232-59); *idem, Leviticus,*
1966, pp. 229 ff.

reminiscent of the patriarchal traditions, and the prophetic words recall the promises of territory and descendants. The theophanies that take place in the presence of the patriarchs, of which we hear much, can easily be associated with a state of mild ecstasy like that of a *kāhin*. The *kāhin* can also carry out priestly functions, as would be required of the patriarchs when they founded cults. Finally, the *kāhin*, as a result of his authority, can achieve the position of leader of his clan or tribe, a position like that we may assume for the patriarchs. Like the *kāhin*, then, the patriarchs conform to the type of inspired leaders, such as appear repeatedly in specialized form in the later history of Israel.

§ 3 CANAANITE RELIGION

J. AISTLEITNER, *Die mythologischen und kultischen Texte aus Ras Schamra*, 2nd ed., 1964; W. F. ALBRIGHT, "Syrien, Phönizien und Palästina," in *Historia mundi*, II (1953), 331-76; *idem*, "The Role of the Canaanites in the History of Civilization," in *The Bible and the Ancient Near East* (Albright Festschrift), 1961, pp. 328-62; F. BAETHGEN, *Beiträge zur semitischen Religionsgeschichte*, 1888; W. W. GRAF BAUDISSIN, *Studien zur semitischen Religionsgeschichte*, I-II, 1876-78; H. BAUER, "Die Gottheiten von Ras Schamra," *ZAW*, LI (1933), 81-101; LIII (1935), 54-59; W. BAUMGARTNER, "Ugaritische Probleme und ihre Tragweite für das Alte Testament," *ThZ* III (1947), 81-100; G. CONTENAU, "La Phénicie," in E. DRIOTON, *Les religions de l'Orient ancient*, 1957, pp. 65-70 (English: "The Ancient Religions of Western Asia: Phoenicia," in E. DRIOTON, *Religions of the Ancient East*, 1959, pp. 74-81); S. A. COOK, *The Religion of Ancient Palestine in the Light of Archaeology*, 1930; S. I. CURTISS, *Primitive Semitic Religion Today*, 1902; M. DAHOOD, "Ugaritic Studies and the Bible," *Gregorianum*, XLIII (1962), 55-79; G. R. DRIVER, *Canaanite Myths and Legends*, 1956; R. DUSSAUD, *Les découvertes de Ras Shamra (Ugarit) et l'Ancien Testament*, 2nd ed., 1941; *idem, Les origines cananéennes du sacrifice israélite*, 1941; O. EISSFELDT, "Kanaanäisch-ugaritische Religion," *HdO*, I.8.1 (1964), 76-91; I. ENGNELL, *Studies in Divine Kingship in the Ancient Near East*, 2nd ed., 1967; G. FOHRER, "Die wiederentdeckte kanaanäische Religion," *ThLZ*, LXXVIII (1953), cols. 193-200; T. H. GASTER, *Thespis: Ritual, Myth and Drama in the Ancient Near East*, 2nd ed., 1961; C. H. GORDON, *Ugaritic Literature*, 1949; *idem, Ugaritic Textbook*, 1965; J. GRAY, *The Legacy of Canaan*, 2nd ed., 1965; A. HALDAR, *The Notion of the Desert in Sumero-Accadian and West-Semitic Religions*, 1950; A. HERDNER, *Corpus des tablettes en cunéiformes alphabétiques découvertes à Ras Shamra-Ugarit de 1929 à 1939*, 1963; F. F. HVIDBERG, *Weeping and Laughter in the Old Testament*, 1962; E. JACOB, *Ras Shamra-Ugarit et l'Ancien Testament*, 1960; A. JIRKU, *Kanaanäische Mythen und Epen aus Ras Schamra-Ugarit*, 1962; *idem, Der Mythus der Kanaanäer*, 1966; A. S. KAPELRUD, "Temple Building, a Task for

Gods and Kings," *Or*, XXXII (1963), 56-62; *idem, The Ras Shamra Discoveries and the Old Testament*, 1963; M. J. LAGRANGE, *Études sur les religions sémitiques*, 2nd ed., 1905; R. DE LANGHE, *Les textes de Ras Shamra-Ugarit et leur rapports avec le milieu biblique de l'Ancien Testament*, 1945; M. MATTHIAE, *Ars Syra*, 1962; S. MOSCATI, *Il mondo dei Fenici*, 1966 (English: *The World of the Phoenicians*, 1968); M. J. MULDER, *Kanaänitische goden in het Oude Testament*, 1965; D. NIELSEN, "Die altsemitische Muttergöttin," *ZDMG*, XCII (1938), 504-51; J. H. PATTON, *Canaanite Parallels in the Book of Psalms*, 1944; E. PILZ, "Die weiblichen Gottheiten Kanaans," *ZDPV*, XLVII (1924), 129-68; M. H. POPE and W. RÖLLIG, "Syrien; die Mythologie der Ugariter und Phönizier," in H. W. HAUSSIG, ed., *Wörterbuch der Mythologie*, 1. Abt., I (1965), 217-312; J. B. PRITCHARD, *Ancient Near Eastern Texts Relating to the Old Testament*, 3rd ed., 1970 (especially the section edited by H. L. GINSBERG); C. F.-A. SCHAEFFER, *Le Palais Royal d'Ugarit*, 5 vols., 1955-65; *idem, Ugaritica*, 4 vols., 1939-62; W. H. SCHMIDT, *Königtum Gottes in Ugarit und Israel*, 2nd ed., 1966; A. VAN SELMS, *Marriage and Family Life in Ugaritic Literature*, 1954; W. ROBERTSON SMITH, *Lectures on the Religion of the Semites*, 3rd ed., 1927; R. C. THOMPSON, *Semitic Magic*, 1908; A. VANEL, *L'iconographie du dieu de l'orage dans le Proche-Orient ancien jusqu'au VIIᵉ siècle avant J.-C.*, 1965.

1. *Ugarit and Canaanite religion.* Canaanite religion[1] was mostly *terra incognita* until a few decades ago; the little that was known was mostly secondhand information. Some conclusions could be drawn from statements in the OT (more likely polemic than historically accurate), from the Egyptian execration texts, from the Amarna Letters, and from late Phoenician inscriptions. Additional information could be found in a few Greek writers or others who wrote in Greek, the most important being Philo Byblius (from Byblos; *ca.* A.D. 64-141), a Phoenician scholar, portions of whose *Phoenician History* were borrowed by Eusebius for his *Praeparatio evangelica*.[2] According to Philo himself, his work represents a translation of an original written by Sanchuniaton before the Trojan War, that is, in the thirteenth or fourteenth century B.C. This Sanchuniaton is mentioned in several other sources; according to Porphyry, in a note also cited by Eusebius, he was a native of Beirut, while others locate him in Tyre or Sidon. The accuracy of this information has frequently been doubted; the results of modern excavations, however, allow us to conclude that he did in fact write in Phoenician around or shortly after the middle of the second

[1] *BHH*, II, 926-30; *RGG*, III, 1106-15; V, 360-62; *IDB*, I, 494-98; III, 800-804.
[2] C. Clemen, *Die Phönikische Religion nach Philo von Byblos*, 1939; O. Eissfeldt, "Art und Aufbau der phönizischen Geschichte des Philo von Byblos," *Syria*, XXXIII (1956), 88-98 (= his *Kleine Schriften*, III [1966], 398-406).

millennium B.C.[3] Philo then "translated" these writings; that is, he reworked them, borrowing much from other sources or adding from his own knowledge. Parts of his work, then, are based on ancient and reliable traditions.

Certain features of Canaanite religion could be derived from a new comparative study of the better-known Semitic religions; such a study, however, remains to be written.[4] The elements common to these religions include the following: [5] (a) a number of powerful anthropomorphic gods, usually not too many, whose actions spring from personal will rather than from an abstract idea; (b) astral deities (Sun, Moon, Venus) as the major gods, besides whom a weather god is also found, at least occasionally, though the latter may not belong to the primitive Semitic pantheon; some scholars have suggested the possibility of a high god El standing above the other gods, but this assumption still needs to be investigated; (c) complete dependence of man on the gods, man's sinfulness, and man's reliance on divine mercy; (d) the idea of divine justice and the problem of theodicy (at least in Babylonia); (e) an absence of mysticism, due to Semitic realism, and a gulf between god and man that is felt to be insuperable; (f) originally, it seems, an absence of myths concerning the gods, since Babylonian mythology is rooted mostly in Sumerian mythology, Phoenician and Ugaritic mythology in Hurrian.

Excavations in Palestine have provided a few insights, bringing to light Egyptian representations of Canaanite deities, identified by head covering or by name.[6] They have also yielded a goddess Qadesh, standing on a lion and holding serpents in her hands.[7] Although the Egyptian influence in these representations is unmistakable, native figurines of bronze covered with gold or silver dating from several centuries of the pre-Israelite period have been found at various sites.[8]

---

[3] O. Eissfeldt, *Ras Schamra und Sanchunjaton*, 1939 (cf. *FF*, XIV [1938], 251-52; and *ThBl*, XVII [1938], 185-97 [= his *Kleine Schriften*, II (1963), 127-44]); *idem, Taautos und Sanchunjaton*, 1952; *idem, Sanchunjaton von Berut und Ilumilku von Ugarit*, 1952; F. Løkkegaard, "Some Comments on the Sanchuniaton Tradition," *StTh*, VIII (1955), 51-76.

[4] In the meantime, see O. Eissfeldt, "Götternamen und Gottesvorstellung bei den Semiten," *ZDMG*, LXXXIII (1929), 21-36 (= his *Kleine Schriften*, I [1962], 194-205); S. Moscati, *Le antiche divinità semitiche*, 1958.

[5] *RGG*, V, 1690-93.

[6] See, for example, P. Matthiae, "Note sul deo siriano Rešef," *Oriens antiquus*, II (1963), 27-43.

[7] *ANEP*, 473, 474, 476, 487.

[8] See W. P. Albright, *Archaeology and the Religion of Israel*, 4th ed., 1956,

The excavation of the Phoenician city of Ugarit,[9] which has been underway since 1929, has been especially important for our knowledge and understanding of Canaanite religion. Located on *rās eš-šamra,* "Fennel Head," this city-state was a port on the northern coast of Syria. It flourished in the second half of the second millennium B.C., and was destroyed around 1200 B.C. during the advance of the so-called Sea Peoples. The documents and texts that have been found there, primarily in alphabetic cuneiform and Akkadian, have cast new light on political, social, economic, and artistic questions, as well as contributing to our knowledge of ancient Near Eastern linguistics and the development of writing. Besides documents of secular life, three types of discovery may be cited that have religio-historical significance: (*a*) archaeological monuments such as the remnants of temples; altars; cultic implements; representations of deities in stone, metal, and ivory; burial sites with funerary offerings; and provisions for certain rituals; (*b*) documents of everyday cultic life, such as lists of gods and sacrifices, ritual regulations, and prayers; (*c*) the first remnants of Canaanite religious literature, in the form of poetic epics whose subject matter may be myth, saga, or legend. Now, it seems, the Canaanites of a specific place and time can speak directly to us through the material they left.

Some reservations, however, are in order. In the first place, we are dealing with religious monuments, documents, and texts from a city-state of the fourteenth-thirteenth centuries, which initially at least can illuminate only their own place and period. One must be cautious in drawing conclusions about the Canaanite religion of other places and periods. The population of Ugarit, furthermore, was a motley mixture: beside a basic Canaanite population stratum, residing mostly in satellite villages, there lived, primarily in the city of Ugarit itself, a non-Semitic population that may even have been in the majority, comprising primarily Hurrians, but also Kassites, people of Asia Minor, and other elements.[10] The result—apart from the general influence of Mesopotamia—was surely quite often

pp. 75-76; E. F. Campbell, Jr., "The Fifth Campaign at Balâtah (Shechem) : Field VII," *BASOR,* CLXXX (1965), 24-25; *ANEP,* 466.

[9] *BHH,* III, 2044-46; *RGG,* VI, 1100-1106; *IDB,* IV, 724-32; C. F.-A. Schaeffer, "Les fouilles de Ras Shamra—Ugarit, I. Campagne" and the series of subsequent articles, appearing in *Syria* beginning with volume X (1929). In the following discussion, the texts are cited according to the edition of Cyrus Gordon in *UT.*

[10] M. Noth, "Die syrisch-palästinische Bevölkerung des zweiten Jahrtausends v. Chr. im Lichte neuer Quellen," *ZDPV,* LXV (1942), 9-67; *idem,* "Die Herrenschicht von Ugarit im 15./14. Jh. v. Chr.," *ibid.,* pp. 144-64; A. van Selms.

a Canaanite-Hurrian syncretism and a powerful influence exercised by Hurrian myths.[11] Influences from the western Mediterranean also deserve mention; these affected Ugaritic culture and religion as they affected the entire Syro-Palestinian coastal region, though the effect was not creative, and the Canaanite character was not significantly changed.[12] Finally, in these myths we are dealing with poetic compositions that draw upon the dominant religious notions and customs for subject matter. We may still ask to what extent, despite their internal dependence on tradition, they represent a free and independent development with respect to common religious practice, to what extent they reflect such practice directly, or even to what extent they preserve religious material from the dead past.

These reservations notwithstanding, the Ugaritic texts do allow us to draw some conclusions about Canaanite religion, the religion the Israelites discovered upon entering Palestine, by which they were influenced, and with which they had to come to terms. This is true even though the various provincial and local forms of Canaanite religion diverged more markedly than is usually assumed from the discoveries at Ugarit, and the Ugaritic form itself cannot simply be identified with the forms attested in the OT. This Canaanite religion is the second pre-existing religious element that any history of Israelite religion must take into account.

Canaanite religion exhibits points of contact with and similarities to other Near Eastern religions as distant as those of India.[13] This

---

[11] For instance, the mythological epic of the marriage of the moon god Yeraḫ with the goddess Nikkal is probably based on Hurrian material. Besides Canaanite deities and the pair of Kassite gods Shukamnu and Shumalia (*ṯkmn wšnm*), borrowed indirectly through the Hurrians, Text 1 introduces the Hurrian goddess Ishḫara (*ušḫry*) (1. 13). Text 4. 6-8 equates the Hurrian god Kumarbi with El. O. Eissfeldt, "Mesopotamische Elemente in den alphabetischen Texten von Ugarit," *Syria*, XXXIX (1962), 36-41 (= his *Kleine Schriften*, IV [1969], 39-43); J. Nougayrol, "L'influence babylonienne à Ugarit d'après les textes en cunéiformes classiques," *ibid.*, pp. 28-35.

[12] See C. H. Gordon, *Before the Bible*, 1962; H. Haag, "Homer und das Alte Testament," *Tübinger ThQ*, CXLI (1961), 1-24; idem, "Der gegenwärtige Stand der Erforschung der Beziehungen zwischen Homer und dem Alten Testament," *JEOL*, VI, no. 19 (1965/66), 508-18; J. Hempel, "Westliche Kultureinflüsse auf das älteste Palästina," *PJB*, XXIII (1927), 52-92; R. H. Pfeiffer, "Hebrews and Greeks Before Alexander," *JBL*, LVI (1937), 91-101. Canaanite civilization and religion, on the other hand, exercised a powerful influence on the early history of Greece: the Canaanite pantheon has points of contact with the Homeric Olympus; Greek theogony (Hesiod) and cosmogony are dependent in part on Canaanite mythology; the anthropomorphizing Ugaritic poetry about the gods prepares the way for the Greek Philosophy of religion. This counter-influence is exaggerated, however, by M. C. Astour, *Hellenosemitica*, 1965.

[13] M. Pope, in *Wörterbuch der Mythologie*, p. 239.

does not mean, however, that we should assume a common cultic
schema throughout the entire ancient Near East, within which
Canaanite religion found its place. Quite apart from other considerations, such a hypothesis is disproven by the increasingly evident openness of the ancient Near East to the Mediterranean world
and Asia Minor, as well as the Caucasus, Armenia, and India.[14]
Canaanite religion bears its own unique stamp, which distinguishes
it from other religions. It is a national religion adhered to by a
civilization organized in city-states. It presumes a general condition
of divine favor, which, for the benefit of the people, must be preserved and repeatedly restored. In content it is a religion of renewed
life and fertility; like all such religions, it is sensual, orgiastic, and
cruel.

2. *Canaanite gods.* Earlier notions of the Canaanite pantheon
have had to be corrected on the basis of the Ugaritic texts. These
texts say nothing of sacred rocks, trees, and springs; their mention
in the OT can only indicate the remnants of ancient local cults.
Neither can we assume a primitive polydemonism or the existence
of numerous minor local gods. Of course people believed in demons,
and we do find scattered local deities. Above these, however, stands
a host of high gods, a pantheon like that of Babylonia or Greece,
worshiped in a well-organized temple cult. The dominant figures of
this pantheon are the gods El and Baal, familiar from the OT. The
many epithets attached to them in the OT (e.g., El Olam, Baal
Hermon) do not indicate a multiplicity of local deities; they are
to be understood as expressing local forms of the gods or as geographical designations of their dwelling places or cultic sites.

a El [15] occupies the most important position, although he sometimes
appears already to be a *deus otiosus,* forced somewhat into the background. He stands at the head of the gods as king, and presides
over the divine assembly, the "circle [or: 'totality'] (of the sons)
of El." He is called "father of the gods," "father of mankind," and
"creator of all creatures"; that is, he is the creator and father of
gods and men. Other West Semitic inscriptions also refer to him as
"creator of the earth." The title "king" and the epithet "bull El"
indicate his power and dominion. He is also the eternally wise one,

---

[14] See also S-F, § 2.2.
[15] *BHH,* I, 386-89; *RGG,* II, 413-14; O. Eissfeldt, *El im ugaritischen Pantheon,*
1951; F. Løkkegaard, "A Plea for El, the Bull, and Other Ugaritic Miscellanies,"
in *Studia orientalia Ioanni Pedersen,* 1953, pp. 219-35; M. H. Pope, *El in the
Ugaritic Texts,* 1955.

"the holy one," and "the friendly one, El, the one with feeling."
His dwelling place, to which the gods resort when they want to
seek counsel, lies "at the source of the [two] rivers, between the river-
beds of the [two] deeps" (Text 49, i. 5-6). This probably does not
refer to the waters beneath the earth (Pope), but to the end of the
earth, where the waters above and below the earth meet, and where,
far in the mythical distance, the ancient Near East imagined the
world mountain to stand.

Asherah[16] is the consort of El. She shares his high rank, is worshiped as "creator of the gods," and can intercede effectually with
El on behalf of others. At the request of Anat, for example, she
intercedes for Baal, although she also appears as Baal's opponent.
She appears more as a matron who has passed the age for conception
and childbearing than as a vital and amorous woman (Eissfeldt).
Because of the polarity often encountered in the nature of the
Canaanite gods, this does not prevent her being pictured as giving
birth and nursing.

Since in practice El remains very much in the background, Baal [17]
occupies a dominant position. The word is both a common noun
meaning "lord," "owner," or "husband" and also the name of the
god, who is to be identified with Hadad, the god of storms, rain, and
fertility;[18] he is therefore frequently called "cloud-rider." The

[16] *BHH*, I, 136-37; *RGG*, I, 637-38; *IDB*, I, 250-51.

[17] *BHH*, I, 173-75; *RGG*, I, 805-6; *IDB*, I, 328-29; W. F. Albright, "Baal-
Zephon" in *Festschrift Alfred Bertholet zum 80. Geburtstag*, 1950, pp. 1-14;
R. Dussaud, "Le mythe de Ba'al et d'Aliyan d'après des documents nouveaux."
RHR, CXI (1935), 5-65; O. Eissfeldt, *Baal Zaphon, Zeus Kasios und der Durchzug
der Israeliten durchs Meer*, 1932; A. S. Kapelrud, *Baal in the Ras Shamra Texts*,
1952. For other developments of the Baal figure, see Pope-Röllig, pp. 270-73:
Baal-addir, Baal biq'ah, Baal-chammon, Baal-karmelos, Baal-marqod, Baal-
qarnaim, Baal-Shamen. On the latter, see O. Eissfeldt, "Ba'alšamēm und Jahwe,"
ZAW, LVII (1939), 1-31 (= his *Kleine Schriften*, II [1963], 117-98). The OT
mentions the following forms of Baal, in which the epithet often designates a town
or other geographical site: Baal-berit (Judg. 8:33; 9:4), Baal-gad (Josh. 11:17;
12:7; 13:5), Baal-hamon (Song 8:11), Baal-zebub (= Baal-zebul) (II Kings 1:2-3,
6, 16), Baal-hazor (II Sam. 13:23), Baal-hermon (Judg. 3:3; I Chron. 5:23),
Baal-meon (Num. 32:38; Josh. 13:17; Ezek. 25:9; I Chron. 5:8), Baal-perazim
(II Sam. 5:20; I Chron. 14:11), Baal-zephon (Exod. 14:2, 9; Num. 33:7), Baal-
shalishah (II Kings 4:42), Baal-tamar (Judg. 20:33), as well as Baalath-beer
(Josh. 19:8) and probably Baale-judah (II Sam. 6:2). See also R. Hillmann,
*Wasser und Berg; kosmische Verbindungslinien zwischen dem kanaanäischen
Wettergott und Jahwe*, Dissertation, Halle, 1965.

[18] The two figures are identified in Text 76, ii. 4-5, 32-33; iii. 8-9; and elsewhere. It is not impossible, of course, that the identification is secondary, and
that there were originally two distinct gods (Kapelrud). See H. Klengel, "Der
Wettergott von Ḥalab," *JCSt*, XIX (1965), 87-93; *BHH*, II, 620; *RGG*, III, 7-8.

epithet "Aliyan" designates him as the "mighty" or "powerful" one, "ruler." His power is also shown by the title "Prince Baal," or by the extended form "prince, lord of the earth." [19] Although El is called father of Baal (Text 51, v. 90), Baal is also considered the son of Dagon (Text 49, i. 24). Such inconsistencies point to the gradual growth of the pantheon. The dwelling place of Baal is Mount Zaphon, north of Ugarit. Baal, too, is king; or, more precisely, he must gain his kingdom, secure it by building a temple-palace, and defend it against his enemies; he nevertheless loses it, only to rise as king once more at the end (Schmidt). Unlike El, he is not a creator; he is the preserver of creation, giver of all fertility, and representative of vegetation. When he falls into the hands of the god of death, nature languishes and all growth ceases until the shout "Aliyan Baal lives; the prince, lord of the earth, is here!" announces his return and the revival of nature. Like much else in the religion of Ugarit, it is uncertain whether this takes place annually, every seven years, or at irregular intervals.

Anat [20] is the sister and consort of Baal. She is called "virgin Anat" as an expression of her youth and her inexhaustible powers of life, love, and conception. One side of her nature is thus an exaggerated sexuality; the other is a lust for battle and bloodthirstiness. The latter is revealed in a description of her murderous rage in which she wades in blood up to her knees, nay, to her neck, walks over human skulls, while human hands fly about her like locusts, until she finally washes her hands in flowing blood before advancing to new deeds or atrocities ('nt, ii).

Yam is one of Baal's two opponents. The full form of his name, "Prince Sea, Ruler River," shows that the sea is his domain, since "river" is probably to be understood in the sense of "current." He contests Baal's kingdom by attacking the vegetation of the land with the power of the sea, together with the sea monsters Leviathan, Tannin, and the "twisted serpent," allied to Yam or identified with him.

Mot, "death," whose realm is maturity and death, drought and desert, death and the underworld, is Baal's other and more dreadful

---

[19] On the basis of this title, "zbl b 'l 'ars," II Kings 1:2 ff. has deliberately altered the name of the god of Ekron, changing "Baal-zebul" to "Baal-zebub," "lord of the flies."

[20] BHH, I, 91-92; RGG, I, 356; J. Aistleitner, "Die Anat-Texte aus Ras Schamra," ZAW, LVII (1939), 193-211; U. Cassuto, The Goddess Anath, 1953 (in Hebrew); H. Cazelles, "L'hymne ugaritique à Anat," Syria, XXXIII (1956), 49-57.

opponent, who actually defeats Baal for a limited time, so that nature languishes.

Ashtar[21] was also worshiped at Ugarit, although the texts say little about him. After Baal has been defeated by Mot, he is said to be Baal's successor; but he is not equal to the task, and must resign. This suggests that he may represent artificial irrigation. Like the South Arabian god of the same name, he appears also to be associated with Venus, the evening star. Human sacrifice was offered to him,[22] as the Moabite Mesha Inscription shows; line 17 mentions the god Ashtar-Chemosh instead of Chemosh, whose name occurs elsewhere in the inscription.[23] Either Chemosh (at Ugarit: *UT*, Glossary, 1263 *a*) is a manifestation of Ashtar, or both could simply be equated. The Ammonites apparently worshiped the same god, since the term used for him, "Milkom" (which also occurs in texts 17.11 and 124.17), is not a proper name but the title *"mlk"* with the suffix *"m"* (the definite article in South Arabian dialects), and Judg. 11:24 presupposes that Chemosh was worshiped in the region between the Arnon and the Jabbok, and therefore in Ammon. This equates Ashtar, Chemosh, and Mlkm, with an important bearing on the significance of the OT expression *"mōlek"* (cf. *c* below).

Astarte [24] corresponds to the Babylonian goddess Ishtar and is mentioned quite frequently in the cultic and liturgical texts from Ugarit. She is definitely a fertility goddess with a sexual cult; the warlike and astral aspects of Ishtar retreat into the background. There are numerous pictorial representations of female deities with pronounced sexual attributes; at least a part of these probably represent Astarte. That she also appears as the patron goddess of cities [25] shows her great importance for Canaanite religion.

Dagon[26] was worshiped from the third millennium on in Meso-

---

[21] A. Caquot, "Le dieu 'Athtar et les textes de Ras Shamra," *Syria*, XXXV (1958), 45-60; J. Gray, "The Desert God 'Attr in the Literature and Religion of Canaan," *JNES*, VIII (1949), 72-83.

[22] An episode in the *Life of St. Nilus* at Sinai (cf. J. P. Migne, *Patrologia graeca*, LXXIX [1865], 612, 681, 684) has been erroneously cited as evidence. The narrative is fanciful and without historical basis; the description of a camel sacrifice is in conflict with the rest of our knowledge of ancient Arabian ritual. See J. Henninger, "Ist der sogenannte Nilus-Bericht eine brauchbare religionsgeschichtliche Quelle?" *Anthropos*, LXXX (1955), 81-148.

[23] Cf. *KAI*, Nr. 181.

[24] *BHH*, I, 142-43; *RGG*, I, 661.

[25] At Ashteroth (Gen. 14.5 and elsewhere), Ashkelon or Gath (I Sam. 31:10), and Sidon (I Kings 11:5, 33; II Kings 23:13).

[26] *BHH*, I, 311-12; *RGG*, II, 18-19; *IDB*, I, 756; H. Schmökel, *Der Gott Dagan*, Dissertation, Heidelberg, 1928.

potamia (Mari) and Syria. In Syria, at least, he was considered the god of grain and bestower of fertility (cf. Judg. 16:23; I Sam. 5:2-5); a Phoenician seal shows a head of grain as his symbol. He was worshiped zealously at Ugarit, as is shown by the position of a temple dedicated to him next to that of Baal, his mention in cultic and liturgical texts, the dedication to him of two sacrificial stelae (texts 69 and 70), and the use of his name as an element in personal names. In Palestine, he was a major god of the Philistine region, with temples at Gaza (Judg. 16:23) and Ashdod (I Sam. 5:1-5), as well as elsewhere.

Resheph [27] was worshiped from the third or second millennium on, especially in the Canaanite region, but also far off in Asia Minor and Egypt, as well as at Ugarit, as his appearance in cultic and liturgical texts and in personal names demonstrates. In him we find a combination of destructive violence, like the Babylonian god Nergal, and beneficence, which makes him a god of peace and prosperity (Karatepe Inscriptions).

Astral deities include the sun goddess Lady Shapash (at Ugarit, as in ancient South Arabia, the sun is considered a goddess; in the other Semitic religions, it is considered a god); the moon god Yeraḫ, the "illuminator of the heavens," whose marriage with Nikkal is recounted (text 77); and the gods of dawn and dusk, Shahar and Shalim, "lovely and beautiful," whose birth is described in text 52, and the second of whom was an important god of Canaanite Jerusalem (§ 11.2).

b) There were also numerous other deities; they are less prominent, or more likely have only local significance, or appear as servants of the great gods without being themselves the objects of cultic worship. There is a question whether the clever god Koshar wa-Ḥassis, "skillful and shrewd," who was worshiped cultically, should be counted among the great gods. In any case, the lesser gods include the *rpum* (texts 122.4, 12; 123. 5-6; 124.8-9),[28] who eat and

---

[27] G. Fohrer, *Das Buch Hiob*, 1963, pp. 148-49; B. Grdseloff, *Les débuts du culte de Rechef en Égypte*, 1942; J. Leibovitch, "Quelques nouvelles représentations du dieu Rechef," *Annales du Service des Antiquités de l'Égypte*, XXXIX (1939), 145-60; F. Vattioni, "Il dio Resheph," *Annali dell' Instituto Universitario Orientale di Napoli*, NS XV (1965), 39-74; W. D. van Wijngaarden, "Karakter en voorstellingswijze van den god Rejef," *Oudheidk. Med. Rijksmuseum van Oudh. te Leiden*, NR X:1 (1929), 28-42.

[28] A. Caquot, "Les Rephaim ougaritiques," *Syria*, XXXVII (1960), 75-93; A. Jirku, "Rapa'u, der Fürst der Rapa'uma—Rephaim," *ZAW*, LXXVII (1965), 82-83. In Israel, they were historicized as a pre-Israelite race of giants inhabiting Palestine (Gen. 14:5 and elsewhere) and then reduced to spirits of the dead (Isa. 14:9 and elsewhere).

drink for seven days in the palace of El (texts 121.ii.4; 122.1-4, 8-12; 123.23; 124.21-24). If their name is connected with the verb "to heal," they were considered gods of healing. Gepen wa-Ugar, "vineyard and field," are mentioned as a pair of messengers serving Baal (or only a single messenger may be intended, since double names can refer to a single figure). Another pair, Qadesh wa-Amrar, "holy and blessed," is mentioned as servants of Asherah (again, a single figure may be meant). Other minor divine beings include the Kasharat goddesses, who appear on joyous occasions; the Weeping Woman *(bkyt)* and the Lamenting Woman *(mšspdt)*, who appear at times of death and disaster; and the healing fairy *š'tqt,* who can conjure diseases away.

Other more or less widespread gods, some of whom are mentioned in the Ugaritic texts, include Betel,[29] Eshmun,[30] Horon,[31] Yw,[32] Koshar, Melqart of Tyre,[33] Mikal,[34] Ṣedeq (at Jerusalem),[35] Ṣelach,[36] Ṣid,[37] and the god of Tabor.[38] Later still other gods were added. Scholars have suggested the existence of other deities with varying degrees of probability: Bezeq in the city of the same name

[29] O. Eissfeldt, "Der Gott Bethel," *ARW,* XXVIII (1930), 1-30 (= his *Kleine Schriften,* I [1962], 206-33); J. P. Hyatt, "The Deity Bethel and the Old Testament," *JAOS,* LIX (1939), 81-98; for a different view, see R. Kittel, "Der Gott Beth'el," *JBL,* XXIV (1925), 123-53; *idem,* "Zum Gott Bet'el," *ZAW,* XLIV (1926), 170-72. Originally this god probably represented the deified sanctuary; for another example, see A. Alt, "Ein neuer syrischer Gott," *ZAW,* L (1932), 87-89 (the "god of the dwelling-place").

[30] W. F. Albright, "The Syro-Mesopotamian God Šulman-Ešmun and Related Figures," *AfO,* VII (1931), 164-69.

[31] J. Gray, "The Canaanite God Horon," *JNES,* VIII (1949), 27-34.

[32] J. Gray, "The Canaanite God *Yw* in the Religion of Canaan," *JNES,* XII (1953), 278-83. The name occurs as a doubtful reading in the badly damaged text *'nt* pl. x. iv. 14; it has no connection whatsoever with Yahweh, but may be connected with *Ieuō* of Byblos, mentioned by Philo Byblius. On Ya'u or Yawi, see § 6.1.

[33] R. Dussaud, "Melqart," *Syria,* XXV (1946/48), 205-30; H. Seyrig, "Antiquités Syriennes," *ibid.,* XXIV (1944/45), 62-80. Melqart exhibits some similarities to the Ugaritic god Mot.

[34] L. H. Vincent, "Le baal cananéen de Beisan et sa parèdre," *RB,* XXXVII (1928), 512-43.

[35] W. W. Graf Baudissin, *Adonis und Esmun,* 1911, pp. 247-48; R. Kittel, *Geschichte des Volkes Israel,* I, 5th and 6th eds. [1923], 436. Note the names Adoniṣedeq, Malkiṣedeq, and Ṣadoq (Adoni-zedek, Melchizedek, Zadok) found at Jerusalem. On Ṣedeq and Shalim, see Ps. 85:11 (English: 85:10), where "Shalim" has turned into *"šālôm."*

[36] M. Tsevat, "The Canaanite God Ṣälaḥ," *VT,* IV (1954), 41-49.

[37] Baudissin, *Adonis und Esmun,* pp. 260, 275, 278; E. Meyer, "Untersuchungen zur phönikischen Religion," *ZAW,* XLIX (1931), 8.

[38] O. Eissfeldt, "Der Gott des Tabor und seine Verbreitung," *ARW,* XXXI (1934), 14-41 (= his *Kleine Schriften,* II [1963], 29-54): Baal-Tabor.

(*chirbet ibzīq*) ,[39] Gish (Gilgamesh) ,[40] Kinaru/Kinneret,[41] and others.

c) In many cases we are apparently dealing with titles; it cannot be determined precisely what deities they applied to. Such titles include "Baalat" [42] and "Elyon." [43] The OT term *mōlek* (Lev. 18:21; 20:2-5; II Kings 23:10; Jer. 32:35; LXX occasionally renders as *"moloch,"* hence the alternative English forms "Molech" and "Moloch") should probably be included in this category, although on the basis of Latin and Punic inscriptions from North Africa, Eissfeldt prefers to interpret the term as an expression for child sacrifice rather than as a divine name, which would mean that the sacrifice of firstborn children had a legitimate place in Yahwism until the Deuteronomic reform.[44] The idiom "play the harlot after Molech" (Lev. 20:5) does not fit a kind of sacrifice. Many objections to this interpretation have therefore rightly been made,[45] although these objections cannot prove that the expression is a divine name. We are more likely dealing with the word *"melek,"* "king," used as a title and, like other words pertaining to alien religions, vocalized after the pattern of *"bōšet,"* "shame." [46] The god referred to could be Ashtar, to whom children were sacrificed (cf. *a* above) , or one of his local manifestations.

d) To determine the particular nature of the Canaanite pantheon, we must first investigate the relationship between El and Baal, the two most important gods. Both count as kings, though with an im-

[39] H. W. Hertzberg, "Adonibesek," *JPOS*, VI (1926) , 213-21 (= his *Beiträge zur Traditionsgeschichte und Theologie des Alten Testaments*, 1962, pp. 28-35) .
[40] B. Maisler, "Zur Götterwelt des alten Palästina," *ZAW* L (1932) , 86-87.
[41] A. Jirku, "Gab es eine palästinisch-syrische Gottheit Kinneret?" *ZAW*, LXXII (1960) , 69; *idem*, "Der kyprische Heros Kinyras und der syrische Gott Kinaru (m) ," *FF*, XXXVII (1963) , 211.
[42] *BHH*, I, 176; *RGG*, I, 806.
[43] R. Lack, "Les origines de 'Elyôn, le Très-Haut, dans la tradition cultuelle d'Israel," *CBQ*, XXIV (1962) , 44-64; R. Rendtorff, "El, Ba'al und Jahwe," *ZAW*, LXXVIII (1966) , 277-91.
[44] O. Eissfeldt, *Molk als Opferbegriff im Punischen und Hebräischen und das Ende des Gottes Moloch*, 1935. In *Neue keilalphabetische Texte aus Ras Schamra-Ugarit*, 1965, p. 14, he also calls Ugaritic text 2004 a liturgy for the *mlk* sacrifice (*dbḥ mlk*) ; but the next line goes on to speak of *dbḥ ṣpn*, without referring to a kind of sacrifice.
[45] A. Bea, "Kinderopfer für Moloch oder für Jahwe?" *Bibl*, XVIII (1937) , 95-107; E. Dhorme, "Le dieu Baal et le dieu Moloch dans la tradition biblique," *AnSt*, VI (1956) , 57-61; A. Jirku, "Gab es im Alten Testament einen Gott Molek (Melek) ?" *ARW*, XXXV (1938) , 178-79; M. J. Mulder, *Kanaänitische goden in het Oude Testament*, 1965, 57-64.
[46] A suggestion made long ago by A. Geiger, *Urschrift und Übersetzungen der Bibel*, 1857, pp. 299-308.

portant difference: El is king, Baal becomes king. El's kingship is timeless, changeless, static; Baal's kingship is dynamic, for he gains it, secures it by building a temple, defends it against enemies, loses it, and arises as king once more (Schmidt). Baal's struggle with his enemies for the kingship also decides the fate of man, for whom the rule of Yam or Mot means death, while the rule of Baal, the preserver of creation, means life. El and Baal apparently live peacefully side by side, each having royal rank and status. El is not monarchically superior; neither has Baal displaced him from his sovereign position. For all that, the juxtaposition of these two gods, as well as many absurdities or contradictions in the religion of Ugarit, are best explained historically, on the theory that an earlier group around El and Asherah, corresponding to the Babylonian and South Arabian pantheon, has been combined with a later West Semitic group around Baal, Anat, and Mot (Baumgartner).

One striking feature is the markedly sexual element not only of goddesses but also of gods—not excepting El and, above all, Baal. Many deities exhibit two widely divergent aspects, alone or in combination with another deity. El is the creator and Baal the preserver of creation; Mot is the destroyer. Anat both gives birth to the nations and destroys men. A similar relationship between destruction and creation is found in the Indian pantheon (Shiva—Kali/Durga). In India, however, the two counterbalance each other, while in the Canaanite religion creation is successfully preserved. In the Old Testament, Yahweh is conceived of exclusively as creator; destruction is seen as resulting not from conflict within or between gods, but from human sin.

That Baal should temporarily fall into the power of Mot and then rise again can also be understood as a double aspect. Scholars have therefore been happy to add Baal to the series of dying and rising gods that purportedly begins with the Sumerian god Tammuz (Dumuzi). Recently, however, serious objections have been raised against the view that Tammuz or Marduk are dying and rising gods[47]—partially in the light of new texts. Such an assumption with respect to Baal must therefore be considered questionable, the more so because views concerning the structure and meaning of the crucial

[47] O. R. Gurney, "Tammuz Reconsidered," *JSS*, VII (1962), 147-60; F. R. Kraus, "Zu Moortgat, 'Tammuz,'" *WZKM*, LII (1953/55), 36-80; W. von Soden, "Gibt es ein Zeugnis dafür, dass die Babylonier an die Wiederauferstehung Marduks geglaubt haben?" *ZA*, LI (NF XVII [1955]), 130-66; L. Vanden Berghe, "Réflexions critiques sur la nature de Dumuzi-Tammuz" *NC*, VI (1954), 298-321; E. M. Yamauchi, "Tammuz and the Bible," *JBL*, LXXXIV (1965), 283-90.

Baal myth are widely divergent. For the time being, the only sure evidence for dying and rising gods dates from the Christian era; therefore the significance of Mot's victory over Baal and Baal's reappearance must remain an open question. Perhaps Baal can be termed a vegetation god, who withers and is then restored.

3. *Canaanite myths and legends. a*) The most extensive cycle of myths from Ugarit pertains to Baal. The texts, however, are fragmentary, in some cases poorly preserved, and uncertain as to sequence; we are apparently dealing with a complex of several myths. Interpretations therefore diverge widely.[48] The situation with the other Ugaritic texts is no different.

According to one episode of the complex, Yam, having built a palace, tries to make himself lord over all the gods; he demands that they hand over Baal, who opposes him. Baal inspires new courage in the gods, who were ready to give in; only El is prepared to hand him over. Then Koshar wa-Ḥassis promises him victory and gives him two magic clubs, which rout Yam. The outcome reads: Yam is dead, Baal is king (text 68.32).

Another episode deals with the construction of a temple palace for Baal, who seeks thereby to gain recognition for his kingship. Both Anat and Asherah exert themselves to gain El's consent. Once El has given permission for the building to be constructed, Koshar wa-Ḥassis does the building. When it is finished, it is dedicated with great sacrifices and a festal banquet of the gods. Baal alone will now rule, "that gods and men may grow fat, indeed, that the multitude of the earth may grow fat" (text 51.vii.49).

A third episode deals with Baal's struggle for dominion with Mot, the god of death. Baal submits to Mot's threats and descends to him in the underworld, whence messengers bring the announcement of his death to the face of the earth. Despite Baal's sojourn in the underworld, Anat seeks out his body and buries it on Mount Zaphon. Ashtar is installed as the new king, but he proves a failure.

[48] U. Cassuto, "Baal and Mot in the Ugaritic Texts," *IEJ*, XII (1962), 77-86; J. Gray, "The Hunting of Baal," *JNES*, X (1951), 146-55; V. Jacobs and I. Rosensohn, "The Myth of Môt and 'Al'eyan Ba 'al," *HThR*, XXXVIII (1945), 77-109; A. S. Kapelrud, "Ba'al's kamp met havets fyrste i Ras Sjamra-Tekstene," *NTT*, LXI (1960), 241-51; F. Løkkegaard, "The House of Baal," *AcOr* (Copenhagen), XXII (1955), 10-27; *idem,* "Baals Fald," *DTT*, XIX (1956), 65-82; J. Obermann, "How Baal Destroyed a Rival," *JAOS*, LXVII (1947), 195-208; *idem, Ugaritic Mythology,* 1948; S. E. Loewenstamm, "The Ugaritic Fertility Myth—the Result of a Mistranslation," *IEJ*, XII (1962), 87-88; W. Schmidt, "Baals Tod und Auferstehung," *ZRGG*, XV (1963), 1-13.

In the meantime, Anat's yearning for Baal increases. When Mot refuses to give him back, she takes vengeance on him by cracking him like grain, winnowing him, burning him, grinding him, and strewing him on the ground, where the birds devour him. Because Baal has taken the rain with him, the earth suffers. Then El dreams that "the heavens rain oil and the streams overflow with honey" (text 49.iii.6-7, 12-13) —a sign that Baal lives. He slays the sons of Asherah and, after seven years, fights a fierce battle with Mot, who reappears once more, finally conquering Mot.

b) The Legend of Aqhat [49] begins by telling how King Danel requests and is granted a son (Aqhat), and later receives from Koshar wa-Hassis a bow that he gives to his son. Anat demands the bow, but Aqhat refuses to give it to her. This angers her so that she has him killed, destroying the fertility of the earth. When Danel receives news of the death of his son, he is able to persuade Baal to seek out the murderers. The search is fruitless, and so Danel's daughter arms herself and finds out the murderer, who boasts drunkenly of his deed. The text mentions a continuation and then breaks off. It may be that the girl goes on to slay the murderer. In some fashion fertility must also be restored to the earth.

c) The Legend of Keret [50] tells how King Keret, who has lost his wife and children, wins a new wife, the daughter of the king of Udm, who bears him many sons and daughters. Then he falls seriously ill, until El's magical rites break the power of death, so that Keret regains his health and his throne. One of Keret's sons requests him to abdicate in his favor; Keret calls upon some of the gods to punish his son. This text, too, is probably incomplete. In any event, its subject matter is the situation of a king who is apparently semidivine and immortal, but in reality is sick and incapable of ruling. It also deals with the question of a father's being succeeded or supplanted by his son.

d) Other Ugaritic texts describe the marriage of the moon god Yerah with Nikkal, and the conception and birth of the gods Shahar and Shalim. In addition, there is a considerable number of frag-

---

[49] U. Cassuto, "Daniel et son fils dans la tablette II D de Ras Shamra," *REJ*, NS V (1940), 125-51; J. Obermann, *How Daniel Was Blessed with a Son*, 1946.
[50] K.-H. Bernhardt, "Anmerkungen zur Interpretation des KRT-Textes von Ras Schamra-Ugarit," *WZ Greifswald*, V (1954/55), 102-21; U. Cassuto, "The Seven Wives of King Keret," *BASOR*, CXIX (1950), 18-20; H. L. Ginsberg, *The Legend of King Keret*, 1946; J. Gray, *The Krt Text in the Literature of Ras Shamra*, 2nd ed., 1964; J. Pedersen, "Die Krt-Legende," *Berytus*, VI (1941), 63-105.

ments, some of them unpublished.[51] At Ugarit and in the rest of
Canaan there were surely other myths and legends. For several of
them we can at least determine the subject matter. This holds true
especially for the sanctuary and cult legends that have been incorporated into Genesis: the revelation of El Roi (Genesis 16); the
replacement of human sacrifice by animal sacrifice at a sanctuary
whose name is no longer recorded (Genesis 22:1 ff.); the discovery of
holy places at Bethel and Penuel on the Jabbok (Gen. 28:10 ff.;
32:25 ff.). Historical reminiscences like the memory of a looting
expedition by people from the East and of King Melchizedek of
Jerusalem were preserved (and incorporated in Genesis 14). In addition, regulations like the rule against combining two different
things (Lev. 19:19) or the rule governing the fruit of newly planted
trees (Lev. 19:23-25) can well be Canaanite, at least in subject
matter.

4. *Canaanite worship and religious life.* The Canaanite cult was
highly developed. It was carried out at numerous sacred sites on the
"high places" with their green trees (for Moab, see Isa. 15:2; 16:12;
for Israel, see I Kings 3:2; II Kings 12:4 [English: 12:3]; and elsewhere), where burial rites apparently also took place.[52] In ancient
times these sacred high places were officially recognized in Israel
(I Sam. 9:12); they were brought into disrepute, however, by prophetical polemic and finally by Deuteronomistic theology. More important were the temples,[53] whose construction was part of the recognition given a high god. In them the cult reached its climax with
festal eating and drinking (cf. Judg. 9:27 and the Ugaritic descriptions of the banquet of the gods). Excavations in Syria and in the
pre-Israelite cities of Palestine have brought such temples to light.
Their modifications and renovations show how they were adapted
to varying needs over the course of generations. Besides minor
cultic utensils, used primarily for the offering of sacrifice, the sanctuaries were outfited with altars,[54] images or symbols of the gods,[55]

[51] See the latest survey by O. Eissfeldt, *Neue keilalphabetische Texte aus Ras Schamra-Ugarit*, 1965 (his earlier survey is now available in his *Kleine Schriften*, II [1963], 330-415).
[52] *BHH*, II, 736-37; *IDB*, II, 602-4; W. F. Albright, "The High Place in Ancient Palestine," *VTSuppl*, IV (1957), 242-58; L. H. Vincent, "La notion biblique du haut lieu," *RB*, LV (1948), 245-78.
[53] *BHH*, III, 1940-41; *RGG*, VI, 681-84; *IDB*, IV, 560-68.
[54] *BHH*, I, 63-65; *RGG*, I, 251-53; *IDB*, I, 96-100.
[55] *BHH*, I, 249-50; *IDB*, II, 673-75. Examples from Palestine include representations of Baal from Tell ed-Duweir and of Anat from Beth-shan.

masseboth[56] representing a deity (some were officially recognized in Israel, as at the sanctuary of Arad;[57] they were legitimized by being reinterpreted, as in Exod. 24:4; later, however, there was increasingly violent opposition to them, e.g. Exod. 23:24; Deut. 7:5) , and sometimes also a wooden post, called an asherah, which symbolized the goddess of the same name (cf. Judg. 6:25; I Kings 14:23) .[58]

According to the Legend of Aqhat and the Legend of Keret, in the early heroic period performance of the cult was primarily the right of the king. In the period for which historical data are available, however, the king had only minor functions.[59] At Ugarit, the cult was carried out by a large group, hierarchically organized: a high priest, twelve families of priests *(khnm)*, subordinate to these a group of sacred persons not further defined *(qdšm)*, and apparently also a group of singers *(šrm)*. In addition, the lists mention many craftsmen who were obviously in the service of the temple. The education of the priests was supported by a school for scribes and a library of clay tablets, located near the temples of Dagon and Baal.

The variety of sacrifices offered can be seen in the different terms used for them; some of these are identical with those in the OT, or correspond in practice: *šrp*, "burnt offering" (not found in most Semitic cults; borrowed from the indigenous population in Syria and Palestine) ; *dbḥ*, "sacrifice" (OT *zbḥ*) ; *šlm*, meaning uncertain, as in the OT (possibly "concluding sacrifice" [60]) ; *ndr*, "vow." Sacrifices seem also to have been offered as a collective act of propitiation (text 2) ; disaster was considered the consequence of ethical or cultic sin, consciously or unconsciously committed, which had to be acknowledged and expiated,[61] a practice similar to the communal laments and penances of the Israelites. Caution is warranted, however, in comparing the Ugaritic evidence with that of the OT, because there are no parallels in the OT to some of the Ugaritic ex-

[56] *BHH*, II, 1169; *IDB*, III, 815-17. A massebah is not a sacred stone kept in its natural form and sacred as such, but a stone whose significance lies in having been shaped to represent a deity.

[57] There is an Israelite sanctuary with three masseboth within the fortress; see Y. Aharoni and R. Amiran, "Arad, a Biblical City in Southern Palestine," *Archaeology*, XVII (1964) , 43-53.

[58] *BHH*, I, 136-37; *RGG*, I, 637-38; *IDB*, I, 251-52.

[59] Cf. Melchizedek of Jerusalem (Gen. 14:17-18) .

[60] G. Fohrer in G. Kittel, ed., *Theological Dictionary of the New Testament*, VII, 1022-23.

[61] A. Caquot, "Un sacrifice expiatoire à Ras Shamra," *RHPhR*, XLII (1962) , 201-11; Gray, pp. 204-7. See also the letter of Ribaddi of Byblos published by J. A. Knudtzon, *Die El-Amarna-Tafeln*, 1908-15, no. 137.33.

pressions and practices, and conversely the cultic acts of the OT do not always have Ugaritic equivalents.[62]

As in the OT, the most common sacrificial animals are cattle, sheep, goats, and pigeons. Wild species like the gazelle and ibex were also considered suitable for sacrifice. When lists of such animals occur in mythological texts, however, the question arises as to whether and when such regulations were in force. Excavations in the Late Neolithic stratum at Gezer and the Bronze Age stratum at Tirzah show that pigs were sacrificed in Palestine, probably since the pre-Semitic period. The extent to which human sacrifice was practiced in the Canaanite religion is still unknown.[63] While it is not mentioned at Ugarit, it is presupposed by the OT, and had not yet died out by the third century B.C. among the Carthaginians of North Africa. At least the cults of Ashtar and related gods seem to have involved child sacrifice (cf. 2a), though Genesis 22 confirms its early replacement by animal sacrifice at an unknown sanctuary. Not unknown was the practice of using children for a foundation sacrifice, offered at the laying of a cornerstone or at the completion of a building (I Kings 16:34, on which Josh. 6:26 depends). Such remains have been discovered in the course of excavation, but the high rate of infant mortality raises the question whether children who were already dead may not often have been substituted for the actual sacrifice.

Canaanite religion, being a fertility cult, was familiar with the sacral prostitution that was widespread throughout the ancient Near East.[64] It must be understood from the perspective of an agricultural religion and its needs. In such a religion it served to strengthen the deity and keep the powerful forces of life active. This custom nevertheless was a weak point of Canaanite religion, the more so since, as in Babylonia, the distinction between sacral and secular prostitution was easily obliterated.

Dance also played some rôle in the cult.[65] The OT records the festal dance of the girls at Shiloh (Judg. 21:21), the vintage dance

---

[62] See, for example, D. Kellermann, " 'āšām in Ugarit?" *ZAW*, LXXVI (1964), 319-22 and the arguments against Dussaud and Gaster in Gray, pp. 196 ff.

[63] *BHH*, II, 1191; *RGG*, IV, 867-68; *IDB*, IV, 153-54; see also F. M. T. de Liagre Böhl, "Das Menschenopfer bei den alten Sumerern," in his *Opera minora*, 1953, pp. 163-73; J. Henninger, "Menschenopfer bei den Arabern," *Anthropos*, LIII (1958), 721-801.

[64] *BHH*, III, 1948-49; *RGG*, V, 643-45; *IDB*, III, 931-34; W. Krebs, "Zur kultischen Kohabitation mit Tieren im Alten Orient," *FF*, XXXVII (1963), 19-21.

[65] *BHH*, III, 1931-32; *IDB*, I, 760-61.

of men (Judg. 9:27), and processional dances like that when the ark was brought to Jerusalem (II Sam. 6:14).

Some of the Ugaritic texts give us an idea of the prayers and hymns. There is a prayer directed to El in time of need (text 107), a hymn to the sun goddess (text 62), and the originally Canaanite texts incorporated in the OT: Pss. 19:2-7 (Eng. 19:1-6); 29; and parts of 68. Such poetry, like the myths, was recited in the cult with music and singing, as the regulations in text 52 show. The Ethan, Heman, Calcol, and Darda mentioned in I Kings 5:11 (Eng. 4:31) were probably Canaanite singers.[66]

As befits a fertility religion, the entire ritual was markedly influenced by magical conceptions; the forms often appear unrefined and immature. One must not forget, however, that the Canaanite religion had its own set of values, which were determined by its relationship to nature. It produced an intimacy between man and nature that must have been attractive to nomads settling in Palestine. It sought to elevate and establish human life by involving man in the preservation of the world and compensating for his dependence on the deity by considering him the helper of the gods. Among the early Israelites, therefore, this religion was able to reinforce the element of reciprocity between God and man and make possible the element of God's rule as king.

§ 4 THE RELIGION OF THE EARLY ISRAELITES IN PALESTINE

A. ALT, Die Landnahme der Israeliten in Palästina, 1925 (= his Kleine Schriften zur Geschichte des Volkes Israel, I [1953], 89-125; English: Essays on Old Testament History and Religion, 1966, pp. 133-70); idem, "Erwägungen über die Landnahme der Israeliten in Palästina," PJB, XXXV (1939), 8-63 (= his Kleine Schriften, I [1953], 126-75); M. NOTH, "Gilead und Gad," ZDPV, LXXV (1959), 14-73; J. VAN DER PLOEG, "Les anciens dans l'Ancien Testament," in Festschrift Junker, 1961, pp. 175-91; H. H. ROWLEY, From Joseph to Joshua, 1950; M. WEIPPERT, Die Landnahme der israelitischen Stämme, 1967; see also the various histories of Israel.

1. The occupation and its consequences. The occupation of Palestine by the Israelites was not the accomplishment of all Israel under a single leader; it took place in several stages over a considerable period of time. The patriarchal clans, whose territorial narratives constitute the nucleus of the traditions recorded in Genesis 12 ff.,

---

[66] See CBL, 294-95, 491.

probably settled down gradually as early as the fourteenth century. The major portion of the Israelites followed, primarily in the thirteenth century; once in Palestine, they were organized as a group of tribes. Their immigration apparently took place in four waves, corresponding, so to speak, to the four original tribes named after Jacob's wives and their maidservants: Leah from the south, Zilpah from the southeastern Transjordan, Rachel from the same region, and finally Bilhah from an unknown direction. The occupation narrative of the central or Rachel group, having undergone much revision, is now found in the Joshua tradition, with its few hero sagas and its numerous etiological sagas referring to the Palestinian situation.[1] It has displaced the tradition of how the Moses group established themselves in the settled territory west of the Jordan. This latter group arrived in Palestine toward the end of the thirteenth century at the earliest. Numbers 13–14, which tells how the tribe of Caleb occupied the city of Hebron, shows that still other nomads were infiltrating. These and other narratives or brief notices testify to the diversity of the historical events.

It is seldom possible to make out details, which explains why there has been so much discussion of whether the occupation took place peacefully or involved much fighting.[2] The answer probably differs for different regions and periods. A survey of the later locations of the Israelite tribes shows that they often settled in those parts of Palestine that were then uninhabited or only thinly populated. Where they laid claim to land that was still uncleared and therefore ownerless, their settling was essentially peaceful, although there may have been occasional minor encounters with neighboring Canaanite city-states. Elsewhere, however, sizable battles must have taken place. The best evidence for such battles is not the destruction of cities in the last part of the thirteenth century: some, like Bethel or Tell Beit Mirsim, were destroyed by conflagrations; others, like Lachish, were not resettled at all for two hundred years after their destruction; still others, like Hazor, were too large and strong for a small group of Israelites. The possibilities to be considered in

---

[1] See S-F, § 30.
[2] Most unlikely is the recent thesis of G. E. Mendenhall, "The Hebrew Conquest of Palestine," *BA*, XXV (1962), 66-87, according to which there was no significant invasion of Palestine by large numbers of people, but rather a revolt of the peasants against the network of city-states that covered the land, caused by the religious movement of a small group of about seventy families after their flight from Egypt. For a more accurate picture, see J. B. Pritchard, "Arkeologiens plats i studiet av Gamla Testamentet," *SEA*, XXX (1965), 5-20.

such cases can best be seen by a study of Megiddo's situation.[3] The best evidence for major battles is the fact that the tribes of Reuben, Simeon, and Levi were almost totally exterminated, and that the tribe of Dan (and probably also Naphtali) was unable to hold its own against the superior force of the Canaanite and Philistines in the hill country west of the Jordan, and had to find new regions to settle in the north.

After they settled in Palestine, the nomadic organization of clans and tribes was out of date. In their new situation the clans and tribes turned into regional associations. A person no longer belonged to a clan or tribe by virtue of his birth; what mattered was his settling in a certain town or territory. Thus it became possible to incorporate members of other tribes and Canaanites; on the other hand, Israelites also came to settle in Canaanite cities. In addition, a new structure determined by economic considerations gradually came into being. The elders of the clan lost their influence; their place was taken by those who owned the most land. The latter reduced the local inhabitants with small or moderate property holdings to a state of dependency, occupied the official positions, and often developed into a kind of nobility. At first most of the Israelites were peasants living in closed communities; a portion of them finally arrived at a truly urban economy.[4] This is one of the reasons for the later enmity between city and countryside, to the extent that it was not rooted, like the antipathy of the rural population of Judah toward Jerusalem, in the fact that the majority of the city-dwellers were Canaanites.

2. *The encounter between nomadic and Canaanite religion.* The Israelite groups brought their clan religions with them to Palestine. Simple small sanctuaries were certainly laid out in or near the towns; the altar law in Exod. 20:24-26 may have applied to such installations. In addition, Israelites gained admittance to some Canaanite sanctuaries. The clan gods were soon linked to these sanctuaries rather than to the clan, which had now settled permanently; deities of the road became deities of specific places. As a consequence it became necessary to transplant the traditions con-

cerning the recipients of revelation, founders of cults, and inspired leaders to Palestinian soil and adapt them to the new situation. All that endured was what could still be relevant to the new way of life in Palestine. As a result, what lived on from the nomadic period was primarily the cults themselves and the names of their founders, while the cultic sagas, which had no connection with Palestine, fell into oblivion. Gradually even some of the cults died out, because they were not relevant to life in settled regions. Only some few were preserved in the body of Israelite tradition because they were associated with important sanctuaries.

The ancient cultic sagas were replaced by the sanctuary and cult legends of the various Canaanite sanctuaries, which were made to refer to the founders of the cults and their gods. This was the necessary consequence of joint use of the sanctuaries, and at the same time provided the religious basis and justification for such joint use.

Above all, at least in the case of sites sacred to El, the clan gods were equated with the local god. Tradition accordingly always locates the encounters of the patriarchs with El in Palestine. This, following the worship of clan gods, is the second stage of early Israelite religion. As a result, the tradition preserved the names of various local manifestations of El. The following sanctuaries deserve mention:

Beer-lahai-roi, in the Negeb, associated with El Roi, whose sanctuary legend has been incorporated into Gen. 16:7-14, and with whom the god of the Isaac clan was sometimes associated (cf. Gen. 24:62; 25:11b).

Beer-sheba,[5] associated with El Olam, whose sanctuary legend has been incorporated into Gen. 21:14-19, and with whom the gods of the Abraham and Isaac clans were associated (cf. Gen. 21:33; 26:23-25, a legitimation of the sanctuary).[6]

Mamre[7] was considered to be legitimized by Abraham's building an altar there (Gen. 13:18), and perhaps also by the theophanies in Genesis 15 and 18. Later, however, it was rejected, so that no sanctuary legend has been preserved. This rejection appears to be connected at least in part with a special tree mentioned in Gen. 18:4, 8 and in the plural elsewhere in the Masoretic text; the text also misleads the reader concerning the location by associating the trees with Hebron[8] (Gen. 13:18) and finally equating Mamre explicitly with Hebron (Gen. 23:19; 35:27). Thus Hebron, more acceptable to a later generation, was to replace Mamre. For the

[5] BHH, I, 211; RGG, I, 956-57; IDB, I, 375-76; W. Zimmerli, Geschichte und Tradition von Beerseba im Alten Testament, 1932.

[6] The inclusion of Jacob through Gen. 46:1-4 is secondary.

[7] BHH, II, 1135-36; IDB, III, 235; F. Mader, Mamre, 1957.

[8] BHH, II, 669-70; RGG, III, 110; IDB, II, 575-77.

64   The Religious Background

original situation, accordingly, we must see in El Shaddai (perhaps "El of the plain" [9]) the god of Mamre, not of Hebron.

Bethel,[10] associated with El Bethel, whose sanctuary legend has been incorporated into Gen. 28:10-22, and with whom the god of the Jacob clan was associated (cf. Gen. 31:5b, 13; 35:1 ff.).

Shechem[11] was the sanctuary of El Israel.[12]

Gen. 22:1-4, 19 contains what was originally a Canaanite cult legend telling how animal sacrifice replaced human sacrifice. Gunkel ingeniously associated this legend with a sanctuary called Jeruel or Jeriel, to be found in the wilderness of Judah.[13]

Penuel [14] on the Jabbok has been associated with the transjordanian Jacob group through reinterpretation of its ancient sanctuary and cult legend in Gen. 32:25-32.

Gilgal [15] in the Jordan valley, located east of Jericho according to Josh. 4:19, was likewise a pre-Israelite sanctuary; the local deity is never mentioned, however, nor can it be determined from the place name as in the case of Jeruel and Penuel. No patriarchal clan is associated with Gilgal, but rather the central Palestinian Rachel group or the Ephraimites together with the later Benjaminites, who took with them an ark that was first set up there (Josh. 4:18-19; 7:6; cf. § 10.1). The name of the cultic site derives from the "circle" of stones that delimited it. The twelve stones supposedly set up by Joshua were probably in fact stelae. Gilgal was therefore a stele sanctuary like those discovered by excavations at Gezer and Hazor.

The equation of the clan gods with El laid the groundwork for the borrowing of various aspects of Canaanite religion; later the further equation of El with Yahweh incorporated this material into Yahwism. It is not impossible that the names of some of the Israelite tribes should be interpreted as divine names. There is evidence for the use of "Gad" as an epithet meaning "(god of) good fortune" for various gods and goddesses in Syria and Palestine.[16] "Dan," with

[9] M. Weippert, "Erwägungen zur Etymologie des Gottesnamens 'Ēl Šaddaj," ZDMG, CXI (1961), 42-62; for a different view, see E. C. B. MacLaurin, "Shaddai," Abr-Nahrain, III (1961/62), 99-118.

[10] BHH, I, 231-32; RGG, I, 1095-96; IDB, I, 391-93.

[11] BHH, III, 1781-83; RGG, VI, 15; IDB, IV, 313-15.

[12] See H. Seebass, Der Erzvater Israel und die Einführung der Jahweverehrung in Kanaan, 1966.

[13] H. Gunkel, Genesis, 6th ed., 1964, ad loc. According to II Chron. 20:16, Jeruel forms part of the wilderness between Tekoa and En-gedi. The association of the narrative with Moriah (Gen. 22:2), identified by II Chron. 3:1 with the mountain on which the Jerusalem Temple was built, is secondary.

[14] RGG, V, 217-18; IDB, III, 727.

[15] BHH, I, 572-73; RGG, II, 1577-78; IDB, II, 398-99; K. Galling, "Bethel und Gilgal," ZDPV, LXVI (1943), 140-55; LXVII (1944/45), 21-43; H.-J. Kraus, "Gilgal," VT, I (1951), 181-99; J. Muilenburg, "The Ancient Site of Gilgal," BASOR, CXL (1955), 11-27; E. Sellin, Gilgal, 1917.

[16] This usage is best known from the Hauran, Phoenicia, and Palmyra; but

the meaning "ruler, judge," may have been the title of a Canaanite deity. "Asher" or "Ašer" may be a masculine counterpart of Asherah. "Zebulun" recalls the name "Baal-zebul." All this remains mere speculation, but in any case the process of assimilation and integration began very early, before the Palestinian Israelites became acquainted with Yahwism.[17]

Finally, there was yet another significance to the equation of the clan gods with El. It preserved the remnants of the ancient clan cults and the conceptions associated with them. Above all, when the sanctuaries at which these gods were worshiped were later adopted by Yahwism, the traditions about some of the founders of the clan religions became a part of the religion of Yahweh and were further elaborated in the new context, forging a continuity in Israel's history and relationship to Yahweh.

---

it is also found in place-names such as Baal-gad (Josh. 11:17) and Migdal-gad (Josh. 15:37).

[17] Because this period has left few traces in the tradition, many highly improbable hypotheses have been advanced: H. G. May, "The Evolution of the Joseph Story," *AJSL*, XLVII (1930/31), 83-93 (Joseph was originally the fertility god of Shechem); J. Morgenstern, "The Divine Triad in Biblical Mythology," *JBL*, LXIV (1945), 15-37 (the Israelites worshiped the North Semitic triad Eloah or Elyon [highest heaven], Shaddai [atmospheric heaven], and El [earth/sea]).

CHAPTER TWO: MOSAIC YAHWISM, THE FIRST INFLUENCE

§ 5 Traditions, Events, and Figures

E. AUERBACH, *Moses*, 1953; G. BEER, *Mose und sein Werk*, 1912; W. BEYER-LIN, *Herkunft und Geschichte der ältesten Sinaitraditionen*, 1961 (English: *Origins and History of the Oldest Sinaitic Traditions*, 1966); M. BUBER, *Moses*, 2nd ed., 1952 (English [translated from 1st ed.]: *Moses*, 1946); W. CASPARI, "Neuere Versuche geschichtswissenschaftlicher Vergewisserung über Mose," *ZAW*, XLII (1924), 297-313; D. DAUBE, *The Exodus Pattern in the Bible*, 1963; G. FOHRER, *Überlieferung und Geschichte des Exodus*, 1964; F. GIESEBRECHT, *Die Geschichtlichkeit des Sinaibundes*, 1901; H. GRESS-MANN, *Mose und seine Zeit*, 1913; C. A. KELLER, "Vom Stand und Aufgabe der Moseforschung," *ThZ*, XIII (1957), 430-41; S. E. LOEWENSTAMM, *The Tradition of the Exodus in Its Development* (Hebrew), 1965; E. MEYER, *Die Israeliten und ihre Nachbarstämme*, 1906; *Moïse, l'homme de l'alliance*, 1961; E. OSSWALD, *Das Bild des Mose in der kritischen alttestamentlichen Wissenschaft seit Julius Wellhausen*, 1962; H. SCHMID, "Der Stand der Moseforschung," *Judaica*, XXI (1965), 194-221; F. SCHNUTENHAUS, *Die Entstehung der Mosetraditionen*, Dissertation, Heidelberg, 1958; H. SEEBASS, *Mose und Aaron, Sinai und Gottesberg*, 1962; E. SELLIN, *Mose und seine Bedeutung für die israelitisch-jüdische Religion*, 1922; R. SMEND, *Das Mosebild von Heinrich Ewald bis Martin Noth*, 1959; P. VOLZ, *Mose und sein Werk*, 2nd ed., 1932; A. S. VAN DER WOUDE, *Uittocht en Sinaï*, 1961.

1. *Traditions concerning the beginnings of Yahwism*. The OT contains different views about the beginnings of Yahwism. The source stratum J traces the origin of Yahwism all the way back to the third generation of men: "At that time men [Samaritan: 'he,' viz., Enosh] began to call upon the name Yahweh" (Gen. 4:26).[1] He was thenceforth worshiped under this name. The source stratum N also uses the name "Yahweh" from the beginning. How the use of this name became established remains obscure; the name itself is not revealed, nor is its meaning explained. The men of that age or Enosh used it in this way, and that is the end of the matter. For J and N, therefore, it goes without saying that the god who spoke to all later generations and acted on their behalf is Yahweh. This

---

[1] F. Horst, "Die Notiz vom Anfang des Jahwekultes in Gen 4,26," in *Libertas christiana* (Delekat Festschrift), 1957, pp. 68-74. Horst sees here the integration of the creator god El with the cult god Yahweh.

also applies to Moses. In Exod. 3:16, J nevertheless expressly equates Yahweh with "the God of your fathers, the God of Abraham, of Isaac, and of Jacob." This identification already formed part of the tradition used by J, so that the link between Yahweh and the pre-Yahwistic clan gods equated with El was forged not by the narrator, but long before him. Of course J's statement in Gen. 4:26 is not true in the sense that Yahweh worship from the beginnings of mankind is certainly inconceivable. But it is true in the sense that the Mosaic period does not mark the appearance of a "new" and hitherto unknown god; instead, a god already worshiped elsewhere became henceforth the God of a band of Israelites.

The tradition attaches much more weight to the narratives of E than to the theory of J. These narratives transfer the origin of Yahwism to the southern part of the ancient Near East and consider it to be based on a revelatory event, in which a god hitherto unknown by name to the Israelites,[2] the "God of your fathers, the God of Abraham, the God of Isaac, and the God of Jacob" (Exod. 3:15), appears and reveals his name, which is known from this time forward. Exod. 3:14 adds an explanation of the meaning of God's name. The origin of this explanation is unclear. Exod. 3:15 follows directly upon 3:13, giving the desired answer to the question asked there, "What is his name?" Exod. 3:14 interrupts this continuity, introducing two additional statements by God. We are therefore compelled to see in 3:14a and 3:14b two admittedly very ancient interpolations, one of which may go back to E itself. It is no longer possible to determine whether E or a later hand is responsible for the well-known explanation of the name "Yahweh" through the statement " *'ehyeh 'ăšer 'ehyeh.*" In Exod. 6:2 ff., which again equates Yahweh with the God of the patriarchs, P states even more clearly than E that the name of Yahweh was revealed for the first time in the Mosaic period; for this reason he uses the formula of self-introduction. The importance of these traditions is increased by the association of Yahweh with the deliverance of the Israelites at the exodus and by the events at Sinai or the mountain of God. This raises the question of the historical background behind the tradition concerning these events.

[2] For differing views, see R. Abba, "The Divine Name Yahweh," *JBL*, LXXX (1961), 320-28; J. P. Hyatt, "Yahweh as 'the God of my Father,'" *VT*, V (1955), 130-36; S. Mowinckel, "The Name of the God of Moses," *HUCA*, XXXII (1961), 121-33.

2. *Historical development.* The OT tradition considers the events associated with the figure of Moses, which involve the exodus and the adoption of Yahwism by the refugees from Egypt, as fundamental to the period that followed. The details of these events, however, can be made out only in part or not at all. The reason is primarily that only a small fraction of the later people of Israel experienced them. The tradition nevertheless made them apply to the entire nation, so that traditions of other tribes have been added to the ancient narrative nucleus. OT scholarship has therefore long been concerned to analyze the traditions of the Mosaic period in order to illuminate the events and processes that were so important for the history of Israel's religion. In recent times these efforts have often led to negative results and general impugnment of the historical reliability of the traditions.

a) The question was raised whether the exodus narrative took shape in association with the annual celebration of the Passover. Pedersen, for instance, on the basis of Exodus 12–13, interpreted the entire body of Exodus 1–15 as a Passover festival legend, holding that it came into being over the course of centuries through an alternation of narrative and dramatic representation.[3] Noth adopted this theory for Exodus 1–13.[4] In this view the Passover ritual was primary; its sacrifice of the firstborn was the point of departure for the narrative concerning the apotropaic protection of the Israelites' firstborn and the slaying of the firstborn of the Egyptians. These interpretations are not correct, however. The regulations governing Passover, the Feast of Unleavened Bread, and the consecration of the firstborn (Exod. 12:1-20, 24-27*a*; 13:3-16) belong to the late source strata D and P, and could not have been the point of departure for the narrative that existed centuries earlier. Furthermore, the firstborn of animals were not sacrificed at the Passover,[5] especially since in the pre-Deuteronomic period, according to Exod. 22:29 (Eng. 22:30), this sacrifice was to be offered on the eighth day after birth. The protection of the Israelite firstborn and the slaying of the Egyptian cannot therefore be derived from the Passover. In addition, before Deut. 16:1-8 the Feast of Unleavened Bread was historicized in Exod. 23:15; 34:18 and associated with the exodus;

[3] J. Pedersen, "Passahfest und Passahlegende," *ZAW*, LII (1934), 161-75; *idem*, *Israel, Its Life and Culture*, III-IV (1940), 384-415, 728-37; this theory was already attacked by S. Mowinckel, "Die vermeintliche 'Passahlegende' Ex 1–15 in Bezug auf die Frage: Literarkritik und Traditionskritik," *StTh*, V (1951), 66-88.
[4] M. Noth, *Das zweite Buch Mose, Exodus*, 1959, pp. 70-77 (English: *Exodus*, 1962, pp. 87-93).
[5] This point is correctly made by E. Kutsch, "Erwägungen zur Geschichte der Passafeier und des Massotfestes," *ZThK*, LV (1958), 1-35; N. Nicolsky, "Pascha im Kulte des jerusalemischen Tempels," *ZAW*, XLV (1927), 174-76; R. de Vaux*, II, 390 (Eng. p. 489); J. A. Wilcoxen, "The Israelite Passover: Some Problems," *Biblical Research*, VIII (1963), 13-27.

the same does not hold true for the Passover, which furthermore lost all its importance some time after the occupation and was not restored until the Deuteronomic reform of the cult. Finally, the Passover ritual of N was not chosen for Exod. 12:21 because of interest in the Passover, but because it was a nomadic blood ritual. Exodus 1–15, then, does not represent a cult legend; it is based on historical reminiscences.

b) Mowinckel had termed the Sinai narrative a "description" or "reproduction" of a cultic festival.[6] Von Rad modified this thesis by suggesting that the narrative was the festival legend of the covenant renewal at the autumn festival at Shechem.[7] In this case it is not easy to explain why from the Exile on the Sinai narrative and the so-called "covenant concept" came instead to be associated with the Feast of Weeks. Above all, there is no record anywhere of a "covenant" renewal festival, nor can the existence of such a festival be derived from Exodus 19; Josh. 8:34; 24; Deuteronomy 27; 31, texts dating in part from a late period (Deuteronomy 27) or subject to revision (Joshua 24). The OT gives no cause to assume the existence of such an annual festival,[8] above all if the so-called "covenant concept" did not play an important rôle in the pre-Deuteronomic period (see § 8.3).

c) Interpretation of the exodus and Sinai narratives as festival legends leads scholars to separate them and ascribe both the traditions and the events to different groups of Israelites. A further cause of this is the schematic division of the Pentateuch into individual "themes," although only the Song of Moses (Exod. 15:1-19, a later interpolation) gives the impression of a major diversion falling between the exodus and the events that followed. When the Song of Moses is disregarded, it can be seen at once that we are dealing not with two "themes" but with a single complex. Even if the exodus and Sinai narratives had been transmitted in different contexts, this would not necessarily mean that they derive from different groups and have no historical background. Many complexes of ideas and traditions can retain their vitality only in certain situations or at certain times.[9] Traditio-historical analysis of the Sinai narrative shows that it was originally associated with the exodus narrative (Beyerlin); the converse also holds true (Fohrer). All the essential elements of the tradition are inseparable from the very outset: Moses' sojourn in Midian, the revelation at Sinai or the mountain of God, the deliverance promised there, the appointment of Moses to proclaim or carry out this deliverance, the reference to later events at Sinai, the exodus with its deliverance from pursuit (however the latter is to be explained), the journey to Sinai or the moun-

---

[6] S. Mowinckel, *Le décalogue*, 1927, p. 129.

[7] G. von Rad, *Das formgeschichtliche Problem des Hexateuch*, 1938 (= his *Gesammelte Studien zum Alten Testament*, 1958, pp. 9-86 [English: *The Problem of the Hexateuch, and Other Essays*, 1966, pp. 1-78]). Von Rad also suggests that the earliest form of the occupation tradition is to be found in Deut. 26:5 ff. as the festival legend of the Feast of Weeks at the sanctuary of Gilgal; on this question, see § 10.3.

[8] Cf. E. Kutsch, *Das Herbstfest in Israel*, Dissertation, Mainz, 1955.

[9] See A. Hultkrantz, "Configurations of Religious Beliefs," *Ethnos*, 1956, pp. 194-95.

70   Mosaic Jahwism, the First Influence

tain of God, and events there. The exodus and Sinai traditions constitute a
single complex.[10]

d) These considerations at the same time lead us to reject the view that,
on the basis of historical and traditio-historical analysis of the individual
traditions, attaches little importance to Moses if not condemning him to
complete insignificance; only the tradition of his burial place (which is
in fact completely unknown; cf. Deut. 34:6) revives the figures of Moses,
so that he gradually dominates the tradition. For the details of this approach
we refer the reader to the full retrospective studies of Osswald and Smend,
and, for the most recent developments, the presentation of Schmid. The
disintegration of the figure of Moses through analysis of the individual
traditions in isolation leads ultimately to the exclusion of Moses from the
growth and development of Yahwism, which, contrary to all religio-historical
probability, is claimed to be the product of accumulated traditions and
historical constellations.[11] In contrast to this approach, we must remain
alert to the total context of the individual traditions. If Moses, according
to the various individual analyses, was associated from the beginning with
the exodus,[12] with Midian, Kadesh, and the events at Sinai,[13] as well as
with the occupation of Transjordan,[14] it is perfectly clear that the Moses
tradition as a whole, which comprises a synthesis of exodus-Midian-Kadesh-
Sinai-occupation, is not so far from historical probability as is sometimes
supposed.

First, we may assume as a historical fact the sojourn in Egypt of
a group of nomads that for simplicity's sake will be called the
Moses host, after their later leader. This group must be distinguished from the Israelite tribes, most of which were already engaged in the occupation of Palestine; it must also be distinguished
from the "house of Joseph," since the Joseph novella constitutes a
secondary connecting link between the patriarchal and Mosaic traditions. The Moses host may not even have been of Aramean blood;
at least from the exodus on a great variety of non-Aramean ele-

[10] The observation that many OT texts mention only the exodus and occupation, but not Sinai, is not a sufficient counterargument. Recollection of the deliverance from Egypt was so fundamental that it was mentioned again and again.
It had many consequences, one of which was the commitment at Sinai, another
the occupation, the attainment of the goal set by the exodus. Failure to mention
Sinai does not mean that the texts are unacquainted with what happened there,
but that the commitment at Sinai did not play the rôle for them that is ascribed
to it today.

[11] K. Koch, "Der Tod des Religionsstifters," *KuD*, VIII (1962), 100-23; for
a contrary view, see F. Baumgärtel, *ibid.*, IX (1963), 223-33.

[12] A. H. J. Gunneweg, "Mose in Midian," *ZThK*, LXI (1964), 1-9; R. Smend,
Jahwekrieg und Stämmebund, 1963 (English: *Yahweh War & Tribal Confederation*, 1970).

[13] Beyerlin; Seebass.

[14] M. Noth, *Überlieferungsgeschichte des Pentateuch*, 2nd ed., 1960, pp. 172-91;
idem, *Geschichte Israels*, 5th ed., 1961, pp. 45 ff. (English: *History of Israel*,
2nd ed., 1961, p. 136).

ments attached themselves to it. According to Egyptian evidence, such groups of Asiatic nomads frequently sought refuge in Egypt in the period between 1500 and 1200 B.C., and the Egyptians brought 'Apiru back with them as prisoners and slaves.[15] There is also no reason to suspect the statements that the Moses host was sent to live in the land of Goshen (Wadi et-Tumelat) and that after some time they, like Egyptians, were forced to provide compulsory labor for the building projects of the Pharaoh, the more so since Ramses II (1301-1234) built the store cities Pithom and Raamses (Tanis) mentioned in Exod. 1:11, and used 'Apiru for the work. Such labor must have seemed the worst kind of oppression to the nomads.

Their circumstances were changed by the appearance of Moses,[16] one of their own people, born in Egypt and obviously not unfamiliar with Egyptian ways. His name is a component of theophorous Egyptian names, which designate their bearer as the son (ms) of a deity or represent him as the human likeness of the deity (". . . is born," e.g., Thut-mose or Ra-mses). Also historical is his marriage to an alien woman, which resulted in his having Jethro, a Midianite priest, as his father-in-law (J).[17] Another tradition (N) refers to Jethro as a Kenite, Hobab the son of Reuel; this is merely one of many instances in which persons or places are called by different names. It is probably due to N's having borrowed a tradition of the Kenites,[18] who were neighbors of the Israelites and known to be worshipers of Yahweh. Moses stayed temporarily in the land of Midian, east of the Gulf of Aqabah.[19] There or somewhere thereabouts he came to know the god Yahweh, most likely as an originally Midianite god. From Midian he brought to his suffering compatriots the promise of a land "flowing with milk and honey." Since J uses this phrase only from Exod. 3:8 on, it may go back to Moses or the Moses host, who were looking for a land of their own as prosperous as the land of Egypt.

This promise was the final incentive that caused the nomads to

[15] See the texts in M. Greenberg, The Ḫab/piru, 1955, pp. 56-57.
[16] BHH, II, 1239-42; RGG, IV, 1151-55; IDB, III, 440-50.
[17] BHH, II, 866; IDB, II, 896-97.
[18] BHH, II, 918, 940; RGG, III, 1243; IDB, III, 2, 6-7; H. Heyde, Kain, der erste Jahwe-Verehrer, 1965; B. Mazar, "The Sanctuary of Arad and the Family of Hobab the Kenite," Eretz-Israel, VII (1964), 1-5; JNES, XXIV (1965), 297-303; H. Schmökel, "Jahwe und die Keniter," JBL, LII (1933), 212-29; W. Vischer, Jahwe, der Gott Kains, 1929.
[19] BHH, II, 1214; RGG, IV, 939-40; IDB, III, 375-76; L. E. Binns, "Midianite Elements in Hebrew Religion," JThSt, XXXI (1929/30), 337-54; H. St. J. Philby, The Land of Midian, 1957.

escape. In the years 1234-1230 B.C. Egypt was under attack from various quarters; since the external situation was favorable, their attempt was successful. It is associated with the recollection of a miraculous experience: deliverance from the pursuing Egyptians at Lake Sirbonis on the Mediterranean coast.[20] The Song of Miriam[21] in Exod. 15:21, which certainly dates from the same period as the events themselves, attests to the deliverance and Yahweh's responsibility for it. Throughout the following centuries all Israel attached its own interpretation to this event, glorifying the God who had thereby shown Israel to be his people, who had crushed the power of Egypt and proven himself mightier than the other gods.

The historical development of Mosaic Yahwism was basically the same as the development of the clan religions of ancient times (§ 2.4). Like the so-called patriarchs, Moses was first and foremost a recipient of revelation, founder of a cult, and inspired leader of a nomadic (or semi-nomadic) group that achieved solidarity on the basis of its new religion and sought to realize the promise of territorial possession. The escape from Egypt took place under the aegis of this new religion. Its successful outcome, which was ascribed to Yahweh, was a major reason that Mosaic Yahwism did not remain a mere variant of the clan religions. In the deliverance from Egypt, which later always plays a crucial rôle in any discussion of the relationship between Yahweh and Israel, there was a sense of that irrational element that allowed Yahwism to progress from being the religion of a group of nomads to a world religion.

It seems that when the Moses host had escaped from Egypt they journeyed to the oasis of Kadesh (see Exod. 15:22 ff.; Judg. 11:16), about fifty miles south of Beer-sheba,[22] which was to serve as the base for their advance into Palestine. This plan failed, however, as a result of their defeat at the hands of the Amalekites (Num. 14:40 ff.). They even had to quit Kadesh, though not without taking along some of the priests of the famous sanctuary there; these were the Levites (see Exod. 32:26-29; Deut. 33:8-11).[23] These priests

[20] O. Eissfeldt, *Baal Zaphon, Zeus Kasios und der Durchzug der Israeliten durchs Meer*, 1932.
[21] *BHH*, II, 1219; *RGG*, IV, 962-63; *IDB*, III, 402.
[22] *BHH*, II, 917-18; *IDB*, III, 1-2.
[23] *BHH*, II, 1077-79; *RGG*, IV, 336-37; *IDB*, III, 880-81; recent studies include A. H. J. Gunneweg, *Leviten und Priester*, 1965; E. Nielsen, "The Levites in Ancient Israel," *ASTI*, III (1964), 16-27. The Levites were associated with Moses by representing him as a descendant of Levites (Exod. 2:1) and as ancestor of the Levitical priests (Judg. 18:30). For arguments to the contrary, see T. J. Meek, "Moses and the Levites," *AJSL*, LVI (1939), 113-20; Meek thinks Moses was a

became adherents of Yahwism either directly or by equating Yahweh with the deity of Kadesh. They brought with them their own form of obtaining an oracle by casting lots, became Moses' picked troops against the enemies of Yahweh, and in Palestine contributed significantly to the spread of Yahwism.

From Kadesh the Moses host journeyed to the mountain of Yahweh, which the OT refers to as Sinai (J), the mountain of God (E), or Horeb (especially Deuteronomy).[24] Since the tradition was obscure even as early as the period of the Israelite monarchy, and since there was no cult associated with the mountain that would have required precise transmission of its name and location, it cannot be located with certainty. At any rate, this was the site where the relationship between Yahweh and the Moses host was finally determined, constituting this host as the community of Yahweh's worshipers (see § 6.2).

The statement that the mountain of Yahweh was located in the southern part of the Sinai Peninsula[25] goes back to the fourth century c.e. The date itself is suspicious, since many attempts were being made in that period to localize sacred sites, with usually erroneous results. Furthermore, it is highly unlikely that the Moses host would have ventured into the vicinity of the Egyptian copper mines in this area, where they would have been in danger of running into Egyptian troops. The vicinity of Kadesh is also out of the question,[26] because no ancient tradition points to Kadesh. All the evidence in fact points to the territory of Midian; even Deut. 33:2-3; Judg. 5:4-5; Hab. 3:7; Ps. 68:9 (Eng. 68:8) refer to the region southeast rather than south of Palestine. If Yahweh was originally a Midianite god, his holy mountain must have been in Midianite territory or somewhere nearby. The itinerary in Num. 33:3-49 could also point this way, if its terminus was in fact Sinai, which would then lie in northwest Arabia.[27] One possibility is Chala' l-Bedr in northwest Arabia, since all the data in the tradition can be made to agree with this site.[28] The compara-

---

member of the tribe of Levi. On Dedan as the supposed place of origin of the Levites, see H. Grimme, "Der südarabische Levitismus und sein Verhältnis zum Levitismus in Israel," Le Muséon, XXXVII (1924), 169-99; R. de Vaux, " 'Lévites' minéens et lévites israélites," in Lex tua veritas (Junker Festschrift), 1961, pp. 265-73 (= Bible et orient, 1967, pp. 277-86).

[24] BHH, I, 594; II, 647; III, 1801-2; RGG, VI, 44-45; IDB, IV, 376-78.

[25] See the recent discussion by Y. Aharoni in B. Rothenberg, Y. Aharoni, and A. Hashimoni, Tagliot Sinai, 1957/58 (English: God's Wilderness, 1961).

[26] See the recent discussion by J. Gray, "The Desert Sojourn of the Hebrews and the Sinai-Horeb-Tradition," VT, IV (1954), 148-54; S. Mowinckel, "Kadesj, Sinai og Jahwe," Norsk Geografisk Tidsskrift, IX (1942), 1-32.

[27] M. Noth, "Der Wallfahrtsweg zum Sinai (4. Mose 33)," PJB, XXXVI (1940), 5-28.

[28] This suggestion was already made by W. J. Pythian-Adams, "The Mount of God," PEFQSt, 1930, pp. 135-49, 192-209; idem, "The Volcanic Phenomena of

tively great distance of this site from the central area of Midian might be a counterargument, except that in Exodus 18 J and E expressly state that Sinai or the mountain of God lay outside the main territory of the Midianites, who traveled to it (Exod. 18:5-6, 27); according to both source strata, Moses once crossed the steppe to get there (Exod. 3:1). The suggested location therefore has considerable support.

After a stay of some time at the mountain of Yahweh, the Moses host set out for Palestine in pursuance of their earlier plan. Their route took them through Transjordan, where Moses died before 1200. Deprived of their leader, the group continued across the Jordan and was absorbed into the group of tribes occupying central Palestine. From there Yahwism spread among the Israelites.

3. *The significance of Moses.* Tradition is correct in associating the beginnings of Israelite Yahwism with the figure of Moses. Both the exodus and the new religious understanding are inconceivable without him; he helped bring the events about, interpreted them brilliantly, and sought to keep alive the religious forces awakened by these events, guiding them into proper channels. Repeated efforts were therefore made in Israel to understand and depict Moses in light of his significance. But the description of him as a magician, miracle worker, priest, or prophet hardly does him justice,[29] any more than do many modern descriptions, which characterize him as one of the few truly great founding figures in the history of religions. That Yahwism achieved the status of a world religion is less the accomplishment of Moses than the result of a development over the course of centuries. On the other hand, Moses' rôle as founder of a religion can hardly be restricted to that of a prototype for the "office" of judge or prophet, nor can it be completely denied, in disregard of all observations in the history of religions.

Like the so-called patriarchs, Moses is a figure from an early culture, in which the totality of political, legal, social, and cultic activity is neither specialized and apportioned to different persons nor kept separate from the direct inspiration and enthusiastic action

the Exodus," *JPOS*, XII (1932), 86-103; for more recent discussion, see J. Koenig, "La localisation du Sinaï et les tradition des scribes." *RHPhR*, XLIII (1963), 2-31; XLIV (1964), 200-35; *idem*, "Itinéraires sinaïtiques en Arabie," *RHR*, CLCVI (1964), 121-41; *idem*, "Le Sinaï montagne de feu dans un désert de ténèbres," *ibid.*, CLXVII (1965), 129-55; see also H. Gese, "Tò dè Hagàr Sinà ŏros estín en tē̃ Arabía (Gal 4,25)," in *Das ferne und nahe Wort* (Rost Festschrift), 1967, pp. 81-94.

[29] For a different view, see J. R. Porter, *Moses and Monarchy*, 1963; according to Porter, Moses is depicted in terms of the Israelite monarchy.

of a man under the influence of the deity. Like the patriarchs, Moses must be understood as a receiver of revelation, founder of a cult, and inspired leader of a nomadic (or semi-nomadic) group. As such he founded a religion that, at its outset, resembled the early Israelite clan religions. It contained, however, a creative nucleus that was to go on developing in the ages that followed—not least in conflict with the existing religious elements, conflict that led either to rejection or integration—so that acquaintance with a deity who was originally a Midianite mountain god, joined with a nomadic clan religion, developed into a new faith of historic importance, a major religion.

§ 6 Mosaic Yahwism

G. FOHRER, "Das sogenannte apodiktisch formulierte Recht und der Dekalog," *KuD*, XI (1965), 49-74; K. GALLING, *Die Erwählungstraditionen Israels*, 1928; O. GRETHER, *Name und Wort Gottes im Alten Testament*, 1934; E. O. JAMES, "The Development of the Idea of God in the Old Testament," *ET*, XLVII (1935/36), 150-54; E. KUTSCH, "Gesetz und Gnade," *ZAW*, LXXIX (1967), 18-35; V. MAAG, "Das Gottesverständnis des Alten Testaments," *NThT*, XXI (1966/67), 161-207; H. H. ROWLEY, "Mose und der Monotheismus," *ZAW*, LXIX (1957), 1-21; C. F. WHITLEY, "Covenant and Commandment in Israel," *JNES*, XXII (1963), 37-48.

1. *Yahweh. a)* The name of the God of Moses[1] is attested in the form *"yhwh"* in the OT, the Moabite Mesha inscription (ninth century), and the Lachish ostraca (588/587).[2] The pronunciation "yahve" (rhymes with "Ave"; not "yahvo"[3]) is sufficiently attested by Greek transcription, like the forms *"Iabe"* and *"Iaouai"* found in Theodoret and Clement of Alexandria, as well as other evidence.[4] The short form "Yahu" is not an earlier form from which "Yahweh" developed; such a development is philologically unlikely, while the opposite process is easy to explain.[5] Thus "Yahu" is an abbreviated

---

[1] *RGG*, III, 515-16; *IDB*, II, 408-11.

[2] Moabite Stone, line 18; Lachish ostraca, no. 2, lines 2, 5; no. 3, lines 3, 9; no. 4, line 1; no. 5, lines 1, 8; no. 6, lines 1, 12; no. 9, line 1.

[3] W. Vischer, "Eher Jahwo als Jahwe," *ThZ*, XVI (1960), 259-67; L. Waterman, "Method in the Study of the Tetragrammaton," *AJSL*, XLIII (1926), 1-7.

[4] B. Alfrink, "La prononciation 'Jehova' du tétragramme," *OTS*, V (1948), 43-62; O. Eissfeldt, "Neue Zeugnisse für die Aussprache des Tetragramms als Jahwe," *ZAW*, LIII (1935), 59-76 (= his *Kleine Schriften*, II [1963], 81-96); G. J. Thierry, "The Pronunciation of the Tetragrammaton," *OTS*, V (1948), 30-42.

[5] See among other studies C. F. Burkitt, "On the Name Yahweh," *JBL*, XLIV (1925), 353-56; G. R. Driver, "The Original Form of the Name 'Yahweh': Evidence and Conclusions," *ZAW*, XLVI (1928), 7-25; B. D. Eerdmans, "The Name Jahu," *OTS*, V (1948), 1-29; M. Jastrow, Jr., "The Origin of the form *yh* of the Divine Name," *ZAW*, XVI (1896), 1-16; E. König, "Die formell-genetische Wechselbeziehung der beiden Wörter Jahweh und Jahu," *ibid.*, XVII

form of "Yahweh," just as "Yah" and "Yô" are probably themselves abbreviated forms of "Yahu." Of these, "Yah" occurs in the OT as an independent divine name (e.g., Exod. 15:2; 17:16; Isa. 12:2) ; "Yahu (Yahô) " and "Yô" occur as components of personal names.[6]

It has often been suggested that the name "Yahweh"—albeit in a different form—is to be found in Old Babylonian documents, in early Aramaean names from Mari, or in Syro-Aramaic names of the eighth century.[7] But the names "Ja-ú/wu-um-ilu" and "Ja-ah-wi-ilum" mean "mine is the god" and "God is";[8] they have nothing to do with Yahweh.

There is no agreement on the meaning of the name "Yahweh." The number of opinions and attempted interpretations is legion: it would be an almost hopeless undertaking to try to summarize them all. The usual point of departure is either the word "Yahweh" itself or the explanation of it in Exod. 3:14, which may be the work of E. It was formerly common to explain the name as meaning "the falling (or 'felling') one," on the grounds that Yahweh was originally a god of lightning, storm, and tempest; more recently, the following interpretations have been proposed: "O He!" (*ya-huwa*) , as a cultic shout;[9] "He who creates" (hiphil of *hāyâ*) , as a term of the creator God;[10] "Preserver";[11] "I will passionately love whom I love";[12] emphasis on the reality of God,[13] his unchanging presence,[14]

(1897), 172-79; *idem*, "Ja-u und Jahu," *ibid.*, XXXV (1915), 45-52; E. C. B. MacLaurin, "YHWH, the Origin of the Tetragrammaton," *VT*, XII (1962), 439-63.

[6] The members of the Jewish military colony at Elephantine never called their God Yahu. In the magical literature of the first century after Christ such forms as "*Iaō*" often occur as the name of the Jewish God.

[7] See F. M. Cross, Jr., "Yahweh and the God of the Patriarchs," *HThR*, LV (1962), 225-59; F. Delitzsch, *Babel und Bibel*, I (1902), 47 (English: *Babel and Bible*, 1903, pp. 133-34) ; G. R. Driver, "The Original Form of the Name 'Yahweh' "; A. Finet, "Iawi-Ilâ, roi de Talḫayûm," *Syria*, XLI (1964), 117-42; J. Gray, The Legacy of Canaan, 2nd ed., 1965, pp. 181-82; K. G. Kuhn, "jw, jhw, jhwh; Über die Entstehung des Namens Jahwe," in *Orientalistische Studien Enno Littmann*, 1935, pp. 25-42; A. Murtonen, *The Appearance of the Name* YHWH *outside Israel*, 1951.

[8] W. von Soden, "Jahwe 'Er ist, Er erweist sich,' " *WdO*, III:3 (1966), 177-87.

[9] S. Mowinckel, "The Name of the God of Moses," *HUCA*, XXXII (1961), 121-33.

[10] C. F. Burkitt, "On the Name Yahweh"; F. M. Cross, Jr., "Yahweh and the God of the Patriarchs"; D. N. Freedman, "The Name of the God of Moses," *JBL*, LXXIX (1960), 151-56.

[11] J. P. Hyatt, "Yahweh as 'the God of my Father,' " *VT*, V (1955), 130-36 ("Preserver of . . .") ; J. Obermann, "The Divine Name YHWH in the Light of Recent Discoveries," *JBL*, LXVIII (1949), 301-23.

[12] S. D. Goitein, "YHWH the Passionate," *VT*, VI (1956), 1-9.

[13] J. Hänel, "Jahwe," *NkZ*, XL (1929), 608-41; J. Lindblom, "Noch einmal die Deutung des Jahwenamens in Ex 3,14," *ASTI*, III (1964), 4-15.

[14] R. Abba, "The Divine Name Yahweh," *JBL*, LXXX (1961), 320-28.

his actuality and existentiality,[15] his indeterminable fullness of being;[16] "Being";[17] "Being" in the sense of "active existential being";[18] "He is";[19] "'I am'—that is what I am";[20] "He is, He proves himself to be," as a thanksgiving name.[21]

According to the only Israelite explanation, that found in Exod. 3:14, the name means that this God is one of whom *hāyâ* can be fully predicated.[22] Since this verb in Hebrew refers not merely to static existence, but to dynamic and effectual presence, the name ascribes dynamic, powerful, effectual being to Yahweh. Yahweh's nature, as expressed by his "name," is a union of being, becoming, and acting—an effectual existence that is always becoming and yet remains identical with itself. This relatively late Israelite explanation is certainly right in deriving the word "Yahweh" from the verb *hāyâ* or *hāwâ*. Since it represents neither a noun, nor a participle, nor a causative hiphil form of this verb, being instead an archaic qal form,[23] it means "He is," in the sense of active and effectual existence. We are therefore not dealing with a proper name in the strict sense at all. The term "Yahweh" instead characterizes the God of Moses as an active and effectual power; this activity refers primarily to the life and destiny of nations and men, and only later to nature and creation. Like the title "Baal" applied to the god Hadad, this term came to be used almost as a proper name.

b) Unlike most deities of the ancient Near East, Yahweh stands alone. He neither heads nor belongs to a pantheon—merely a heavenly court is later ascribed to him—nor is he given a consort, son, or daughter. This isolation is so characteristic of his nature that the later attempt to associate him with a goddess was unsuccessful (I Kings 15:13).

Like the patriarchal gods, Yahweh is not restricted to a fixed place of residence. He is not a local or territorial god, but the God who

[15] T. C. Vriezen, " 'Ehje 'ᵃšer 'ehje," in *Festschrift Alfred Bertholet,* 1950, pp. 498-512.

[16] O. Eissfeldt, " 'Äh°yäh 'ᵃšär 'äh°yäh und 'Ēl 'ôlām," *FF,* XXXIX (1965), 298-300 (= his *Kleine Schriften,* IV [1969], 193-98).

[17] L. Köhler (and W. Baumgartner), *Lexicon in Veteris Testamenti libros,* 1953, pp. 368-69.

[18] R. Mayer, "Der Gottesname Jahwe in Lichte der neuesten Forschung," *BZ,* NF II (1958), 26-53.

[19] E. Dhorme, "Le nom du Dieu d'Israël," *RHR,* CXL (1952), 5-18.

[20] W. A. Irwin, "Exod. 3:14," *AJSL,* LVI (1939), 297-98.

[21] W. von Soden, "Jahwe 'Er ist, Er erweist sich.' "

[22] C. H. Ratschow, *Werden und Wirken,* 1941.

[23] W. von Soden, "Jahwe 'Er ist, Er erweist sich,' " pp. 182-83.

accompanies the group associated with him or hastens to their side; later he is the God of a people. When the ancient period thinks of his dwelling place at all, it is the heavens, from which he descends to appear upon the mountain of God, to accompany those who worship him during their wanderings, or to perform his deeds in settled territory, by the sea, or in the steppes.

Yahweh will not tolerate any other gods among the people associated with him; he claims his worshipers for himself alone. He is justified in this prerogative because he accompanies the Moses host on their journey and because he is more powerful than the other gods, as was shown at the exodus. Other nations may have other gods, but Yahweh surpasses them all, and the Moses host must worship him alone. Mosaic Yahwism therefore knew nothing of a theoretical monotheism that denies the existence of other gods. Neither is the oft-used term "henotheism" appropriate, since it refers to belief in several individual gods who alternately rank supreme.[24] It would be more correct to speak of monoyahwism or practical monotheism.[25]

Yahweh is conceived solely as having human form—a later theology reversed the notion, seeing man created in Yahweh's image (Gen. 1:26-27)—while the ancient Near Eastern gods appear also or only in forms that range from the astral world to the world of plants and animals. In addition, Yahweh is conceived as possessing human features like love and hate, joy and sorrow, forgiveness and vengeance. This was important for the unsophisticated Israelite, who needed concrete images. His God understood his human/all-too-human feelings and actions, because his God himself could love and hate. Unlike the Homeric gods, however, Yahweh did not incorporate any human weaknesses and failings. He could not be ridiculed like them, for he never ceased to be an exalted deity.[26]

Yahweh also has traits that appear negative. He is passionate and wrathful, often characterized not by his calm and secret governance, but by the blazing violence of his intervention. This violence has even led some to speak of the "demonic" element in Yahweh.[27] It

---

[24] *RGG*, III, 225.

[25] See also B. Balscheit, *Alter und Aufkommen des Monotheismus in der israelitischen Religion,* 1938; V. Hamp, "Monotheismus im Alten Testament," *BEThL,* XII (1959), 516-21; W. L. Wardle, "The Origins of Hebrew Monotheism," *ZAW,* XLIII (1925), 193-209.

[26] J. Hempel, "Die Grenzen des Anthropomorphismus Jahwes im Alten Testament," *ZAW,* LVII (1939), 75-85.

[27] P. Volz, *Das Dämonische in Jahwe,* 1924.

would be more appropriate to understand these features as expressing the irrational aspect of Yahweh: in contrast to the ephemeral human world, Yahweh possesses the energy of all-prevailing divine power.

Yahweh is also a God of moral purpose, who requires unconditional faith and absolute obedience. He is a God of righteousness and justice, of ethics and morality. His demands concern not only a man's relationship to him, but also to his fellowman and the society in which he lives.

Thus characterized, the God of Mosaic Yahwism certainly differs significantly from the Midianite mountain god whom Moses came to know. About the only elements they have in common are: (1) the name "Yahweh," which may have been used in this or similar form alongside the unrecorded name of the Midianite god; (2) the site of the original revelation; and (3) possibly certain passionate and violent features. The association of Moses with Egypt suggests that he may possibly have drawn on Egyptian religion[28] (1) for the notion of a single god for an individual or a nation, and (2) for the notion of divine sovereignty that transcends local and even earthly bounds. Finally, there are points of contact with the religion of the early Israelite nomads: (1) the association of theophanies with mountains and storms, which nomads especially must have felt to be manifestations of the divine; (2) the close association between the deity and his worshipers, expressed, for example, in personal names; and (3) the permanent relationship between the deity and his circle of worshipers, expressed in terms of family and clan.

What sets Yahweh apart from the gods of the ancient Near East is not the features based on such points of contact, but two special facts. First, Yahweh does not act within the cycle of nature so as to be indistinguishable from it; his acts concern the fate of men and nations directly. He can always act, not just at certain seasons of the year; he thus interrupts the cycle of nature. Secondly, Yahweh is a God of ethical demands. Man cannot satisfy him in a cult or avail himself of God's power cultically. Yahweh instead requires trust and obedience, thus making his claim and demanding a decision.

[28] More far-reaching hypotheses are unlikely. D. Völter ("Die Herkunft Jahwes," ZAW, XXXVII [1917/18], 126-33) suggests that Yahweh is identical with Sopd, originally a nomadic god; N. Walker ("Yahwism and the Divine Name 'YHWH,'" ibid., LXX [1958], 262-65) suggests that "Yahweh" derives from a translation of the Egyptian "moon" with the addition of "one," thus meaning "One Yah."

2. *The relationship between God and man.* The view is widespread that the relationship between Yahweh and the Moses host was constituted definitively by the "covenant" that, according to tradition, was concluded at the mountain of Yahweh. The definitive establishment of this relationship is in fact intimately associated with the events that took place at that mountain, but it was not established by means of a "covenant" *(bᵉrît)*. More likely the cultic meal described by N in Exod. 24:9-11 served this purpose. It is true that both J and E expressly mention a *bᵉrît,* J in the context of the so-called cultic decalogue in Exod. 34:10, 27-28, E in the context of the people's acceptance of their obligation in Exod. 24:7-8. But the Hebrew word does not mean "covenant, treaty, contract"; in such a religious setting it refers either to Yahweh's obligation of himself in the form of a promise or the obligation placed upon man by Yahweh (Kutsch). J and E clearly intend the latter: the obligation placed upon Israel at the mountain of Yahweh. J defines the content of this obligation by means of the so-called cultic decalogue (Exod. 34:14-26); E defines it by means of the so-called ethical decalogue (Exod. 20:1-17, to which Exod. 24:7-8 originally referred).

This definition of the term makes untenable the comparison with the Hittite vassal treaties that have recently been cited, and from which certain scholars have derived a literary type for "covenant" documents, the "covenant formulary," on the basis of a supposed parallelism between their schema and certain OT texts, especially the decalogues in Exodus 20 and 34, as well as Deuteronomy 4; 29–30, and Joshua 24.[29] According to this theory, the vassal treaties and "covenant formulary" comprise an opening formula, the antecedent history of the treaty relationship, a statement of substance, individual stipulations, a list of witnesses, blessings, and curses. In the Old Testament, this form of the "covenant," which resembles the vassal treaties, remains constant from the earliest to the latest period.

Quite apart from the fact that the word *bᵉrît* does not mean "treaty, covenant," there is really no parallelism: the Sinai tradition is not modeled after a treaty form.[30] Again, quite apart from the fact that we are not dealing with a treaty form limited to the Hittite Empire, but common to the entire ancient Near East,[31] so that a "covenant" concept could be based on the contemporary circumstances of a much later period, and any parallels in the Sinai narratives could be due to their revision and

[29] Especially K. Baltzer, *Das Bundesformular,* 1960 (English: *The Covenant Formulary,* 1972); G. E. Mendenhall, *Law and Covenant in Israel and the Ancient Near East,* 1955. See the surveys in *RGG,* I, 1513-15 and D. J. McCarthy, *Der Gottesbund im Alten Testament,* 1966.
[30] See especially F. Nötscher, "Bundesformular und 'Amtsschimmel,'" *BZ,* NF IX (1965), 181-214.
[31] D. J. McCarthy, *Treaty and Covenant,* 1963.

alteration, it is hard to imagine the Moses host in the desert of northern Arabia as having access to Hittite, Mesopotamian, or Syrian foreign treaties. Examination shows that the texts referring to the purported "covenant" at Sinai are not based on the treaty pattern, and the purported parallels are questionable. The first person introduction "I am Yahweh" (Exod. 20:2) is not formally similar to "Thus (says) the Sun Mursilis"; the parallel would be "Thus says Yahweh." Neither is the mention of the exodus analogous to the antecedent history of the treaty relationship (e.g., "Although you were sick, I the Sun appointed you to take the place of your father"), nor does the relationship between Yahweh and Israel correspond to that between lord and vassal. That the Sinai tradition derives from another context can, finally, be seen from the fact that, despite the legal and political basis for a treaty theory, no Sinai "covenant" played any rôle during the following centuries in Palestine.[32]

The Sinai event can only be understood in the same terms as the identical act in the early Israelite clan religions, to which Mosaic Yahwism was most similar. It was a single unique event intended to establish a permanent relationship between Yahweh and the Moses host in the sense of an ongoing community. The community constituted at the mountain of Yahweh was thought of as a blood relationship, in which the Moses host represents the 'am of Yahweh, that is, his clan or family. There is therefore much to suggest that they brought this very expression, "clan, family, people" of Yahweh, with them to Palestine.[33] It is striking that the suffixed forms of 'am, in which the suffix refers to Yahweh, are especially frequent in the exodus tradition (Exod. 3:7, 10; 5:1, 23; 7:16; 8:16 ff. [Eng. 8:20 ff.]; 9:1, 13; 10:3).

Several features typify the structure of the relationship thus constituted between Yahweh and his circle of adherents. These features remained peculiar to Yahwism throughout its subsequent history:

a) The personal structure of the relationship, already encountered in the clan religions, and seen most clearly later in the prophetical movement;

b) The juxtaposition on the one hand of Yahweh's dominion over the people associated with him, expressed in his claim to sole

[32] A. Jepsen, "Berith," in *Rudolph Festschrift*, 1961, pp. 161-79; R. Kraetzschmar, *Die Bundesvorstellung im Alten Testament in ihrer geschichtlichen Entwicklung*, 1896; J. J. P. Valeton, "Bedeutung und Stellung des Wortes ברית im Priestercodex," *ZAW*, XII (1892). 1-22; idem, "Das Wort ברית in den jehovistischen und deuteronomischen Stücken des Hexateuchs, sowie in den verwandten historischen Büchern," *ibid.*, pp. 224-60; idem, "Das Wort ברית bei den Propheten und in den Ketubim.—Resultat," *ibid.*, XIII (1893), 245-79.
[33] R. Smend, *Die Bundesformel*, 1963, p. 16.

82   Mosaic Jahwism, the First Influence

recognition by them, which later developed into a claim to dominion over all the world; and on the other of the communion between him and his worshipers (or, later, all who acknowledge him) ;

c) Yahweh's acting in the lives of the nations and individuals whose destinies he governs and determines, just as the interpretation of the exodus witnesses to his power over Egypt;

d) The correlation between what Yahweh does, the consequent decision and conduct of man, and the measures undertaken in response by Yahweh; there is harmony between the purposes, decisions, and acts of both, since all actions of the one are undertaken with respect to the other, so that the history of man in his relationship to Yahweh represents a history of decisions.

3. *Worship and ethics. a*) An important restriction stands at the beginning of our discussion of the cult: the lack of images in Mosaic Yahwism, which remained one of its basic features through subsequent ages.[34] Just as no proper name for Yahweh is mentioned, so too there can be no representation of him in visible and tangible form. Just as knowledge of a name might give the initiate magical power over its bearer, so the manageable concentration of "power" in an image of God might be made to serve human purposes by means of the cult. In Palestine there were certainly occasional lapses from the principle that forbade images, such as the image of Micah (Judges 17), the bronze serpent (Num. 21:8-9; II Kings 18:4), or the bull images of Jeroboam I (I Kings 12:28-29), which the narrative of the golden bull at the mountain of God (Exodus 32), a retrojection into the desert period, is intended to condemn. In all such cases foreign influence, especially Canaanite, seems to have been at work; after varying periods of time this influence aroused resistance and was suppressed.

Caution is advisable with respect to other concrete suggestions concerning the cult of the Moses host. The regulations in Exod. 34:14 ff. and the so-called Covenant Code in Exod. 20:24-23:9—with the possible exception of Exod. 20:24-26 (see § 4.2)—came into being in Palestine during the monarchy; those in Deut. 27:15 ff. did not come into being until the period of Deuteronomic theology. They are in part the product of a compromise between Yahwism, the remnants of the clan religions, and Canaanite religion, so that they yield no information about Mosaic Yahweh worship.

[34] K.-H. Bernhardt, *Gott und Bild*, 1956; A. Kruyswijk, "*Gen gesneden beeld . . . ,*" 1962.

Use was certainly made of the Urim and Thummim, the oracular casting of lots kept in a pocket, which the Levites had brought with them.[35] It is the simplest form of oracle, in which a question answerable by "yes" or "no" was brought before the deity; the appearance of the first oracle meant a negative answer ('*ûrîm,* "cursed"), while the appearance of the second meant a positive answer (*tummîm,* "innocent[?]").

Notwithstanding opinions to the contrary in Jer. 7:22 and Amos 5:25 (the latter possibly Deuteronomistic), sacrifices were probably offered. Sacrifice was an important means of presenting a gift to the deity in order to pay him homage or request something of him (for a detailed discussion, see § 16.4). Sacrifice accompanied every important occasion. In the form of animal sacrifice it also represented intimate communion between the deity and the person sacrificing, a communion established by the eating of the sacrificial animal and the simultaneous offering of part of the animal to the deity. Of course sacrifice did not play as important a rôle as it later did in Palestine, where further types of sacrifice, such as the burnt offering, were added, and the ritual was elaborated.

Although there are several views on the origin of the ark, it is not uncommonly regarded as a sacred item belonging to the Moses host, for the protection of which a tent was set aside. Within this tent, encounters with Yahweh took place for the very reason that it contained the ark.[36] P, however, was the first to associate the ark with the tent, also called "tent of meeting" or "tabernacle."[37] Furthermore, the ark does not in fact appear to have been a palladium of the Moses host; it belongs in a totally different context (see § 10.1). The situation is different with respect to the tent, which can be thought of as a kind of portable sanctuary; Arab

[35] *BHH,* I, 420; II, 1103; *RGG,* IV, 1664-66; VI, 1193-94; *IDB,* IV, 739-40; E. Robertson, "The 'Urîm and Tummîm; What Are They?" *VT,* XIV (1964), 67-74.

[36] R. de Vaux, "Arche d'alliance et Tente de réunion," in *A la rencontre de Dieu* (Gelin Denkschrift), 1961, pp. 55-70 (= his *Bible et Orient* [1967], pp. 261-76).

[37] M. Haran, "The Tent of Meeting," *Tarbiz,* XXV (1955/56), 11-20; *idem,* "The Nature of the ''Ohel Mô'ēdh' in Pentateuchal Sources," *JSS,* V (1960), 50-65; G. von Rad, "Zelt und Lade," *NkZ,* XLII (1931), 476-98 (= his *Gesammelte Studien zum Alten Testament,* 1958, pp. 109-29 [English: *The Problem of the Hexateuch and Other Essays,* 1966, pp. 103-24]); L. Rost, "Die Wohnstätte des Zeugnisses," in *Festschrift Friedrich Baumgärtel,* 1959, pp. 158-65; E. Sellin, "Das Zelt Jahwes," in *Alttestamentliche Studien Rudolf Kittel zum 60. Geburtstag dargebracht,* 1913, pp. 168-92.

parallels suggest that it was small and empty. It served primarily
as a place of revelation, where lots were cast or a divine decision
was sought in difficult questions and cases.

Mosaic Yahwism undoubtedly had some cultic practices. The cult
was not so prominent among the Moses host in its nomadic setting
as it was in the religions of the settled parts of the ancient Near East
and later Palestinian Israel; there were enough features, however, to
provide starting points for subsequent development that led to a
markedly cultic religion (§ 13.4).

b) Ever since Alt's distinction between apodictically and casuistically formulated law,[38] it has been common to interpret Mosaic
ethics according to the principle that the laws termed apodictic,
which have been preserved primarily in longer or shorter series of
laws exhibiting identical structure, are uniquely and genuinely
Israelite and Yahwistic, and that their categorical directives reflect
their strict reference to the divine will. Sometimes they are referred
to briefly and incautiously as divine law. The following points, however, can be considered demonstrated since the appearance of Alt's
monograph: (1) such laws are not genuinely Israelite and Yahwistic, but can be found elsewhere—whether in Mesopotamian and
Hittite texts or even as an expression of the clan ethos through the
entire Semitic world,[39] or universally as a prototype of human
legislation; (2) there is considerable evidence for the continued construction of series of commandments or prohibitions, with a prefer-
ence for ten elements, within the nomadic or semi-nomadic world
of the ancient Near East (cf. Lev. 18:7 ff.; § 2:4); (3) these series
actually comprise not laws but rules of conduct; they thus agree
with one of the characteristics of Yahwism, which is not a religion

---

[38] A. Alt, *Die Ursprünge des israelitischen Rechts*, 1934 (= his *Kleine Schriften
zur Geschichte des Volkes Israel*, I [1953], 278-332 [English: *Essays on Old
Testament History and Religion*, 1966, pp. 79-132]); K. Rabast, *Das apodiktische
Recht im Deuteronomium und im Heiligkeitsgesetz*, 1948; H. Graf Reventlow
goes even further in his "Kultisches Recht im Alten Testament," *ZThK*, LX
(1963), 267-304.

[39] G. J. Botterweck, "Form- und überlieferungsgeschichtliche Studie zum
Dekalog," *Concilium*, I (1965), 392-401; F. C. Fensham, "The Possibility of the
Presence of Casuistic Legal Material at the Making of the Covenant at Sinai,"
PEQ, XCIII (1961), 143-46; C. Feucht, *Untersuchungen zum Heiligkeitsgesetz*,
1964; E. Gerstenberger, *Wesen und Herkunft des "apodiktischen Rechts,"* 1965;
G. Heinemann, *Untersuchungen zum apodiktischen Recht*, Dissertation, Hamburg,
1958; R. Hentschke, "Erwägungen zur israelitischen Rechtsgeschichte," *Theologia
viatorum*, X (1965/66), 108-33; R. Kilian, "Apodiktisches und kasuistisches
Recht im Licht ägyptischer Analogien," *BZ*, NF VII (1963), 185-202.

of law, but a religion of life according to sanctified rules expressing God's will.[40]

Of course it is impossible to ascribe to Moses with assurance even a single rule of life and conduct in apodictic form. The so-called ethical decalogue (Exod. 20:1-17) is often cited in this connection, but—apart from the elimination of later expansions—major alterations must be undertaken in the text to produce a proto-decalogue of ten identically structured commandments, representing either a short recension in which each commandment consists of two words [41] or a uniform longer recension in which the short prohibitions are expanded and the commandments transformed.[42] It is a more likely assumption that the decalogue was assembled secondarily, perhaps by E, as a selection of material from three other series.[43] The first three prohibitions may derive from the time of Moses:

> You shall have no *other* god.[44]
> You shall not make yourself a graven image.
> You shall not take the name of Yahweh in vain.

Regulations prohibiting child sacrifice, magic, and sodomy as components of religious ceremonies may also go back to Moses. One must, however, reckon with the possibility that large portions of the apodictic rules of conduct were not brought to Palestine by the Moses host, but either, like Lev. 18:7 ff., derive from a non-Yahwistic nomadic environment and were integrated into Yahwism, or else did not come into being until after the settlement in Palestine, as an imitation of ancient forms.

In any case, such regulations constituted the first steps along a path that led to a goal Moses can hardly have had in mind: a comprehensive system of commandments and prohibitions regulating the entire life of the nation and the individual, such as the Jewish religion of the law envisions.

4. *Further development.* Mosaic Yahwism, after the basic Canaanite and nomadic elements, was the first influence on the history of Israelite religion. It formed this religion in contention with the

---

[40] G. Fohrer.
[41] B. Couroyer, *L'Exode*, 1952, p. 97.
[42] A. Alt and K. Rabast (n. 38).
[43] G. Fohrer; S-F, § 8.2.
[44] The words "before me" or "besides me," which now conclude the sentence, are a later addition.

two pre-existing elements, opposing all attempts at an extensive assimilation to the latter. At first it was the faith of a small nomadic band; but it soon proved to be so vital and vigorous that it won the allegiance of the Israelite tribes in Palestine.

Its greatest strengths, however, were slow in developing. On the one hand, its cult provided a starting point for the growth of a Yahweh religion that was purely cultic; on the other hand, the comparatively minor rôle played by the cult opened the possibility of a faith that saw its goal not in cultic celebration, transcending the demands of the day by entering the sphere of the divine, but in surrender to God's will in everyday life according to the ethical principle of Yahweh's nature. In addition, the ordering of life by means of apodictic regulations did not necessarily lead to a legalistic religion. The prohibitions, mostly in negative form, could challenge Israel to concentrate its principles in the great positive requirements that express the totality of the divine will. In either case, small groups first pursue the second course, but the great individual prophets are the first to see and reach the goal. The dynamics of the continued pursuit of Yahwism's own proper course and the conflict with other elements are characteristic of the history of Yahwism in Palestine before the Israelite state and during the period of the monarchy.

CHAPTER THREE: YAHWISM IN PALESTINE BEFORE THE ISRAELITE STATE

§ 7 THE HISTORICAL AND RELIGIOUS BACKGROUND

J. DUS, "Ein richterzeitliches Stierbildheiligtum zu Bethel? Die Aufein-anderfolge der frühisraelitischen Zentralkultstätten," *ZAW*, LXXVII (1965) 268-86; G. FOHRER, "Altes Testament—'Amphiktyonie' und 'Bund'?" *ThLZ*, XCI (1966), 801-16, 893-904; C. H. J. DE GEUS, "De richteren van Israël," *NThT*, XX (1965), 81-100; S. HERRMANN, "Das Werden Israels," *ThLZ*, LXXXVII (1962), 561-74; F. HORST, "Zwei Begriffe für Eigentum (Besitz): נחלה und אחזּה," in *Rudolph Festschrift*, 1961, pp. 135-56; W. H. IRWIN, "Le sanctuaire central israélite avant l'établissement de la monarchie," *RB*, LXXII (1965), 161-84; M. NOTH, *Das System der zwölf Stämme Israels*, 1930; H. M. ORLINSKY, "The Tribal System of Israel and Related Groups in the Period of the Judges," *Oriens antiquus*, I (1962), 11-20; T. H. ROBINSON, "Some Economic and Social Factors in the History of Israel," *ET*, XLV (1933/34), 264-69, 294-300; H. SEEBASS, *Der Erzvater Israel und die Einführung der Jahweverehrung in Kanaan* 1966; H.-J. ZOBEL, *Stammesspruch und Geschichte*, 1965; A. H. VAN ZYL, "The Relationship of the Israelite Tribes to the Indigenous Population of Canaan According to the Book of Judges," *OuTWP*, 1959, pp. 51-60.

1. *Adoption and expansion of Yahwism.* At a late stage in the settlement of Palestine by the Israelite tribes, the Moses host arrived there, bringing Mosaic Yahwism with them; they were absorbed in the central group of tribes belonging to the "house of Joseph." This group appears soon to have accepted the new faith, which proved itself in the fighting entailed by the occupation and self-assertion of the tribes, thus showing that it was the "true" faith. In consequence of the political and military superiority of the central Palestinian group, as well as the activity of the Levites, who acted as missionaries of Yahwism throughout the land, Yahwism was rapidly acknowledged among the other Israelite tribes. This process was probably essentially complete as early as the middle of the twelfth century.

The tradition of Joshua gives us some insight into how this took place in the central Palestinian group of tribes. Joshua,[1] whose as-

---

[1] *BHH*, II, 894-95; *RGG*, III, 872-73; *IDB*, II, 995-96; A. Alt, "Josua," in BZAW, LXVI (1936), 13-29 (= his *Kleine Schriften zur Geschichte des Volkes Israel*, I [1953], 176-92).

sociation with Moses is secondary and dates from a later period, was a member of that group during the twelfth century B.C. The meager points of historical reference in the tradition reveal nevertheless the important rôle he played in the battle at Gibeon and Aijalon. There he gained a victory under the aegis of the God Yahweh, who, the warriors believed, intervened personally in the contest (Josh. 10:1-15). In addition, Josh. 17:14-18 tells how the central Palestinian group of tribes turned to Joshua to expand their territory; this account appears to presuppose that Joshua was a tribal leader. Like other "judges," then, he was a tribal hero and military commander, whose successes could raise him to the position of tribal leader. Thus he was finally able to achieve the adoption of Yahwism by his own tribe, if not by the whole central Palestinian group, as recounted by the original version of Joshua 24. In its present form, of course, the narrative is Deuteronomistic; it is based on an earlier account that, like the other sagas in the book of Joshua, presupposes "all Israel" unified under the leadership of Joshua. Ultimately, however, it goes back to a tribal narrative. This latter did not refer to a regularly celebrated "covenant festival" at Shechem, but depicted a historical event: Joshua's engagement of his own tribe or group of tribes to follow Yahweh, in whose name he had achieved his victories and risen to become tribal leader.

Not long afterward there was another acknowledgment of Yahweh by reason of a military victory: after the battle with the Canaanites in the valley of Jezreel, celebrated by the stirring religious victory song in Judges 5. Under the leadership of Barak and Deborah, the oppressed tribes of Issachar, Naphtali, and Zebulun, in alliance with Benjamin, Ephraim, and Machir—according to Judges 4, only Naphtali and Zebulun—won a victory because, as they believed, Yahweh had intervened with all his might on behalf of the Israelites. This victory was attributed directly to Yahweh, and obviously made a deep impression on the tribes that took part, and possibly on other Israelite tribes as well. Yahweh was mightier than the gods of the Canaanites—that is the assurance that informs the entire victory song. If the ancient narrative in Judg. 4:4a, 5*, 6-10, 12-16 is correct in assigning Deborah to central Palestine, her summons to Barak to come from Naphtali and fight at Yahweh's command, and Barak's desire for her to go along, can be considered a kind of parallel to the conduct of Joshua. Just as Joshua conquered in the name of Yahweh, Deborah offered the same opportunity to Barak, who was not yet a follower of Yahweh, and accompanied him as a guarantee of divine aid. If this interpretation is correct, the victory song in Judges 5 is also the acknowledgment of Yahweh on the part of his new converts. Thus one tribe after the other came to accept Yahwism: through its introduction as a tribal religion (central Palestine), as a consequence of sudden conviction following unexpected victory (northern Palestine), or by gradual extension from clan to clan and from city to city. Nor is it at all impossible that after Yahwism was adopted as a tribal religion individual families and clans continued to worship their clan gods, equated with El.

2. *The problem of the sacral tribal league and Israel as the people of Yahweh.* The theory is often heard that, after the acceptance of Yahwism, the Israelites constituted a sacral tribal league (perhaps taking the idea from smaller pre-Yahwistic leagues); this league is supposed to have flourished primarily in the period before the Israelite state and, together with its institutions, to have had an enduring influence. Some scholars think of it, comprising a varying number of tribes, as a military league with Yahweh as its war god, guarantor of social order, and dispenser of material prosperity.[2] Others, on the analogy of Greek and Italian amphictyonies, assume a fixed membership of twelve tribes, finding the nucleus of the league in worship at a central sanctuary and in law, both uncodified customary law and codified amphictyonic law regulating the cultus and the mutual relationships of the members; war could be waged against a member only in exceptional cases, specifically when there was a breach of the amphictyonic law.[3] The two theories are often combined: in the latter, ten tribes only are counted as members;[4] the sacral institution of holy war against external enemies is also ascribed to this amphictyony;[5] or the league is expanded into a political organization of the tribes with a leader and a college of elders.[6]

Numerous other phenomena have been derived from or associated with

[2] M. Weber, *Gesammelte Aufsätze zur Religionssoziologie*, III, 2nd ed. (1923), 90 ff.
[3] M. Noth, *Das System der zwölf Stämme Israels*, 1930.
[4] S. Mowinckel, *Zur Frage nach dokumentarischen Quellen in Josua 13–19*, 1946, pp. 20 ff.; *idem*, " 'Rahelstämme' und 'Leastämme,' " in *Von Ugarit nach Qumran* (Eissfeldt Festschrift), 1958, pp. 129-50; see also A. Weiser, "Das Deboralied," *ZAW*, LXXI (1959), 96; K.-D. Schunck, *Benjamin*, 1963, pp. 48 ff.
[5] G. von Rad, *Der Heilige Krieg im alten Israel*, 4th ed., 1965.
[6] J. Dus, "Die 'Ältesten Israels,' " *Communio viatorum*, III (1960), 232-42; *idem*, "Die 'Sufeten Israels,' " *ArOr*, XXXI (1963), 444-69.

such a sacral tribal league; there is little left in Israel's history that has not been considered an amphictyonic institution or the derivative of such an institution. The so-called minor judges, for example, are thought of as representatives of a central office of judge or as political leaders; the $n^e\acute{s}i\bar{\imath}m$ are considered official representatives of their tribes in the assembly of the league; the prophets fill a Mosaic and amphictyonic office that involves the proclamation and transmission of the law; apodictic or divine law (cf. § 6.3), supposedly genuinely Israelite and Yahwistic, is identified as amphictyonic law, leading up to Deuteronomic law and the Holiness Code; even the origin of Yahwism, disassociated from the work of Moses is connected with the tribal league. In view of all these theories, one might almost ask whether Yahweh is not an invention or a numinous personification of the tribal league.

Apart from a few moderating voices,[7] the hypothesis of a sacral tribal league has often been fundamentally questioned and rejected for various reasons.[8] Such reasons include the doubtful character of the analogy with European institutions, the narrow understanding of the "twelve" tribes, the postulate of a (rotating) central sanctuary and the debatable function of the ark, the dubious interpretation of certain Old Testament texts, and the erroneous assessment of the situation during the period before the Israelite state. Since objections to the hypothesis of a sacral tribal league outweigh what has been said in its favor, it must be considered unproven and improbable; it cannot be used as the basis for a presentation of the history of Yahwism in the period before the state and the monarchy.

a) While the Greeks coined the term "amphictyony" for their sacral league, there is no corresponding Hebrew term, although there are Hebrew expressions for all conceivable institutions and areas of life; one would certainly expect such a basic institution as a tribal league to have its own designation. The term "Israel," a word compounded with the name of the Canaanite god El, cannot possibly be considered as a substitute for such a term within an institution based on Yahwism. The terminological lacuna raises doubts about the existence of a tribal league.

b) The existence of Greek and Italic amphictyonies does not imply the existence of a similar Israelite institution. The former provide neither analogy nor model for an Israelite tribal league; they correspond better to the loose confederation of the five Philistine city-states.[9] The amphictyony

---

[7] S. Herrmann; B. D. Rahtjen, "Philistine and Hebrew Amphictyonies," *JNES*, XXIV (1965), 100-104; R. Smend, *Jahwekrieg und Stämmebund*, 1963 (English: *Yahweh War & Tribal Confederation*, 1970).

[8] O. Eissfeldt, "The Hebrew Kingdom," in *The Cambridge Ancient History*, II, chap. 34 (1965), pp. 16-17; G. Fohrer; H. M. Orlinsky; for different reasons, Y. Kaufmann, *The Religion of Israel*, 1960, p. 256; M. H. Woudstra, *The Ark of the Covenant from Conquest to Kingship*, 1965.

[9] B. D. Rahtjen, "Philistine and Hebrew Amphictyonies."

is an institution native to Indogermanic tribes; its existence among Semitic tribes cannot simply be assumed. There is in fact no evidence for any amphictyony in the ancient Near East,[10] not even among the Phoenician city-states, which were familiar with the eastern Mediterranean world. Furthermore, however one classifies the sociological structure of the Greek and Italic tribes before and after their permanent settlement, they were certainly not nomads or semi-nomads after the manner of the Semitic tribes. The sociological differences imply far-reaching consequences for the total way of life, differences that render comparison almost impossible.

c) Apart from the twelve ancestors of the Israelite tribes the OT mentions other Semitic groups of six or twelve: the twelve sons of Nahor, the ancestors of Aramean tribes (Gen. 22:20-24); the twelve sons of Ishmael, the ancestors of Ishmaelite tribes (Gen. 25:13-16); the twelve or thirteen ancestors of the Edomite tribes descended from three wives of Esau (Gen. 36:10-14); the six sons of Abraham and Keturah, the ancestors of Arabic tribes (Gen. 25:2); and perhaps also the six or seven ancestors of Horite tribes from the mountains of Seir (Gen. 36:20-28). It is most unlikely that the very tribes farthest removed from Greece, and living, unlike the Greeks, not in settled territory but outside or on the fringes of the settled regions, should have been familiar with the Greek institution or have evolved it independently. In addition, the regular transhumance of such tribes would have rendered the permanent maintenance of a central sanctuary impossible.

d) In the period before the state, Israel did not have a rotating central sanctuary with the ark as its cultic symbol at Shechem, Bethel, and Shiloh. There is no mention of the ark in connection with Shechem,[11] and it is associated with Bethel only in the late interpolation Judg. 20:27-28, which is intended to explain why the Israelites sought an oracle from Yahweh at Bethel, which had come to be hated as the state sanctuary of the Northern Kingdom. And just as the narrative of Joshua 24 in its original form does not refer to the establishment of a tribal league, but to the acceptance of Yahwism by the tribe or group of tribes associated with Joshua, so the journey from Shechem to Bethel ascribed to the Jacob tribe (Gen. 35:1-5) naturally has nothing to do with the transfer of an amphictyonic Yahweh

---

[10] W. W. Hallo, "A Sumerian Amphictyony," *JCSt*, XIV (1960), 88-114 does not produce evidence of a Sumerian amphictyony, but of an obligation placed on several cities to provide for the temple at Nippur; this parallels Solomon's division of Northern Israel into administrative districts.

[11] Furthermore, the episode of Judges 9 with Abimelech, who must be termed a Canaanite rather than an Israelite, presupposes that the population of Shechem was Canaanite. After Abimelech's destruction of the city, which archaeological evidence dates in the first half of the twelfth century, the site appears to have remained unsettled for a considerable period. See E. F. Campbell, Jr., "Excavation at Shechem, 1960," *BA*, XXIII (1960), 102-10; L. E. Toombs and G. E. Wright, "The Third Campaign at Balâṭah (Shechem)," *BASOR*, CLXI (1961), 11-54; *idem*, "The Fourth Campaign at Balâṭah (Shechem)," *ibid.*, CLXIX (1963), 1-60. One can therefore think at most in terms of a Yahwistic tree sanctuary east of Shechem (cf. Gen. 12:6-7; 33:20; 35:4; Josh. 24:26-27; Judg. 9:37); such a sanctuary does not appear exactly appropriate as the focal point of an Israelite amphictyony.

sanctuary. Shiloh, however, after Gilgal (Josh. 4:18-19; 7:6), was the site of the ark before it was lost to the Philistines. It is not easy to see what else might have qualified Shiloh to be a central sanctuary; until well into the period shortly before its destruction by the Philistines (about 1050), it does not play an important rôle. Above all, there is a real question whether the ark actually served as the palladium of a sacral tribal league. Since this question is associated with other questions about the origin and significance of the ark, its discussion must be put off until later (§ 10.1); there we shall find that the answer is negative, and that Shiloh, too, is eliminated as a potential central sanctuary of a tribal league. Such a sanctuary never existed.

e) Neither do any OT texts mention a sacral tribal league or report its actions. The victory song in Judges 5 and the narrative of the campaign against the Benjaminites in Judges 19–21 have been cited in this connection; but Judges 5 names only ten tribes (Judges 4 only two!) and is concerned with a battle against Canaanites, which cannot have been an ampictyonic war. The only tribes actually involved in the events described in Judges 19–21 were Ephraim and Benjamin; Benjamin's transgression was political in nature, and consisted in the revolt of Benjamin or some southern Ephraimite cities against the Ephraimite heartland, and in the separation of Benjamin from Ephraim.[12]

f) It is certainly true that the Israelite tribes were always numbered as twelve. In itself, however, this schema does not imply an amphictyony; we find similar patterns in the Egyptian, Greek, and Italic systems of twelve gods, or in the twelve tables of the Roman law. Twelve is above all the round number of a totality.[13] The counting of twelve Israelite tribes therefore shows only that this pattern was in each case meant to designate the totality of Israel.

g) Gen. 29:31 ff.; 49; Numbers 1, 26; Deuteronomy 33 reveal three forms of the schema of twelve. In the first, the tribes are arranged in four groups, according to the wives of Jacob and their handmaidens. In the second and third forms, some names are omitted and new ones added:

	First form	Second form	Third form
Leah:	1. Reuben	1. Reuben	1. Reuben
	2. Simeon	2. Simeon	2. Simeon
	3. Levi	3. Levi	
	4. Judah	4. Judah	3. Judah
	5. Issachar	5. Issachar	4. Issachar
	6. Zebulun	6. Zebulun	5. Zebulun
	7. Dinah		
Bilhah:	8. Dan	7. Dan	6. Dan
	9. Naphtali	8. Naphtali	7. Naphtali

---

[12] O. Eissfeldt, "Der geschichtliche Hintergrund der Erzählung von Gibeas Schandtat," in *Beer Festschrift*, 1935, pp. 19-40 (= his *Kleine Schriften*, II [1963], 64-80).

[13] See F. Heiler, *Erscheinungsformen und Wesen der Religion*, 1961, pp. 171-72 (additional bibliography *ibid.*, pp. 161-62).

	First form	Second form	Third form
Zilpah:	10. Gad	9. Gad	8. Gad
	11. Asher	10. Asher	9. Asher
Rachel:	12. Joseph	11. Joseph	10. Ephraim
			11. Manasseh
		12. Benjamin	12. Benjamin

If we follow Noth, who takes no account of the first form, in dating the second form in the earliest period before the state and the third form in the second half of this period, then the first form derives from the period immediately after the immigration of the last Israelite tribes or clans. In this period the Moses host was still on its way to Palestine. Since the latter group brought Yahwism with them, before their arrival—that is, at the time of the first form of the schema—it was simply impossible to constitute a sacral tribal league on the basis of Yahwism.

h) If the schema of twelve were an amphictyonic list, one would expect it to be updated; the destruction of Reuben and Simeon, as well as the rise of Machir, should have been registered. That such is not the case shows once more that there was no amphictyony in Israel; it is probably connected with the completion of the process of settlement, after which the territories or districts took over the rôle previously played by the tribes. In the final analysis, then, the schema reflects the situation of the tribes before they became permanently settled, just as do the other lists of six or twelve nomadic tribes cited in (c) above.

The schema of the twelve tribes of Israel, then, does not point to a sacral tribal league; it means precisely what the OT says it means: it is a genealogical list recording descent and relationship. The various clans or families within a tribe trace their descent to a common ancestor and count as his "sons"; they therefore consider themselves related, as "brothers" in the broader sense. The same holds true in the relationship of several tribes to one another. Their relations are likewise framed in the categories of kinship, so that two tribes express what they have in common by tracing their ancestry back to two men who were really brothers. Just as the living generation of a tribe considers itself related to its supposed ancestor and shares a common life on this basis, so too it considers itself related to other tribes whose ancestors appear as brothers of its own ancestor. In this way several tribes are able to live side by side in peace, use a common sanctuary, and occasionally cooperate in military ventures.

The schema of the twelve tribes of Israel is therefore intended to comprehend the totality of Israel living together in Palestine in a single genealogical list that declares them to be descendants of twelve related ancestors, themselves descended from a single ancestor. This schema does not resemble the learned genealogies of P, Chronicles, and Islam:[14] it is a survival of earlier, popular tradition. It represents an abbreviated popular genealogy, and constitutes the totality of Israel as a whole united in blood relationship, established by their tribal ancestor Jacob/Israel and ultimately, through the genealogical chain of the patriarchs, by Abraham. They are the 'am of Israel. Thus begins the process that forges of them one people, the 'am Israel.

None of this means that Yahwism, once adopted by the Israelite tribes, did not likewise function as a unifying force binding them together. Indeed, it was precisely by its assimilation of the Moses host, constituted as the 'am of Yahweh, and by its adoption of Yahwism that the 'am Israel as a whole became the 'am of Yahweh and were drawn into community with Yahweh. On the one hand, the Moses host was assimilated into the 'am Israel; on the other, Israel was assimilated into the 'am of Yahweh. This observation helps us understand why Israel preserved the patriarchal traditions even after the adoption of Yahwism and equated the clan gods, in the form identified with local manifestations of El, with Yahweh. Israel thus established continuity, so that the 'am Israel descended from Jacob/ Israel could appear from the very outset as the 'am of Yahweh. At the same time, this procedure made it possible to continue using kinship categories for the relationship between Yahweh and Israel; these categories were natural to both the clan religion and Israel's own self-understanding.

3. *The period before the Israelite state.* The lack of any all-inclusive religious institution corresponds to the political and military life of the Israelite tribes. They had migrated separately into Palestine and occupied the land separately; in the period before the state, the so-called period of the judges, there was no advance beyond a juxtaposition of tribes without common leadership. Even military actions were usually undertaken by individual tribes or clans. Exceptions include Deborah's battle against the Canaanites and action against the Philistines of a coalition based at Shiloh (I Samuel 4); in these cases vastly superior opponents forced groups of tribes to work together. Otherwise, however, the consolidation of the tribes into territories or districts and the establishment of satellite settlements by larger cities threatened to lead to fragmentation. This tendency worked directly contrary to any sense of representing the

---

[14] F. Wüstenfeld, *Genealogische Tabellen der arabischen Stämme und Familien,* 1852.

totality of the people Israel and, as such, the people of Yahweh. That the consequences were not totally destructive was primarily due to the fact that the period from the occupation to the establishment of an Israelite state was too short and turbulent for independent Israelite territories or city-states to consolidate their positions. Examination in restrospect makes the tendencies in this direction appear more like preliminary stages leading to a state embracing all Israel.

a) The tradition shows[15] that when Israel was in this situation a series of figures came to the fore who were tribal heroes, military leaders of various tribes, or are otherwise not sufficiently identified: Othniel, Ehud, Shamgar, Deborah, Gideon, Jephthah, Abimelech, and Samson. Of these, Shamgar was probably a non-Israelite with a Hurrian name from the Canaanite city of Beth-anath in Galilee (Judg. 3:31; cf. Josh. 19:38; Judg. 1:33); Abimelech was a Canaanite adventurer (Judges 9); the puzzling basis of the tradition makes it impossible to give any details about Ehud (Judg. 3:7-11). Like these, the other figures are called "judges," i.e., agents of justice, helpers, rulers, although they are all military heroes, or else referred to as "charismatic" leaders, although this term, since overused, derives from a completely different age and environment, and has long been in need of examination to see whether it is really applicable to ancient Israel.

Later ages at least understood the unusual personal courage and military success of these men as a consequence of Yahweh's being with them in their deeds; it is doubtful, however, that their contemporaries interpreted this courage and success in the sense of the term "charisma" as a direct gift of grace from God. Such can hardly be the case when the elders of Gilead offer Jephthah the rôle of temporary leader for a military campaign in his territory on account of his talents as head of a gang of freebooters (Judg. 11:6), and when he in turn capitalizes on the situation and succeeds in having himself appointed to the dignity of permanent head of the militia (Judg. 11:11). It therefore appears better to avoid the term "charismatic" for the military heroes of the period before the state, and also for other figures belonging to the later history of Israel.

The heroes of this period were embroiled in internal wars against Canaanites (the battle fought by Deborah), had to defend against new incursions and claims in the east (Ehud, Gideon, and Jephthah), or where drawn into the incipient conflict with the Philistines, who were striving for sovereignty over Palestine (Samson). All these cases

96   Yahwism in Palestine Before the Israelite State

involve resistance and defense, not conquest of additional territory.

b) Tola, Jair, Ibzan, Elon, and Abdon constitute a second group of judges, for whom the tradition preserves only a brief mention. Similar mention is made of Gideon and Jephthah. These brief statements are patterned after the notices concerning Saul and the later kings, so that these "judges" are represented as rulers, just as the verb *šāpaṭ*, usually translated "judge," can also mean "rule." [16] Judicial activity on the part of these men could be understood as part of their function as rulers. In addition, Judg. 10:1-5; 12:8-15 associate the first five not with tribes but with cities. Their supposed order of succession is secondary; they may have ruled as contemporaries or at different times in the cities mentioned, or perhaps even throughout an entire region (Jair in Gilead). They resemble the kings of the Canaanite city-states, and mark the transition from a government based on tribes to one based on city-states. Seen in this light, the statement in Judg. 8:22-23 that Gideon was offered the kingship does not appear at all exaggerated, to the extent that the offer is placed in the mouths of the men of Manasseh and not all Israel.[17] Samuel, too, may belong in this series: he is described as a Nazirite, priest, and prophet, but I Sam. 7:2-17, in a pre-Deuteronomistic recension, depicts him as a "judge" who functions as both tribal leader and also ruler of his city or tribe, as in the case of Gideon and Jephthah.

In the period before the Israelite state, then, apart from a few common actions we see the developing territories or districts and the independent cities going their own ways politically, militarily, and religiously. To paint a precise picture of the Yahwism of this period would require abundant evidence from all these individual regions. The extant tradition, however, casts only spotty illumination on the religious situation of the period, and archaeology does not contribute much more on the basis of the scanty settlements. One central feature can be recognized: the conflict of Yahwism with the existing elements of nomadic life and Canaanite religion. This conflict, and the new requirements of life in a settled civilization, resulted in a form of Yahwism more inclusive than that of the Mosaic period.

[16] W. Richter, "Zu den 'Richtern Israels,'" *ZAW*, LXXVII (1965), 40-72; for discussion of the traditional view, see H. W. Hertzberg, "Die Kleinen Richter," *ThLZ*, LXXIX (1954), 285-90 (= his *Beiträge zur Traditionsgeschichte und Theologie des Alten Testaments*, 1962, pp. 118-25).

[17] G. H. Davies, "Judges VIII, 22-23," *VT*, XIII (1963), 151-57 even suggests an acceptance on the part of Gideon, cloaked in the humble form of a refusal.

§ 8 THE CONFLICT BETWEEN YAHWISM AND NOMADISM

G. H. W. BREKELMANS, *De herem in het Oude Testament*, 1959; O. EISSFELDT, "Jahwe, der Gott der Väter," *ThLZ*, LXXXVIII (1963), 481-90 (= his *Kleine Schriften*, IV [1969], 79-91) ; s. NYSTRÖM, *Beduinentum und Jahwismus*, 1946.

1. *God's sovereignty and power*. The conflict between Yahwism and nomadism began quite naturally within the Moses host; to the extent that remnants of the conceptual world of nomadism survived in Palestine, the conflict continued there.

That the God Yahweh is exalted and mighty, as well as dangerous, is a frequently noted element of Yahwism. It can still be seen in the narrative of the transfer of the ark to Jerusalem: during the first attempt, Uzzah died because he had touched the ark (II Sam. 6:6-7). This dangerous side of Yahweh's nature engenders fear, trembling, and awe in his worshipers, who must beware of approaching him. For this reason the Moses host were not even allowed to touch the mountain of Yahweh when Yahweh had descended upon it; to touch it meant death (Exod. 19:12-13). No one can approach the sovereign with impunity except by specific permission. He instills in the nomad a respectful fear that warns him to keep proper distance.

This distance was increased by the lack of images in Yahwism. The Israelite could not see Yahweh and grasp him in his form; he could not comprehend Yahweh's nature. The irrational or numinous element in Yahweh eluded him, so that he could only bow in humility, unlike the Greek, who lost his respect for gods who could be rationally comprehended. This humility could only increase when Yahweh, with a power transcending all reason, showed himself a God who performs wonders. This is how men experienced him repeatedly, ever since the particularly impressive deliverance from the pursuing Egyptians at the Exodus.

The varied experience of Yahweh's sovereign power exerted its influence in the context of the nomadic way of life. The Israelite had to learn the meaning of fear of God and respect for him. He had to learn to take his place at a proper distance from the divine sovereign and bow before him.

2. *God's association with his people*. At the mountain of Yahweh the Moses host became the 'am of Yahweh. The 'am Israel, genealogically defined, entered into this relationship, which was originally conceived in terms of kinship, and thus became the people of Yahweh.

There was thus an intimate association between Yahweh and Israel, which the prophets still continued to describe in the terminology of kinship.

This association is not a fact of nature; it comes into being at a moment in history through the will of Yahweh. The conduct of Yahweh in this relationship is characterized by *ḥesed* and *'emet* (Gen. 24:27; Exod. 34:6; and *passim*). The first of these terms[1] expresses the bond of solidarity that one manifests toward a member of one's family or tribe, or toward a friend. The second expresses its continuity and its permanence. Yahweh, too, exhibits this permanent association in many ways—most strikingly, for the Israelite of the period before the state, by his intervention in battle. This intervention is limited to a brief period of time, but it expresses Yahweh's continual guidance of the fortunes of Israel on the basis of his solidarity with his people.

In this association it is Yahweh who gives and Israel who receives. Confidence in one's own might is replaced by confidence in the mighty help of Yahweh; one's own will is replaced by obedience to the will of Yahweh; striving for one's own glory is replaced by glorification of Yahweh; and pride in one's own generosity is replaced by gratitude for the generosity of Yahweh. Thus new values displace the nomadic ideal.

3. *Religious consequences and changes. a*) Not a few OT narratives are directed, sometimes almost in the manner of a polemic, against the nomadic way of life with its confidence in one's own might or its striving for one's own glory, demanding instead humility, loyalty, and obedience. A similar tendency is exhibited when human activity recedes into the background or is not mentioned at all, and Yahweh appears more or less in isolation as the agent of what takes place.

A few examples will show clearly how nomadic ideals are abrogated by Yahwism. After Deborah's battle, for instance, Jael, a nomadic woman, murdered Sisera, the Canaanite general, who had sought refuge in her tent (Judg. 4:18 ff.; 5:24 ff.). By doing so she grossly violated the nomadic principle of hospitality and refuge. In the conflict of duties between this principle and radical affirmation

---

[1] N. Glueck, *Das Wort Ḥesed im alttestamentlichen Sprachgebrauch*, 2nd ed., 1961; A. R. Johnson, "HESED and ḤĀSÎD," in *Interpretationes ad Vetus Testamentum pertinentes* (Mowinckel Festschrift), 1955, pp. 100-112; H. J. Stoebe, "Die Bedeutung des Wortes *ḥäsäd* im Alten Testament," *VT*, II (1952), 244-54.

of Yahweh she did as her faith bade her in the struggle between Yahweh and his enemies. For the enemies of Yahweh there is no refuge.

It often turns out that the law of blood vengeance was no longer in full force. The principle was maintained, but since vengeance is Yahweh's, it was no longer necessary for a man to avenge himself in order to increase his own glory and avoid the disgrace that would follow his failure to take vengeance. Compromise, monetary compensation for the blood of a slain man, was made easier. This may also explain the peaceableness ascribed to the patriarchs. Although the situation more than once called for vengeance, they never took revenge, nor do they seem even to have considered revenge. The way they are depicted obviously bears the stamp of Yahwism.

It is possible that the ancient taboo of the *ḥerem* or "curse" was given a new meaning when it became "setting apart for Yahweh." The curse was now directed against the enemy of the God who had given victory, and to whom the enemy and his possessions were now dedicated. Outwardly, the change from taboo to dedication changed little or nothing, but it entailed as a necessary consequence the less frequent application of the *ḥerem,* because total destruction of the conquered enemy by the victor did not accord with the nature of Yahwism. This removed one of the roots from which war sprang. In fact the *ḥerem* was carried out only very rarely (Brekelmans cites Num. 21:1-3; Joshua 6–7; I Samuel 15); the wars of the period before the state were not aggressive wars of conquest, but defensive battles.

Finally, the remnants of the clan god cults, to the extent that they had survived fusion with the religion of El, lost their remaining support when worship of Yahweh was accepted in Israel. Yahwism spread itself over the ancient religious strata and adopted for itself the traditions concerning the recipients of revelation and the founders of the cults of the clan gods. In the meantime, the clan gods had been identified with the local manifestations of El. As a result, the continuity between Yahweh and Israel was established from the time of Abraham. Another consequence was the transformation of the sanctuaries already used by Israelites into Yahweh sanctuaries, so that Yahwism gained a footing at ancient and venerable sites.

b) **The** destruction of nomadic conceptions and institutions affected even Yahwism itself, when it adapted itself to the situation of a settled civilization. It had to divest itself of everything no longer appropriate to the new circumstances that could not continue to exist through a change of function.

The first point to mention is the $b^e r\hat{\imath}t$ concept. In the period before the state the Israelites were certainly familiar with the Sinai $b^e r\hat{\imath}t$ (and also, in part, the Abraham $b^e r\hat{\imath}t$) ; what was basic to Israel, however, was not the $b^e r\hat{\imath}t$ but the deliverance from Egypt. The Sinai $b^e r\hat{\imath}t$ was an event of the past, of which people became less and less conscious. The rare mentions of it in the OT books that depict Israel before the state and during the monarchy, such as Judg. 2:20; I Kings 19:10, 14, all date from a later period. The people of Yahweh, identified with Israel in the Song of Deborah (Judg. 5:13, emended) and by later periods,[2] preserved the tradition of the Sinai $b^e r\hat{\imath}t$, so that it is recorded in the book of Exodus; but the $b^e r\hat{\imath}t$ was no longer something to live by when the circumstances of nomadism no longer obtained. The change in the situation makes it easy to understand why the $b^e r\hat{\imath}t$ concept took a back seat. Now begins a hiatus that was to last for centuries, until the rise of Deuteronomic theology. Meanwhile what counted was to maintain and nurture the outcome of the Sinai event: the permanent association between Yahweh and Israel. The purpose was served by the cult practiced in the settled territories and by retention of the kinship categories according to which the people Israel, defined genealogically, constitute as a whole the people of Yahweh.

The situation is similar with regard to the Passover—if we can assume that this nomadic festival was actually celebrated by the Moses host and incorporated into Yahwism. In the centuries from the settling of the Moses host in Palestine to the time of King Josiah it does not seem to have been celebrated, as II Kings 23:21-22 indicates:

And the king commanded all the people, "Keep the Passover to Yahweh your God, as it is written in this book of the law." For such a [LXX: *this*] Passover had not been kept since the days of the *judges* who ruled Israel, or during all the days of the kings of Israel or of the kings of Judah.

In fact there is no mention of Passover during the period indicated. Josh. 5:10-12 is a very late addition, already familiar with the Deuteronomic combination of Passover with the Feast of Unleavened Bread and with the designation of the fourteenth day of the month as a festival, mentioned by P in Exod. 12:6. It is true that the so-called cultic decalogue of J mentions the Passover in Exod. 34:25, but the

[2] See the citations in R. Smend, *Die Bundesformel*, 1963, p. 19.

words "sacrifice of the feast of the Passover" are probably Deuteronomistic;[3] one of the major reasons for this conclusion is the striking
use of the term *ḥag*, "pilgrimage feast," which was not applicable to
the Passover until after Deuteronomy had associated it with the
Feast of Unleavened Bread. Thus the ancient pastoral festival, which
had become meaningless in the context of Palestinian agriculture,
soon ceased to be celebrated after the occupation. It was not revived
until the Deuteronomic law associated it with the Feast of Unleavened Bread and provided it with historical basis in the exodus
(Deut. 16:1-8).

In like manner the portable sanctuary of the Moses host, the tent
of revelation, became superfluous in the settled territory with its local
sacred sites. There is no early evidence for its continued existence
in Palestine. The tent David provided for the ark in Jerusalem is
not the same, and passage such as Josh. 18:1; 19:51 that mention the
tent derive from a much later period. Above all, P's association of the
tent with the ark forged a new construct that caused some embar-
rassment to the Chronicler, who situated the tent in Gibeon. The
tent of the Moses host was either lost during the occupation of
Palestine or discarded shortly thereafter.[4]

§ 9 THE CONFLICT BETWEEN YAHWISM AND CANAANITE RELIGION

G. W. AHLSTRÖM, *Aspects of Syncretism in Israelite Religion*, 1963; R. DUS-
SAUD, *Les origines cananéennes du sacrifice israélite*, 1941; O. EISSFELDT,
"Ba'alšamēm und Jahwe," *ZAW*, LXII (1939), 1-31 (= his *Kleine Schriften*,
II [1963], 171-98); *idem*, "El and Yahweh," *JSS*, I (1956), 25-37 (= his
Kleine Schriften, III [1966], 386-97 [German translation]); J. FICHTNER,
"Die Bewältigung heidnischer Vorstellungen und Praktiken in der Welt

---

[3] E. Kutsch, "Erwägungen zur Geschichte der Passafeier und des Massotfestes,"
ZThK, LV (1958), 7. Whether Exod. 23:18 refers to the Passover is at best
uncertain.—Additional bibliography on the Passover: G. B. Gray, "Passover and
Unleavened Bread, the Laws of J, E and D," *JThSt*, XXXVII (1936), 241-53;
H. G. May, "The Relation of the Passover to the Festival of Unleavened Cakes,"
JBL, LV (1936), 65-82; N. Nicolsky, "Pascha im Kulte des jerusalemischen
Tempels," *ZAW*, XLV (1927), 174-76; L. Rost, "Weidewechsel und altisraelitischer
Festkalender," *ZDPV*, LXVI (1943), 205-16 (= his *Das kleine Credo und andere
Studien zum Alten Testament*, 1965, pp. 101-12); J. B. Segal, *The Hebrew
Passover from the Earliest Times to A.D. 70*, 1963; A. C. Welch, "On the Method
of Celebrating Passover," *ZAW*, XLV (1927), 24-29; see also H.-J. Kraus, *Gottes-
dienst in Israel*, 2nd ed., 1962, pp. 65-66 (English: *Worship in Israel*, 1966,
pp. 45-54).

[4] Cf. also J. Maier, *Das altisraelitische Ladeheiligtum*, 1965, pp. 1-2; R. de
Vaux*, II, 114 ff. For a different view, see S. Lehming, "Erwägungen zur Zelttradi-
tion," in *Gottes Wort und Gottes Land* (Hertzberg Festschrift), 1965, pp. 110-32.

des Alten Testaments," in *Festschrift Friedrich Baumgärtel,* 1959, pp. 24-40
(= his *Gottes Weisheit,* 1965, pp. 115-29); J. GRAY, "Cultic Affinities
Between Israel and Ras Shamra," *ZAW,* LXII (1949/50), 207-20; *idem, The
Legacy of Canaan,* 2nd ed., 1965; R. HILLMANN, *Wasser und Berg; kosmische
Verbindungslinien zwischen dem kanaanäischen Wettergott und Jahwe,*
Dissertation, Halle, 1965; S. H. HOOKE, "The Mixture of Cults in Canaan
in Relation to the History of Hebrew Religion," *JMEOS,* XVI (1931),
23-30; *idem, The Origins of Early Semitic Ritual,* 1938; F. F. HVIDBERG,
Weeping and Laughter in the Old Testament, 1962; W. KORNFELD, "Frucht-
barkeitskulte im Alten Testament," in *König Festschrift,* 1965, pp. 109-17;
V. MAAG, "Jahwäs Begegnung mit der kanaanäischen Kosmologie," *Asiatische
Studien/Études asiatiques,* XVIII/XIX (1965), 252-69; J. MAIER, "Die
Gottesvorstellung Altisraels und die kanaanäische Religion," in *Bibel und
zeitgemässer Glaube* I (1965), 135-58; M. J. MULDER, *Ba'al in het Oude
Testament,* 1962; R. RENDTORFF, "El, Ba'al und Jahwe," *ZAW,* LXXVIII
(1966), 277-92; J. N. SCHOFIELD, "The Religion of the Near East and the Old
Testament," *ET,* LXXI (1959/60), 195-98; T. WORDEN, "The Literary
Influence of the Ugaritic Fertility Myth on the Old Testament," *VT,* III
(1953), 273-97.

1. *Basic considerations.* The conflict with Canaanite religion was
more bitter, protracted, and momentous than that with nomadism,
which was in any case bound to decline if not die out entirely once
the Israelites settled in Palestine. Its outcome was also different. It
began while there was as yet no Israelite state, but continued for
centuries to place its stamp on the internal history of Israel. The
great individual prophets still felt compelled to intervene in this
conflict. Thus the period of contact, mutual influence, and differentia-
tion lasted from the twelfth well into the seventh century.

The nature of Yahwism and the situation of the Israelites in
Palestine made the conflict inevitable. On the one hand, Yahweh
appeared as a God who seizes and constrains men, mighty and exalted
above all else, a God of ethical will demanding radical obedience,
who claims the sole allegiance of his worshipers. On the other hand,
after the occupation of Palestine the Israelite way of life became
increasingly like that of the Canaanite population, as the Israelites
adopted agriculture and then life in cities. Although they still felt
the Canaanite world to be alien, they necessarily developed closer
and closer relationships to it. They could not attain the achievements
of settled civilization and use the new language they had adopted
without also sharing the thoughts and experiences on which they
were nurtured. The new way of life was intimately associated with
the ideas and conduct the Israelites found among the indigenous

population. Inescapably they began to approximate the Canaanite way of life, cultic practices, and religious background.

Taken as a whole, despite the resistance and rejection on the part of the Israelites which must be taken into account, the influence of Canaanite civilization on the Israelites can hardly be pictured in powerful and comprehensive enough terms. The constant infiltration of Canaanite practices and ideas could not be stemmed. Of course between determined rejection and ready acceptance of this alien material there were many gradations of partial appropriation, assimilation to Israelite practice, integration into Israelite faith, successful transformation, or victorious assertion of the Israelite way of life. The end result of all this, however, was a profound alteration in the unique character of Israel. Yahwism, too, was involved in this change. The process cannot simply be termed Canaanization or syncretism, examples of which occur in the official religious policies of the period of the monarchy. Apart from these, however, we are dealing with a necessary historical process in which Yahwism on the one hand developed along the lines of its own inner genius and on the other was subject to constant transformation under the influence of an alien factor, Canaanite religion. In this process, which is not sufficiently described in terms of progress and development, the Yahwism of the period before the Israelite state constitutes no more than a transitional stage.

2. *Yahweh and the gods of Canaan.* Israel saw its God Yahweh in opposition to other gods that were equally real powers. The existence of these other gods was freely admitted; just as Yahweh was the God of Israel, so they were naturally and unreservedly viewed as the lords of the other nations (cf. Judg. 11:21 ff.; I Sam. 26:19). The Israelites believed in other divine powers beside Yahweh, as can be seen, for instance, from the regulation in Exod. 21:6, according to which a slave who does not desire his freedom after six years of service but wants to remain in his position is to be brought by his master "to the god" at the door or the doorpost, where his ear will be bored through as a sign of his permanent association with the house. The "god" in this case is surely not Yahweh, but a minor door deity. For this reason the regulation was altered in Deut. 15:17.[1] It is not impossible that in this period the *bᵉnê* (*hā-*) *'ĕlōhîm/'ēlîm* were considered by the Israelites to be a particular group of major

---

[1] O. Eissfeldt, "Gott und Götzen im Alten Testament," *ThStKr,* CIII (1931), 151-60 (= his *Kleine Schriften,* I [1962], 266-73).

gods.[2] Whether they were subordinate to Yahweh from the very beginning, as the Ugaritic gods were subordinate to El, must remain open, as must the question of whether they were really worshiped alongside Yahweh. In any case, during the period of the monarchy they were considered a group subordinate to Yahweh; after Yahweh had been given the title of king, they were viewed as his court and as lower beings of the heavenly world (§ 14.2-3). On the other hand, there seems to have been a permanent cult devoted to the goddess Asherah.[3]

It is therefore not astonishing that El, already identified with the earlier clan gods, was equated with Yahweh, and that the religion of El and Yahwism began to coalesce. This is the third stage—after the worship of the clan gods and their identification with El—in the development of the Israelite idea of God. Outwardly, this stage did not manifest itself until centuries later in the exilic and post-exilic periods, when Deutero-Isaiah claimed the name El for Yahweh alone, to the exclusion of other gods (Isa. 40:18; 43:13; 45:22), when "El" was used naturally to refer to Yahweh (Josh. 22:22; Ps. 104:21; Job), and Abraham was depicted offering worship to the artificial construct El Elyon (Gen. 14:18 ff.).[4] The first steps, however, were taken in the period before the Israelite state. Eissfeldt assumes that in this period El was even occasionally acknowledged by Yahweh as having superior authority; there is not sufficient evidence, however, for this conclusion. Deut. 32:1-43, from which Eissfeldt cites vss. 8-9, dates from the exilic period,[5] and belongs to the passages mentioned above that mark the end of the process of fusion. Psalm 82, which he also cites, is admittedly pre-exilic and incorporates Canaanite mythological material; but it represents a judgment discourse of Yahweh (spoken by a cult prophet) in the "divine council" (not "council of El"), comprising invective, admonition, and threat. It attacks the Canaanite pantheon and proclaims the universal lordship of Yahweh (vs. 8). Though Yahweh was not subordinate to El, Yahwism did not combat the religion of El, striving instead for an accommodation. Thus El, the god identified with the clan gods, was conceived as a past revelation of the God who

[2] W. Herrmann, "Die Göttersöhne," ZRGG, XII (1960), 242-51.

[3] R. Patai, "The Goddess Ashera," JNES, XXIV (1965), 37-52.

[4] H. S. Nyberg, "Studien zum Religionskampf im Alten Testament," ARW, XXXV (1938), 329-87, sees in El Elyon one of several variant names for a god 'Al, whom he conceives as the territorial god of the entire western portion of the Near East, with his primary dwelling place at Jerusalem.

[5] S-F, § 27.4.

later made himself known as Yahweh. This paved the way for Yahweh to borrow considerably from El. Cultic material like sacrificial practices and hymns was included in this borrowing. Above all, the dangerous, sinister, and passionate features of Yahweh, which appeared beside his beneficent features, were supplemented by characteristics typical of El: prudence and wisdom, moderation and patience, forbearance and mercy (Eissfeldt).[6] Thus a stronger bond between the polar characteristics of Yahweh was forged. Later, the functions of creator and king were added.

In contrast to El, Baal gradually came to be apprehended and opposed as a rival to Yahweh. Of course this does not imply that many Israelites did not worship this god in addition to or instead of Yahweh, or that features or expressions peculiar to Baal were not applied to Yahweh, as can be observed down to the time of Elijah.[7] Immediately after the spread of Yahwism, for example, the name "Baal" was used as a designation for Yahweh and as a theophorous element in Israelite personal names (Saul's son Ishbaal). When Ps. 68:5 (Eng. 68:4) introduces Yahweh as *rōkēb bā'ărābôt*, we are reminded of the epithet *rkb 'rpt*, "rider on the clouds," applied to Baal in the Ugaritic texts. The riding or sitting of Yahweh on a cherub or cherubim is to be understood analogously; the cherubim personify the storm clouds (cf. Ps. 18:11 [Eng. 18:10] and the designation of Yahweh as "he who sits upon the cherubim"). Many Israelites in fact thought of Baal at first as the god of fertility and worshiped him so that he would cause their fields to prosper. According to Judg. 6:11-32, for instance, a Baal-shalom appears to have been known at Ophrah as giver of prosperity and increase. The story at the same time intimates that the Israelites were already divided in their attitude: one group, whose position is reflected in 6:11-24, maintained that this Baal could be reconciled with Yahweh; another group, according to 6:25-32, demanded that his cult be eradicated.[8] Apart from rare exceptions or reverses, this rejection and hostility increased during the early period.

3. *Worship.* The same juxtaposition of borrowing and rejection is found in the cultic sphere (Fichtner). Under the influence of

[6] F. Løkkegaard, "A Plea for El, the Bull, and Other Ugaritic Miscellanies," in *Studia orientalia J. Pedersen dicata*, 1953, pp. 219-35.

[7] S. Linder "Jahwe und Baal im alten Israel," in *In piam memoriam Alexander von Bulmerincq*, 1938, pp. 98-107.

[8] O. Eissfeldt, "Neue Götter im Alten Testament," in International Congress of Orientalists, *Atti del XIX. Congresso Internazionale degli Orientalisti (Rome, 1935)*, 1938, pp. 478-79 (= his *Kleine Schriften, II* [1963], 145-46).

Canaanite rites and ceremonies the cult of Yahweh was constantly
elaborated. In particular, the Canaanite sacrificial system was largely
adopted; the notion of food and drink for the gods played an important rôle in this process.[9] Another Canaanite practice that was
borrowed was to forgo the gleaning of sheaves in the fields and fruit
on the boughs, because they had once been considered sacrifices to
Baal, the giver of fertility.[10] The saga of Rahab in Joshua 2–6*
alludes to a family of Canaanite origin living in Jericho, an Israelite
city, where they were engaged in sacral prostitution at the local
Yahweh sanctuary.[11] The dances of the girls in the vineyards of
Shiloh during the feast of Yahweh were Canaanite in nature, and
even suggest the existence of orgiastic worship (Ahlström). The
saga of the sacrifice of Jephthah's daughter provided a later justification for what was originally a four-day Canaanite festival during
which the women of Gilead mourned the departed spring (Judg.
11:40).[12] The original regulations in Deut. 20:5-7 determining who
is forbidden to participate in a military campaign appear also to be
based on Canaanite conceptions.[13] On the other hand, the law in
Exod. 34:26 against boiling a kid in its mother's milk is directed
against a Canaanite practice alluded to in Urgaritic text 54.14.

§ 10 ISRAELITE RELIGION BEFORE THE ISRAELITE STATE

W. W. GRAF BAUDISSIN, *Die Geschichte des alttestamentlichen Priestertums,*
1889; H. DREYER, *Tradition und heilige Stätten,* Dissertation, Kiel, 1952;
H. FREDRIKSSON, *Jahwe als Krieger,* 1945; A. VON GALL, *Altisraelitische Kult-
stätten,* 1898; A. JIRKU, *Das weltliche Recht Israels,* 1927; J. MAIER, *Das
altisraelitische Ladeheiligtum,* 1965; K. MARTI, "Jahwe und seine Auffassung
in der ältesten Zeit, *ThStKr,* LXXXI (1908), 321-33; A. MENES, *Die
vorexilischen Gesetze Israels,* 1928; M. NOTH, *Die Gesetze im Pentateuch,*
1940 (= his *Gesammelte Studien zum Alten Testament,* pp. 9-141 [English:
The Laws in the Pentateuch and Other Studies, 1966, pp. 1-107]); G. WEST-
PHAL, *Jahwes Wohnstätten nach den Anschauungen der Hebräer,* 1908.

1. *Yahweh and the ark.* a) Since the fusion of Yahweh with El
had just begun in the period before the state, this fusion was not

[9] W. Herrmann, "Götterspeise und Göttertrank in Ugarit und Israel," *ZAW,*
LXXII (1960), 205-16.
[10] A. von Gall, "Ein vergessenes Baalsopfer," *ZAW,* XXX (1910), 91-98.
[11] G. Hölscher, "Zum Ursprung der Rahabsage," *ZAW,* XXXVIII (1919/20),
54-57.
[12] *Ibid.*
[13] W. Herrmann, "Das Aufgebot aller Kräfte," *ZAW,* LXX (1958), 215-20.

yet able to influence the notion of God significantly. There remained two sides to his behavior: the beneficent and the terrifying (see § 9.2). Yahweh brings about the destruction of all his enemies, but makes those who love him like the sun as he rises in his might (Judg. 5:31). Against the latter he achieves his triumphs of deliverance (Judg. 5:11) or sends forth others in the strength of his spirit (Judg. 6:34; 11:29; 14:6). He thus guarantees Israel his powerful aid, at the same time lighting upon Israel's enemies. And just as he bestows on the heroes of Israel the strength they need through his spirit so too he brings disaster upon the Canaanites by sending an evil spirit that sets them at variance and leads them to attack each other (Judge. 9:23). With these two sides to his nature, Yahweh continues to govern the destinies of nations and individuals. It is due both to the circumstances of the period and the selectivity of the tradition that this takes place primarily through war and battle, and that the warlike features of God's activity are therefore emphasized. The element of ethical demand also remained, but it was supplemented and modified in large measure by the developing cultus. It was this cultus above all by means of which Israel strove to preserve and cultivate its association with Yahweh.

Yahweh was spoken of as coming to earth and appearing to men.[1] Often this took place in the form of visions during the waking state, which can be termed hallucinatory experiences (e.g., Exod. 24:9 ff.; Judg. 6:11 ff.; I Sam. 3:10).[2] The Song of Deborah in particular contains the first and for a long time the only description of Yahweh's appearance and coming to battle accompanied by tumult of nature (Judg. 5:4-5); the association of a theophany with particular natural phenomena probably derives from the world surrounding Israel. In this case, at least, the theophany introduces the victory song and is intimately connected with it. This connection and the allusion to natural phenomena can be explained by the assumption that a storm actually made possible the victory of the Israelites over the Canaanites, who were better equipped.

b) Scholars frequently assume that the expressions "Yahweh

---

[1] See J. Barr, "Theophany and Anthropomorphism in the Old Testament," *VTSuppl*, VII (1960), 31-38; J. Jeremias, *Theophanie*, 1965; P. D. Miller, Jr., "Fire in the Mythology of Canaan and Israel," *CBQ*, XXVII (1965), 256-61; F. Schnutenhaus, "Das Kommen und Erscheinen Gottes im Alten Testament," *ZAW*, LXXVI (1964), 1-22.

[2] J. Lindblom, "Theophanies in Holy Places in Hebrew Religion," *HUCA*, XXXII (1961), 91-106.

Sabaoth" and "he who sits upon the cherubim" originated in this period; according to this theory, these expressions were first associated with the ark and then with the sanctuary at Shiloh, where the ark was located, and finally came to Jerusalem with the ark. Thus we come to the questions surrounding the origin and significance of the ark and the date of these terms for Yahweh.

The origin, function, and purpose of the ark are hotly disputed.[3] Much will always remain unclear, because the ark appears only four times in the light of history: it was brought along when the Israelites crossed the Jordan and, according to the later account, effected a miracle similar to the one performed by Yahweh when he delivered the Israelites from Egypt by the sea (Joshua 3-4); according to the first section of the ark narrative (I Sam. 4:1-7:1),[4] it was brought into the camp of the Israelite army from the temple at Shiloh, fell into the hands of the Philistines when the Israelites were defeated, and gradually sank into oblivion after it was returned; David brought the ark to Jerusalem (II Samuel 6); Solomon transferred it to the temple he had built (I Kings 8). Beyond these facts not much can be gleaned from the tradition.

[3] *BHH*, II, 1038-41; *RGG*, IV, 197-99; *IDB*, I, 222-26; W. R. Arnold, *Ephod and Ark*, 1917; C. Brouwer, *De ark*, 1955; K. Budde, "Die ursprüngliche Bedeutung der Lade Jahwe's," *ZAW*, XXI (1901), 193-97; idem, "War die Lade ein leerer Thron?" *ThStKr*, LXXIX (1906), 489-507; idem, "Ephod und Lade," *ZAW*, XXXIX (1921), 1-42; L. Couard, "Die religiös-nationale Bedeutung der Lade Jahves," *ZAW*, XII (1892), 53-90; M. Dibelius, *Die Lade Jahves*, 1906; J. Dus, "Der Brauch der Ladewanderung im alten Israel," *ThZ*, XVII (1961), 1-16; idem, "Noch zum Brauch der 'Ladewanderung,'" *VT*, XIII (1963), 126-32; O. Eissfeldt, "Lade und Stierbild," *ZAW*, LVIII (1940/41), 190-215 (= his *Kleine Schriften*, II [1963], 282-305); idem, "Lade und Gesetztafeln," *ThZ*, XVI (1960), 281-84 (= *ibid.*, III [1966], 526-28); H. Gressmann, *Die Lade Jahves und das Allerheiligste des salomonischen Tempels*, 1920; M. Haran, "The Ark and the Cherubim," *IEJ*, IX (1959), 30-38; idem, "'Otfe, Mahmal and Kubbe," in *Neiger Memorial Volume*, 1959, pp. 215-21; R. Hartmann, "Zelt und Lade," *ZAW*, LVII (1917/18), 209-44; W. B. Kristensen, *De ark van Jahwe*, 1933; J. Maier, *Das altisraelitische Ladeheiligtum*, 1965; H. G. May, "The Ark—a Miniature Temple," *AJSL*, LII (1935/36), 215-34; J. Morgenstern, "The Ark, the Ephod, and the Tent of Meeting," *HUCA*, XVII (1942/43), 153-266; XVIII (1943/44), 1-52; E. Nielsen, "Some Reflections on the History of the Ark," *VTSuppl*, VII (1960), 61-74; G. von Rad, "Zelt und Lade," *NkZ*, XLII (1931), 476-98 (= his *Gesammelte Studien zum Alten Testament*, 1958, pp. 109-29 [English: *The Problem of the Hexateuch and Other Essays*, 1966, pp. 103-24]); H. Schmidt, "Kerubenthron und Lade," in *Gunkel Festschrift*, I (1923), 120-44; W. Seeber, *Der Weg der Tradition von der Lade Jahwes im Alten Testament*, Dissertation, Kiel, 1956; H. Torczyner (Tur-Sinai), *Die Bundes-Lade und die Anfänge der Religion Israels*, 2nd ed., 1930; M. H. Woudstra, *The Ark of the Covenant from Conquest to Kingship*, 1965.

[4] For a discussion of the ark narrative, see S-F, § 32.3.

The tradition that the ark was constructed at Sinai under the direction of Moses (Exod. 37:1 ff.; Deut. 10:1 ff.) is of quite late date, and is unknown to the ealy source strata JNE. The ark does not date from the wanderings of the Moses host. The portable sanctuary of this group was the tent of revelation, which had no connection with the ark (§ 6.3). In addition, Num. 10:33*b* and the ostensible ark-sayings in Num. 10:35-36 are later interpolations, and Num. 14:44*b* is an addition to the text. It is therefore frequently assumed that the ark was a sacred object of the permanently settled region or did not come into being until the Israelites had settled permanently. Dibelius, Gressmann, von Rad, and others maintain its Canaanite origin; Nielsen thinks it was a sacred object of the Benjaminites in Palestine; Maier considers it a Palestine Israelite symbol of an anti-Philistine tribal alliance, if it did not in fact originate earlier. These theories are quite uncertain.

The theory that the ark did not come into being until the Israelites were in Palestine is contradicted by the fact that in the three early source strata JNE, which also occur in the book of Joshua,[5] the ark has an essential place in the narrative of the crossing of the Jordan (Joshua 3-4) and cannot be eliminated from it. That is was not originally associated with Yahweh is suggested by the earliest name for it, which does not contain the name "Yahweh" at all: *'ărôn (hā) 'ĕlōhîm*, "ark of Elohim" or "ark of God" (I Sam. 3:3; 4:11, and *passim*). Of course the ark was associated with Yahweh at least by the time it was placed in the temple at Shiloh; in other words, "Elohim" was considered to be none other than Yahweh. With respect to the origin of the ark, the two observations just made suggest a home outside Palestine and a date before the Israelites adopted Yahwism; an immigrating group of Israelites presumably brought it to Palestine with them (Schmidt, Seeber, and others) — most likely the group that preserved the tradition of immigrating by route of the Jordan valley, with which the name of Joshua is associated: the central Palestinian group, or the Ephraimites and the later Benjaminites, who went with them. This theory explains both the mention of the ark in the narratives of the book of Joshua and its final resting place at Ephraimite Shiloh, after an apparently brief stop at Gilgal.

Many scholars have considered the ark an empty throne (Dibelius, Eissfeldt, Nielsen, von Rad, and others; disputed by Budde, Haran, Maier, Seeber, and others) or footstool (Haran, Torczyner) for God. This theory is contradicted by its placement in the Jerusalem Temple with its narrow side toward the entrance, and above all by

[5] See S-F, § 30.

the term "box" or "chest." The ark must probably be considered a container, the only explanation that accounts for its being shaped like a block (Exod. 25:10). Of course it is impossible even to guess what it may once have contained: stones representing the deity (Couard), one or more divine images (Budde, Gressmann), documents (Sellin*), or some kind of oracle (Arnold) —to mention only the less reckless hypotheses.[6] We simply do not know for what the early Israelites used the chest. At Shiloh, after the association with Yahweh had been established, the ark seems to have become the symbol of a short-lived military alliance formed in response to the Philistine threat; it may have served at the same time as a receptacle for the document or symbol of the alliance (Maier). In any case the ark was not a military palladium, since the Israelites did not automatically take it into their camp, but brought it in as a last resort. Neither did it represent Yahweh, since the statement in II Sam. 7:6 to the effect that Yahweh had not dwelt in a house since the exodus would be impossible after the placement of the ark in the temple at Shiloh. It could only be considered a symbol of the joint campaign against the Philistines and a guarantee of divine aid.

The association of the ark with Yahweh is therefore secondary, and dates from the time the ark was at Shiloh, when it was used as the symbol of a military alliance. This makes it doubtful whether the terms "Yahweh Sabaoth" and "he who sits upon the cherubim" could have come into being in association with the ark. That they in fact did not is shown by the narrative describing the transfer of the ark to Jerusalem in II Sam. 6:2:

And David arose and went with all the people who were with him to *Baalat* in Judah, to bring up from there the ark of God, which is *there*[7] called by the name of Yahweh Sabaoth, who sits enthroned on the cherubim.

This passage reveals that the receptacle was called "the ark of God" until it was brought to Jerusalem by David, and had another name at Baalat. In other words, the Yahwistic terms associated with the ark there had not been connected with it earlier when it was at Shiloh. These terms appear rather to correpond to a new function of the ark, linked to its earlier use, and to have come into being

---

[6] Hartmann suggests it was the coffin of Joseph, brought from Egypt; Kristensen suggests a coffin containing the dead god and a symbol of the earth; May suggests it was a miniature temple.

[7] Instead of the repeated *šēm*, "name," we follow numerous manuscripts in vocalizing one as *šām*, "there."

in the time of David. We shall therefore investigate their meaning
in another context (§ 14.1).

2. *Worship.* a) In the period before the state there came to be
many sanctuaries of Yahweh in Palestine. After the identification
of Yahweh with the clan gods and El, the sanctuaries that had been
shared in the pre-Yahwistic period were dedicated to Yahweh. Other
sanctuaries, originally Canaanite, were also associated with Yahweh.
In addition, new Yahweh sanctuaries came into being at previously
unused sites, of which Shiloh was the best known, but not the
only one.

Beer-sheba[8] seems to have acquired a certain importance as a consequence of its situation on the boundary between the settled territory and
the Negeb. This can be seen from Samuel's appointment of his sons to be
rulers there (I Sam. 8:1-2). The sanctuary was accessible primarily to the
groups in southern Judaea that were gradually absorbed into the tribe of
Judah; but it also had a certain attraction for the Israelites of central
Palestine, who were still going on pilgrimages there during the monarchy
(Amos 5:5) and swore by the *dôd*, "darling," of Beer-sheba (Amos 8:14,
emended).

It is impossible to tell whether the Israelies had already begun to reject
the sanctuary at Mamre and replace it with Hebron, with which it is
identified in Gen. 23:19; 35:27.[9] For this period we should probably assume
that a double sanctuary, Hebron-Mamre, constituted the cultic focus of
Judah. Hebron alone was already the site of David's coronation and his
first official residence (II Sam. 2:4; 5:3, 5a).

In the hill country of western Judaea was located the Yahweh sanctuary
of Zorah,[10] which first belonged to Dan and later to Judah. Its sanctuary
legend has been transferred to the father of Samson (Judges 13).

The ancient sanctuary of the sun god at Beth-shemesh[11] was legitimized
as a Yahweh sanctuary by the narrative in I Sam. 6:10-14, which tells how
the cows that pulled the cart with the ark were sacrificed on the "great
stone" there, the local altar.

The high place of Gibeon,[12] which may have been located atop *nebi
samwil*, north of Jerusalem, apparently looked back on a long history, and
was still flourishing in the time of Solomon (cf. I Kings 3:4 ff.). No
sanctuary legend or legitimation has been preserved. Since the execution
of Saul's descendants took place *at Gibeon on the mountain* of Yahweh,
as II Sam. 21:6 should be read, we are probably dealing with what had
originally been a Canaanite ritual, so that the cult of Yahweh continued
an earlier cult.

[8] See § 4, n. 5.
[9] See § 4, n. 7-8.
[10] *IDB*, IV, 963.
[11] *BHH*, I, 229-30; *IDB*, I, 401-3.
[12] *BHH*, I, 568-69; *RGG*, II, 1567; *IDB*, II, 391-93.

Whether the tree sanctuary at Shechem[13] continued to have some importance after the city was destroyed and not resettled must remain an open question.

The sanctuary of Bethel [14] clearly continued to exist and was visited by pilgrims (I Sam. 10:3).

The same holds true for Gilgal,[15] which was probably frequented by several tribes—Benjamin, Ephraim, Manasseh—and was highly regarded in the time of Samuel, Saul, and David, as well as in the time of Elijah and Elisha.

Shiloh[16] is the first Yahweh sanctuary for which we have explicit mention of a temple (I Samuel 1–3). This temple, the pilgrimage festival taking place in the fall, and the dances in the vineyards (Judg. 21:19 ff.) show how much this sacred site, apparently newly established, stood under the influence of Canaanite religion and its fertility cult.

Like Gilgal, the sanctuary of Mizpah in Benjamin,[17] which is mentioned in Judges 20–21, played an important rôle in the time of Samuel and Saul (I Sam. 7:5-12, 16; 10:17 ff.). It may have been the central sanctuary of Benjamin since it was there that Saul was chosen by lot to be king.

Judg. 6:11-32, describing the situation at Ophrah,[18] gives us some insight into the conflicts surrounding the assignment of a sanctuary to Baal or to Yahweh (§ 9.2). The altar of Yahweh that was evidently set up there was apparently tolerated at first, as we may assume on the basis of Judg. 8:27. At the same time, this brief notice reveals that the ephod made this small sanctuary offensive to a latter period.

A Yahweh sanctuary also came into being on Mount Tabor,[19] an ancient Canaanite site (§ 3.2). It was used by the tribes of Issachar and Zebulun (Deut. 33:19), on whose common border it was located (Josh. 19:22). It was apparently also used by Naphtali, as suggested by the assembly of troops there under the leadership of Barak, from Naphtali, before the battle fought by Deborah (Judg. 4:6).

At Dan was located the sanctuary belonging to the tribe of the same name,[20] after they had finally settled in northern Palestine. The background of this sanctuary is narrated in Judges 17–18, albeit in hostile form: the sanctuary came by its image through a double theft! There was of course no such theft in the original recension of the narrative, which recorded the tradition of how the tribe of Dan moved about in Palestine.

[13] See § 4, n. 11.

[14] See § 4, n. 10.

[15] See § 4, n. 15.

[16] *BHH*, III, 1794-95; *RGG*, VI, 35; *IDB*, IV, 328-30; O. Eissfeldt, "Silo und Jerusalem," *VTSuppl*, IV (1957), 138-47 (= his *Kleine Schriften*, III [1966], 417-25); M. Haran, "Shiloh and Jerusalem: the Origin of the Priestly Tradition in the Pentateuch," *JBL*, LXXXI (1962), 14-24.

[17] *BHH*, II, 1228; *RGG*, IV, 1065; *IDB*, III, 407-9.

[18] *BHH*, II, 1353; *RGG*, V, 1659-60; *IDB*, III, 606-7; S. A. Cook, "The Theophanies of Gideon and Manoah," *JThSt*, XXVIII (1926/27), 368-83.

[19] *BHH*, III, 1962-63; *RGG*, VI, 598; *IDB*, IV, 508-9.

[20] *BHH*, I, 317; *IDB*, I, 759-60.

In Transjordan, beside Penuel,[21] there existed the sanctuary of Mahanaim,[22] north of the Jabbok, which the account in Gen. 32:2-3 of the appearance of Yahweh's armed camp to Jacob is intended to legitimize, and the sanctuary of Mizpah in Gilead,[23] with which the tradition of Jephthah is associated (Judg. 11:11, 34). In addition, the narrative in Josh. 22:7 ff., which has undergone major revision, mentions (vss. 10-11, 34) an altar for Reuben and Gad on the west side of the Jordan "near the stone circles." We may have here an echo of a temporary sanctuary.

This account does not exhaust the list of Yahweh sanctuaries. In general, even in this period every settlement that was totally or predominantly Israelite possessed a site dedicated to Yahweh and laid out after the model of Canaanite cultic sites (see § 3.4). The OT calls such a site a *bāmâ*, "high place." [24] This expression does not necessarily mean that the sanctuary was situated on a hill, since it could also be located within a town, at a city gate, or in a valley (cf. I Kings 13:32; II Kings 23:8; Jer. 7:31). What is meant is, rather, a small elevation for cultic use; it could be natural but in most cases was constructed artificially (I King 11:7 and *passim*). Archaeological excavations have uncovered some of these sanctuaries: at Megiddo an oval platform twenty-five to thirty feet in diameter, dating from the middle of the third millennium; at Nahariya, near Haifa, a roughly circular heap of stones twenty and later forty-five feet in diameter, together with a small sanctuary from the eighteenth or seventeenth century; at Hazor a platform from the thirteenth century; in the citadels of Hazor and Arad rectangular sites from the early Israelite monarchy and the ninth or eighth century; and on a ridge southwest of Jerusalem sites with diameters up to eighty feet, dating from the seventh or sixth century. These discoveries clearly exhibit the continuity in the establishment of such cultic sites throughout the Canaanite and Israelite periods. These high places appear also to be associated in some way with the heaps of stones that were occasionally set up as funeral mounds (II Sam. 18:17), so that on the one hand deserted high places could be explained as funeral mounds of an earlier age (Josh. 7:26; 8:29), and on the other funeral rites could be performed as part of the cult at the high places.

b) The sanctuaries were also fitted out like their Canaanite

[21] See § 4, n. 14.
[22] *BHH*, II, 1123-24; *IDB*, III, 226-27.
[23] *BHH*, II, 1228-29; *RGG*, IV, 1065; *IDB*, III, 407.
[24] *BHH*, II, 736, 1021-22; *IDB*, II, 602-4.

prototypes (see § 3.4).[25] Each probably had an altar, massebah, asherah, libation vessels, and water jars (for cultic ablutions). At Dan we know there was the image mentioned above. The cultic paraphernalia also included ephod and teraphim.[26] Originally the ephod was probably a garment placed on a divine image; this is the explanation that best fits Judges 17–18, while the great weight indicated in Judg. 8:26-27 is more suggestive of a metal covering laid over a wooden core (cf. Isa. 30:22). Then an empty vestment came to be kept by the priest exclusively for oracular purposes; he would get it and put it on as occasion demanded (I Sam. 2:28; 14:3; 23:9; 30:7). In addition, "ephod" refers to the linen loin cloth that formed part of the official vestments of a priest (I Sam. 2:18; 22:18; II Sam. 6:14). In the post-exilic period the word refers to part of the vestments of the high priest. In the word "teraphim" we have a collective noun used with scornful connotations for images (in I Sam. 15:23 it is paired with sorcery). In the Jacob story a small image of a household god in human form may be meant; elsewhere the expression probably designates a cultic mask used as a symbol of God (I Sam. 19:13, 16). Such masks dating from the Canaanite period have been discovered at Hazor; they constituted part of the paraphernalia of the sanctuary (Judg. 17:5; 18:17 ff.; Hos. 3:4), and were used for obtaining oracles (Ezek. 21:26 [Eng. 21:21]; Zech. 10:2).

c) The priests[27] were the most important group of cultic personnel: the Elides at Shiloh, who boasted descent from the Moses host; the Aaronides at early Bethel; the priests at Nob, all of whom (with the exception of Abiathar, who escaped) were executed by Saul for favoring David (I Samuel 21–22); and the Levitical priests at Dan, who traced their descent to the son of Moses. Other sanctuaries no doubt had other families of priests, with sons inheriting the

[25] RGG, III, 158; VI, 686-87.
[26] BHH, I, 420; III, 1952; RGG, II, 521-22; VI, 690-91; IDB, I, 118-19; P. R. Ackroyd, "The Teraphim," ET, LXII (1950/51), 378-80; W. E. Barnes, "Teraphim," JThSt, XXX (1928/29), 177-79; G. Dahl, "The Problem of the Ephod," AThR, XXXIV (1952), 206-10; H. J. Elhorst, "Das Ephod," ZAW, XXX (1910), 259-76; K. Elliger, "Ephod und Choschen," VT, VIII (1958), 19-35 (also published in Festschrift Friedrich Baumgärtel, 1959, pp. 9-23); M. Haran, "The Ephod According to Biblical Sources," Tarbiz, XXIV (1954/55), 38-91; G. Hoffmann and H. Gressmann, "Teraphim," ZAW, XL (1922), 75-137; C. J. Labuschagne, "Teraphim—a New Proposal for Its Etymology," VT, XVI (1966), 115-17; E. Sellin, "Efod und Terafim," JPOS, XIV (1934), 185-93; H. Thiersch, Ependytes und Ephod, 1936.
[27] BHH, III, 1486-90; RGG, V, 574-78; IDB, III, 876-89.

occupation of their fathers. We do not know to what extent
Canaanite priests were accepted into the cult of Yahwism.

Only in the case of Dan do we have evidence that Levites[28] were
permanent priests at a specific sanctuary. With this exception, no
priests in this period were called Levites, nor were any Levites
called priests. There was clearly a difference between the two groups,
although we can no longer make out what this difference was, the
more so because both performed the same duties. It is possible that
the Levites were not associated with a specific sanctuary, but rather
moved about the countryside ministering at the minor cultic sites
that were without priests.

The duties of priests and Levites consisted in offering sacrifice
at the altar, offering incense, instructing people in cultic, ethical, and
legal torah, and obtaining decisions or oracles from God by means
of ephod and Urim-Thummim.[29] They could therefore claim a
portion of the sacrifice for themselves. It is important to note, however, that the priests and Levites were not the only ones permitted
to perform cultic acts; at least the head of every family had the
privilege of offering sacrifice (Judg. 6:25 ff.; 13:15 ff.) or instituting
a cult (Judg. 8:27; 17:5).

In addition to priests and Levites, early forms of the prophets also
existed: seers and nabis, who are equated in I Sam. 9:9 from the
perspective of a later phase. In the period before the state, however,
there can be no question of a fusion of these various types of prophet.
The confusion that came about in this regard results in Samuel's
being characterized not only as a ruler, priest, and Nazirite, but also
as a seer and nabi. The early history of the prophetical movement
will be treated in detail in a larger context (§ 18).

d) At the cultic sites sacrifices were offered, which from this
period on steadily increased in importance, the more so because,
until the centralization of the cult at Jerusalem introduced by the
Deuteronomic reform, all animal slaughter was sacrificial. Sacrifice
is frequently mentioned in this period: offered by priests (Eli and
his sons, I Sam. 2:12 ff.), by other men (Gideon, Judges 6; Manoah,
Judges 13; Samuel's father, I Sam. 1:21), and by Samuel described
ambiguously (I Sam. 7:9-10; 9:12-13).

Since the Israelite sacrificial system will be treated thoroughly in
another context (§ 16.4), we shall here merely indicate the peculiari-

[28] See § 5, n. 23; G. R. Berry, "Priests and Levites," *JBL*, XLII (1923), 227-38.
[29] See § 6, n. 5; J. Lindblom, "Lot-casting in the Old Testament," *VT*, XXII
(1962), 164-78.

ties of the period before the state. Of the various modes of offering
the simplest was still familiar: the depositing of gifts intended as
food for the deity at a sacred site (Judg. 6:19), a mode that continued
in use for the bread of the Presence (e.g., I Sam. 21:7 [21:6]). Drink
offering, which later came to be merely a supplementary form, was
still independent; it involved libations of oil (Gen. 28:18; 35:14),
wine (Exod. 29:40), or water (I Sam. 7:6; II Sam. 23:13 ff.). Besides
the slaughtering of animals for consumption, the Israelites also
practiced burnt offering, in which the sacrificial animal was burned
whole. The burnt offering was a Syro-Palestinian practice, originally
non-Semitic, which the Israelites encountered and borrowed in
Palestine.

The purpose of food and drink offering is primarily alimentation
of the deity. Animal sacrifice and burnt offering correspond to two
basic features of Yahwism. The former strengthens and renews the
communion between Yahweh and his worshipers, who at a cultic
banquet devour the sacrifice from which Yahweh also receives his
portion. The latter is simply a sacrifice of homage, expressing recognition of Yahweh's dominion over his worshipers.

e) Although no calendar dating from the period before the state
has been preserved, it is possible to identify several festivals that were
celebrated in Israel.[30] The feast of Passover is not reckoned among
these, since the Israelites ceased temporarily to celebrate it when
they settled in Palestine (§ 8.3).

As is true wherever time is reckoned by the moon (in months),
the day of the new moon was a festival.[31] This is the day on whose
(preceding) evening the crescent moon becomes visible once more.
When we find this festival in the OT it is already a Yahweh festival.
Because it was a day of rest, it is often mentioned in association
with the Sabbath.

The Sabbath[32] is the last day of the seven-day week, on which work

[30] *BHH*, I, 471-74; *RGG*, III, 910-17; *IDB*, II, 260-64.
[31] F. Wilke, "Das Neumondfest im israelitisch-jüdischen Altertum," *Jb der
Gesellschaft für die Geschichte des Protestantismus in Österreich*, LXVII (1951),
1-15.
[32] *BHH*, III, 1633-35; *RGG*, V, 1258-60; *IDB*, IV, 135-41; K. Budde, "The
Sabbath and the Week," *JThSt*, XXX (1928/29), 1-15; W. W. Cannon, "The
Weekly Sabbath," *ZAW*, XLIX (1931), 325-27; J. Hehn, *Siebenzahl und Sabbat
bei den Babyloniern und im Alten Testament*, 1907; E. Jenni, *Die theologische
Begründung des Sabbatgebotes im Alten Testament*, 1956; E. J. Kraeling, "The
Present Status of the Sabbath Question," *AJSL*, XLIX (1932/33), 218-28; J. and
H. Lewy, "The Origin of the Week," *HUCA*, XVII (1942/43), 1-152; J. Mein-
hold, *Sabbat und Woche im Alten Testament*, 1905; *idem*, "Die Entstehung des

ceased. It very early became a Yahweh festival, if it was not so from the very outset (Exod. 20:10; Deut. 5:14; and *passim*). The OT contains no historically accurate information about its origin. The Deuteronomist explains it on the basis of the exodus (Deut. 5:15); P derives it from Yahweh's resting when he had finished creating the world (Exod. 20:11; 31:17b); Ezek. 20:12, 20; Exod. 31:13, 17a interpret it as a sign of the obligation placed on Israel by Yahweh.

Many attempts have been made to derive the Sabbath from non-Israelite practices: Budde and others suggest that it was a day of Saturn borrowed from the Kenites, a tribe of smiths, a suggestion which cannot be supported by the late text Exod. 35:3 and Num. 15:32-36; Meinhold suggests that it was the day of the full moon, on the basis of the similar word *šab/pattu* used by the Babylonians for the fifteenth day of the month, although there is no evidence that this was a day of rest; others suggest that it was analogous to the days marking the phases of the moon known to have occurred in some of the Assyro-Babylonian months, although such days, unlike the Sabbath, were considered "evil" days; Jenni suggests that it was a market day, although work and trade were specifically forbidden; Lewy derives the week from a supposed schema of fifty days, Tur-Sinai from a "fifth of a month," although the calculation does not work out evenly for lunar months. We are left at best with the hypothesis that as in other instances seven was used as a small round number to determine regular small divisions of time (weeks), the last day of which was set apart as the Sabbath, in which case the name would derive from *šābat*, "cease" (Kutsch, in *RGG*).

Just as Judg. 9:27 tells of a Canaanite vintage festival in the fall, so Judg. 21:19 ff.; I Sam. 1:3 ff. speak of an analogous Israelite festival in the vineyards and at the temple at Shiloh. This suggests the hypothesis that in this period the Israelites borrowed from the Canaanites the three pilgrimage festivals of the settled territory that are mentioned in the later festival calendars and celebrated them as Yahweh festivals. Since we will discuss them later (§ 16.3), we will merely list them here: the Feast of Unleavened Bread in the spring, the Feast of Harvest (Feast of Weeks) with the offering of first fruits, and the vintage festival in the fall (Feast of Booths).

There is no evidence for other feasts; despite the fertile fantasy of exegetes, their existence is unlikely. But many isolated or variable events were probably celebrated—for the most part presumably at a sanctuary and accompanied by the offering of sacrifices. Such events included for the family or clan the weaning of a child (Gen. 21:8),

Sabbats," *ZAW*, XXIX (1909), 81-112; R. North, "The Derivation of Sabbath," *Bibl*, XXXVI (1955), 182-201; N. H. Tur-Sinai, "Sabbat und Woche," *BiOr*, VIII (1951), 14-24; T. C. Vriezen, "Kalender en Sabbat," *NThS*, XXIII (1940), 172-95.

perhaps also its circumcision (cf. Genesis 17), a marriage (Gen. 29:22 ff.; Judg. 14:10 ff.), and a burial (II Sam. 3:31 ff.), in the framework of the agricultural year the shearing of the sheep (I Sam. 25:2 ff.; II Sam. 13:23 ff.), in the realm of politics a victory (cf. I Sam. 15:12 and the songs in Exod. 15:20-21; I Sam. 18:7) or a general disaster (later marked by public lamentation and fasting). We must probably assume that the whole of life was religiously permeated and accompanied by cultic acts..

This observation also applies to war,[33] which is frequently viewed as "holy" war, being a sacral institution of ancient Israel.[34] Despite basic agreement, Ringgren* has objected that the accounts of the early wars have been influenced in part by later theories and stylized accordingly, and that the "holy" war is more likely associated with nomadic life than with settled life in Palestine. Now there were certainly religious conceptions and practices based on the effort to gain victory and avert defeat through divine aid. These gave rise to more or less fixed proverbs and idioms.[35] Like everything in life, the conduct of war was surrounded by religious conceptions and accompanied by religious rites. But these do not make it a "holy" war and a sacral institution any more than the religious conceptions, rites, and formulas that surround birth, weaning, marriage, death, and sheep-shearing make them holy. A "holy" war as a sacral institution of the ancient period is nothing more than the result of a late systematization of the actual religious conduct of an early cultural stage, conditioned by religious hostility to everything alien. One can speak of a "war of Yahweh" only in those cases in which the Israelites believed Yahweh had personally intervened in the battle. Since these were exceptional cases, we are usually faced with nothing more than the fact that the practices associated with the conduct of war were included in the general religious permeation of life.

3. *Historical traditions and law*. a) Although there is no direct evidence, literary and traditio-historical analysis of the Hexateuch reveals that the historical traditions were considerably elaborated

---

[33] C. H. E. Brekelmans, *De ḥerem in het Oude Testament*, 1959; A. Malamat, "Der Bann in Mari und in der Bibel," in *Kaufmann Festschrift*, 1960, pp. 149-58; E. Nielsen, "La guerre considérée comme une religion et la religion comme une guerre," *StTh*, XV (1961), 93-112; R. Smend, *Jahwekrieg und Stämmebund*, 1963 (English: *Yahweh War & Tribal Confederation*, 1970).

[34] G. von Rad, *Der Heilige Krieg im alten Israel*, 4th ed., 1965.

[35] S-F, § 8.1.

in the period before the state.[36] Some of the originally independent territorial claim and occupation narratives of the various clans, groups, and tribes achieved a general significance for Israel and were gradually assembled in a first basic narrative strand that was current in oral tradition. Cultic and didactic forces played a special part in shaping it, as well as delight in narrative elaboration; there was as yet no dominant interest in the presentation of the total course of history.

The genealogical linking of the patriarchal traditions represented an importaant step forward; Abraham, Isaac, and Jacob/Israel were placed in father-son relationship. In addition, the traditions concerning the patriarchs were connected with the Moses tradition. This took place at first without the interpolation of the Joseph novella, so that the narrative apparently progressed directly to the story of how Jacob and his family migrated to Egypt, as Deut. 26:5 still presupposes. Finally the Joshua tradition was appended in an early, simple form, so that it constituted a continuous narrative with the patriarchal and Moses tradition. In this narrative the patriarchal tradition emphasized the element of promised territory; the Joshua tradition was intended primarily to depict the realization of the promise. The Moses tradition, supplementing the promise and its realization, was made to justify Yahweh's claim upon Israel and describe Israel's obligations toward Yahweh.

Neither the occupation tradition nor the Hexateuch as a whole grew out of a cultic creed, like the so-called "short historical creed" (the festival legend of the Feast of Weeks at Gilgal) von Rad has claimed to find in Deut. 26:5 ff.[37] This has been repeatedly demonstrated by new studies of Deut. 26:5 ff. and similar passages.[38] In Deut. 26:1 ff. there is no mention of any feast for the offering of the first of all the fruit of the ground, at which the so-called creed is to be recited; the variability of harvest time would make such a feast almost impossible. Furthermore the text is more like a prayer or catechism intended not only to provide Yahwistic legitimation for the agricultural ritual but to incorporate it into the historical

---

[36] S-F, § 19.4-5.

[37] G. von Rad, Das formgeschichtliche Problem des Hexateuch, 1938 (= his Gesammelte Studien zum Alten Testament, 1958, pp. 9-86 [English: The Problem of the Hexateuch and Other Essays, 1966, pp. 1-78]).

[38] C. H. W. Brekelmans, "Het 'historische Credo' van Israël," Tijdschrift voor Theologie, III (1963), 1-10; L. Rost, "Das kleine geschichtliche Credo," in his Das kleine Credo und andere Studien zum Alten Testament, 1965, pp. 11-25; T. C. Vriezen, "The Credo in the Old Testament," OuTWP, 1963, pp. 5-17; A. Weiser, Einleitung in das Alte Testament, 5th ed., 1963, pp. 79 ff.; A. S. van der Woude, Uittocht en Sinaï, 1961; see S-F, § 18.5.

traditions of Yahwism. In other words, it belongs to the later period, as the analogous ceremony at the Feast of Unleavened Bread and Passover shows. In addition, the text presupposes a knowledge of the historical traditions; it is not their nucleus, but rather a later summary intended for didactic purposes.

As the first basic narrative was being formed, many other early traditions were incorporated: lists (Gen. 22:20-24; 25:1-6; 36:31-39) ; narratives concerning the history of tribes and nations (Gen. 16:4-14; 19:30-38; 21:8-21; 25:21-26a, 29-34; 29–30; 34; 38:27-20) ; nature sagas (Genesis 19; Exodus 16–17; Numbers 11; 20) ; short stories (Gen. 12:10 ff.; 20; 24; 26) ; proverbs and songs (Gen. 9:6; 25:23; 27:27-29, 39-40) ; and sanctuary and cult legends, most of which were originally Canaanite. New narratives were also composed, some as elaborations or expansions of the extant body of tradition (e.g., Exod. 5:5-21; 7:14–10:29; 32; 34:29-35; Num. 11:14 ff.; 16–17).

The primary narrative of the Hexateuch recounted in outline the following: the departure of Abraham (and Lot) from their homeland, the promise of territory and descendants made to them, the destruction of Sodom and the deliverance of Lot, the announcement of the birth of Isaac, the endangering of Sarah, the expulsion of Hagar, the birth of Isaac, the promise to Isaac, Jacob-Esau, Jacob-Laban, Jacob's return and sojourn at Shechem and Bethel, Esau's wives and descendants, Jacob's migration to Egypt, the oppression of the Israelites, the introduction of Moses, his sojourn in Midian and his marriage, his call in Midian and return to Egypt, the slaying of the Egyptian firstborn and the escape of the Israelites, pursuit and deliverance at the sea, the journey to the mountain of Yahweh, events at Sinai, the unfortunate incident there followed by the command to depart, the continuation of the journey, the miraculous provision of water, manna, and quails, the rebellion of Aaron and Miriam or Dathan and Abiram, spying out of the land (Caleb) and its consequences, Edom's refusal of permission to pass, continued advance and victory over the Amorites, repeated murmuring and apostasy of the people, the death of Moses, short statements and narratives concerning the successes and failures of the Israelites in Palestine (Judges 1 and the nucleus of 2:1-5), and the nucleus of the Joshua tradition. This presentation was further elaborated in the Davidic-Solomonic period (§ 11.6).

b) Since early Israelite nomadic law was to a large extent no longer appropriate for the circumstances of the settled regions and did not suffice for the situation there, during this early period in

Palestine the Israelites borrowed Canaanite law, which was related to the law of the other Semitic peoples. It was adapted as necessary to the Israelite situation and underwent further development. Henceforth the apodictically formulated rules of conduct, assembled in series, the roots of which go back to the nomadic period (§ 2.4), and to which new rules had been added in Palestine, stood side by side with casuistically formulated laws treating individual cases. Both were later grounded on the authority of Yahweh and Moses. For the time being, Yahwism was still a religion of life and conduct according to hallowed rules expressing God's will. But the adoption of Canaanite law began a process that was to lead in later centuries to a religion of legalism.

It is hardly possible to determine in detail which laws can be ascribed to the period before the state. In any case the so-called Covenant Code as a whole (Exod. 20:24–23:9) does not date from it.[39] This hypothesis probably holds true, however, for the archaic material in the Covenant Code: in the section dealing with bodily injury (21:18-36), the talion formula with its principle of exact retribution (21:23-25),[40] the taboo theory of the goring ox (21:28),[41] and the evaluation of a slave as physical property (21:32);[42] some material in the section on offences against property (21:37–22:16), in which 22:8 (Eng. 22:9) betrays an archaic perspective; perhaps also the regulations governing lawsuits (23:1-9). At least the substance and nucleus of the regulations governing procedure in the case of murder by an unknown hand (Deut. 21:1-9) and the law of the assembly (Deut. 23:2-9)[43] derive from an early period. For the most part, we are dealing with orally transmitted customary law, which can no longer be determined in detail.

4. *Consequences.* How are we to look upon the transitional stage of religion in the period before the state, with respect to both Mosaic Yahwism and later historical developments? It was an organic development, maintaining the central ideas of God's sovereignty and

---

[39] S-F, § 20.2.

[40] A. Alt, "Zur Talionsformel," *ZAW*, LII (1934), 303-5 (= his *Kleine Schriften zur Geschichte des Volkes Israel*, I [1953], 341-44); A. S. Diamond, "An Eye for an Eye," *Iraq*, XIX (1957), 151-55.

[41] A. van Selms, "The Goring Ox in Babylonian and Biblical Law," *ArOr*, XVIII/4 (1950), 321-30.

[42] P. Heinisch, "Das Sklavenrecht in Israel und im Alten Orient," *StC*, XI (1934/35), 201-18.

[43] K. Galling, "Das Gemeindegesetz in Deuteronomium 23," in *Festschrift Alfred Bertholet*, 1950, pp. 176-91.

communion with God, of Yahweh's acting in the lives of men and nations, and of emphasis on the ethical requirements of living according to the rules that express God's will. At the same time, Yahwism, by assimilating and integrating Canaanite concepts and practices, was caught up in a transformation that enabled the nomadic Yahwism of the Mosaic period to survive in a settled civilization. Thus a new settled form of Yahwism began gradually to take shape, which was adapted to the changed circumstances and could be practiced as part of the new way of life. But the emphasis on the cultic element, by means of which the Israelites came increasingly to represent and cultivate their relationship with Yahweh, together with the adoption of Canaanite law, which the Israelites later traced back to Yahweh, marked the first dangerous steps toward degrading the nucleus of Yahwism and an aberrant development.

PART TWO

The Religion of the Monarchy

CHAPTER ONE: KINGSHIP, THE SECOND INFLUENCE

§ 11 EVENTS AND FIGURES

G. W. AHLSTRÖM, *Aspects of Syncretism in Israelite Religion*, 1963; A. ALT, "Jerusalems Aufstieg," *ZDMG*, LXXIX (1925), 1-19 (= his *Kleine Schriften zur Geschichte des Volkes Israel*, III [1959], 243-57); *idem, Die Staatenbildung der Israeliten in Palästina*, 1930 (= *ibid.*, II [1953], 1-65 [English: *Essays on Old Testament History and Religion*, 1966, pp. 171-238]); *idem*, "Das Königtum in den Reichen Israel und Juda," *VT*, I (1951), 2-22 (= *ibid.*, II [1953], 116-34 [English: *ibid.*, pp. 239-60]); *idem*, "Die Weisheit Salomos," *ThLZ*, LXXVI (1951), 139-44 (= *ibid.*, II [1953], 90-99); *idem*, "Der Anteil des Königtums an der sozialen Entwicklung in den Reichen Israel und Juda," in his *Kleine Schriften zur Geschichte des Volkes Israel*, III (1959), 348-72; S. AMSLER, *David, roi et messie*, 1963; W. CASPARI, *Aufkommen und Krise des israelitischen Königtums*, 1909; A. CAUSSE, "La crise de le solidarité de la famille et du clan dans l'ancien Israël," *RHPhR*, X (1930), 24-60; O. EISSFELDT, "Der Gott Bethel," *ARW*, XXVIII (1930), 1-30 (= his *Kleine Schriften*, I [1962], 206-33); *idem*, "Ba'alšamēm und Jahwe," *ZAW*, LVII (1939), 1-31 (= *ibid.*, II [1963], 171-98); G. FOHRER, "Israels Staatsordnung im Rahmen des Alten Orients," *Österreichische Zeitschrift für Öffentliches Recht*, VIII (1957), 129-48; *idem*, "Zion-Jerusalem im Alten Testament," *ThW*, VIII, 292-318; K. GALLING, *Die israelitische Staatsverfassung in ihrer vorderorientalischen Umwelt*, 1929; M. J. MULDER, *Ba'al in het Oude Testament*, 1962; *idem, Kanaänitische goden in het Oude Testament*, 1962; E. NEUFELD, "The Emergence of a Royal-Urban Society in Ancient Israel," *HUCA*, XXXI (1960), 31-53; E. NICHOLSON, "The Centralisation of the Cult in Deuteronomy," *VT*, XIII (1963), 380-89; M. NOTH, "Jerusalem und die israelitische Tradition," *OTS*, VIII (1950), 28-46 (= his *Gesammelte Studien zum Alten Testament*, 1957, pp. 172-87 [English: *The Laws in the Pentateuch and Other Studies*, 1966, pp. 132-44]); J. VAN DER PLOEG, "Les anciens dans l'Ancien Testament," in *Lex tua veritas* (Junker Festschrift), 1961, pp. 175-91; H. H. ROWLEY, "Hezekiah's Reform and Rebellion," *BJRL*, XLIV (1961/62), 395-431 (= his *Men of God*, 1963, pp. 98-132); J. N. SCHOFIELD, "Religion in Palestine During the Monarchy," *JMEOS*, XXII

124   Kingship, the Second Influence

(1938), 37-52; J. SCHREINER, *Sion-Jerusalem, Jahwes Königssitz*, 1963; R. B. Y. SCOTT, "Solomon and the Beginnings of Wisdom in Israel," *VTSuppl*, III (1955), 262-79; J. A. SOGGIN, *Das Königtum in Israel*, 1967; E. W. TODD, "The Reforms of Hezekiah and Josiah," *SJTh*, IX (1956), 288-93; E. VOEGELIN, *Order and History, I: Israel and Revelation*, 1956; G. WALLIS, "Die Anfänge des Königtums in Israel," *WZ Halle-Wittenberg*, XII (1963), 239-47; M. WEINFELD, "Cult Centralization in Israel in the Light of a Neo-Babylonian Analogy," *JNES*, XXIII (1964), 202-12; A. WEISER, *Samuel*, 1962; H. WILDBERGER, "Samuel und die Entstehung des israelitischen Königtums," *ThZ*, XIII (1957), 442-69.

1. *Saul's kingship.* When Saul[1] was advanced to the rank of king, Israel took a crucial step that not only had political, national, cultural, economic, and military consequences, but also had a significant effect on the history of Yahwism. Kingship, therefore, must be called a second influence, following Mosaic Yahwism, because of the positive and negative effects it had on the form of Yahwism that was developing in the settled territory of Palestine.[2] Of course the kingship of Saul was merely a transitional stage between the tribal or city-state form of government of the so-called period of the judges and the establishment of a true state. Saul's rule did not extend over a continuous territorial state, nor did he apparently exercise any domestic political functions; he was primarily a military king called on in time of need. In this he resembles the military leaders of the period before the state; but he stood at the head not of a single tribe but of several tribes, who chose him successively (I Sam. 8; 10:17-27 tells of his election by lot at Mizpah; 9:1–10:16 recounts his anointing as *nāgîd* at Ephraim;[3] 11 describes his acclamation as king at Gilgal). Samuel's rôle in all this must remain uncertain, since tradition depicts him as Nazirite, priest, and prophet, as well as "judge."[4] He may have played a part in bringing his own tribe of Ephraim under the leadership of Saul.

The nature of the OT tradition does not permit us to determine the religio-historical facts. On the one hand, the narrative cycle in I Sam. 9:1–10:16; 11; 13–14 (omitting 13:7b-15bα); 31, which tells of Saul's rise and downfall, is informed by reverence for the king, awareness of his difficult task, and respect for his temporary successes. On the other hand, the narrative in I Sam. 8; 10:17-27, which recounts Saul's elevation to the kingship, in its present form takes

[1] *BHH*, III, 1677-78; *RGG*, V, 1375-77; *IDB*, IV, 228-33.
[2] *BHH*, II, 978-81; *RGG*, III, 1709-14; *IDB*, III, 11-17.
[3] W. Richter, "Die *nāgîd*-Formel," *BZ*, NF IX (1965), 71-84.
[4] *BHH*, III, 1663-64; *RGG*, V, 1357-58; *IDB*, IV, 201-2.

a critical position toward the kingship. The narratives of Saul's rejection (I Samuel 15, on account of his failure to destroy all the spoil taken from the Amalekites; I Sam. 13:7b-15α, on account of his unauthorized offering of sacrifice) as well as the story of his visit to the medium at Endor (I Samuel 28) bear the stamp of a hostile attitude toward the king. These critical and negative voices, however, do not belong to the period of Saul; they are characteristic of a theological interpretation of history represented by later prophetical and priestly circles. This view arose out of conflict with a monarchy that followed its own interests in the realm of nationalism and power politics, and stresses the opposition between secular power and God's power. Saul's own age does not appear to have found such a monarchy to represent a threat to Yahwism, looking on it rather as a necessity in the perilous situation of the Israelites if the nation and Yahwism were to be preserved. There can be no doubt that the monarchy was not imposed in opposition to Yahwism, but came into being in the interests of Yahwism and with the furtherance of its representatives.

2. *David and Solomon. a*) Already in consequence of David's[5] actions the kingship began to develop in a different direction and entail different religious consequences from those envisioned by its first proponents and adherents. Despite many questionable or condemnable actions (e.g., II Sam. 8:2, 4; 11), David was certainly a devout worshiper of Yahweh in the sense that he lived according to the Yahwistic cult (see § 13.4); in his understakings he gladly submitted to Yahweh's guidance through priestly oracles and the dicta of cult prophets. There is furthermore no reason to doubt the tradition that he devoted his artistic talent to the service of the cult and composed psalms, even though it is highly doubtful whether any of his songs—probably only few in number—have been preserved.[6] In addition, after the conquest of Jerusalem, he took the ark, the symbol of an anti-Philistine tribal association and the guarantee of divine aid (§ 10.1), which had fallen into the hands of the Philistines and then been discarded by them, called it "by the name of Yahweh Sabaoth, who sits enthroned on the cherubim," and transferred it to Jerusalem, his capital city (II Samuel 6). Later, at least, the ark was considered the palladium of the God who was superior to all other

---

[5] *BHH*, I, 324-29; *RGG*, II, 48-50; *IDB*, I, 771-82.
[6] The laments for Saul and Jonathan in II Sam. 1:19-27 and the lament for Abner in II Sam. 3:33-34, however, probably do derive from David.

beings of the divine realm and a symbol of David's election; in other words, it acquired theological and dynastic significance.[7] Its association with Yahweh implied that he, the distant God, was linked to the residence of the king; this laid the groundwork for his being considered the deity of the Israelite state.

But the transfer of the ark also had another side, which probably betrays Canaanite influence: besides the offering of sacrifices, there took place a solemn procession accompanied by music and cultic dancing, the latter led by the king himself exercising a priestly function. David first housed the ark in a tent that he pitched beside the spring Gihon. He intended later to follow Canaanite example and build a temple, the privilege and task of victorious kings,[8] in which to house the ark. But he had to submit to the violent opposition that arose in the name of Yahweh, which was communicated to David through Nathan the seer (II Sam. 7:1-7, 17); the time was not yet ripe for such a step.[9]

Despite this victory achieved by the supporters of an unadulterated Yahwism, Canaanite influence gained a large measure of success in Jerusalem. The ancient Canaanite city, which had been and continued to be occupied by the Jebusites, joined gradually by a sizable number of Judeans, became the private property of David and his dynasty after being taken, and had a special constitutional status alongside Judah and Israel. David inherited the privileges and obligations of the earlier Canaanite city kings, at the same time acquiring the priestly functions that were rooted in Canaanite tradition—perhaps as successor of the last city king Melchizedek (cf. Gen.

---

[7] J. Maier, *Das altisraelitische Ladeheiligtum*, 1965, pp. 63-64, suggests instead that the ark was the palladium of the militias of Judah and Israel, which were so successful under David's leadership, and a symbol of David's election, making the significance of the ark political and dynastic.

[8] A. S. Kapelrud, "Temple Building, a Task for Gods and Kings," *Or*, XXXII (1963), 56-62.

[9] G. W. Ahlström, "Der Prophet Nathan und der Tempelbau," *VT*, XI (1961), 113-27; H. van den Bussche, "Le Texte de la Prophétie de Nathan sur la Dynastie Davidique," *ALBO*, II:7 (1948); H. Gese, "Der Davidsbund und die Zionserwählung," *ZThK*, LXI (1964), 10-26; E. Kutsch, "Die Dynastie von Gottes Gnaden," *ibid.*, LVIII (1961), 137-53; S. Mowinckel, "Natanforjettelsen 2 Sam. kap 7," *SEA*, XII (1947), 220-29; E. S. Mulder, "The Prophecy of Nathan in II Samuel 7," *OuTWP*, 1960, pp. 36-42; M. Noth, "David und Israel in II Samuel 7," in *Mélanges Bibliques Robert*, 1957, pp. 122-30 (= his *The Laws in the Pentateuch and Other Studies*, 1966, pp. 250-59); M. Simon, "La prophétie de Nathan et le Temple (Remarques sur II Sam 7)," *RHPhR*, XXXII (1952), 41-58; A. Weiser, "Die Tempelbaukrise unter David," *ZAW*, LXXVII (1965), 153-68.

14:18-20; Ps. 110:4).[10] Thus through his relationship to the figure of the sacral king in other ancient Near Eastern cultures he came to occupy a special place in the Jerusalem cult. As a consequence this cult borrowed and adopted the Canaanite forms; in fact, the outcome seems to have been an actual fusion of Yahwism with the Canaanite cult of Jerusalem, whether the latter was devoted to El, Ṣedeq, or Shalim. This is already suggested by the fact that, in contrast to the names of David's sons who were born at Hebron, none of the names of the eleven or twelve born at Jerusalem have "Yahweh" as a theophorous element, although "El" occurs in several cases (cf. II Sam. 5:14-16), and David's son Jedidiah, "beloved of Yahweh," adopted or was given the name "Solomon," which, like the name of David's son Absalom, is connected with the divine name "Shalim" contained in the name "Jerusalem." There is the further unmistakable evidence that the Canaanite priestly family of Zadok[11] officiated as priests of Yahweh, at first alongside Abiathar, who came with David,[12] and later alone.

Thus the door was opened to the influx of other Canaanite ideas, the adoption of which in many cases determined the official religious policies of the state during the monarchy.[13] Hitherto Yahwism had developed historically in the settled territory as an independent entity, with some changes due to Canaanite influence (§ 9.1). From the time of David on we encounter a second movement with a tendency toward syncretism, toward a deliberate coalescence of Yahwism with the Canaanite cults. This tendency was politically determined: in the united kingdom of David and Solomon and afterward in the divided kingdoms the Israelites and Canaanites living side by side had to be placed on an equal footing if tensions were to be avoided. This resulted in an attempt to create an ideological basis

[10] S-F, § 27.1; see also *BHH*, II, 1185-86; *RGG*, IV, 843-45; *IDB*, III, 343; H. W. Hertzberg, "Die Melkisedek-Traditionen," *JPOS*, VIII (1928), 169-70 (= his *Beiträge zur Traditionsgeschichte und Theologie des Alten Testaments*, 1962, pp. 36-44); G. Levi della Vida, "El 'Elyon in Genesis 14:18-20," *JBL*, LXIII (1944), 1-9; R. Rendtorff, "El, Ba'al und Jahwe," *ZAW*, LXXVIII (1966), 277-91.

[11] *BHH*, III, 2200; *RGG*, VI, 1860; *IDB*, IV, 928-29; E. Auerbach, "Die Herkunft der Ṣadokiden," *ZAW*, XLIX (1931), 327-28; K. Budde, "Die Herkunft Ṣadok's," *ibid.*, LII (1934), 42-50; *idem*, "Noch einmal: Die Herkunft Ṣadok's," *ibid.*, p. 160; H. H. Rowley, "Zadok and Nehushtan," *JBL*, LVIII (1939), 113-41; *idem*, "Melchizedek and Zadok (Gen 14 and Ps 110)," in *Festschrift Alfred Bertholet*, 1950, pp. 461-72.

[12] *BHH*, I, 360; *IDB*, I, 6-7.

[13] J. A. Soggin, "Der offiziell geförderte Synkretismus in Israel während des 10. Jahrhunderts," *ZAW*, LXXVIII (1966), 179-204.

common to all, that is, a state religion, through a fusion of Yahwism and Canaanite religion—an attempt only temporarily interrupted or reversed by the so-called reforms of some of the kings. The politically motivated attitude of toleration toward the Canaanites had religious consequences that were bound to appear suspect to many. At the same time, the elevation of Jerusalem to the status of official residence of the Davidic dynasty, the transfer of Yahweh's presence thither, and the expansion of Yahwism through the adoption of Canaanite concepts laid the groundwork for the gradually increasing importance of the city, which reached its culmination only many centuries later.[14]

b) The reign of Solomon[15] marked a significant step forward. Since David had raised him to the position of coregent and successor by a kind of coup d'état and without previously consulting the representatives of the people (I Kings 1),[16] he sought a different kind of official legitimation: within the framework of a royal novella following Egyptian example, he derived his legitimation from Yahweh himself (I Kings 3:4-15).[17] Solomon actually based his installation as king on the narrative, which is therefore placed at the beginning of the account of his reign. It takes as its point of departure the moment of the coronation day in the Egyptian royal novella when the new ruler is granted the titles and names of his kingship in an encounter with the deity. In Solomon's case, therefore, divine legitimation took the place of political acknowledgment through a treaty between king and people. This legitimation, however, referred only to the person of Solomon, so that it had to be renewed or extended for his successors. In this way there came to be divine recognition and guarantees for the ruler and the Davidic dynasty.

Furthermore Solomon succeeded where David had failed: in building a temple. Immediately to the north of the ancient Jebusite city of David he established a new quarter, which made it possible to build a new royal residence and relieved the overcrowding suffered by the growing population. There, after the manner of the residence temple of the Egyptian New Kingdom, palace and temple were built

[14] *BHH*, II, 820-50; *RGG*, III, 593-96; *IDB*, II, 843-66.
[15] *BHH*, III, 1651-53; *RGG*, V, 1336-39; *IDB*, IV, 339-408.
[16] G. Fohrer, "Der Vertrag zwischen König und Volk in Israel," *ZAW*, LXXI (1959), 1-22.
[17] S. Herrmann, "Die Königsnovelle in Ägypten und Israel," *WZ Leipzig*, III (1953/54), 51-62; H. Brunner, "Das hörende Herz," *ThLZ*, LXXIX (1954), 697-700.

together as a single complex. The construction of the Temple was of enormous significance for the period that followed. The location of the palace and Temple in the same city, surrounded by a wall, stated clearly that the Temple was the property of the Davidic dynasty and a state sanctuary, in which the private sacrifices of the king were offered and the official state cult was performed. Thus Yahweh became the official deity of the territory ruled by Solomon and his successors, inhabited primarily by Israelites and Canaanites; Jerusalem was declared its chief and most distinguished cultic site. Since the building was erected with Phoenician help and according to Canaanite model, and since it marked the final victory of the practice of having fixed cultic sites in certain localities, as was usual in the settled areas, the sanctuary itself became a sacred site in its own right, opening the door to additional Canaanite ideas and practices. The ark, it is true, was transferred to the Temple, and in the time of Solomon the so-called ark narrative (I Sam. 4:1–7:1; II Sam. 6; 7:1-7, 17) was probably assembled out of its original component narratives and expanded to demonstrate the legitimacy of Jerusalem as the site of the ark; the power of the ark was expressly emphasized in this context.[18] The ark nevertheless quickly lost its earlier importance, while the Temple cult underwent further elaboration after the Canaanite model. As a result, there was an increasing tendency toward syncretism. In addition, after the beginnings made in the time of David, a new change took place in the form of Yahwism, with more emphasis on the cult and religious nationalism (§ 13.4-5). The subsequent historical rôle of Jerusalem was also significantly affected by the building of the Temple and the transfer to it of the cult, which had previously been performed in the city of David. The presence of Yahweh, who now like a "king" had his own "house," was associated with the Temple, so that from Solomon's dedication of the Temple on (I Kings 8:12-13) we find the idea that Yahweh "dwells" at Jerusalem. At first this notion was associated with the Temple itself, later with the mountain on which it was built (Isa. 8:18).

Besides Solomon's tolerant attitude toward the Canaanites belonging to his kingdom and his politically motivated accommodation with Canaanite religion, his diplomatic and economic relations with the international world of the ancient Near East led to the fostering of intellectual and cultural exchange, in consequence of which wisdom

[18] S-F, § 32.3.

teaching above all was borrowed from Egypt. This served in Jerusalem for the instruction of the royal officials who became necessary with the developing administration. At the school that presumably existed in Jerusalem from the time of Solomon on, as in other cities and royal residences of the ancient Near East,[19] among other subjects two forms of wisdom were taught, which can be ascertained from I Kings 5:12-13 (Eng. 4:32-33) :

He [Solomon] also uttered three thousand proverbs; and his songs were a thousand and five. He spoke of trees, from the cedar that is in Lebanon to the hyssop that grows out of the wall; he spoke also of beasts, and of birds, and of reptiles, and of fish.

When we make allowance for the exaggeration of court style, which ascribes all achievements to the ruler himself, and for the erroneous association of the large numbers with proverbs and songs, we can observe two forms of wisdom teaching or learning: academic wisdom, reduced to the form of lists; and practical wisdom, expressed in proverbs or songs. After its beginnings in the time of Solomon, the latter came to play an important rôle especially during the reign of Hezekiah, and developed into an independent approach to life (§ 13.6). Like Canaanite law, which was also borrowed, it became necessary during the transition to an urban civilization and the development of the governmental system, when the customs and practices of the nomads and peasantry could no longer be accepted without question and new realms opened up to which the customs of the past could make no contribution. This practical wisdom, with its sagacious rules for the conduct of life, was gradually integrated into Yahwism, because Yahwism was a religion of life and conduct according to hallowed rules expressing God's will.

Finally, we must note that Solomon admitted alien cults for those of his wives that came from other peoples, and apparently permitted sanctuaries of other gods to be built (I Kings 11:7). Thus the Jerusalemites could become familiar with other cults at first hand.

3. *To the beginning of Assyrian ascendancy.* The historical picture from the division of the kingdom after the death of Solomon to about 750 B.C., some two centuries in all, can be summarized briefly. In the cities Canaanite elements penetrated increasingly into Yahwism, until by around 750 the latter was not much more than one variety of the Canaanite cults; syncretism to all intents and purposes had won the day. The reactions against these tendencies—in Judah

[19] See K. Galling, *Die Krise der Aufklärung in Israel,* 1952.

under Asa and Jehoshaphat and in both states under Joash and Jehu—constituted merely delaying actions. In the countryside, however, where the population was often in open opposition to their own particular capital or official cultic center, the beginning of our period witnessed merely the further development of the Yahweh cult, until finally syncretism made inroads there as well.

a) In Jerusalem after the division of the kingdom syncretism first continued to develop under Rehoboam and Abijah, not least in consequence of the marriage policies of the royal house. Rehoboam's mother was an Ammonite whose name indicates the worship of an alien goddess. Asa's mother, who came from the family of Absalom, the son of David who married an Aramean princess from northern Transjordan, set up an "abominable image" (*mipleṣet*) for the goddess Asherah; such terms elsewhere refer to sexual symbols (I Kings 15:13).[20]

The Davidic dynasty did not, however, intend to renounce Yahwism. In fact, the dynasty asserted its divine legitimation by expanding II Samuel 7 through the addition of the core of vss. 8-16, 18-29, according to which Yahweh guarantees the continued existence of the royal house. The promises made to Solomon personally in I Kings 3:4-15 were now extended to the entire dynasty. This most likely took place in the time of Rehoboam. The coronation ritual expressed concretely the legitimation of each individual king. Somewhat later, because tinged with prophetical thought, is the legitimation of the Davidic dynasty against other claims by means of the narrative in I Sam. 16:1-13, in which Samuel anoints David. Furthermore, occasional efforts were made in Jerusalem to purify the religion of Yahweh. This took place under Asa,[21] who, among other things, did away with the male temple prostitutes that had existed alongside the female prostitutes[22] in Jerusalem; again under Jehoshaphat;[23] and finally a third time under Joash,[24] after a period

[20] On the position of the queen mother in the Old Testament, see H. Donner, "Art und Herkunft des Amtes der Königinmutter im Alten Testament," in *Friedrich Festschrift*, 1959, pp. 105-45; G. Molin, "Die Stellung der Geʙira im Staate Juda," *ThZ*, X (1954), 161-75. The importance of the queen mother is best explained by the legal custom of documenting the transfer of rule to a new king by having him take official possession of his predecessor's harem (cf. II Sam. 16:21 ff.); in this fashion the queen mother, as the most important person in the harem, legitimized the right of her son to rule.
[21] *BHH*, I, 133-34; *IDB*, I, 243-44.
[22] *BHH*, III, 1948-49; *RGG*, V, 642-43; *IDB*, III, 932-33.
[23] *BHH*, II, 886-88; *RGG*, III, 858-59; *IDB*, II, 815-16.
[24] *BHH*, II, 868; *IDB*, II, 909-10.

of marked syncretistic tendencies in consequence of Judah's dependence on the Northern Israelite dynasty of Omri and the predominance of the Baal cult during the reign of Queen Athaliah.

b) In the countryside of Judah the sanctuaries were apparently served primarily by Levitical priests. These rural priests were much more cautious about adopting alien elements than the Jerusalemites were. They sought to introduce into the faith and cult only those elements that were not at odds with the basic nature of Yahwism, though in the process of doing so they undoubtedly helped Yahwism develop into a cultic religion. In this period the first ritual regulations were laid down. For example, the directives concerning special days of the year (Exod. 34:18*a*α, 21*a*, 22*a*α, 26*a*) and sacrificial matters (34:20*b*β, 25*a*, 25*b*, 26*b*) contained in the so-called cultic decalogue of the Yahwist may well go back to regulations for the sanctuaries of Judah, presupposing the situation of Canaanite Palestine.

Of course the line between cultic Yahwism and the Canaanite cults was not always and everywhere sharply drawn. The distinction was sometimes obscured, so that the cultic tendency came very close to syncretism, and it may have been hard to distinguish baalized Yahwism from a Baalism with Yahwistic overtones.

c) In the Northern Kingdom of Israel, the first king, Jeroboam I,[25] established two state sanctuaries at Bethel and Dan after the division of the kingdom. The former continued a long tradition of sacred sites located there since before the Israelites, while the latter was associated with the establishment of a sanctuary by the tribe of Dan, as recounted by the original redaction of Judges 17–18, which underwent a Jerusalemite revision toward the end of the monarchy, tracing the sanctuary to a reprehensible double theft.[26] At these sanctuaries rather than at Jerusalem the North Israelites were supposed to worship the God who brought Israel up out of Egypt, symbolized by images of golden bulls (I Kings 12:28-29). The story of the bull image at the mountain of God (Exodus 32), a polemic against such symbols, and the equally sharp words of Hosea (Hos. 8:4*b*-6; 10:5-6*a;* 13:2) suggest not cultic standards[27] but wooden sculptures in the shape of bulls covered with plates of gold. These

[25] *BHH,* II, 819-20; *RGG,* III, 591-92; *IDB,* II, 840-42.

[26] M. Noth, "The Background of Judges 17–18," in *Israel's Prophetic Heritage,* 1962, pp. 68-85.

[27] O. Eissfeldt, "Lade und Stierbild," *ZAW,* LVIII (1940/41), 190-215 (= his *Kleine Schriften,* II [1963], 282-305).

did not constitute a pedestal for the invisible deity to stand on, but rather represented him in animal form.[28]

If this is a sign of Canaanite influence, it increased during the rule of the dynasty of Omri,[29] whose policies toward their Israelite and Canaanite subjects had as their goal equal rights for both groups. This amounted in practice to a promotion of Canaanite culture, which had hitherto been at a disadvantage in the Northern Kingdom. In addition, as a consequence of their close association with Phoenician Tyre, the Omrides adopted and propagated the cult of Tyrian Baal.

The revolution of Jehu[30] constituted a temporary reverse. He stamped out and prohibited the Canaanite cult. His campaign never went beyond superficial political measures, however, with the result that the tensions were not resolved and the internal Canaanization continued. In the time of Jeroboam II [31] the cult of Baal and other Canaanite deities was apparently even practiced publicly once again (see Hos. 2:15 [Eng. 2:13]; 8:4b-5; 10:5; Amos 3:14, 8:14, emended), although Yahwism remained the official cult. Of course this Yahwism had been so transformed by fusion with Canaanite elements that it differed almost only in name from the Baal cult (see, for example, Hos. 4:12-14). Typical of the situation are Israelite personal names found on ostraca that may date from the period of Jeroboam II: only a third contain "Yahweh" as their theophorous element; two thirds are compounded with "Baal." This means that either the parents of only a third of the people named were true worshipers of Yahweh or the term "Baal" was also used uncritically for Yahweh.

d) In any case, the situation was serious for Yahwism. It is therefore understandable that religious considerations in consciously Yahwistic circles produced an attitude of rejection and intolerance toward the Canaanites. The Yahwist and Elohist, and later Deuteronomy, express this attitude, demanding that the Canaanites be driven out or destroyed (Yahwist: Exod. 34:11-12; Elohist: 23:28, 32-33). The Yahwist expresses this position most clearly, having Yahweh say:

Observe what I command you this day. Behold, I will drive out before you the Amorites, the Canaanites, the Hittites, the Perizzites, the Hivites, and the Jebusites. Take heed to yourself, lest you give assurances to the

[28] See M. Weippert, "Gott und Stier," ZDPV, LXXVII (1961), 93-117.
[29] BHH, II, 1341-42; RGG, IV, 1630; IDB, III, 600-601.
[30] BHH, II, 808-10; RGG, III, 574-75; IDB, II, 817-19.
[31] BHH, II, 820; RGG, III, 592-93; IDB, II, 842.

inhabitants of the land whither you go, lest it become a snare in the midst of you.

Form and motif analysis reveals three elements in this passage: (1) Yahweh's driving out of the Canaanites, in order to realize the promise of territory; (2) a warning to the Israelites not to admit exceptions through assurances and the treaties embodying them; (3) the motivating threat that the Canaanites will otherwise tempt the Israelites ino apostasy from Yahweh. In content, though not in form, the third motif is dominant: religious danger. In the view of the narrator, this danger would have been avoided if Israel had refused to give any assurances allowing the Canaanites to remain, and had instead driven them out to the last man. This shows that the syncretism promoted by the attitude of political toleration was the cause of the contrary hostile religious attitude toward the Canaanites.

4. *The period of Assyrian ascendancy.* While the Northern Kingdom of Israel soon fell to the Assyrians, the Yahweh cult was kept up for more than a century at the newly restored sanctuary of Bethel, albeit at the instigation of the Assyrians themselves.[32] The Kingdom of Judah continued to exist. Since Ahaz, its king,[33] had become an Assyrian vassal, he had to introduce the cults of Assyrian gods at Jerusalem as a token of submission. From this time forward, in contrast to the situation during the reign of the dynasty of Omri, which had carried out the cult of Tyrian Baal voluntarily to promote the alliance with Tyre, alien cults of Assyrian deities, followed later by Babylonian and Egyptian, were compulsorily introduced into Judah as a consequence of policies that either could not be evaded or were actually enforced, usually as an expression of dependence on the ruling great power. There is little point therefore in joining with Deuteronomic theology to condemn the kings of Judah; usually their only choice was between vassalage, which implied introduction of the cults of the sovereign, and the even worse fate of incorporation into the Assyrian or Babylonian provincial system, which would mean deportation of the upper classes. Thus the period from about 735 to 587 B.C. is dominated by the repeated influence of foreign cults. As a consequence, not only were Canaanite elements able to proliferate

[32] The cult was discontinued with the fall of the Assyrian Empire when Josiah annexed the territory and suppressed it in favor of the Jerusalem cult. It was reinstituted under Babylonian rule until the sanctuary was destroyed in the period between 555 and 540.

[33] *BHH,* I, 49-50; *RGG,* I, 190; *IDB,* I, 64-66.

unhindered, but other alien elements also infiltrated Yahwism. The period of exclusive Canaanite influence was over. After Ahaz took his oath of allegiance to the Assyrian king at Damascus, he used an Aramean bronze altar there as model for an identical altar, which he ordered built in the Jerusalem Temple for the Assyrian cult.

His successor Hezekiah[34] sought once more to peruse nationalistic policies, with the goal of making Judah independent of Assyria. This attempt furnishes the setting for his cultic reformation, which was intended to purify the Jerusalem cult of all non-Israelite elements, and replace syncretism with a cultic piety compatible with Yahwism. This was the purpose behind the removal of the bronze serpent (the symbol of a beneficent demon), the masseboth, and the asheroth, and probably also accounts for the new altar set up by Ahaz. We are dealing here with political measures, one element in the renunciation of foreign sovereignty and the striving for independence. Hezekiah's attitude toward the sanctuaries throughout the countryside of Judah cannot be determined with certainty. He certainly did not eliminate them utterly, as the Deuteronomistic author of Kings asserts (II Kings 18:4); at most we should think in terms of a purifaction of their cults through the removal of foreign elements.

But the two revolts against Assyria in which Hezekiah took part miscarried, and even led to temporary loss of large portions of the countryside of Judah. In 701, Sennacherib even tried to subjugate Jerusalem; against all expectations, it was saved by his sudden departure (see II Kings 18–19; Isaiah 36–37). Although the detailed circumstances cannot be made out, since several reasons for Sennacherib's retreat are stated or implied (II Kings 19:7, 8-9, 35), the occasion served to increase considerably the significance of Jerusalem and its Temple: Jerusalem, as the event was later interpreted, was the rock on which the almost invincible Assyrian foundered. The Isaiah legends together with the prophetical discourses they contain, which certainly do not derive from Isaiah but from a much later period, show that this deliverance led to the belief, which later became almost a dogma, that Jerusalem could not be taken (see Jer. 7:4).

In the religious sphere, Hezekiah's failure meant reversion to the unfortunate situation that had prevailed earlier. Under Manasseh,[35]

---

[34] F. L. Moriarty, "The Chronicler's Account of Hezekiah's Reform," *CBQ*, XXVII (1965), 399-406; see also *BHH*, II, 729-30; *RGG*, III, 366-68; *IDB*, II, 598-600.

[35] *BHH*, II, 1137; *RGG*, IV, 707-8; *IDB*, III, 254-55; M. Haran, "The Dis-

Assyrian and other non-Yahwistic cults were practiced once more in Jerusalem. Baal, Astarte, and the goat deities of the fields were worshiped, masseboth and asheroth were set up once more, a special place was set aside in the Valley of Hinnom[36] for child sacrifice, a symbol of the goddess Ishtar was set up in the Temple, in her honor sacral prostitution was practiced, for which even a special house was built; in the outer courts stood altars for the Assyrian astral deities and a throne chariot for the procession of the sun-god Shamash; even the worship of Tammuz, originally a Sumerian god, was carried on in Jerusalem for several decades. In this religious mishmash the uniqueness of Yahwism threatened to smother completely.

At the same time an opposition was forming against a monarchy and its policies that permitted such a state of affairs. Manasseh had to contend with considerable resistance in Judah during his reign, and was only able to silence public opposition by violent measures. The resistance movement continued on in secret, finally merging into the political and religious reforms of Josiah, which we shall discuss elsewhere (§ 21). Upon the sudden death of the latter king, foreign cults once more made inroads in Jerusalem (see Jer. 7:16-20; Ezekiel 8).

Nevertheless, in contrast to the earlier Canaanite influences, these left no permanent marks. This is true in the first place because they were predominantly politically motivated, so that the intensity of their effect varied with the political situation; they frequently encountered rejection or hatred. Unlike the Canaanite cults, they did not determine the atmosphere in which the Israelites lived and from which they could not escape. In addition, the movements within Yahwism that had not been weakened by syncretism had so fortified themselves that they were no longer subject to fundamental change by outside influences. Among them the prophetical movement, beginning in the eighth century, deserves special mention for its part in the increasing resistance, now much stronger than during the earlier period of the monarchy.

5. *The beginning of the Diaspora.* We cannot paint a clear picture of the subsequent existence of the upper classes of the Northern

---

appearance of the Ark," *IEJ*, XIII (1963), 46-58; E. Nielsen, "Politiske forhold og kulturelle strømninger i Israel og Juda under Manasse," *DTT*, XCII (1966), 1-10.

[36] *BHH*, II, 723; *IDB*, II, 606.

Kingdom of Israel, whom the Assyrians had deported.[37] During the reign of Manasseh the foundation seems to have been laid for the Israelite military colonies in Egypt. Most of our knowledge about these colonies is due to the papyri from Elephantine, an island in the Nile, which date from a later period. On this island a temple was built (before 525 B.C.), in which both Yahweh and the god Bethel in threefold form were worshiped (see § 14.2).

6. *Literary consequences. a)* The first basic narrative of the Hexateuchal traditions, which was transmitted orally, was expanded during the early period of the monarchy into a second basic narrative; when the kingdom was divided after the death of Solomon, it was probably extant in written form. The most important sections added at this time were the following: the wooing of Rebecca, Jacob's reconciliation with Esau, the Joseph novella, Moses' first interview with Pharaoh, the preliminary Egyptian plagues, the introduction of a judicial system on the advice of Moses' father-in-law, the story of Balaam, the designation of territories for Gad and Reuben, and the appointment of Joshua to succeed Moses. The revision may have taken place at Jerusalem, in line with the incipient nationalism of the Davidic and Solomonic periods with their growing historical consciousness. After the kingdom was divided, the second basic narrative split into a southern and a northern form. About 850-800 B.C., the former became the source stratum of the Yahwist (J); before the middle of the eighth century, the latter became the source stratum of the Elohist (E). If we think in terms of a third ancient source stratum (J[1], L, N), we may assume that it developed out of the first basic narrative about 800 B.C. or shortly later. Two motives were primarily responsible for the production of these source strata: the intention to survey and portray a specific historical period that was important to Israel, and the endeavor to permeate the account with religion and understand the events theologically.

In addition, during the early or middle period of the monarchy the traditions about the heroic figures of the period before the state, which comprised individual narratives and narrative cycles and had already been adapted so as to apply to Israel as a whole, were brought together into a pre-Deuteronomistic Book of Judges, a loose and unorganized collection. The essential traditions about Saul and David also had already come into being during the early monarchy:

[37] W. F. Albright, "An Ostracon from Calah and the North-Israelite Diaspora," *BASOR*, CXLIX (1958), 33-36.

the narratives of Saul's rise and downfall, of David's rise, and of his succession. While the story of Saul's rise and downfall is popular in nature, the authors of the other two narratives probably resided at the courts of David and Solomon. In the period that followed, other narratives were added, in which prophetical and priestly thought took issue with the early story of the monarchy, so that these later narratives often conflict with the earlier tradition: the so-called story of Samuel's boyhood, the nucleus of the narrative of Israel's conversion and Samuel's victory over the Philistines, a narrative of Saul's elevation to the kingship, the original form of Samuel's farewell address, the two versions of the rejection of Saul, and the narrative of Saul's visit to the medium. Primarily at the royal courts, less frequently at the temples, were produced the annals, which contain official records of important events occuring each year; the chronicles, which record the dates of the kings and notes about their deeds and fates; and the other documents expressly mentioned in the Books of Kings: the Acts of Solomon, the Chronicles of the Kings of Israel, and the Chronicles of the Kings of Judah, which clearly comprised extracts from the court annals and must have been accessible to the public. In addition, in the late post-exilic period the Chronicler recorded or adapted a series of notes concerning the fortifications and military conduct of the kings of Judah, which undoubtedly derive from an ancient source.[38]

b) The institution of kingship naturally had an effect on jurisprudence. Thus the so-called Covenant Code (Exod. 20:24–23:9) and Proto-Deuteronomy (Deut. 4:44–11:32*; 12; 14–26*; 27:1-10; 28:1-68), like their ancient Near Eastern parallels, can be termed royal legal codes. They are not intended to record current customary law but to furnish the basis for a legal reform by using new regulations or judgments in particular cases to change earlier decisions. The so-called Covenant Code most likely came into being in the Northern Kingdom of Israel during the ninth century, perhaps in the context of Jehu's revolution; Proto-Deuteronomy probably originated in the same place during the first half of the eighth century, perhaps during the reign of Jeroboam II.

c) In addition, the practical wisdom that was taught in the royal schools was gradually collected and preserved for posterity. In the collection constituting Prov. 10–22:16, some of the aphorisms and minor collections, perhaps even the basis of the two major components (10–15; 16–22:16), may derive from the period of the monar-

[38] S-F, § 31–35.

chy. The superscription of the collection in Proverbs 25–29, which places its origin in the reign of Hezekiah, has the aura of credibility. *d*) Finally, royal songs of religious and cultic nature were composed; some have been preserved in the Psalter. Several belonged to the coronation ritual of the king.[39] They typically derive the subordinate power of the king from the power of Yahweh. Oracles play a rôle in some of these songs, for instance Psalm 2, an accession song, Psalm 110, a collection of oracles, and Psalm 45, a wedding song. Others are laments or songs of thanksgiving that refer to a war, for instance Psalms 18B; 20; 44; 89B; and 144. Also worthy of mention are Psalm 21, intended for an annual commemoration, Psalm 72, with its prayer for a blessing for the king, Psalm 101, with its exposition of the principles according to which the king rules, and Psalm 132, intended for the founding day of the Jerusalem Temple.

§ 12 THE RELIGIOUS CONCEPTION
AND SIGNIFICANCE OF THE MONARCHY

A. ALT, "Das Königtum in den Reichen Israel und Juda," *VT*, I (1951), 2-22 (= his *Kleine Schriften*, II [1953], 116-34 [English: *Essays on Old Testament History and Religion*, 1966, pp. 239-60]) ; B. BALSCHEIT, *Gottesbund and Staat*, 1940; K.-H. BERNHARDT, *Das Problem der altorientalischen Königsideologie im Alten Testament*, 1961; W. BEYERLIN, "Das Königscharisma bei Saul," *ZAW*, LXXIII (1961), 186-201; G. COOKE, "The Israelite King as Son of God," *ZAW*, LXXIII (1961), 202-25; I. ENGNELL, *Studies in Divine Kingship in the Ancient Near East*, 2nd ed., 1967; K. F. EULER, "Königtum und Götterwelt in den altaramäischen Inschriften Nordsyriens," *ZAW*, LVI (1938), 272-313; G. FOHRER, "Der Vertrag zwischen König und Volk in Israel," *ZAW*, LXXI (1959), 1-22; J. DE FRAINE, *L'aspect religieux de la royauté israélite*, 1954; idem, "Peut-on parler d'un véritable sacerdoce du roi en Israël?" *BEThL*, XII (1959), 537-47; H. FRANKFORT, *Kingship and the Gods*, 1948; K. GALLING, *Die israelitische Staatsverfassung in ihrer vorderorientalischen Umwelt*, 1929; J. GRAY, "Canaanite Kingship in Theory and Practice," *VT*, II (1952), 193-220; R. HALLEVY, "Charismatic Kingship in Israel," *Tarbiz*, XXX (1960/61), 231-41, 314-40; idem, "The Place of the Monarchy in Israelite Religion," *ibid.*, XXXII (1962/63), 215-24; S. H. HOOKE, ed., *Myth, Ritual, and Kingship*, 1958; E. O. JAMES, "Aspects of Sacrifice in the Old Testament," *ET*, L (1938/39), 151-55; A. R. JOHNSON, "The Rôle of the King in the Jerusalem Cultus," in S. H. HOOKE, ed., *The Labyrinth*, 1935, pp. 75-111; idem, *Sacral Kingship in Ancient Israel*, 2nd ed., 1967; A. A. KOOLHAS, *Theocratie en Monarchie in Israël*, 1957;

---

[39] G. von Rad, "Das judäische Königsritual," *ThLZ*, LXXII (1947), 211-16 (= his *Gesammelte Studien*, 1958, pp. 205-13 [English: *The Problem of the Hexateuch and Other Essays*, 1966, pp. 222-31]) .

140   Kingship, the Second Influence

H.-J. KRAUS, *Die Königsherrschaft Gottes im Alten Testament*, 1951; E. KUTSCH, *Salbung als Rechtsakt im Alten Testament und im Alten Orient*, 1963; R. LABAT, *Le caractère religieux de la royauté assyro-babylonienne*, 1939; F. M. T. DE LIAGRE BÖHL, *Nieuwjaarsfeest en Koningsdag in Babylon en Israël*, 1927; A. LODS, "La divinisation du roi dans l'Orient méditerranéen et ses répercussions dans l'ancien Israël," *RHPhR*, X (1930), 209-21; C. R. NORTH, "The Old Testament Estimate of the Monarchy," *AJSL*, LXVIII (1931/32), 1-19; *idem*, "The Religious Aspect of Hebrew Kingship," *ZAW*, L (1932), 8-38; M. NOTH, "Gott, König und Volk im Alten Testament," *ZThK*, XLVII (1950), 157-91 (= his *Gesammelte Studien*, 1957, pp. 188-229 [English: *The Laws in the Pentateuch and Other Studies*, 1966, pp. 145-78]); H. RINGGREN, "König und Messias," *ZAW*, LXIV (1952), 120-47; C. S. RODD, "Kingship and Cult," *London Quarterly and Holborn Review*, 1959, pp. 21-26; E. I. J. ROSENTHAL, "Some Aspects of the Hebrew Monarchy," *JJS*, IX (1958), 1-18; *The Sacral Kingship*, 1959; H. SCHMIDT, *Der Mythos vom wiederkehrenden König im Alten Testament*, 1925; J. A. SOGGIN, "Zur Entwicklung des alttestamentlichen Königtums," *ThZ*, XV (1959), 401-18; *idem*, "Charisma und Institution im Königtum Sauls," *ZAW*, LXXV (1963), 54-65; *idem, Das Königtum in Israel*, 1967; T. C. G. THORNTON, "Charismatic Kingship in Israel and Judah," *JThSt*, NS XIV (1963), 1-11; R. DE VAUX, "Le roi d'Israël, vassal de Yahvé," in *Mélanges E. Tisserant*, I (1964), 119-33; G. WIDENGREN, *The King and the Tree of Life in Ancient Near Eastern Religion*, 1951; *idem, Sakrales Königtum im Alten Testament und im Judentum*, 1955; *idem*, "King and Covenant," *JSS*, II (1957), 1-32.

1. *Consequences of the monarchy.* We have already stated that the effect of the kingship on the history of Yahwism justifies its being called a second influence (§ 11.1). The first effect was the rôle accorded Yahwism in the structure of the state: it was the official religion. On the one hand, it was a temple religion; the Jerusalem Temple was the dwelling place of Yahweh, and any other temples—especially in the Northern Kingdom of Israel—were of lesser significance. On the other hand, it was an ideology that placed Israelite and Canaanite citizens under a common obligation and bound them together. For this purpose of reconciling Israelites and Canaanites, Yahwism was guided in the direction of syncretism until well into the eighth century, despite all resistance and reaction.

In this context the significance of Jerusalem came to exceed by far that of a capital city and royal residence. Not only the Temple, but gradually also the mountain on which the Temple was built and the city as a whole came to be considered the dwelling place of God, and therefore holy (Isa. 31:4; 48:2; Pss. 15:1; 24:3; 46:5 [Eng. 46:4]; 48:2-3; 87). In eschatological prophecy and the Chronicler's theology this estimation will rise even higher (§ 26.1-2; 27.4).

Moreover, the Davidic dynasty played a religious rôle. In consequence of the divine legitimation and guarantee that its kings invoked, and the loyalty to it that the Jerusalem priesthood sought to inculcate in the people, it was able to stay in power until the downfall of the state of Judah, while in the Northern Kingdom of Israel several dynasties and individual kings followed in rapid succession. The result was a particularly intimate association between Yahwism and the Davidic dynasty; the primary outcome of this association was the Messianic expectation of the post-exilic period (§ 26.3). In addition, the Davidic kings not only supervised the cult of the Jerusalem Temple, which was the private temple of the dynasty (de Fraine), but also surely had priestly functions by virtue of being city kings of Jerusalem and for the performance of the cult on special state occasions (Hallevy *et al.*). Ps. 110:4, for example, terms the king a priest after the manner of the Canaanite king Melchizedek; Ahaz offers sacrifice at the dedication of his new altar (II Kings 16:12-13); and even the princes seem to have had priestly functions (II Sam. 8:18).

In addition, in the period of the Davidic and Solomonic Empire the foundations were laid for two religious movements and approaches to life that later became more highly developed. Rejecting syncretism and hostile toward the Canaanites, representatives of a Yahwism as free as possible from adulteration constituted a movement of religious nationalism that is expressed above all in the source strata J and E (§ 13.5). Such a movement would be inconceivable apart from the current existence of the Empire with its concomitant inclusion of all the Israelite tribes. The same period marks the growing influence of wisdom instruction, which was gradually integrated into Yahwism (§ 13.6). It, too, owes its existence and growth in Israel primarily to the presence of the monarchy and the state.

Finally, the monarchy both directly and indirectly promoted the development and formation of historical traditions, law, and literature. No small portion of the Old Testament writings came into being as a consequence of the monarchy (§ 11.6).

Thus although the monarchy produced many impulses that spelled advance as well as danger for Yahwism, it was also able to impugn the basic conception of Yahwism. Syncretism and the further introduction of alien cults threatened Yahweh's claim to exclusive worship and the principle of divine sovereignty. The political and military plans of the kings were often at odds with faith in Yahweh's

action in the life and destiny of nations, as we can see especially in
Isaiah's opposition to the measures taken by Ahaz and Hezekiah
during the Syro-Ephraimite War and in the two revolts against
Assyria, as well as in Jeremiah's conflict with Zedekiah and anti-
Babylonian circles. Finally, the king and his officials could be
inclined to substitute shrewd calculation for the ethical claims of
Yahwism, which required men to conduct their lives according to
the rules expressing God's will, thus alienating the everyday conduct
of men from its religious basis; Isa. 5:20, 21; 10:1-3 attack this
tendency. Yahwism, however, was already so securely established that
such threats simultaneously aroused the forces of opposition and
resistance.

2. *The nature of kingship in Israel.* Despite the comparatively
long duration of the monarchy, its consequences, the accounts concerning it, and the criticism of it, it remains difficult to determine its
unique character in contrast to the ancient Near Eastern conceptions
of kingship and, correspondingly, the conceptions—possibly quite
different—in the two states representing Israel divided. The discussion of this question has been dominated by two contrary opinions:
one places the Israelite monarchy totally within the framework of
ancient Near Eastern kingship as a whole; the other interprets it as
a charismatic Yahwistic kingship.

a) The first opinion is based on the assumption of an ancient Near
Eastern divine kingship with a cultic pattern of the widest possible distribution; it derives the divinity of the king from his position as representative
in the cult of a dying and rising god (Engnell, Hooke, Widengren, *et al.*).
Sometimes the ritual associated with this conception is viewed as one of the
central cults in ancient Near Eastern religions; at other times, though the
hypothesis is basically accepted, a distinction is made between the Near
Eastern conception of kingship and the basically different conception
found in Egypt (Frankfort, Labat). Sometimes the idea of the primal man
as a mythological cosmic figure is associated with the royal ideology.[1]
Expansion of a one-sidedly cultic interpretation of the Psalms leads to an
interpretation of Israelite kingship within the framework of ancient Near
Eastern conceptions, where it is viewed merely as a special case of the
ancient Near Eastern idea of divine kingship (Widengren *et al.*). This
view is based in particular on the following three elements: (1) the prominent position of the king in the Psalms, which depict not particular but
typical situations; (2) the Jerusalem royal or enthronement ritual, follow-

[1] According to Schmidt, and above all A. Bentzen, *Messias, Moses redivivus,
Menschensohn,* 1948. For a criticism of this view, see S. Mowinckel, "Urmensch
und 'Königsideologie,'" *StTh,* II (1948), 71-89.

ing the ancient Near Eastern cultic pattern, within the New Year's festival as the *Sitz im Leben* of the Psalms; (3) the position of the king as the central figure in the ritual, comprising dramatic representations of the sacred, in which the king not only appeared as representative of the people but also played the rôle of Yahweh.

Some scholars (Rodd, Rosenthal), while accepting the basic ideas of these hypotheses, have disputed the extensive rôle and function ascribed to the king and insisted on the uniqueness of Yahwism. A more numerous group have subjected these ideas to fundamental criticism (Bernhardt, Gray, McCullough, Noth). In basic agreement with this criticism, the following points may be cited:

1) Within the ancient Near East there were significant differences in the notion of kingship.[2] Egypt was familiar with divine kingship as an institution. There the king at first stood above other gods as the god Horus or the sun-god Re or Re's son; from the Fifth Dynasty on his status was lower, but he remained a god from birth, was worshiped in temples of the dead after his death, and while on earth was both priest of the gods and bestower of fertility. His divinity did not depend on his political power.

In Mesopotamia, the cultic divinization of the king found among the Sumerians must be distinguished from the self-deification of the Akkadian king. To the Sumerians the king was only a "great man" (*lú-gal*), the agent of the gods. In the cities the cults were under the direction of the local governor (*ensi*). A special cultic act in which the king participated was probably the re-enactment of the marriage of Tammuz and Inanna, through which, from the Third Dynasty of Ur on, he became a god. Temples were built to him and hymns were sung in his honor. The Semitic kings of Accad, on the contrary, were led by an exaggerated sense of power to identify themselves with the city god. The Babylonians and Assyrians also assumed that the monarchy was divinely established, but their kings were never divinized, even when the Assyrian Sargonids degraded certain divine predicates and applied them to themselves in a secular sense. Neither was the New Year's festival an enthronement festival.

The kings of the Hittites were high priests, responsible for the religious condition of the land; they had more cultic duties than elsewhere in the ancient Near East, so that many festivals could be celebrated only with their participation. Nevertheless, despite the title "my Sun," borrowed from Egypt, they were not considered gods while they lived. Only after they died were they divinized and offered ancestral sacrifices; their king did not *die,* but *became a god.*

There is no unambiguous evidence for divine kingship in Syria-Palestine. The Ugaritic legends of Aqhat and Keret have no bearing on the historical period, and the Amarna Letters apply divine predicates only to the Egyptian king. Canaanite kingship clearly developed in its own individual way (see also Gray).

Israel, too, knew nothing of divine kingship. All the characteristic features are lacking: identification of god and king or divinization of the king, either posthumously or by his own claim; the king as object of the cult; and his

[2] Our discussion follows W. von Soden in *RGG*, III, 1712-14.

power over the forces of nature. We find instead that on many occasions kingship is rejected in various ways; there is no trace of this tendency in other ancient Near Eastern cultures, and there is no place for it in an ideology of divine kingship.

2) There are many reasons for rejecting the hypothesis of a uniform cultic pattern extended as widely as possible. From the perspective of today, ancient Near Eastern civilization can appear as uniform as present-day European civilization may to later observers. But just as European civilization is in fact highly differentiated and in part contradictory, so too the civilizations of the ancient Near East had their individualities, differences, and contrasts. Comparison of these civilizations with one another reveals this clearly.[3] Furthermore, the presupposition behind this hypothesis, namely that the ancient Near East constituted a consistent and unified whole, has been increasingly questioned. Even the Hittites do not really fit in. Above all, interpretation of the excavations at Ugarit reveals that the Near East was open to the influence of the eastern Mediterranean world. There was an analogous relationship between its eastern regions and India. Furthermore, the alleged uniform cultic pattern cannot be shown to exist in its entirety in any single civilization of the ancient Near East. Each reveals only a few characteristics, which must be assembled from everywhere to constitute the whole. The texts brought together for comparison are also too hastily declared to be parallel; the same word can have different meanings and connotations in different cultures. Finally, the alleged discovery of a wealth of echoes of the supposed cultic pattern in late (!) texts of the OT presupposes an incredible knowledge of the history of religions on the part of the individual Israelite.

3) Restriction of the *Sitz im Leben* of the OT Psalms to the cult of the pre-exilic Temple and the ritual of its festivals means an unjustified limitation, even when the important rôle of the cult in official Yahwism is taken into account. An original association of the Psalms with a royal ritual and a subsequent "democratization" into their present form cannot be made even remotely probable, any more than can a compilation of the assumed situations of the royal ritual to form a great autumnal or New Year's festival, in which the repeated enthronement of the king was associated with that of Yahweh, and the king played the central rôle as representative of Yahweh.[4]

b) Against this comparison with ancient Near Eastern kingship we may set the theory, primarily developed by Alt, that the Israelite monarchy developed out of the charismatic leadership typical of the period before the state, that by and large the idea of charismatic kingship was best preserved in the Northern Kingdom, but was ousted by the dynastic principle in Judah, that this dynastic monarchy nevertheless acquired religious and theological significance through the notion of the eternal "covenant" con-

---

[3] See, for example, H. Schmökel, ed., *Kulturgeschichte des Alten Orient*, 1961.
[4] For a detailed discussion, see E. Kutsch, *Das Herbstfest in Israel*, Dissertation, Mainz, 1955. Kutsch's reservations also apply to the "royal Zion festival" postulated by Kraus, which combines a premonarchic amphictyonic covenant festival with the royal cult of Jerusalem.

cluded with David by Yahweh, which legitimized the Davidic house's dominion for all the years to come (II Sam. 7:8 ff., and *passim*), and that the divergence from charismatic to dynastic kingship—which even took place in the Northern Kingdom under Omri and Jehu—was brought about by the possession of a capital city belonging to the king personally, in which the king was not bound by the laws of Israel.[5] Many scholars have adopted this interpretation. Soggin, it is true, finds the charismatic element too narrow a basis and feels called upon to add two further elements: the "democratic" principle of having a popular assembly elect the king and the tendency to institutionalize the kingship, each working in the opposite direction. Hallevy considers only the first two kings to be charismatic figures; from Solomon on, individual ability replaced charisma, and in the fourth generation of the monarchy its charismatic nature was completely lost.

It is in fact difficult to look upon the kings of Judah and Israel as being endowed with a charisma, a direct gift of divine grace; the estimate of the prophets and the Deuteronomist is quite the reverse. Neither do the kings and their courts appear to have looked upon themselves in this light. It is therefore better to avoid applying the term "charismatic" to the Israelite kings, as well as the military heroes of the period before the state (§ 7.3), especially since the conception of the king's power is not rooted in the notion of a charisma, but in the original idea of the king as a person endowed with mana, i.e., an extraordinary power conceived in impersonal terms.[6] The most one can say is that a portion of Israel considered the monarchy, a dynasty, or a particular king as being ordained by God, and on occasion as having divine legitimation. Further conclusions find no support in the tradition of the OT.

The Israelite view of kingship can be presented in three aspects, which hold good for the united monarchy and at least for the separate state of Judah.

a) The conception of the kingship of the Davidic dynasty is described by means of the terms "son" of God and "anointed of Yahweh," which are applied to the king; the North Israelite conception is obscure.[7]

The OT three times refers to the king as God's son (II Sam.

[5] Thornton, on the other hand, would derive the royal offices from the political situation, which allowed the development of a dynastic mystique only in the small and homogeneous state of Judah.

[6] See W. Eichrodt, *Theologie des Alten Testaments*, I, 6th ed. (1959), 296 (English: *Theology of the Old Testament*, I [1961], 306).

[7] It might find expression in Ps. 45:7 (Eng. 45:6), if in fact the king is really addressed as *'ĕlōhîm*, "divine one," in this verse. But this point remains uncertain, because *'ĕlōhîm* could have been substituted for *yhwh*, a misreading of *yihyeh*; and vs. 7 (Eng. vs. 6) may contain a condensed idiom, "your throne is (like) the (throne) of God," or *'ĕlōhîm* can be interpreted as modifying *kissē'*, "your divine (mighty) throne."

7:14; Ps. 2:7; 89:27-28 [Eng. 89:26-27]).[8] In the expansion of the Nathan prophecy, in which Yahweh guarantees the unshakable endurance of the Davidic dynasty (§ 11.3), he declares concerning David's posterity: "I will be his father, and he shall be my son" (II Sam. 7:14a); he will be chastened for his iniquities, but will not be rejected (7:14b-15). The immediate image is that of the human father-son relation as an example or model, but II Sam. 7:8-16, 18-29 is in fact concerned primarily with divine legitimation of the Davidic dynasty as a whole. Just as a father (or his principal wife) could recognize as legitimate the child of a concubine or slave, Yahweh goes beyond the dynastic principle to legitimize each individual king by designating him his son, granting him a share in the sovereignty that is rightfully his as father.

Ps. 89:4-5, 20-38 (Eng. 89:3-4, 19-37) depicts this divine legitimation in poetic terms; the lament that follows prays for the alleviation of some distress and for the deliverance of the king from his foes. In this context vss. 27-28 (Eng. 26-27) say concerning David what also holds true for his successor:

> He shall cry to me, "Thou art my Father,
> my God, and the Rock of my salvation."
> And I will make him the first-born,
> the highest of the kings of the earth.

Since the emphasis on the king's humanity in vs. 20 (Eng. 19) makes it impossible to think of the king as Yahweh's own son in the physical sense, these verses correspond to the declaration in II Samuel 7, though with this difference, that the king of Judah has the priority of the firstborn among all rulers. This emphasizes his claim to pre-eminence, and is directed against the claims of others. The psalm uses the notion of Yahweh's legitimation of the Judahite king in order to request his aid for the legitimate king.

This fundamental legal legitimation, which is probably to be distinguished from adoption,[9] was given concrete form in the Judahite coronation ritual.[10] The king could exercise his authority once

---

[8] See also the corrupt text of Ps. 110:3. Ps. 22:11 (Eng. 22:10); 27:10 do not refer to the king.

[9] See G. Fohrer, "huiós . . . ," ThW, VIII, 340-54.

[10] G. von Rad, "Das judäische Königsritual," ThLZ, LXXII (1947), 211-16 (= his Gesammelte Studien zum Alten Testament, 1958, pp. 205-13 [English: The Problem of the Hexateuch and Other Essays, 1966, pp. 222-31]); K. H. Rengstorf, "Old and New Testament Traces of a Formula of the Judaean Royal Ritual," NT, V (1962), 229-44.

Yahweh had acknowledged him as his son, declared his complete royal name (II Sam. 7:9; I Kings 1:47), granted him a first request (cf. Ps. 2:8; 20:5; 21:3, 5 [Eng. 21:2, 4]), and bestowed the crown on him (II Kings 11:12; Ps. 21:4 [Eng. 21:3]; 110:2). This is the sense in which the ritual of Ps. 2:7 is to be understood:

> He said to me, "You are my son,
> today I have begotten you."

Although the Psalm as a whole probably derives from a perilous situation like that presupposed by Ps. 89, justifying the authority of the king over other nations, vs. 7, with its "He said . . ." formulation, refers back to the divine declaration at the coronation. Its first part, "You are my son," might be taken as an adoption formula, but "today begotten" can be interpreted this way only with difficulty. The more likely assumption is therefore that the statement is based on a wife's recognition of a child borne on her behalf by a slave: "You are my son, today I have borne you myself." This inferred formula has been modified so as to apply to a father, and then incorporated into the coronation ritual.

In the Judahite view, accordingly, the king was not the son of God by nature; neither did he enter the divine sphere of his own accord at his accession. He was instead recognized as son by an express declaration of Yahweh's will, and in this fashion received a portion in Yahweh's dominion, property, and heritage. That the concept of sonship was used to express this situation is due primarily to the dependence of the Judahite coronation ritual on the Egyptian in which the Pharaoh was proclaimed son of god. The Jerusalemite ritual however transformed the Egyptian notion of physical sonship into one of legal legitimation. This was rendered possible or at least easier by the fact that the calling of the king "son of God" was also rooted in the idiom that referred to Israel as son of God (§ 15.3). The election of Israel and Yahweh's promises to it in the events surrounding the exodus and Sinai provided the form and foundation for the notion of the election of David and his house, as well as the promises made to them. In like fashion, the notion of Israel's sonship furnished an appropriate model for the relationship between Yahweh and the Davidic dynasty.

The term "Yahweh's anointed," apart from its application to Saul (I Sam. 24:7, 11 [Eng. 24:6, 10]; 26:9 ff.; II Sam. 1:14, 16), is accorded primarily to David and his descendants: David (I Sam. 16:6; II Sam. 19:22; 23:1), Solomon (II Chron. 6:42), and kings not mentioned by name (I Sam. 2:10, 35; II Sam. 22:51 [= Ps. 18:51 (Eng. 18:50)]; Hab. 3:13; Ps. 2:2; 20:7 [Eng. 20:6]; 28:8; 84:10 [Eng. 84:9]; 89:39, 52 [Eng. 89:38, 51]; 132:10, 17). It is nevertheless striking that the act of anointing is performed by the people or their representatives. On the other hand, we also read that the anointing was performed by Yahweh or upon his commission by a prophet in the case of Saul (I Sam. 9:16; 10:1; 15:1), David (I Sam. 16:12-13; II Sam. 12:7), Jehu (II Kings 9:3ff.; II Chron. 22:7), and in Ps. 45:8 (Eng. 45:7). Kutsch has explained the situation as follows: the accounts of the anointing of the kings by the people, which corresponds to Hittite usage, are found in historically reliable annals; those of an anointing by Yahweh, which corresponds to the Egyptian practice of having the Pharaoh anoint high officials and vassal princes, are found in historically unreliable prophet legends, in which at best the anointing of Jehu may be based on historical fact.

Since there is therefore no question of any anointing by Yahweh or at his behest, the expression "Yahweh's anointed" must be understood as referring not to the act but to the effect of anointing. It refers to the relationship between Yahweh and the king that follows upon the anointing, and is a theological concept expressing Yahweh's delegation of sovereign authority to the king.

b) The king was considered monarch of the world (Galling). In this notion we find echoes of a universalism dating from the empire of David and Solomon. For instance, Ps. 72:8-11 salutes the king as follows:

> May he have dominion from sea to sea,
>   and from the River to the ends of the earth!
> May his foes bow down before him,
>   and his enemies lick the dust!
> May the kings of Tarshish and of the isles
>   render him tribute,
> may the kings of Sheba and Seba
>   bring gifts!
> May all kings fall down before him,
>   all nations serve him!

The expression of such claims is not due simply to the exaggerated court style of the ancient Near East. There speaks in them rather a nationalistic and religious hope that feeds on the memory of an empire that was.

c) The king is the governor of the social order (Galling), and embodies divine justice. For example, Ps. 45:7 (Eng. 45:6) describes a North Israelite king as follows:

> Your royal scepter is a scepter of equity,
> you love righteousness and hate wickedness.
> Therefore *Yahweh* your God has anointed you.

In Ps. 101, a proclamation is placed in the mouth of a Judahite king at his accession that reads as follows (vss. 2*a*, 5, 7) :

> I will give heed to the way that is blameless,
> *faithfulness dwells with me.*
> Him who slanders his neighbor secretly
> I will destroy.
> The man of haughty looks and arrogant heart
> I will not endure.
> No man who practices deceit
> shall dwell in my house.

Even when, as in Psalm 72, the poet is speaking of the ruler of the world, he interrupts himself twice to mention the king's succor to the poor and destitute (vss. 4, 12). Therefore the elementary requirement placed on the king is always that he rule justly and promote justice. Side by side with a warning against injustice we find one against profiteering from the tribute of plundered subjects (Prov. 29:4).

3. *Limitation and rejection.* The complex picture of the monarchy, which depended on Yahwism for legitimation and support, and in turn meant both profit and danger for Yahwism, would be incomplete without mention of the limitation and rejection of the monarchy, or at least criticism of it, that was in part an outgrowth of Yahwism.

a) Apart from the right of the people to participate in the appointment of a king and the determination of the contractual stipulations involved (Fohrer), which finally under Josiah led to a kind of constitution (Galling), the limitation placed on the monarchy was primarily determined by the claim of divine sovereignty. The unique position of Yahweh rendered any deification of the king impossible, allowing only the possibility of legitimizing the king as God's son, as the son of a concubine or slave might be legitimized. It is for this reason that Ezekiel no longer views the expected future ruler as an independent king, but as a *nāśi'* ("prince") of lower rank, dependent on Yahweh, who will be a shepherd subordinate to the divine supreme shepherd (Ezek. 34:23-24). By the same token there were no first-person royal accounts in Israel, such as constituted the bulk of historical tradition elsewhere in the ancient Near East. Neither were there songs glorifying the king in either first or third person; on the contrary, in the royal songs of the Psalter, Yahweh, not the king, is the center of attention. Less is said about the power and achievements of the king than about what Yahweh promises him, what he asks of Yahweh, or for what he thanks Yahweh. In other areas, too, limitations could be placed on the monarchy in the name of Yahweh, as we see in the appearance of Elijah following the judicial murder of Naboth (I Kings 21) and the appearance of Jeremiah when Jehoiakim was building his palace (Jer. 22:13-19).

b) Peculiar to Israel is the repeated fundamental rejection of kingship, in which religious motives are frequently combined with the freedom of the nomadic ideal. Thus kingship might be rejected as the unlawful despotism of a particular individual, for example in Jotham's fable mocking superfluous and pernicious kingship (Judg. 9:8-15) and in the "royal prerogatives" of the Saul tradition (I Sam. 8:11 ff.). Or it might be viewed as apostasy from Yahweh and condemned on these grounds, for example in Gideon's statement (Judg. 8:23), in one of the narratives about Saul's elevation to kingship (I Sam. 8:7, 9-10, 19-22), and perhaps also in the polemic of Hosea, even though one cannot say definitely whether Hosea's verdict on the kings of his period is based on these considerations or is of a more fundamental nature (cf. Hos. 8:4; 10:3; 13:11).

In the following period the situation changed. Isaiah and Jeremiah merely turned against individual evil kings, but did not attack the institution itself. Isaiah awaited political disorder and the downfall of the monarchy as Yahweh's judgment, bringing destruction and death (Isa. 3:1-9), while he looked upon the reign of David as the ideal period (Isa. 1:21-26). Deuteronomic and Deuteronomistic criticism also was not directed against the Davidic monarchy as such, but only against particular representatives who did not meet the Deuteronomic requirements (especially with respect to centralization of the cult at Jerusalem), while other kings, above all Hezekiah and Josiah, were judged positively. Only the greater distance of the post-exilic period permitted significant mitigation of the critical attitude. The important thing is that religious considerations could in fact lead to criticism and rejection of the monarchy.

CHAPTER TWO: YAHWISM
IN THE PERIOD OF THE MONARCHY

§ 13 RELIGIOUS MOVEMENTS

W. F. ALBRIGHT, "Some Canaanite-Phoenician Sources of Hebrew Wisdom," *VTSuppl*, III (1955), 1-15; A. ALT, "Die Weisheit Salomos," *ThLZ*, LXXVI (1951), 139-44 (= his *Kleine Schriften zur Geschichte des Volkes Israel*, II [1953], 90-99); J. J. VAN AS, *Skuldbelydenis en Genadeverkondiging in die Ou Testament*, Dissertation, Utrecht, 1961; J. BARR, "Revelation through History in the Old Testament," *Interpr*, XVII (1963), 193-205; A. CAUSSE, "Sagesse égyptienne et sagesse juive," *RHPhR*, IX (1929), 149-69; J. B. CURTIS, "A Suggested Interpretation of the Biblical Philosophy of History," *HUCA*, XXXIV (1963), 115-23; B. DUHM, *Die Gottgeweihten in der alttestamentlichen Religion*, 1905; O. EISSFELDT, "Jahwe-Name und Zauberwesen," *ZMR*, XLII (1927), 161-86 (= his *Kleine Schriften*, I [1962], 150-71); J. FICHTNER, *Die altorientalische Weisheit in ihrer israelitisch-jüdischen Ausprägung*, 1933; idem, "Die Bewältigung heidnischer Vorstellungen und Praktiken in der Welt des Alten Testaments," in *Festschrift Friedrich Baumgärtel*, 1959, pp. 24-40 (= his *Gottes Weisheit*, 1965, pp. 115-29); G. FOHRER, "Die zeitliche und überzeitliche Bedeutung des Alten Testaments," *EvTh*, IX (1949/50), 447-60; H. GESE, *Lehre und Wirklichkeit in der alten Weisheit*, 1958; J. DE GROOT, *De Palestijnsche achtergrond van den Pentateuch*, 1928; M.-L. HENRY, *Jahwist und Priesterschrift*, 1960; H.-J. HERMISSON, *Sprache und Ritus im altisraelitischen Kult*, 1965; P. HUMBERT, *Recherches sur les sources égyptiennes de la littérature sapientiale d'Israël*, 1929; F. JAMES, "Some Aspects of the Religion of Proverbs," *JBL*, LI (1932), 31-39; A. JIRKU, *Die Dämonen und ihre Abwehr im Alten Testament*, 1912 (= his *Von Jerusalem nach Ugarit*, 1966, pp. 1-107); idem, *Mantik in Altisrael*, Dissertation, Rostock, 1913 (= *ibid.*, pp. 109-62); idem, *Materialien zur Volksreligion Israels*, 1914 (= *ibid.*, pp. 163-318); A. LODS, "Magie hébraïque et magie cananéenne," *RHPhR*, VII (1927), 1-16; B. LUTHER, *Die Persönlichkeit des Jahvisten*, 1906; J. MEINHOLD, *Die Weisheit Israels*, 1908; S. MOWINCKEL, *Psalmenstudien I. Awän und die individuellen Klagepsalmen*, 1922; idem, "Psalms and Wisdom," *VTSuppl*, III (1955), 205-24; R. E. MURPHY, "The Concept of Wisdom Literature," in J. L. MCKENZIE, ed., *The Bible in Current Catholic Thought*, 1962, pp. 46-54; N. NICOLSKY, *Spuren magischer Formeln in den Psalmen*, 1925; N. W. PORTEOUS, "Royal Wisdom," *VTSuppl*, III (1955), pp. 247-61; G. VON RAD, " 'Gerechtigkeit' und 'Leben' in den Psalmen," in *Festschrift Alfred Bertholet*, 1950, pp. 418-37 (= his *Gesammelte Studien zum Alten Testament*, 1958, pp. 225-47 [English: *The Problem of the Hexateuch and Other Essays*, 1966, pp. 243-66]); H. H. SCHMID, *Wesen und Geschichte der Weisheit*, 1966; H. SCHMÖKEL, "Die jahwetreuen Orden in Israel," *ThBl*, XII (1933),

327-34; R. B. Y. SCOTT, "Solomon and the Beginnings of Wisdom in Israel," *VTSuppl*, III (1955), 262-79; H. W. WOLFF, "Heilsgeschichte—Weltgeschichte im Alten Testament," *Der evangelische Erzieher*, XIV (1962), 129-36; *idem*, "Das Kerygma des Jahwisten," *EvTh*, XXIV (1964), 73-98 (= his *Gesammelte Studien zum Alten Testament*, 1964, 345-73); W. ZIMMERLI, "Zur Struktur der alttestamentlichen Weisheit," *ZAW*, LI (1933), 177-204; *idem*, "Ort und Grenze der Weisheit im Rahmen der alttestamentlichen Theologia," in *Les Sagesses du Proche-Orient ancien*, 1963, pp. 121-37 (= his *Gottes Offenbarung*, 1963, pp. 300-315).

1. *Basic considerations.* It would be a gross oversimplification to say that the period of the monarchy is characterized by the cultivation of Yahwism as an official religion, primarily at the royal sanctuaries, and by its lengthy subjection to a pernicious syncretism more or less vigorously promoted for the sake of reaching an accommodation with the Canaanite element of the population (§ 12). While this was going on, there existed or developed a series of other religious movements of very different and sometimes contradictory sorts. Many Israelite circles sought to preserve Mosaic Yahwism in as unadulterated a form as possible; others in various ways continued the transformation of Yahwism, begun in the period before the state, into a form more adapted to the settled territory through the assimilation and integration of Canaanite material and the simultaneous development of Yahwism's own potential. We may also note other movements that conflicted with Yahwism or could be assimilated into it only gradually. The resulting picture is complex and variegated—more so even than the following discussion can depict. For on the one hand, the boundaries between the religious movements were fluid, and on the other, two movements such as cultic emphasis and religious nationalism could join together in combination.

2. *The survival of ancient Yahwism and the conservative approach to life.* a) Many traditions, figures, and institutions of the period before the state, such as the Song of Deborah (cf. Judg. 5:4-5), Samuel, and occasionally the sanctuary at Shiloh, whose priests apparently traced their lineage back to the Moses host (cf. I Sam. 2:27), suggest that certain circles preserved Yahwism unchanged alongside the new form that was developing in the settled territory. This tendency continued in the period of the monarchy. Nathan's opposition to David's plans for building a temple is a sign of its continued vitality. There continued to be more or less sizable groups

of Israelites who were attached to the ancient form of their faith.[1]
They belonged primarily to circles that also remained faithful to
their old way of life and raised livestock. Certainly not all Israelites
made the transition at once from the old nomadic life to the new
life of farming, and not all of those who did make it concluded at
once that the transition meant a new form of Yahwism. They were
not interested in an agricultural religion, and were therefore also
not interested in the sanctuaries with their symbols of God and
increasingly elaborate cult that served this religion. Instead they
remained faithful to the Yahweh of Sinai and the desert. Though
they only rarely made an appearance and had little influence on the
people as a whole, they were nevertheless present. Their criticism of
the religious situation in Palestine is later taken up in a new and
more intense form by the great individual prophets, the first of
whom, Amos, was significantly also a herdsman.

b) A Nazir or Nazirite[2] was originally a man who dedicated himself as an individual to Yahweh and placed his whole life at Yahweh's
service. The oath was later recast; lifelong dedication was replaced
by a temporary obligation, primarily of an ascetic nature, modeled
on priestly regulations (Num. 6:1-21). The original field of activity
of the Nazirite was the Yahweh war, in which he performed heroic
deeds while in a state of warlike ecstasy (cf. Gen. 49:23-24; Deut.
33:16-17; Judg. 15:14); later he appears also to have dwelt at sanctuaries. His life is determined on the one hand by perpetual battle on
behalf of Yahweh, on the other by rejection of Canaanite civilization.
Refusal to drink wine (Amos 2:11-12)[3] is a symbol for rejection of
agricultural civilization and its accompanying cult. Also of ancient
origin is the prohibition against cutting one's hair; this prohibition
is not connected with any cult of the dead or of the sun, but is a
mark of the nomadic life style. Through such measures—and presumably others like them of which nothing is recorded—the Nazirites
proclaimed their belief that Canaanite civilization was incompatible
with the ancient form of Yahwism. For them Yahwism and the
nomadic life style went together.

Time passed the Nazirites by. Their mode of existence lost its
raison d'être during the monarchy through the growth of a professional army, the obligation of private citizens to serve in the militia,
and the new technology of war. The Nazirites gradually turned into

[1] *RGG*, III, 365-66.
[2] *BHH*, II, 1288-89; *RGG*, IV, 1308-9; *IDB*, III, 526-27.
[3] *RGG*, VI, 1572-73.

figures of fun, whom the people mocked by trying to make them drunk (Amos 2:12).

c) The Rechabites[4] are first mentioned in connection with the revolution of Jehu (841 B.C.); they continued to exist until the conquest of Jerusalem (587 B.C.). They likewise represent a conservative movement. They constituted a fellowship that can be called a kind of religious order devoted to Yahweh. The order was probably founded by Jonadab ben Rechab,[5] who was recognized during his lifetime as its head; their duty was "zeal for Yahweh." Jeremiah 35 records their rules of life: they renounced ownership of fields and vineyards, did no farming, drank no wine, and built no houses, but rather lived in tents. This shows that their purpose was to preserve or return to the simplicity of nomadic life, even in the settled territory. Only in this way did they believe they could remain faithful to their God.

In other words, the Rechabites wanted to associate Yahwism with a specific form of civilization, even though this form was out of date and could never be brought back. They also resisted the discovery that every faith continues to develop and evolve, and must seek new answers to new questions if it is to remain alive. They sought instead to maintain the civilization and faith of the desert period.

d) Finally, conservative and reactionary conceptions can be heard in the third early source stratum of the Hexateuch, whose existence many scholars have tried to prove.[6] Even the primal history in this narrative strand exhibits hostility toward, or even rejection of, the advances of settled civilization. The true man and the true believer is the nomad. Therefore Israel should actually have stayed at the mountain of God in the desert, from which Yahweh unwillingly dismissed them because of their impetuosity. For the settled territory with its sanctuaries is only an imperfect substitute for the true homeland of Israel: the desert with the mountain of God.[7] Therefore the Israelites deserted Yahweh as soon as they came in contact with the settled territory (Num. 25:1-5). At this point we hear clearly conservative nomadic criticism of the civilized form of Yahwism influenced by Canaanite religion.

[4] *RGG*, V, 951-52; *IDB*, IV, 14-16.
[5] *BHH*, III, 1559.
[6] S-F, § 24.
[7] O. Eissfeldt, *Einleitung in das Alte Testament*, 3rd ed., 1964, p. 259 (English: *The Old Testament*, 1965, p. 196).

3. *The magical approach to life*.[8] In Palestinian Israel the magical
approach was primarily shaped by the Canaanite vegetation and fertility cults, whose basis was largely magical. Only in the conceptual
world of magic can one expect to strengthen the deity and maintain
the mysterious forces of life by means of sexual rites, or to reawaken
the rhythm of nature each year and render the earth fertile through
rites centering on a deity that fades away and then revives. Therefore
the Israelites adopted many Canaanite magical practices. They had
also brought others along out of their own nomadic past (§ 2.3);
this made the invasion of Canaanite magic easier, just as conversely
the old magical heritage of Israel could revive in this environment.
All this, finally, was reinforced by the borrowing of foreign cults,
primarily in consequence of the alliance policies or vassal status of
Judah during the later monarchy (§ 11.4), since these cults were
partially or totally saturated with magic. It is true that Yahwism pro-
scribed magical practices (cf. Exod. 20:7; 22:17 [Eng. 22:18]; I Sam.
28:9; in later terms Lev. 20:27; Deut. 18:10 ff.), but in daily life
there was often little resistance.

Like the Canaanites, the Israelites sensed the presence of demons
everywhere—not only in the desert, so that an annual apotropaic
sacrifice to one of them seemed necessary (Leviticus 16), but also in
the settled territory, where the fertility of the fields, the security of
the house, and the health of man depended at least in part on them
(cf. § 14.3). There were men and women skilled in the dangerous
technique of gaining influence over such powers or rendering them
subservient. The many names the OT uses for them show how various this group was. They could exorcize diseases, impose or release
a spell, bring about unlucky days, make rain, and practice
necromancy. The people were probably more devoted to magic than
is usually assumed. Men feared the perpetual threat of demons and
the magical powers of their neighbors. They therefore performed

[8] *BHH*, I, 9-11, 19, 52, 90-91, 209, 225-26, 598-99; III, 1867-68, 1894-95, 2204-5,
2209-10; *RGG*, I, 1321; IV, 258, 595-601, 727-29, 1628-29; VI, 604-5, 1525-26,
1871-75; *IDB*, III, 223-25; J. Döller, *Die Wahrsagerei im Alten Testament*, 1923;
H. J. Elhorst, "Eine verkannte Zauberhandlung (Dtn 21,1-9)," *ZAW*, XXXIX
(1921), 58-67; F. C. Fensham, "Salt as Curse in the Old Testament and the
Ancient Near East," *BA*, XXV (1962), 48-50; P. Humbert, *La "terou'a", analyse
d'un rite biblique*, 1946; S. Iwry, "New Evidence for Belomancy in Ancient
Palestine and Phoenicia," *JAOS*, LXXXI (1961), 27-34; S. Reinach, "Le souper
chez la sorcière," *RHR*, LXXXVIII (1923), 45-50; I. Trencsényi-Waldapfel,
"Die Hexe von Endor und die griechisch-römische Welt," *AcOr* (Budapest),
XI (1960), 201-22; F. Vartioni, "La necromanzia nell' Antico Testamento,"
Augustinianum, III (1963), 461-81.

magical actions to protect themselves and injure their foes. In many Psalms we can still catch echoes of the notion that the disaster afflicting a man is due to a spell that must be broken by a counter-spell. Excavations, too, have brought various magical devices to light: execration tablets containing curses upon the enemy; small figurines with hands and feet bound, intended to bind the enemy through imprisonment, sickness, or death; numerous amulets like blue pearls against the evil eye, small silver hands for the protection of children, and symbols of gods or demons to assure their patronage. And just as in the early period, words of blessing and cursing were considered to have magical power, as were corpses, whose power was averted by funerary rites.

Thus the daily life of the Israelites was replete with a great number of magical practices, even though tradition has often disguised their character. A woman might seek by their aid to overcome her husband's aversion (Gen. 30:14), a herdsman might seek to influence the litter of his sheep (Gen. 30:37-38). Harmful springs were to be made wholesome by means of salt, poisonous food by means of meal (II Kings 2:19 ff.; 4:38 ff.). Men interpreted dreams and constellations (Deut. 13:2 ff.; Jer. 10:2) or predicted the future by omens (Lev. 19:26; Deut. 18:10; II Kings 17:17; 21:6): water was used by observing bubbles and refraction (Gen. 44:5), arrows were drawn from a receptacle or shaken, the livers of sacrificial animals were examined for color and shape (Ezek. 21:26 [Eng. 21:21]). In this way people thought they could recognize, influence, or control the great forces of life in order to be masters of their own lives, protect themselves against danger, and make the most of their existence.

4. *The cultic approach to life. a*) In contrast to syncretism and the magical approach, the cultic approach to life is characterized by its refusal to adopt Canaanite ideas and practices without careful consideration; it sought rather to incorporate into Yahwism only those elements that were viable and not antithetical to Yahwism. This middle way between radical rejection of Canaanite religion and complete accommodation of Yahwism to it therefore exhibits a juxtaposition of suppression and compromise.

Magic and sorcery, with all their accompanying manifestations, were prohibited and bitterly attacked. Since sorcery called into question the sole worship of Yahweh as recognition of divine sovereignty, it was usually punished with death. Certain specifics were also forbidden, such as funerary practices (Lev. 21:1 ff.; Deut.

14:1-2) and sacrificial customs (Exod. 34:26; see § 9.3) based on magic. Besides some of the kings, the high priest Jehoiada introduced a cultic reform at Jerusalem when he attacked the Baal cult of Queen Athaliah (II Kings 11).

In addition, what appeared necessary and acceptable in the new situation of the settled territory was borrowed and assimilated. Following Canaanite example, the Israelites built sanctuaries and temples, regulating their trappings and cult (see § 9.3; 16). In the cult, in which communion between Yahweh and Israel was cultivated, Yahweh came to assume the features of the local gods and to be worshiped as they were. The intense ethical will of the ancient conception of God retreated in favor of the mysterious power of the deity over life and his operation in the realm of nature. Instead of the terrible exaltation of Yahweh, the mediation of divine blessing was stressed. According to this belief Yahweh no longer protected his people only on special occasions in time of war, intervening in the battle in storm and tumult, but perpetually vouchsafed his blessing to his people in order that the flocks and fruits of the earth might flourish. Gradually, therefore, all the incidents of agricultural life became associated with Yahweh.

In the view of those who shared the cultic approach, through the cult one could participate in the divine sphere, caught up in emotional rapture or ecstatic exaltation. This cult, however, was neither grounded on a divine revelation nor created by the Israelites themselves; it was an outgrowth of the cult proper to the land that had been occupied, for it had to satisfy the requirements of the land. The men admitted to participation in the cult accordingly assembled at the sanctuaries to celebrate the great annual agricultural festivals for and with the divine bestower of blessing (§ 16.3). If Yahweh vouchsafed his blessing to the farmer, the latter in return would offer sacrifice as prayer and thanksgiving. He sat at table with Yahweh, happy in the confidence that in the following year, too, he could once more be richly blessed if he could retain his God's favor. The primary purpose of the cult was to obtain something from Yahweh. Since the aim was preservation of the existing order, the cultic approach was essentially conservative.

b) Priestly cultic theology combined cultivation of communion with God through the cult with a consciousness of man's distance and God's unapproachability, corresponding to the principle of divine sovereignty. To make the disparity outwardly visible, the sacred precincts and sanctified objects were marked off from the realm of secular life. To divorce Israel from other divine or demonic powers, whose realm was to be avoided as unclean, rules of purity and abstinence were set up that permeated all life. Thus the groundwork was laid for what was to be increasingly stressed in later times: the absolute transcendence of God on the one hand, and the separation of the holy people on the other.

In order to maintain a real relationship between the two quantities, priestly cultic theology stressed the importance of the law more than Mosaic Yahwism had. The priesthood itself cultivated and extended the existing law, with the result that in the post-exilic period an independent devotion to the law came into being. The law represented the sovereign will of Yahweh in concrete form; in it this will left the sphere of the divine and invaded the earthly realm. As lawgiver Yahweh demonstrated his power over men by regulating their lives and keeping them in perpetual dependence.

The cultic laws were based on the notion that within Israel everything is Yahweh's property. The nature of the cult had to conform to this notion, so that festivals, sacrifices, and other rituals served to make men recognize Yahweh's sovereignty, bringing home to the individual Israelite that his life was dedicated to this God and determined by him even in its outward manifestations. The cultic forms were frequently intended to be morally educational: see, for instance, the priestly instruction concerning the principles of social conduct in Ps. 15; 24:3-6. Other forms, like the hymns and prayers of the temple, the words of Yahweh, and blessings, might serve to express the relationship of the nation and the individual to Yahweh.

Everyday life and conduct were also drawn into the sphere of the law. Since the law as a whole was considered the concrete embodiment of God's will, the man who framed his life according to its prescripts was rendering obedience to the demands of Yahweh himself. The specific actions of a man were the crucial factor, because they were considered the visible expression of a corresponding inner attitude that as such cannot be discerned. Thus the righteous man who obeyed the divine commands was at the same time the devout man.

Of course all this was only the theology of the priestly cult and therefore theoretical. In many ways reality bore a different aspect, as the religio-historical course of the monarchy (§ 11) and the indictments of the prophets (§ 20.2) showed.

5. *The nationalist approach to life.* Like the magical notions and practices of popular religion, the popular tradition of the narratives from Israel's early history provoked a certain amount of criticism. This criticism resulted in the final recension of the second groundwork of the Hexateuch[9] on the part of the great editors and framers of the source strata J and E.[10] They both represented individual clearly defined theological points of view.

J affirmed the agricultural civilization of Palestine and the Yahwism that went with it as an inseparable unity, as is shown especially by the so-called cultic decalogue (Exod. 34:1-28). He looked with favor on national power, the state, and the monarchy (Gen. 27:29; Num. 24:3-9, 15-19). Israel accordingly leaves Sinai gladly, and expectantly enters the land "flowing with milk and honey" (Exod. 3:8 and *passim*); Yahweh goes along to dwell in this land. At the same time, by prefixing the primal history in Genesis 1–11,[11] J as a kind of warning depicted the whole course of history from the perspective of sin as the dissolution of communion with God and of judgment as the vindication of God's sovereignty over against the sinner. Thus the whole account took on the character of a story of decision.

E likewise exhibits a marked Israelite self-awareness; in his case, in fact, an approach to universalism found in J, according to which the other nations can share in the blessing bestowed on Israel, fell victim to concentration on religious nationalism. God's sovereignty and communion were essentially restricted to Israel. Nevertheless the nationalistic element was not so immediately associated with the religious element as in the case of J; instead theology tends to displace nationalism. The crucial elements are the religious side of Israel's election by Yahweh and the separation associated with this selection (Num. 23:9b). The emphasis is on Israel's religious heritage and religious purpose: they are a nation singled out from the Gentile world and placed in the service of Yehweh. This notion transcends mere materialistic nationalism. In the story of the golden calf at the mountain of God, E can even take a negative attitude toward Israel: in contrast to J's account, E concludes the story on a menacing note, since Israel is sent away from the mountain of

[9] S-F, § 19.
[10] S-F, § 21–23.
[11] See W. G. Lambert, "New Light on the Babylonian Flood," *JSS*, V (1960), 113-23.

God and judgment is proclaimed against the generation of the desert (Exod. 32:34).

Such differences notwithstanding, J and E represented a form of Yahwism distinct from the cultic approach. Characteristic of their thought was the association of religion with nationalism in the sense of national solidarity of a people on the basis of religion. Like the cultic approach, religious nationalism was conservative, since it sought to preserve the existing order.

Fundamental is the belief that Yahweh has chosen Israel from among the nations of mankind, although the Deuteronomic term *bāḥar* does not yet appear. E's account accordingly begins with Abraham and his election. J, too, in whose story the primal history constitutes the gloomy background to the election of the patriarchs, was primarily interested in the chosen people. Subsidiary branches were quickly excluded while the main line was pursued. Many narratives deal with the passing danger that the chosen clan will die out because a female ancestor is barren (Sarah, Rachel) or imperiled by an alien (Gen. 20; 26:1-11), while others are intended to show how Yahweh brought his purpose to happy fruition despite the command to sacrifice Isaac, the flight of Jacob, and the threat to Joseph. God's repeated promises of territory made to the patriarchs lay the groundwork for Israel's claim as a nation to the settled territory they occupied.

A further reason for the emphasis on the patriarchal tradition was the notion of "all Israel." In the period of the divided monarchy, J and E laid the foundation in Israel's prehistory for the ideal, realized only in the empire of David and Solomon, of a national state encompassing all Israelites: a single genealogy, a single nation. Therefore national and religious boundaries coalesce. Yahweh may cross the boundaries of the land, but not those of the nation. J accordingly refuses to have the name of Yahweh, which he uses from the very outset, pronounced in the presence of or by non-Israelites.

Thus Yahweh was confined not only within the bounds of the cult but also within the bounds of the nation. The Israelite believed that his life was made secure not only through performance of the cult but also by virtue of his belonging to the chosen people. Just as the cultic approach gradually led to an increasing proliferation of ritual and law, so the nationalistic approach led Israel to expect divine aid for the success of the Israelite state and its sovereignty, until the revolts in the period of Roman domination brought about a final catastrophe.

6. *The wisdom approach to life.* Ever since the time of Solomon wisdom instruction was indigenous to Israel.[12] It was cultivated at the royal court and among the increasingly numerous officials; above and beyond this, it was the contemporary form of intellectual training and education quite generally. When we notice its influence outside official circles, as in the case of some of the prophets, this means nothing more than that we are dealing with educated men of common sense. Nevertheless Isaiah's criticism of the "wise," with their schemes and programs that appear shrewd but are actually pernicious,[13] shows that as late as the second half of the eighth century wisdom instruction still basically represented the training and morality of high officialdom in the wider sense. Only from the end of the seventh century do we find evidence of a broader base. Deut. 1:13, 15; 16:19 include minor officials and administrators of justice in the circle of the "wise." Jer. 8:8-9 calls the priests "wise men" as dispensers of the law, while 18:18 speaks of a separate class of wise men whose function is to give counsel. Thus from the end of the seventh century on, wisdom instruction evolved from the training and morality of an official class into a view shared by extensive circles without social or sociological restriction.

In addition, there had always been a practical familiarity, based on experience, with certain laws of nature and realms of activity, since man is always confronted with the task of mastering his environment and making the most of his life in the world. But it is out of place to speak of ancient clan wisdom as a special form of wisdom. Always and everywhere it is necessary to seek order and regularity in the multiplicity of events and phenomena, an order to which man can adapt himself and which he can use his own purposes. This takes place above all in the popular proverbs that simply record scraps of knowledge and experience, leaving it to the in-

---

[12] *BHH,* III, 2153-55; *RGG,* VI, 1574-77; *IDB,* IV, 852-61; E. G. Bauckmann, "Die Proverbien und die Sprüche des Jesus Sirach," *ZAW,* LXXII (1960), 33-63; L. Dürr, *Das Erziehungswesen im Alten Testament und im antiken Orient,* 1932; J. Fichtner, "Zum Problem Glaube und Geschichte in der israelitisch-jüdischen Weisheitsliteratur," *ThLZ,* LXXVI (1951), 145-50 (= his *Gottes Weisheit,* 1965, pp. 9-17); G. Fohrer, "*sophía* B, Altes Testament," *ThW,* VII, 476-96; A. Lods, "Le monothéisme israélite a-t-il eu des précurseurs parmi les 'sages' de l'ancien Orient?" *RHPhR,* XIV (1934), 197-205; P. A. Munch, "Die alphabetische Akrostichie in der jüdischen Psalmendichtung," *ZDMG,* XC (1936), 702-10; *idem,* "Die jüdischen 'Weisheitspsalmen' und ihr Platz im Leben," *AcOr* (Copenhagen), XV (1936), 112-40; W. Richter, *Recht und Ethos,* 1966.

[13] J. Fichtner, "Jesaja unter den Weisen," *ThLZ,* LXXIV (1949), 75-80 (= his *Gottes Weisheit,* 1965, pp. 18-26).

dividual to draw the proper conclusions concerning his own conduct (I Sam. 24:14 [Eng. 24:13]; Prov. 11:2a; 16:18; 18:22). The statement can be paradoxical or contradictory (Prov. 11:24; 20:17; 25:15; 27:7), without any apparent attempt to derive a universally valid principle or erect a system. Although such proverbs were handed down in the context of wisdom literature, and were later often expanded by the addition of a second line with a corresponding reference to the human realm (Prov. 25:23; 26:20; 27:20), it is expedient to reserve the term "wisdom" for the training and morality of official circles, subdivided in turn into theoretical and practical wisdom.

This doctrine is based on an ideal of training and forming the whole man, since its purpose is not merely to determine the order and regularity of nature and of life, but also to educate men on this basis. The ideal is similar to Egyptian teaching: the man with a cool spirit (Prov. 17:27) in contrast to the hothead (Prov. 15:18; 22:24; 29:22), the man who is slow to anger in contrast to the man with a hasty temper (Prov. 14:29), the man of tranquil mind, who does not give way to devouring passion (Prov. 14:30) but controls his emotions and impulses.

We encounter theoretical wisdom in the ancient Near East in the form of scholarly lists; lacking an Israelite example, we may cite the onomasticon of Amen-em-opet (ca. 1100 B.C.). As preserved, it furnishes a list of 610 key words: heavenly beings and objects, things found in the water and upon earth, divine and royal figures, courtiers, officials, professions, classes, tribes and types of men, cities, buildings, and their constituent parts, estates, grain and grain products, food and drink, parts of an ox and types of meat. We are therefore dealing with a universal encyclopedia in the form of a lexicon arranged by subject. Such lists also existed in Israel: they were utilized in Genesis 1; Psalms 104; 108, as well as in Prov. 6:16-19; 30, and other numerical sayings. Extended poems appear to follow such lists in their structure (Job 24:5-8, 14-16a; 28; 30:2-8; 36:27–37:13; 38:4–39:30; 40:15-24; 40:25–41:26 [40:25–41:34]).

More important was practical wisdom with its rules in the form of proverbs or songs. This form of wisdom provided truths that apply to human life, according to which a man can guide his conduct. It was always lucid and sensible, frequently prosaic, practical, and intended to be put to use. Its purpose was mastery of one's own life; it taught that it is possible to avoid all offense and escape all danger if one observes the wise established rules that govern life. For even the deity obeys the laws of nature and guarantees their validity,

so that the wise man is able to make himself a part of the substance
and system of this universal order. The representative of this
optimistic attitude is therefore sagacious and upright; he stands in
devout awe of God, but has full confidence in his ability to control
his life and fulfill his human needs. He draws a sharp and scornful
line between himself and the fool who does not possess such insight.[14]

Adaptation to Israelite life and accommodation to Yahwism left
their marks on wisdom instruction. Although from the outset a
morality for official circles, it did not restrict itself to a specific class
as definitely as was the case elsewhere, especially in Egypt, but was
more applicable to all men. Hence the emphasis on the duties of
children toward their parents, the relatively high status accorded
women, the strong condemnation of fornication and adultery, the
high value placed on friendship, and the concern for the poor and
weak. Within the framework of Yahwism as a religion of human
conduct according to certain definite rules, wisdom instruction became
anthropologized: the human self came to replace the world as the
crucial factor. Above all the concept of "wisdom" was gradually so
transformed that wisdom, righteousness, and piety came to constitute
an indissoluble unity, and the rules of conduct were associated with
the God of Israel and grounded in him. In this context the notion
of retributive justice carried out by Yahweh during a man's earthly
life gained new significance.

7. *Shared characteristics.* Markedly distinct as the approaches out-
lined above were, they all nevertheless exhibit two common features
that typify non-prophetical Yahwism of the monarchy:

a) The spiritual well-being of the nation or the individual is
presupposed; it is not a goal to be achieved or a gift from Yahweh.
It is presupposed in the life of nomadic Yahwism as well as that of
the Mosaic period; in the cult with its festivals in which the worshiper can participate in the divine realm, in agricultural society,
and in political life; or in the wise rules of conduct that permit a
man to make the most of his life. Even the magical approach, without any obligation to Yahweh, rests on a similar basis.

b) This state of well-being can be upset for the whole group or
for an individual through concrete lapses in consequence of specific
acts or omissions. It is not, however, destroyed, but can be recovered
or restored, above all through appropriate acts of expiation.

[14] W. Zimmerli, *Die Weisheit des Predigers Salomo*, 1936, p. 11.

This generally accepted view, according to which Israel lived by nature in a state of spiritual well-being that could be upset temporarily but restored at any time, was bitterly contested by the great individual prophets from the eighth century on (§ 20.1).

§ 14 YAHWEH AND THE DIVINE REALM

K.-H. BERNHARDT, *Gott und Bild*, 1956; T. CANAAN, *Dämonenglaube im Lande der Bibel*, 1929; G. COOKE, "The Sons of (the) God (s)," *ZAW*, LXXVI (1964), 22-47; E. DHORME, "La démonologie biblique," in *maqqél shâqédh, Hommage à W. Vischer*, 1960, pp. 46-54; H. DUHM, *Die bösen Geister im Alten Testament*, 1904; H. FREDRIKSSON, *Jahwe als Krieger*, 1945; G. W. HEIDT, *Angelology of the Old Testament*, 1949; A. JIRKU, *Die Dämonen und ihre Abwehr im Alten Testament*, 1912 (= his *Von Jerusalem nach Ugarit*, 1966, pp. 1-107); H. KAUPEL, *Die Dämonen im Alten Testament*, 1930; A. KRUYSWIJK, "*Geen gesneden beeld . . . ,*" 1962; C. J. LABUSCHAGNE, *The Incomparability of Yahweh in the Old Testament*, 1966; E. LANGTON, *The Ministries of the Angelic Powers*, 1937; idem, *Essentials of Demonology*, 1949; J. RYBINSKI, *Der Mal'ak Jahwe*, 1930; F. STIER, *Gott und sein Engel im Alten Testament*, 1934; M. T. UNGER, *Biblical Demonology*, 1952; A. S. VAN DER WOUDE, "mal'ak Jahweh: een Godsbode," *NThT*, XVIII (1963/64), 1-13.

1. *Yahweh and his manifestations.* a) During the monarchy the notion of God was extended and expanded in many ways, as can be seen most immediately from the new epithets and titles accorded Yahweh. The first of these to deserve mention are the two based on II Sam. 6:2 (see § 10.1): "Yahweh Sabaoth" (full form: "Yahweh, God of Sabaoth"), and "he who sits enthroned on the cherubim." The phrase "Yahweh (God of) Sabaoth" is hard to interpret, since, as is so often the case, the OT offers no explanation. Suggested interpretations fall into three groups: (1) "Sabaoth" refers to the military hosts of Israel or the combined militias of Judah and Israel [1]; (2) it refers to the hosts of heaven, whether the stars, the angels or other heavenly beings, the degraded Canaanite pantheon, or subjugated demons;[2] or (3) it stands for "powers" in some non-concrete

[1] E. Kautzsch, "Die ursprüngliche Bedeutung des Namens צבאות יהוה," *ZAW*, VI (1886), 17-22.
[2] A. Alt, "Gedanken über das Königtum Jahwes," in his *Kleine Schriften zur Geschichte des Volkes Israel*, II (1953), 354-55; V. Maag, "Jahwäs Heerscharen," *Schweiz. Theol. Umschau*, XX (1950), 27-52. Unlikely are the suggestions of J. P. Ross, "Jahweh S̥ebā'ôt in Samuel and Psalms," *VT*, XVII (1967), 76-97, that the expression "Sabaoth" originally referred to a Canaanite god, and of M. Tsevat, "Studies in the Book of Samuel, IV," *HUCA*, XXXVI (1965), 49-58, that the term depicted Yahweh as the militia of Israel.

sense, such as an abstract plural "Sabaoth-ness" meaning omnipotence.[3] The first view is supported by the fact that I Sam. 17:45 calls Yahweh "God of the armies of Israel"; but this belongs to a later elaboration of the narrative. Any reference to the militias of Judah and Israel would be possible only in the period of the Davidic and Solomonic empire. For the following period, after the division of the kingdom, the second view appears appropriate, especially since Josh. 5:14 presupposes a celestial army (singular) of Yahweh, whose leader appears to Joshua, and Isa. 24:21 refers to a "host of heaven" that Yahweh will call to account. But no precise definition of the idea is possible. The "hosts" might be the heavenly army (Josh. 5:13-15), the beings that make up the heavenly court (I Kings 22:19; Job 1:6), the celestial beings who lead or judge nations on earth (Dan. 4:14 [Eng. 4:17]; 10:13, 20-21; 12:1), the constellations (Isa. 40:26) as astral deities worshiped by men (Deut. 4:19; Jer. 19:13). But just as the boundary between the stars and astral spirits or deities was vague, so that the constellations could be thought of as living beings (Judg. 5:20), so, following Babylonian example, they could be identified with heavenly beings (Job 38:7). In any case, the phrase "Yahweh (God of) Sabaoth" expresses a significant extension of Yahweh's power, since it implies the subordination of the heavenly beings to him. In later use the term lost this concrete significance; its popular use in post-exilic prophecy most likely corresponds to the third interpretation, which sees in the phrase a reference to the fullness of Yahweh's power.

The additional designation of Yahweh as "he who sits enthroned on the cherubim" corresponds to his being called "rider on the clouds" (§ 9.2). For the cherubim, depicted as winged sphinges, were considered either bearers of all kinds of objects (including thrones) or the embodiment of storm clouds.[4] In the Davidic period, Yahweh came on them (Ps. 18:11 [Eng. 18:10]) as the God hastening to battle in the midst of the storm. After the completion of Solomon's Temple this concept was reinterpreted. The pair of cherubim in the holy of holies symbolized the throne of God, upon which Yahweh was conceived as sitting "enthroned on the cherubim." This inter-

[3] O. Eissfeldt, "Jahwe Zebaoth," *Miscellanea Academica Berolinensia*, II.2 (1950), 128-50 (= his *Kleine Schriften*, III [1966], 103-23); B. N. Wambacq, *L'épithète divine Jahvé Sébaot*, 1947; G. Wanke, *Die Zionstheologie der Korachiten*, 1966, pp. 40-46.
[4] But cf. also P. Dhorme and H. Vincent, "Les Chérubins," *RB*, XXXV (1926), 328-58, 481-95.

pretation is therefore associated with the use of the title "king" for Yahweh.

Opinions differ widely concerning the origin and above all the date of the application of the title "king" to Yahweh.[5]

While Buber assumes that Israel was originally theocratic and believed in Yahweh's kingship from the beginning, Alt interprets this kingship as the notion of Yahweh enthroned in the midst of a host of subordinate divine beings, a concept dating from the premonarchic period in Palestine. Weiser reaches the same conclusion on the basis of the name "Malchishua" (a son of Saul) and of Exod. 15:18; Num. 23:21; Deut. 33:5.[6] Rost, on the other hand, maintains that J, whom he dates in the period of David and Solomon, still rejected the notion of Yahweh's kingship. Von Rad, too, thinks the notion came into being sometime after the development of the Israelite monarchy.[7]

Although the earliest explicit literary evidence (Isa. 6:5; cf. Num. 23:21 [E]) dates only from the eighth century, the use of the title "king" for Yahweh is undoubtedly earlier and represents a Canaanite heritage. It combines the notion of the timeless, immutable, "static" kingship of El with that of the "dynamic" kingship of Baal, which must be won, secured, and defended (Schmidt). As in Isa. 6:5, so, too, in Jer. 46:18; 48:15; 51:57; Ps. 24:9-10 the royal title is associated with the term "Yahweh Sabaoth" and thus with the ark (§ 10.1). While the connection between the latter two was established during the period of David, it seems likely that the title "king" was adopted at the latest following the construction of Solomon's Temple as the earthly likeness of God's heavenly palace and the transfer to it of the ark. In any case, the application of the royal title to Yahweh is frequently associated with Jerusalem (e.g., Isa. 52:7; Jer. 8:19), and the Davidic kingship is practically equated with the kingship of God (I Chron. 17:14; 28:5; 29:3; II Chron. 9:8; 13:8). But such official use does not exclude the possibility that the title was used

[5] A. Alt, "Gedanken über das Königtum Jahwes"; M. Buber, *Königtum Gottes*, 3rd ed., 1956 (English: *Kingship of God*, 1967); O. Eissfeldt, "Jahwe als König," *ZAW*, XLVI (1928), 81-105 (= his *Kleine Schriften*, I [1962], 172-93); J. Gray, "The Hebrew Conception of the Kingship of God," *VT*, VI (1956), 268-85; *idem*, "The Kingship of God in the Prophets and Psalms," *ibid.*, XI (1961), 1-29; V. Maag, "Malkût Jhwh," *VTSuppl*, VII (1960), 129-53; L. Rost, "Königsherrschaft Gottes in vorköniglicher Zeit," *ThLZ*, LXXXV (1960), 721-24; W. H. Schmidt, *Königtum Gottes in Ugarit und Israel*, 2nd ed., 1966.

[6] A. Weiser, "Samuel und die Vorgeschichte des israelitischen Königtums, I Sam 8," *ZThK*, LVII (1960), 141-61. But the three passages cited are considerably later and do not contain traditions of the period before the state.

[7] *ThW*, I, 567.

earlier and elsewhere as a more or less private form (I Sam. 14:49). The essential point throughout is that the royal title does not refer to Yahweh's sovereignty over the gods, as in the case of El and Baal, but to his sovereignty over Israel. The extent of this sovereignty does not, of course, remain constant; it expands continually with the passage of time, until it includes all nations and the entire world.

The term "shepherd" proclaimed above all help and protection. In Israel, however, it was applied only hesitantly to Yahweh, because it was burdened by being used already for the Sumerian Dumuzi (Tammuz) and the ancient Near Eastern king. We do not find it applied to Yahweh until the eighth century in Gen. 48:15 (E) and Hos. 13:5-6, emended; its use becomes more frequent from the end of the seventh century on (Jer. 23:1ff.; Ezek. 34; Ps. 23; and *passim*).

b) God's dwelling place was never identified by Israel with Sinai; not even the expressions "he of Sinai" (Judg. 5:5; Ps. 68:9 [Eng. 68:8]) and "mountain of God" can be taken in this sense. The reference is only to Yahweh's appearance or descent upon the mountain, not to his permanent dwelling there. The mountain serves as a temporary place of revelation or as the point of departure for Yahweh's further journey toward Palestine (Judg. 5:4-5; Deut. 33:2; Hab. 3:3-4; Ps. 68:18 [Eng. 68:17]). Neither were the sanctuaries and cultic sites of Palestine considered places where Yahweh dwelt permanently. He was believed present only at the moment of his revelation there. For a period that cannot be determined precisely the Jerusalem Temple constituted an exception: according to Solomon's prayer of dedication, it was intended as a temple for God to dwell in (I Kings 8:12-13). The question nevertheless arises whether this does not refer to the dwelling of God's likeness, just as the Temple itself was considered the likeness of God's heavenly palace.[8] In this palace, built upon the firm vault of heaven and above the heavenly ocean, Yahweh was thought to dwell (e.g., Gen. 11:5; 19:24; 21:17; 22:11; 24:7; 28:12; Exod. 19:18; Ps. 2:4; 18:7 [Eng. 18:6]), although even in this respect a later voice notes cautiously that heaven itself cannot contain him (I Kings 8:27). This is nevertheless the dominant conception. The primary interest, however, is less in localization for its own sake than in the omniscience (Ps. 11:4; 14:2; 33:13 ff.; and *passim*) and omnipotence (Isa. 40:22 ff.) of Yahweh symbolized thereby.

---

[8] The later period furthermore restricted this notion to the dwelling of Yahweh's *kābód* or name.

Yahweh comes from heaven to appear in various forms at Sinai or the sanctuaries. Apart from the mythico-anthropomorphic form (e.g., Genesis 18) and appearance in dreams (e.g., Gen. 46:2), which need no further explanation, the theophany deserves first mention.[9] In their early form, the accounts of theophanies comprise the two motifs of Yahweh's coming and the effect of his coming (e.g., Judg. 5:4-5; Mic. 1:3-4). The effect can be exhibited on the one hand in the fear it engenders in men (the Sinai theophany), on the other in tumult of the elements. Since the latter effect apparently derives from non-Yahwistic accounts common throughout the ancient Near East, the former, which furthermore comports with the personal nature of Yahwism, must be considered original. The Sinai theophany can therefore be considered the basis for the accounts of other theophanies. Jeremias has recently shown that origin from a Jerusalem festival cult is out of the question; but the victory song that he considers the *Sitz im Leben* of the theophany is probably itself impossible, because Judges 5 constitutes too narrow a basis and itself already exhibits the later form of the effect upon nature of Yahweh's coming.

Occasionally the "face" or "countenance" (*pānîm*) of Yahweh is used in the sense of a manifestation[10]—that is, neither in the original sense of an image of God nor in the transferred sense of participation in the cult at a sanctuary ("looking on the face of Yahweh"). What is meant is rather that Yahweh's presence is a firm guarantee, but at the same time can be endured by man. The expression was used in this sense primarily with reference to Yahweh's leading Israel through the desert (Exod. 33:14-15; Deut. 4:37; Isa. 63:9; cf. Ps. 21:10 [Eng. 21:9]; 80:17 [Eng. 80:16]; Lam. 4:16).

In addition, beside its other meanings, the term *kābôd* [11] came in priestly theology to mean a manifestation of Yahweh—the reflected splendor of the transcendent God, the visible aspect of the invisible, and the presence of the deity, not unique or transitory, but perpetual. The deity makes his presence known symbolically through his "glory," though Yahweh himself is not bound to any earthly site.

[9] *RGG*, VI, 841-43; *IDB*, IV, 619-20; J. Jeremias, *Theophanie*, 1965.

[10] E. Gulin, *Das Antlitz Gottes im Alten Testament*, 1923; A. R. Johnson, "Aspects of the Use of the Term פנים in the Old Testament," in *Eissfeldt Festschrift*, 1947, 155-59; F. Nötscher, "*Das Angesicht Gottes schauen*" *nach biblischer und babylonischer Auffassung*, 1924.

[11] H. Kittel, *Die Herrlichkeit Gottes*, 1934; B. Stein, *Der Begriff K⁰bod Jahweh und seine Bedeutung für die alttestamentliche Gotteserkenntnis*, 1939.

Finally, the "spirit" (*rûaḥ*) [12] could be considered a manifestation —albeit impersonal—of Yahweh, filling men with might, animating them, and bestowing religious gifts. In particular it can inspire a prophet, press him to speak his message, and induce him to communicate his revelation to others (Num. 24:2; II Sam. 23:2; Isa. 42:1; 61:1; Ezek. 11:5; Mic. 3:8; Zech. 7:12; and *passim*).

c) Yahweh's appearance does not seem to be a problem often considered by Israel. The statements that no man can see him (Exod. 33:20) and that he is spirit, not flesh (Isa. 31:3) of course do not mean that he is formless or invisible, but rather that man cannot endure the sight of him (cf. Judg. 13:22) and that, in contrast to transitory "flesh," he possesses an eternal vitality. But the prohibition against images (Exod. 20:4) [13] contributed decisively to checking all speculation about Yahweh's appearance. Neither the bull sculptures at the sanctuaries of Bethel and Dan, which symbolized and represented him in animal form (§ 11.3), nor the metaphorical comparisons with other animals,[14] which refer to the nature of his activity (e.g., Deut. 32:11; Hos. 5:14; 11:10; 13:7; Lam. 3:10), say anything about his form. All the evidence suggests that from the outset Yahweh was conceived in human form (cf. § 6:1), just as conversely for a later theology man is an image resembling God (Gen. 1:26-27): God walks about in his garden and converses with men (Genesis 3), he shuts the door of the ark after Noah (Gen. 7:16), he comes down to inspect the city and tower being built (Gen. 11:5), he visits Abraham (Genesis 18). The call visions of Isaiah and Ezekiel likewise presuppose that Yahweh's appearance is human (Isa. 6:1; Ezek. 1:26-27). This conception made it possible to use anthropomorphisms and anthropopathisms in speaking of Yahweh.

d) Much more important was the polymorphism in which Israel experienced the uniqueness of the divine nature and activity. For example, Yahweh was "holy" and "the Holy One of Israel." Although the notion of holiness appears to derive from the Canaanite realm,[15] it came to be of fundamental importance, as above all its triple

---

[12] J. Hehn, "Zum Problem des Geistes im Alten Orient und im Alten Testament," *ZAW*, XLIII (1925), 210-25.

[13] K.-H. Bernhardt, *Gott und Bild*, 1956; A Kruyswijk, "*Geen gesneden beeld . . . ,*" 1962.

[14] See J. Hempel, "Jahwegleichnisse der israelitischen Propheten," *ZAW*, XLII (1924), 74-104 (= his *Apoxysmata*, 1961, pp. 1-29).

[15] W. Schmidt, "Wo hat die Aussage: Jahwe 'der Heilige' ihren Ursprung?" *ZAW*, LXXIV (1962), 62-66.

aspect in Isaiah 6 shows: it denotes the exaltedness and unapproachability of Yahweh, his absolute omnipotence (*kābôd* as the "energy"
that fills the world), and the power of his ethical will (Isa. 6:5).
Persons or objects are termed holy because they are associated with
Yahweh and belong to him as his property. When a man is called
upon to make himself holy or to be holy, this can signify both cultic
purity and obedience to ethical commandments (cf. Lev. 19:2 ff. and
passim).

Yahweh is a "righteous" God (cf. § 6.1). The Hebrew term *ṣdq*
refers to God's sovereign and judicial governance. Yahweh is
righteous when he vanquishes his enemies and brings deliverance to
Israel, when he rewards the just and punishes—or spares—the sinner.
A later period sees this governance operating in the order of nature
(Joel 2:23; Ps. 85:12-13).

Yahweh can be a God of wrath,[16] expressing his displeasure without any particular reason, so that a man can be suddenly struck
down in consequence of God's displeasure. Sometimes Yahweh's
wrath is frankly incomprehensible; David, for instance, suspects that
Yahweh has stirred up Saul against him (I Sam. 26:19), and II Sam.
24:1 traces David's disastrous census to Yahweh's wrath against the
Israelites (cf. on the contrary I Chron. 21:1, according to which
Satan incited David!). Usually, however, the anger is ethically based;
its source is found in human sin. In the non-prophetical view this
refers to individual transgressions and is therefore transitory; in the
prophetical view, however, God's anger is aroused by the totally sinful nature of man, and it therefore flames with terrible ferocity.

But beside God's wrath stands the statement that Yahweh is gracious: "a God merciful and gracious, slow to anger, and abounding
in steadfast love and faithfulness" (Exod. 34:6). His grace and faithfulness were refuge in difficult situations (Gen. 24:12; I Kings 3:6),
they were invoked on behalf of one about to depart or found to be
loyal (II Sam. 2:6; 15:20), they were mentioned in liturgical formulas used in prayers of petition and thanksgiving: "Give thanks to
Yahweh, for he is good; for his steadfast love endures for ever" (Ps.
106:1; 107:1).

But Yahweh is also a jealous God ('*ēl qannā*'),[17] that is, accord-

[16] H. M. Haney, *The Wrath of God in the Former Prophets*, 1960.

[17] H. A. Brongers, "Der Eifer des Herrn Zebaoth," *VT*, XIII (1963), 269-84;
F. Küchler, "Der Gedanke des Eifers Jahwes im Alten Testament," *ZAW*,
XXVIII (1908), 42-52; B. Renaud, *Je suis un Dieu jaloux*, 1963; G. D. Richard-
son, "The Jealousy of God," *AThR*, X (1927), 47-55.

ing to the basic meaning of *qn':* one who asserts his own rights over against others without regard for their rights. The expression therefore characterizes Yahweh as a God who seeks recognition of his sovereign will and refuses to share his sovereignty with anyone (cf. Exod. 20:5; 34:14). Though not the earliest, this is the most striking formulation of Yahweh's claim to sole worship.

Of course Yahweh is a powerful God. Israel believed that it experienced this power first and most impressively in Yahweh's warlike acts (Fredricksson). These were therefore extolled in the earlier hymns (Exod. 15:21; Judges 5), and appropriate attributes were ascribed to Yahweh: "a warrior, mighty and highly exalted, terrible and glorious in holiness, mighty and a worker of wonders." For the Israelite also experienced Yahweh's power as a miraculous creative and vitalizing force—from the nature miracles of the desert period to the longed-for harmony of nature expected in the age of eschatological deliverance. Above all, the influence of Canaanite religion led to recognition of God's miraculous governance in the quiet regularity of natural processes, in the alternation of seasons, in the circling of the constellations, and in the appearance of new life. Just as Yahweh demonstrated his power by maintaining the world and all things living, so too he demonstrated his power in creation. The creation narrative in Gen. 2:4b ff. (J) shows that this belief was current at least from the ninth century on. Finally, Yahweh was considered powerful as the savior and deliverer of Israel, helping the nation and the individual when they were in need, and, according to the message of some of the prophets, even redeeming the guilty and mortally depraved existence of man (§ 20.1).

Yahweh is a living God, not limited in time or space and not a fading and reviving vegetation god, but always at work and accessible to man. He is not dependent on life as a superordinate category; he is lord over all life and the source of all life (Ps. 36:10 [Eng. 36:9]).

In all these aspects Yahweh is an eternal God. The concept of a theogony was always inconceivable to the OT; the world had a beginning, but not Yahweh (Ps. 90:2). It is true that Yahweh's eternity is especially emphasized in post-exilic literature (e.g., Ps. 9:8 [Eng. 9:7]; 10:16; 29:10; 33:11; 92:9 [Eng. 92:8]; 93:2; 102:13 [Eng. 102:12]; 145:13), but before this notion was conceptualized it lived in the direct knowledge that the unique reality of Yahweh is not temporally limited, but eternal.

2. *Yahweh and the gods.* Mosaic Yahwism already assumed that in
Israel Yahweh could claim exclusive devotion. This principle was
continually championed, even though it was often enough transgressed in practice, and in the official worship of the deities of foreign
overlords had of necessity to be transgressed in the Jerusalem Temple
(§ 11.4). But Israelite monoyahwism or practical monotheism did
not rule out the natural assumption that there were other gods for
other nations or lands; after preparatory steps taken by Jeremiah and
Ezekiel, Deutero-Isaiah was the first representative of theoretical
monotheism.[18] In the earlier period, by way of contrast, the Moabites
were termed the people of Chemosh (Num. 21:29), and their territory was distinguished from that of the Israelites as being given by
Chemosh rather than by Yahweh (Judg. 11:23-24). II Kings 3:27
presupposes that every people and land has its own tutelary deity, so
that in a foreign land one must serve a foreign god (I Sam. 26:19).
Yahweh nevertheless was considered the greatest and most powerful
God (Ps. 89:6-9), who can act effectively within the sphere of influence of other gods—both in Palestine (Gen. 20:1 ff.) and in Egypt
(Gen. 12:10 ff.; Exod. 7:8 ff.). This is all the more true for the universalistic view of the prophets.

In addition, drawing especially on its Canaanite environment,
Israel adopted the notion of a pantheon and a divine assembly. According to this theory there existed a series of divine beings (cf.
§ 9.2), among whom at least some of the gods of other nations were
at times included; they were subordinate to Yahweh, the supreme
God. The evidence comprises several Psalms in which this interpretation of *bᵉnê hā'ĕlōhîm* and similar expressions as referring to
individual gods can be perceived behind the present interpretation
of them as referring to heavenly ministers (see the discussion in the
next section of Ps. 29:1; 82:1, 6-7; 89:6-8 [Eng. 89:5-7]).

Finally, individual Israelites or groups of Israelites went so far in
their recognition of other gods beside Yahweh that they accepted
and worshiped such gods of their own accord. Beside El and Baal,
for whom this fact is generally recognized, there were widespread
cults of mother-goddesses, above all Asherah,[19] suggested by the
frequent mention of asheroth, wooden posts serving as the symbol of

---

[18] The contrary view has recently been espoused once more by B. Hartmann,
"Es gibt keinen Gott ausser Jahwe. Zur generellen Verneinung im Hebräischen,"
ZDMG, CX (1960), 229-35. According to Hartmann, theoretical monotheism be-
gins no later than the ninth century.

[19] R. Patai, "The Goddess Ashera," *JNES*, XXIV (1965), 37-52.

the goddess, and Astarte, as indicated by the numerous finds of pictorial representations (see § 3.2). Also mentioned are worship of Bethel (Amos 3:14),[20] the "queen of heaven" (Ishtar; Jer. 7:18; 44:17 ff.), Tammuz (Ezek. 8:14), the sun-god (II Kings 23:5, 11; Jer. 8:2; Ezek. 8:16), and the constellations (II Kings 21:3; Jer. 8:2), as well as local deities such as Ashimah of Samaria and Dod of Beersheba (Amos 8:14 emended), the former of which is mentioned in II Kings 17:30 as the god of Hamath. But the worship of other gods beside Yahweh was constantly exposed to severe criticism.[21]

Only in the Israelite military colony on the island of Elephantine in the Nile was a Yahwistic-Canaanite pantheon worshiped officially in the temple, built some time before 525 B.C. Beside Yahweh, the gods *ḥrm-betel*, *'nt-betel*, and *'šm-betel*[22] were worshiped there. But this remained an exception.

3. *Heavenly beings and demons.*[23] a) With the notion of Yahweh as the God of heaven is linked that of figures belonging to the heavenly world, called *bᵉnê hā'ĕlōhîm*, "divine beings," by virtue of their relationship to the divine realm and *mal'ākîm*, "messengers," by virtue of their function. As a group they were referred to as *'ădat 'ēl*, "the divine council" (Ps. 82:1), as *qāhāl*, "assembly," and *sôd*, "intimate circle," of the *qᵉdōšîm*, "holy ones," those who sit "round about" him (Yahweh) (Ps. 89:6, 8 [Eng. 89:5, 7]). Originally gods foreign to Yahwism, within Yahwism they were gradually turned into beings completely subordinate to Yahweh, constituting a part of his court and of his armies.

The yahwistically edited fragment in Gen. 6:1-4 is based on an originally mythological narrative in which the divine beings mated with human women. While the myth originally dealt with gods, the intervention of Yahweh (vs. 3) shows that the present narrator was thinking in terms of subordinate heavenly beings.

Behind Ps. 29:1; 89:6-8 (Eng. 89:5-7) stands the notion of a pantheon headed by a supreme god, to whom the subordinate gods pay homage, and

[20] For details, see O. Eissfeldt, "Der Gott Bethel," *ARW*, XXVIII (1930), 1-30 (= his *Kleine Schriften*, I [1962], 206-33).

[21] This criticism is minimized by R. H. Pfeiffer, "The Polemic Against Idolatry in the Old Testament," *JBL*, XLIII (1924), 229-40.

[22] The names are difficult to interpret. The first may signify the (hypostatized) "holiness of Bethel," the second the "sign" (actual presence) or "will of Bethel" or the (goddess) "Anat of Bethel," the third the "name of Bethel" or "Ashim-Bethel."

[23] *BHH*, I, 315-16, 410-11; *RGG*, II, 1301-3; *IDB*, I, 128-34, 817-24.

who holds sway over them in a reign of terror. Psalm 29 is obviously based on a Cannaanite hymn, into which Yahweh has been interpolated in the rôle of heavenly king. In Ps. 29:1 the original interpretation of the heavenly beings as gods is more evident; in Ps. 89:6-8 (Eng. 89:5-7) we see their power stripped by Yahweh.

Canaanite concepts are even more evident in Psalm 82: vs. 1 refers to the divine beings as *ʿădat ʿēl,* "the divine council" (perhaps originally "the council of El") and as *ʾĕlōhîm,* "gods"; vs. 6 calls them *bᵉnê ʿelyôn,* "sons" or "companions of Elyon." The end with which they are threatened in vs. 7 may go back to a mythological episode concerning the fall of a member of the divine council (cf. Isa. 14:12). But Yahweh has replaced Elyon as supreme judge in the heavenly council.

These heavenly beings are usually sent forth to carry out Yahweh's bidding. A man may see in a dream at a sacred spot how they go up and down a stairway connecting heaven and earth (Gen. 28:12). Among their duties may be the protection and preservation of men (Ps. 34:8 [Eng. 34:7]; 91:11-12). But they can also come as angels of destruction and death (Ps. 78:49; Exod. 12:23; II Sam. 24:16), just as an evil or lying spirit can go forth from Yahweh (Judg. 9:23-24; I Sam. 16:14; I Kings 22:21).

There is frequent mention of the *malʾak yhwh,* the "angel" or "messenger of Yahweh." Although it is not quite clear whether this refers to a specific figure, as is usually assumed, or simply to some heavenly being (van der Woude), the evidence tends to support the former view. This messenger appears as a bearer of revelation and of aid. He rescues Hagar as she flees from Sarai (Gen. 16:7 ff.), reveals himself to Moses as a flame in a thorn bush (Exod. 3:2), summons Gideon to deliver the Israelites (Judg. 6:11 ff.), announces the birth of Samson (Judg. 13:3 ff.), fortifies Elijah (I Kings 19:7), and vanquishes the Assyrian army (II Kings 19:35). He is always a subordinate minister of Yahweh, although he frequently appears to be practically identical with Yahweh, so that the expressions "angel of Yahweh" and "Yahweh" are mutually interchangeable. In other instances he comes close to the ancient Near Eastern notion of the heavenly vizier who carries out on earth the will of the supreme god at his behest. Thus he is appointed to bring the Israelites safely to Palestine (Exod. 23:20 ff.), he appears to Joshua as leader of the heavenly army (Josh. 5:13), he calls down curses on those that have not come to Yahweh's aid (Judg. 5:23), and he designates those that are to be spared by the heavenly beings following him (Ezek. 9:2 ff.).

More humble services were assigned to the cherubim and seraphim.[24] On the one hand, the cherubim were thought of as throne bearers or as personifications of thunder-clouds (see section 1 above), from which lightning can blaze forth (cf. Gen. 3:24). On the other hand, they appear in Ezekiel 1 and 10 as beings of mixed human and animal nature, such as are familiar primarily from Babylonian representations. The seraphim mentioned in Isaiah 6 are similar hybrids: they have human voices, hands, and (probably) faces, as well as wings and a serpentine body (cf. Num. 21:6; Isa. 14:29; 30:6).

In Yahwism none of these heavenly beings had any independent significance; they were accepted as a kind of auxiliary notion. Depending on the rôle they played, they might symbolize Yahweh's exaltation, his beneficent power, or his judgmental and punitive intervention.

b) Belief in demons was essentially alien to true Yahwism. Impressed by the notion of Yahweh's uniqueness, it refused to recognize any other powers. Mysterious, awful, and horrifying phenomena were incorporated into the picture of God himself, or else were associated with a heavenly being or spirit sent by Yahweh. In consequence Yahweh took on "demonic" features (Gen. 32:23-32 [Eng. 32:22-31]; Exod. 4:24-26)[25]—or, more accurately, came to appear in an irrational and numinous light—and the boundary between heavenly beings and demons was obscured. Demons are therefore seldom mentioned. It was forbidden to offer them sacrifice (Lev. 17:7) and relations with them were prohibited, without any denial of their existence.

To extensive groups in Israel, however, demons symbolized the mysterious aspect of the world; they surely played an important rôle in popular religion. Ruins and waste places, felt to be sinister, were thought of as their dwelling places; foreign gods, relegated to an inferior position, were counted among them; and demons from other religions invaded the Israelite conceptual world. Many of these notions finally took such firm root that they could not be eliminated, but could only be reinterpreted within the framework of Yahwism. These included ideas and practices associated with sexual conduct (Lev. 12:1 ff.; Deut. 23:10 ff.; 24:1-4; 25:11-12; Song 3:8), sickness (Leviticus 13; Num. 21:9), agriculture (Lev. 19:9, 23; Deut. 22:9), thresholds (I Sam. 5:5; Zeph. 1:9), and other causes (Deuteronomy 20).

The most important demons mentioned in the OT (without

----

[24] *BHH,* I, 298-99; III, 1776-77.
[25] See P. Volz, *Das Dämonische in Jahwe,* 1924.

distinguishing between the pre-exilic and post-exilic periods) are: (1) hairy demons in the form of goats, inhabiting the open countryside (*ś^eʿîrîm*; Lev. 17:7; II Kings 23:8, emended; Isa. 13:21; 34:14; II Chron. 11:15) ; (2) the black demons (*śēdîm*), i.e., sinister demons, probably former pagan gods (Deut. 32:17; Ps. 106:37) ; (3) the dry demons (*ṣiyyîm*) inhabiting waterless regions (Isa. 13:21; 34:14; Jer. 50:39) ; the desert animals mentioned in the same context are probably conceived as demons in animal form; (4) Azazel, a demon living in the desert, who was thought to receive the scapegoat released in the ceremony of the great Day of Atonement (Leviticus 16) ; (5) demons bringing sickness, striking by day or night (Ps. 91:5-6) ;[26] (6) Lilith, by origin probably an Assyrian storm demon, then considered a nocturnal demon because of the similarity to the Hebrew word for "night." Belief in demons took on greater importance in later Judaism than in the OT.

§ 15 Yahweh and the Earthly Realm

P. ALTMANN, *Erwählungstheologie und Universalismus*, 1964; K.-H. BERNHARDT, "Zur Bedeutung der Schöpfungsvorstellung für die Religion Israels in vorexilischer Zeit," *ThLZ*, LXXXV (1960), 821-24; S. G. F. BRANDON, *History, Time and Deity*, 1963; R. C. DENTAN, ed., *The Idea of History in the Ancient Near East*, 1955; W. EICHRODT, *Das Menschenverständnis des Alten Testaments*, 1947; I. ENGNELL, *Israel and the Law*, 1946; G. FOHRER, "Prophetie und Geschichte," in his *Studien zur alttestamentlichen Prophetie (1949-1965)*, 1967, pp. 265-93; K. GALLING, *Die Erwählungstraditionen Israels*, 1928; H. GESE, "Geschichtliches Denken im Alten Orient und im Alten Testament," *ZThK*, LV (1958, 127-45; H. GUNKEL, *Schöpfung und Chaos in Urzeit und Endzeit*, 2nd ed., 1921; J. HASPECKER, "Religiöse Naturbetrachtung im Alten Testament," *BiLe*, V (1964), 116-30; *idem*, "Natur und Heilserfahrung in Altisrael," *ibid.*, VII (1966), 83-98; J. HEMPEL, "Gott, Mensch, und Tier im Alten Testament mit besonderer Berücksichtigung von Gen 1-3," *ZSTh*, IX (1931), 211-49 (= his *Apoxysmata*, 1961, pp. 198-229) ; *idem*, *Das Ethos des Alten Testaments*, 2nd ed., 1964; M.-L. HENRY, *Das Tier im religiösen Bewusstsein des alttestamentlichen Menschen*, 1958; F. HESSE, "Erwägungen zur religionsgeschichtlichen und theologischen Bedeutung der Erwählungsgewissheit Israels," in *Vriezen Festschrift*, 1966, pp. 125-37; E. JACOB, *La tradition historique en Israël*, 1946; A. JIRKU, *Das weltliche Recht Israels*, 1927; R. KNIERIM, *Die Hauptbegriffe für Sünde im Alten Testament*, 1965; K. KOCH, "Zur Geschichte der Erwählungsvorstellung in Israel," *ZAW*, LXVII (1955),

[26] R. Caillois, "Les démons du midi," *RHR*, CXV (1937), 142-73; CXVI (1937), 143-86.

205-26; L. KÖHLER, *Der hebräische Mensch*, 1953; N. LOHFINK, "Freiheit und Wiederholung; zum Geschichtsverständnis des Alten Testaments," in *Die religiöse und theologische Bedeutung des Alten Testaments*, n.d., 79-103; A. MENES, *Die vorexilischen Gesetze Israels*, 1928; C. R. NORTH, *The Old Testament Interpretation of History*, 1946; M. NOTH, *Die Gesetze im Pentateuch*, 1940 (= his *Gesammelte Studien zum Alten Testament*, 1957, pp. 9-141 [English: *The Laws in the Pentateuch and Other Studies*, 1963, 1-107]); G. ÖSTBORN, *Yahweh's Words and Deeds*, 1951; W. PANGRITZ, *Das Tier in der Bibel*, 1963; G. PIDOUX, *L'homme dans l'Ancien Testament*, 1953; G. VON RAD, "Das theologische Problem des alttestamentlichen Schöpfungsglaubens," in *Werden und Wesen des Alten Testaments*, 1936, pp. 138-47 (= his *Gesammelte Studien zum Alten Testament*, 1958, pp. 136-47 [English: *The Problem of the Hexateuch and Other Essays*, 1966, pp. 131-43];) H. H. ROWLEY, *The Biblical Doctrine of Election*, 2nd ed., 1964; R. SMEND, "The Chosen People," *AJSL*, XLV (1928/29), 73-82; W. STAERK, "Zum alttestamentlichen Erwählungsglauben," *ZAW*, LV (1937), 1-36; W. ZIMMERLI, "Das Gesetz im Alten Testament," *ThLZ*, LXXXV (1960), 481-98.

1. *Nature, creation, and primordial events. a*) From time immemorial Israel believed that Yahweh could bestow certain gifts of nature and make use of the forces and processes of nature in his activity. First among the gifts bestowed is the land, the promise of which plays such an important rôle in the patriarchal and Moses traditions, and the conquest and control of which constitute the focus of the tradition behind Joshua and Judges.[1] Yahweh can also bring about the increase of nature. The flocks of Abraham and Lot, for example, increased beyond what the land could support (Gen. 13:2 ff.). Even in a year of famine Isaac could reap a hundredfold because Yahweh blessed him (Gen. 26:1-3, 12). Jacob, too, attributed to Yahweh his rise from nothing to prosperity (Gen. 32:11 [Eng. 32:10]; 33:11). This accords with the blessing Isaac pronounces over him:

See, the smell of my son
is as the smell of a field
which Yahweh has blessed!
May God give you
of the dew of heaven,
and of the fatness of the earth,
And plenty of grain and wine.   (Gen. 27:27-28)

[1] G. von Rad, "Verheissenes Land und Jahwes Land im Hexateuch," *ZDPV*, LXVI (1943), 191-204 (= his *Gesammelte Studien zum Alten Testament*, 1958, 87-100 [English: *The Problem of the Hexateuch and Other Essays*, 1966, pp. 79-93]); H. Wildberger, "Israel und sein Land," *EvTh*, XVI (1956), 404-22.

After the Deluge Yahweh guaranteed the regular fertility of the fields (Gen. 8:21-22); on special occasions he also bestowed miraculous gifts of nature, such as the manna and quails given to the Israelites for food while journeying through the desert, and the water given them to drink.

Yahweh can likewise make use of the forces of nature to accomplish his purpose or will. The Egyptian plagues were conceived as natural catastrophes that befell Egypt because Pharaoh would not agree to release the Israelites. Even the destruction of the Egyptians pursuing the Israelites when they finally escaped or were released took place by means of a natural event, even though the individual source strata have differing conceptions of what happened.

For Palestinian Yahwism the crucial question was to whom the Israelite farmer owed the fertility of his fields: Yahweh or the Canaanite god Baal. Especially in the early period many Israelites quite artlessly favored the latter, but the final answer can be seen in the statements concerning the blessing of the patriarchs, retrojected into the early period of Israel's history: it is Yahweh, not Baal, who bestows or denies fertility. Elijah appears to have been the first to represent this point of view, by interpreting an unusually extended drought as Yahweh's punishment and also ascribing to Yahweh the reappearance of rain (I Kings 17:1; 18:1-2). It was a significant step when the prophet claimed for Yahweh the capacity to bring rain, so important for life in Palestine, or at least lent his authority to this view if it was already current. He expanded Yahwism's picture of God and rejected the claims of the Canaanite cults: the people owe the natural bounty of the land to their God Yahweh alone, who can not only guarantee assistance and protection against enemies in the hour of need but also place them under his constant blessing.

The viewpoint represented by Elijah soon carried the day. A century later the source stratum J (Gen. 2:5 and passim), as well as the prophets Amos and Hosea (Amos 4:6-12; Hos. 2:10-11, 23-25 [Eng. 2:8-9, 21-23]), accepted it as a matter of course. Later theology went on to associate Yahweh's sovereignty over nature with his speaking.[2] The divine word became the principle behind the creation and

---

[2] L. Dürr, Die Wertung des göttlichen Wortes im Alten Testament und im antiken Orient, 1938; M.-L. Henry, "Das mythische Wort als religiöse Aussage im Alten Testament," in D. Müller Festschrift, 1961, pp. 21-31; K. Koch, "Wort und Einheit des Schöpfergottes in Memphis und Jerusalem," ZThK, LXII (1965), 251-93; according to W. Gerhardt, Jr., "The Hebrew/Israelite Weather Deity," Numen, XIII (1966), 128-43, Yahweh was a weather-god; this view is highly unlikely.

preservation of the world, as well as the activity of nature: it creates
the world and lays down its fundamental laws (Gen. 1:1–2:4a; Isa.
44:24; 48:13; Ps. 33:6, 9; 104:7), it provides manna (Deut. 8:3), it
maintains or alters the world (Isa. 40:26; 50:2; Ps. 147:4, 15-18; 148).
Thus God's activity in nature was incorporated into the theology of
creation.

b) Belief that Yahweh created man and the world [3] likewise
meant an expansion of the concept of God through the adoption of
non-Yahwistic ideas. For belief in creation is not a unique characteristic of Yahwism. That the deity created the world was rather an
article of faith throughout the ancient Near East;[4] we even find the
notion of creation through the word of the deity. In the Babylonian
creation epic Enuma Elish, it is true, this notion plays only a minor
rôle, since the god Marduk demonstrated this ability on an object in
order to prove his divine power. It was an important part of ancient
Egyptian Memphite theology, according to which Ptah, the god of the
universe, acted as creator with the aid of "heart and tongue," i.e.,
through his word.[5] In Psalm 104, the influence of the Egyptian Hymn
to Aton shows how Egyptian descriptions of creation could be borrowed. Canaanite religion, too, which may have thought in terms of
generation of the earth by the god El,[6] but certainly conceived its
origin as being in a battle with chaos, exercised a certain influence.[7]

The earliest Israelite evidence for belief in creation is the narrative
of the source stratum J in Gen. 2:4b-25.[8] It does not speak of creation
of heaven and earth, but presupposes the existence of a dry desert

[3] *BHH*, III, 1710-14; *RGG*, V, 1473-76; *IDB*, I, 725-32.

[4] R. Amiran, "Myths of the Creation of Man and the Jericho Statues,"
BASOR, CLXVII (1962), 23-25; G. J. Botterweck, "Die Entstehung der Welt in
den altorientalischen Kosmogonien," *BiLe*, VI (1965), 184-91; S. G. F. Brandon,
Creation Legends of the Ancient Near East, 1963; *Die Schöpfungsmythen*, 1964.

[5] See W. Erichsen and S. Schott, *Fragmente memphitischer Theologie in
demotischer Schrift*, 1954; Junker, *Die Götterlehre von Memphis*, 1940. In Egypt
creation was conceived as an emanation of the deity, in Mesopotamia as an
evolution.

[6] For the limitation to the earth, see R. Rendtorff, "El, Ba'al und Jahwe,"
ZAW, LXXVIII (1966), 277-91.

[7] See, among other discussions, O. Eissfeldt, "Gott und das Meer in der Bibel,"
in *Studia orientalia Ioanni Pedersen*, 1953, 76-84; F. Hvidberg, "The Canaanite
Background of Genesis I–III," *VT*, X (1960), 285-94; O. Kaiser, *Die mythische
Bedeutung des Meeres in Ägypten, Ugarit und Israel*, 2nd ed., 1962.

[8] The narrative in Gen. 1:1–2:4a, as well as most of the Psalms (themselves
difficult to date) that speak of Yahweh as creator, and the doxologies in Amos
4:13; 5:8; 9:5-6 either date from a later period or were borrowed then. For a
discussion of Gen. 14:19, see the article by Rendtorff mentioned in note 6 above.

into which water is introduced, through which life is made possible. Then Yahweh created man (*'ādām*) "of dust from the ground" and made him a living being by breathing into him the breath of life. He planted for man a garden in Eden with all kinds of trees and placed man there to cultivate and guard the garden. Then Yahweh sought for man "a helper fit for him," i.e., a partner, and for this purpose created the animals and birds, which man named, thus placing them in his service.[9] When they turned out to be unsuitable, Yahweh caused a deep sleep to fall on the man and took a rib from him. From this rib he formed woman (*'iššâ*), whom man (*'iš*) acknowledged as a fit partner in a kinship formula (Gen. 2:23).

Later this belief in creation was elaborated (cf. § 28.2). But from the very beginning it presupposed the cosmology accepted throughout the ancient Near East.[10] The world was thought of as a self-contained structure; in Israel, it was first conceived of as bipartite (heaven—earth) and later, under Mesopotamian influence, as tripartite (heaven—earth—abyss). Heaven represents a gigantic bell-shaped dome inverted over the earth; above it are the waters of heaven and the heavenly palace of the deity, below it the stars and constellations move about. The earth is a flat surface with four corners or, on account of the horizon, a round disc; it rests on posts or pillars. The latter are fixed in the waters of the abyss under the earth; this water feeds the springs and watercourses of the earth, until it possibley returns once more to the abyss. Within or beneath the abyss lies the realm of the dead, which is usually thought of as belonging to the third portion of the world.

c) Yahweh intervened decisively in the primordial events following creation. The addition of this so-called primal history in Genesis, which did not form a part of the groundwork narratives of the Pentateuch, was the work of the source stratum J. It traced the course of human history downward into sin and judgment immediately after creation:[11] from the Fall and its attendant curse, through Cain's murder and punishment, to the almost total destruction of sinful

[9] On the significance of naming, see W. Schulz, "Der Namenglaube bei den Babyloniern," *Anthropos*, XXVI (1931), 895-928.

[10] *BHH*, III, 2161-63; *RGG*, III, 1615-18.

[11] P. Humbert, *Études sur le récit du paradis et de la chute dans la Genèse,* 1940; T. C. Vriezen, *Onderzoek naar de Paradiesvorstelling bij de oude semitische volken,* 1937; A. Weiser, "Die biblische Geschichte vom Paradies und Sündenfall," *Deutsche Theologie,* 1937, pp. 9-37 (= his *Glaube und Geschichte im Alten Testament,* 1961, 228-57).

mankind by the Deluge, after which the human race multiplied once more, though without any prospects for improvement. Although the structure of the narrative followed the Mesopotamian prototype of the Atrahasis Epic,[12] its result was to trace history back to its beginnings, viewing its entire course from the perspective of sin as the dissolution of communion with God and of judgment as the vindication of God's sovereignty over the sinner.

The primal history of the source stratum N exhibits a unique and characteristic rhythm. Man repeatedly comes into contact with civilization or achieves corresponding cultural progress: he lives in the garden of God, founds a nomadic civilization with musicians and smiths, discovers viticulture, and builds a city and a ziggurat. Repeatedly the unruly creature goes astray or finds himself in the position of overstepping his boundaries and limitations, appropriating divine powers, or taking heaven by storm: the tree of life in the garden of God, the marriages of divine beings with human women, the building of the city and tower. Repeatedly, therefore, Yahweh must intervene and restrain his creature, expelling him from the garden, shortening his life, and dispersing mankind, now become numerous.

Thus since creation there has been reciprocity between human and divine action. Just as the sequence and structure of the primordial drama in J follow the pattern of a Mesopotamian myth, so individual narratives like the story of the Deluge or narrative motifs like man's failure to attain equality with God are influenced by or borrowed from other myths. But they were not taken over unchanged. Their incorporation into Yahwism involved a transformation: they were detached from their polytheistic background and made to refer to the one God of Israel; they were removed from the exclusively divine realm and applied to the belief in creation and the relationship of Yahweh to life and the fortunes of mankind. They served to depict the relationship existing at a given moment between God and man. It is therefore incorrect to say that in Yahwism myth was "historicized"[13] or history "mythologized" (Ringgren*).[14] The original

[12] S-F, § 12.2; cf. J. Laessøe, "The Atraḫasis Epic: a Babylonian History of Mankind," *BiOr*, XIII (1956), 90-102; W. G. Lambert, "New Light on the Babylonian Flood," *JSS*, V (1960), 113-23.

[13] M. Noth, "Die Historisierung des Mythus im Alten Testament," *ChuW*, IV (1928), 265-72, 301-9.

[14] See also J. Barr, "The Meaning of 'Mythology' in Relation to the Old Testament," *VT*, IX (1959), 1-10; K.-H. Bernhardt, "Elemente mythischen Stils in der alttestamentlichen Geschichtsschreibung," *WZ Rostock*, XII (1963), 295-97; B. S. Childs, *Myth and Reality in the Old Testament*, 1960; G. H. Davies, "An Ap-

mythological element was instead disarmed by being transferred to the personal relationship between God and man.

2. *Yahweh as governor of history.* From the beginning there was one feature typical of Yahwism that is intimately related to three other primitive features—its personal structure, its juxtaposition of divine sovereignty and communion, and its correlation between God and man: Yahweh's activity in the lives of men and nations, whose destinies he governs and determines (§ 6.2). Even Yahweh's operation in nature, creation, and the events of primordial history was seen from this perspective. He grants or denies the gifts of nature to specific persons, and makes use of the forces of nature in his dealings with them; everything on earth he actually created for the sake of man, his first and noblest creation; and in the primal history he must constantly concern himself with sinful or unruly mankind. Ever since, he has continued to govern and determine the destinies of men and nations—above all, of course, the destiny of Israel. Demonstration of this fact is the real purpose of the various historical narratives from the period of the monarchy.

This feature of Yahwism is frequently termed "Yahweh's acting in history." That Yahwism is definable as a theology of history, that all the basic confessional statements of the OT refer to history as the locus of Yahweh's actions, and that his revelation or activity takes place in or through history seems to be the characteristic principle for the so-called historical books of the OT and for prophecy. In this linkage with history we seem to see the true difference between Yahwism and other religions, with their timeless or non-historical basis, and thus the revelatory nature of Yahwism. In fact this interpretation is merely a contribution to the apologetic requirements of the nineteenth century. By its means the materialistic, skeptical, and immanent philosophies of history that threatened to relativize the biblical faith were repulsed, on the grounds that no one took history as seriously as the Bible.[15] Several objections can be raised to this interpretation:

a) The view that Yahweh acts in or through history is one-sided, and comprehends only a single aspect of the totality and fullness of Yahwism. Quite apart from the fact that it does not hold true for wisdom literature,

proach to the Problem of Old Testament Mythology," *PEQ,* LXXXVIII (1956), 83-91; J. Hempel, "Glaube, Mythos und Geschichte im Alten Testament," *ZAW,* LXV (1953), 109-67; J. L. McKenzie, "Myth and the Old Testament," *CBQ,* XXI (1959), 265-82; *idem, Myths and Realities,* 1963.

[15] J. Barr, "Revelation Through History in the Old Testament," *Interpr,* XVII (1963), 193-205.

a major portion of the Psalms, and the later law, and perhaps also not for apocalypticism, it encounters serious problems even in the so-called historical books. We find many mythological conceptions and motifs of quite unhistorical nature that are not at all "historicized." The framework sections of the book of Judges, which surround and unite the individual episodes, are based on a cyclic view of history that conforms to naturalistic thought linked to the recurring seasons. Finally, the concept of "history" must be overextended if it is to unite such disparate narratives as those of creation, the Deluge, Jacob's dream at Bethel, the exodus, or the downfall of the northern and southern kingdoms. Furthermore, such an approach breaks down the higher unity of the narratives, because each individual narrative stands in a different relationship to what can be called "history": the result is the well-known conflict between the OT view of history and that of historical-critical scholarship. One can escape these difficulties by following the lead of the OT text itself and saying that the narratives depict Yahweh as acting and man as responding in appropriate situations.

b) The notion of acting in history is conceptually imprecise, because Yahweh does not act retroactively in the past. It would be more accurate to speak of his acting in each present moment—whether with reference to a present that is now past, with reference to the present that now is, or with reference to a present that will be. It should be noted in passing that, according to one common OT view, Yahweh does not act constantly, uninterruptedly, and continuously, but may at first observe passively only to intervene "suddenly" (Isaiah 18); he may apparently not intervene directly at all, but determine the course of events almost imperceptibly (Isa. 8:5-8); he may incline human hearts toward a specific action (Genesis 24).

c) Above all, this approach does not grasp the one feature of Yahwism that distinguishes it from other religions of the ancient Near East. Among the peoples surrounding Israel, too, historical events were interpreted as divine acts; they were sometimes ascribed to the operation of the divine word, the deity was believed to act purposefully and methodically in what took place, and such events were even understood as divine revelation.

d) Finally, belief in creation and in Yahweh's operation in the natural realm furnished elements that could no longer be incorporated into the concept of "history." Yahweh acts rather throughout the whole realm of the world and life, so that it is impossible to draw a distinction between history and nature, man and beast, Israel and the nations in order to absolutize one of these aspects. Hosea, who thinks and argues throughout in "historical" terms, at the same time and as a matter of course views the relationship between Yahweh and Israel within the framework of a chain of blessing that comprehends heaven, earth, and the bounty of nature (Hos. 2:23-25 [Eng. 2:21-23]), and depicts it as growing and flourishing like a plant (Hos. 14:2-9). All are aspects of one and the same life and belong together.

Yahweh's actions in the lives and destinies of men and nations at each present moment are the theme of the historical narratives that

came into being or attained their final form in the period of the
monarchy (see § 11.6; 13.5). In the narratives and narrative cycles
of the later book of Judges this theme appears in the heroic figures
of the pre-monarchic period, aroused by Yahweh. It appears in the
narrative of Saul's rise and downfall, in the story of David's rise and
his court history, in the critical accounts of the early monarchy,
framed under the influence of prophetical and priestly ideology. The
same situation obtains in the general presentations of early history
in the pre-exilic source strata of the Hexateuch, which extend from
creation or the call of Abraham to the occupation of Palestine. The
prophets, too, refer to events of the past. For them the two major
factors necessary to understand this period are Israel's sin on the one
hand, and on the other the calamities sent by Yahweh as warnings
and admonitions, as well as his other efforts on Israel's behalf. Since,
however, all has been in vain, the prophets, looking back on Yahweh's actions in the past, declare that and why he must and will
act once more in the present, intervene radically and punish Israel
with destruction if it does not return to him, or—more rarely—that
and why he will nevertheless act with mercy and forgiveness. In the
past, after an initial happy beginning and despite the help, admonitions, and punishments sent by God, Israel lost the opportunity to
establish and accept the sovereignty of God and communion with
him. Now, on the basis of a decision facing Israel in the present—on
the one hand repentance or patient hope in deliverance, on the other
final rejection of Yahweh—the immediate future will bring conclu-
sive recognition of the loss through an act of Yahweh that will destroy the rebellious, or miraculous restoration through divine intervention that breaks down all resistance. The great individual
prophets of the pre-exilic period overwhelmingly sensed that their
God was obliged to decree downfall and destruction as the final and
inescapable fate of Israel. In any case, it is God who intervenes
actively in history.

3. *Yahweh and Israel. a)* During the period of the monarchy, belief in Israel's election was espoused above all by religious nationalism (§ 13.5).[16] According to this belief, Yahweh's special relationship
to Israel was based on his election of the nation; this election was
first associated with the deliverance from Egypt in the Mosaic period

[16] *BHH,* I, 435-36; III, 2051-52; *RGG,* II, 610-13; VI, 1160-62; *IDB,* II, 76-82.

and later with the patriarchs. Election was always viewed against the universalistic background of the inhabited world, involving the three quantities Yahwe—Israel—nations.[17] Yahweh, the God whose power extended over the entire world, set Israel apart from the other nations by election, making Israel a peculiar people. As the elect nation, Israel occupied a unique position in the eyes of this mighty God.

The source stratum J made this clear through the statements that Abraham was to become a great and mighty nation, in which all the nations of the earth should bless themselves (Gen. 18:18), and that the descendants of Jacob would be numerous as the dust of the earth and spread abroad in all directions, and that in him and his descendants all the families of the earth would bless themselves (Gen. 28:14.[18] The election of Israel is indeed to yield a blessing for the other nations, but Israel is the nation blessed above all others. The nationalistic consciousness that echoes through these statements cannot be missed: Israel is the crucial element in the world of all the nations; the fate of the others depends on their relationship to Israel.

The source stratum E exhibits a somewhat different understanding of election, as can be seen from the reinterpretation of Yahweh's promise to Abraham: Yahweh will bless him and make his descendants very numerous; while they occupy the gate of their enemies, all the nations of the earth shall bless themselves by invoking these descendants (Gen. 22:17-18; cf. 26:4-5). The restriction to formulas of blessing shows that Israel's election has no direct significance for the world of the nations, just as the selection of Israel becomes a separation (Num. 23:9b). This is the result of E's concentrated religious nationalism.

Belief in Israel's election must have played an important rôle in the period of the monarchy even before the advent of Deuteronomic theology, which introduced the term bāḥar for it. This can be seen from the way the prophets criticized the idea. Amos ironically rejected the confidence in a sense of election that was flaunted before him:

---

[17] On the relationship between Yahweh and the nations, see M. Peisker, *Die Beziehungen der Nichtisraeliten zu Jahve nach der Anschauung der altisraelitischen Quellenschriften*, 1907; A. Rétif and P. Lamarche, *Das Heil der Völker*, 1960; H. Schmökel, *Jahwe und die Fremdvölker*, 1934.

[18] An expanded form of this notion has been introduced in Gen. 12:3 as an addition to N, in which Yahweh merely says to Abraham, "Be a blessing," without reference to the other nations.

Indeed, you are my "chosen people"
upon earth.
Therefore—I will punish you
for all your iniquities.[19]   (Amos 3:2)

He dealt equally ironically with Israel's claim to be the "first of the
nations" (Amos 6:1-7), and refused to ascribe any primacy to Israel
by virtue of its deliverance from Egypt, because Yahweh had led
other nations in similar fashion (Amos 9:7). Hosea correspondingly
condemns a sense of election oriented toward the patriarchal traditions (Hos. 12:3 ff.). And Micah violently attacked the erroneous
conclusion, based on election, that Yahweh was essentially well disposed toward Israel (Mic. 2:6-9). When the ground was cut from
under belief in election, the idea of Israel's uniquely favorable position also fell. Israel instead took on a negative rôle, becoming the
key nation that Yahweh would call to account before a universal
forum (Isa. 1:2-3; Mic. 1:2 ff.) ; the sentence would be carried out by
the other nations (Isa. 7:18-19; 5:26 ff.; Hos. 10:10; Amos 6:14;
Zeph. 1:7).

b) Contrary to the usual assumption, the relationship between
Yahweh and Israel was not understood in terms of a "covenant"
during the monarchy. Quite apart from the fact that the word b⁼rît
probably does not even have this meaning, the notion of a b⁼rît
played no rôle in the centuries between the early nomadic period
and the advent of Deuteronomic theology (§ 8.3). Instead the ancient notions of Israel as Yahweh's 'am and the use of kinship categories were preserved and extended.

Although we do not yet encounter the full formula of association,
stating that Yahweh is the God of Israel and Israel the people of
Yahweh, their mutual solidarity is expressed in partial formulas
(Smend) : "I am Yahweh, your God"; "Yahweh, our God"; "Yahweh,
God of Israel"; "our/your God"; "my people"; "my people Israel";
"the people of Yahweh"; etc. (See Exod. 20:2; I Sam. 9:16-17; 13:14;
15:1; II Sam. 5:2; 6:21; 7:8; I Kings 14:7; 16:2; II Kings 9:6). The
formula "God of Israel" was used practically as a formal title, especially in solemn discourse: in oaths (I Sam. 20:12; 25:34; I Kings
1:30; 17:1), in invocations (I Sam. 23:10-11; II Sam. 7:27; II Kings
19:15), in praise (I Kings 1:48), and in the introductory formulas

---

[19] The translation follows E. Balla, *Die Botschaft der Propheten*, 1958, p. 85.
The verb *yāda'* is rendered in the sense of the notion flaunted before Amos (cf.
also Jer. 1:5); of course this loses the complementary tone of intimate communion.

of Yahweh's discourse (I Sam. 2:30; II Sam. 12:7; I Kings 11:31; 17:14; II Kings 9:6). We can accordingly say that during the monarchy Israel thought of Yahweh as its God and of itself as Yahweh's people, and thus sensed a mutual solidarity. Even in Amos Yahweh uses the phrase "my people," albeit in the context of threatened judgment (Amos 7:8, 15; 8:2); we find similar usage in Isaiah (Isa. 1:3; 5:25), although he preferred the derogatory phrase "this people" (Isa. 6:9; 8:6, 11; 28:11; 29:13-14). In Hosea both formulas occur: "your/our/their God"; "my people" (Hos. 4:6, 8, 12; 5:4; 11:7; 12:7, 10; 13:4; 14:2, 4). In Hosea, in fact, the ground is laid for the full solidarity formula when Yahweh's command to name the prophet's third child is based on the statement "For you are not my people and I am not your God" (Hos. 1:9), and the threat is subsequently annulled by the statement "I will say to Not my people, 'You are my people'; and he shall say, 'Thou art my God' " (Hos. 2:25 [Eng. 2:23]). It is admittedly not clear in all cases whether 'am still has its ancient meaning of "kinship" or "family," or means "people" or "nation"; the latter is probably true in the majority of cases.

But kinship categories also continued in use to describe the relationship between Yahweh and Israel. For Isaiah, Yahweh was the beloved or bridegroom who had made abundant preparations for his "vineyard" (Isa. 5:1 ff.); in Amos 3:2, the verb yāda' contains echoes of the notion of an intimate marriage-like relationship between Yahweh and Israel. Hosea and Jeremiah looked on this relationship primarily as one of marriage (Hos. 1; 2:18 [Eng. 2:16]; 3; Jer. 2:2; 3:6 ff.); Hos. 1:2 even refers naturalistically to the land rather than the people inhabiting it as the wife of Yahweh. More frequently the father-son relationship is used.[20] Yahweh speaks of Israel as his first-born son (Exod. 4:22; Jer. 31:9), whom he called out of Egypt (Hos. 11:1), as his darling child (Jer. 31:20), and exalted above his other sons, the nations (Jer. 3:19)—none of this being based on any "election" of Israel, but on the personal relationship of Yahweh's love. By analogy Yahweh is referred to as Israel's father (Jer. 3:4; then Deut. 32:6, 18), and the Israelites as a body are considered his sons and daughters (in a later period: Deut. 14:1; 32:5, 19; Isa. 43:6; 45:11; Hos. 2:1 [Eng. 1:10]), born to him by his wife Israel (Hos. 2:4 [Eng. 2:2]) or Jerusalem (Ezek. 16:20). Although in Exod. 4:22 and in the image of marriage between Yahweh and Israel, as the offspring of which the Israelites may be considered (Hos. 2:4 [Eng.

[20] BHH, III, 2071-72; RGG, VI, 1233-34.

2:2]), there is an echo of physical sonship, the father-son relationship is never intended to express a relationship between Yahweh and Israel that exists by nature and is indissoluble. Israel or the Israelites are not Yahweh's son or sons in the physical sense; they were recognized and legitimized by Yahweh on the basis of his own free divine decision and authority. The father-son relationship thus served to characterize two aspects of the relationship between Yahweh and Israel. On the one hand, the distance separating them and the subordination of Israel to Yahweh were emphasized in terms of the father's authority in matters of both personal relationship and property, and the concomitant subordination of the son. On the other hand, the notion also expressed Yahweh's goodness and love, since these characterized the conduct required of a father (Ps. 103:13). Thus the notion of sovereign authority was linked with that of solidarity and communion.

c) Taken as a whole the characteristic features of primitive Yahwism continued to operate in the relationship between Yahweh and Israel (§ 6.2) : the personal structure of the relationship, the juxtaposition of God's sovereignty and communion with God, Yahweh's acting to shape Israel's destiny, and the interrelation between Yahweh's actions and the conduct of Israel.

4. *Man before Yahweh.* a) The twofold notion of sovereignty and communion that was basic to the relationship between God and man determined the religious attitude of man before Yahweh. There are always two complementary reactions or notions: fear and love, absolute trust and communion, dependence and sharing in God's sovereignty.

If Yahweh is Lord, man is his slave or servant (*'ebed*), whose duty is to serve (*'ābad*).[21] The proper attitude for this service is fear or reverence (*yir'â*),[22] so that both terms are frequently coupled (Deut. 6:13; 10:12-13; Ps. 2:11). In addition, obedience to the Lord's demands is required; thus Abraham is said to "fear God" when he is prepared at Yahweh's behest to sacrifice his son (Gen. 22:12). This fear is at times awe before the all-powerful sovereign; at other times it is true dread, fear and trembling, especially when Yahweh appears in a theophany (Exod. 20:18-19; cf. Ps. 76:8-9 [Eng. 76:7-8]), so that when God appears he usually begins by saying, "Do not fear" (e.g.,

[21] C. Lindhagen, *The Servant Motif in the Old Testament*, 1950.
[22] J. Becker, *Gottesfurcht im Alten Testament*, 1965; S. Plath, *Furcht Gottes* 1963.

Judg. 6:23). In addition, "fear" can stand for the religious attitude in general, especially in the wisdom literature (Prov. 1:7; 9:10; Job 1:1).—Only in the later period was love toward Yahweh stressed, particularly in the parenetic discourses of Deuteronomy (Deut. 6:5; 10:12), less frequently in the Psalms (Ps. 18:2 [Eng. 18:1]), where other expressions and idioms are preferred (cf. Ps. 90:14-15).

Human confidence is also associated with Yahweh's sovereignty throughout the world. The terms *he'ĕmîn* and *bāṭaḥ* in particular are used for this idea. Just as Abraham believed the far-reaching promise of Yahweh, and this belief was recognized as the appropriate attitude (Gen. 15:6 [E]), so Isaiah demanded such faith in the sole power of Yahweh to intervene on Israel's behalf, rather than confidence in military might and political alliances (Isa. 7:9; 30:15). Anyone who trusts in ephemeral man rather than in the eternal power of Yahweh commits apostasy (Jer. 17:5; cf. Ps. 62:9-10; 118:8-9).— This confident dependence corresponds to an intimate solidarity between man and God, for which the terms *ḥesed*, "steadfast love," [23] and *yāda'*, "be familiar, enjoy communion," [24] are primarily employed:

> For I desire steadfast love and not sacrifice,
> communion with God, rather than burnt offerings.
> (Hos. 6:6)

For Hosea, what was basically wrong with Israel was that it did not possess such faithful and steadfast love and intimate knowledge of God (Hos. 4:1, 6). Many Psalms suggest that this intimate communion, which probably is not to be identified with some mystical union with God, could also exist between Yahweh and a particular individual (e.g., Ps. 25:14; 63:9 [Eng. 63:8]; 73:23 ff.; 91:14).[25]

Finally, man is to be conscious of his total dependence on Yahweh. This follows from belief in creation. At creation Yahweh gave the breath of life to the man "of dust," thus making him a living being

---

[23] See the bibliography in § 8, n. 1.

[24] E. Baumann, "ידע und seine Derivate," *ZAW*, XXVIII (1908), 22-40; G. J. Botterweck, *"Gott erkennen" im Sprachgebrauch des Alten Testaments*, 1951; S. Mowinckel, *Die Erkenntnis Gottes bei den alttestamentlichen Propheten*, 1941; for a different view, see H. W. Wolff, "'Wissen um Gott' bei Hosea als Urform von Theologie," *EvTh*, XII (1952/53), 533-54 (= his *Gesammelte Studien zum Alten Testament*, 1964, pp. 182-205). See also the discussion with E. Baumann, *ibid.*, XV (1955), 416-25, 426-31.

[25] This relationship can also be expressed in the use of "my God" as a form of address; cf. O. Eissfeldt, "'Mein Gott' im Alten Testament," *ZAW*, LXI (1945/48), 3-16 (= his *Kleine Schriften*, III [1966], 35-47).

(Gen. 2:7). Without this breath of life man is dead; with it, alive (Ps. 104:29-30). Man is infinitely small and ephemeral in comparison to Yahweh (Ps. 8:5 [Eng. 8:4]; 90:4-6), and therefore completely dependent on him.—Parallel to this basic notion, which is found throughout the entire OT, is the other idea that man stands closer to his creator God than does any other creature, that he shares in the divine sovereignty by virtue of delegated authority, and as a consequence is exalted above all other beings. This is stated with particular clarity in Gen. 1:27-28 and Ps. 8:6-9; but even J states in Gen. 2:20 that man has authority over the beasts, and in Gen. 3:20 that the male has authority over the female, as a consequence of giving them names. Thus on the one hand man is far inferior to his creator and at all points dependent on him; on the other, man is closely associated with him and shares in his sovereign authority.

b) From the very outset Yahweh was considered a God of ethical purpose, demanding complete obedience. Yahwism was a religion of life and conduct according to the rules expressing God's will. These rules, in which God's will assumed concrete form, include above all the apodictically formulated rules of conduct (§ 6.3), often summarized in groups of ten or twelve. Of these the following deserve special mention:[26]

1) The series, pre-Yahwistic in origin, prohibiting sexual intercourse with certain females (§ 2.4). This was later reinterpreted as an ordinance of Yahweh prohibiting the permanent relationship of marriage within certain degrees, and finally as a general law against unchastity, in order to guarantee the holiness and cultic purity of the community.

2) The so-called ethical decalogue in Exod. 20:3-17, composed of three series (five long commandments, three short commandments, two commandments), the first three of which at most may derive from the Mosaic period (§ 6.7):[27]

[26] See G. Fohrer, "Das sogenannte apodiktisch formulierte Recht und der Dekalog," *KuD,* XI (1965), 49-74; E. Auerbach, "Das Zehngebot—allgemeine Gesetzesform in der Bibel," *VT,* XVI (1966), 255-76.

[27] *BHH,* I, 331-32; *RGG,* II, 69-71; *IDB,* IV, 569-73; A. Jepsen, "Beiträge zur Auslegung und Geschichte des Dekalogs," *ZAW,* LXXIX (1967), 277-304; R. Knierim, "Das erste Gebot," *ZAW,* LXXVII (1965), 20-39; J. Meinhold, *Der Dekalog,* 1927; S. Mowinckel, *Le décalogue,* 1927; E. Nielsen, *Die zehn Gebote,* 1965; H. Graf Reventlow, *Gebot und Predigt im Dekalog,* 1962; H. Schmidt, "Mose und der Dekalog," in *Gunkel Festschrift,* I (1923), 78-119; J. Schreiner, *Die Zehn Gebote im Leben des Gottesvolkes,* 1966; J. J. Stamm and M. E. Andrew, *The Ten Commandments in Recent Research,* 1967.

    I   You shall have no *other* god.
   II You shall not make yourself a graven image.
 III You shall not take the name of Yahweh in vain.
 IV Remember the sabbath day.
   V Honor your father and your mother.
 VI You shall not kill.
 VII You shall not commit adultery.
VIII You shall not steal.
 IX You shall not bear false witness against your neighbor.
   X You shall not covet your neighbor's house.

3) The so-called cultic decalogue in Exod. 34:14-26, which—apart from the first two prohibitions, which correspond to the first two in Exodus 20—is composed of two series, the first dealing with special days of the year (commandments), the second dealing with sacrificial regulations (prohibitions); the series in Exod. 23:10-19 is dependent on this series:

    I   You shall worship no other god.
   II You shall make for yourself no molten gods.
 III The feast of unleavened bread you shall keep.
 IV *You shall not* appear before me with empty hands.
   V Six days you shall work, but on the seventh day you shall rest.
 VI You shall observe the feast of weeks.
 VII You shall not offer the blood of my sacrifice with leaven.
VIII The sacrifice shall not be left until the morning.
 IX You shall bring the best of the first fruits of your ground to the house of Yahweh.
   X You shall not boil a kid in its mother's milk.

4) The plural decalogue in Lev. 19:3-12, which, because of the primacy given to the commandment to revere mother and father, may possibly be termed a domestic "catechism."

5) The later singular decalogue in Lev. 19:13-18, with its requirements in the realm of social ethics: the weak and in fact all "neighbors" are to be protected against infringements in daily life and before the bar.

6) Several short series, among which the regulations concerning taboo persons in Exod. 22:17-21, 27 (Eng. 22:18-22, 28) and those concerning exemption from military service in Deut. 20:5-8 may be quite ancient, at least in content.

God's will could also be pronounced in the concrete *tôrâ* ("instruction," "teaching") imparted by a priest or cult prophet.[28] Cultic

---

[28] *BHH*, III, 1494-95; *RGG*, VI, 950-51; *IDB*, IV, 673.

192   Yahwism in the Period of the Monarchy

instruction dealt with questions of cultic conduct, e.g. the distinctions between clean and unclean, sacred and profane (cf. Hag. 2:10-14). Legal instruction informed the ignorant about general legal principles or determined a difficult and ambiguous case referred to the priest. Entrance instruction or liturgy tested whether the conditions for admission to the sanctuary had been fulfilled; for this purpose it might use a "guide for self-examination," [29] as is obviously the case in Ps. 15 and 24:3-6 (for the most part ethical conditions).[30] Other individual divine ordinances or commandments could also be called torah (cf. Exod. 16:28; 18:16; Hos. 8:12, emended). The word finally came to be a collective designation for all Yahweh's instructions, including the juristic regulations of casuistic law and the precepts formulated apodictically (the so-called *môt-yûmāt* series, originally perhaps in Exod. 22:19; Lev. 24:16; Exod. 21:12, 16, 17; Lev. 20:10-13, 15; and the series of curses in Deut. 27:15-26).[31] The process produced the torah as "law," as first the Deuteronomic code (Deut. 1:5; 4:8; 17:18; etc.) and later the entire Pentateuch came to be called.[32]

Prophecy undertook to transcend the multiplicity of regulations and the primarily negative formulation of the commandments and express the totality of the divine will as a comprehensive positive requirement: "Seek good, and not evil" (Amos 5:14), "Cease to do evil, learn to do good" (Isa. 1:16-17), "Do justice, love kindness, and walk humbly with your God" (Mic. 6:8). These attempts were in line with the tendencies of primitive Yahwism.

The man who does God's will practices justice (*mišpāṭ*) and righteousness (*ṣᵉdāqâ*).[33] "Justice" includes both social justice and the impartial administration of justice; it refers to the conduct a person owes toward the God of the people to which be belongs, the principle by which men's conduct toward one another and their attitude toward their God is measured and judged, and the claim

[29] *BHH*, I, 213.
[30] This provided the model for the instruction concerning the relationship between Yahweh and Israel given in a liturgical framework in Psalms 50, 81, and 95. Prophetical imitations are found in Isa. 33:14-16; Mic. 6:6-8.
[31] Cf. also *BHH*, III, 1559-61; *RGG*, V, 820-21; *IDB*, III, 77-89; F. Horst, "Recht und Religion im Bereich des Alten Testaments," *EvTh*, XVI (1956), 49-75 (= his *Gottes Recht*, 1961, pp. 260-91).
[32] *BHH*, I, 559-60; *RGG*, II, 1513-15.
[33] K. H. Fahlgren, צדקה *nahestehende und entgegengesetzte Begriffe im Alten Testament*, 1932; H. W. Hertzberg, "Die Entwicklung des Begriffes משפט im AT," *ZAW*, XL (1922), 256-87; K. Koch, "Wesen und Ursprung der 'Gemeinschaftstreue' im Israel der Königszeit," *ZEE*, V (1961), 72-90.

made by Yahweh's requirements upon his worshipers. "Righteousness" refers to exoneration and innocence before the court, life according to the norms obtaining in a society, social conduct that both assumes and creates the harmony of life within society, obedience to Yahweh in fulfilling one's duties toward him and toward one's neighbor,[34] and the order imposed on human life and the cosmos by the deity, to which the wise man will accommodate himself. Finally, in the order and norms imposed by Yahweh's will on the course of the world and the ethical conduct of life, in the way men order their lives with respect to God and their neighbors, and in Yahweh's judgment upon their conduct we are dealing with various aspects of justice and righteousness.

c) The OT is for the most part of the opinion that man can freely decide in favor of proper religious and ethical conduct and live according to his decision. He is able to fear God and to love him, to trust in him and live in communion with him, to practice obedience and to do what is good. "For this commandment which I command you this day is not too hard for you, neither is it far off . . . . But the word is very near you; it is in your mouth and in your heart, so that you can do it" (Deut. 30:11, 14). Just as Ezekiel presupposes that man is able to practice righteousness (Ezek. 18:21-32), so Job repeatedly declares himself sinless and guiltless, even declaring his innocence upon oath (Job 31).

This freedom to decide of course does not mean that man in fact decides rightly. The OT makes something like the contrary assertion. In Genesis 3, J depicts the origin of sin: tempted by the serpent, the man and woman eat of the forbidden fruit of the tree of knowledge in order that they may know everything, both good and evil, and thus become like Yahweh. J's purpose is to describe the process which repeats itself in the dawning consciousness of every man, the almost necessary fall of every man into sin, which takes place at the very moment when man seeks to carry out his commission to rule over the earth. Thus "the imagination of man's heart is evil from his youth" (Gen. 8:21). Just as there is no man who does not sin (I Kings 8:46; cf. Ps. 103:3; Prov. 20:9), so the individual is totally sinful (Jer. 17:9; Ps. 51:7 [Eng. 51:5]). This same assumption is made by all the great pre-exilic individual prophets of Israel.[35]

There are various Hebrew words for sin. The verb *ḥāṭā'* and its

---

[34] J. Fichtner, "Der Begriff des 'Nächsten' im Alten Testament," *WuD*, NF IV (1955), 23-52 (= his *Gottes Weisheit*, 1965, pp. 88-114).
[35] *BHH*, III, 1890-92; *RGG*, VI, 478-82; *IDB*, IV, 361-67.

derivatives are based on a social relationship that the sinner fails to observe, which he bypasses and against which he transgresses. The word *pešaʿ* refers to concrete transgressions and legally definable offences, so that it is most accurately translated as "offence." Finally, the word *ʿāwôn* refers both to transgression, perversion, and folly, as well as to the result of this lapse: guilt. Nevertheless, too much emphasis should not be placed on the differences between these terms, because often two or even all three of the words are used together in such a way as to appear synonymous.

More important is the distinction that gradually came to be made between deliberate transgressions and unconscious sins (cf. Ps. 19:13) or unwitting sins (Lev. 4:2, 13, 22).[36] In addition, beside a concrete and objective understanding of sin as a conscious or unconscious transgression of a specific divine law, there developed a personal understanding, which included, together with the awareness of having transgressed a commandment, a feeling of responsibility.

d) In every case the right or wrong religious and ethical conduct of man involves certain positive or negative consequences—both for the individual and for society.[37] The decision confronting man means choice between blessing and curse, life and death (cf. Deuteronomy 28; 30:15 ff.).[38]

The consequences of right conduct are a long and rich life (Exod. 20:12; Ps. 34:13 ff. [Eng. 34:12 ff.]; 91:16); *šālôm* in the sense of wholeness and harmony, good fortune, well-being, and peace; and finally blessing, which includes everything that constitutes the richness of a successful and happy life. The consequence of wrong conduct is disaster—Yahweh's punishment for sin. This punishment falls upon man as sickness[39] and suffering of all sorts. This fate, too, which often comes as a punishment that fits the crime, is based on divine retribution. Well-being and disaster were always ascribed to Yahweh (cf. Exod. 20:5-6; Deut. 28:1 ff., 15 ff.; Job 34:11).

This statement must nevertheless be temporally qualified. During

[36] *BHH*, II, 774-75.
[37] Z. W. Falk, "Collective Responsibility in Bible and Aggada," *Tarbiz*, XXX (1960/61), 16-20; K. Koch, "Gibt es ein Vergeltungsdogma im Alten Testament?" *ZThK*, LII (1955), 1-42; H. G. May, "Individual Responsibility and Retribution," *HUCA*, XXXII (1961), 107-20; E. Pax, "Studien zum Vergeltungsproblem der Psalmen," *LA*, XI (1960/61), 56-112; G. Sauer, *Die strafende Vergeltung Gottes in den Psalmen*, Dissertation, Basel, 1957; M. Weiss, "Some Problems of the Biblical 'Doctrine of Retribution.'" *Tarbiz*, XXXI (1961/62), 236-63; XXXII (1962/63), 1-18.
[38] *BHH*, I, 487-88; III, 1757-58; *RGG*, V, 1649-51; *IDB*, I, 446-48, 749-50.
[39] *BHH*, II, 997-99; *IDB*, I, 847-51.

the period of the monarchy, this doctrine of retribution was developed almost exclusively in the negative direction. Yahweh's punitive retribution was emphasized (e.g., Genesis 18–19; Judg. 9:23-24; I Sam. 15:2-3; II Kings 1), while little stress was placed on the idea of reward for right conduct. Not until Deuteronomic theology was the doctrine of two-sided retribution developed clearly: Yahweh's blessing came as a reward for man's obedience, devastating punishment as recompense for man's disobedience. This doctrine furthermore came to typify practical wisdom, which repeatedly inculcated the notion that the devout man might expect reward, the wicked man punishment (e.g., Prov. 11:21, 31; 19:17). This notion is not merely the heritage of the general OT view of man's position before Yahweh, but also originates in ancient Near Eastern practical wisdom, in which the idea of retribution played a crucial rôle. Not until the post-exilic period did the author of Job violently attack such views.

It must nevertheless be noted that non-prophetical Yahwism was based on the assumption that man basically stood in Yahweh's favor; this status could be disturbed by transgressions, but could be restored or recovered by means of appropriate propitiatory measures. Such measures were primarily cultic.

§ 16 Worship

A. ARENS, Die Psalmen im Gottesdienst des Alten Bundes, 1961; E. AUERBACH, "Die Feste im alten Israel," VT, VIII (1958), 1-18; G. A. BARTON, "A Comparison of some Features of Hebrew and Babylonian Ritual," JBL, XLVI (1927), 79-89; W. GRAF BAUDISSIN, Die Geschichte des alttestamentlichen Priestertums, 1889; A. BERTHOLET, "Zum Verständnis des alttestamentlichen Opfergedankens," JBL, XLIX (1930), 218-33; F. M. T. BÖHL "Priester und Prophet," NThS, XXII (1939), 298-313; T. A. BUSINK, "Les origines du temple de Salomon," JEOL, XVII (1963), 165-92; R. E. CLEMENTS, God and Temple, 1965; E. DHORME, "Prêtres devins et mages dans l'ancienne religion des Hébreux," RHR, CVIII (1933), 111-43; G. FOHRER, "Zion-Jerusalem im Alten Testament," ThW, VII, 292-318; L. GAUTIER, Prêtre ou sacrificateur? 1927; J. VAN GOUDOEVER, Biblical Calendars, 2nd ed., 1961; G. B. GRAY, Sacrifice in the Old Testament, 1925; A. H. J. GUNNEWEG, Leviten und Priester, 1965; F. JEREMIAS, "Das orientalische Heiligtum," Angelos, IV (1932), 56-69; H.-J. KRAUS, Gottesdienst in Israel, 2nd ed., 1962 (English: Worship in Israel, 1966); E. KUTSCH, Das Herbstfest in Israel, Dissertation, Mainz, 1955; A. LODS, "Israelitische Opfervorstellungen und -bräuche," ThR, NF III (1931), 247-66; J. C. MATTHES, "Die Psalmen und der Tempeldienst," ZAW, XXII (1902), 65-82; K. MOHLENBRINK, Der Tempel

Salomos, 1932; J. L. MYERS, "King Solomon's Temple and Other Buildings and Works of Art," *PEQ*, LXXX (1948), 14-41; C. R. NORTH, "Sacrifice in the Old Testament," *ET*, XLVII (1935/36), 250-54; W. O. E. OESTERLEY, *Sacrifices in Ancient Israel*, 1937; A. PARROT, *Le Temple de Jérusalem*, 1954 (English: *The Temple of Jerusalem*, 1955); O. PLÖGER, "Priester und Prophet," *ZAW*, LXIII (1951), 157-92; G. QUELL, *Das kultische Problem der Psalmen*, 1926; H. RINGGREN, *Sacrifice in the Bible*, 1962; H. H. ROWLEY, "The Meaning of Sacrifice in the Old Testament," *BJRL*, XXXIII (1950/51), 74-110 (= his *From Moses to Qumran*, 1963, pp. 67-107); J. SCHREINER, *Sion-Jerusalem, Jahwes Königssitz*, 1963; J. B. SEGAL, "The Hebrew Festivals and the Calendar," *JSS*, VI (1961), 74-94; N. H. SNAITH, "Worship," in *Record and Revelation* (Robinson Festschrift), 1938, pp. 250-74; *idem*, "Sacrifices in the Old Testament," *VT*, VII (1957), 308-17; A. SZÖRENYI, *Psalmen und Kult im Alten Testament*, 1961; R. DE VAUX, *Les sacrifices dans l'Ancien Testament*, 1964 (English: *Studies in Old Testament Sacrifice*, 1964); H. VINCENT, "Le caractère du temple salomonien," in *Mélanges Bibliques Robert*, 1957, pp. 137-48; A. WENDEL, *Das Opfer in der altisraelitischen Religion*, 1927; G. WIDENGREN, "Aspetti simbolici dei templi e luoghi di culto del Vicino Oriente Antico," *Numen*, VII (1960), 1-25.

1. *General considerations.* Although OT tradition gives few hints of the fact, the Yahweh cult of the monarchy was highly varied. It took place at the official sanctuaries of Jerusalem, Bethel, and Dan, at the sanctuaries of the early period set apart by venerable traditions, and at the many small local sanctuaries. It took on many forms. It was an official state cult, celebrating not only the usual cultic events but also special events in the life of the state such as the investiture of a king (see Psalms 2, 72, 101, 110) or the prayers, thanksgivings, or laments that accompanied war (prayer: Psalms 20, 44, 144; thanksgiving: Psalm 18B; reproach: Psalm 89B). It was an affair involving the whole population, as on the occasion of a day of lamentation and penance proclaimed in a time of distress (see Jer. 36:9). It was the cultic act of the inhabitants of a village when they thought they had occasion to offer sacrifice (see I Sam. 9:12 ff.). It was a clan or family festival (see I Sam. 20:6), or the act of a single individual who wanted to offer his petitions or thanksgiving before God or to obtain an oracle. In addition, men might visit the sanctuary as a place of judgment (see Exod. 22:7), as a place of asylum (see I Kings 1:50 ff.),[1] or to receive a revelation in a dream (incubation; see I Sam. 21:8 [Eng. 21:7]).[2]

----

[1] *BHH*, I, 143-44; *RGG*, I, 666-68; *IDB*, IV, 24; L. Delekat, *Katoche, Hierodulie und Adoptionsfreilassung*, 1964; M. Greenberg, "The Biblical Conception of Asylum," *JBL*, LXXVIII (1959), 125-32; M. Löhr, *Das Asylwesen im Alten Testament*, 1930.

[2] E. L. Ehrlich, *Der Traum im Alten Testament*, 1953; E. Preuschen, "Doeg

The cult served to cultivate the communion between Yahweh and Israel as Yahweh's people. It vouchsafed to those who attended the sanctuary participation in the sphere of the divine, so that they were overcome with emotional rapture or ecstatic exaltation. On the great agricultural festivals of the year it gave the farmer opportunity to turn to Yahweh in prayer and thanksgiving so as to continue to receive Yahweh's blessing. Finally, through its propitiatory actions on behalf of the people or an individual, it made possible the restoration of God's favor in case it had been lost through a transgression. We can sum up by saying that the cult was intended to promote recognition of God's sovereignty, and to strengthen and deepen communion with God.

For a long time Israel refrained from asserting that Yahweh had established or inaugurated the cult.[3] Only later was such a claim made, and then only in part (P ascribes to God the institution of the Sabbath in Gen. 2:1-3 and of circumcision in Genesis 17). At first the cult was merely thought to be regulated by divine command once it was already in existence, as the ordinances of the various decalogues placed in the mouth of Yahweh show (see § 15.4). Nevertheless toward the end of the monarchy there seems to have been some support for a claim of divine revelation, as Jeremiah's denial in Jer. 7:22 suggests. Perhaps Deuteronomic theology laid the groundwork for this development.

2. *Cultic sites.* a) A large portion of the sanctuaries of the early period (§ 4.2; 10.2) continued to exist during the monarchy. In addition, most if not all the villages had local cultic sites.[4] They have left no more archaeological trace than have the temple structures that we may assume served as official sanctuaries, and for which there is some evidence. Only at one site—Arad, east of Beer-sheba—have excavations brought to light the sanctuary of the local Judean fortress.[5]

---

als Inkubant," *ZAW*, XXIII (1903), 146; A. Resch, *Der Traum im Heilsplan Gottes*, 1964; W. Richter, "Traum und Traumdeutung im Alten Testament," *BZ*, NF VII (1963), 202-20.

[3] There is even less reason in general to term the cult a locus of divine revelation, as R. Gyllenberg does in his "Kultus und Offenbarung," in *Interpretationes ad Vetus Testamentum pertinentes* (Mowinckel Festschrift), 1955, pp. 72-84.

[4] *BHH*, II, 1121-22; *RGG*, III, 156-60; *IDB*, II, 602-4; see also W. F. Albright, "The High Place in Ancient Palestine," *VTSuppl*, IV (1957), 242-58.

[5] Y. Aharoni and R. Amiran, "Arad, a Biblical City in Southern Palestine," *Archaeology*, XVII (1964), 43-53.

The sanctuary at Arad seems to have been in existence at least since the ninth century B.C., and to have been destroyed in the second half of the eighth century B.C. It was a sizable building consisting of three rooms arranged in sequence, such as are usually assumed for the Solomonic Temple at Jerusalem. As in the latter, the entrance was at the east end, the "holy of holies" at the west end. Three steps led up to the entrance of the latter; it was flanked by two stone altars with a gutter between them. Within the room itself there was a raised platform of stone (bāmâ), about which stood three stelae or masseboth. To all appearances we are dealing here with a royal or official sanctuary; this raises the question whether all Judean (and Israelite) fortresses may not have had similar arrangements.

b) On account of its historical importance the Jerusalem Temple provokes the greatest interest.[6] The earliest preserved portions belong to the Herodian Temple; of the post-exilic Temple, as of the Solomonic, nothing remains. Only the sacred rock, the natural foundation of the entire structure, over which at one time the rear room or holy of holies was erected,[7] is still visible as the center of the Islamic Dome of the Rock. Thus the Solomonic Temple represented an "enclosed rock," but the enclosure was built in such a way that the rock was incorporated into the foundation.[8]

For our knowledge of the Temple that was built at the time of Solomon and remained in use until the end of the monarchy we have only literary data at our disposal: first the description in I Kings 6–7, apparently revised and expanded by several hands, and then the vision account in Ezekiel 40–42, which for the most part represents the prophet's recollection of how the building looked in the late pre-exilic period. Comparison of the two descriptions shows that architectural changes were undertaken in the course of the monarchy,[9] including especially the construction of the three-storied surrounding structure with its chambers (in I Kings 6:1-10, probably only 6:2-4, 9 are original). Furthermore, I Kings 6–7 especially is so ambiguous at many points that there is a great disparity of views

[6] *BHH,* III, 1940-47; *RGG,* VI, 684-86; *IDB,* IV, 534-47; H. Mayer, "Das Bauholz des Tempels Salomos," *BZ,* NF XI (1967), 53-66.
[7] H. Schmidt, *Der heilige Fels in Jerusalem,* 1933. According to II Sam. 24:18 ff., this is more likely than the assumption that the altar of burnt sacrifice stood on the rock. For still another view, see H. W. Hertzberg, "Der heilige Fels und das Alte Testament," *JPOS,* XII (1932), 32-42 (= his *Beiträge zur Traditionsgeschichte und Theologie des Alten Testaments,* 1962, pp. 45-53); according to Hertzberg, there is in the OT a mere clue to the special position of the rock.
[8] Cf. H. Bruns, "Umbaute Götterfelsen," *Jb des Deutschen Archäologischen Instituts,* LXXV (1960), 100-111, and the Roman temple on the *qal'a* of Amman.
[9] See also L. A. Snijders, "L'orientation du Temple de Jérusalem," *OTS,* XIV (1965), 214-35.

with respect to the plan and possible model of the Temple. Did it represent a longitudinal building with three rooms, or a hall with an open porch and a built-in wooden chest (for the ark and cherubim)? [10] Was it constructed according to Syro-Palestinian models— either with three rooms or one room with an open porch—or was it a uniquely Israelite creation? [11]

It is probably safe to assume that the Temple, like the sanctuary at Arad, represented a longitudinal building comprising three sections, porch, holy place, and rear room (later termed the "holy of holies"), and that it was constructed after the pattern of tripartite temples. Such temples include the (non-axial) Early Bronze sanctuary at et-Tell (Ai),[12] the Middle to Late Bronze temple at Hazor,[13] the temple at Tell Tainat, dating from the ninth or eighth century B.C.,[14] and the more distantly related temples at Tell Chuera in north-eastern Syria,[15] some of whose porches are open, others enclosed. Reference may also be made to the later "Syrian temple type." [16]

The porch of the Solomonic Temple was about 17 feet deep and 33 feet wide. It was entered from the east—if we are not dealing with an enclosed porch, through an open passageway. On both sides of the entrance stood the bronze pillars Jachin and Boaz,[17] whose names may be a prayer ("May he [God] make secure [the Temple, the dynasty] in strength") or else refer to their architectural function ("May it [the pillar] give security—in it is strength"). Leaving the porch, one passed through a double door of cypress into the holy place, about 67 feet deep, 33 feet wide, and 50 feet high, illuminated

[10] This is suggested by H. Schult, "Der Debir im salomonischen Tempel," *ZDPV*, LXXX (1964), 46-54. See also A. Kuschke, "Der Tempel Salomos und der 'syrische Tempeltypus,'" in *Das ferne und nahe Wort* (Rost Festschrift), 1967, pp. 124-32.

[11] This is the view of J. Brand, "Remarks on the Temple of Solomon," *Tarbiz*, XXXIV (1964/65), 323-32.

[12] J. Marquet-Krause, *Les fouilles de 'Ay*, 1949, pl. XCIII-XCIV; *ANEP*, p. 730.

[13] See *IEJ*, VIII (1958), 11-14; IX (1959), 81-84.

[14] See C. W. McEwan in *AJA*, XLI (1937), 9 ff.; D. Ussishkin, "Solomon's Temple and the Temples of Hamat and Tell Tainat [Hebrew]," *Yediot*, XXX (1966), 76-84.

[15] A. Moortgat, *Tell Chuēra in Nordost-Syrien*, 1962.

[16] A. Alt, "Verbreitung und Herkunft des syrischen Tempeltypus," *PJB*, LV (1939), 83-99 (= his *Kleine Schriften zur Geschichte des Volkes Israel*, II, [1953], 100-115).

[17] W. Kornfeld, "Der Symbolismus der Tempelsäulen," *ZAW*, LXXXIV (1962), 50-57; H. G. May, "The Two Pillars Before the Temple of Solomon," *BASOR*, LXXXVIII (1942), 19-27; R. B. Y. Scott, "The Pillars of Jachin and Boas," *JBL*, LVIII (1939), 143-49.

by light coming through windows in the upper half of the wall. In the holy place were located the altar of incense, the table for the so-called "bread of the Presence," on which bread was placed before Yahweh, and the two-times-five lampstands. A second double door of cedar closed off the rear room,[18] an elevated chamber in the shape of a cube 33 feet on a side. In it were located two figures of cherubim, thought of as supporting the throne, and the ark, whose sacral function was not architectural (such as a throne or a footstool), but to symbolize Yahweh's association with the royal residence of the Davidic line and thus legitimize the dynasty.[19] The doors and paneled walls of the Temple were decorated with cherubim, palms, and garlands of flowers in bas-relief. In the inner court, separated by a wall from the outer court, stood the altar of burnt offering, the gigantic bronze sea[20]—obviously originally a representation of the primal flood, later interpreted as a basin for washing (II Chron. 4:2 ff.)—and the ten lavers[21]—originally associated with the bronze sea, later interpreted as vessels for rinsing off the meat of the burnt offerings (II Chron. 4:6).

The Temple was thought of as an earthly copy of Yahweh's heavenly palace and as his official seat as "king," as an allotment of the land over which he reigned and which he had granted Israel, and as the official state sanctuary for all Israel and later for Judah, in which Yahweh dwelled because there, in the cult, he manifested his presence. But gradually the mountain on which the Temple had been built within the framework of the palace complex came to assume, on account of the rock of God it enclosed, the significance of the mountain of God, otherwise located by ancient Near Eastern tradition in the northern regions of the earth. In the course of time, the Temple gave to Jerusalem the prestige of being God's residence and city, the site of the cult and the Temple city (Fohrer; see also § 11.2).

[18] K. Galling, "Das Allerheiligste in Salomos Tempel," *JPOS*, XII (1932), 43-46; H. Schult, "Der Debir im Salomonischen Tempel."

[19] J. Maier, *Das altisraelitische Ladeheiligtum*, 1965; M. Noth, "Jerusalem und die israelitische Tradition," *OTS*, VIII (1950), 28-46 (= his *Gesammelte Studien zum Alten Testament*, 1957, pp. 172-87 [English: *The Laws in the Pentateuch and Other Studies*, 1966, pp. 132-44]); R. de Vaux, "Les chérubins et l'arche d'alliance, les sphinx gardiens et les trônes divins dans l'ancien Orient," *MUB*, XXXVII (1961), 93-124.

[20] *BHH*, I, 372; A. Segré, "Il mare fusile del Tempio di Salomone," *RSO*, XLI (1966), 155.

[21] *BHH*, II, 944.

Beyond this, scholars have assumed the existence of a Jerusalem cult tradition, which originated through the transference to Yahweh of a series of elements belonging to the pre-Israelite religion of El. This tradition is supposed to have left its deposit in several passages from the Psalms and the prophets. Schmid [22] included among these elements the notion of El as creator, lord over the gods, and God of the universe; the idea of a mountain of God; and the tradition of a battle with chaos. Others added such motifs as the battle with the nations,[23] the pilgrimage of the nations to Jerusalem,[24] and the inviolability of Jerusalem.[25]

Wanke[26] has shown, however, that although the ideas or motifs cited by Schmid can claim great antiquity, and are rooted in non-Israelite literature, we are not dealing with a unified tradition, but with isolated notions or motifs that did not enter into Israelite thought until very late, and that the additional motifs mentioned above have no origin outside Israel. Since the ancient mythological motifs were not borrowed by Israel until late, in the post-exilic period, and the OT evidence for them applies only to this period, and since above all the motif of the battle with the nations is non-mythological, and is likewise a product of the late period, the hypothesis of an independent Jerusalem cult tradition cannot be maintained. The supposed elements of this tradition did not play any rôle until the development, primarily observable in the post-exilic period, of the notions associated with Zion-Jerusalem. For the entire period of the monarchy there is no evidence for the existence of such a tradition.

3. *Feasts and festivals. a*) From Exod. 34:14-26 we can conclude that there were in Israel during the monarchy catalogs of feasts, listing the festivals to be observed regularly (see § 15.4). Into this passage have been incorporated four regulations from a series of ordinances for the special days of the year. They mention the Sabbath, the presentation of first fruits, the Feast of Unleavened Bread, and the Feast of Weeks (Exod. 34:18aα, 21a, 22aα 26a). Later the Feast of Ingathering was added as the third agricultural festival (vs. 22b), and, by Deuteronomic hand, Passover (vs. 25b). Exod. 23:10-19, which depends on Exodus 34, mentions all these observances —calling the Feast of Weeks the Feast of Harvest—and adds the fallow year. Additional cultic regulations derive from the Deuteronomic, exilic, and post-exilic periods (see § 22.2; 23.3; 28.4).

[22] H. Schmid, "Jahwe und die Kulttraditionen von Jerusalem," *ZAW*, LXVII (1955), 168-97.

[23] E. Rohland, *Die Bedeutung der Erwählungstraditionen Israels für die Eschatologie der alttestamentlichen Propheten*, Dissertation, Heidelberg, 1956.

[24] H. Wildberger, *Jesaja*, 1965- , p. 80.

[25] J. L. Hayes, "The Tradition of Zion's Inviolability," *JBL*, LXXXII (1963), 419-26.

[26] G. Wanke, *Die Zionstheologie der Korachiten*, 1966.

b) Besides the Sabbath and the day of the new moon (§ 10.2), the regularly observed feasts included the three agricultural festivals, but not Passover, which was not revived until the Deuteronomic period (§ 8.3).[27]

The Feast of Unleavened Bread [28] was originally a Canaanite agricultural festival, which the Israelites adopted. They incorporated it into Yahwism by referring it to Yahweh and associating it with the exodus from Egypt (Exod. 23:15; 34:18). It took place at the beginning of the barley harvest in the month of Abib (the first month) and lasted seven days; since it began "on the morrow after the Sabbath" (Lev. 23:11, 15), it coincided exactly with a week. A more precise date could not be fixed, because the festival depended on the ripening of the grain. It was a pilgrimage festival like the other two agricultural festivals. The farmers journeyed to the sanctuaries, there to enjoy bread made from new grain without leaven, i.e., without any addition from the old harvest. At the same time further thank offerings and sacrifices were surely presented to the deity.

The Feast of Harvest or Feast of Weeks[29] was celebrated seven weeks after the beginning of the Feast of Unleavened Bread, and thus came in the third month. As Exod. 34:22 explains, it was actually the festival—originally Canaanite—of the wheat harvest. During this pilgrimage festival the first fruits of the harvest were offered (Exod. 23:16; 34:22); later there was also a cereal offering of two loaves of bread made from new flour, baked with leaven (Lev. 23:16-17; Num. 28:26). Although it was a joyous festival full of gladness and rejoicing, in the period of the monarchy it seems to have acquired no great importance. In consequence it long remained unassociated with any specific act on the part of Yahweh. The first association was made by P, who dated the events at Sinai on the Feast of Weeks (cf. Exod. 19:1).

The Feast of Ingathering[30] is the third Canaanite festival that

---

[27] *BHH*, I, 471-74; *RGG*, II, 910-17; *IDB*, II, 260-64.

[28] H.-J. Kraus, "Zur Geschichte des Passah-Massotfestes im Alten Testament," *EvTh*, XVIII (1958), 47-67; E. Kutsch, "Erwägungen zur Geschichte der Passafeier und des Massotfestes," *ZThK*, LV (1958), 1-35; *BHH*, II 1169-70.

[29] H. Grimme, *Das israelitische Pfingstfest und der Plejadenkult,* "Studien zur Geschichte und Kultur des Altertums," I.1, 1907; E. Lohse in *ThW*, IV, 45-46; *BHH*, II, 1440-41.

[30] Kutsch; *BHH*, II, 1052-53; *pace* R. Kittel, "Osirismysterien und Laubhüttenfest," *OLZ*, XXVII (1924), 385-91, the festival is not to be associated with a Canaanite festival of Osiris-Adonis.

Israel adopted and associated with Yahweh. Like the Feast of Un-leavened Bread, it coincided with a week, taking place "at the end of the year" (Exod. 23:16) or "at the turn of the year" (Exod. 34:22), when the last of the harvest had been gathered in and the labor of the threshing-floor and the winepress had been finished. It was the most important feast of the year, and was therefore known simply as "the feast of Yahweh" (Judg. 21:19; Lev. 23:39) or "the feast" (I Kings 8:2, 65; 12:32; and *passim*); it was dominated by the thought of the harvest and festal rejoicing. According to a late note, Jeroboam I is said to have moved it a month later (I Kings 12:32-33); but even after the conquest of Jerusalem (587 B.C.) people from the region of the former Northern Kingdom were still coming to Jerusalem on pilgrimages in the seventh month, i.e., to the Feast of Ingathering (Jer. 41:4-5). From the time of the Deutero-nomic legislation it was called the Feast of Booths (Deut. 16:13, 16), because the week of dwelling in booths was considered the most important observance. Whether this practice was followed from the outset or was introduced during the course of the monarchy cannot be determined. In any case, it derives from the booths that were erected in orchards and vineyards during the harvest. This custom was later used to associate the feast with the desert period: the Israelites are to dwell in booths during the feast as they did then (Lev. 23:42-43). In the desert, however, the people lived not in booths but in tents. This shows that we are dealing with a late explanation.

An additional regular observance was the annual celebration of the dedication of the Jerusalem Temple. According to I Kings 8:1-2, the Feast of Ingathering had provided the occasion for the dedication of the Solomonic Temple; the annual festival, probably referred to in Psalm 132, therefore coincided with the Feast of Ingathering.

The situation is different with respect to the regulation in Deut. 31:10-11 that requires the recitation of the law every seven years at the Feast of Booths. Deut. 31:1-13 is one of the supplements to the second, later con-clusion of the book, which were added in the exilic period at the earliest, and probably in the post-exilic period.[31] That such a ceremony actually took place is doubtful; the regulation may have come into being following the recitation of the law by Ezra, in order to legitimize it.

Neither can the designation of every seventh year as a fallow year,[32]

[31] S-F, § 25.
[32] It is also known as the year of release and the sabbatical year; *BHH*, I, 429-30; *RGG*, II, 568-69; *IDB*, II, 263; F. Horst, *Das Privilegrecht Jahwes*,

required by Exod. 23:10-11, be considered an actual practice. The inclusion of vineyards and olive orchards and the charitable motivation are surely not original. The more recent explanations in terms of the cult or agricultural economy are also dubious. It is likewise uncertain whether the practice is to be derived from the nomadic or Canaanite environment. There is no evidence for actual observance until the second century B.C. (I Macc. 6:49, 53). This therefore raises the question whether the Deuteronomic regulation canceling debts every seven years (Deut. 15:1 ff.) is not primary and the regulation requiring a fallow year secondary.

The lack of other data about Israelite festivals during the monarchy has led a one-sided cult-historical approach, which considers worship to be the central phenomenon of religion, to postulate a series of festivals unknown to OT tradition. These include a "New Year's festival of Yahweh" parallel to the Babylonian New Year's festival at the beginning of the new year in the fall, to celebrate the power shown by Yahweh in creation and in the establishment of his people;[33] the "enthronement festival of Yahweh" associated with the New Year's festival, in which Yahweh annually regained his sovereignty over his people and all creation after his victory over the forces of chaos;[34] the "covenant festival" or "covenant renewal festival" sometimes associated with the "enthronement festival," possibly having a "cultic theophany" as its climax;[35] the "royal Zion festival" to celebrate Yahweh's election of Jerusalem and the Davidic dynasty (reshaped after the Exile into the enthronement festival of Yahweh) ;[36] and an "election festival" based on Exod. 19:3-8.[37] All these hypotheses, however, are most unlikely. The autumnal festival (Feast of Ingathering) was a harvest festival, not a New Year's festival; no mythical notions such as a battle with chaos, the creation of the world, etc. were associated with it, while the connection with the desert period was a product of the post-exilic period. The so-called enthronement psalms are monotheistic hymns dependent on Deutero-Isaiah,[38] in which the phrase *yhwh mālak* means "it is Yahweh that reigns as king." Above all, there can be no question of any involvement of the Israelite king and of his "sacral marriage," especially since the

---

1930, pp. 56 ff. (= his *Gottes Recht*, 1961, pp. 79 ff.) ; *idem*, "Das Eigentum nach dem Alten Testament," in *Kirche und Volk*, II (1949) , 87-102 (= *ibid.*, pp. 203-21) ; R. North, "Maccabean Sabbath Years," *Bibl*, XXXIV (1953) , 501-15.

[33] P. Volz, *Das Neujahrsfest Jahwes*, 1912.

[34] S. Mowinckel, *Psalmenstudien*, II, 1922; *idem*, *The Psalms in Israel's Worship*, I (1963) , 106-92; H. Schmidt, *Die Thronfahrt Jahves am Fest der Jahreswende im alten Israel*, 1927.

[35] S. Mowinckel, *Psalmenstudien; The Psalms in Israel's Worship;* G. von Rad, *Das formgeschichtliche Problem des Hexateuch*, 1938 (= his *Gesammelte Studien zum Alten Testament*, 1958, pp. 9-86 [English: *The Problem of the Hexateuch and Other Essays*, 1966, pp. 1-78]) ; A. Weiser, *Die Psalmen*, 4th ed., 1955 (English: *The Psalms*, 1962) ; *idem*, "Zur Frage nach den Beziehungen der Psalmen zum Kult," in *Festschrift Alfred Bertholet*, 1950, pp. 513-31 (= his *Glaube und Geschichte im Alten Testament*, 1961, pp. 303-21) .

[36] H.-J. Kraus, *Die Königsherrschaft Gottes im Alten Testament*, 1951.

[37] H. Wildberger, *Jahwes Eigentumsvolk*, 1960.

[38] S-F, § 39.2.

assumption is misguided that the Song of Songs represents a collection of garbled songs to accompany such a ceremony. The "covenant" or "covenant renewal festival" vanishes when one realizes that *b°rît* does not mean "covenant" at all; the assurances given by Yahweh or the acceptance of obligation on the part of Israel that we may assume instead did not need to be renewed annually. Furthermore, the Sinai tradition was not associated with the autumnal festival but with the Feast of Weeks. And just as the exegetical basis for the hypothetical Zion festival is insecure, so the election festival is based on a text of the late post-Deuteronomic monarchic period in Judah.[39]

c) Irregular public ceremonies included the ritual enthronement of the king (I Kings 1:32-48; II Kings 11:12-20).[40] The cultic action took place within the sanctuary: the king was presented with the diadem and the royal protocol in which Yahweh acknowledged the king as his son, entrusted him with sovereignty over the people, named his throne name, etc.; in many instances the king was anointed; finally all those present gave their acclamation (see § 12.2). Later a secular ceremony took place in the palace: the king sat upon the throne, delivered his inaugural address, received the homage of the officials, and confirmed them in their offices.

Sacred sites were also the scene of victory celebrations, supplications, and lamentations, whose form varied according to the occasion and situation. Only during or after the Exile were there fixed dates for communal laments; before then, these and other such observances were carried out as occasion demanded (see I Kings 21:9-10; Jer. 36:9).[41] From the post-exilic period, Joel 1–2 records the words spoken by cultic prophets on days of lamentation and penance.[42]

4. *Performance of the cult. a*) The cultic ceremonies were carried out according to specific regulations and ordinances.[43] Therefore the individual sanctuaries very early reduced their cult to rules that were punctiliously observed by all who attended and took part in the cult. Above all an official sanctuary like that in Jerusalem would possess a recognized cultic code. It would be wrong, however, to conclude that there was uniformity of ritual. There can be no

[39] S-F, § 27.3.
[40] G. von Rad, "Das judäische Königsritual," *ThLZ*, LXXII (1947), 211-16 (= his *Gesammelte Studien zum Alten Testament*, 1958, pp. 205-13 [English: *The Problem of the Hexateuch and Other Studies*, 1966, pp. 222-31]).
[41] *BHH*, I, 290-92; *IDB*, II, 261-62; see also H. W. Wolff, "Der Aufruf zur Volksklage," *ZAW*, LXXVI (1964), 48-56.
[42] S-F, § 62.
[43] K. Koch, *Die Priesterschrift von Exodus 25 bis Leviticus 16*, 1959; R. Rendtorff, *Die Gesetze in der Priesterschrift*, 1954.

doubt that quite divergent cultic regulations came into being; the more sanctuaries there were, the greater was the ritual variety.

Specific cultic ordinances have been incorporated into the books of Leviticus and Numbers; these are instructions governing the service performed by the priests, regulating their activity or defining the criteria by which they are to decide cases. Among other things, they contain directions for the various kinds of sacrifice (e.g., Leviticus 1–3). The original form can often be restored by removing the introductory formulas and by changing direct address and second person forms into third person forms. At least the nucleus of these regulations derives from the period of the monarchy.

Other instructions and regulations, likewise intended for priests, contain portions of priestly professional lore (e.g., Leviticus 15). These differ from the cultic ordinances in that they represent short isolated fragments assembled in collections without formal or substantial continuity.

b) The most important cultic act was the offering of sacrifice.[44] We may ask what types of sacrifice there were, how frequently they were offered, and what purposes they served.

The sacrifice of a slaughtered animal (*zebaḥ*) was a communion sacrifice, for which cattle, sheep, or goats could be used. The animal sacrificed was consumed in a communal meal.[45] The meat was divided between Yahweh and the worshipers; after some date that can no longer be determined it was also shared with the priest. Yahweh received the most valuable parts of the slaughtered animal, the fat portions, which were burned upon the alter. After he had received his share of the food in this fashion, the actual meal could begin, in the course of which—after the breast and right shank had been removed as the priest's portion—the worshiper, together with his family and invited guests, devoured the meat. Those who partook had to be ritually clean. Since all slaughtering was sacrificial, and since almost no meat was eaten in regular meals, such a festive meal at the sanctuary took on a special character. The primary purpose of this type of sacrifice was communion: communion of those who shared the meal with one another, and communion of the whole group with Yahweh.

Such a sacrificial meal was also associated with the type of sacrifice called *šelem* or *šᵉlāmîm*. In light of the double translation used by

---

[44] *BHH*, II, 1345-50; *RGG*, IV, 1641-47; *IDB*, IV, 147-59.

[45] The term "fire offering" in I Sam. 2:28 apparently refers to this type of sacrifice; *RGG*, IV, 607-8.

the LXX, it is usually understood as meaning "salvation offering" or "peace offering," less frequently as having some other meaning.[46] A more appropriate derivation would be from the piel of *šlm* in the admittedly uncommon sense "make complete"; the meaning would then be "concluding offering." In lists, this sacrifice always occupies the last place (e.g., II Kings 16:13) and seems originally to have concluded a celebration consisting of burnt offerings (Exod. 20:24; Judg. 20:26; 21:4; I Sam. 13:9; II Sam. 6:17-18; 24:25; I Kings 8:64), in order to add, through its sacrificial meal, the notion of communion. Because of this ritual it was associated quite early with sacrificial slaughter, so that we find mention of "sacrifices that are concluding offerings" (Exod. 24:5; I Sam. 11:15). In the later period, especially after the Exile, sacrificial slaughter lost its importance; the concluding offering, similar to it in ritual, first neutralized and then replaced it.

The burnt offering (*'ōlâ*), of non-Semitic origin (see § 10.2), was a whole offering.[47] The worshiper, who had to be ritually clean, brought the sacrifical animal (or birds) to the priest for approval and laid his hand on the animal's head—either to confirm that it was really offered by the worshiper or to transfer sin, curse, etc. to the animal.[48] The worshiper then slaughtered it, the priest poured the blood around the altar and burned the pieces of the dismembered animal upon the altar, so that its smoke "went up" (*'ālâ*) to Yahweh; neither the worshiper nor the priest received a portion. Such burnt offerings honored Yahweh and paid him homage (I Sam. 6:14); they were therefore offered in the Temple cult at the annual festivals (I Kings 9:25). But also the prayers of the congregation (Jer. 14:12) and of the king (Ps. 20:4-5 [Eng. 20:3-4]) were offered during the burnt offerings.

In contrast to the other offerings, the thank offering (*tôdâ*) might include leaven (Amos 4:5). This sacrifice was offered primarily in the course of thanksgiving celebrations, in which the community or an individual would give thanks for deliverance from calamity.

[46] For a detailed discussion, see G. Fohrer in *ThW*, VII, 1022-23; R. Schmid, *Das Bundesopfer in Israel*, 1964, translates as "covenant offering."
[47] L. Rost, "Erwägungen zum israelitischen Brandopfer" in *Von Ugarit nach Qumran* (Eissfeldt Festschrift), 1958, pp. 177-83; W. H. Stevenson, "Hebrew *'olah* and *zebach* Sacrifices," in *Festschrift Alfred Bertholet*, 1950, pp. 488-97.
[48] S. H. Hooke, "The Theory and Practice of Substitution," *VT*, II (1952), 2-17;P. Volz, "Die Handauflegung beim Opfer," *ZAW*, XXI (1901), 93-100; for a different view, see J. C. Matthes, "Der Sühnegedanke bei den Sündopfern," *ZAW*, XXIII (1903), 97-119.

The guilt offering (*'āšām*) was apparently known at least toward the end of the monarchy, since the Holiness Code, which mentions it in Lev. 19:20 ff., can be traced back to a pre-exilic nucleus.[49] This sacrifice was intended to expiate minor transgressions or instances of uncleanness.

From time immemorial offerings of food and drink (libations) were customary; the bread of the Presence also belongs in this category (see I Sam. 21:3-7 [Eng. 21:2-6]). Originally the term "gift" (*minḥā*) referred to all sacrificial rituals involving animals or vegetable substances; it was later restricted to the latter, including grain, plants, oil, and wine. In this sense the word occurs alongside sacrificial slaughter (I Sam. 2:29; 3:14; Isa. 19:21), concluding offering (Amos 5:22), and burnt offering (Jer. 14:12; Ps. 20:4 [Eng. 20:3]).

Incense offering is attested for the entire period of the monarchy by the mention and discovery of incense altars.[50] Incense, which was introduced from South Arabia, is first mentioned in Jer. 6:20, but this does not mean that it was not used earlier. Other resins were also available.[51]

From Canaanite religion Israel borrowed the practice of dedicating the firstborn to the deity.[52] Just as the first fruits of the field were offered at the harvest festivals, so too the male firstborn of the cattle were to be offered (Exod. 34:19). The extent to which this requirement originally applied to human firstborn cannot be determined; in any event, even the Canaanite precursor of the story of Abraham's journey to sacrifice his son (Genesis 22) seems to have been designed to justify the substitution of animal sacrifice for human sacrifice. In Israel the offering of firstborn animals served to acknowledge Yahweh's sovereign and proprietary rights and to express dependence on Yahweh and thanksgiving to him.

The cultic tithe[53] is attested only for the Northern Kingdom during the period of the monarchy. Amos 4:4 mentions it for Bethel and Gilgal; Gen. 28:22 (E) justifies it for Bethel by tracing the

---

[49] P. D. Schötz, *Schuld- und Sündopfer im Alten Testament*, 1930; N. H. Snaith, "The Sin-offering and the Guilt-offering," *VT*, XV (1965), 73-80.

[50] M. Haran, "The Use of Incense in the Ancient Israelite Ritual," *VT*, X (1960), 113-29; M. Löhr, *Das Räucheropfer im Alten Testament, eine archäologische Untersuchung*, 1927.

[51] See *BRL*, pp. 325-66.

[52] *BHH*, I, 434; *RGG*, II, 608-10; *IDB*, II, 271.

[53] *BHH*, III, 2208-9; *RGG*, VI, 1878-79; O. Eissfeldt, *Erstlinge und Zehnten im Alten Testament*, 1917.

practice back to Jacob. The justification for Jerusalem found in
Gen. 14:20 dates from a considerably later period. More precise
regulations appear to have been laid down only by Deuteronomy
and in the post-exilic period.

The sacrificial cult was taken for granted. There is therefore
almost nothing preserved concerning the frequency and regularity
of sacrifice. We do not know whether sacrifice was limited to specified
dates and special occasions, whether it was offered regularly, perhaps
even daily, or whether it took place whenever the worshiper felt
like it. Only II Kings 16:15 mentions regular sacrifice at the Jerusalem Temple: a burnt offering every morning and a cereal offering
every evening.

The offering of sacrifice could serve various purposes, but all are
associated with the basic notion of God's sovereignty and communion
with God. That sacrificial slaughter and concluding offering served
to establish mutual fellowship and communion with Yahweh among
those who partook of the sacrificial meal has already been mentioned.
Another purpose, especially associated with burnt offering, was to
offer Yahweh a gift; in this fashion the worshiper acknowledged
the majesty of the divine sovereign, paid homage to him, and showed
his respect. Sacrifice could furthermore reinforce a petition or express
thanks for help that had been received. But sacrifice could also
serve to appease God's wrath or expiate human transgressions against
Yahweh.[54] It brought before Yahweh a pleasing odor (*rēaḥ nîḥōaḥ*)
to appease his wrath (Gen. 8:21; I Sam. 26:19), or was a propitiatory
gift in substitution for the human life that was theoretically forfeit
(cf. Mic. 6:7).[55] Finally, it was possible for an individual—perhaps
during a festival—to offer a freewill offering (Amos 4:5), for which
even a deformed animal might be used (Lev. 22:23).

c) Although the offering of sacrifice played an important rôle,
it was far from constituting the whole of the cult. The OT records
a series of other cultic acts or acts taking place in the cultic realm;
these included ancient religious material (§ 2.3). The vow[56] was
a rite of consecration. It was usually made for the fulfillment of

---

[54] *RGG*, VI, 507-11; *IDB*, I, 310; IV, 16-17; S. Herner, *Sühne und Vergebung in
Israel*, 1942; J. J. Stamm, *Erlösen und Vergeben im Alten Testament*, 1940.

[55] L. Moraldi, *Espiazione sacrificiale e rite espiatori nell' ambiente biblico*,
1956; R. J. Thompson, *Penitence and Sacrifice in Early Israel Outside the
Levitical Law*, 1963.

[56] *BHH*, I, 541-42; *RGG*, II, 1322-23; *IDB*, IV, 792-93; W. H. Gispen, "De
gelofte," *GThT*, LXI (1961) 4-13, 37-45, 65-73, 93-107; A. Wendel, *Das israelitisch-
jüdische Gelübde*, 1931.

a petition or request (Gen. 28:20-22; Judge. 11:30-31; I Sam. 1:11; II Sam. 15:8), more rarely as an expression of thanks (Jonah 1:16). In the course of time the making and fulfilling of vows was increasingly incorporated into the cult, and the priesthood became involved (see Lev. 7:16; 22:21; 27:2-8; Num. 6:2-21; 15:8).

Rites of purification or desecration were necessary when a person came in close contact with something unclean or sacred.[57] For example, such rites were necessary when a woman became unclean by giving birth, or when a priest became holy by offering sacrifice. The person in question had to be purified or desecrated before returning to everyday life. Sacrifice might be offered for this purpose, for instance by a woman eight days after giving birth (Lev. 12:1-8), by a leper (Lev. 14:10-32), or by someone sexually unclean (Lev. 15:14-15, 29-30); ablutions with water might serve to purify vessels, clothing, or persons defiled by contact with something unclean (Lev. 11:24-25, 28, 32, 40; 15). In many cases we are dealing with ancient customs or conceptions that survived reinterpreted in the cultic sphere.

Priests had special authority to pronounce blessings and curses; when they put the name of Yahweh "upon the people of Israel" during a cultic ceremony, divine blessing was effected (Num. 6:27). What had originally been a magical blessing or curse formula generally became a wish associated with Yahweh: "May so-and-so be blessed (or cursed) by (or before) Yahweh." An oracle served to discover God's response, which would determine the course of events.[58] Psalms 45 contains such an oracle, spoken by a cult prophet on the occasion of a royal wedding. Suspicious acts or persons were tested by ordeal (cf. Num. 5:11 ff.).[59] Pronouncements by cult prophets could also be part of a cultic ceremony. Psalm 82, for example, represents a prophetical judgment discourse spoken by Yahweh, comprising invective, admonition, and threat directed against the divine realm of the Canaanites. The cult prophets Nahum and Habakkuk most likely pronounced their threats against the

---

[57] *BHH*, III, 1578-79, 2052-53; *RGG*, V, 942-44, 47-48; VI, 1549; *IDB*, I, 648; W. H. Gispen "The Distinction Between Clean and Unclean" *OTS*, V (1948), 190-96.

[58] *BHH*, I, 598-600; *RGG*, IV, 1664-66; F. Küchler, "Das priesterliche Orakel in Israel und Juda," in *Baudissin Festschrift*, 1918, pp. 285-301; J. Begrich, "Das priesterliche Heilsorakel," *ZAW*, LII (1934), 81-92 (= his *Gesammelte Studien zum Alten Testament*, 1964, pp. 217-31).

[59] *BHH*, I, 600; *RGG*, II, 1808-9; R. Press, "Das Ordal im alten Israel," *ZAW*, LI (1933), 121-40, 227-55.

Assyrian Empire within the cultic context of the Jerusalem Temple.[60]
Hymns and prayers accompanied the cultic ceremonies.[61] The few
Psalms that can be dated in the period of the monarchy with some
probability are—apart from the royal songs, which are quite distinct
—primarily cultic prayers of the individual: laments (Ps. 3; 27:7-14;
28; 42/43; 54; 57; 59; 61), thanksgivings (Ps. 30; 63), or combina-
tions of the two (Ps. 31:1-9; 31:10-25; 56). The only other types are
the two cultic entrance liturgies (Ps. 15; 24) and the noncultic
individual songs of confidence (Ps. 11; 27:1-6). The laments, represented in striking number, presuppose that man should normally
be in a state of favor with God, a state interrupted by human
failure or divine wrath. The prayer of lament was a petition to
Yahweh that he put an end to the interruption and restore the
petitioner to his favor.[62] The prayer was sometimes spoken in standing position (see I Sam. 1:26; I Kings 8:22; Jer. 18:20), more frequently kneeling (see I Kings 8:54); the hands might be raised
to heaven (I Kings 8:22; 54; Isa. 1:15) or the forehead lowered to the
ground (Ps. 5:8 [Eng. 5:7]; 99:5, 9; the Hebrew word translated
"worship" actually means "prostrate oneself"). This is the same
posture taken before the king or before a person to be honored (see
I Sam. 24:9 [Eng. 24:8]; II Sam. 9:8; I Kings 2:19; II Kings 1:13;
4:37).

Finally, we may mention cultic dancing (II Sam. 6:5) and proces-
sions (Isa. 30:29; Ps. 42:5 [Eng. 42:4]); there is no evidence of
cultic drama, and such performances are unlikely.

5. *Cultic personnel.* Unlike the prophets, the priests[63] received
no call; they assumed their ministry as members of a priestly family.
Originally, there was no ritual by which a priest was consecrated;
he simply assumed his office, and his ministry sanctified him (for the
later procedure, which differed somewhat, see Exod. 28:41). He was
thus set apart from the secular sphere and everyday life, and had
to remain so. He was therefore subject to many prohibitions and
regulations concerning purity, which became increasingly rigorous
in the course of time (see Exod. 28:42-43; 30:17-21; 40:31-32; Lev.

[60] See S-F, § 67–68.
[61] *BHH*, I, 518-22, 554-55; II, 1258-62; *RGG*, II, 1213-17; IV, 1201-5; *IDB*,
III, 857-62.
[62] D. R. Ap-Thomas, "Some Notes on the Old Testament Attitude to Prayer,"
SJTh, IX (1956), 422-29; A. Wendel, *Das freie Laiengebet im vorexilischen
Israel*, 1932.
[63] *BHH*, III, 1486-89; *RGG*, V, 574-78; *IDB*, III, 876-89.

8:6; 10:8-11; 21:1-7; Num. 8:7).[64] Belonging by birth to a specific priestly family, he was appointed to serve at the sanctuary to which the family belonged, and shared its fortunes with his family. Thus just as the Jerusalem Temple gained precedence over the other sanctuaries, so its priesthood acquired pre-eminence over the priests of the countryside.

The functions of the priests included above all the oversight of oracles and ordeals, instruction, and the pronouncing of blessings and curses. Originally they played only a minor part in the sacrificial ritual: they poured out the blood, placed the portions intended for Yahweh on the altar, and offered incense. Later the former functions diminished in importance or vanished entirely, while the sacrificial ritual was increasingly reserved for the priesthood and became a priestly monopoly. In his various functions, a priest represented Yahweh to man (oracle, ordeal, instruction, blessing and cursing) and also man to Yahweh (sacrifice). Thus he functioned in his office as a mediator.

The ancient idiom for the installation of a priest, "to fill his hand" (Judg. 17:12), probably refers to the priestly right to a portion of the sacrificial offerings and the income of the sanctuary. It was generally true that the priest lived from the altar: except for the burnt offering, he received a portion of the sacrificial animals, and probably also a portion of the cereal offerings and first fruits, as well as the tithes. That these privileges were abused can be seen from I Sam. 2:12-17 and Hos. 4:8.

The Zadokite priesthood maintained itself in Jerusalem until the Exile,[65] although the list of Zadok's successors in I Chron. 5:34-41 (Eng. 6:8-15) represents an artificial structure. If the text can in fact be analyzed into lists of twelve names, it sets up an intentional parallel between the twelve generations of Zadok's ancestors before the building of the Temple (I Chron. 5:29-34 [Eng. 6:3-8]) and the twelve generations of priests from the building of the Solomonic Temple to its rebuilding after the Exile.[66] The Jerusalem priests were royal officials; the chief priests belonged to the class of high officials (I Kings 4:2), who were appointed and deposed by the

[64] W. Falk, "Endogamy in Israel," Tarbiz, XXXII (1962/63), 19-34.
[65] A. Bentzen, "Zur Geschichte der Ṣadoḳiden," ZAW, LI (1933), 173-76.
[66] For a different view, see H. J. Katzenstein, "Some Remarks on the Lists of the Chief Priests of the Temple of Solomon," JBL, LXXXI (1962), 377-84; cf. also J. Bowman, "La Genealogioj de la Ĉefpastroj en la Hebrea kaj la Samaritana Tradicioj," Biblia Revuo, V (1966), 1-16.

king (I Kings 2:27, 35) and received their instructions from him
(II Kings 12:5-17 [Eng. 12:4-16]; 16:10-16). Of course there were
also conflicts, since the priests tried to restrict the authority of the
king over the Temple and its cult.

The Jerusalem priesthood—and probably the priesthood at other
great sanctuaries as well (cf. Amos 7:10) —was hierachically organized. At its head stood "the priest" (I Kings 4:2 and *passim*),
or "chief priest" (II Kings 25:18), who supervised the other priests
and was in turn responsible to the king. After him came the "second
priest" (II Kings 23:4; 25:18), who in Jer. 29:24 ff. bears the title
"overseer of the Temple" and had the Temple police under him.
The "keepers of the threshold" also occupied major priestly offices
(II Kings 23:4); according to II Kings 25:18, there were three of
them. In consequence of the ramification of the priesthood, there
were the "senior priests," the heads of the priestly families (II Kings
19:2; Jer. 19:1).

The Levites[67] are scarcely mentioned during the monarchy. We
see only Jeroboam I accused of appointing non-levitical priests to
the state sanctuary in Bethel (I Kings 12:31; 13:33). But we may
assume that Levites continued to minister at the rural sanctuaries
(see § 10.2; 11.3).

Cult prophets could also make their appearance at the sanctuaries,
although they were only loosely associated with them. They will be
discussed in another context (§ 19.1).

The singers and doorkeepers may be termed auxiliary personnel.
Since Ezra 2:41-42 mentions their return from the Exile, there must
have been such persons before the Jerusalem Temple was destroyed.
Their existence in the Northern Kingdom is also presupposed (Amos
5:23). The early adoption of temple singers from the Canaanite
cults is suggested by the names "Ethan," "Heman," and "Jeduthun"
(in the superscriptions to the Psalms; I Kings 5:11; I Chron. 6:18-32
[Eng. 6:33-47]; 25:1), which are not Israelite names. They were
considered artists ("wise men"); sometimes they are termed Ezrahites,
that is, indigenes or Canaanites, and referred to as members of a
guild of musicians (*māḥôl*).

Finally, the Jerusalem Temple had slaves, who performed the
simpler tasks; according to Josh. 9:27 the Gibeonites were condemned
to be hewers of wood and drawers of water. The *nᵉtînîm* mentioned

---

[67] *BHH*, II, 1077-79; *RGG*, IV, 336-37; K. Möhlenbrink, "Die levitischen
Überlieferungen des Alten Testaments," *ZAW*, LII (1934), 184-231.

in Ezra 2:43 ff.; 8:20 among those who returned from the Exile were such Temple slaves.

While there is mention of women who sang and danced at religious festivals (Exod. 15:20; Judg. 21:21; Ps. 68:26 [Eng. 68:25]), and Israel had both prophetesses (II Kings 22:14; Isa. 8:3) and occasionally sacral prostitutes (contrary to the principles of Yahwism), there was no female cultic personnel in the strict sense of the word.

6. *Further development and criticism.* The Deuteronomic centralization and reform of the cult, followed by the destruction of the Jerusalem Temple and the Exile, marked a decisive turning point that had a major effect in the realm of the cult. In many respects the post-exilic cult took on its own peculiar form, differing more or less markedly from the pre-exilic cult (see § 28.4). But since the cult of Yahwism was not a fixed constant but was involved in continuous change, it did not escape criticism, at least from the eighth century onward. We refer here to the criticism of the cult, in part striking at its very roots, pronounced by the great individual prophets, especially Amos, Hosea, Isaiah, and Jeremiah, and to a lesser degree Micah and Zephaniah. We shall return to this topic below (§ 20.2).

§ 17 LIFE AND DEATH

A. BERTHOLET, *Die israelitischen Vorstellungen vom Zustand nach dem Tode,* 2nd ed., 1914; E. DHORME, "L'idée de l'au-delà dans la religion hébraïque," *RHR,* CXXIII (1941), 113-42; L. DÜRR, *Die Wertung des Lebens im Alten Testament und im antiken Orient,* 1926; A. F. FEY, "The Concept of Death in Early Israelite Religion," *JBR,* XXXII (1964), 239-47; G. FOHRER, "Das Geschick des Menschen nach dem Tode im Alten Testament," *KuD,* XIV (1968), Heft 4; A. R. JOHNSON, *The Vitality of the Individual in the Thought of Ancient Israel,* 2nd ed., 1964; R. MARTIN-ACHARD, *De la mort à la résurrection d'après l'Ancien Testament,* 1956; G. QUELL, *Die Auffassung des Todes im Alten Testament,* 1925; J. SCHARBERT, *Fleisch, Geist und Seele im Pentateuch,* 1966; J. SCHREINER, "Geburt und Tod in biblischer Sicht," *BiLe,* VII (1966), 127-50; F. SCHWALLY, *Das Leben nach dem Tode nach den Vorstellungen des alten Israel und des Judentums,* 1892; L. WÄCHTER, *Der Tod im Alten Testament,* 1967.

1. *Man as a living creature in this world.* a) When Yahweh formed man "of dust," he breathed into him the breath of life,

thus making him a "living being" (Gen. 2:7).[1] The word used by J, *"nepeš,"* originally meant "throat," then the "breath" that passes through the throat and the "life" that can be recognized through the presence of breath, which is in the blood, and by extension "man," "human being," "self," but also the "soul" as the locus and bearer of dispositions and sensations (for example, longing). This shows clearly that the term usually refers to man as a whole. Yahweh did not create the body and add to it a "soul"; man is to be understood as a living whole, not as a dichotomy or trichotomy.

On the one hand, this man (*'ādām*) is taken from the soil (*'ădāmâ*). While this explanation by J is probably a play on the similarity of the two words, the emphasis lies on the fact that man is "dust" (Gen. 2:7; 3:19) or made from clay (Job 10:9; 33:6), and that he must therefore return to dust (Ps. 90:3). Thus man's transitoriness and mortality are expressed. In addition, man is "flesh" (*bāśār*);[2] Yahweh, however, is spirit (Gen. 6:3; Isa. 31:3). This antithesis does not refer to the contrast between what is material and what is spiritual; it emphasizes that man is weak but God is strong (Jer. 17:5; Isa. 31:1-3), that man is transitory but God lives eternally (Gen. 6:3; Isa. 40:6, 8).

On the other hand, what makes the weak and transitory man of dust into a living being is the divine vitalizing energy that is given him as breath (*n*e*šāmâ*) or spirit (*rûaḥ*).[3] Without breath or spirit there is no life, and therefore no emotions, sensations, or feelings. Besides the soul, various organs are identified as the locus of mental states: the heart, as the organ of thought and feeling, receiving impressions, framing plans, awakening courage and will, and evolving religious understanding; also the kidneys, liver, and bowels, as elsewhere in the ancient Near East.

b) Man is utterly restricted to life in this world; Yahwism is characterized by its complete and unqualified this-worldliness. Just as Yahweh's words and acts come to pass in the momentary present, so human life in its relationships to God and the world is linked

[1] *BHH*, II, 1055-57; *IDB*, III, 124-26; J. H. Becker, *Het begrip nefesj in het Oude Testament*, 1942; D. Lys, *Nèpèsh*, 1959.

[2] *RGG*, II, 974-75; *IDB*, II, 276.

[3] J. Hehn, "Zum Problem des Geistes im Alten Orient und im Alten Testament," *ZAW*, XLIII (1925), 210-25; P. van Imschoot, "L'esprit de Jahvé, source de vie, dans l'Ancien Testament," *RB*, XLIV (1935), 481-501; D. Lys, *Rûach*, 1962; J. H. Scheepers, *Die gees van God en die gees van die mens in die Ou Testament*, 1960; P. Volz, *Der Geist Gottes und die verwandten Erscheinungen im Alten Testament und im anschliessenden Judentum*, 1910; M. Westphal, *La ruach dans l'Ancien Testament*, Dissertation, Geneva, 1958.

exclusively to this life on earth. Only here is meaningful human existence possible. Therefore man must order his present life in such a way that it takes on its full significance here and now. This life does not serve as a preparation for the next, nor is it completed by an existence in the beyond; it takes its value from the present, irretrievable moment, where alone man can experience and learn what there is to be experienced and learned.

Therefore the Israelite wished to die "in a good old age" or "old and full of days" (Gen. 15:15; 25:8; 35:29; Judg. 8:32; Job 42:17; I Chron. 23:1; 29:28), that is, having lived out in peace man's allotted span (Gen. 6:3; Ps. 90:10) and after a full and satisfying life. It was bad for a man to have to die the early death of the godless (II Sam. 3:33) and to be taken "in the midst of his days" (Ps. 102:25 [Eng. 102:24]), the more so because premature and sudden death was considered a divine punishment (I Sam. 25:38; 26:10; Jer. 17:11; Ps. 26:9).

The relationship between man and Yahweh was also limited to this world. For he is the God of the living, not of the dead. The dead are separated from him; therefore he stands by the living who serve him and acknowledge his sovereignty, who allow themselves to be won by him and are called on to live in communion with him:

> For Sheol cannot thank thee,
>   death cannot praise thee.
> Those who go down to the pit cannot hope
>   for thy faithfulness.   (Isa. 38:18)

This was in the mind of the suppliant as he lamented his misfortune to Yahweh and prayed to him for help, asking Yahweh not to let him die. If he fell victim to his sickness, he had no future expectation. There remained only a shadowy existence in darkness and oblivion:

> Dost thou work wonders for the dead?
> Do the shades rise up to praise thee?
> Is thy steadfast love declared in the grave,
>   or thy faithfulness in the realm of the dead?
> Are thy wonders known in the darkness,
>   or thy saving help in the land of forgetfulness?
>   (Ps. 88:11-13 [Eng. 88:10-12])

Departure from these ideas is extremely rare (Ps. 22:30 [Eng. 22:29]).

2. *Life and death.* Despite the contrast between life and death, the Israelite did not think of them as strictly separate realms, but

as fluid and changing fields of force that could interpenetrate and interact: the power of death can invade the sphere of human life and there spread its influence. Then the force of life weakens until finally it is completely extinguished or with renewed impetus vanquishes the power of death.

Thus Isa. 3:1-9 depicts how, after the threatened deportation of the upper classes from Jerusalem, chaos and anarchy will break out as a further consequence among those left behind. This represents a severe threat to life, which is generally based on traditional law and traditional order. Things fall apart because all bands are broken, all order dissolved; life degenerates into confusion and anarchy, loses its vigor, and gradually perishes. Even the women are sucked into the maelstrom: most of the men having been slaughtered, they put all shame aside, throw themselves at the first man they find, and even renounce their right to maintenance (Isa. 3:25–4:1). The situation is the same for the individual Israelite, for whom sickness or oppression by enemies represents an irruption of death into his life and foretaste of death itself, so that he can see himself already in the underworld (Isa. 38:10; Ps. 18:5-6 [Eng. 18:4-5]; 88:4-6 [Eng. 88:3-5]). Such plaintive descriptions are not poetic exaggeration; they express the general OT understanding of the relationship between life and death. Equally serious is the prayer that Yahweh will restore life to the suppliant and bring him up from the depths of the earth (Ps. 71:20). The consequent deliverance from sickness or peril is extrolled as deliverance from the grave and the underworld (Ps. 30:4 [Eng. 30:3]; 86:13).[4]

3. *After death. a*) Many conceptions and practices associated with death are extremely ancient; in part their significance was originally magical (see § 2.3). The corpse, for instance, was considered unclean, and whoever touched it likewise became unclean; this may be based on ancient taboo ideas.

Mourning customs[5] were originally intended to convey new vital force to the departed or to avert the harm he threatened; gradually

[4] C. Barth, *Die Errettung vom Tode in den individuellen Klage- und Danklieder des Alten Testaments*, 1947.

[5] *BHH*, III, 2021-22; *RGG*, VI, 1000-1001; *IDB*, III, 452-54; H. J. Elhorst, *Die israelitischen Trauerriten*, 1914; P. Heinisch, *Die Trauergebräuche bei den Israeliten*, 1931; N. Lohfink, "Enthielten die im Alten Testament bezeugten Klageriten eine Phase des Schweigens?" *VT*, XII (1962), 260-77; J. C. Matthes, *Die israelitischen Trauergebräuche*, 1905.

they took on the significance of "inferiority rites." [6] The mourner sat or lay upon the ground (Isa. 3:26; 47:1; Jer. 6:26), wept and fasted (II Sam. 1:12), rent his garments (Gen. 37:29, 34) and put on "sackcloth," a mourning garment made of dark goat or camel hair (Gen. 37:34; II Sam. 3:31; 21:10), went barefoot, loosened his turban, and covered his beard (Ezek. 24:17), smote his thighs and his breast (Isa. 32:12; Jer. 31:19), scattered dirt or ashes on his head (I Sam. 4:12; II Sam. 1:2; Ezek. 27:30). In addition, the mourner cut his hair and chopped his beard (Isa. 22:12; Jer. 7:29; Amos 8:10) or cut his skin (Jer. 16:6; 41:5). Although these latter practices, whose Canaanite origin was all too apparent (see I Kings 18:28; Jer. 47:5), were frequently forbidden (Lev. 19:27-28; 21:5; Deut. 14:1), they were able to survive for a long time.

Mourning was expressed by muffled lament (Amos 5:16) and such cries as "Alas, my brother!" "Ah sister!" or "Alas, lord!" (I Kings 13:30; Jer. 22:18; 34:5), which were originally rooted in the cult of the dead or in the cult of vegetation deities.[7] Lament for the dead also included the dirge,[8] which was sung to the sound of the flute by the dead man's family or by professional mourning women. Two such dirges, ascribed to David, lament Saul and Jonathan (II Sam. 1:19-27) and Abner (II Sam. 3:33-34). Jeremiah proposes to teach the mourning women a new dirge (Jer. 9:19-21 [Eng. 9:20-22]).

Worship of the dead[9] was rejected by Yahwism (as can be seen indirectly from Lev. 19:31; 20:6, 27; Deut. 18:11). There are a few signs of such a cult, like necromancy, involving prostration before the spirits of the dead (I Sam. 28:13-14; cf. II Kings 21:6; Isa. 8:19), and the provision of offerings (implicit in Deut. 16:14) or sacrificial meals (Ps. 106:28) for the dead, but these are scanty. Such conduct was always considered apostasy from Yahweh. Neither was there any notion that the dead were judged.[10]

Burial,[11] to which the corpse was borne on a bier (II Sam. 3:31), usually took place on the day of death. It was followed by the strict

[6] E. Kutsch, " 'Trauerbräuche' und 'Selbstminderungsriten' im Alten Testament," in K. Lüthi, E. Kutsch, and W. Dantine, *Drei Wiener Antrittsreden*, 1964, pp. 25-42.

[7] S-F, § 40.6.

[8] P. Heinisch, *Die Totenklage im Alten Testament*, 1931; H. Jahnow, *Das hebräische Leichenlied*, 1923.

[9] J. Frey, *Seelenglaube und Seelenkult im alten Israel*, 1898; A. Lods, *La croyance à la vie future et le culte des morts dans l'antiquité israélite*, 1902; cf. *RGG*, VI, 961-62.

[10] H. Cazelles, in *Le judgement des morts*, 1961, pp. 103-42.

[11] *BHH*, I, 211-12; *IDB*, I, 474-76.

observance of seven days of mourning (I Sam. 31:13), a period that could be extended in special cases (Gen. 50:3; Deut. 34:8).

b) The OT usually assumes that man is not completely annihilated after death, but continues in a certain sense to exist. Naturally this existence should not be termed "life" in the full sense of the word, but more a kind of vegetating. The important point is that we are once again dealing with man as a whole, not with his "soul" or some other part of him. At his death, a shadow of his person becomes detached and continues to vegetate in the underworld. Its existence obviously depends on the corpse and, after its decomposition, on the bones. To a degree that cannot be defined more precisely, these constitute the concrete earthly base for the shadowy image. For this reason, cremation was unknown, and the burning of bones was considered sacrilege (Amos 2:1). The bones were therefore collected in a pit within the tombs, which were often used for many generations; later they were kept in ossuaries.

The grave, then, was of crucial importance for the fate of men after death: it was the repository for corpse and bones, the base on which the shadow rested. It is therefore incorrect to see either an evolution or a contradiction when both grave and underworld are mentioned. There is simply no evidence to support any development along the lines of single grave—many graves—large tomb—underworld. Neither is the juxtaposition of the grave as repository and place of union with one's fathers, and the underworld as the "house appointed for all living" (Job. 30:23) an unresolved contradiction. The grave, rather, contains the base on which the shadow rests as it vegetates in the underworld.

This underworld [12] is comparable neither to the Hades of the Greeks nor to hell and purgatory. The Hebrew term $š^{e\prime}\hat{o}l$ probably means "non-land," the realm in which there is nothing active and dynamic, the land that therefore "does not exist" in the Israelite sense. It was conceived as an enclosed space within the abyssal ocean beneath the earth, or even beneath the waters (Job 26:5). The realm of total impotence, closed by barred gates (Isa. 38:10; Ps. 9:14 [Eng. 9:13]; Job 38:17), is entered by the shade that frees itself from the departed, there to lead the ghostly existence that traditionally typifies the fate of men after death. The term $r^{e}p\bar{a}\hat{\imath}m$, "spirits of the dead," which echoes the verb $r\bar{a}p\hat{a}$, "grow weak," "collapse," is probably meant to characterize the total impotence of the shades. In silence,

[12] *BHH*, III, 2014-15; *RGG*, III, 403-4; VI, 912-13; *IDB*, I, 787-88.

calm, and impotence something like the former life runs its course. Rank and status still count. The dead man still occupies the position he had as he went to his death or in which he was buried. Kings sit enthroned with the tokens of their dignity (Isa. 14:9 ff.); warriors appear in full armor; prophets appear wrapped in their robes (I Sam. 28:14). Only the man who is denied honorable burial is forced to lie upon maggots and be covered with worms (Isa. 14:11, 19-20). And just as miscarriages and the uncircumcised, the murdered and the executed, were flung aside away from the regular places of burial or at best given hasty burial there, so in the underworld their shades were assigned a separate place of residence—unclean, inglorious, and disgraceful.[13]

But even man's normal fate is hard. The impotence of the shades renders any real and effective life impossible. Therefore the dead can only chirp (Isa. 8:19; 29:4). There is no mutual fellowship among the dead, and so there is no hope of reunion with others. The dead do not even know about events in the world of the living (Job 14:21).

Last but not least, human shades are separated from God. When a man dies, God's sovereignty over him and his communion with God come to an end; they do not continue for the shade in the underworld. For all that God's power may even extend to the underworld (Isa. 7:11; Amos 9:2; Ps. 139:8; Job 26:5-6), the fate of men after death is separation from God. Although the idea of divine sovereignty and the notion of communion with God constitute a basic feature of Yahwism, for more than a millennium this religion associated them exclusively with the living, denying any relationship between Yahweh and the fate of men after death. It was religion of this world, of impressive consistency and coherence. That this involved picturing man's fate after death as even more dismal and hopeless than it is anyway was accepted. Awareness that God's sovereignty and communion with God were so abundantly provided in this life so surpassed the limitations implied by vegetating in the underworld that the latter did not even count in comparison.

Although there is no return from the underworld, a certain continued presence and influence of the departed upon earth was conceivable. Like Gilgamesh, who failed in his attempt to gain the plant of life, he might live on in a great and enduring work, such as the

[13] A. Lods, "La mort des incirconcis," *CRAI*, 1943, pp. 271-83; O. Eissfeldt, "Schwerterschlagene bei Hesekiel," in *Studies in Old Testament Prophecy* (Robinson Festschrift), 1950, pp. 73-81 (= his *Kleine Schriften*, III [1966], 1-8).

city wall of Uruk, because the work remains and is greater than its maker, who is condemned to death. He might live on in his descendants—especially if they bore so-called "surrogate names," i.e., personal names expressing the view that their bearer re-embodied a departed family member, or that the departed had reappeared or come to life once more in the bearer of the name.[14] This is why it was thought so terrible when a man's sons were extirpated and the family name was snuffed out (Isa. 14:20-21; Ps. 109:13). Only to the devout eunuchs did the prophet, in Yahweh's name, give the comfort of an everlasting name (Isa. 56:4-5). But all this remained cold and inadequate comfort in view of the inexorable fate of the shades in the underworld. Even a man like Job at the ultimate pitch of despair could only momentarily find something good to say about the underworld (Job 3).

c) Only rarely during the monarchy do we find deviations from the traditional notion of man's fate after death; this also remained the case later.

In the belief of the legends surrounding the prophets Elijah and Elisha, restoration of the dead to life marked a temporary escape from the fate awaiting men after death. Thus I Kings 17:17-24 tells how Elijah revived the son of a widow of Zarephath; II Kings 4:18-37 tells how Elisha revives the son of a Shunammite woman. The latter legend exhibits the most archaic features: First the prophet sent his staff to be laid on the face of the dead child, that the staff's magical power might restore him to life. When this failed, he stretched himself twice upon the child, mouth to mouth, eye to eye, hand to hand, to transmit to the child his own vital force. The first time the boy's body grew warm; the second time he sneezed, opened his eyes, and was restored to life. In the Elijah legend, the magical features are toned down: Elijah stretched himself three times upon the dead child and called upon Yahweh, who caused life to return to the dead. Even the bones of such a prophet can miraculously restore the dead to life (II Kings 13:20-21). These and other remarkable features occur in the account of prophets in the books of Kings, which clearly credit the prophets with the same powers as mantics and magicians. This notion of the virtually magical powers possessed by "men of God" and prophetical masters may reflect the original undivided nomadic culture before the advent of specialization, in which the tribal magician was identical with the tribal prophet, poet, and priest

[14] See, with many examples, J. J. Stamm, "Hebräische Ersatznamen," in *Landsberger Festschrift*, 1965, pp. 413-24.

(see § 2.5). In any case, the first narratives that speak of raising the dead exhibit an archaic background and sense of magic, albeit attenuated by incorporation into Yahwism. This survival of the forbidden element of magic explains why the hope for at least a temporary escape from the jaws of the underworld until the recurrence of inexorable death plays no rôle in the OT apart from the prophetical legends just described.

Another possibility is offered by the search for immortality, the goal pursued by Gilgamesh in the early Mesopotamian epic. Like Gilgamesh, however, according to the account of the source stratum N, early mankind failed in this pursuit. Before man could eat from the tree of life and thus gain eternal life, Yahweh drove him away from the tree, over which he then set strict guard (Gen. 3:22b-24). And when the marriages of divine beings with human women began to cause an influx of the full divine spirit of life into mankind, Yahweh limited the human life span to 120 years, that his vital force might not abide in man for ever (Gen. 6:1-4).

Finally, the notion that a man might ascend to God while still alive, a fate ascribed by the OT tradition only to Enoch and Elijah (Gen. 5:24; II Kings 2:11), which could not become a general expectation, appears to be based on alien ideas. The total length of Enoch's life is 365 years, and corresponds to the number of days in a solar year. He also parallels the seventh antediluvian Mesopotamian king, Enmeduranna, whose capital was the ancient center of the sun-god of Sippar. Just as this explains the correspondence between the years of Enoch's life and the number of days in a solar year, so too it presumably explains his translation. In any case, the chariot of fire with horses of fire in which Elijah ascends to heaven in a whirlwind is obviously connected with the chariot and horses of the sun, in which the sun-god pursues his course through the heavens. This chariot bears Elijah away. One may ask whether the translation takes place through the power of the sun-god, to the sun-god, or even as the sun-god. In the OT we are clearly no longer dealing with such conceptions, but with translation to the divine realm. But the mythological background is unmistakable.

Revival of the dead, immortality, translation—there were never more than a handful who pondered these possible hopes or were associated with them by tradition. They never affected the fundamental notion of the shades vegetating in the underworld.

CHAPTER THREE: PROPHECY,
THE THIRD INFLUENCE

§ 18 PROPHECY IN THE ANCIENT NEAR EAST AND IN ISRAEL TO THE NINTH CENTURY B.C.

E. BALLA, *Die Botschaft der Propheten*, 1958; W. CASPARI, *Die israelitischen Propheten*, 1914; A. CAUSSE, *Les prophètes d'Israel*, 1913; K. H. CORNILL, *Der israelitische Prophetismus*, 7th ed., 1912; B. DUHM, *Israels Propheten*, 1916; G. FOHRER, "Neuere Literatur zur alttestamentlichen Prophetie," *ThR*, NF XIX (1951), 277-346; XX (1952), 192-27; 295-361; *idem*, "Zehn Jahre Literatur zur alttestamentlichen Prophetie," *ibid.*, XXVIII (1962), 1-75, 235-97; 301-74; *idem*, "Die Propheten des Alten Testaments im Blickfeld neuer Forschung," in his *Studien zur alttestamentlichen Prophetie (1949-1965)*, 1967, pp. 1-17; *idem*, "Prophetie und Magie," *ibid.*, pp. 242-64; F. GIESEBRECHT, *Die Berufsbegabung der Propheten*, 1897; A. GUILLAUME, *Prophecy and Divination Among the Hebrews and Other Semites*, 1938; H. GUNKEL, *Die Propheten*, 1917; A. HALDAR, *Associations of Cult Prophets in the Ancient Near East*, 1945; J. HEMPEL, *Worte der Propheten*, 1949; G. HÖLSCHER, *Die Profeten*, 1914; A. JEPSEN, *Nabi*, 1934; A. R. JOHNSON, *The Cultic Prophet in Ancient Israel*, 2nd ed., 1962; H. JUNKER, *Prophet und Seher*, 1927; C. KUHL, *Israels Propheten*, 1956; J. LINDBLOM, *Prophecy in Ancient Israel*, 1962; F. NÖTSCHER, "Prophetie im Umkreis des alten Israel," *BZ*, NF X (1966), 161-97; J. PEDERSEN, "The Rôle Played by Inspired Persons Among the Israelites and the Arabs," in *Studies in Old Testament Prophecy* (Robinson Festschrift), 1950, pp. 127-42; R. RENDTORFF, "Erwägungen zur Frühgeschichte des Prophetismus in Israel," *ZThK*, LIX (1962), 145-67; N. H. RIDDERBOS, *Israëls profetie en "Profetie" buiten Israël*, 1955; H. H. ROWLEY, "The Nature of Old Testament Prophecy in the Light of Recent Study," *HThR*, XXXVIII (1945), 1-38 (= his *The Servant of the Lord*, 2nd ed., 1965, pp. 95-134); J. SCHARBERT, *Die Propheten Israels bis 700 v. Chr.*, 1965; W. R. SMITH, *The Prophets of Israel*, 2nd ed., 1895; B. VAWTER, *Mahner und Künder*, 1963.

1. *Prophecy in the ancient Near East.* Although in Israelite prophecy as embodied in Elijah and in the great individual prophets from Amos on we encounter a unique phenomenon, a new and distinct religious movement and approach to life that was of immense importance for the history of Yahwism and even beyond, prophecy as such was not uniquely Israelite or Yahwistic. Prophets appear in many religions and cultures, including those of the

ancient Near East.[1] The evidence for this is scanty, but this is probably due primarily—quite apart from the chance nature of archaeological discoveries—to the fact that prophets proclaimed their message orally, and it was usually not recorded in writing any more than was the torah delivered by priests. Therefore the few remarks and traditions concerning ancient Near Eastern prophets are all the more important, showing conclusively that such figures did indeed make their appearance. We can say more precisely that we have to do with two forms of prophecy, corresponding to the two types of religious background, nomadic religion and the religion of the settled area. The corresponding prophets were seers and nabis.

a) One form of prophecy was rooted in the nomadic world. On the basis of later Arab examples, we may assume that among the nomads of the ancient Near East the figure of the seer played an important rôle (Pedersen). For the early period, it is true, we have few allusions and no direct accounts. But the persistency of nomadic institutions in the bedouin world makes it likely that men of God or inspired persons appeared as seers among the nomads, proclaiming divine instructions primarily on the basis of dreams and presentiments. Thus the patriarchs or Balaam (Numbers 22–24) may correspond to the Arabic *kāhin*.

The seer was not necessarily associated with a sanctuary, as was typical of other prophetical figures. Neither, of course, was there any opposition between the seer and the sanctuary attendant, since both exercised similar powers. Indeed, in early nomadic culture the activities of priest, magician, and clan leader might coincide with those of the seer in a single person held to be inspired. As the word itself suggests, the seer's primary contact with the other, higher world was through the sense of vision; hearing played a lesser rôle. Oracles were usually based on what came into view and what the seer observed. This was true of Balaam, who had to see the Israelites before he could curse them. Like a *kāhin* in other recorded cases, he opened his soul and his spirit, ready to receive the first impression given him by outward appearances.

Finally, the poetic form of OT prophetic discourse may owe more to the deliberate and artistically composed speech of the seer than to the ecstatic stutterings of the nabi. It seems to be the case that no

---

[1] *RGG*, V, 608-13; A. F. Puukko, "Ekstatische Propheten mit besonderer Berücksichtigung der finnisch-ugrischen Parallelen," *ZAW*, LIII (1935), 23-35; H. H. Rowley, *Prophecy and Religion in Ancient China*, 1956; W. Zimmerli, *Le prophète dans l'Ancien Testament et dans l'Islam*, 1945.

Israelite prophet purporting to speak in the name of Yahweh could gain a hearing unless he clothed his speech in poetic form. Though the OT contains no explanation of this fact, the *kāhin* was often so intimately associated with a deity or demon that delivery of a seer discourse in meter was considered the mark of a person associated with the powers of the supernatural world. The ability to speak in poetic form was a remnant of this association.

b) Another form of prophecy had its roots in the settled area of the ancient Near East, and was obviously linked to the stimulating vegetation and fertility cults. We are here dealing with ecstatic prophets at sanctuaries or royal courts, who are best designated by the OT expression *nābî'*. The OT itself mentions the ecstatic prophets of the god Baal (I Kings 18:19 ff.; II Kings 10:19), and presupposes the existence of prophets as an internationally known phenomenon (Jer. 27:9).

Until very recently, the earliest evidence for the appearance of such prophets dated from about 1100 B.C.; it was therefore assumed at times that in Palestine we are dealing with the consequence of a great ecstatic movement originating about a century earlier in the course of the Aegean migration. According to this theory, this movement spread from its focus among the Thracian and Phrygian peoples and from Asia Minor throughout the rest of the ancient Near East and into southern Europe, everywhere laying the emotional groundwork for ecstatic prophecy. In the meanwhile, however, significantly earlier evidence for such prophecy has appeared; by 1100 it had long been a familiar phenomenon in the ancient Near East.

Even the Sumerians had a term for ecstatics; it probably means "the man who enters heaven." [2] In the eighteenth century B.C., in a letter from Aleppo, an ambassador of Zimrilim, king of Mari, mentions an *āpilum*, "answerer," who had a feminine counterpart and normally performed his duties at a sanctuary. [3] For the period around 1700, a series of letters from Mari, on the middle Euphrates, testifies to the appearance of male and female prophets termed *āpilum* or *muḫḫûm* and *muḫḫûtum*. [4] They belonged to a class of men and

---

[2] V. Christian, "Sum. lú-an-ná-ba-tu = akkad. maḫḫû 'Ekstatiker,'" *WZKM*, LIV (1957), 9-10.

[3] A. Malamat, "History and Prophetic Vision in a Mari Letter," *Eretz-Israel*, V (1958), 67-73.

[4] A. Lods, "Une tablette inédite de Mari, intéressante pour l'histoire ancienne du prophétisme sémitique," in *Studies in Old Testament Prophecy* (Robinson Festschrift), 1950, pp. 103-10; A. Malamat, " 'Prophecy' in the Mari Documents," *Eretz-Israel*, IV (1956), 74-84; *idem*, "Prophetic Revelations in New Documents from Mari and the Bible," *VTSuppl*, XV (1966), 207-27; M. Noth, *Geschichte und Gotteswort im Alten Testament*, 1949 (= his *Gesammelte Studien zum*

women who received mandates from the deity with whose temple they were associated through omens, dreams, or visions and ecstatic experiences, which they transmitted in the form of oracles. In the following period,[5] too, there were in Babylonia priests and priestesses who supported the king with "spoken dreams." For Assyria, we know of another type of ecstatic prophecy, exercised by priestesses known by name, especially those associated with the Ishtar Temple at Arbela. In the fifteenth century b.c., a letter of Rewašša of Taanak mentions an *ummânu* of Astarte who was expert in magic and could foresee the future.[6] The Egyptian Wen-Amon or Un-Amun tells of a voyage along the Syro-Palestinian coast (about 1100), departing from the city of Byblos: "When he [the king of Byblos] offered sacrifice to his gods, the god seized one of his older boys and drove him mad, and he said: Summon up the god, summon the messenger who has the god with him; it is Amon who sent him, it is he who caused him to come."[7] Finally, the inscription of Zakir, king of Hamath (about 800), speaks of seers and men who could foretell the future.[8] Only in Egypt is there no certain evidence for the appearance of prophets; it is still doubtful whether the texts cited are really relevant.[9] Nevertheless, Pliny reported in his *Historia naturalis* viii. 185 that during the cultic ceremony around the Apis bull young men were seized by frenzy and predicted future events.

The Mari letters deserve special attention. They tell in each case how a man or woman came without being summoned to a governor or other high official of the king, bringing a demand or message from the deity to be transmitted to the king. In most cases we are dealing with the god Dagan, in one case with the weather-god Hadad (see § 3.2). The letters frequently state that the ecstatics received

---

Alten Testament, 2nd ed., 1960, pp. 230-47; H. Schult, "Vier weitere Mari-Briefe 'prophetischen' Inhalts," *ZDPV,* LXXXII (1966), 228-32; W. von Soden, "Verkündigung des Gotteswillens durch prophetisches Wort in den altbabylonischen Briefen aus Mâri," *WdO,* I.5 (1950), 397-403; C. Westermann, "Die Mari-Briefe und die Prophetie in Israel," in his *Forschung am Alten Testament,* 1964, pp. 171-88.

  [5] *AOT,* pp. 281-84.

  [6] W. F. Albright, "A Prince of Taanach in the Fifteenth Century B.C.," *BASOR,* XCIV (1944), 12-27.

  [7] *AOT,* pp. 71-77; *ANET,* pp. 25-29.

  [8] *AOT,* pp. 443-44; *ANET,* pp. 501-2; *KAI,* No. 202.

  [9] G. Lanczkowski, "Ägyptischer Prophetismus im Lichte des alttestamentlichen," *ZAW,* LXX (1958), 31-38; *idem, Altägyptischer Prophetismus,* 1960; C. C. McCown, "Hebrew and Egyptian Apocalyptic Literature," *HThR,* XVIII (1925), 357-411; for the contrary argument, see S. Herrmann, "Prophetie in Israel und Ägypten," *VTSuppl,* IX (1963), 47-65.

the instructions (once the word "oracle" is used) of the deity in a dream; no distinction is made between dreams and vision, which are also mentioned. The requirements of the deity were addressed to the king and referred to quite diverse matters: the deity's instructions about the strategic situation when the king was at war, the construction of a city gate, the provision of sacrificial animals and the observance of sacrificial occasions. Two extracts are given by way of example:

1) Speak to my lord: Thus says your servant Itūr-asdu: On the day on which I sent this letter of mine to my lord, Malik-dagan, a man from Sakka, came to me and reported as follows: "In my dream, I and a man who was with me from the district of Sagarātum in the upper region wanted to go to Mari. In my vision I went to Terqa and immediately upon entering went into the temple of Dagan and prostrated myself before Dagan. As I lay on my knees, Dagan opened his mouth and spoke to me as follows: 'Have the sheiks ("kings") of the Benjaminites and their people made peace with the people of Zimrilim, who came forth?' I said: 'They have not made peace.' When I was on the point of leaving, he spoke again to me as follows: 'Why do the emissaries of Zimrilim not stay constantly in my presence, and why does he not give me a complete account (of everything)? Otherwise I would days ago have given the sheiks of the Benjaminites into the hand of Zimrilim. Now go. I have sent you; to Zimrilim you shall speak as follows: Send your emissaries to me and give me a complete account. Then I will cause even the sheiks of the Benjaminites to wriggle in a fish-trap and place them before you.' " This is what that man saw in his dream and said to me.

2) In oracles Hadad, the Lord of Kallassu, (spoke) as follows: "Am I not [Had]ad, lord of Kallassu, who brought him (i.e. Zimrilim) up upon my lap and placed him upon the throne of his father's house? When I had placed him upon the throne of his father's house, I also gave him a dwelling place (i.e. his palace). And now, just as I placed him upon the throne of his father's house, I shall take Neḫlatum out of his hand. If he will not give it up, I am lord of throne, earth, and city: I shall take away what I gave. If that is not the case, and if he is willing to give what I wish, I shall give to him throne upon throne, house upon house, earth upon earth, city upon city. And I shall give to him the land from the rising of the sun to its setting."

The next extract is of a different sort; in this case the *āpilum* apparently promised the king victory and dominion over other nations without any special conditions. He delivered an oracle against foreign nations concerning the imminent destruction of the enemy, thus indirectly promising salvation and deliverance of his own people; it is therefore possible to speak of nationalistic optimistic prophecy:

3) Speak to my lord: Thus (says) Mukanniŝum your servant: I had offered the sacrifices to Dagan for the life of my lord. The "answerer" of Dagan of Tutul arose; thus he spoke, namely: "Babylon, what are you still up to? I will drive ('assemble') you into the snare (?) . . . . The houses/families of the seven partners and whatever their possessions (are) I shall put into the hand of Zimrilim . . . ."

The parallels to a certain type of Israelite prophecy are unmistakable. The *āpilum* or *muḫḫûm* corresponds to the nabi; like the nabi, he used the form of the short prophetical saying. He demanded that the divine command be transmitted to the king without regard for whether it pleased the king. He criticized the king's conduct without regard for the fact that vassals of the king learned of this criticism. He delivered admonitions and warnings. If a promise was conditional, as in the first example, he expected the king to obey the divine command; but he could also promise unconditionally, as in the third example. All in all, this is very like the professional prophecy of Israel.

2. *Early Israelite prophecy*.[10] *a*) The presence in ancient Israel of both forms of ancient Near Eastern prophecy is shown by a remark in I Sam. 9:9: "He who is now called a prophet [nabi] was formerly called a seer." This suggests that the originally nomadic Israelites brought with them to Palestine the institution of the seer as represented by the patriarchs in the pre-Yahwistic period (see § 2.5), but discovered the institution of the nabi in Palestine and borrowed it. The same passage shows furthermore that the two distinct forms began to coalesce and that something new was coming into being. OT prophecy is certainly not the mere amalgamation and continuation of the two original forms; it transformed what it had borrowed and preserved into something unique and different. This took place under the influence of Yahwism, which made a crucial contribution to the existing elements—as much so in the development of prophecy as in the rest of the religious realm. Thus began a long and complicated process that was still in full swing about 1000 B.C. In this period Yahwistic seers (Nathan) and nabis (I Sam. 10:5) still existed side by side as representatives of separate phenomena. Their gradual coalescence produced OT prophecy in the strict sense, first in transi-

[10] *BHH*, III, 1496-1512; *RGG*, V, 613-18; *IDB*, III, 896-910.

tional forms that are hard to make out, more clearly in Elijah and Elisha. Following the practice of the seers, such prophets could make their appearance as individual figures independent of sanctuary and cult and without ecstatic experiences. Like the nabis, the prophets could also make their appearance in groups or bands, associated with a sanctuary and the cult, and sharing deliberately induced ecstatic experiences.

b) A few representatives of the transitional form of prophecy are preserved in the tradition. This tradition, however, has in part been subject to revision, so that it often remains an open question how much real reminiscence the tradition contains.

In the time of Solomon, Ahijah of Shiloh[11] assured the rebellious Jeroboam by means of a symbolic action that he would rule over the ten northern tribes (I Kings 11:29-31) and later predicted the death of the sick child of Jeroboam, who had meanwhile become king (I Kings 14:1-18 *).

Shemaiah [12] is said to have restrained Rehoboam from going to war against the Northern Kingdom after the division of the kingdom (I Kings 12:21-24; but cf. 14:30).

An anonymous prophet from Judah is reported to have pronounced a threat against the altar at Bethel (I Kings 12:32–13:10); but this narrative presupposes the cultic reform of Josiah. The same prophet is later said to have accepted the invitation of another prophet at Bethel contrary to Yahweh's command; on his return, he was killed by a lion and buried at Bethel (I Kings 13:11-32).

When the Israelite king was making inquiry of his prophets concerning a campaign against the Arameans, a certain Zedekiah[13] is singled out, who made iron horns and promised the king victory (I Kings 22:11). Micaiah ben Imlah,[14] on the other hand, predicted defeat and death for the king on the same occasion (I Kings 22:13-28).

Finally, II Kings 21:10-15 contains an anonymous prophetical threat against Manasseh and Jerusalem; but this is a later addition to the text.

There were surely transitional prophets beside those mentioned in the tradition. This conclusion is supported by many summary passages, although the numbers given are not to be taken literally (see I Kings 18:4; 22:6; II Kings 21:10; and the Elisha legends).

[11] *BHH*, I, 50-51; *IDB*, I, 67-68; A. Caquot, "Ahiyya de Silo et Jéroboam Iᵉʳ," *Semitica*, XI (1961), 17-27.
[12] *BHH*, III, 1769-70; *IDB*, IV, 322.
[13] *BHH*, III, 2206; *IDB*, IV, 947-48.
[14] *BHH*, II, 1210; *IDB*, III, 372.

3. *Elijah.*[15] a) Six originally independent Elijah narratives reporting his activities have been assembled in I Kings 17–19; 21; II Kings 1:1-17, together with several legendary anecdotes. These tell of a drought broken by rain, of divine judgment on Mount Carmel, of an encounter with Yahweh at Horeb, of the call of Elisha, of the judicial murder of Naboth, and of Ahaziah's request for an oracle. According to these stories, Elijah appeared in the Northern Kingdom during the period of kings Ahab and Ahaziah, i.e., between 874 and 852 B.C. He represented the class of wandering prophets, not being associated with any sanctuary or living as a member of a prophetical guild. He was obviously more like seer than a nabi.

He exercised his ministry primarily against the background of the policies pursued by Ahab, who was seeking to overcome the problem of integrating both Canaanites and Israelites into his kingdom by means of a neutral approach that accorded both groups parity and equal rights. Since Canaanite civilization had previously been checked or repressed, this policy meant in practice that it would now be promoted, which favored the advance of Canaanite religious ideas and practices. Furthermore Ahab, who considered himself a dynastic ruler of the ancient Near Eastern sort, wanted to replace the Israelite conception of kingship with the absolute monarchy typical of the ancient Near East and introduce into Israel the kind of royal law associated with absolute monarchy.

Elijah opposed Ahab on both points. He succeeded in having the Carmel region with its mixed population treated as Israelite rather than Canaanite territory, so that Yahweh alone would be worshiped there. In the case of Naboth, he supported the continued recognition of the ancient Israelite law of land ownership, rejecting the notion that the king has power over the life and property of his subjects. Finally, in such questions as who bestowed rain on the land and to whom a sick man should turn to be healed he insisted on Yahweh's unique authority, refusing Baal any recognition.

b) Elijah's message was characterized first by the assertion of traditional elements of Yahwism that were to continue to be recognized in Palestine. He supported Yahweh's claim to sole sovereignty in Israel, and showed himself a vigorous guardian of the religio-

[15] *BHH*, I, 396-97; *RGG*, II, 424-27; *IDB*, II, 88-90; G. Fohrer, *Elia*, 2nd ed., 1968; H. Gunkel, *Elias, Jahve und Baal*, 1906; C. A. Keller, "Wer war Elia?" *ThZ*, XVI (1960), 298-313; G. Molin, "Elijahu," *Judaica*, XVIII (1952), 65-94; H. H. Rowley, "Elijah on Mount Carmel," *BJRL*, XLIII (1960/61), 251-76 (= his *Men of God*, 1963, pp. 37-65).

ethical way of life that refused to let even the king infringe upon basic human rights and violate the divine command of justice, and required anyone anxious for his health or his life to turn to Yahweh rather than taking refuge in Canaanite vitalism.

In the second place, Elijah introduced new elements into the faith of Yahwism to preserve its viability within the context of an advanced civilization and political order and keep it from declining into syncretism. Thus he declared that it was Yahweh, not Baal, who bestowed or withheld rain and thereby the fertility of the land (cf. § 15:1), and turned from the notion of Yahweh as a god of war and battle to a conception of God in which Yahweh's activity is not represented by awesome eruptions and raging storms, but is characterized by quiet governance, comparable to the calm after a storm, just as Yahweh also reveals himself through his word (I Kings 19:11 ff.). It is easy to see how these influences led tradition to compare him to Moses in many points and to depict him as a new, second Moses.

Elijah differs from the later great individual prophets in that he still considered Israel to be fundamentally in a state of favor with God, which it was incumbent on the nation to maintain or to restore after an interruption. But he paved the way for those prophets by reasserting Yahweh's claim to sovereignty in such terms that they could measure Israel's failure and guilt against it.

4. *Elisha*.[16] The Elisha tradition is found in reasonably coherent form in II Kings 2; 3:4-27; 4:1-8:15; 9:1-10; 13:14-21. Its first strand comprises a narrative cycle of popular miracle stories, whose common element is their association with Gilgal, where Elisha usually lived (II Kings 4:38). This cycle brings together what were originally independent anecdotes reflecting real acts of power performed by Elisha or associating him with widespread motifs. A second group comprises a series of individual narratives of diverse character; all they have in common is their reference to the contemporary political and historical background against which Elisha played his rôle.

The anecdotes and narratives reveal two aspects of Elisha's activity. On the one hand, they show the effect he had on daily life and events within the circle of his prophetical guild and the ordinary people with whom he came in contact. On the other hand, they extend their horizon to include the authoritative figures of the politi-

[16] *BHH*, I, 399-401; *RGG*, II, 429-31; *IDB*, II, 91-92; W. Reiser, "Eschatologische Gottessprüche in den Elisalegenden," *ThZ*, IX (1953), 321-38.

cal world; in the conflict between Israel and the Arameans and in Elisha's attitude toward the reigning Israelite dynasty they agree with contemporary history. Those narratives that exhibit the prophet's hostility to the reigning dynasty (II Kings 3:4-27; 8:7-15) point to the time of Joram, the last king of the Omride dynasty. The turning point was marked by the revolution of Jehu, the intellectual authors of which included Elisha (II Kings 9:1-10), although he retreated completely into the background after it began. According to the rest of the narratives he was friendly to the reigning dynasty and hostile to the Arameans (II Kings 5; 6:8-23; 6:24–7:20; 13:14-19); these events took place in the period of Jehu's dynasty.

Unlike Elijah, Elisha gathered a guild of prophets about him with whom he usually lived in a fixed location. Although there is no mention of any permanent association with a sanctuary, this mode of life approximates that of the cult prophets. Like them, Elisha was furthermore associated with the political life of his nation and stood ready to provide oracles for the king, whom he even accompanied on a military campaign (II Kings 3:11). He therefore had political influence, which he was able to exercise on behalf of those in trouble (II Kings 4:13). Apart from this care for the needy, which was in line with the purposes of the later prophets, the significance of Elisha lay in the spirit of zeal for Yahwism that filled him–albeit not in the depth and purity of thought and action that characterized Elijah. The title of honor accorded him (II Kings 13:14) summarized the experiences of the dynasty of Jehu with him.

5. *Primitive features. a*) In the narratives about the early prophets we have just discussed we not uncommonly encounter primitive features that show that at least for popular tradition there was a certain connection between prophecy and magic.

The legends of the prophets frequently mention features reminiscent of divination, whether these features are correctly ascribed to the prophets or not. The wife of Jeroboam went in disguise to the blind prophet Ahijah to obtain an oracle about her sick son; as soon as Ahijah heard her steps, he knew who was coming to him (I Kings 14). Elijah foresaw the imminent death of Ahaziah (II Kings 1:2 ff.). Elisha knew where water could be found in the desert (II Kings 3:16-17), knew that Gehazi was hastening after Naaman (II Kings 5:25-26), knew where the Arameans were lying in ambush (II Kings 6:9), knew that the kings had given orders to kill him (II Kings 6:32), knew what the king of Damascus said in his bedchamber

(II Kings 6:12), and knew that he must die and that Hazael would be his successor (II Kings 8:10-13).

Furthermore, the prophetical legends often exhibit miraculous features that are of frankly magical nature. It does not matter whether and to what extent this sort of material is based on actual events. The tradition makes it clear that for a time such activity could be expected of prophets and viewed as one of their characteristics. Naaman, for example, assumed that Elisha would call upon Yahweh, wave his hand, and in this fashion cure him of his sickness (II Kings 5:11). A prophet could make use of visible means to perform a miracle: he could use salt to make the water of a spring wholesome (II Kings 2:19-22), meal to counteract poisoned food (II Kings 4:38-41), a cut piece of wood to retrieve the iron head of an axe from a river as though with a magnet (II Kings 6:1-7), or his staff, laid upon the face of a dead man, to restore him to life through its magical power (II Kings 4:29). If this did not succeed, he would stretch himself upon the dead man so as to transmit his own vital force (I Kings 17:21; II Kings 4:34-35). Even a prophet's bones could still miraculously restore life (II Kings 13:20-21). He was likewise able to feed a multitude with scant provisions (II Kings 4:42-44), cause the oil from a single jar to fill many jugs (II Kings 4:1-7), and prevent meal and oil from running out (I Kings 17:14-16). But he could also afflict men with sickness and blindness (II Kings 5:27; 6:18), cause bears to attack people (II Kings 2:23-25), or lightning to strike them (II Kings 1:9-12). He could even destroy an altar by means of word and sign (I Kings 13:1-5).

Some symbolic actions like those more frequently performed by the later prophets are also ascribed to the early prophets: Ahaijah of Shiloh tore his garment into twelve pieces, ten of which he gave to Jeroboam (I Kings 11:29-31); Elijah cast his mantle upon Elisha (I Kings 19:19-21); Zedekiah made himself iron horns (I Kings 22:11); Elisha had king Joash shoot an arrow toward the east and strike the ground with a bundle of arrows (II Kings 13:14-19). Here, too, we hear the echo of magical elements (§ 19.2).

Finally, there was a general belief that the word of Yahweh as spoken by a prophet possessed a kind of effectual power like that ascribed words of magic. When Jehu's arrow struck the fleeing king, it marked the realization of the word of Yahweh proclaimed by Elijah and the messenger of Elisha (I Kings 21:19; II Kings 9:25). A prophet's prediction of death and destruction in the name of Yahweh spelled inexorable doom for the wicked (cf. I Sam. 2:27-34;

4:11; and I Kings 2:26-27; II Sam. 12:11-18; I Kings 13:20-24; 14:12-18; and *passim*). Conversely, predicted deliverance was sure to come to pass (cf. I Kings 11:31-32 and 12:20; II Kings 19:6-7, 35; 20:5 ff.; and *passim*).

In view of all this, one may ask whether these conceptions about prophecy and this acquaintance with the virtually magical power of the "men of God" and prophetical masters were not an echo of ancient nomadic civilization, undifferentiated and unspecialized. This hypothesis would explain many phenomena: the special dress worn by the prophets, which seems to follow nomadic practice; possible ritual tonsure (II Kings 2:23), based on the notion that a man's hair is a locus of power; the term *'îš* (*hā-*) *'ĕlōhîm,* which ascribes to its bearer "El powers," powers superhuman and divine; and the invulnerability of these men, at least of the great masters, which could cause the death of anyone who raised his hand against them (II Kings 1:9-12; 2:23-25).

Remarkably often it is the prophet himself in the examples given who brings about the result by word or deed. In some cases, however, we can begin to make out a discontinuous or dialectical relationship of the prophet to magic. In these cases it was not the prophet himself who knew or divined the unknown; it was Yahweh who revealed it to him (I Kings 13:2; 14:5; II Kings 3:16-17). He did not act on his own authority but at Yahweh's behest (I Kings 13:3) or by appeal to Yahweh's will (II Kings 4:43). He might act by speaking Yahweh's word (I Kings 17:14 ff.) or Yahweh himself might act (II Kings 6:15 ff.; 7:1 ff.). Or the miracle might take place after or during a prayer to Yahweh (I Kings 17:20 ff.; II Kings 4:33). Here we see the surviving magical element and its significance for prophecy defined: it is the notion that prophetical words and actions are effectual—effectual because based on the will and on the power of Yahweh.

b) Ecstasy, found more frequently among the nabis, was likewise based on primitive conceptions and modes of conduct.[17] It was characterized by violent motor agitation, a kind of "frenzy," associated with a rush of speech, and occasionally accompanied by a sense of

---

[17] On the following discussion, see W. Lange-Eichbaum and W. Kurth, *Irrsinn und Ruhm,* 6th ed., 1967, pp. 209-10; also B. Baentsch, "Pathologische Züge in Israels Prophetentum," *ZWTh,* L (1907), 77-85; H. Hackmann, "Die geistigen Abnormitäten der alttestamentlichen Propheten," *NThT,* XXIII (1934), 26-48; H. Heimann, *Prophetie und Geisteskrankheit,* 1956; W. Jacobi, *Die Ekstase der alttestamentlichen Propheten,* 1920; F. Maass, "Zur psychologischen Sonderung der Ekstase," *WZ Leipzig,* III (1953/54), 297-301.

being filled and "possessed" by the deity. The early prophets—often after preparation through asceticism and isolation, by means of music, dance, or other rhythmic movement (cf. I Sam. 10:5-6; I Kings 18:26 ff.) —would deliberately use autosuggestion to achieve a state of dulled and narrowed consciousness; at times narcotics were probably made use of.[18] Primitive mechanisms could then easily take over: rolling about, rising up, paroxysms and convulsions—all meant to express the ultimate degree of emotional intoxication. Further automatisms such as do not occur in a state of full consciousness when the ego is "in control" would commence: obscure speech, "prophecies," speaking in tongues. In ancient times psychotics or epileptics thought to be holy were models for this type of ecstasy. Even the prophets themselves were sometimes called "mad." Hosea, for instance, had to face the accusation:

> The prophet is a fool,
> the man of the spirit is mad. (Hos. 9:7b)

And Shemaiah wrote to a priest at Jerusalem who was to have oversight over "every madman who prophesies" in the Temple (Jer. 29:26). It is in fact quite possible that the mentally ill occasionally were members of prophetical guilds or appeared as prophets. But ecstasy is primarily nothing more than the release of primitive elements subject to artistic and poetic exaggeration; it need not have been a symptom of mental illness in every case.

§ 19 ISRAELITE PROPHECY IN THE EIGHTH AND SEVENTH CENTURIES B.C.

L. DÜRR, Wollen und Wirken der alttestamentlichen Propheten, 1926; H. GUNKEL, Die Propheten, 1917; F. HÄUSSERMANN, Wortempfang und Symbol in der alttestamentlichen Prophetie, 1932; J. HEMPEL, "Prophet and Poet," JThSt, XL (1939), 113-32 (republished in German in his Apoxysmata, 1961, pp. 287-307) ; S. H. HOOKE, Prophets and Priests, 1938; E. JENNI, Die alttestamentliche Prophetie, 1962; W. C. KLEIN, The Psychological Pattern of Old Testament Prophecy, 1962; S. MOWINCKEL, " 'The Spirit' and the 'Word' in the Pre-Exilic Reforming Prophets," JBL, LIII (1934), 199-227; idem, Die Erkenntnis Gottes bei den alttestamentlichen Propheten, 1941; O. PLÖGER, "Priester und Prophet," ZAW, LXIII (1951), 157-92; N. W. PORTEOUS, "Prophecy," in Record and Revelation, 1938, pp. 216-49; A. C. WELCH, Prophet and Priest in Old Israel, 2nd ed., 1953; G. WIDENGREN,

---

[18] A. H. Godbey, "Incense and Poison Ordeals in the Ancient Orient," AJSL, XLVI (1929/30), 217-38; J. Hempel, Mystik und Alkoholekstase, 1926.

Literary and Psychological Aspects of the Hebrew Prophets, 1948; see also the bibliography of § 18.

1. The later history of pre-exilic prophecy.[1] Just as prophecy has a history that reaches back much further than had earlier been supposed, so too Israelite prophecy of the eighth and seventh centuries is a more extensive and complex phenomenon than is suggested by the misleading term "literary prophets" or "writing prophets," which has been commonly applied to the prophets beginning with Amos.

a) From the transitional types of prophets there gradually developed a large comprehensive group representing the dominant state of prophecy. This group was not homogeneous; it was as diverse and varied as the possibilities and demands of life itself. Considered as a whole, it is best called popular cultic professional prophecy. Apart from independent prophets who wandered about the countryside, two forms can be distinguished, although in practice they largely coincide. First were the cult prophets, found throughout the country participating in cultic observances at the sanctuaries alongside the priests or Levites. Discourses of such cult prophets are found in some Psalms or verses of Psalms (Psalms 2; 21; 81; 110; 132) and prophetical books (Nahum, Habakkuk). There were also court prophets, who exercised their ministry at the royal court—and probably also in the vicinity of other important national figures. To the extent that they were associated with a royal sanctuary, they are identical with the cult prophets. They might promise the king his desired victory before a military campaign (I Kings 22) or, like Hananiah, support the king's policies against dissenters (Jeremiah 28). This large group of professional prophets includes those condemned as false prophets in the OT.

Since there were still professional prophets in the post-exilic period, we are dealing with a professional class that maintained its existence for several centuries and played an important rôle in Israel. The function of these prophets was primarily to provide divine oracles, whether in answer to an inquiry or simply whenever the "spirit" of Yahweh came upon them, thus proclaiming Yahweh's will or instructions. Conversely, they would intercede with Yahweh as representatives of the king, the people, or a single individual. In this ministry they, like the priests, were mediators between God and man.

Theologically, the professional prophets adhered largely to the

[1] *RGG,* V, 618-27.

cultic approach and that of religious nationalism (§ 13.4-5), although they must not be forced into a Procrustean schema, and allowance must be made for various emphases. In Nahum the nationalistic element was dominant; in Habakkuk, it took second place to the cultic and truly prophetical elements. The fundamental fact is that these various religious tendencies coalesced to form a new unity in the professional prophets. The individual elements can be determined by exegetical analysis; but they cannot be eliminated from the total context in case they appear theologically suspect in order to yield a purified cult-prophetical discourse. For these prophets did not merely support cultic or nationalistic ideas on certain occasions; they integrated these ideas completely into their theology.

b) More important than the professional prophets—indeed, second only to Moses in importance for the history of Yahwism—is the small group comprising the great individual prophets, including Amos and Hosea, Isaiah and Micah, Zephaniah and Jeremiah, Ezekiel and in part Deutero-Isaiah. They did not exercise their prophetical ministry as members of a profession but on the basis of a special call that snatched them from their original profession. In them Israelite prophecy reached its summit; and although they are lumped with other forms under the common heading of "prophecy," there is more to distinguish them from than to identify them with these forms. They came forward among their people not as members of a guild or of a class, not as representatives of a tribe or of a clan, not as functionaries of a sanctuary or of the king, but as conscious representatives and messengers of their God.

We must therefore keep constantly in mind that prophecy meant something different to the Israelite of the monarchy than it does to our retrospective vision. The Israelite thought primarily of the professional prophets as the prophetical class; alongside them the great individual prophets made their appearance as extraordinary figures only in isolation and in part at very different times. Beginning with the Babylonian Exile this perspective began to change: people realized that these few prophets had been right and all the professional prophets wrong. In the post-exilic period therefore cult prophecy more and more lost its importance, while the discourses and accounts of the great individual prophets were collected whenever possible, and these collections gradually took on the character of holy writ. By contrast only a relatively few discourses of professional prophets were preserved.

Up to this point, our survey of the history of prophecy shows that

Prophecy, the Third Influence

the great individual prophets constitute only a very small fraction of prophecy as a whole, albeit the most important fraction theologically. In the following discussion, therefore, when we speak of "prophets" we are usually referring to these great individual prophets.

2. *Prophetical experience and ministry.*[2] *a*) A prophet's ministry began with his call experience (see Isa. 6; Jer. 1:4-10; Ezek. 1:1–3:15).[3] It might be pursued continuously despite opposition or rejection on the part of his listeners (e.g., Hos. 9:7*b*; Ezek. 12:21 ff.) ; it might be broken off by external coercion (Amos 7:10 ff.) or by the prophet himself on account of failure (Isa. 8:16-18) ; or on account of his inward conversion to a new message (Ezek. 3:22-27; 24:25-27; 33:21-22) it might be temporarily interrupted. The prophet's words were usually spoken to those for whom his message was intended. The discourses were therefore primarily meant to be recited orally; preservation in written form usually took place subsequently. In addition, the prophets frequently performed symbolic actions, which constituted a second form of proclamation supplementary to prophetical discourse.

b) Prophetical discourse usually took shape through a process of some length involving at least four steps.

The first stage, and thus the ultimate source of prophetical activity, was a moment of deep personal contact with God, in which the "spirit" or "word" of Yahweh came upon the prophet. Among the early nabis and the cult prophets, the spirit was an impelling force, but ambiguous and diffuse. The great individual prophets, on the other hand, usually looked with suspicion on the gift of the spirit, precisely because it gave rise to the words of the cult prophets, which were often objectionable. The individual prophets appealed rather to the word of Yahweh, which encountered them as an alien force, imposed itself against their personal wishes and inclinations, showing itself to be God's word through its persuasive content and consistent demands, which shatter the ordinary human response to life, giving rise to a new approach that differs from what went before not only in degree but in essence. In such a moment of contact

[2] J. Hempel, "Prophetische Offenbarung," *ZSTh*, IV (1926), 91-112; F. Horst, "Die Visionsschilderungen der alttestamentlichen Propheten," *EvTh*, XX (1960), 193-205; J. Lindblom, "Die Gesichte der Propheten," *StTh*, I (1935), 7-28; S. Mowinckel, "Ecstatic Experience and Rational Elaboration in the Old Testament Prophecy," *AcOr* (Leiden), X (1935), 264-91; I. P. Seierstad, *Die Offenbarungserlebnisse der Propheten Amos, Jesaja und Jeremia,* 2nd ed., 1965.
[3] *BHH*, I, 222-23; *RGG*, I, 1084-86.

with God the prophet had a "secret experience" (Gunkel). Apart from dreams,[4] which, like the gift of the spirit, were suspect (Jer. 23:25 ff.), we can recognize four types of such experiences, which took place at least partially in abnormal psychic states: visions (internal sight, e.g., Isaiah 6);[5] auditions (internal hearing, e.g., Jer. 4:5-8, 13-16, 19-22); sudden inspiration (e.g., Isa. 7:10-17); and miraculous knowledge (e.g., the "foe from the north" in the early period of Jeremiah's ministry). Visions and auditions often occurred together.

Often the secret experiences of even the great individual prophets were obviously accompanied by ecstatic experiences, such as are best observed in the case of Ezekiel. But ecstasy had no independent significance in its own right and was not an isolated phenomenon; it merely accompanied the secret experience. Furthermore, although it might occur in this context, it was not obligatory. Thus it came about as a possible accompanying phenomenon to secret experiences, exposing the prophet to more or less powerful agitation and emotion. If it occurred, the mind reeled, fear and trembling overwhelmed the prophet, his hair stood on end, and his feet refused to obey (Isa. 21:1-10).

The second stage was the prophet's interpretation of his experience. This interpretation was completely dominated by the faith through which the prophet lived, which was now intensified and reshaped by the force of the new experience. For the new experience was interpreted in such a way that the particular experience was incorporated into the existing picture of Yahweh's nature and will, making it come alive afresh.

As the third stage there was added the rational processing of the experience. If the content of the secret experience was to be articulated as the divine obligation required so that it could become effectual in the outward world, it had to be translated into rational and comprehensible words; it could not remain the babbling of glossolalia. This translation was so much a matter of course that the faith of the prophet himself often contributed the appropriate motivation, or that the logical consequences of the experience were incorporated into the words spoken by Yahweh.

The fourth stage, which paralleled the third, was reduction of the message to artistic form; this likewise was a matter of course. According to the belief of the period, all oracles—including propheti-

[4] *BHH*, III, 2023-25; *RGG*, VI, 1001-5; *IDB*, I, 1868-69.
[5] *BHH*, III, 2109-10; *RGG*, VI, 1409-10; *IDB*, IV, 791.

cal oracles—had to be communicated in poetically structured form. There is therefore no genuine prophetical saying not in the form of poetry.

From this description we may see how the phenomenon known as false prophecy[6] came into being. Either there was no secret experience giving rise to it, so that everything said was without foundation, or the secret experience was erroneously interpreted by the prophet or wrongly applied.

c) The prophets performed the following symbolic actions:[7]

Hos.	1:2-9	Hosea's first marriage and naming of his children;
Hos.	3	Hosea's second marriage;
Isa.	7:3	presupposed naming of one of Isaiah's children;
Isa.	8:1-4	naming of another child of Isaiah;
Isa.	20	wearing the clothing of a captive;
Jer.	13:1-11	hiding of a waistcloth;
Jer.	16:1-4	Jeremiah's renunciation of marriage and children;
Jer.	16:5-7	Jeremiah's renunciation of mourning;
Jer.	16:8-9	Jeremiah's renunciation of feasting;
Jer.	19:1, 2a, 10-11a, 14-15	breaking of a flask;
Jer.	27:1-3, 12b	bearing a yoke;
Jer.	28:10-11	breaking of the yoke (Hananiah);
Jer.	32:1, 7-15	buying a field;
Jer.	43:8-13	burying of stones at Tahpanhes;
Jer.	51:59-64	sinking in the Euphrates of a book containing prophecies of disaster;
Ezek.	3:16a; 4:1-3	portrayal of a city under siege;
Ezek.	4:4-8	Ezekiel's lying motionless;
Ezek.	4:9-17	baking of bread;
Ezek.	5:1-14	cutting, division, and destruction of hair;
Ezek.	12:1-11	departure like a deported exile;
Ezek.	12:17-20	trembling while eating and drinking;
Ezek.	21:11-12 (Eng. 21:6-7)	collapse and sighing;
Ezek.	21:23-29 (Eng. 21:18-24)	marking and distinction of ways;
Ezek.	24:1-14	boiling and tempering of a pot;
Ezek.	24:15-24	omission of mourning customs;
Ezek.	3:22-27; 24:25-27; 33:21-22	dumbness and renewal of speech;
Ezek.	37:15-28	joining of two inscribed sticks;
Zech.	6:9-15	coronation of Zerubbabel.

[6] E. Osswald, *Falsche Prophetie im Alten Testament,* 1962; G. Quell, *Wahre und falsche Propheten,* 1952; G. von Rad, "Die falschen Propheten," *ZAW,* LI (1933), 109-20.

[7] G. Fohrer, *Die symbolischen Handlungen der Propheten,* 2nd ed., 1968; idem, "Die Gattung der Berichte über symbolische Handlungen der Propheten," in his *Studien zur alttestamentlichen Prophetie (1949-1965),* 1967, pp. 92-112.

These actions were really performed, as the occasional remarks about their performance, the astonished questions of the people, and the reply of the prophet show. They were carried out deliberately and with full awareness, not as involuntary responses to subconscious drives, because they often extended over several years. They were performed for a specific purpose; they did not originate in a whim or caprice of the prophet.

These actions accompanied the words of spoken prophecy as a kind of variant, resulting from a prophetical act. Far more than any words could, they emphasized that the message of the prophets was to be an effectual message. This becomes clear when we inquire into the origin of the symbolic actions. It turns out that they were based on magical actions, i.e., actions whose performance was intended to achieve a specific purpose. Anciently this purpose was in fact thought to be achieved by the action. Thus striking examples from the magical realm can be cited for all the prophetical actions. These examples, however, show not only the originally intimate association between magic and the symbolic acts of the prophets, but also the clear difference between them. According to the belief of the prophets, their actions did not produce the symbolized events mechanically *ex opere operato*. For the prophets, assurance that the event would take place was grounded in the power of Yahweh and his will to realize in truth what the symbolic acts declared. Therefore accounts of symbolic acts often include Yahweh's directive to perform them and his promise to realize what they proclaim.

The prophets thus considered their symbolic acts effectual not in consequence of magically coercive power but as God's declaration through his authorized representatives of what he was about to do. Indeed, the prophets not only declared God's intent but also through their actions brought about the events announced. And their contemporaries, all of whom undoubtedly knew of such symbolic acts, understood them as effectual proclamation.

d) The literary types enshrining the prophetical message are discussed in introductory studies.[8] They may be summarized in three groups: prophetical sayings; prophetical accounts; and imitations of rhetorical forms deriving from other fields.

The prophetical sayings are intended to declare Yahweh's will as it

[8] S-F, § 53.4.

determines the future in consequence of man's present attitude and conduct. They include:

> prophetical oracles;
> sayings proclaiming disaster or threats;
> sayings proclaiming deliverance or assurances;
> invectives;
> admonitions or warnings.

The prophetical accounts do not represent a later group of forms; some exhibit primitive forms that later lost their importance. They include:

> narrative seer sayings;
> accounts of visions;
> accounts of auditions;
> accounts of visions and auditions (summons narratives);
> accounts of symbolic actions.

The imitative forms, some of which exhibit extensive development, derive primarily from the realms of daily life, the cult, wisdom instruction, historical narrative, and law. The striking frequency of their use shows clearly the altered situation of the prophets that employed them: the traditional, purely prophetical forms no longer sufficed the great individual prophets and the later eschatological prophets for the proclamation of their message, so that they had to have recourse to forms as yet uncommon.

e) Our previous mention of ecstasy and symbolic acts shows that even the great individual prophets still exhibited primitive characteristics. This also helps explain the belief in the effectuality of the words spoken by Yahweh through the prophets. Even the sayings formulated by the prophets in their own right and not ascribed to Yahweh could claim a similar power. Unlike ineffectual dreams, the divine word is like a hammer that breaks the rock in pieces (Jer. 23:29). It hews like a sword and slays (Hos. 6:5); it lights upon Israel so that the entire nation feels it (Isa. 9:7-8 [Eng. 9:8-9]); in the prophet's mouth it becomes a fire that devours the people like wood (Jer. 5:14); therefore the land cannot bear this word at will (Amos 7:10). For when Yahweh lifts his voice and roars, the pastures and the forests of Carmel wither (Amos 1:2).

Primitive conceptions were still at work in the borrowing of rhetorical forms with a magical background (taunt song and dirge;

ideas, images, and phrases deriving from ancient Near Eastern curses) ; in the geographical arrangement of oracles against foreign nations, a variant of the schema used by the Egyptian execration texts; and in the written recording and transmission of the spoken word in order to preserve its effectiveness.

It is true that total association of prophetical words and actions with Yahweh did not absolutely overcome the original magical element. It can still be glimpsed behind the notion of the effectuality of these words and actions, in knowledge of the future, and above all in the power of the prophets to influence the future—but this effectual power was grounded in the will and power of Yahweh.

3. *Amos.*[9] a) Amos came from Tekoa, located about twelve miles south of Jerusalem in the fringe between settled territory and steppe. He lived there as a herdsman or shepherd (1:1; 7:14), and apparently also engaged in the cultivation of sycamore trees (7:14), so that he may even have been a property owner. In any case, he led an independent, thoroughly "middle class" existence until he felt himself snatched from it by the personal call of Yahweh (7:15). There is no reason to think of Amos as an occasional or permanent cult prophet or functionary on account of the apparently ambiguous statement in 7:14a or on the basis of form-critical analyses.[10] In 7:14a, Amos is merely telling the high priest Amaziah, who sends him to earn his living in Judah, that the profession from which Yahweh has called him and sent him to Israel provides his subsistence, and that he does not have to rely on income from his prophetical ministry. Form-critical study does not furnish any extensive insights for our understanding of Amos. The mere use of certain rhetorical forms proves very little, since they can always take on a function totally different from that corresponding to their original *Sitz im Leben.*

[9] K. Cramer, *Amos,* 1930; J. L. Crenshaw, "The Influence of the Wise upon Amos," *ZAW,* LXXIX (1967) , 42-52; F. Dijkema, "Le fond des prophéties d'Amos," *OTS,* II (1943) , 18-34; R. Fey, *Amos und Jesaja,* 1963; P. Humbert, "Quelques aspects de la religion d'Amos," *RThPh,* NS XVII (1929) , 241-55; A. S. Kapelrud, *Central Ideas in Amos,* 1956; L. Köhler, *Amos,* 1917; V. Maag, *Wortschatz und Begriffswelt des Buches Amos,* 1951; A. Neher, *Amos,* 1950; H. Graf Reventlow, *Das Amt des Propheten bei Amos,* 1962; H. Schmidt, *Der Prophet Amos,* 1917; R. Smend, "Das Nein des Amos," *EvTh,* XXIII (1963) , 404-23; S. Terrien, "Amos and Wisdom," in *Israel's Prophetic Heritage* (Muilenburg Festschrift) , 1962, pp. 108-15; J. D. W. Watts, *Vision and Prophecy in Amos,* 1958; A. Weiser, *Die Profetie des Amos,* 1929; H. W. Wolff, *Amos' geistige Heimat,* 1964.
[10] For a detailed discussion, see S-F, § 63.1.

Amos exercised his prophetical ministry during the reign of Jeroboam II (786/82 to 753/46; 1:1; 7:9 ff.). The subject matter of his discourses suggests that Israel was then enjoying political, economic, and cultural prosperity, and could boast of important successes (6:1, 13). This comports with the middle or closing period of Jeroboam's reign, so that Amos' ministry can be dated between 760 and 750 B.C.

Although he was a Judahite, his mission sent him to the Northern Kingdom of Israel. He probably made his first appearance in Samaria, the capital (see 3:9 ff.; 4:1 ff.; 6:1-2) ; then he put in his most important appearance in the course of a festival at the royal sanctuary of Bethel. But his ministry lasted only a short time. Since his words hit the mark, the high priest accused him before the king of inciting to riot, and he was banished from the kingdom (7:10-17). Thereupon he probably returned to his home, without appearing again as a prophet.

Of Amos' message there have been preserved five vision accounts, one extended series of discourses (1:3–2:16), and twenty-seven individual discourses, mostly short, comprising primarily invectives and threats. To these have been added several later passages deriving from the exilic or post-exilic period (1:2, 9-12; 2:4-5; 3:7; 4:13; 5:8-9; 8:8; 9:5-6, 8-15).[11]

b) Fundamental to Amos' message is his "No!" to social conditions in Israel, to its cult, to its understanding of history, and to its way of life in general. Israel does not automatically live in a state of favor with Yahweh; therefore it cannot claim any superiority on the basis of its election by Yahweh (3:2) or its deliverance from Egypt (9:7) —except possibly swifter retribution for its wickedness. For Yahweh has led other nations as he has led Israel:

> "Are you not like the Ethiopians to me,
> O people of Israel?" says Yahweh.
> "Did I not bring up Israel
>   from the land of Egypt,
> and the Philistines from Caphtor
> and the Syrians from Kir?" (9:7)

There are therefore fundamental rules expressing God's will for the relationship between nations; Yahweh punishes transgressions of these rules even when Israel is not involved:

[11] For a detailed discussion, see S-F, § 63.3-4.

> For three transgressions of Moab,
>   and for four, I will not revoke the punishment;
> because he burned to lime
>   the bones of the king of Edom.[12]   (2:1)

Yahweh will likewise punish the sins of Israel, which has committed apostasy despite its obligation to obey—thanks, for instance, to the raising up of Nazirites and prophets (2:11). As the primary evidence of this apostasy Amos cited the social and cultic transgressions that constitute his principal points of attack:

> Woe to those who are at ease in Zion,[13]
>   and to those who feel secure on the mountain of
>   Samaria,
> the notable men of the first of the nations,
>   *the lords* of the house of Israel!
> O you who put far away the evil day,
>   and bring near *devastation and* violence.
> Woe to those who lie upon beds of ivory,
>   and stretch themselves upon their couches,
> and eat lambs from the flock,
>   and calves from the midst of the stall;
> who sing idle songs to the sound of the harp,
>   and like David invent for themselves *all kinds* of music;
> who drink wine in bowls.
>   and anoint themselves with the finest oils.
> Therefore they shall now be the first of those to go into
>   exile,
>   and the revelry of those who stretch themselves shall
>   pass away.   (6:1-7)

> I hate, I despise your feasts,
>   and I take no delight in your solemn assemblies.
> Your offerings do not please me,
>   the concluding offerings of your fatted beasts I will not
>   look upon.
> Take away from me the noise of *your* songs,
>   to the melody of *your* harps I will not listen.
> But let justice roll down like waters,
>   and righteousness like an ever-flowing stream. (5:21-24)

---

[12] With respect to this procedure, otherwise unknown in the ancient Near East, see the discovery in Nabatean (formerly Edomite) territory reported by G. and A. Horsfield, "Sela-Petra, the Rock of Edom and Nabatene III, The Excavations," *QDAP*, VIII (1938, 87-115.

[13] "Zion" here does not refer to Jerusalem, but stands in parallel to "the mountain of Samaria" as a general term for the site of a capital.

A third, less frequent point of attack was the worship of foreign gods:

> "You have taken up *Sakkuth*
> and *Kaiwan* your images,
>   which you made for yourselves.
> Therefore I will take you into exile
> far beyond Damascus,"
>   says Yahweh.   (5:26-27; cf. 3:14; 8:14, emended)

Yahweh nevertheless tried repeatedly to bring Israel to its senses. He is the source of all disasters (3:3-6); he thus sent various plagues, easily comprehensible admonitions to repent—but in vain (4:6-11). Now, therefore, Israel is faced with destruction on the Day of Yahweh, the traditional beneficent significance of which Amos turned on its head (5:18-20). Israel will perish utterly unless the repentance and conversion that it has hitherto refused take place at the last minute—interpreted by Amos as seeking Yahweh (5:4) and doing good (5:14). Even in this case Yahweh preserves his freedom of action: Israel's repentance does not oblige Yahweh to forgive:

> Seek good, and not evil,
>   that you may live;
> and so Yahweh will be with you,
>   as you (now) say.
> Hate evil, and love good,
>   and establish justice in the gate;
> it may be that Yahweh
>   will be gracious to the remnant of Joseph.
>   (5:14-15)

4. *Hosea.*[14] a) Like Amos, Hosea exercised his ministry in the Northern Kingdom of Israel. Unlike Amos, he was probably also a native of the Northern Kingdom. Little else can be determined about his origin except that he belonged to the educated class, as is shown by his knowledge of the past, his verdict upon history and the

---

[14] F. Buck, *Die Liebe Gottes beim Propheten Osee,* 1953; A. Caquot, "Osée et la royauté," *RHPhR,* XLI (1961), 123-46; W. Eichrodt, "'The Holy One in Your Midst,' the Theology of Hosea," *Interpr,* XV (1961), 259-73; E. Jacob, "L'héritage cananéen dans le livre du prophéte Osée," *RHPhR,* XLIII (1963), 250-59; *idem,* "Der Prophet Hosea und die Geschichte," *EvTh,* XXIV (1964), 281-90; H. G. May, "The Fertility Cult in Hosea," *AJSL,* LXVIII (1931/32), 73-98; H. S. Nyberg, *Studien zum Hoseabuche,* 1935; G. Östborn, *Yahweh and Ba'al,* 1956; N. H. Snaith, *Mercy and Sacrifice,* 1953; T. C. Vriezen, *Hosea: profeet en cultuur,* 1941; H. W. Wolff, "Hoseas geistige Heimat," *ThLZ,* LXXXI (1956), 83-94 (= his *Gesammelte Studien zum Alten Testament,* 1964, pp. 232-50).

present, and his style. Since his language also exhibits wisdom influence, he may well have been educated at a wisdom school, such as served primarily for the training of royal officials.

We might gain further insight into his personal circumstances from the accounts of his marriage and children if their interpretation were not so disputed. According to the first account (1:2-9), Hosea was to marry "a wife of harlotry" named Gomer Bath Diblaim and beget children, who were given the symbolic names Jezreel, Not Pitied, and Not My People. According to the second account (3:1-5a), he was to marry "again," this time "a woman who is an adulteress," so as to keep her locked up from the rest of the world, not even visiting her himself. The very offensiveness of these proceedings has led to many suggested interpretations,[15] of which the following is probably the most likely: The two accounts refer to two marriages of Hosea with two different women, and are to be understood in the context of the symbolic acts performed by the prophets. First he married a prostitute, probably a sacral prostitute, and begot children by her whose symbolic names were intended to proclaim the calamitous future destiny of Israel. He later contracted a second marriage with another woman; this marriage was intended to proclaim Yahweh's gracious treatment of Israel in place of annihilating judgment. The difference between the two symbolic actions shows how the prophet of judgment became the prophet of hope and redemption. Using this change as a point of departure we cannot distinguish well-defined periods in Hosea's ministry, but it is possible to make out a gradual transformation of his message.

Hosea's prophetical ministry lasted nearly three decades. It began while the dynasty of Jehu was still on the throne, probably during the reign of Jeroboam II (cf. 1:1, 4), and extended through the period of internal confusion and regicide following the fall of this dynasty, as well as the Syro-Ephraimite War (736-733), into the days of Hoshea, the last king of Northern Israel (cf. 7:11-12; 12:2); but it ended before the fall of the Northern Kingdom. As the period of Hosea's ministry we may therefore assume the years from between 755 and 750 to 725 B.C. Besides his appearances at Samaria, he may have put in an occasional appearance at a sanctuary such as Bethel or Gilgal.

The text of Hosea's discourses, which were rescued and brought to Judah after the fall of the Northern Kingdom and there revised,

---

[15] For a detailed discussion see S-F, § 61.2; G. Fohrer, *Die symbolischen Handlungen der Propheten*, 2nd ed., 1968.

has suffered considerably in transmission. It is also difficult to define the basic units, because introductory and concluding formulas are often lacking. The opinion of scholars has therefore varied: some assume numerous very short sayings; others think in terms of fewer but longer sayings or complexes. A great variety of rhetorical forms occurs: besides the traditional prophetical sayings, we may mention prophetical judgment discourse, historical analysis, prophetical liturgy, and argument. Later additions have also been included in the Hosea tradition (apart from minor glosses, 2:1-3, 6-7, 8-9, 12, 14 [Eng. 1:10–2:1, 4-5, 6-7, 10, 12]; 4:15; 5:5; 7:13*b*-14; 11:11; 12:1; 14:10 [Eng. 14:9]).[16]

b) Hosea's message is dominated by the severe tension between Yahweh's conduct toward Israel and the conduct of Palestinian Israel toward Yahweh, between their once unclouded relationship and the relationship that has for centuries been practically destroyed. The Israelites are Yahweh's sons, whom he called from Egypt as a father (11:1). The relationship between Yahweh and Israel is like marriage (1:2 ff.; 2:18 [Eng. 2:16]; 3). This relationship, which is traced back to the deliverance from Egypt (12:10 [Eng. 12:9]; 13:4), is not based on any "election" of Israel; in line with the images and similes from the realm of family and personal relations, it is based on love (11:1). But this unclouded relationship that existed in the Mosaic and desert period came to an end when the Israelites became acquainted with Canaanite religion and the luxury of civilization—not because Israel lived thereafter within the realm of agricultural and urban civilization, but because within the realm of this civilization it fell prey to Baal:

> Like grapes in the wilderness
> I found Israel.
> Like the first fruit on the fig tree
> I saw *their* fathers.
> But they came to Baal-peor,
>   and consecrated themselves to *Baal,*
> and became detestable like their lovers.   (9:10)

> It was I who *pastured them* in the wilderness,
>   in the land of drought.
> *When I had pastured them* they became full;
>   they became full and their heart became
>   presumptuous.   (13:5-6)

[16] For a detailed discussion, see S-F § 61.3-4.

The whole subsequent history of Israel in Palestine is characterized by apostasy from Yahweh and faithlessness toward him. Despite the warnings of the prophets and the word of Yahweh (6:5), the people remained rebellious down to the time of Hosea (1:4; 9:9; 10:9). Israel as a woman committed adultery and fornication; to illustrate this fact and its consequences Hosea began his ministry with the symbolic action of marrying a prostitute and giving his children ominous names (1:2-9).

Amos rejected the cult as a means of salvation primarily on ethical grounds, opposing it to the practice of justice in daily life. Hosea attacked the cult because it was in fact not directed toward the God of Israel, but to a baalized Yahweh or to Baal himself, and was therefore sinful:

> Because Ephraim has multiplied altars for sinning,
>   they have become to him altars for sinning.
> Were I to write for him *my laws by ten thousands,*
>   they would be regarded (merely) as the laws of a stranger.
> *They love sacrifice, therefore they sacrifice,*
>   flesh, and therefore they eat it.   (8:11-13*a*)

The second point attacked by the prophet was Israel's domestic and foreign policy. The political convulsions of his time left a deep mark on him, and they re-echo through his discourses. He announced the end of the monarchy, which had become a plaything in the hands of pro- and anti-Assyrian power blocs, and looked upon the great powers of his age—Assyria and Egypt—as the forces that would bring about Israel's downfall:

> *Where* now is your king, to save you;
>   *where are all your princes,* to give you justice?
> I will indeed give you a king in my anger,
>   and take him away in my wrath.   (13:10-11)

> Ephraim is like a dove,
>   silly and without sense,
> calling to Egypt for help,
>   going to Assyria.
> Whenever they go, I will spread
>   my net over them;
> I will bring them down like birds of the air;
>   *I will catch them with the throwing-stick.*   (7:11-12)

All this suggests that at first Hosea expected only divine judgment:

destruction like that which befell Admah and Zeboiim (11:8) or
revocation of the exodus and new enslavement (9:1-6; 11:1-7):

> Shall I ransom them from the power of Sheol?
> Shall I redeem them from Death?
> O Death, *where* are your plagues?
> O Sheol, *where* is your destruction?
> Compassion is hid from my eyes. (13:14)

Only return to Yahweh offers a possibility of deliverance (5:15–6:6),
to which he will respond with mercy (10:12-13*a*; 14:2-9 [Eng. 14:1-8]):

> Return to your God, O Israel,
>   for you have stumbled because of your iniquity.
> Take with you words
>   and return to Yahweh.

Say to him:

> *"You can take away all iniquity*
>   *so that we receive* what is good.
> Assyria shall not save us,
>   we will not ride upon horses;
> and we will say no more, Our God,
>   to the work of our hands."

> I will be as the dew to Israel;
>   he shall blossom as the lily,
> he shall strike root as the *poplar;*
>   his shoots shall spread out;
> his beauty shall be like the olive,
>   and his fragrance like Lebanon.
> What has Ephraim to do with idols?
>   I am now *his Anat* and *Asherah;*
> I am like an evergreen cypress,
>   from me comes *his fruit.* (14:2-9 [Eng. 14:1-8])

But when Hosea was forced to recognize that man cannot free
himself at will from the disaster into which he has plunged himself
(5:3-4; 13:12-13), that man's guilt indeed imposes restrictions even
on Yahweh (6:11*b*–7:2), he took an audacious and crucial step
toward belief in redemption: [17] God's grace does not wait for man's

[17] G. Farr, "The Concept of Grace in the Book of Hosea," *ZAW*, LXX (1958),
98-107; G. Fohrer, "Umkehr und Erlösung beim Propheten Hosea," in his *Studien
zur alttestamentlichen Prophetie (1949-1965)*, 1967, pp. 222-41.

conversion before it takes effect; on the contrary, it precedes, while man's response and action follows. Hosea's belief in redemption expressed itself first in the expectation that Israel would be led back to its pre-Palestinian situation and thus quite concretely to the sources of its faith, there to make a new beginning (12:10 [Eng. 12:9]; 3). Yahweh will actually woo Israel into accepting help and then once more lead Israel into Palestine to live in intimate, unbroken communion with him as in the days of her youth—this time in the midst of civilization (2:16-25 [Eng. 2:14-23]) :

> Therefore, behold, I will allure her,
>   and bring her into the wilderness and speak tenderly to her.
> And then I will give her back her vineyards,
>   and make the valley of Achor a door of hope.
> She shall *go up* as in the days of her youth,
>   as at the time when she came out of the land of Egypt.
>   (2:16-17 [Eng. 2:14-15])

Thus at the end will stand blessing, grounded in the redemptive grace of Yahweh, who brings about the complete transformation of Israel:

> In that day I will answer the heavens,
>   and they shall answer the earth;
> and the earth shall answer the grain and wine,
>   and they shall answer "Jezreel."
> I will sow him once more in the land;
> I will have pity on Not Pitied,
>   and I will say to Not My People, "You are my people";
>   and they shall say, "My God."   (2:23-25 [Eng. 2:21-23])

5. *Isaiah*.[18] a) Isaiah came from Jerusalem and grew up there. He was apparently of noble birth (cf. Isa. 7:3; 8:2; 22:15-16). That he received a corresponding formal education can be concluded from his use of wisdom forms and expressions. He was married to a woman referred to explicitly as a "prophetess" (8:3). His sons Shear-jashub

[18] S. H. Blank, *Prophetic Faith in Isaiah*, 1958; K. Budde, "Über die Schranken, die Jesajas prophetischer Botschaft zu setzen sind," *ZAW*, XLI (1923), 154-203; *idem, Jesajas Erleben*, 1928; B. S. Childs, *Isaiah and the Assyrian Crisis*, 1967; R. Fey, *Amos und Jesaja*; J. Fichtner, "Jahves Plan in der Botschaft des Jesaja," *ZAW*, LXIII (1951), 16-33 (= his *Gottes Weisheit*, 1965, pp. 27-44) ; S. M. Gozzo, *La dottrina teologica del Libro di Isaia*, 1962; G. Hölscher, "Jesaja," *ThLZ*, LXXVII (1952), 683-94; O. St. Virgulin, *La "Fede" nella profezia d'Isaia*, 1961; T. C. Vriezen, "Essentials of the Theology of Isaiah," in *Israel's Prophetic Heritage* (Festschrift Muilenburg) , 1962, pp. 128-46; *idem, Jahwe en zijn stad*, 1962; F. Wilke, *Jesaja und Assur*, 1905.

("Remnant That Returns"; 7:3) and Maher-shalal-hashbaz ("Speed-spoil Haste-prey"; 8:3) were involved in his prophetical ministry through their symbolic names.

Isaiah experienced his call to be a prophet in the year King Uzziah (Azariah) died, 746 or 740 B.C. (6:1). He exercised his ministry during the reigns of Jotham, Ahaz, and Hezekiah, a time of political turmoil; his last discourses date from the year 701. In the first period of his ministry, from his call to the time just before the Syro-Ephraimite War (746 or 740 to 736), he devoted himself primarily to controversy concerning the domestic situation in Judah following a period of political and economic prosperity. The second period encompasses the Syro-Ephraimite War, during which Damascus and the Northern Kingdom of Israel tried to force Judah to join their anti-Assyrian alliance (736-733). Isaiah opposed both this alliance and the policies of Ahaz, the king of Judah, who wanted to declare himself an Assyrian vassal and summon the Assyrians to help repel the aggressor. When this nevertheless took place, Isaiah withdrew for several years following his failure (8:16-18). Only when Hezekiah made his first attempt in league with other states to free himself from vassal status (716-711) did Isaiah come forward again for a third period of activity, uttering new warnings against the policies embarked upon. After the revolt collapsed he fell silent once more. The fourth period falls in the years of Hezekiah's second attempt to restore the independence of Judah through a general revolt in Palestine with the support of Egypt (705-701). This attempt led to the devastation of Judah, the loss of extensive regions, a threat to Jerusalem, and the complete submission of Hezekiah. According to an apocryphal legend, Isaiah died a martyr under Manasseh, the next king.

The Isaiah tradition constitutes only a part of the book of Isaiah, namely chapters 1–39; the book as a whole became a storehouse of later anonymous prophetical discourses.[19] The discourses and reports of Isaiah, in part fragmentary, are contained in the following sections: 1:2-31; 2:6–4:1; 5:1-24 + 10:1-3; 6:1–8:22; 9:7-20 [Eng. 9:8-21] + 5:25-29; 10:5-15, 27b-32; 14:24-32; 17:1-6; 18; 20; 22:1-19; 28:1–32:14 (after deletion of the later additions 3:10-11; 7:23-25; 8:9-10; 29:17-24; 30:18-26; 32:1-8).

The most important extensive complexes containing sayings from a later period are the oracles against the foreign nations in 13:1–14:23; 15–16; 19;

[19] For a detailed discussion, see S-F, § 56.3-5.

21; 23, the so-called Isaiah Apocalypse in 24–27, the prophetical liturgies in 33, eschatological discourses in 34–35, and the unhistorical Isaiah legends in 36–39 (taken, with some alterations and additions, from II Kings 18:13; 18:17–20:19). Important late individual sayings are 2:2-4 (= Mic. 4:1-3); 9:1-6 (Eng. 9:2-7); 11:1-9, 10, 11-16; 17:12-14.

b) In the first years of his ministry Isaiah devoted most of his message to attacks on the social and ethical situation in Judah and Jerusalem, even making serious remonstrances against the king and government:

> My people—*their autocrat is a child,*
> *usurers* rule over them.
> O my people, your leaders mislead you,
> and confuse the course of your paths.

> Yahweh has taken his place to contend,
> he stands to judge *his people.*
> Yahweh enters into judgment
> with the elders and princes of his people:

> "It is you who have devoured the vineyard,
> the spoil of the poor is in your houses.
> What do you mean by crushing my people,
> by grinding the faces of the poor?"   (3:12-15)

He likewise attacked the upper class, for example the great land-owners:

> Woe to those who join house to house
> who add field to field,
> until there is no more room,
> and you are made to dwell alone in the midst of the
> land.   (5:8)

No one will be able to escape the threatened judgment. All will be subject to it (2:12-17; 3:1-9), even the women (3:16-24; 3:25-4:1). The cult offers no escape, because it is displeasing to Yahweh (1:10-17). There can be only one salvation: doing good, being willing and obedient (1:17, 19-20).

But Isaiah changed his theme in the second peeriod of his ministry. From this time on his prophecy reflects the attacks of the Assyrians upon the political structure of Syria and Palestine and the attempts of the states attacked to defend themselves. Isaiah's discourses accordingly returned again and again to the themes of Yahweh's activity in the world of men and nations and the relationship between religion and politics: Yahweh governs the course of history and acts in history, albeit gently and quietly (8:5-8). Man is not intended to gaze passively upon this activity or to proceed arbitrarily on his own; he is rather to accept the tension and uncertainty of perseverance, trusting in Yahweh's universal sovereignty. This also applies to politics. Therefore in the Syro-Ephraimite War Isaiah advised against calling on Assyria for help, demanding exclusive reliance on confident faith:

> Thus says Yahweh:
> "It shall not stand and it shall not come to pass!
> For the head of Syria is (only) Damascus
> and the head of Damascus is Rezin.
> And the head of Ephraim is (only) Samaria,
> and the head of Samaria is the son of Remaliah.
> If you will not believe,
> surely you shall not be established." (7:7-9)

Ahaz nevertheless intended to go his own political way without listening to Isaiah, and rejected a sign offered to assure him of Yahweh's power. The prophet thereupon burst forth prophesying a sign of disaster from Yahweh:

> Behold, a young woman is pregnant,
> and shall bear a son,
> and shall call his name
> God Is With Us.
> He shall (have to) eat curds and honey
> when he knows how to refuse the evil
> and choose the good.

> For before the child knows how
> to refuse the evil
> and choose the good,
> the land will be deserted.
> Yahweh will bring such days
> as have not come since the day
> that Ephraim departed from Judah. (7:14b-17)

Later Isaiah at first looked upon the Assyrian king as Yahweh's appointed servant and admonished Hezekiah to be a loyal subject, while at the same time cautioning the "wise" politicians of Judah against autocratic power politics and alliance with Egypt. Instead—

and once more in vain—he recommended quiet confidence in Yahweh, who, unlike Egypt, can really help (31:1-3) :

> For thus said
> Lord Yahweh,
>   the Holy One of Israel:
> "In turning (from war) and respecting your commitments
>   you can be helped,
> in quietness and in trust
>   shall be your strength."
> But you would not,
>   and refused.
> "We will speed upon horses!"—
>   therefore you shall speed away!
> "We will ride upon swift steeds!"—
>   therefore your pursuers shall be swift!
> At the mere threat of five
>   you shall flee
>   till you are left
> like a flagstaff on the top of a mountain,
>   like a signal on a hill.   (30:15-17)

But when the Assyrian king overran Palestine, Isaiah was forced to recognize that he had no notion of being the instrument of Yahweh, but rather was seeking the increase of his own power (10:5-15). Isaiah therefore proclaimed judgment against him, while once more exhorting Judah to persevere, confident in the invisible God:

> Yahweh Sabaoth has sworn:
>   "As I have planned, so shall it be;
>   and as I have purposed, so shall it stand.
>   I will break the Assyrian in my land,
>   and upon my mountains trample him under foot."
>   (14:24-25)

Jerusalem was in fact delivered from the Assyrians in 701, but not in consequence of its faith in God. Then Isaiah accused the triumphant city of sinning in its rejoicing: because it had not proclaimed a day of mourning and turned to Yahweh, all would have to undergo the penance of death (22:1-14).

Throughout Isaiah's ministry his message bore the fundamental stamp of his call, in which he experienced Yahweh as the Holy One (6:3), unique and distinct from everything earthly, who fills the world with his glory and governs it, confronting man with the power of personal will, so that man comes to sense his mortal sinfulness

(6:5). This God insists upon his sole sovereignty. Anyone opposing it is condemned to judgment on the Day of Yahweh, when Yahweh will show himself exalted high above all else (2:12-17). Therefore in the name of Yahweh Isaiah threatened the Assyrian Empire, which was promoting its own sovereignty; but he also attacked the social and political sins of Judah as rebellion against Yahweh (1:2-3): oppression of the poor (3:12-15), luxury (3:16-24) and debauchery (5:11-13, 22), injustice (5:1-7, 23) and theft of land (5:8-10), vying for the favor of the great powers (8:5-8; 30:1-5, 6-7; 31:1-3, 4-9) and trust in one's own power (30:15-17). Isaiah condemned the seemingly shrewd politicians (5:21; 28:14-22; 29:15) and the priests and cult prophets who mocked him (28:7-13). He likewise attacked self-righteousness and arrogance (2:6-22), as well as faithless despair (7:1-9). All these represent respect for powers that are earthly and transitory ("flesh"), rather than divine ("spirit") (31:3). In this fashion man opposes his cleverness to the unique wisdom of God (31:2), rebelling against him (10:15).

Therefore judgment threatens to destroy the sinful way of life that opposes God's holy will. This threat recurs throughout Isaiah's preaching, from his call (6:11) to his last discourses (22:1-14; 32:9-14). He occasionally proclaimed it as a refining and purifying judgment (1:21-26), but usually as a destroying judgment by means of war (3:25–4:1), enslavement (3:24), and anarchy (3:1-9). Only the complete transformation of Israel and adherence to the divine will, only obedience and the penitent return demanded and offered through the name of the prophet's son could save (1:17, 18-20; 7:3). But this return means faith, that is, absolute trust in the promises of the God who invisibly governs the course of history, although their realization is not yet in view (7:9); it means quietness and confident awaiting of Yahweh's intervention (30:15). Thus throughout his entire ministry Isaiah was a prophet of penitent return to God. But he was invariably disappointed, so that even his final discourse was a threat:

> You women who are at ease,
>   hear my voice;
> you complacent daughters,
>   give ear to my speech.
> In little more than a year
>   you will shudder, you complacent women;
> for the vintage will fail,
>   the fruit harvest will not come.

Tremble, you women who are at ease,
  shudder, you complacent ones;
strip, and make yourselves bare,
  beat upon your breasts
for the pleasant fields,
  for the fruitful vine,
for all the joyous houses
  in the joyful city.

For the palace will be forsaken,
  the populous city deserted;
the hill and the watchtower
  will become dens for ever,
a joy of wild asses,
  a pasture of flocks.   (32:9-14)

6. *Micah.*[20] *a)* Micah came from the small town of Moreshet-Gath in the hill country of Judah southwest of Jerusalem. He was probably a free peasant well acquainted with the abuses emanating from the capital, possibly suffering from them himself. It is certain that he appeared during the reign of Hezekiah (cf. Jer. 26:18). Since 1:2-9 attacks Samaria, which is still in existence, Micah's activity must have begun before its destruction, while he clearly knows nothing of the Assyrian campaigns in 711 and 701. Therefore his ministry can probably be dated in the period from 725 to some time before 711 B.C.

The Micah tradition is not extensive; it is found in eight discourses contained in chapters 1–3 of the book (1:16; 2:4-5, 10, 12-13 are later additions). The other sections of the book probably derive from the post-exilic period.[21]

b) Although in 1:10-15 and 2:1-3 Micah appears to have been influenced by Isaiah, he was nevertheless a powerful and striking figure bearing a unique stamp. Through his own personal experience he knew the abuses he attacked, especially the Jerusalem-initiated annulment of the ancient agrarian laws for the benefit of the large landowners. The unusual violence and bitterness of his attacks and threats are explained by his compassion for the sufferings of the

[20] W. Beyerlin, *Die Kulttraditionen Israels in der Verkündigung des Propheten Micha,* 1959; B. A. Copass and E. L. Carlson, *A Study of the Prophet Micah,* 1950; E. Hammershaimb, "Einige Hauptgedanken in der Schrift des Propheten Micha," *StTh,* XV (1961), 11-34 (translation in his *Some Aspects of Old Testament Prophecy from Isaiah to Malachi,* 1966, pp. 29-50).

[21] For a detailed discussion, see S-F, § 66.2-6.

peasants and his contempt for the professional prophets, who flattered
the rich for profit:

> Hear, you heads of Jacob,
>   and rulers of the house of Israel!
> Is it not for you to know justice?—
>   you who hate the good and love the evil.
> They eat the flesh of my people,
>   and flay their skin from off them,
> they chop it up *like meat* in a kettle,
>   like flesh in a caldron.   (3:1-3)

> Thus says Yahweh concerning the prophets:
>   "They lead my people astray,
>   for when they have something to eat
>   they cry, 'Peace!'
>   But when someone gives them nothing to eat,
>   they declare war against him."   (3:5)

To this Micah contrasted his sense of his own mission: with power,
justice, and might he was to declare Israel's sin (3:8). On the basis
of his knowledge of the righteousness willed by God, he attacked
the false security of those who thought they enjoyed Yahweh's favor
and therefore felt safe from all disaster. This reliance on being
Yahweh's people he rejected summarily: "You are by no means 'my
people'!" (2:6-8). Therefore Micah's sole message was inescapable
disaster:

> Therefore because of you Zion
>   shall be plowed as a field;
> Jerusalem shall become a heap of ruins,
>   and the Temple mountain a wooded height.   (3:12)

7. *Zephaniah.*[22] a) Zephaniah was a Judahite, and probably lived
in Jerusalem; the long genealogy recorded in 1:1 is probably intended
to avoid the impression that his father Cushi was an Ethiopian. The
prophet made his appearance during the reign of Josiah. Since foreign
gods were still being worshiped in Jerusalem (1:4-5), we must think
in terms of the years preceding the Deuteronomic reformation. And
since 1:8 mentions merely the king's sons and not the king himself,
the period of the king's minority must be considered for at least
some of the discourses of Zephaniah. His ministry can therefore be
dated around 630 B.C.

[22] G. Gerleman, *Zephanja,* 1942.

From Zephaniah we have six discourses against and about Judah and Jerusalem (1:4-5, 7-9, 12-13, 14-16; 2:1-3; 3:11-13) and three discourses against other nations (2:4, 13-14; 3:6-8). The remaining discourses of the small book derive from a significantly later period.[23]

b) In his preaching Zephaniah followed Amos, Isaiah, and Micah; in particular, he extended and expanded the interpretation of the Day of Yahweh represented by the first two. He attacked idolatry, the imitation of practices based on foreign religions, and self-confident doubt that Yahweh would display his wrath. The terrible judgment that Zephaniah announced so impressively that it still echoes in the *Dies irae,* the Latin poetic version of 1:14-16, would strike the wicked upper class of Judah and Jerusalem, but also of other nations:

> The great day of Yahweh is near,
>   near and hastening fast.
> *The day of Yahweh is swifter than a runner*
>   and speedier than a mighty man.
> A day of wrath is that day,
>   a day of distress and anguish,
> a day of ruin and devastation,
>   a day of darkness and gloom,
> a day of clouds and thick darkness,
>   a day of trumpet blast and battle cry
> against the fortified cities
>   and against the lofty battlements.   (1:14-16)

But if people will use the time remaining to recall the commandments of Yahweh, if they return to righteousness and humility (2:1-3), only a judgment of purification will take place. In this judgment a portion of Israel will be left, like the remnant of an army escaped from a terrible defeat; as in the days of the fathers they will dwell humbly and obscurely but faithfully upon Mount Zion, where they will do no wrong and live in peace:

> On that day you shall not be put to shame because of the deeds
>   by which you have rebelled against me;
> for then I will remove from your midst
>   your proudly exultant ones,
> and you shall no longer be haughty
>   in my holy mountain.
> For I will leave in the midst of you
>   a people humble and lowly.

[23] For a detailed discussion, see S-F, § 69:2-3.

They shall seek refuge in the name of Yahweh,
    those who are left in Israel;
they shall do no wrong
    and utter no lies,
nor shall a deceitful tongue be found
    in their mouth.
For they shall pasture and lie down,
    and none shall make them afraid.   (3:11-13)

8. *Jeremiah.*[24] *a*) Jeremiah came from a priestly family that resided at Anathoth, northeast of Jerusalem. He experienced his call to be a prophet in the year 626 B.C. (see Jer. 1:2; 25:3). Recently several scholars have espoused the hypothesis that he did not become a prophet until after the death of Josiah, some two decades later; but this assumption founders on the express dating of his call, the assignment of 3:6-13 to the period of Josiah, and the assumption in 2:18 that the Assyrian Empire, which collapsed in 612, was still in existence. Since Jeremiah termed himself a "youth" at the time of his call (1:6), he was probably born about 650 or shortly thereafter. We may conclude from 16:1-2 that he never married. Tradition records considerably more detail concerning his fate and personality than is true for any other prophet.

Jeremiah exercised his prophetical ministry for more than four decades, with interruptions. His ministry can be divided into four periods, whose message reflects both the internal situation of Judah and the crucial events of world politics, which also determined Jeremiah's personal condition. The first period comprised the years from Jeremiah's call to shortly before Josiah's reformation was finished (626-622 B.C.). After an apparently brief period of activity at Anathoth, Jeremiah went to Jerusalem, where he pilloried the sins of his people in the cultic, ethical, and political realms. When he was forced to recognize the failure of his message, he considered his mandate ended (see 6:10-11, 27-29) and kept silent for many years. The second period of his ministry fell in the reign of Jehoiakim; it involved the prophet in serious conflicts (608-597).

[24] S. H. Blank, *Jeremiah*, 1961; H. W. Hertzberg, *Prophet und Gott*, 1923; J. P. Hyatt, *Jeremiah*, 1958; J. W. Miller, *Das Verhältnis Jeremias und Hesekiels*, 1955; A. Neher, *Jeremias*, 1961; H. Ortmann, *Der alte und der neue Bund bei Jeremia*, Dissertation, Berlin, 1940; H. Graf Reventlow, *Liturgie und prophetisches Ich bei Jeremia*, 1963; P. Volz, *Der Prophet Jeremia*, 2nd ed., 1930; A. C. Welch, *Jeremiah*, 1928; H. Wildberger, *Jahwewort und prophetische Rede bei Jeremia*, 1942.

In the first years of this period he primarily attacked the Temple and the cult, exhorting the people as before to repent and return to Yahweh because judgment was approaching. But he found bitter opponents, especially the king and the priests, who threatened and attacked him: accusations of blasphemy, deceitful assaults on his life, scourging, and exclusion from the Temple. As a final warning Jeremiah had Baruch write down his earlier discourses and recite them in the Temple; then the king ordered his arrest; and he had to go into hiding until the king's death. The third period of his activity comprised the years from the accession of Zedekiah after the first deportation until after the fall of Judah and Jerusalem (597-586). Despite the inclinations of the king, Jeremiah was unable to carry the day against the nationalistic anti-Babylonian party and the nationalistic prophets of Yahweh's favor. Indeed, following the siege of Jerusalem by the Babylonians he was once more in mortal peril and escaped death by a hair (37–38). After the fall of Jerusalem he remained in Palestine; but after the murder of Gedaliah, the commissar appointed by the Babylonians, by a group of refugees, he was forced to accompany them to Egypt (42–43). There he exercised his ministry for a brief fourth period, and there he vanished from sight; according to legend, he suffered a martyr's death.

A significant portion of the Jeremiah tradition[25] was contained in the scroll that Jeremiah dictated to Baruch and had rewritten after the king destroyed it. The bulk of it is found in 2–9 and 11; it is still quite coherent and generally in chronological order. Some discourses from it were included in chapters 13–14; 18; 25; and 46. Other discourses outside the scroll include the laments or confessions of Jeremiah (distributed through chapters 11–20); sayings concerning the dynasty and individual kings (in 21:1–23:2), prophets (23: 9-40), and salvation to come (30–31); other individual discourses and reports are scattered throughout the book. In addition, Baruch recorded a series of narratives concerning Jeremiah, in order to show that the predictions made by Jeremiah, for which he had to suffer so much, were finally fulfilled (19*+20:1-6; 26; 27*–28; 29; 34*; 36–45; 51:59-64). Scattered throughout the entire book of Jeremiah we find a great number of sayings by other authors. These cannot be listed; only the oracles against the foreign nations constitute a unified section (46:13–51:58).

b) There is no evidence that at the beginning of Jeremiah's

---

[25] For a detailed discussion, see S-F, § 59:3-6.

ministry he considered himself a nabi prophesying against the nations, or that later he occasionally appeared as a cult prophet interceding for the people or leading worship, not to mention holding permanent liturgical office. Neither is he completely subject to tradition; his message bears his personal stamp more than that of any other prophet. It is true that he drew upon the theological terminology of his time when he used the Deuteronomic *b^erît* concept (31:31-34),[26] and the solidarity formula to describe the relationship between Yahweh and Israel (11:1 ff.; 24:7). In addition, however, he maintained the earlier prophetical description of this relationship, using kinship terminology to describe its personal nature. Like Hosea, he depicted it as a marriage relationship (2:2; 3:6 ff.) and called the Israelites Yahweh's sons (3:19, 22; 4:22). Like Hosea, he traced the relationship back to the deliverance from Egypt (2:6); unlike Deuteronomic theology, however, he did not base this deliverance on any "election" of Israel, but on Yahweh's love. Like Hosea, he limited the period of unclouded relationship between Israel and Yahweh to the Mosaic and desert period (2:20), when sacrifice was not yet offered (7:22). It was in the settled territory that apostasy from Yahweh began (2:7), apostasy that Jeremiah preferred to describe in natural rather than historical images (8:4-7), depicting it in classic terms:

> Go and proclaim in the hearing of Jerusalem:
> Thus says Yahweh:
> I remember the devotion of your youth,
>   your love as a bride,
> how you followed me in the wilderness,
>   in a land not sown.
> Israel was *a* holy *possession* to Yahweh,
>   the first fruits of his harvest.
> All who ate of it became guilty;
>   evil came upon them.

> Then I brought you into a plentiful land,
>   to enjoy its fruits and its good things.

[26] The traditional translation of *b^erît* as "covenant" has been proven erroneous by new studies. The word actually means "obligation": the obligation a person undertakes for himself, the obligation a person can impose on another, and mutual obligation. For a discussion, see G. Fohrer, "Altes Testament—'Amphiktyonie' und 'Bund'?" *ThLZ*, XCI (1966), 801-16, 893-904 (= his *Studien zur alttestamentlichen Theologie und Geschichte* [*1949-1966*], 1969, pp. 84-119); E. Kutsch, "Gesetz und Gnade," *ZAW*, LXXIX (1967), 18-35; *idem*, "ברית *b^erît* Verpflichtung," in *Theologisches Handwörterbuch zum Alten Testament*, I (1971), 339-52.

> But when you came in you defiled my land,
>   and made my heritage an abomination.
> The priests did not say, "Where is Yahweh?"
>   Those who handle the law did not know me.
> The shepherds transgressed against me;
>   the prophets prophesied by Baal,
>   and went after things that do not profit.   (2:2-3, 7-8)

> I thought
>   how I would set you among my sons
> and give you a pleasant land,
>   a heritage most beauteous.
> And I thought *you* would call me Father
>   and would not turn from following me.
> *But as* a woman becomes faithless on account of her friend,
>   so have you been faithless to me, O house of Israel.
>   (3:19-20)

Apostasy from Yahweh continues down to the present. Jeremiah saw the sins of his age that he attacked in the political, cultic, and ethical realm:

> What do you gain by going to Egypt,
>   to drink the water of the Nile?
> Or what do you gain by going to Assyria,
>   to drink the water of the Euphrates?   (2:18)

> How can you say, "I am not defiled,
>   I have not gone after the Baals"?
> Look at your way in the valley;
>   know what you have done—
> a restive young camel interlacing her tracks,
>   *breaking loose in the wilderness.*
> In *her* heat she sniffs the wind!
>   Who can restrain her lust?
> None who seek her need weary themselves;
>   in her month of heat they will find her.
> Keep your feet from going unshod
>   and your throat from thirst!
> But you said, "No, it is hopeless,
>   I love strangers,
>   and after them I will go!"   (2:23-25)

> To what purpose does frankincense come to me,
>   or sweet cane from a distant land?
> Your burnt offerings are not acceptable,
>   nor your sacrifices pleasing to me.   (6:20)

> Run to and fro through the streets of Jerusalem,
>   look and take note!
> Search her squares to see
>   if you can find a man,
> one who does justice
>   and seeks truth.
> Though they say, "As Yahweh lives,"
>   they *surely* swear falsely.
> Thou hast smitten them, but they felt no anguish;
>   they refused to take correction.
> They made their faces harder than rock:
>   they have refused to repent.   (5:1-3)

On account of all these sins annihilating judgment impends; Yahweh would not even heed the intercession of a Moses or Samuel (15:1). Jerusalem and Judah simply do not live in a basic state of favor with Yahweh, which can quickly and easily be restored if interrupted; their situation is basically one of alienation from Yahweh:

> From the least to the greatest of them,
>   every one is greedy for unjust gain;
> and from prophet to priest,
>   every one deals falsely.
> They have healed the wound of my people
>   lightly, saying,
> "Peace, peace."
> But there is no peace!   (6:13-14)

Like his predecessors, Jeremiah saw the only possibility of deliverance from the impending disaster in repentance and return to Yahweh, which he urgently demanded (e.g. 3:6-13; 3:21–4:2; 4:3-4):

> Break up the fallow ground,
>   and sow not among thorns.
> Circumcise yourselves to *your God,*
>   remove the foreskin of our hearts,
> lest my wrath go forth like fire,
>   and burn with none to quench it,
>   because of the evil of your doings.   (4:3-4)

In the year 605 Jeremiah could even sum up all his previous message as a call to return to Yahweh:

> From the thirteenth year
> of Josiah, the son of Amon,
> king of Judah,
> to this day,
> for twenty-three years
> I have spoken to you
> late and early:

> Turn now, every one of you, from his evil way
> and wrong doings,
> and you shall dwell upon this land
> which Yahweh gave
> to you and your fathers
> from of old and for ever.
> Yet you have not listened to me.   (25:3, 5, 7)

But when such return had been proven impossible and the judgment upon Judah had begun with the first deportation, Jeremiah came to expect a supporting and redeeming intervention on the part of Yahweh on behalf of the afflicted deportees from Judah and the earlier deportees from the Northern Kingdom (24; 30–31*). His future hope was sober and far removed from the extravagance of the later eschatological prophets (see 31:6; 32:15; 35:18-19). The crucial point was that Yahweh would give his people a heart to know him; the obligations of Sinai, once broken, would not be renewed— Yahweh would instead instill the divine will into man and write it on his heart, so that it would be known and done naturally:

> The days are coming
> when I will make a new *b*ᵉ*rît* [obligation]
> with the house of Israel—
> not like the *b*ᵉ*rît* [obligation] which I made with their fathers
> when I took them by the hand
> to bring them out of the land of Egypt,
> my *b*ᵉ*rît* [obligation] which they broke.

> But this is the *b*ᵉ*rît* [obligation]
> which I will make with Israel
> after those days:
> I will put my law within them,
> and I will write it upon their hearts;
> and I will be their God,
> and they shall be my people.

And no longer shall each man teach his neighbor
and each his brother, saying:
"Know Yahweh."
For they shall all know me,
from the least of them to the greatest.
For I will forgive their iniquity,
and I will remember their sin no more.   (31:31-34)

All in all, Jeremiah developed the message of his predecessors along his own lines: a personal relationship with God proceeding from the tension between God and man, a communion with God based on reciprocal interaction, finding its expression especially in prayer, a profound surrender of the whole man to God, a surrender refined through crisis; a fundamental understanding of sin not as an individual lapse but as a basic perversion of human life; thus all the more imperatively the call to repentance and then, since God is not only righteousness but also and above all love, the change to a belief in redemption that anticipates a genuine communion with God, at the same time achieving the goal of God's sovereignty.

c) We know of a few other prophets belonging to the period of Jeremiah, three of whom must be briefly mentioned.

Nahum[27] primarily voiced threats against Nineveh, the Assyrian capital (shortly after 626). His preaching exhibited genuinely prophetical insights when he acknowledged Yahweh as lord of the nations, spoke of Assyria's mandate to punish Judah, and rebuked Assyrian policies as being contrary to God's will, threatening an end to the Assyrian Empire. But he was primarily a representative of optimistic prophecy with a strongly nationalistic bias, which outweighted the cultic element. To his way of thinking Yahweh acted exclusively with reference to Judah, promoting its interests for the benefit of all Israel. In many ways Nahum came suspiciously close to the line dividing false from true prophecy.

Habakkuk,[28] who also prophesied the downfall of Assyria, may be dated a little later than Nahum, but still prior to 622. He was a cult prophet to whom Judah was the "righteous" (2:4), to whom he promised help but without requiring humble penitence and return to Yahweh. He did not look upon Yahweh's righteousness as a demand upon his people, but as being directed solely against the wicked powers of the world. Especially when his discourses are com-

---

[27] A. Haldar, *Studies in the Book of Nahum*, 1946; S-F, § 67.
[28] P. Humbert, *Problèmes du livre d'Habacuc*, 1944; S-F, § 68.

pared with the contemporaneous discourses of Jeremiah (Jeremiah 1–6) a certain measure of nationalistic prophetical optimism cannot be overlooked. In contradistinction to Nahum, however, the nationalistic element was not the basis of his prophecy, but rather dismay at the moral injustice of secular power and concern for Yahweh's demonstration of his righteousness in history. Habakkuk shared the genuinely prophetical awareness of Yahweh's majesty, looking on Yahweh as the defender of the oppressed, having power over all nations, raising them up or bringing them low, and using them as instruments of his will. On the basis of these insights he calls on the faithful to reject outward appearances and wait patiently, trusting in Yahweh (2:1-4).

Hananiah[29] came forward to oppose Jeremiah when the latter wore a yoke as a symbolic act demanding permanent subjection to the Babylonians (Jeremiah 27). After a message of salvation, in which he predicted the breaking of the Babylonian yoke and the return of the deportees, and the rejection of this prophecy by Jeremiah, he broke Jeremiah's yoke in an antithetical symbolic act. Jeremiah at first withdrew in defeat and later returned pronouncing a threat against Hananiah. Baruch's account (Jeremiah 28) shows the bitterness of the conflict between prophets proclaiming antithetical messages in the name of Yahweh.

§ 20 The Approach to Life of the Great Prophets

E. L. ALLEN, *Prophet and Nation*, 1947; M. BUBER, *Der Glaube der Propheten*, 1950 (English: *The Prophetic Faith*, 1949) ; J. HÄNEL, *Das Erkennen Gottes bei den Schriftpropheten*, 1923; E. W. HEATON, *Die Propheten des Alten Testaments*, 1959; A. J. HESCHEL, *The Prophets*, 1962; J. HESSEN, *Platonismus und Prophetismus*, 2nd ed., 1956; P. HUMBERT, "Les prophètes d'Israël ou les tragiques de la Bible," *RThPh*, XXIV (1936), 209-51; J. P. HYATT, *Prophetic Religion*, 1947; J. LINDBLOM, "Die Religion der Propheten und die Mystik," *ZAW*, LVII (1939), 65-74; S. MOWINCKEL, *Die Erkenntnis Gottes der alttestamentlichen Propheten*, 1941; A. NEHER, *L'essence du prophétisme*, 1955; T. H. ROBINSON, *Prophecy and the Prophets in Ancient Israel*, 2nd ed., 1953; R. B. Y. SCOTT, *The Relevance of the Prophets*, 1947; G. F. WHITLEY, *The Prophetic Achievement*, 1963; W. G. WILLIAMS, *The Prophets, Pioneers to Christianity*, 1956; see also the bibliographies to § 18 and § 19.

[29] H.-J. Kraus, *Prophetie in der Krisis*, 1964; W. Staerk, "Das Wahrheitskriterium der alttestamentlichen Prophetie," *ZSTh*, V (1927), 76-101.

268   Prophecy, the Third Influence

1. *The content of the prophetical message.*[1] The faith of the great individual prophets (§ 19.1), based on the continuing influence of Mosaic Yahwism, was grounded in a new understanding of Yahweh born out of the mystery of personal experience. According to the prophets, this experience could be shared in some fashion by every man. He then experiences God as a holy passion and blazing fire consigning to destruction all that opposes his will. When he senses how this will invades his life and convulses it, all that remains appears to be humble renunciation of all self-willed action and total subjection to Yahweh. But the prophets in fact learned that God's holy power does not reduce man to involuntary servitude, making him grovel in the dust, but rather confronts him with a personal decision: the decision whether he will say Yes or No to Yahweh and Yahweh's will, whether he will become a totally new man or remain totally the man he has been.

With this as their starting point the prophets disputed the usual human approach to life: the desire for security, calm, and satiety instead of the joyful confidence and utter surrender that Yahweh requires. They warned against such a life and its consequences, summoning men to decide for the new life in which they already lived, a life open to all who desire it.

The prophets warned against the old life because it is characterized by human guilt vis-à-vis Yahweh and the world, and represents the source of other false ideas, words, and actions. Since they were not philosophers or theologians, they proceeded in the first instance by reproving the individual sins that met their eyes. In the process they attacked the various classes and strata of their people with unprece-

---

[1] E. Balla, "Der Erlösungsgedanke in der israelitisch-jüdischen Religion," *Angelos,* I (1925), 71-83; R. E. Clements, *Prophecy and Covenant,* 1965; W. Cossmann, *Die Entwicklung des Gerichtsgedankens bei den alttestamentlichen Propheten,* 1915; E. K. Dietrich, *Die Umkehr (Bekehrung und Busse) im Alten Testament und im Judentum,* 1936; J. Fichtner, "Die 'Umkehrung' in der prophetischen Botschaft," *ThLZ,* LXXVIII (1953), 459-66 (= his *Gottes Weisheit,* 1965, pp. 44-51); J. H. Grønbaek, "Zur Frage der Eschatologie in der Verkündigung der Gerichtspropheten," *SEÅ,* XXIV (1959), 5-21; S. Herrmann, *Die prophetischen Heilserwartungen im Alten Testament,* 1965; J. Lindblom, "Gibt es eine Eschatologie bei den alttestamentlichen Propheten?" *STTh,* VI (1952), 79-114; H.-P. Müller, "Zur Frage nach dem Ursprung der biblischen Eschatologie," *VT,* XIV (1964), 276-93; A. Neher, "Fonction du prophète dans la société hébraïque," *RHPhR,* XXVIII/XXIX (1948/49), 30-42; E. Rohland, *Die Bedeutung der Erwählungstraditionen Israels für die Eschatologie der alttestamentlichen Propheten,* Dissertation, Heidelberg, 1956; H. W. Wolff, "Das Thema 'Umkehr' in der alttestamentlichen Prophetie," *ZThK,* XLVIII (1951), 129-48 (= his *Gesammelte Studien zum Alten Testament,* 1964, pp. 130-50).

dented candor, hurling such words at them as they had never heard before. They turned against all in whom they found offence: the king and his administration, the rich and aristocratic, judges and elders, large landowners and merchants, priests and cult prophets, but also the simple and poor. The whole nation has come to ruin by the perfidious course it has taken.

But all individual transgressions are rooted in a man's fundamental and universal attitude, which gives rise to the particular violations. This attitude is the refusal of the joyful confidence and utter surrender that Yahweh requires, rebellion against him and apostasy from him. Herein lies man's guilt at the most profound level. Amos saw it in ingratitude, Hosea in inward aversion and hostility toward Yahweh, Isaiah in arrogance and presumption, Jeremiah in mendacious malice and wickedness. All these exercise such fearsome power over man that often the possibility of change seems a hopeless prospect. Obdurate refusal to accept the divine will turns into active hostility to Yahweh.

Thus the prophets opposed traditional piety and theology, which felt confident of God's favor. They recognized man's deep guilt toward Yahweh, which could not be removed by the promise of peace and salvation, because there is none (Jer. 6:14). They had to learn themselves that Yahweh not only chastizes for a time, as was asserted, but that he destroys (Isa. 6:11). They therefore saw man in a state of fundamental alienation from God, in which, however, man is still confronted with a crucial either/or, like that formulated by Jer. 22:1-5 for the king of Judah and by Isa. 1:19-20 for the whole nation: either righteousness and justice will prevail, followed by salvation, or they will not prevail, and disaster will follow.

Since the prophets were of the opinion that sin prevailed, they expected a terrible punitive judgment to overtake their nation. This judgment would not come unexpectedly, since it had been preceded by many admonitions, warnings, and minor reverses. But since these had been in vain, the bitter end was expected imminently, from which no one could escape. The prophets depicted this judgment in various forms; differing views can even be found within the writings of a single prophet. The judgment would be accomplished by natural catastrophes, by devastating war and deportation, by revolution and anarchy, or by the Day of Yahweh. In any case its advent was so certain that the dirge could and should be sounded at once, because later there would be no one left to raise it and bury the last corpses of his people.

Two terms and conceptions deserve special discussion: the "Day of Yahweh" and the "remnant of Israel."

a) In the OT, the term "Day of Yahweh" [2] refers to the coming great day of judgment on which Yahweh will reveal himself visibly and summon Israel or the nations to judgment. The same day is also called the "day of vengeance" (Isa. 34:8), "day of disaster" (Jer. 17:16-17), "day of calamity" (Jer. 46:21), "day of punishment" (Jer. 50:27; Mic. 7:4), or simply "the day" (Ezek. 7:7). Independent of this expression but probably not uninfluenced by it is the term "his day" for the day on which the fate of a man, especially an evil-doer, is sealed (I Sam. 26:10; Ezek. 21:30 [Eng. 21:25]; Ps. 37:13; Job 18:20).

The expectation of the Day of Yahweh has a long history. Its roots lie in the belief of the ancient period that on the day of battle Yahweh intervened on behalf of Israel and came to its aid (Judges 5). But even before the earliest explicit mention of the Day of Yahweh by Amos, this belief had been extended to become a more comprehensive hope including an expectation of salvation for Israel: it was believed that on such a Day of Yahweh a great light would shine forth, because Yahweh would become visible in his wondrous glory; the traditional phenomena accompanying a theophany were also included. This day was expected to be a glorious and happy event, since catastrophe would befall the enemies of Israel, while Israel itself would benefit from the salutary effects of Yahweh's appearance.

The prophets transformed this expectation. Amos proclaimed that the Day of Yahweh meant not "light" (salvation) but "darkness" (disaster) for sinful Israel (Amos 5:18-20). Isaiah saw the consequence of the glorious theophany on the Day of Yahweh likewise as destruction for Judah, when tempest would rage from the mountains and forests at the northern boundary of Palestine to the Red Sea in the south, and the earth would quake, so that the proud and haughty man would perish together with his works (Isa. 2:12-17). According to Zephaniah, on the Day of Yahweh the sinners in Jerusalem would be the fitting sacrifice for Yahweh at his theophany (Zeph. 1:7-9); in ever-changing terminology he describes the terrible judgment (cf. Zeph. 1:14-16), which Ezek. 7:5 ff., 10 ff. also threaten for Judah and Ezek. 30:1-9 for Egypt and its allies.

This threat was taken up by the later prophets, who reinterpreted the concept of the Day of Yahweh in eschatological terms. Having seen the threatened judgment carried out in the fall of Judah and the Exile, in the eschatological age to come they expected new salvation for the remnant of Israel and disaster for powers of the world hostile to God, or a last judgment extending to all nations. To describe this they used, among other

---

[2] L. Černý, *The Day of Yahweh and Some Relevant Problems*, 1948; R. Largement and H. Lemaître, "Le Jour de Yahweh dans le contexte oriental," *BEThL*, XII (1959), 259-66; S. Mowinckel, "Jahwes dag," *NTT*, LIX (1958), 1-56; G. von Rad, "The Origin of the Concept of the Day of Yahweh," *JSS*, IV (1959), 97-108; K.-D. Schunk, "Strukturlinien in der Entwicklung der Vorstellung vom 'Tag Jahwes,'" *VT*, XIV (1964), 319-30; M. Weiss, "The Origin of the 'Day of Yahweh' Reconsidered," *HUCA*, XXXVII (1966), 29-71.

things, the expectation of the Day of Yahweh (Isaiah 13; 24; 34; Joel; Obadiah 15 ff.; Zechariah 14). According to this view, there will be a fundamental change in the course of history; it marks the end, not of the world as a whole, but of the age dominated by a power hostile to God. This radical transformation, together with the eschatological last judgment, constitutes the prerequisite for the coming of a new eschatological world.

b) Originally, "remnant" [3] referred to the lesser portion that remained after destruction (cf. Exod. 10:12; Lev. 5:9; Josh. 11:22). The same was true for pre-exilic prophecy, for which the idea of a remnant was not associated with expected salvation, but accompanied threats of judgment and exhortations to return to Yahweh. Isaiah, for instance, used it in the sense of the pitiful survivors of a battle, who merely attest the seriousness of the catastrophe (Isa. 1:8; 6:11-12; 17:3, 5-6; 30:14, 17) ; Amos 5:3 clearly uses it in the same sense. The situation is no different in the case of Jeremiah and Ezekiel (cf. Jer. 24:8-9; 42:2-3; Ezek. 9:8; 17:21). When a remnant is mentioned in an exhortation, it can refer to the entire nation. In this sense the name of Isaiah's son Remnant That Returns (Isa. 7:3) meant that when judgment had overtaken Samaria and Damascus, the guilty parties, Judah would remain like the survivors of a battle, if the Judahites would repent and return to Yahweh.

The idea of a holy remnant intended to constitute the future people of Yahweh and experience new salvation was unknown to the great individual prophets of the pre-exilic period. It first appears in eschatological prophecy dating from the end of the exilic period. Then the deportees in exile interpreted the concept of the remnant in such a way that it referred to a portion of Israel singled out to be a new people of Yahweh. The term came to be applied both humbly and proudly to those who had escaped alive from the divine judgment; they were no longer considered worthless runaways, but the elect representatives of God's saving future (Isa. 4:3; 10: 20-21; 11:11, 16; 28:5; 46:3-4; Mic. 7:18; Hag. 2:2; Zech. 8:6). The extent to which the term changed its meaning can be seen from its equation with "a strong nation" (Mic. 4:7) and its comparison to a rampaging lion (Mic. 5:7 [Eng. 5:8]), which are directly contrary to its original meaning.

The prophets did not consider the judgment of Yahweh that they were predicting to be simply the legally prescribed punishment for guilt, and certainly not divine caprice, despotism, and brutality. For the guilt is rooted in man's false striving for security, and consists in living a secure life based on the created natural order, which is transitory, rather than confidence and surrender to the divine will. Therefore guilt leads necessarily to downfall and catastrophe, because the natural created order is transitory. Life set going on the wrong course must as a logical consequence come to grief. Occasionally sin and judgment are so closely linked that guilt itself is judgment, for

[3] S. Garofalo, La nozione profetica del "Resto d'Israele," 1942; W. E. Müller, Die Vorstellung vom Rest im Alten Testament, Dissertation, Leipzig, 1939; R. de Vaux, "Le 'Reste d'Israël' d'après les prophètes," RB, XLII (1933) , 526-39.

example in Isaiah's image of the cracked wall that finally collapses (Isa. 30:8-14).

But the prophets invariably came at some time to realize that judgment is not Yahweh's real will. Ezekiel gave this notion classical expression:

Have I any pleasure in the death of the wicked,
and not rather that he should turn from his way and live?   (Ezek. 18:23)

Therefore judgment cannot be inescapable, any more than the wrong approach to life is invincible. The prophets also glimpsed the possibility of a new salvation: the possibility of man's fulfilling the will of Yahweh so completely that Yahweh would in fact rule the world.

It must be noted, of course, that though we find a series of discourses prophesying salvation in the great individual pre-exilic prophets, these are fewer in number than the invectives and threats. Many optimistic passages were interpolated into the prophetical books at a later period. But when the prophets did consider salvation possible, they saw it primarily in the inward renewal of man. They expected no outward splendor; like Zephaniah, they even spoke of a poor and insignificant people, living however in true faith. Just as they were themselves brought to this faith by their call, so too others could all be brought to this faith. Then Yahweh will put his will into the hearts of men so that they carry it out, as it were, by nature (Jer. 31:31-34).

The prophets almost never anticipated the distant future. What they expected to happen they usually expected to happen imminently—even the post-exilic prophets. Everything was on the point of taking place, and there was just time to alert men and challenge them to draw the proper conclusions with respect to the present. In particular the words of God's favor spoken by the great individual prophets had nothing to do with the distant future, but constituted the sublime *Or* to the *Either* of threatened judgment; the imminent fulfillment of both was equally possible. The prophets' message spoke of imminent events and proximate history. And the only reason it spoke of proximate history was to influence the present. The present in which they lived was the prophets' real concern.

The first crucial principle for an understanding of the great individual prophets is therefore this: the prophets' intention was not to predict the distant future but to influence and shape their own present age. This is why they censured wickedness, warned against the threatened destruction to follow, and called men to new life in God's favor.

The second crucial principle follows: the theme of the prophets' message was the possible deliverance of man, despite the guilt that subjected him to death.

The first answer to the question of how such deliverance might take place was the summons to repentance and return to Yahweh that we find in all the great prophets. "Return!"—that means turn away from the perfidious life of sin, turn to the special life of confidence and surrender to God's sovereignty and communion with God. If man will return, Yahweh will be merciful and gracious to him. This call to repentance was issued to the prophet's contemporaries, and they were confronted with a decision: to become totally new or to remain totally as they had been—with all the consequences that entailed.

A second strand runs from Hosea (see § 19.4) through Jeremiah (see § 19.8) and Ezekiel to Deutero-Isaiah and beyond. Its keynote is not return but redemption. Everything was expected to flow from Yahweh's redeeming act, which would be followed by man's response. The crucial point was the decision to accept Yahweh's offer of forgiveness and redemption and to be brought by him into a new life. Thus Ezekiel promised a new heart of flesh instead of stone, associated with the gift of the divine spirit that forms and determines man's new life (Ezek. 36:25-27).

Of course repentance and redemption should not be sharply distinguished; they are certainly not mutually exclusive. For both signify a transformation of man, and are only two different ways of describing this transformation, with emphasis either on what man does or what Yahweh does. Repentance means that man himself redeems what he has lost through sin, of his own accord turns from his wicked way of life, and centers all his thoughts and actions on Yahweh. Redemption means that Yahweh causes everything within a man that leads the man away from him to return to him, and centers all the man's thoughts and actions on their proper focus.

In view of all this the prophets demanded that men make the right decision because Yahweh would act correspondingly—if he does not expressly ignore man's decision, doing or not doing something for the sake of his honor or love. Usually, however, God does not act apart from human intention, although Yahweh is certainly not dependent on man's choice. Isaiah frequently based his appeal on the harmony between what Yahweh does and what man does (see Isa. 1:19; also, for example, Jer. 7:1-15; 18:1-11; 22:1-5). Yahweh's readiness to forgive and man's willingness belong together and in the last analysis constitute two aspects or components of a single process: the deliverance of the sinful man subject to death, who grasps the possibility of repentance or the offer of redemption. Conversely, there is a similar harmony in the deadly crisis of the man who will not believe and rejects Yahweh: his own unwillingness and Yahweh's closing of his eyes and ears cause the recalcitrant sinner to become ever more deeply entangled in his own destruction (see Isa. 6:9-10; 29:9-10).

On this basis we can summarize the substance of the prophets' message in a few points. It starts (1) with the necessary transformation of man through repentance or redemption. This brings about (2) the realization of God's sovereignty in the life of the man who has returned to Yahweh or been redeemed, which leads (3) to a real communion with God in a new life and transforms (4) man's entire way of life, since he now fulfills God's will. Finally (5) the individual believers join together in a community that is the true people of God. The task of each individual and of the community of the faithful is to realize God's sovereignty and communion with God on this earth through their lives here and now.

2. *Prophetical criticism. a)* The prophets took basic issue with the history of their people.[4] Even their point of departure differed from the traditional view. For they saw in Yahweh's treatment of Israel merely one segment of his actions in the lives and destinies of all men and nations—albeit a special case of his universal operation, determined by his intimate relationship with Israel. The difference between the prophetical view and that of tradition was even greater

---

[4] G. F. Allen, "The Prophetic Interpretation of History," *ET*, LI (1939/40), 454-57; G. H. Davies, "The Yahvistic Tradition in the Eighth-Century Prophets," in *Studies in Old Testament Prophecy* (Robinson Festschrift), 1950, pp. 37-51; G. Fohrer, "Prophetie und Geschichte," in his *Studien zur alttestamentlichen Prophetie (1949-1965)*, 1967, pp. 265-93; J. Hempel, *Die Mehrdeutigkeit der Geschichte als Problem der prophetischen Theologie*, 1936; O. Procksch, *Die Geschichtsbetrachtung bei den vorexilischen Propheten*, 1902; A. F. Puukko, "Die Geschichtsauffassung der alttestamentlichen Propheten," in International Congress of Orientalists, *Actes du XX Congrès International des Orientalistes*, 1940, p. 296; J. Rieger, *Die Bedeutung der Geschichte für die Verkündigung des Amos und Hosea*, 1929; H. W. Wolff, "Das Geschichtsverständnis der alttestamentlichen Propheten," *EvTh*, XX (1960), 218-35 (= his *Gesammelte Studien zum Alten Testament*, 1964, pp. 289-307).

when the course of history itself is considered. It did indeed begin with an initial possibility of favor offered by Yahweh and a limited period of an unclouded relationship between Yahweh and Israel, which Hosea and Jeremiah identified with the Mosaic and desert period and Isaiah extended into the period of David and Solomon. But the subsequent course of history was utterly and absolutely sinful. Israel rebelled against Yahweh and remained rebellious down to the prophets' own time. And since Yahweh was never willing to accept this state of affairs, the history of Israel was also a history replete with calamities sent by God to admonish Israel and warn it of the annihilating judgment to come. Thus Isaiah, surveying the history of the Northern Kingdom of Israel from the wars with the Philistines and Arameans down to a severe earthquake in the immediate past, saw in it the raging voice and hand of wrath, because the people repeatedly refused to return to him who smote them (Isa. 9:7-20 [Eng. 9:8-21]; 5:25-29). For the prophets, Israel's sin and Yahweh's admonishing and warning calamities as well as his other efforts were the two major factors necessary for an understanding of Israel's history in Palestine.

Israel's history was therefore not *Heilsgeschichte*. This frequently encountered term is used by theology in various senses, but none of its senses reflects the prophetical view. Not even the supposed idea of a primordial "plan" of Yahweh encompassing judgment and salvation can be cited to support it. The expressions interpreted in this sense occur in Isaiah only in threats of judgment, never in promises of salvation; and even if discourses of later prophets in Isaiah 1–35 are drawn on to construct a plan of salvation, it exhibits many discrepancies. Furthermore, such "planning" would obviously have been remarkably vacillating. Isaiah first looked upon the Assyrians as Yahweh's instrument, but later considered them repudiated as such; in like fashion he repeatedly offered deliverance and preservation to the Judahites, condemned to the fate of Sodom and Gomorrah, if they would repent; finally, when they disappointed him after the Assyrian withdrawal from Jerusalem associated with Hezekiah's payment of tribute, he condemned them irrevocably (Isa. 22:1-14; 32: 9-14). In view of this, it is impossible to speak of a primordial "plan" associated with *Heilsgeschichte*. We should speak rather of a "purpose" or "resolve" that can be framed in each particular case and abrogated if necessary.

It is quite possible to speak of Yahweh's purposeful activity; for the earlier source strata of the Hexateuch this culminates in the occupation of Palestine; for P it culminates in the final establishment of the sacral ordinances and—for their realization—the distribution of Palestine; for eschatology it culminates in a state "without history." To this purposeful activity with a limited positive goal there corresponds, however, a parallel activity with negative results (see the Deuteronomic judgment upon the period of the monarchy and the prophets' judgment upon the history of Israel) or even with a negative goal, Yahweh's threatened annihilating judgment. At the very least, *Heilsgeschichte* and the history of sin or disaster counterbalance each other. More precisely, Yahweh's saving and destroying activity and man's predominantly sinful activity are all interwoven.

Whether moving toward salvation or disaster, history was always a history of crisis; in the general prophetical estimation of Israel's experiences, the present moment was always a critical situation for individual and nation, who had to decide for continued or renewed apostasy from Yahweh or return to him. Previous decisions—apart from the often assumed period of unclouded relationship between Yahweh and Israel—are without exception termed wrong, so that Israel has forfeited its chance for happiness:

> O that you had hearkened to my commandments!
> Then your peace would have been like a river,
> and your prosperity like the waves of the sea.   (Isa. 48:18)

But Israel was disobedient, and so the promises could not be fulfilled. The resultant history of apostasy and sin now determines the present situation, in which annihilating judgment is imminent, and demands for this very reason a new decision in the present moment, which will in turn determine the future:

> If you are willing and obedient,
>   you shall eat the good of the land;
> But if you refuse and rebel,
>   you shall be devoured *by the* sword.   (Isa. 1:19-20)

b) Rarely has a religious institution been subjected to such bitter, almost limitless criticism as that leveled by the prophets against the Israelite cult:[5] The popular cult is apostasy from Yahweh

[5] R. Dobbie, "Sacrifice and Morality in the Old Testament," *ET*, LX (1958/59), 297-300; *idem*, "Deuteronomy and the Prophetic Attitude to Sacrifice," *SJTh*, XII (1959), 68-82; R. Hentschke, *Die Stellung der vorexilischen Schriftpropheten zum Kultus*, 1957; H. W. Hertzberg, "Die prophetische Kritik am Kult," *ThLZ*, LXXV (1950), 219-26 (= his *Beiträge zur Traditionsgeschichte und*

and sin, and therefore itself the cause of the coming judgment (Hos. 2:15 [Eng. Hos. 2:13]). Altars, masseboth, and sacrificial slaughter are sin (Hos. 8:11-13; 10:1-2). The statues of bulls set up as symbols of the deity are sin (Hos. 8:4b-6). This cult is adultery and fornication; no wonder, then, that the spirit of unchastity comes to pervade all life and conduct, and women and girls prostitute themselves, led astray by the men who should be wise and nevertheless go aside with sacral prostitutes (Hos. 4:12-14). No less guilty are the priests, who lead the people astray by means of the cult, which they promote for the profit they make from it (Hos. 4:7-10; 5:1-2).

The prophets attacked the cult not only because Canaanite elements lived on in it, because Yahweh was subjected to tangible constraint and access to him was sought by material and magical means, but also because it misled the people into being content with the performance of their cultic obligations, supposing that they had thus fulfilled their service to Yahweh. They observed the outward forms that they had learned and thought that they had thus demonstrated complete obedience (Isa. 29:13-14). Frequent participation in the cult, the generous offering of sacrifice, vouchsafe a feeling of security and gratification that Amos already attacked bitterly (Amos 4:4-5).

The prophets' wrath against the operation of the cult was primarily aroused by their realization that the people were not taking Yahweh's ethical requirements seriously, supposing instead that they came near to Yahweh and gained his protection in the cult or in the Temple (Jer. 7:1-15). Therefore the prophets opposed to the cult the ethical requirements that were supposed to shape and determine the course of daily life (Amos 5:21-24),[6] bluntly rejecting the cult as a means of salvation (Isa. 1:10-17). They did not reject all cultic observance on principle and a priori. They sought rather to state

---

Theologie des Alten Testaments, 1962, pp. 81-90) ; J. P. Hyatt, *The Prophetic Criticism of Israelite Worship*, 1963; R. Rendtorff, "Priesterliche Kulttheologie und prophetische Kultpolemik," *ThLZ*, LXXXI (1956), 339-42; K. Roubos, *Profetie en cultus in Israël*, 1956; H. H. Rowley, "Ritual and the Hebrew Prophets," *JSS*, I (1956), 338-60 (= his *From Moses to Qumran*, 1963, pp. 111-38); *idem*, "Sacrifice and Morality: a Rejoinder," *ET*, LX (1958/59), 341; M. Schmidt, *Prophet und Tempel*, 1948.

[6] E. Hammershaimb, "On the Ethics of the Old Testament Prophets," *VTSuppl*, VII (1960), 75-101 (= his *Some Aspects of Old Testament Prophecy from Isaiah to Malachi*, 1966, pp. 63-90); N. W. Porteous, "The Basis of the Ethical Teaching of the Prophets," in *Studies in Old Testament Prophecy* (Robinson Festschrift), 1950, 143-56; C. Tresmontant, *Sittliche Existenz bei den Propheten Israels*, 1962; U. Türck, *Die sittliche Forderung der israelitischen Propheten des 8. Jahrhunderts*, Dissertation, Göttingen, 1935.

plainly that it is blasphemous to act contrary to Yahweh's will in daily life and still offer sacrifice, that this blasphemy must lead to destruction, and that in this situation the cult cannot be used to avert judgment. Yahweh is not to be sought in his sanctuary but in good works (Amos 5:4-6, 14-15); he is not to be served in the cult, but in righteousness and justice (Amos 5:21-24).

This attitude has sometimes been understood as meaning that the prophets demanded an ethical religion without cultic accretions, but this conclusion is wrong. They criticized and attacked the cult, but did not simply oppose it to ethics. This antithesis was instead typical of wisdom instruction, whose ideal is frequently ethical religiosity without cultic observance. The prophets, however, did not stress ethical requirements because they were valuable in their own right or required by law, but because they expressed the claim of God's will upon man, because Yahweh's will stands behind them, and because obedience to them is a mark of the believer.

Prophetical criticism of the cult sprang from the same source. The prophets inveighed against it because it appeared to them an attempt to deceive Yahweh. The people were not taking their God seriously, were not letting his power determine their lives; they were pursuing a course contrary to God's will. The cult could exist only if man's entire conduct were correct. Since devotion was restricted to the cult, in flagrant contradiction to the rest of life, the prophets condemned the cult as sinful and demanded repentance, righteousness, and justice.

What mattered to the prophets was not the cult or ethics per se, but the individual believer depending on Yahweh and sustained by him. Therefore they attacked the cult because in it the unbeliever claimed to have rights over against Yahweh instead of acknowledging and obeying Yahweh's will. They summoned men to do good, to practice righteousness and justice, because such conduct was the primary expression of commitment to Yahweh. If God's sovereignty and communion with God had determined the way men lived, finding expression in justice and love for one's fellowman, a certain cult would have been justifiable as an expression of this faith and as worship of Yahweh's exalted majesty. Only the worship offered by the believer whose whole life is shaped by God's will would be pleasing to Yahweh.

None of the pre-exilic prophets suggested what a proper cult of the faithful might be like. Obviously they considered the question unreal and meaningless so long as their nation had not demonstrated

through observance of the ethical requirements that it had returned
to Yahweh. Such repentance and return was all-important. Therefore
it was not the prophets' purpose to improve the cult but to bring
about a transformation of men's total lives through surrender to the
divine will. Only after judgment had actually been visited upon
Judah and Jerusalem and a portion of the nation had gone into exile
did Ezekiel consider himself commissioned to lay out the program
for a new cult to be observed by an Israel purified through judgment
and deportation.

c) The prophetical attitude in questions of social justice[7] was
above all characterized by denunciation of disregard for and transgression of the law. Such conduct, especially for the representatives
of Yahwism, must have appeared not only as a clear sign of political
and moral deterioration but also of disrespect for Yahweh, who
legitimized the law, and apostasy from him. The law is disregarded
when a man has inwardly declared himself independent of Yahweh
and will have nothing to do with God's sovereignty and communion
with God.

Above all the prophets relentlessly exposed the transgressions of
the upper classes and property owners: They defraud others in com-
merce and can hardly wait to begin again after a holiday (Amos
8:4-7). They abhor justice and commit outrages and bloody deeds
(Mic. 3:9-10). They hate the man who can give true evidence in
court that conflicts with their interests (Amos 5:7, 10-11). They take
bribes to acquit the guilty and condemn the innocent (Isa. 5:23).

It is not sufficient, however, to observe the laws in force. Perhaps
this is what Amos already meant when he accused men of heartlessly
using for their own benefit the pledged garment of the poor man,
which should cover him at night, of drinking the wine collected in
place of money, and selling the poor into slavery on account of a
trifle (Amos 2:6-8). Although the laws in force may provide for such
conduct, it is still a sin to proceed brutally according to the letter in
every case, neither inquiring into the sense and spirit of a law nor
listening to one's own heart speak against its superficial and wooden
application (Isa. 29:13). Even in the realm of law and justice man
is called on to submit totally to Yahweh's claim, basing his conduct
not on objective performance and outward observance of the law but

[7] A. Causse, "Les prophètes et la crise sociologique de la religion d'Israël,"
RHPhR, XII (1932), 93-140; H. Donner, "Die soziale Botschaft der Propheten
im Lichte der Gesellschaftsordnung in Israel," *Oriens Antiquus*, II (1963), 229-
45; E. Gillischewski, "Die Wirtschaftsethik der israelitischen Propheten," *Jb für
jüdische Geschichte und Literatur*, XXV (1923/24), 32-61.

on personal surrender and an attitude in harmony with God's will. For this reason the principle *"fiat justitia, pereat mundus"* must give way before human rights, willed and given by God. For the prophets were guardians of human rights long before these rights were discovered for political applications.

An example of proper human conduct according to a comprehensive principle is given in Isa. 1:16*b*-17:

> Cease to do evil,
>   learn to do good;
> seek justice,
>   guide *the oppressed;*
> defend the fatherless,
>   plead the case of the widow.

Such intervention on behalf of the oppressed, orphans, and widows was originally a duty of the king, as the Code of Hammurabi (Rev. xxiv. 60-61), Ugaritic texts (I Aqht i. 23-25; II Aqht v. 7-8; 127. 33-34, 45-47), and for Israel Ps. 72:2, 4 show. Then it was declared to be the duty of every Israelite (Exod. 22:20-23; cf. the later texts Deut. 10:18; 24:17; 27:19). Isaiah went a step further in another direction. His first and basic requirement was: Do good and not evil! The specific individual requirements that follow served to elucidate the basic requirement; they were practical examples of how the basic principle should be applied. The individual ordinances of the old law, which the prophets interpreted as mere examples, were replaced by a single concentrated requirement claiming the total man: do good. The attitude so described was to evidence its presence and effects in the detailed conduct of daily life.

When Israel refused to accept this fundamental claim, it was unavoidable that the prophets should find themselves in opposition to merely outward or erroneous application of the law, coupled with blindness to the fundamental requirement and attitude. And the danger associated with erroneous understanding of law and justice finally resulted in opposition to the content of the law itself. The true will of Yahweh, transformed into a lie by the pen of the scribe, was contrasted to the written law (Jer. 8:8). The many regulations of the state, which the officials never tired of issuing in the name of the king, were condemned because they merely laid new burdens upon the people and robbed them of their rights (Isa. 10:1-3) In contrast to these regulations stands the living will of God for the present moment, which demands man's total surrender. From this surrender flow knowledge of the concrete requirement and its application in personal decision and responsibility, and in opposition to the existing legal order. As subsequent treatment of the prophets' message in Deuteronomy and elsewhere shows, to the basic requirement of justice must be added as an inseparable principle the law of love. Justice alone cannot and must not rule; justice and love together must determine and shape the life men live together.

d) Finally, the prophets directed their criticism against the state and its policies,[8] above all against the monarchy, which represented the state and espoused its policies. Since it was responsible to Yahweh and owed him strict accounting, it was necessarily open to violent attacks when catastrophe threatened to follow in its wake. If it refused correction, it and consequently the entire nation were threatened by disaster. Then the monarchy was transformed from a blessing into a curse, from a gift of Yahweh to a punishment, so that the nation could expect no benefit from it. Yahweh even used it as a rod to chastise his people. For this purpose he appointed kings, removed them, and replaced them with others if they did not wreak enough havoc (Hos. 13:9-11), so that the monarchy became an instrument of his judgment.

The state was vulnerable at many points to the prophets' criticism. They frequently condemned the vicious methods employed in pursuit of domestic policies (e.g., Isa. 3:12-15; Jer. 22:13-17), including religious policies. Obviously they did not support the elevation of Yahwism to the status of an established religion and the alliance between throne and altar, which were associated with syncretism. Their attack on the cult was probably based in part on the fact that its observance fostered the established religion and that it was used in support of official policies that were pursued with its aid. In addition, the prophets condemned Israelite foreign policy—that treacherous and deceitful back and forth by means of which the small states of Judah and Israel sought to play a rôle between the great powers. In the last analysis, such policies exhibit abysmal stupidity and corruption of the statesmen, who even so cannot evade the will of Yahweh (Hos. 7:11-12). For all politics that would play

[8] H. Donner, *Israel unter den Völkern*, 1964; K. Elliger, "Prophet und Politik," *ZAW*, LIII (1935), 3-22 (= his *Kleine Schriften zum Alten Testament*, 1966, pp. 119-40); N. K. Gottwald, *All the Kingdoms of the Earth*, 1964; J. Hempel, *Politische Absicht und politische Wirkung im biblischen Schrifttum*, 1938; E. Jenni, *Die politischen Voraussagen der Propheten*, 1956; H.-J. Kraus, *Prophetie und Politik*, 1952; F. Weinrich, *Der religiös-utopische Charakter der "prophetischen Politik,"* 1932.

a rôle in the vain struggle for power on the stage of this world while ignoring the true Lord of the world is condemned to failure from the outset. Even war can no longer be considered a political implement. The prophets considered it rather an expression of Israel's sinfulness, just good enough to serve as a devastating admonition to repent or to be threatened as punishment on the day of judgment. Thus for the prophets peace was not a breathing space between two wars, but the natural condition of the world. Since war, which is waged with confidence in one's own power and that of one's allies, is sinful, peace should in fact always reign. Since this is not the case, man is to blame. Peace is taken away, but the war that replaces it becomes man's judgment. Only repentance could prevent this from happening. But since none of the prophets found the people willing to repent, they spoke of peace to come in the time after Yahweh's judging or redeeming intervention (Zeph. 3:12-13; Hos. 2:20 [Eng. 2:18])—an expectation extended by later eschatological prophecy into eternal peace.

The prophets did not direct their criticism against government per se; Isaiah could even see judgment taking effect in the collapse of government, in anarchy (Isa. 3:1-9). The state was certainly acknowledged as a form of ordered human life together. But the prophets disputed the naïve identification of the king's actions and the policies of his officials with the governance of Yahweh, and thus introduced into public life the tension between man's will and God's will. They showed the ambiguous position of the state, which has a function to perform for human life together and is itself neither divine nor demonic when it performs this function, but which can depart all too easily from this course, claiming for itself divine authority and the power to make ultimate decisions. When this happens it must be resisted and made once more to respect its limitations.

The prophets did not want faith to be dependent on politics; neither did they seek to have the political actions of the state under the tutelage of representatives of the faith. Instead, like Isaiah confronting Ahaz (Isa. 7:1-9), they demanded faithful statesmen who would dare to make their decisions on their own responsibility because in political questions—as in all life—they acted as faithful believers, and not, like the Assyrian king reproached by Isaiah, on the basis of their own might and arrogance (Isa. 10:5-15).

3. *Relationship to tradition.* In the great individual prophets the religious impulses of the Mosaic period came to life once more—if

not in identical shape, then in purified and expanded form. They re-experienced Yahweh's miraculous activity and his inflexible will, requiring a decision. Crucial for them was their own experience, above all what was revealed to them in their "secret experiences" (see § 19.2). Now we must face the question of their relationship to traditions, especially Israelite tradition. We may ask whether they restricted themselves to using such traditions in their preaching and how this was done, or whether they were completely dominated by traditions, lived within them, depended on them, and recited, actualized, or radicalized them.

The simplest solution of this much-discussed problem is to assume that the prophets merely adapted the ancient traditions to each new situation and made practical application of them.[9] But they rejected the traditional religious movements more than they accepted and acknowledged them, and dealt with the traditions in ways not usually imputed to them. Jeremiah did not announce the adaptation of Israel's ancient commitments to the present age, but rather a totally new commitment (Jer. 31:31-34).

The view that prophecy is rooted in tradition has been most vigorously espoused by von Rad.[10] He sees the prophets as being associated with three great comprehensive complexes of tradition, those of the exodus, David, and Zion, all of which are election traditions. To these Deutero-Isaiah added the creation tradition. The differences between the prophets depend accordingly on which tradition they stood in and which of its aspects they emphasized. Furthermore, it is important to note that they interpreted the election traditions eschatologically, resulting in the vision of Yahweh's new saving acts to come in future history.

This view runs up against a basic difficulty that von Rad gets around by treating the historical traditions separately. During the time of the pre-exilic prophets, the historical traditions to which he refers existed only in fragmentary and inchoate form. The very traditions that receive the greatest theological emphasis were also the latest: the Deuteronomistic tradition and the priestly source stratum of the Hexateuch. They could not have exercised any significant influence on the prophets, but were rather influenced themselves by prophetical theology, as Vriezen has shown using the Deuteronomic notion of election as an example.[11] Of course they incorporated much earlier material, but the special religious and theological emphasis that they place on certain aspects is the final element that went into their shaping.

Even apart from this consideration, von Rad's thesis that the roots of the prophets' message are to be found in these three election traditions is contestable. For instance, he considers Isaiah's two themes to be the peril or

---

[9] As is done, for example, by J. Bright, *History of Israel*, 1959.
[10] G. von Rad, *Theologie des Alten Testaments*, II, 4th ed., 1965 (English: *Old Testament Theology*, 1962).
[11] T. C. Vriezen, *Die Erwählung Israels nach dem Alten Testament*, 1953.

safety of Zion and the Davidic messiah. It is dubious, however, whether the two messianic passages Isa. 9:1-6 (Eng. 9:2-7) and 11:1-9 should be assigned to Isaiah. The contrary view is not infrequently espoused, but the evidence is by no means so convincing that half of Isaiah's traditional roots can be traced to these messianic texts. Furthermore, according to Isaiah's preaching Jerusalem is not to be simply delivered or preserved. There is not a single discourse from Isaiah promising anything of the sort. Even when the prophet repudiated the Assyrians as an instrument of divine punishment there was no alteration of his threat against the city; even after the Assyrians withdrew from Jerusalem in 701 the threat was if anything intensified (Isa. 22:1-14; 32:9-14). Isaiah always made deliverance dependent on radical repentance for sin and return to Yahweh. For the necessity of such repentance and return as an indispensable prerequisite for deliverance, see vs. 4 in 29:1-8, vs. 15 in 30:15-17, and vs. 6 in 31:4-9. And in Isa. 1:19-20 the great "either/or" is unmistakably clear. Similar arguments apply to the interpretation of the other prophets.

The situation is no different with regard to the hypothesis that the prophets were rooted in legal or wisdom traditions. In the case of Amos, the scattered references to so-called apodictic law[12]—which in fact represented not "divine law" but rules of conduct (see § 6.3)—are totally insufficient to demonstrate dependence. The same is true in the case of Micah, in whose case Mic. 6:8 has been cited.[13] Apart from the fact that 6:1-8 can hardly be assigned to Micah himself, but is considerably later, it is impossible to claim that *"mišpāṭ"* is a term for "amphictyonic law" and *"higgîd"* for its "cultic proclamation." Furthermore, 6:8 is not addressed to the Israelite but to "man" (*'ādām*); its perspective transcends Israel. The suggestion that Amos is rooted in ancient clan wisdom[14] is seen to be highly questionable when the details are examined more closely.[15] In Amos and above all in Isaiah the connection with wisdom instruction basically means no more than that they had a particular kind of formal education; thus the appearance of elements from and points of contact with wisdom signifies only that the prophet in question was an educated man with common sense.

Of course in everything the prophets said and did they stood within a long and extensive tradition—including not only prophetism, but also the civilization and religion of the ancient Near East and Israel. But this does not mean that they can be assigned a place in some hypothetical civilization found throughout the ancient Near East and equated with Mesopotamian or Canaanite cult prophets.

[12] R. Bach, "Gottesrecht und weltliches Recht in der Verkündigung des Propheten Amos," in *Dehn Festschrift*, 1957, pp. 23-34.
[13] W. Beyerlin, *Die Kulttraditionen Israels in der Verkündigung des Propheten Micha*, 1959.
[14] H. W. Wolff, *Amos' geistige Heimat*, 1964.
[15] J. L. Crenshaw, "The influence of the Wise upon Amos," *ZAW*, LXXIX (1967), 42-52; G. Wanke, "אוי und הוי," *ZAW*, LXXVIII (1966), 215-18.

Neither can they be understood as mere quardians of an Israelite tradition they might reform, to which they might recall people, or whose immediate relevance they might proclaim. Their relationship to the traditions was different. It is true that they were linked with the religious tradition of Israel and through it with the more comprehensive tradition of the ancient Near Eastern nations. But this connection is not what actually determined their approach to life, but rather their own experience of Yahweh. That is what made the prophets a unique phenomenon. They gave up the religious forms that had arisen through compromise with other ideas and practices, acting instead on a truth they discovered existentially. In the process they did not exclude tradition, but made use of it for their preaching. The ancient traditions, however, were not fundamental to their faith; they were reshaped for the prophets' message, interpreted and understood afresh, in order that with their aid the prophets might express what they wanted to say. This is the way Isaiah handled the notion of the Day of Yahweh (Isa. 2:12-17, following Amos 5:18-20), the confident terms "rock" and "stone" applied to Yahweh, which would instead cause men to stumble and fall (Isa. 8:14), the epithet "who dwells on Mount Zion," guaranteeing the destruction of the city (Isa. 8:16-18), and the memory of Yahweh's victorious battles under David, which would soon be repeated—but against Judah (Isa. 28:21). These ideas were based on Isaiah's call experience. His question "How long?" addressed to Yahweh presupposed, according to the traditional view of his age, that Yahweh would torment but not destroy. But Yahweh in his answer predicted utter desolation (Isa. 6:11). Thus tradition was dashed to pieces for Isaiah, and he was set on a new course.

This helps explain why the prophets were not restricted by traditions and were not dependent on them, but rather used them freely for specific purposes implicit in their message. Despite all their common Israelite traits, each possessed an unmistakable individuality; in like fashion, they were not concerned with the common traditions, but with the particular message that each had to proclaim. They therefore used the traditions in the interests of this message. More precisely, the traditions and their interpretation were not among the primary elements of the prophets' discourses, but belonged to their later stages: the interpretation of the secret experience in the context of prophetical faith or the rational analysis of the experience necessary for its proclamation.

Within this framework, the reason the prophets used the traditions and their interpretation was to render the living word of Yahweh comprehensible for preaching and to illustrate their new insight into man's relationship to Yahweh and to the world. Because of this new insight the prophets did not recall men to tradition; by interpreting it and unfolding its meaning they pointed the way to a new relationship with Yahweh. The change undergone by tradition corresponded to the inward and outward change in the sinner when transformed into a new man.

4. *Relationship to other religious attitudes.* The great individual prophets attacked more or less explicitly and in detail the other religious movements they found about them. An isolated exception, in a certain sense, was religious conservatism, which played only a minor rôle and could not claim special attention. The prophets, like Jeremiah, acknowledged the seriousness and pure intent of the representatives of this movement (Jeremiah 35), but did not for a moment consider preserving Yahwism in its most ancient form or even viewing the nomadic way of life as a desirable religious ideal. Nevertheless the real purpose of this school was fulfilled in the prophets' message in a new and different way: the maintenance of Yahwism in all its purity. But its association with an antiquated way of life was surmounted.

What is merely hinted at here both characterized and determined the relationship of the prophetical approach to the other ascertainable approaches: again and again other religious forms were surmounted, while their actual purposes were fulfilled.

a) First, the prophets both surmounted and fulfilled magic. The example of their symbolic actions makes this clear. These originated from magical actions such as are found among all races. Such magical actions are expected to have their own efficacy and produce the desired effect by means of their own magical power. The prophet, on the contrary, did not assume that the objects with which he performed his action were imbued with power and that its performance was effectual—in other words, he did not expect that the result would automatically follow the performance of his action. Instead he symbolized the desired outcome; its realization was left to Yahweh.

Though the magical element was thus surmounted and eliminated, the prophet nevertheless performed his action in full certainty that the event symbolized would in fact take place. The symbolic action was the effectual announcement of an event because it was Yahweh's will to bring it about. Thus in the symbolic action magic was not only surmounted but also fulfilled: what was symbolized could take place.

b) The prophets also surmounted and fulfilled cultic religion. They removed the cultic barriers intended to render life secure, especially in the face of its total questioning through the living experience of Yahweh. The cult is not a means of salvation (Isa. 1:10-17); when it is employed in this fashion it must perish. Everything that people had thought could be used to preserve or attain God's favor—temple and priesthood, images and altars, sacrifices and hymns, songs and dances, vows and festivals—everything was useless as a means of securing Yahweh's blessing. Indeed, it could be seen throughout the land that ultimately this cult served only the cause of sin, that it was itself fundamentally sinful, because by its aid men evade God's claim instead of surrendering to it. As long as this is the case, the cult does not bring about God's favor but is rather a sign of the human corruption that must submit to God's judgment.

The prophets not only surmounted cultic religion but fulfilled its real purpose in prayer. True worship of Yahweh takes place in the prayer of the believer. The most characteristic example is the life of Jeremiah, which is filled with three types of prayer: inward struggle with Yahweh (laments or confessions of Jeremiah), intercession on behalf of his erring nation, and absorption of the prophet in Yahweh, whereby Yahweh's will in each situation was made clear to him. Here the self-centered cultic attitude was surmounted and fulfilled most profoundly in prayer.

c) The prophets also surmounted the approach of religious nationalism, breaking down its nationalistic barriers. For the God they preached refuses to place himself at the disposal of a people or nation, and is not the guarantor of national power or culture. Before his will, people and nation, monarchy and election, favorable alliances and victorious armies pale into insignificance. On this basis we may understand the prophets' criticism of the monarchy; the same holds true for their condemnation of the nation. Yahweh's exclusive association with Israel was surmounted. According to the faith of the prophets, Yahweh holds sway in the destinies of all peoples and nations.

The national God became Lord of the world. The history of the nation expanded into the history of the world and was viewed within that framework. History looked beyond the boundaries of the nation and became religious interpretation of all that took place in the world. Thus the nationalistic faith was also fulfilled. It had seen Yahweh's revelation not in the cycle of the seasons and the fertility of the soil, but in the events that make up the lives of men and nations, transcending natural processes. All that remained necessary was to surmount the restriction to the Israelite people and their national experience, and to recognize Yahweh as Lord of all nations. This is precisely what took place with the prophets. Now Yahweh's will pertained to all nations. This is why the prophets so often addressed Yahweh's word to them; this is why they, too, were threatened with judgment if they had disobeyed his commands—even if it was only the Moabites wronging the Edomites (Amos 2:1-3). For the later eschatological prophecy, all nations will even share in eschatological salvation.

d) The wisdom approach to life was surmounted by Isaiah, the only prophet to concern himself expressly with this movement. He attacked the "wise" who arrogantly based their political plans on their own wisdom, trusting in their own insight and the power of their Egyptian allies while doubting Yahweh's wisdom. Their self-confident wisdom is closed to the true wisdom of God. But Yahweh alone is wise and frustrates the cleverness of those whose wisdom is worldly. The whole point is not to be clever and prudent, looking right and left for a way out, but to act on faith, to repent, and to trust in Yahweh (Isa. 7:9; 30:15). Thus the wisdom approach is also surmounted, but its purpose—deliverance and strength—fulfilled.

e) The legal approach, which we encounter toward the end of the pre-exilic period and which is often associated with the cultic approach, may likewise be said to have been surmounted by the prophetical movement. Seen from the viewpoint of the prophets' message, fulfillment of the law appeared as merely a further attempt on the part of the devout individual to place Yahweh under an obligation through his own actions. One must not stop at the letter of the law, but recognize and fulfill its spirit. Personal commitment must replace objective performance and merely outward obedience. In the schema of performance and reward man asserts his rights vis-à-vis Yahweh instead of acknowledging Yahweh's will, before which he is nothing. Therefore the prophetical message excluded legalistic piety even in its more refined form, not to mention its grosser manifestations.

Of course the prophets themselves repeatedly pronounced ethical admonitions, though not as individual laws, but as specific applications of Yahweh's basic requirements, adapted to each situation. Above all, their position was different: they are the consequence of living rightly in the world before Yahweh, not the foundation on which such a life is built. Their observance without ulterior motives is the outward expression that a man is in the grip of Yahweh and has surrendered to him in faith.

This helps explain why Jeremiah did not welcome the reformation of Josiah joyfully, but at first took a "wait and see" attitude, possibly even critical, and said nothing. For even though many grounds of prophetical complaint were removed, the cultic and legal interest was still there. Later Jeremiah openly expressed his criticism. Neither did Ezekiel look on the Deuteronomic attitude as a way to salvation. He did not see Jerusalem preserved by the reformation but condemned to destruction as before. Above all, he picked up the Deuteronomic idea of Israel's election, which in its original setting—without gainsaying the seriousness of the situation—was meant to be a primary idea helping summon the people to a new life and deliver the entire nation. By taking up this notion and then depicting Israel's constant apostasy from Yahweh (Ezek. 20:1 ff.), the prophet showed that he considered the Deuteronomic experiment unsuccessful.

f) We may now summarize our conclusions. The relationship of the prophetical approach to the other religious movements shows that all of them were surmounted by the prophets, and at the same time fulfilled in their most profound and authentic purposes. Comparison reveals the superiority of the prophets' faith. Of course we find this attitude not only in the few great individual prophets, but more or less plainly almost everywhere in the OT. It was indeed grounded in Mosaic Yahwism, from which authentic influences were at work even in the cultic approach and that of religious nationalism. The prophetical message itself in turn exercised a strong influence: on the narrative historians with their nationalistic attitude, on the representatives of Deuteronomic theology, on later wisdom instruction and the whole post-exilic period.

5. *The place of the great prophetical figures in the history of religions. a)* The prophets' approach to life marked the transition from what was still predominantly an early religion to a fully developed high religion. It is noteworthy that this transition took place elsewhere as well, during the same period.[16] In the Greek world, the

---

[16] R. Otto, *Vischnu-Nārāyana,* 1923, pp. 203-29: "Das Gesetz der Parallelen in der Religionsgeschichte."

period between roughly 800 and 500 B.C. witnessed the transition from *mythos* to *logos,* from mythology to theology. At the beginning of this process stood the cosmological speculations of Hesiod; the multiplicity of gods developed into the unity of the *theîon.* This beginning split into a theistic line from Anaxagoras to Aristotle and a mystical line leading to the universal identity of the Eleatic School, Plato, and the Stoa. But both led to a unity of the absolute and thus to high religion.

In India, the early religion of the Veda contained the seeds of the later development that took place roughly 800-500 B.C., which found expression in the literature of the Upanishads. There the early substratum of sacrificial speculation and mythology is still discernible, but the unity of the absolute is gradually appearing. Buddha constituted the climax.

In China, as in Greece, comprehension of the absolute took two ways, defined by the two outstanding founders of religion in the East: the theistic way by Confucius, the mystical way by Lao-tzu. Both lived about 500 B.C.

Finally, a similar process took place in Israelite prophetism. For in Israel it was the prophets who led the way to a fully developed high religion in the period roughly 800-500 B.C. Its first element, experience of the one absolute God in a practical monotheism, was already largely present, although Deutero-Isaiah was the first to draw its full conclusions in a theoretical monotheism. But the second element originated in prophetism itself: it concerned man, and was the discovery, rooted in that absolute experience of God, of an existential state of alienation from God to which he was exposed. This is not found previously; therefore the prophetical high religion was superior to the other religious movements, which at best constituted a first stage in the transition from early to high religion.

b) The prophetical approach furthermore marked the transition from a national religion to a world religion, in which the national community was no longer identical with the religious community. The individual believer was now the bearer of faith; he could join with others to form a particular religious community. Religion focused on the individual, who had become independent and whose life had developed its own internal problems. In the national religion the individual could lose his salvation if he broke the ties that bound him to the community; now the situation was reversed: existential alienation from God was seen as the fundamental situation in which the individual found himself; salvation was something to be gained, not preserved. The focus of attention was always on the individual person, human existence, a personal need of purely religious nature, independent of all ties with nation and people. Therefore the prophets included other nations in their preaching. Accordingly the message of the prophets, like that of every world religion, was universal: corresponding to the universal distress and need there was a universal message that would lead to universal salvation. For the universality of the message meant not only that it was proclaimed to all and addressed to all, but also that it spoke of a universal subject: the possibility and necessity of life under God's sovereignty and in communion with God, and the way leading to this life. There was a universal offer (transformation through repentance or redemption), acceptance of which laid the groundwork for salvation (a new life). The matter was truly of vital importance: man's existence or nonexistence hung in the balance. For the prophets' message and its efficacy there was no limit within man, no limited area. As a world religion, the prophetical faith was concerned with the very center of the inmost being of human personality, from which all the other realms of human existence derived their new meaning and virtue. In addition, unlike mysticism, the prophetical faith sought to influence all the realms of human life and of the world on the basis of this center, and to shape the course of events through this new association with Yahweh.

CHAPTER FOUR: DEUTERONOMIC THEOLOGY, CONSEQUENCE AND FOURTH INFLUENCE

§ 21 RELIGIOUS DEVELOPMENTS

A. ALT, "Die Heimat des Deuteronomiums," in his *Kleine Schriften zur Geschichte des Volkes Israel*, II (1953), 250-75; W. BAUMGARTNER, "Der Kampf um das Deuteronomium," *ThR*, NF I (1929), 7-25; A. BENTZEN, *Die josianische Reform und ihre Voraussetzungen*, 1926; K. BUDDE, "Das Deuteronomium und die Reform Josias," *ZAW*, XLIV (1926), 177-224; R. FRANKENA, "The Vassal-Treaties of Esarhaddon and the Dating of Deuteronomy," *OTS*, XIV (1965), 122-54; H. GRESSMANN, "Josia und das Deuteronomium, *ZAW* XLII (1924), 313-37; A. JEPSEN, "Die Reform des Josia," in *Festschrift Friedrich Baumgärtel*, 1959, pp. 97-108; S. LOERSCH, *Das Deuteronomium und seine Deutungen*, 1967; N. LOHFINK, "Die Bundesurkunde des Königs Josia," *Bibl*, XLIV (1963), 261-88, 461-98; V. MAAG, "Erwägungen zur deuteronomischen Kultzentralisation," *VT*, VI (1956), 10-18; G. VON RAD, *Deuteronomium-Studien*, 2nd ed., 1948 (English: *Studies in Deuteronomy*, 1963) ; D. W. B. ROBINSON, *Josiah's Reform and the Book of the Law*, 1951; M. WEINFELD, *The Provenance of Deuteronomy and the Deuteronomic School*, Dissertation, Jerusalem, 1964.

1. *Background and early history. a*) Although under the regime of Manasseh, which was totally dependent on Assyria, the opposition in Judah was condemned to silence, its resistance to the growing syncretism continued *sub rosa*. The two major opposition movements, the levitical country priests and prophetical circles, appear to have formed an alliance on the basis of their conservative cultic attitude. Both saw the tragedy of their age in Judah's apostasy from Yahweh. Both saw increasing danger in the numerous unsupervised sanctuaries throughout the land, which were exposed to the influence of Canaanite cults, as well as in Assyrian worship at Jerusalem and the various minor cults. If all these could be done away with, pure Yahwism might be successfully restored to its place of honor. One might hope that in consequence the political, social, and cultural damage could be repaired.

The prerequisite for the realization of these goals came to pass in the latter part of the reign of Ashurbanipal, king of Assyria (d. 626 B.C.), and after his death, when the Assyrian Empire began to fall apart. As a result, Assyrian pressure on the minor states of Syria and Palestine was reduced, so that for a while they were for all practical purposes without a sovereign. In Judah, this made possible the ascendancy of those political and religious forces that operated as a kind of national freedom party, seeking to liberate the land from Assyrian domination and uphold the sovereignty of their own state rather than depending on Egypt. Part of this program was the purification of life and the cult through elimination of foreign accretions.

They were able to gain the support of King Josiah for their goals. By the year 622 B.C. at the latest, he had severed his ties with Assyria. Rejection of Assyrian sovereignty meant also rejection of the Assyrian religion; the latter was inconceivable without the former. It is disputed whether all measures were taken at once or were carried out more cautiously in several stages lasting several years. It appears most likely that Josiah's measures began soon after the death of Ashurbanipal and culminated in the cultic reform of 622 B.C. In any case we are dealing with a continuous coherent process that was both a political and a religious undertaking, even in the concluding reformation. The reformation removed from the cult everything that could not be squared with Yahwism, and was an acknowledgment of Yahweh on the part of the state as the sole ruler of his people. The reformation was on the one hand anti-Assyrian, on the other a conservative revolution with nationalistic, cultic, and legalistic tendencies.

b) The basis for the cultic reform was a law code that was presented to Josiah. It is almost universally recognized that this was an early form of the book of Deuteronomy, the so-called Proto-Deuteronomy; therefore Josiah's reformation has also been called the Deuteronomic Reformation.[1] The reasons for identifying the legal code of the reformation with Proto-Deuteronomy are compelling, the more so since this law book went beyond removal of the cult of the Assyrian state gods from the Jerusalem Temple, adding other measures that are mentioned in II Kings 22–23 and are required only in Deuteronomy: suppression of all sanctuaries apart from the Jerusalem Temple, elimination of all alien cults from the Temple, and celebration of Passover in the Temple. We thus have the following points of agreement between the account of the reformation and Deuteronomy:

[1] BHH, I, 336-38; RGG, II, 101-3; IDB, I, 831-38.

Cultic centralization	II Kings	23:8-9, 19	Deut. 12:13 ff.
Abolition of the astral cult		23:11-12	17:3
Removal of the cult prostitutes		23:7	23:18
Extirpation of the necromancers		23:24	18:11 ff.
Prohibition of child sacrifice		23:10	18:10
Celebration of Passover in the Temple		23:21 ff.	16:1 ff.

The only discrepancy is the difference between II Kings 23:8-9 and Deut. 18:6 in the ranking of the priests from the country sanctuaries, which can be explained by local circumstances.

It is difficult to determine the scope and therefore the content of Proto-Deuteronomy or the law book of the reformation. It can only be defined in broad outline; the wording can no longer be determined at all, because later revision was very thorough. In any case, the law book possessed an introduction and conclusion in addition to the legal corpus, probably the present internal framework of Deuteronomy. We can probably make the following reconstruction:[2]

1. Introduction, sanctioning the law book as Yahweh's will, together with parenetic expansions and solemn admonitions: 4:44–11:32 (omitting 9:7–10:11);
2. Ordinances concerning cultic centralization: 12; 14:22-29; 15:19-23; 16: 1-17; probably also 17:8-13; 26:1-15.
3. Casuistically framed ordinances dealing with "civil" law: nucleus of 21–25;
4. Abomination laws, whose concluding formula declares that such and such an action is an abomination to Yahweh: 16:21–17:1; 18:9-14; 22:5; 23:19; 25:13; possibly also 22:9-12;
5. So-called humanitarian laws: 22:1-4; 23:16-17, 20-21 (Eng. 23:15-16, 19-20); 24:6–25:4; perhaps also the "military laws": 20; 21:10-14; 23:10-15 (Eng. 23:9-14), mostly placed in group 3;
6. Ordinances derived from the so-called Covenant Code (Exod. 20:22–23:19), to the extent these are not contained in the groups already listed: 15:1-11, 12-18; 16:18-20; 19:1-13, 16-21;
7. Conclusion, with the stipulation that the law is to be written upon great stones on Mount Gerizim and an altar is to be built, as well as the pronouncement of blessings and curses: 27:1-10; 28:1-68.

This law book exhibits a complex history.[3] In particular, its relationship to the so-called Covenant Code and the source stratum E suggests the Northern Kingdom of Israel as an answer to the question of where the first law book originated. It must have been composed there before the fall of the state of Israel, in other words, probably not later than the first half of the eighth century B.C. The last period of prosperity under Jeroboam II

[2] See S-F, § 25.3.
[3] See S-F, § 25.4-5.

may have provided the occasion. After the fall of Israel, it found its way
to Jerusalem together with other literature from Israel where it was subject
to an initial revision as early as the time of Hezekiah or on the part of the
opposition reform movement during the reign of Manasseh. At this time
the parenetic and hortatory material was added to the legal corpus, and the
framework, consisting of introduction and conclusion, was composed. The
basic character of the law book was nevertheless preserved, as is shown by
the example of other ancient Near Eastern law codes with introduction and
conclusion (Code of Lipit-Ishtar; Code of Hammurabi). This is the form
in which the law book was used in the time of Josiah.

2. *Josiah's reformation.* According to the account of the reformation in II Kings 22–23, which appears to be based for the most
part on official annals, while II Chronicles 34–35 is less reliable,
the high priest Hilkiah discovered the law book or Proto-Deuteronomy in the Jerusalem Temple. This statement has been interpreted in various ways. But there can be no question of a priestly
fraud or a "discovery" in the sense of legendary origins to legitimize
newly composed documents. We must assume that a scroll was actually discovered after having been in the Temple for a considerable
period. This could result from the custom of depositing important
documents in the Temple (I Sam. 10:25; II Kings 19:14). But if
Proto-Deuteronomy originated as a law book composed in the Northern Kingdom and revised in Jerusalem, it is reasonable to assume
that it was kept in the Temple after being revised and—perhaps in
the context of the initial measures taken against the Assyrian cults—
was rediscovered more or less accidentally.

Hilkiah delivered the scroll to the king, who—dismayed and
terrified at the impending wrath of Yahweh because the ordinances
of the law book had not been obeyed—commanded that inquiry be
made of Yahweh. The prophetess Huldah thereupon predicted disaster, albeit not during Josiah's lifetime. The king took counsel with
the elders of Judah and convoked a general assembly of the people
in the Temple precincts. The book was publicly recited and the
assembly accepted it as new law. Thus its regulations became binding on all. Since it touched on many areas besides cultic questions—
the rights of the king, the appointment of new officials, the disposi-
tion of the army, the treatment of enemies, social and ethical conduct, etc.—and must needs affect the life of the state, the people,
and each individual citizen, its acceptance meant its acknowledgment
as constitution and fundamental law.

Following acceptance of the law book, Jerusalem and its environs
together with the Temple were purified. The paraphernalia of the

Assyrian cults were removed or destroyed, to the extent that this had not already been done: the image of Ishtar, the chariot and horses of the sun-god, and the corresponding altars. The same was done with the furnishings and paraphernalia of the Canaanite and other foreign cults, with the sanctuary of the goat-demons and the site for child sacrifice in the valley of Hinnom. The second act was the centralization of the cult in Judah: all the sanctuaries throughout the countryside were made cultically unclean, and all the priests of Yahweh were ordered to report to Jerusalem. But although Deut. 18:6-7 explicitly gave these priests the same status as the Jerusalem priests, at Jerusalem they were only given the right to live off the income of the priesthood; they were not allowed to officiate at the altar (II Kings 23:9).[4] This is explained by the understandable efforts of the Jerusalem priesthood to avoid carrying out a regulation that was inimicable to their interests. The culmination of all these measures was a Passover celebrated according to the new provisions, such as had not been celebrated since the period of the Judges (II Kings 23:22). Later, when Josiah was able to occupy a few portions of what had been the Northern Kingdom, he extended his reforming measures to them.

Josiah's reformation appears to have been a complete success during his lifetime; at the same time the revision of Proto-Deuteronomy was continued (see § 22.3). After his death, of course, his successors were no longer bound to the law book, so that Jehoiakim—apart from cultic centralization—could simply ignore it. But this did not prevent it from being supplemented in the exilic and post-exilic period until reaching its present form, and it continued to have a powerful effect through its theology.

§ 22 Theology and Life According to Deuteronomic Principles

P. ALTMANN, Erwählungstheologie und Universalismus im Alten Testament, 1964; A. CAUSSE, "La transformation de la notion d'alliance et la rationalisation de l'ancienne coutume dans la réforme deutéronomique," RHPhR, XIII (1933), 1-29, 289-323; F. DUMERMUTH, "Zur deuteronomischen Kulttheologie und ihren Voraussetzungen," ZAW, LXX (1958), 59-98; A. R. HULST, Het karakter van den kultus in Deuteronomium, 1938; A. JEPSEN, Die Quellen des Königsbuches, 2nd ed., 1956; B. MAARSINGH, Onderzoek naar de Ethiek van de Wetten in Deuteronomium, 1961; R. MARTIN-ACHARD,

[4] J. A. Emerton, "Priests and Levites in Deuteronomy," VT, XII (1962), 129-38; G. E. Wright, "The Levites in Deuteronomy," ibid., IV (1954), 325-30.

"La signification théologique de l'élection d'Israël," *ThZ*, XVI (1960), 333-41; M. NOTH, *Die Gesetze im Pentateuch* (= his *Gesammelte Studien zum Alten Testament*, 1957, pp. 9-141 [English: *The Laws in the Pentateuch and Other Studies*, 1962, pp. 1-107]); *idem, Überlieferungsgeschichtliche Studien*, I, 1943; G. VON RAD, *Das Gottesvolk im Deuteronomium*, 1929; T. C. VRIEZEN, *Die Erwählung Israels nach dem Alten Testament*, 1953; M. WEINFELD, "The Origen of the Humanism in Deuteronomy," *JBL*, LXXX (1961), 241-47; *idem*, "The Change in the Conception of Religion in Deuteronomy," *Tarbiz*, XXXI (1961/62), 1-17; H. W. WOLFF, "Das Kerygma des deuteronomistischen Geschichtswerks," *ZAW*, LXXIII (1961), 171-86 (= his *Gesammelte Studien zum Alten Testament*, 1964, pp. 308-24).

1. *Deuteronomic theology.* Deuteronomic theology is dominated by three basic ideas. The first is the unity of Yahweh in contrast to the tendency toward plurality that had been imported into the conception of God by the multiplicity of sanctuaries with their various traditions and theologies.[1] The various epithets applied to El and Baal at the individual sanctuaries of the Canaanites could emphasize certain aspects so strongly that they almost produced new local deities. So likewise the danger had arisen that the conception of Yahweh might split up and finally produce several Yahwehs. The symbolization of Yahweh by means of bull images in the Northern Kingdom had been a first step in this direction. But if there was only a single cultic center, a unified conception of God could be realized there. Therefore Deuteronomic theology demanded centralization of the cult at a single sanctuary.

The second basic idea is that of Yahweh's jealousy. This expression, which we have already encountered (see § 14.1) was employed most frequently by Deuteronomic theology. It expresses striving for recognition of one's sovereign will and individual rights against and to the exclusion of others. In it we clearly hear Yahweh's claim to be worshiped alone. In fact, according to Deuteronomic theology Yahweh's jealousy is directed against Israel's worship of other gods, especially against the influences of the Canaanite cults.

The third basic idea is borrowed from the prophets: the love of Yahweh, who ever since the days of the patriarchs has looked with inexplicable grace and favor upon Israel, although Israel has exhibited no qualities to warrant this favor. This love finds its counterpart on the one hand in Israel's love for Yahweh, which, after scattered earlier references (Exod. 20:6; Judg. 5:31; Jer. 2:2-3), came to

[1] W. F. Bade, "Der Monojahwismus des Deuteronomiums," *ZAW*, XXX (1910), 81-90.

play an important rôle in Deuteronomic theology,[2] and on the other in love for one's neighbor. In this respect Israel is today once more faced with decision, as in the days of Moses.

Deuteronomic theology placed all life under the sign of Yahweh's loving and demanding will. To this end it took up the term *b*ᵉ*rît* (see § 2.4; 6.2; 8.3),[3] which had fallen into disuse for centuries and was preserved only in the Abraham and Moses traditions, making use of its double meaning "assurance/obligation" by applying it on the one hand to Yahweh's promise to the fathers and those who keep his commandments (Deut. 7:9, 12; 8:18; later 4:31; 29:11-12 [Eng. 29:12-13]) and on the other to the obligation placed on the people in the decalogue and the Deuteronomic law (Deut. 5:2; later 4:13, 23; 9:9, 11, 15; 10:8; 17:2; 28:69 [Eng. 29:1]; 29:8 [Eng. 29:9]). Above all the term became significant in the latter sense. Even in the earlier introduction to Deuteronomy it refers to obedience to the decalogue and the Deuteronomic laws (Deut. 5:2-3), which are also mentioned explicitly in Deut. 28:69 (Eng. 29:1); 29:8 (Eng. 29:9). According to this account, Moses gave these laws to the Israelites after they transgressed the Sinai laws in Moab. The new Deuteronomic interpretation of the term differed from the earlier nomadic interpretation in two ways. First, in view of the breach of the old obligation, the Deuteronomic laws refer with special emphasis to the permanent and eternal character of the new obligation, threatening terrible curses in case it is transgressed. Furthermore, they are framed to a much greater extent in legal and juridical terms, especially since the Deuteronomic law book sought to regulate many different aspects of daily life. In this context Deuteronomic theology also developed the idea of double recompense on the part of Yahweh: reward for observing the law, punishment for transgressing it (see § 15.4).[4]

The subjection of all life to the will of Yahweh was directed against the secularization of life and the state that had accompanied cultural development. To this extent Deuteronomic theology was an extension of the earlier cultic and nationalistic religious movements (see § 13.4-5); at the same time, it took a critical attitude toward

[2] J. Coppens, "La doctrine biblique sur l'amour de Dieu et du prochain," *ALBO*, IV.16, 1964.

[3] *BHH*, I, 282, 287; *RGG*, I, 1513-16; *IDB*, I, 714-21; A. Jepsen, "Berith," in *Rudolph Festschrift*, 1961, pp. 161-79; E. Kutsch, "Gesetz und Gnade," *ZAW*, LXXIX (1967), 18-35; N. Lohfink, "Die Wandlung des Bundesbegriffes im Buch Deuteronomium," in *Rahner Festschrift*, 1964, pp. 423-44.

[4] M. Weinfeld, "The Source of the Idea of Reward in Deuteronomy," *Tarbiz*, XXX (1960/61), 8-15.

rationalistic, enlightened, and "secular" wisdom (see § 13.6). The divine sovereignty that was the new aspiration of this theology was to be symbolized concretely in the central sanctuary with its cultic mass activities; the way of life ordained by God was to be based on the written record of God's will. In this way men hoped to avoid human wickedness and the judgment threatened by the prophets as its consequence. For Deuteronomic theology adopted the prophetical criticism of the theory that Israel lived essentially in a state of favor with God. But unlike the prophets, who generally took an extremely negative view of Israel's future chances, this theology attempted to preserve the nation as a whole from the threatened catastrophic judgment, without attempting to cover up the seriousness of the situation. To this end it addressed itself to men as individual sinners, requiring them to accept the obligations of the Deuteronomic law. If each individual would obey it and all would decide for Yahweh, the nation as the sum of all these individuals could be saved. If this reversal would take place, Yahweh's love for Israel would remain. The curse need not take effect, the prophets' threats of judgment would go unrealized. This Deuteronomic attempt at a synthesis between cultic and nationalistic theology on the one hand and prophetical theology on the other, while excluding secularism, was a notable theological accomplishment.

The keynote was the concept of election, for which Deuteronomic theology employed the verb *bāḥar* as a technical term, focusing on this concept in order to summon the entire nation to a new way of life.[5] This lent Israel's self-understanding a markedly nationalistic and particularistic coloration: Israel is Yahweh's own holy people, and is therefore meant to eliminate the other peoples from Palestine and not intermarry with them (Deut. 7:1-6). In similar fashion, a text from this period emanating from priestly circles and influenced by this notion predicts that Yahweh will create a holy nation dedicated to him, with a priestly monarchy or king (Exod. 19:6).[6]

Deuteronomic theology exerted a powerful influence on the future and the subsequent development of Yahwism, above all through the concepts of legal obligation and the election of Israel. It can therefore be termed another influence on Yahwism. Whether this influence was favorable and desirable is another question. Jeremiah in any case did not welcome the Deuteronomic law, and did not pro-

[5] *BHH*, I, 435-36; *RGG*, II, 610-13; *IDB*, II, 76-82.
[6] G. Fohrer, "'Priesterliches Königtum,' Ex. 19,6," *ThZ*, XIX (1963), 359-62; H. Wildberger, *Jahwes Eigentumsvolk*, 1960.

claim its ordinances as an obligatory b*rît* replacing the Sinai obligation that had been broken; he proclaimed instead a new b*rît* embodying Yahweh's promise, which would be established not in a law book but in the communication of Yahweh's will to the inmost heart of man (Jer. 31:31-34). In addition, Deuteronomic theology with its interest in the codified will of Yahweh paved the way for an authoritative canon[7] and marked the beginning of the development of a "religion of the book," a faith that could be taught and learned (see Deut. 7:6 ff.; 30:11 ff.).

2. *Life under the Deuteronomic law. a*) In the cultic realm, the Deuteronomic law bitterly and energetically attacked Canaanite institutions and practices, as well as those connected with other alien religions. It prohibited, often on pain of death, the worship of gods other than Yahweh, holy trees and masseboth, sacral prostitution and child sacrifice, divination, sorcery, and necromancy. The prohibitions against transvestism and mingling of unlike things, as well as the exclusion of eunuchs, are probably directed against alien religious practices (Deut. 22:5, 9-12; 23:2). Yahwism was to be preserved in all its purity. Of course it was not the Yahwism of Moses or of the great individual prophets, but the religion that developed in the course of the monarchy, with cultic and nationalistic emphasis and enriched through the addition of much that was originally Canaanite. The wrath of those who championed the Deuteronomic law was directed only against alien institutions and practices that had not yet been assimilated or could never be assimilated. What the prophets had criticized was not reformed.[8]

As a consequence of cultic centralization the significance of the Jerusalem Temple increased, and the city itself grew in importance. There was now only the one sanctuary at Jerusalem, which Yahweh had singled out. Even for Jerusalem and its Temple Deuteronomic theology had introduced this notion of election, associated with the idea of Yahweh's dwelling in the Temple. On account of the special position Jerusalem occupied as the chosen city and site of the Temple, it became the cultic center for all Israelites.

---

[7] In late additions Deuteronomy is itself already thought of as "scripture"; see Deut. 17:18; 28:58, 61; 29:19-20 (Eng. 29:20-21).

[8] For a discussion of the difference between the prophets and Deuteronomy, see R. Dobbie, "Deuteronomy and the Prophetic Attitude to Sacrifice," *SJTh*, XII (1959), 68-82.

Yahweh chose Jerusalem and the Temple in order to "cause his name to dwell" there (Deut. 12:5). Thus the materialistic notion of the deity's actually dwelling in the sanctuary was surmounted. A distinction was drawn between the supramundane God and the revelation of his governance through his name at the appropriate site. This site of Yahweh's revealed presence was the Temple.

Deut. 16:1-17 contains the Deuteronomic festival calendar with three festivals (see § 16.3)[9] to be celebrated henceforth exclusively in the Jerusalem Temple. Concerning the Feast of Weeks and the Feast of Ingathering, now called the Feast of Booths, nothing more need be said. But what had been the Feast of Unleavened Bread was obviously combined with the reintroduced Passover to constitute a single feast; contrary to the nomadic practice, Passover was transformed into a pilgrimage and Temple festival.[10]

b) The Deuteronomic attitude toward other peoples and nations is likewise based on religious considerations.[11] In its attitude toward the Canaanites it depended on the nationalistic views of the source strata J and E (see § 13.5), but intensified them. While J and E spoke mostly of driving the Canaanites out and only occasionally of annihilating them (Joshua 9), Deuteronomy required primarily that the Canaanite be slain, exterminated, and annihilated—especially through the *ḥerem*[12]—as well as also being driven out. But for all practical purposes by the end of the seventh century B.C. this stricter and more radical requirement was purely theoretical. It served primarily to express fundamental rejection of the Canaanite cults and syncretism.

Ammonites and Moabites were to be excluded from the congregation of Yahweh (Deut. 23:4 [Eng. 23:3]), originally probably because their origin was unacceptable to Israel (see Gen. 19:30 ff.); later other reasons were given for their exclusion (Deut. 23:5-7 [Eng. 23:4-6]). The same applied to others of obscure or dubious origin (23:3). On the other hand, Israel's brothers the Edomites and former

[9] E. Auerbach, "Die Feste im alten Israel," *VT*, VIII (1958), 1-18; H. J. Elhorst, "Die deuteronomischen Jahresfeste," *ZAW*, XLII (1924), 136-45.

[10] N. Füglister, *Die Heilsbedeutung des Pascha*, 1963; H. Guthe, "Das Passahfest nach Dtn 16," in *Baudissin Festschrift*, 1918, pp. 217-32; H. G. May, "The Relation of the Passover to the Festival of Unleavened Cakes," *JBL*, LV (1936), 65-82.

[11] O. Bächli, *Israel und die Völker*, 1962; C. Brekelmans, "Le ḥerem chez les prophètes du royaume du nord et dans le Deutéronome," *BEThL*, XII (1959), 377-83; N. K. Gottwald, "'Holy War' in Deuteronomy, Analysis and Critique," *Review and Expositor*, LXI (1964), 296-310.

[12] *BHH*, I, 193; *RGG*, I, 860-61.

protectors the Egyptians were held in higher esteem (Deut. 23:8-9 [Eng. 23:7-8]).

c) The Deuteronomic law is characterized by a humane tendency that distinguishes it favorably from other legal codes of the ancient Near East. For example, a fugitive slave shall not be returned (23:16-17 [Eng. 23:15-16]); interest shall not be taken from Israelites (23:20-21 [Eng. 23:19-20]); subject to certain limitations, one may satisfy one's hunger with another's grapes or grain (23:25-26 [Eng. 23:24-25]); a mill or portion of a mill may not be taken in pledge (24:6), and a cloak taken in pledge must be returned for use at night (24:12-13); no Israelite must be robbed, mistreated, or sold (24:7); the day-laborer must be given his wages the same day (24:14-15); the relatives of a guilty person must not be punished for his crime (24:16); the rights of aliens, orphans, and widows must not be infringed, and they must be granted the gleanings of fields and orchards (24:17-22); corporal punishment must be moderate (25:1-3). This category also includes the regulations governing the conduct of war, some of which are based on what were originally Canaanite notions (see § 9.3), as well as those dealing with release from military service (20:5 ff.), the prohibition against cutting down fruit trees (20:19-20), and the regulations governing marriage to women taken through battle (21:10 ff.). Not even animals were forgotten (22:1-4; 25:4).

Finally, the law decreed a general remission of debts every seven years (15:1-18), the purpose of which was to make a new beginning possible at regular intervals for those in a weak social position. Nothing is known about the actual enforcement of the regulations concerning remission of debts. Those concerning the release of debtors were obviously not observed, as Jer. 34:8 ff. shows; according to this account, such a release took place only once, as a temporary measure in an especially critical situation, and was afterward revoked. These ordinances—and undoubtedly other Deuteronomic regulations—never became more than a theoretical program. Even so, they remain noteworthy and estimable.

d) The law likewise attempted to regulate and safeguard human life in the realm of social ethics and justice. Since the earlier local judicial assembly in which all full citizens held court together had proved a failure under the changed circumstances, judges were to be appointed throughout the land; they were to exercise their office impartially and without corruption (16:18-20). As before, difficult cases were to be decided by the priests—henceforth the Jerusalem priesthood alone (17:8 ff.). Important also was the protection against blood vengeance that places of asylum were to offer homicides (19:1 ff.).

The law prescribed strict sexual ethics (22:13 ff.); it forbade easy divorce (24:1 ff.) and conduct considered shameless on the part of women (25:11-12).

e) Finally, the state and the monarchy did not escape the effects of the Deuteronomic law.[13] The laws governing the king are characteristic, setting forth primarily what the king is and is not allowed to do (Deut. 17:14 ff.): no foreigners, i.e., preservation of the Davidic dynasty;[14] no multitude of horses or sale of subjects to Egypt to obtain horses, i.e., no expansion of the mercenary army, which had been largely dissipated in the catastrophe of 701, and no wars of aggression; no multitude of wives, i.e., limitation of the king's foreign harem and lessening of alien influences through marriage to the daughters of other rulers; no great wealth, i.e., restrictions on luxury and reduction of taxes. The king of this law is not an absolute sovereign but a popular ruler obligated to obey God's will as laid down in the Deuteronomic law; he is subject to the same law that the popular assembly agreed to obey.

It follows from this equality under God's law that all Israelites are brothers. From among these brothers comes the king as well as the peasant and the merchant; even the Israelite slave is the brother of his master. This sense of political community is undoubtedly nourished by the spirit of the prophets; its legal form exhibits once more the typically Deuteronomic accent.

3. *The pre-exilic Deuteronomistic school. a*) The Deuteronomic reform movement produced a theological school that lasted beyond the death of Josiah and even beyond the collapse of the Judahite state. Already in the time of Josiah this school was continuing the revision of Proto-Deuteronomy by emphasizing its parenetic and hortatory features and introducing into it the militant spirit that was revived in connection with the restoration of the militia composed of all free citizens after the model of the period of ancient Yahwism.

[13] K. Galling, *Die israelitische Staatsverfassung in ihrer vorderorientalischen Umwelt*, 1929.

[14] The legitimation of the dynasty in II Samuel 7* was accordingly interpreted deuteronomistically in II Sam. 23:5 as an eternally valid promise on the part of Yahweh. But see also A. H. J. Gunneweg, "Sinaibund und Davidsbund," *VT*, X (1960), 335-41; L. Rost, "Sinaibund und Davidsbund," *ThLZ*, LXXII (1947), 129-34.

In addition, the series of curses in Deut. 27:15-26, composed in the late pre-exilic period, was incorporated. We are dealing here with a series of legal dicta modeled after the series of apodicitic rules of conduct. In the framework of Deuteronomy, the order of presentation served to give the impression of a (fictitious) cultic action.

The Deuteronomistic school made fewer alterations in the books of Genesis—Numbers. Apart from a few supplementary or redactional notes such as those in the decalogue Exod. 20:1-17, the regulations concerning the Feast of Passover and Unleavened Bread and the firstborn in Exod. 12:24-27a; 13:3-16 may be ascribed to it. The book of Joshua underwent two Deuteronomistic recensions; the major additions apart from brief notices were Josh. 1:3-9, 12-18; 8:30-35; 10:16-43; 11:10-20; 22:1-8; 23. Joshua 24 (E) was also revised. How much of this should be ascribed to the pre-exilic period cannot be determined with certainty. The book of Judges likewise underwent multiple Deuteronomistic revision. The first revision produced the framework comments that were placed around the individual narratives or narrative cycles; according to this framework, there was a constantly repeated schema of Israel's apostasy, Yahweh's punishment, Israel's return to Yahweh, and Yahweh's aid provided through the calling of a deliverer. The resulting course of history is cyclic. The books of Samuel, on the other hand, exhibit only a few Deuteronomistic traces; the major alterations are limited to the revision of I Sam. 2:22-36; 7; 12; and II Sam. 2.

Above all, the books of Kings are a Deuteronomistic product, composed and constructed by the hand of Deuteronomistic authors. Of course their purpose was not to give a detailed presentation of the history of the monarchy, but to provide a religious analysis of history. The Jerusalem Temple, the relationship of the kings to it, and the prophets were to be emphasized. The kings whose reigns were uneventful in this regard received only the minimum necessary coverage; for further details the reader was referred to the historical sources then extant. But all the kings were evaluated according to the criterion of whether or not they had permitted or promoted other cults than that of the Jerusalem Temple. Only Hezekiah and Josiah, on account of their cultic reformations, were honored without reservation; Asa, Jehoshaphat, Joash, Azariah, and Jotham were honored to a lesser degree. Most of the books of Kings was put into writing after 622 B.C.; their composition was concluded before 609, since neither the Babylonian Exile nor Josiah's violent death (cf. II Kings 22:20) are included.

According to another theory, the books of Deuteronomy through Kings constitute a comprehensive Deuteronomistic History (Jepsen, Noth).[15] According to Noth, during the Exile the author of the History assembled sections that had previously been independent and added his own comments. Extensive passages were interpolated later. But his hypothesis raises several objections.

In the first place, Deuteronomy was incorporated into the Pentateuch or Hexateuch after a period of independent existence. This is demonstrated by the continuation of the source strata J, E, and P in Deut. 31:14-17, 23; 33–34, as well as by the incorporation of verses deriving from P in Deut. 1:3; 4:41-43. In addition, Deuteronomy was linked both internally and materially with the Pentateuch or Hexateuch through the later framework narrative. This framework constitutes a unified whole, so that Deuteronomy 1–3 cannot be set apart and considered the beginning of the Deuteronomistic History (Noth). It incorporates Deuteronomy into the Pentateuchal tradition through the supposition of an obligation undertaken by Israel in Moab after its transgression of the obligation undertaken at the mountain of God.

Furthermore, there are clear connections between the Pentateuch and the book of Joshua; these connections were already present in the pre-exilic source strata, as the statements concerning the burial of Joseph's bones (Exod. 13:19; Josh. 24:32) and the introduction of the figure of Joshua show (Exod. 17:8 ff.; 24:13-15; 32:17-18; 33:11; Num. 11:28-29; Deut. 31:14, 23). In addition, the source strata of the Pentateuch continue on in the book of Joshua and the beginning of the book of Judges, as careful analysis shows.

Finally, the books of Judges—Kings differ so markedly that they cannot have constituted portions of a coherent Deuteronomistic History. While only minor Deuteronomistic influence can be detected in the books of Samuel, the book of Judges and the books of Kings exhibit two divergent theories of history, both Deuteronomistic: the course of history in the book of Judges, with its constant repetition, is cyclic; that of the books of Kings is a straight line leading down to catastrophe. This kind of difference cannot be ascribed to a single author or redactor.

That other forces were at work in the same period can be safely assumed at least for the years between the death of Josiah and the fall of the state. In the waning years of the monarchy a first recension of what was later to be the Holiness Code (Leviticus 17–26; see § 23.3) probably came into being, comprising individual collections and complexes. Ezekiel, the product of priestly circles in Jerusalem, was acquainted with this collection there before his deportation. In any case this would explain the agreement between him and the Holiness Code, which can hardly be accidental.[16]

b) The Deuteronomistic account of the period of the Judges and

---

[15] *RGG*, II, 100-101.
[16] See S-F, § 20.3.

the monarchy was intended to demonstrate and elucidate the correctness of Deuteronomic theology. Each episode from the period of the Judges showed how Israel's apostasy was followed by Yahweh's punishment, Israel's repentance by Yahweh's aid. The whole elect nation could therefore be delivered and preserved from destruction if only it would return to Yahweh. But naturally after returning to Yahweh as required by the Deuteronomic law it must not fall into sin once more; to keep this from happening was the very purpose of the law.

The history of the monarchy also illustrated the necessity of radical repentance and return to Yahweh after Israel's sinful failure in the face of God's love. Of course assent and commendation were fitting when the battle against religious abuses was joined as energetically as it was by Hezekiah and Josiah. But to this assent must be contrasted the more or less severe censure of most of the kings, censure intended to admonish and educate. Thus the Deuteronomistic school succeeded in depicting the history of the monarchy as a thousandfold illustration of Israel's unfaithfulness to its own election and in making this unfaithfulness the cause of all misfortunes in the course of that history. This history was to be a textbook for Judah, which must find its way back to the wellsprings of its faith if it was not to perish. The importance of each person's responsibility for the fate of the whole nation was thus reminted into the current coin of popular presentation, while at the same time a new medium was created for the dissemination of religious doctrine.

Of course history was often distorted in the process by gross oversimplification and schematic reinterpretation. That was bound to happen when the kings were evaluated simply according to their attitude toward the Yahweh cult outside Jerusalem, a criterion of which they could have known nothing in their own time. The pedagogical intent of the Deuteronomistic school, in which it made historical tradition serve its own purposes, markedly impaired the worth of its literary activity. But this activity pursued ends that were not historical, but religious and pedagogical.

PART THREE

The Religion of the Exilic Period

§ 23 THE RELIGIOUS SITUATION

A. CAUSSE, "Les origines de la diaspora juive," *RHPhR*, VII (1927), 87-128; *idem*, "Du groupe éthnique à la communauté religieuse," *ibid.*, XIV (1934), 285-335; S. COOK, "Le VI° siècle, moment décisif dans l'histoire du Judaïsme et dans l'évolution religieuse de l'Orient," *ibid.*, XVIII (1938), 321-31; J. DE FRAINE, "Individu et société dans la religion de l'Ancien Testament," *Bibl*, XXXIII (1952), 324-55, 445-75; E. JANSSEN, *Juda in der Exilszeit*, 1956; E. KLAMROTH, *Die jüdischen Exulanten in Babylonien*, 1912; K. KOCH, "Sühne und Sündenvergebung um die Wende von der exilischen zur nachexilischen Zeit," *EvTh*, XXVI (1966), 217-39; A. MENES, "Tempel und Synagoge," *ZAW*, L (1932), 268-76; J. MORGENSTERN, "The Origin of the Synagogue," in *Studi orientalistici G. Levi della Vida*, II (1956), 192-201; M. NOTH, "La catastrophe de Jérusalem en l'an 587 avant Jésus-Christ et sa signification pour Israël," *RHPhR*, XXXIII (1953), 81-103; D. W. THOMAS, "The Sixth Century B.C.: a Creative Epoch in the History of Israel," *JSS*, VI (1961), 33-46.

1. *The situation and the evidence. a)* The collapse of the state of Judah marked a decisive turning point in the historical life of the Israelite nation—a turning point that had a corresponding effect on Yahwism, and began to transform it more markedly than any previous event. This was due on the one hand to the destruction of the Temple, the end of the monarchy, and the general cessation of sacrifice, and on the other to the deportation of part of the population to Babylonia, where they were forced to live in a land considered unclean and surrounded by an alien religion.

The deportations had affected the upper stratum of the population, to the extent that the Babylonians had not already executed its members. It is no longer possible to determine precisely how many were deported; in any case they constituted only a part—albeit an important part—of the total population. The number of those left behind, in spite of the flight of some of them to Egypt in the wake of Gedaliah's assassination, was considerably larger, as Ezek. 33:24 also indicates.

Jerusalem had suffered severe damage. The Temple had been

burned and left in ruins. The Babylonians had destroyed the city walls, albeit not totally, since the later list of those working on the wall speaks almost exclusively of repairs (Nehemiah 3). The city was not uninhabited; quite a number continued to dwell in it (see Lam. 1:4, 11; 5). Of course their condition was wretched: scarcity of victuals (Lam. 1:11), cannibalism (Lam. 2:20; 4:10); suffering on the part of small children (2:11-12, 19); ravishing of women (5:11)·; murder of priests and prophets (2:20); hanging of respected men and degradation of the elders (5:12). The Babylonian administration also involved burdens, above all forced labor (5:13) and taxes (5:4). Only gradually was a certain prosperity restored, so that by the year 520 not a few inhabitants of Jerusalem possessed well-appointed dwellings (Hag. 1:4 ff.).

Understandably enough the situation of the deportees was also difficult, although it varied under the different Babylonian kings. While Nebuchadnezzar exercised a strong hand and pursued his political goals consistantly and constantly, his successor Amel-Marduk was well disposed toward the Judahites and gave King Jehoiachin, who had already been deported in 597, his freedom. It turned out to be advantageous for the deportees to continue to live in enclosed colonies; the Babylonians fortunately let this temporary measure stand. The deportees could build houses, carry on trade, and later even seek out other habitation. Many achieved wealth and prosperity in exile, so that after they were freed by Cyrus only a portion of them took advantage of the offer of being allowed to return to their former homeland.

Various conclusions were drawn from the course of events by those who were left in Judah and those who were deported. Many judged that the way of Deuteronomic reform taken by Josiah was wrong and had angered the other gods; this meant a return to other cults. Others viewed the catastrophe as the judgment of Yahweh that the great individual prophets had threatened, and considered themselves still entangled in guilt because after the death of Josiah the people and the state had once more deserted Yahweh for other cults. Still others doubted whether Yahweh existed at all (see 2a below). Thus the people were divided into several groups.

b) The catastrophe of Judah was reflected in its literature. Apart from contemporary prophecy, which will be discussed elsewhere (§ 24.1-3), the major sources are Lamentations and some of the Psalms.

The five lamentations assembled in one small book[1] were composed by an eyewitness to the fall of Jerusalem some time after the year 587 B.C. It must remain an open question whether the poet dwelt in Jerusalem or in exile. The songs are the elegies of an educated man reflecting on the terrible catastrophe of Jerusalem. While he had apparently once belonged to those circles that hoped for deliverance of the city until the bitter end, its destruction opened his eyes to the deeper context, led him to come to terms inwardly with what had taken place, opened him to the message of the prophets, and made him undertake an attempt to aid his fellow sufferers who had sunk into a crisis of faith. He saw the immediate cause of the disaster in Yahweh's wrath, occasioned in turn by the sinfulness of the people, among whom the priests and cult prophets were the most guilty. The only way of escape from misery and despair was prayer to Yahweh, who would be gracious and merciful to a penitent people.

Several Psalms that can be dated with more or less assurance in the exilic period likewise reflect the difficult situation; these include Psalms 60, 74, and 123, which are communal laments. The individual laments in Ps. 77:1-16 (Eng. 77:1-15) and 102 also refer to these events, showing to what extent they could affect personal piety.

2. *Palestine. a*) There were probably always doubts about Yahweh among the Israelites (cf. Zeph. 1:12), but the fall of Jerusalem intensified them. Events seemed governed by a blind destiny that befell the innocent: "The fathers have eaten sour grapes, but the children's teeth are set on edge" (Jer. 31:29; Ezek. 18:2). Others, to whose objection the poet of Lamentations replied, simply denied Yahweh (Lam. 3:34-36). The consequence was that some of the Judahites in Palestine turned to alien cults. Even in the waning years of the pre-exilic period, after the death of Josiah, such cults had been permitted once more even in the Jerusalem Temple, as can be determined from Ezekiel 8 and other notices. Now the last dikes protecting Yahwism had been breached. And many who did not give Yahweh up and maintained their belief in him as the God of Palestine embraced a syncretistic religion or a multiplicity of cults. For most of the Judahites, Yahweh was merely one god among others, whom they also worshiped.

Thus a popular religion came to prevail with more Canaanite

---

[1] For a detailed discussion, see S-F, § 44.

than Yahwistic features. In addition there was a resurgence of magical practices that had been secretly preserved and transmitted as well as various disreputable cults. This tendency was intensified by the influence of the syncretistic religion, likewise influenced by Canaanite cults, that already existed in the province of Samaria, the heartland of what had previously been the Northern Kingdom of Israel. Yahwism was also invaded by the cults of the transjordanian peoples, small groups of whose adherents settled in what had been Judahite territory. In this mixed religion the Yahweh of Jerusalem cannot have differed much if at all from the Yahweh of Samaria, the Milcom of the Ammonites, or the Chemosh of the Moabites. In addition, of course, Babylonian cults were practiced, finding many adherents as cults of the victors and rulers.

b) Genuine Yahwism nevertheless did not die out, even though it was restricted to a narrower circle than before. Within this circle the catastrophe was understood as the judgment proclaimed by the prophets, which Yahweh had visited upon Judah on account of her sins. Of course the question gradually arose as to how long the judgment would last. The ruined Temple was a mockery of Yahweh —how much longer would it remain so (Ps. 74:9-10)? Or we read in positive terms that it is time for Yahweh to have pity (Ps. 102:14).

Despite all the destruction, the ruins of the Temple still served cultic purposes. According to ancient theory the site remained sacred despite all destruction, so that sacrifice was probably still offered.[2] We do not know whether this took place regularly and whether there was an altar. There is only one mention of men coming to Jerusalem from what had been the territory of Northern Israel bringing cereal offerings and incense (Jer. 41:5-6). Since the sacred site was also the place of lamentation (I Kings 8:33), the ritual lamentations took place there which henceforth, like the festivals, were prescribed for certain dates (cf. Zech. 7:5). According to Zech. 8:19 (cf. II Kings 25:1, 8-9, 25), these rites were to be observed four times a year: in the fourth month on account of the conquest of Jerusalem (June/July), in the fifth month on account of the burning of the Temple (July/August), in the seventh month on account of the assassination of Gedaliah (September/October), and in the tenth month on account of the beginning of the siege of Jerusalem (December/January).

[2] For a different view, see D. Jones, "The Cessation of Sacrifice After the Destruction of the Temple in 586 B.C.," *JThSt*, NS XIV (1963), 12-31.

3. *Exile and Diaspora.*[3] a) The deportation of the Judahite upper class to a foreign land with a superior civilization must have meant a terrible crisis for Yahwism. A sacrificial cult was impossible in an unclean land. Above all the Babylonian god Marduk appeared to be more powerful than Yahweh, because he had conquered Judah by means of the Babylonians. Since it was advantageous to worship the victorious god, and since the Israelites might possibly thus derive advantages from their Babylonian masters, many of the deportees became unfaithful to Yahwism, although there is no way to estimate their number. Others considered at least worshiping the Babylonian gods in addition to Yahweh and setting up images of these gods in their houses (Ezek. 14:1-11). There were also sorceresses who employed Babylonian magic, sewing wrist bands and making veils for the people who came to consult them (Ezek. 13: 18).

Nevertheless, as in Palestine, Yahwism was preserved among the deportees; in fact it took firmer root there than it had before. Thus once more the deportees were enabled to preserve their uniqueness, unlike the Northern Israelites, who for the most part were ethically and religiously absorbed into their new environment. This outcome was further aided by the fact that even in its popular manifestations Yahwism was far superior to the Babylonian cults, not least as a consequence of prophetical influences.

The deportees were most seriously affected by the impossibility of continuing to worship Yahweh in a temple as at Jerusalem. They seem for a time to have looked for a substitute so that they could continue the familiar cult: they wanted to set up an image of "wood and stone," probably copying Babylonian prototypes, but gave up the project after Ezekiel protested (Ezek. 20:32).

Other substitute forms developed instead. The religious school, later to become the synagogue,[4] replaced the temple; in it the people assembled for a simple form of worship that comprised prayer, hymns, and a lecture. The latter, under the influence of the Deuteronomistic school, consisted primarily of historical interpretation. It is frequently assumed that synagogue worship was already fully developed in the Deuteronomic period, but this cannot be proved conclusively. In any case, the class of teachers of the law came to the forefront in this context. It had existed at least since the late pre-exilic period, possibly as a consequence of the Deu-

[3] *BHH*, I, 340-41, 458-60; *RGG*, II, 174-77, 817-19; *IDB*, I, 854-56; II, 186-88.
[4] *BHH*, III, 1906-10; *RGG*, VI, 557-59; *IDB*, IV, 476-91.

teronomic reformation. It had the task of interpreting the law and applying it to the various particular cases arising out of everyday life. The people assembled for worship on the Sabbath, which thus took on new importance.[5] Its observance became the most important substitute for the cult; to keep the Sabbath holy became a crucial religious obligation.

Certain rites and ceremonies received more emphasis during the Exile than they had before. Thus circumcision[6] became an important rite distinguishing Israelites from Babylonians, who were unacquainted with the practice; it symbolized the relationship of the people to Yahweh. In addition, a kind of negative cultus was practiced by fasting in honor of Yahweh and refraining from eating and drinking.[7] This was the manner of observance, above all, of the days of ritual lamentation, which were also observed regularly in the Exile. Finally, the ancient dietary and purity regulations underwent further elaboration.[8] Careful observance of them showed that one did not feel at home in the alien, unclean land, and was the devotee of a different god than its inhabitants. In this way the Exile contributed to the process that linked the nucleus of what had been the Judahite upper class intimately to Yahwism and consolidated Yahwism itself. This consolidation admittedly took a form that the great individual prophets would hardly have approved, although their influence, too, is perceptible. But in the Exile itself some important elements of later Judaism took shape or came to the fore. This faith nevertheless possessed such attraction that during the Exile people belonging to other nations and religions attached themselves to it, presumably for the most part deportees from other nations dwelling in the vicinity of the Judahite settlements. Thus during the very period when Yahwism was totally dependent on a foreign power it demonstrated its victorious strength; during this period, indeed, the notion of Israel's being sent to all nations, the idea of Israel's mission, was born (see § 24.3).

On the other hand, influences from the surrounding world also had an effect, albeit modest, on Yahwism; these were at first of

[5] *BHH*, III, 1634; *RGG*, V, 1259-60; *IDB*, IV, 135-41.
[6] *BHH*, I, 223-24; *RGG*, II, 819; *IDB*, I, 629-31.
[7] *BHH*, I, 465-66; *RGG*, I, 640-41; *IDB*, II, 241-44.
[8] *BHH*, III, 1579, 1828; *RGG*, V, 947-48; VI, 231-32; *IDB*, I, 641-48; J. Döller, *Die Reinheits- und Speisegesetze des Alten Testaments*, 1917; W. Kornfeld, "Reine und unreine Tiere im Alten Testament," *Kairos*, 1965, pp. 134-47; J. Milgrom, "The Biblical Diet Laws as an Ethical System," *Interpr*, XVII (1963), 288-301.

Babylonian origin, toward the end of the Exile of Persian origin.[9] They made themselves felt primarily in the realm of cosmology and belief in angels and demons; beginning with this period these occur in some form everywhere, even in Ezekiel and Deutero-Isaiah. We are not dealing, however, with a new syncretism; the new elements were rather fused with Yahwism, being divested to a greater or lesser degree of their original meaning.

b) The exilic substitute for the earlier cult clearly exhibited a legalistic side such as had already appeared in the Deuteronomic reform movement. After the destruction of the Temple and the cessation of its cult, the deportees, threatened by their new environment, sought something they could hold fast to, some means of protecting themselves against the threat, something into which they could withdraw as into a fortress. They found it in the law.

The primary contribution was that of the exilic Deuteronomistic school. It tried to make clear to the deportees that according to the will of Yahweh everything had to take place as it had happened, that Yahweh had in fact announced everything long before. The important thing, therefore, was to return to Yahweh, because one might then have hope once more. But the possibility of once more attaining God's grace, which had been sealed by oath in the early history of Israel, was given through the law. After the catastrophe there still remained Yahweh's commandments and prohibitions, his regulations and ordinances. Because they had not been obeyed, disaster had struck; if they were now finally obeyed, there was hope of deliverance. The law was the fixed and immovable rock to which one could cling in order to avoid being swept away by the tide of history.

The Deuteronomistic school continued to work on the transmission of scripture. Probably in this period the second framework was added to Deuteronomy, which included as its introduction Deut. 1:1–4:43; 9:7–10:11 and as its conclusion 28:69 (Eng. 29:1) ; 29–30, and served to incorporate Deuteronomy into the Pentateuchal tradition. At the same time the book was given the character of Moses' dying testament or farewell discourse.

In addition, the Deuteronomistic revision of the books of Joshua— Kings was continued. The most important revision was that of the books of Kings by a supplementary hand, which added the references to the Exile along with other supplementary material and the conclusion of the books from II Kings 23:25b on. The new conclusion is the freeing of Jehoiachin.

[9] See, for example, F. Stummer, "Einige keilschriftliche Parallelen zu Jes 40–66," *JBL*, XLV (1926) , 171–89.

The law code contained in Leviticus 17–26 was also given its final form in the Exile. It is called the Holiness Code on the basis of the frequently repeated formula "You shall be holy, for I, Yahweh your God, am holy" (with slight variations).[10] It contains primarily cultic and ethical regulations:

17	Slaughtering of animals and eating their flesh
18	Sexual intercourse
19	Religious and ethical regulations
20	Capital offenses, sexual and otherwise
21	Holiness of priests
22	Holiness of cultic offerings and sacrifices
23	Calendar of feasts
24:1-9	Details of worship in the sanctuary
24:10-23	Israelite law applies to aliens
25:1-55; (26:1-2)	Sabbatical Year and Jubilee Year
26:3-46	Declaration of reward and punishment

The Holiness Code held before the people the requirement that they be holy in the sense of cultic and ethical purity.

It is characteristic that the laws meant for its own age are archaizing; they derive from the desert period as Israel's ideal age, and their illustrations reflect the circumstances of the pilgrim camp. Like Moses and his generation, the people were living outside Palestine and hoping for a new occupation of the land. In addition, all the laws are said to have been given the people through the mediation of Moses at Sinai, so that Moses henceforth became the lawgiver par excellence; he would now have to lend his authority to every law. This principle was carried out even more consistently in P, which was composed later. Despite its archaizing form, the Holiness Code is a program and plan for the reconstruction of national life, albeit not in the prophetical sense of reconstruction through the spirit, but rather through organization and law.

The Sabbatical Year mentioned above (§ 16.3) was prescribed for the first time by Lev. 25:1-7. The exilic situation itself makes it clear that we are dealing with nothing more than a program in the realm of social ethics. It is based on the theory that Yahweh is the real owner of the land of Palestine and the peasant is only his vassal or tenant; the land is actually leased out to the nation as a whole, and its bounty must therefore be made available to those who own no property. There is no mention anywhere of the enforcement of this law at any time during the OT period; since realization of its radical stipulations could hardly have taken place without

---

[10] For a detailed discussion, see S-F, § 20.3.

some response, this silence can be interpreted as an admission that the law was never enforced.

At the same time Lev. 25:8-55 set down the regulations concerning the Jubilee Year,[11] in which the regulations concerning the Sabbatical Year were combined with those of Deuteronomy 15 governing the remission of debts. They, too, remained programmatic.

In this way during the Exile the requirements of the law became the guiding principle of human conduct for a portion of Israel; fulfillment of these requirements was elevated to the status of the optimal way of life. Following the beginnings in the Deuteronomic reform movement, we can now speak of a legal approach to life and a legalistic religion. It is impossible to deny either the deep seriousness or the readiness to obey God's will that informed this approach. It is often possible to sense an inward assent to the law that transcends its letter, nor was there any lack of fulfillment of the law according to its spirit and intent. The individual laws could even be subordinated to the basic standards of conduct toward other Israelites, and this conduct described summarily as love for one's neighbor (Lev. 19:18). Thus help for the weak and oppressed that could not be defined in legal terms was also included.

Though prophetical influence is discernible in this last feature, the legal approach as a whole must be judged in the same terms as the cultic movement. It reduced life to ritual. For the ethical laws received the same emphasis as the ritual laws of the cult, if their importance did not in fact predominate. Life was kept within the narrow bounds of law, regulated, and schematized. The determining factor was the correct outward act, as must be the case with a legalistic orientation. That man was righteous and devout who fulfilled the divine requirements contained in the law.

c) Nothing is known about the Diaspora that already existed in Egypt except that the temple built before 525 B.C. on the island of Elephantine in the Nile was constructed during the exilic period. The Judahites who fled to Egypt after the assassination of Gedaliah may have been lost to Yahwism. At any event they asserted at that time that all the disasters sprang from their failure to continue offering sacrifice to the Queen of Heaven, Ishtar (Jer. 44:17 ff.). According to this view the mistake that had been made in the past and had brought about the catastrophe lay in the Deuteronomic reformation. The elimination of the non-Yahwistic cults had led to

[11] N. M. Nicholskij, "Die Entstehung des Jobeljahres," ZAW, L (1932), 216.

bitter consequences. Therefore the injured deities must be propitiated once more and their cults fostered. This attitude, too, belongs in the picture of the exilic period and illustrates the divisions among the Judahites.

§ 24 Exilic Prophecy and Incipient Eschatology, the Fifth Influence

w. caspari, "Das Ende der alttestamentlichen Prophetie," *NkZ*, XXXVIII (1927), 438-72, 489-500; t. chary, *Les prophètes et le culte à partir de l'exil*, 1955; g. fohrer, "Die Struktur der alttestamentlichen Eschatologie," in his *Studien zur alttestamentlichen Prophetie (1949-1965)*, 1967, pp. 32-58; s. b. frost, "Eschatology and Myth," *VT*, II (1952), 70-80; h. gressmann, *Der Ursprung der israelitisch-jüdischen Eschatologie*, 1906; j. lindblom, "Gibt es eine Eschatologie bei den alttestamentlichen Propheten?" *StTh*, VI (1952), 79-114; c. steuernagel, "Strukturlinien der Entwicklung der jüdischen Eschatologie," in *Festschrift Alfred Bertholet*, 1950, pp. 479-87; t. c. vriezen, "Prophecy and Eschatology," *VTSuppl*, I (1953), 199-299; m. weinfeld, "Universalism and Particularism in the Period of the Exile and Restoration," *Tarbiz*, XXXIII (1963/64), 228-42.

1. *Ezekiel.*[1] *a*) During the course of the exilic period the legalistic approach to life developed and a great change took place in the estimation of the pre-exilic prophets. People turned their backs on the optimistic prophets, and the tradition of the great individual prophets gained in respect and authority. This period also marked the end of the great individual prophets, whose last representative was Ezekiel. The prophets who came after him must be termed epigones. Although many of them were important and innovative figures, they departed at many points from the course set by the great individual prophets. They no longer found the classical answers of the latter to the questions of their time because they were influenced by other movements—nationalistic, cultic, and legalistic.

Ezekiel, who had originally been a priest, was brought to Babylonia with the first group of deportees (597 B.C.). He was settled with others at Tel-abib on the river Chebar, a canal connecting

[1] L. Dürr, *Die Stellung des Propheten Ezechiel in der israelitisch-jüdischen Apokalyptik*, 1923; W. Eichrodt, *Krisis der Gemeinschaft in Israel*, 1953; G. Fohrer, *Die Hauptprobleme des Buches Ezechiel* 1952; idem "Das Symptomatische der Ezechielforschung," *ThLZ*, LXXXIII (1958), 241-50; H. Graf Reventlow, *Wächter über Israel*, 1952; J. Steinmann, *Le prophète Ézéchiel et les débuts de l'exil*, 1953; W. Zimmerli, *Erkenntnis Gottes nach dem Buche Ezechiel*, 1954 (= his *Gottes Offenbarung* 1963, pp. 41-119).

Babylon with Uruk by way of Nippur (1:1; 3:15). His prophetical ministry began in the third year of the deportation and lasted, according to the last date given in his book, until the year 571 (19: 17), extending over something more than two decades. Ezekiel's wife died about 587 before or during the siege of Jerusalem (24:18).

The accuracy of these data in the book of Ezekiel has often been impugned. In opposition to them and going beyond them, scholars have developed various theories about the date and locations of Ezekiel's ministry, his prophetical character and the content of his message, the origin of the book and the history of the text. In particular attempts have been made to date the prophet's ministry and thus the origin of the book in a period different from the one indicated; this usually involves transfer to another location. It has also been assumed that during the period indicated in the book Ezekiel exercised his ministry totally or primarily in Jerusalem or in two places, both in Palestine and in Babylonia. Against such theories we must firmly insist that Ezekiel lived and exercised his prophetical ministry in Babylonia and that he considered himself sent exclusively to the Judahite deportees, to demolish their hopes for any deliverance of Jerusalem and relieve their anguish in the face of its destruction.[2] Of course he did not preach without reference to Jerusalem. By proclaiming judgment against the city through his words and symbolic actions, he contributed, according to the views of his time, indirectly to the realization of this judgment, because such proclamation was considered efficacious. For his contemporaries his long-term significance may have rested on this very fact.

Ezekiel's ministry can be divided into three periods. In the first, which lasted from his call to the fall of Jerusalem (593/92-587), he predicted inescapable disaster for Jerusalem and its Temple, seeking to destroy the people's confidence in their inviolability and an imminent reversal of fortunes in order to dissociate the hopes and anxieties of the deportees from the existence of Jerusalem and its Temple. After a short period of silence following the fall of Jerusalem, Ezekiel changed his message to one of conditional salvation (586/85): salvation for the devout, death for the wicked. The prophet was concerned to comfort those in despair and guide the will to repent into the proper channels. Of course he had to recognize that his demands exceeded the powers of the deportees and that the future could not consist merely in the survival of a few devout souls.

[2] For a detailed discussion, see Fohrer, *Hauptprobleme*.

In the third period of his ministry (after 585) he therefore proclaimed new salvation from which only the deliberate apostates and external enemies of Israel would be excluded: this salvation would involve the transformation of man through Yahweh's redeeming acts, the reunification of Israel, and the return of Yahweh to the restored Temple, from which a river of blessings would flow.

In addition to reports of symbolic actions and ecstatic visions, the Ezekiel tradition contains many discourses, often of considerable length. The minatory forms are most heavily represented, with fifty-six discourses. In addition there are several hortatory and invective discourses, as well as a great number of historical analyses, discussions, instructions, and allegories, which bear witness to the rationalistic and reflective element in Ezekiel's thought. Finally, promises constitute a significant portion of the book. To these were gradually added a series of later discourses deriving from various authors and periods.[3]

b) Ezekiel was the first prophet to draw extensively on non-Israelite traditions of originally mythological character, primarily Canaanite-Phoenician and Mesopotamian material. This phenomenon can frequently be observed from his time on, so that the use of such materials can be considered practically a mark of late origin. The narrative traditions of Israel had less influence on Ezekiel, while he frequently referred to Amos, Hosea, Isaiah, and Micah. He was also rooted in the theology of his age. He thus exhibits frequent points of contact with Jeremiah, on whom he may even be literarily dependent; with Deuteronomic theology in his analysis of history, his estimation of the law, his emphasis on the individual, his demand for unity in the cult and its location, and his evaluation of the monarchy; and with the priestly theology of the Holiness Code and with the cultic ideas and ceremonies familiar to him as a former priest.

But crucial to Ezekiel was his call experience. Contrary to the traditional view that the deity and his land belong together and that the former can only be worshiped in the latter, he came to realize that Yahweh's presence is not limited to a single place, that the believer can experience it wherever he may happen to dwell. This meant a fundamental break with tradition. Life and death are not dependent on whether one abides in his homeland or in a foreign country; they derive from a man's inward attitude or outward con-

[3] For a detailed discussion, see S-F, § 60.4-6.

duct wherever he may dwell and under whatever conditions he may live. Therefore Ezekiel addressed himself especially to the individual.

He also repeatedly examined the history of Israel, rendering an even harsher verdict than the earlier prophets. As his reinterpretation of the images of Israel as a vine (15) and of the marriage between Yahweh and Israel (16) suggests, Ezekiel forged a consistent new interpretation of Israel's entire history by selecting, ignoring, or introducing specific motifs (20:1-32) : already in Egypt the people had worshiped idols, and had therefore sinned from the beginning; ever since then down to the present, despite Yahweh's increasingly harsh threats and actions, they had remained disobedient and rebellious.

With respect to his own age Ezekiel was primarily concerned with the individual Israelite.[4] Everyone is solely responsible for himself and decides personally for salvation or ruin:

> The person that sins shall die.
> The son shall not suffer for the iniquity of the father,
> nor the father suffer for the iniquity of the son.
> The righteousness of the righteous shall be upon himself,
> and the wickedness of *the wicked* shall be upon himself.
>
> (18:20)

What matters is a man's conduct at the crucial moment when Yahweh puts the individual to the test, so that in practice what is done or left undone in any given moment can determine Yahweh's judgment. A man must always be open to Yahweh's admonition to repent and return to him:

> Son of man,
> I have made you a watchman
> for the house of Israel;
> whenever you hear a word from my mouth,
> you shall give them warning from me.
>
> If I say to the wicked, "You shall surely die,"
> and you give him no warning in order to save his life,
> that *wicked man* shall die
> in his iniquity;
> but his blood I will require at your hand.

---

[4] A. Lindars, "Ezekiel and Individual Responsibility," *VT*, XV (1965), 452-67; W. Zimmerli, " 'Leben' und 'Tod' im Buche des Propheten Ezechiel," *ThZ*, XIII (1957), 494-508 (= his *Gottes Offenbarung*, 1963, pp. 178-91); A. H. van Zyl, "Solidarity and Individualism in Ezekiel," *OuTWP*, 1961, pp. 38-52.

> But if you warn *the* wicked,
> and he does not turn from his wickedness or from his wicked
>   way,
> *that wicked man* shall die
> in his iniquity;
> but you will have saved your life.
>
> Again, if a righteous man turns from his righteousness
> and commits iniquity,
> he shall die;
> if you have not warned him,
> his blood I will require at your hand.
>
> Nevertheless if you *warn the righteous man*
> not to sin,
> and he does sin nonetheless,
> *he shall die on account of his sin,*
> but you will have saved your life.   (3:17-21)

Therefore the sins of the present that correspond to the sins of all past history weigh so heavily: "abomination," i.e., the trappings and ceremonies of idolatry; and "blood-guiltiness" and wickedness, i.e., ethical and social offenses. These must of their own necessity lead to the threatened judgment that Ezekiel saw carried out against Jerusalem in the fall of the city.

In the face of sin and judgment Ezekiel first took up the old prophetical admonition to repent, confident that man's own efforts could effect the required transformation:

> Everyone according to his ways
> I will judge you, O house of Israel,
> says Yahweh.
> Repent and turn away from all your transgressions
> so that they *shall not be* a stumbling block of
>   iniquity to you.
>
> Cast away from you
> all the transgressions which you have committed
> and get yourself a new heart
> and a new spirit!
> Why will you die, O house of Israel?   (18:30-31)

Later Ezekiel expected the transformation of man as a consequence of Yahweh's redemptive act: through the forgiveness of guilt that man cannot efface (36:25); through the renewal of the center of life by means of a new heart that is no longer cold, unfeeling, and incapable of change (11:19-20; 36:26); and through the gift of the divine spirit that arouses men to do God's will (11:19; 36:27). Man redeemed and renewed can then will and do what is right as of his own accord, in harmony with the commandments of Yahweh, so that Yahweh's will is done on earth. This new man and his fellowmen constitute a community that lives not only in mutual communion but also and above all in intimate communion with Yahweh (11:20; 36:28):

> I will sprinkle clean water
> upon you, and you shall be clean
> from all your uncleannesses,
> and from all your idols
> I will cleanse you.

> I will give you
> a new heart,
> I will take out of your flesh the heart of stone
> and give you
> a heart of flesh.

> And I will put my spirit within you,
> and cause you
> to walk in my statutes,
> to observe my will
> and to do *it*.

> You shall dwell in the land
> which I gave to your fathers;
> and you shall be my people,
> and I will be
> your God.   (36:25-28)

2. *Other prophets. a*) In the period after the fall of Jerusalem the prophet Obadiah made his appearance with threats against Edom because it had taken the side of Judah's enemies and gloated over the disaster that had befallen it. Five of his discourses constitute the small book named for him (vss. 1*b*-4, 5-7, 8-11, 12-14+15*b*, 15*a*+16-18); to them a post-exilic supplement has been added (19-21).[5]

Obadiah may have been a cult prophet among the Judahites left behind in Palestine; to judge by his message, he was a representative of the optimistic prophetism attacked by Jeremiah. Nevertheless the

---

[5] For a detailed discussion, see S-F, § 64.

decisive element in his thought was not religious nationalism but the ethical seriousness of Yahwism and hope in Yahweh's compensatory justice. Expectation of just revenge, which is clearly expressed in 15*b*, permeates all his discourses. It is linked with the notion of the "Day of Yahweh" as a day of judgment—no longer for Israel, but for the nations. On it Edom above all will receive its just deserts.

b) Another cult prophet may have been the author of Isa. 63:7–64:11. This section, which was probably composed in the first or middle decades of the Exile, is related in content to Deuteronomistic theology, and represents a communal lament beginning with historical analysis. It prays for a change in the situation brought about by the fall of Judah and Jerusalem.

c) Another anonymous prophet composed the prediction of the imminent conquest of Babylon by Elam and Media in Isa. 21:1-10, which came to him in an ecstatic vision and audition. This prophet probably appeared with this message in Palestine around or before 540 B.C., when the nations in question were mobilizing under the leadership of Cyrus to attack the Babylonian Empire:

> And he answered, "Fallen,
> fallen is Babylon,
> and all the images of her gods
> he has shattered to the ground."   (Isa. 21:9*b*)

During the exilic period other prophetical discourses were composed against other nations by anonymous prophets; these were later incorporated into the prophetical books already extant. Such discourses are hard to date, but at least those directed against Babylon must come from the period before the fall of the Babylonian Empire. These include Isaiah 13 and the nucleus of Jer. 50:1–51:58. They primarily bear witness to the hate that the world empire had aroused.

3. *Deutero-Isaiah.*[6] *a*) The anonymous prophet called for convenience Deutero-Isaiah ("Second Isaiah"), whose tradition is contained in Isaiah 40–55, exercised his ministry during the last years

[6] J. Begrich, *Studien zu Deuterojesaja*, 1938, reprinted 1963; P. A. H. de Boer, *Second-Isaiah's Message*, 1956; W. Caspari, *Lieder und Gottessprüche der Rückwanderer*, 1934; L. Glahn and L. Köhler, *Der Prophet der Heimkehr (Jesaja 40–66)*, 1934; E. Hessler, *Gott der Schöpfer*, Dissertation, Greifswald, 1961; S. Porúbčan, *Il Patto Nuovo in Is 40–66*, 1959; C. Westermann, "Sprache und Struktur der Prophetie Deuterojesajas," in his *Forschung am Alten Testament*, 1964, pp. 92-170.

of the Exile among the deportees in Babylonia, when the Babylonian Empire faced destruction and the Persian king Cyrus was awaited as deliverer of the oppressed nations.[7] The prophet also expected Cyrus to liberate the deported Judahites and permit them to return to Jerusalem and rebuild the Temple. In his view Yahweh had called Cyrus, declared him his anointed (45:1), and was making use of him to help Israel.

Some additional information about the prophet may possibly be derived from the discourses concerning the Servant of Yahweh (Ebed Yahweh songs) contained in 42:1-4, 5-7; 49:1-6; 50:4-9; 50:10-11; 52:13–53:12.[8] Interpretation of these songs differs widely, however: the "servant" has been understood collectively as Israel, as it was or idealized, or as the suffering or deported part of Israel; as an individual, with widely divergent theories as to his identity; or in a fluid or integral interpretation combining both theories. If it should turn out to be true that Deutero-Isaiah is himself to be identified with the "servant," some conclusions can be drawn from these discourses. In 42:1-4, 5-7, the prophet gave an account of his commission and ministry for himself and perhaps for others, developing his prophetical self-understanding. Later, in 49:1-6; 50:4-9, like Jeremiah he spoke of his inner doubts and struggles. Perhaps he also felt threatened by the intervention of Babylonian officials, as his anti-Babylonian preaching would lead one to expect. In this situation his life's work and his faith were at stake, so that he sought in his discourses to set forth the meaning of his commission and of his life. By way of contrast 50:10-11; 52:13–53:12 look back upon the life and ministry of the prophet after their conclusion; they presuppose that he was executed after a judicial process. Especially in the last song his adherents apparently tried to reinterpret his life, his sufferings, and his disgraceful death.

In the message of Deutero-Isaiah the characteristic rhetorical forms of pre-exilic prophecy retreated into the background. Other forms come to the fore in his sixty-five or so discourses: the fully developed salvation oracle, the hymn in praise of God's imminent saving act, prophetical forensic argument to demonstrate that Yahweh alone is God, and disputation to combat doubts and objections.

---

[7] E. Jenni, "Die Rolle des Kyros bei Deuterojesaja," *ThZ*, X (1954), 241-56; R. Kittel, "Cyrus und Deuterojesaja," *ZAW*, XVIII (1898), 149-62; C. E. Simcox, "The Rôle of Cyros in Deutero-Isaja," *JAOS*, LVII (1937), 158-71; U. Simon, "König Cyrus und die Typologie," *Judaica*, XI (1955), 83-89.

[8] For a detailed discussion, see S-F, § 57.4.

A few secondary discourses have also found their way into the tradition (40:18-20+41:7; 42:8-9; 44:9-20; 45:18-19; 46:5-8; 48:1-11; 51:11-16; 52:1-6).[9]

b) The message of Deutero-Isaiah is fundamentally dominated by a faith in eschatological redemption.[10] The really new element is suggested by the term "eschatological." While Hosea, Jeremiah, and Ezekiel exhibit a belief in redemption, Deutero-Isaiah was the first prophet to proclaim an eschatological message, since he saw a new era dawning (see below under 4). In his discourses this notion was associated with the outline of a comprehensive theology based on the uniqueness of Yahweh. Up to this time one can speak solely of a practical monotheism that bound Israel to Yahweh alone, notwithstanding the existence of other gods. Deutero-Isaiah, following upon a few hints in Jeremiah, advocated a theoretical monotheism that expressly denies the existence of other gods:[11]

> Thus says the King of Israel
> and his redeemer, Yahweh Sabaoth:
> "I am the first and I am the last;
> besides me there is no god.
> Who is like me? *Let him appear and* proclaim himself,
> let him declare and set it forth before me.
> *Who has announced from of old the things to come?*
> Let them tell *us* what is yet to be.
> Fear not, nor *be afraid;*
> have I not told you from of old and declared it?
> And you are my witnesses! Is there a God
> *or* a rock besides me?"   (44:6-8)

But if only the one God exists, all that takes place, all that manifests itself from the creation of the world [12] to eternity depends on him. Therefore in a single great arc Deutero-Isaiah linked primal

---

[9] For a detailed discussion, see S-F, § 57.3, 5.

[10] A. Jepsen, "Die Begriffe des 'Erlösens' im Alten Testament," in *R. Herrmann Festschrift,* 1958, pp. 153-62; J. J. Stamm, *Erlösen und Vergeben im Alten Testament,* 1940.

[11] R. Mayer, "Monotheismus in Israel und in der Religion Zarathustras," *BZ,* NF I (1957), 23-58; R. A. Rosenberg, "Yahweh Becomes King," *JBL,* LXXXV (1966), 297-307; N. H. Snaith, "The Advent of Monotheism in Israel," *Annual of Leeds University Oriental Society,* V (1963/65), 100-113.

[12] K. Galling, "Jahwe der Weltschöpfer," *ThBl,* IV (1925), 257-61; H.-J. Kraus, "Schöpfung und Weltvollendung," *EvTh,* XXIV (1964), 462-85; R. Rendtorff, "Die theologische Stellung des Schöpfungsglaubens bei Deuterojesaja," *ZThK,* LI (1954), 3-13; C. Stuhlmueller, "The Theology of Creation in Second Isaias," *CBQ,* XXI (1959), 429-67.

history, history, and eschatology, and linked the whole with Yahweh. He and no one else was and is present at creation, in the destiny of men and nations, and in the inauguration of eternal salvation, working his will. Therein rests the guarantee for the future: because Yahweh created the world and mankind and has ever since determined their destiny, he will continue to do so at the coming of the eschaton; and this eschaton is imminent.

Deutero-Isaiah accordingly predicted new salvation for Israel, for which Cyrus would create the necessary political background:

> But now thus says Yahweh,
>   he who created and shaped you, O Israel:
> "Fear not, for I have redeemed you;
>   I have called you by name, you are mine.
> When you pass through the waters I will be with you;
>   and through the rivers, they shall not overwhelm you;
> When you walk through fire you shall not be burned,
>   and the flame shall not consume you.
>
> For I, Yahweh, am your God,
>   the Holy One of Israel is your savior.
> I give Egypt as your ransom,
>   Ethiopia and Seba in exchange for you.
> Because you are precious in my eyes,
>   and honored, and I love you,
> I give *lands* in return for you,
>   peoples in exchange for your life.
>
> I will bring your offspring from the east,
>   and from the west I will gather you;
> I will say to the north, Give up,
>   and to the south, Do not withhold;
> bring my sons from afar
>   and my daughters from the end of the earth,
> every one who is called by my name,
>   whom I created for my glory."   (Isa. 43:1-7)

> Thus says Yahweh to his anointed,
>   to Cyrus, whose right hand I have grasped,
> to subdue nations before him
>   and ungird the loins of kings,
> to open doors before him
>   that gates may not be closed:
> "I will go before you
>   and level the *mountains,*

I will break in pieces the doors of bronze
    and cut asunder the bars of iron,
I will give you the treasures of darkness
    and the hoards of secret places,
that you may know that I am Yahweh,
    who calls you by name—the God of Israel."   (Isa. 45:1-3)

Then those who are set free will march straight through the desert to Palestine—or rather Yahweh will bring them there and rebuild Jerusalem:

"For you shall go out in peace,
    and be led forth in joy;
the mountains and the hills before you
    shall break forth into singing,
and all the trees of the field
    shall clap their hands.

Instead of thorn
    shall come up the cypress;
instead of the brier
    shall come up the myrtle;
and it shall be Yahweh for a memorial,
    for an everlasting sign which shall be cut off."   (55:12-13)

Get you up to a high mountain,
    O herald to Zion;
lift up your voice with strength,
    O herald to Jerusalem!
Say to the cities of Judah,
    "Behold your God!"
Behold, Yahweh
    comes *with might,*
his reward is with him,
    and his recompense before him,
He will feed his flock like a shepherd
    he will gather the lambs in his arms,
he will carry them in his bosom,
    and gently lead those that are with young.   (40:9-11)

O afflicted one, storm-tossed, and not comforted,
    behold, I will set
your stones in antimony
    and lay your foundations with lapis lazuli.
I will make your pinnacles of agate,
    your gates of carbuncles,

and all your wall of precious stones—
all your *architects* are taught by Yahweh.
Great shall be the prosperity of your sons,
and in righteousness you shall be established.

(54:11-14*a*)

Even the other nations will be included in the salvation to come; this provided the impetus for mission in a later period:[13]

Turn to me and be saved,
all the ends of the earth!
For I am God and there is no other.
By myself I have sworn,
and from my mouth goes forth truth,
a word that shall not be overturned:
"To me every knee shall bow,
every tongue shall swear."

Only in Yahweh *for man* is
righteousness and strength;
to him *shall come* and be ashamed
all who were incensed against him.
In Yahweh shall triumph and glory
all the offspring of Israel.   (45:22-25)

It must nevertheless not be overlooked that Deutero-Isaiah's preaching, in consequence of its reliance on the optimistic message of the earlier professional prophets, also contained questionable nationalistic and materialistic elements. Therefore this prophet did not stand at the apex of Israelite prophecy, but marked the beginning of its decline.

4. *Beginnings of eschatology.* However one seeks to describe the fundamental features of the great individual prophets, their message was absolutely non-eschatological. The first decades of the Exile witnessed an incipient movement in the direction of an eschatological reformulation of theological thought (cf. Ezekiel 38–39) ; Deutero-Isaiah was the first to develop this new direction fully, so that eschatology became authoritative for the prophets that followed him and influenced the future development of Yahwism.

[13] J. Hempel, "Die Wurzeln des Missionswillens im Glauben des AT," *ZAW*, LXVI (1954) , 244-72; M. Löhr, *Der Missionsgedanke im Alten Testament*, 1896; R. Martin-Achard, *Israël et les nations*, 1959; E. Sellin, "Der Missionsgedanke im Alten Testament," *Neue Allgemeine Missionszeitschrift*, II (1925) , 33-45, 66-72.

The essential idea in eschatological expectations was the distinction between two ages. Deutero-Isaiah suggests this distinction at once in the three introductory discourses of his corpus (Isa. 40:1-2, 3-5, 6-8). They sketch briefly the end of the transitory age of sin and distress and the beginning of the future age of redemption and deliverance. The distinction is even clearer where the prophet contrasts what is new with the former things of the past (45:18-19), referring to it as a "time of favor" and a "day of salvation" (49:8), or describes the contrast with the aid of the image of a "cup of wrath" and "bowl of staggering" (51:17-23). The prophet saw himself and his generation standing at the end of one age and on the threshold of another. His own day was the moment in which the great transformation began to show clearly or to take place.

The distinction between two ages and the sense of standing on the borderline between them distinguished eschatological prophecy following Deutero-Isaiah not only from traditional Yahwism, which considered Israel to be fundamentally in favor with Yahweh, a state that could be interrupted by isolated transgressions but restored by appropriate propitiatory measures, but also and even more profoundly from the great pre-exilic individual prophets. They did not preach the end of an age of calamity and the beginning of a better age, but the end of the sinful ways of life of Israel and other nations, while the rest of the world went its way. These prophets saw the only possible deliverance in a transformation of man through repentance and return to Yahweh, or through his redemption. They did not speak of two ages, but of the either/or of destruction or deliverance as an ever-recurring decision.

Eschatological prophecy reinterpreted the either/or, making of it a temporal before/after. This reinterpretation took place during the Exile under the continuing influence of the earlier optimistic prophecy that the great individual prophets had rejected. Therefore like the earlier optimistic prophets—albeit in another fashion—they thought in terms of a state of favor that could be restored, and placed one-sided emphasis on God's saving will. At the same time, they understood the fall of Judah and the Exile to be the judgment threatened by the great individual prophets (cf. Isa. 40:1-2). Since this judgment was no longer an imminent possibility but a unique historical event, a final and eternal age of salvation could follow—an "everlasting assurance" (Isa 55:3) with an "everlasting sign" (55:13), "everlasting salvation" (45:17; 51:6, 8), "everlasting love" (54:8), and "everlasting joy" (51:11).

The great transformation was to take place in an eschatological drama that exhibits the following acts in Deutero-Isaiah: (1) the overcoming of the power of oppressive Babylon through Yahweh (43:14-15 and *passim*), his instrument Cyrus (41:24 and *passim*), or through Israel itself (41:14-16); (2) the redemption of Israel through liberation (49:25-26 and *passim*), departure or flight (48:20 and *passim*), return through the desert (55:12-13 and *passim*), arrival in Jerusalem (40:9-11), and assembly of all those scattered throughout the world (41:8-9 and *passim*); (3) Yahweh's return to Zion (40:9-11 and *passim*); (4) the transformation of the earthly situation through rebuilding (44:26 and *passim*), blessings reminiscent of Paradise (51:3), and multiplication of the community (44:1-5 and *passim*); (5) men's realization that their gods are useless and their conversion to Yahweh (51:4-5 and *passim*). In the post-exilic period we frequently encounter these and other features. They plainly reveal the new influence exerted by eschatology.

PART FOUR

The Religion of the Post-Exilic Period

CHAPTER ONE: EARLY POST-EXILIC PERIOD

§ 25 EVENTS AND FIGURES

A. ALT, "Die Rolle Samarias bei der Entstehung des Judentums," in *Procksch Festschrift*, 1934, pp. 5-28 (= his *Kleine Schriften zur Geschichte des Volkes Israel*, II [1953], 316-37); s. H. BLANK, "Studies in Post-Exilic Universalism," *HUCA*, XI (1936), 159-91; A. CAUSSE, "La diaspora juive à l'époque perse," *RHPhR*, VIII (1928), 32-65; T. CHARY, *Les prophètes et le culte à partir de l'exil*, 1955; T. K. CHEYNE, *Das religiöse Leben der Juden nach dem Exil*, 1899; J. DE FRAINE, "Individu et société dans la religion de l'Ancien Testament," *Bibl*, XXXIII (1952), 324-55, 445-75; K. GALLING, *Syrien in der Politik der Achämeniden bis 448 v. Chr.*, 1937; *idem, Studien zur Geschichte Israels im persischen Zeitalter*, 1964; W. KESSLER, "Studie zur religiösen Situation im ersten nachexilischen Jahrhundert und zur Auslegung von Jesaja 55–66," *WZ Halle-Wittenberg*, VI (1956/57), 41-73; K. KOCH, "Sühne und Sündenvergebung um die Wende von der exilischen zur nachexilischen Zeit," *EvTh*, XXVI (1966), 217-39; J. L. MYRES, "Persia, Greece and Israel," *PEQ*, LXXXV (1953), 8-22; W. O. E. OESTERLEY, "The Early Post-Exilic Community," *ET*, XLVII 1935/36), 394-98; M. WEINFELD, "Universalism and Particularism in the Period of Exile and Restoration," *Tarbiz*, XXXIII (1963/64), 228-42.

1. *Return, rebuilding of the Temple, and religious attitude.*
Cyrus' victory over the Neo-Babylonian Empire (538 B.C.) gave the deported Judahites and their offspring the possibility of returning to Palestine. In the design of its new ruler, the Persian Empire was no longer to be a political and military alliance of subject peoples under the leadership of a dominant nation, but a full-fledged state with equal rights for all its citizens. In furtherance of these policies the Judahites, among others, were given permission to return to their homeland. Cyrus allowed them to take back the Temple furnishings that Nebuchadnezzar had brought to Babylonia and gave orders for the rebuilding of the Jerusalem Temple at state expense; this part

of the royal edict, in its original Aramaic, is contained in Ezra 6:3-5.[1]

Only a part of the Judahites living in Babylonia made use of the permission to return. As commissar for the territory of Judea, attached to the province of Samaria, the Persians appointed Sheshbazzar, a descendant of David, who probably laid the cornerstone for the new Temple in 537 B.C. during the Feast of Booths, which was once more being celebrated. In addition, an altar was erected on the Temple grounds, so that the sacrificial cult was restored before the Temple was rebuilt. Sheshbazzar and the other returnees contributed money and offerings for the outfitting of the Temple and the cult; those who stayed behind in Babylonia also contributed. Although the Temple was to be constructed at Persian expense, the situation differed from that during the monarchy. The Solomonic Temple had been royal property, built by the king and belonging to the dynasty. The people paid taxes for its upkeep, but the king once again controlled its use. Now that the Judahite monarchy had been abolished, the support of the new Temple was to be financed by the people and the Temple was to belong to them, so that what had been a royal and official Temple was replaced by a national Temple belonging to the people as a whole. The high priest replaced the chief priest at the apex of the hierarchy.

The situation in Judea nevertheless turned out to be difficult and in part clearly chaotic; there was no sign of the time of salvation that had been predicted. In addition the work on the Temple soon came to a standstill, if it had in fact ever gone beyond the laying of the cornerstone and the erection of the altar. All the returnees had all they could do to build their own houses and produce enough to subsist on.

The situation did not change until the year 520 B.C., when a party took control in Jerusalem that finally sought to finish rebuilding the Temple despite all the difficulties. This movement was favored by internal convulsions in the Persian Empire, which aroused in Judea expectations of an eschatological transformation of all things. The movement was led by the new commissar Zerubbabel, who had recently been appointed, and the high priest Joshua; it received important support from the prophets Haggai and Zechariah.

But all was still not clear sailing. Certain groups wanted to share in the rebuilding of the Temple and participate in the cult, groups

[1] L. Rost, "Erwägungen zum Kyroserlass," in *Rudolph Festschrift*, 1961, pp. 301-7; R. de Vaux, "Les décrets de Cyrus et de Darius sur la reconstruction du Temple," *RB*, XLVI (1937) , 29-57.

that appeared questionable to the strict religious judgment of the returnees, since their form of Yahwism was permeated with alien influences. We should think primarily in terms of descendants of the Judahites who had been left in Palestine at the time of the deportations and of adherents of Yahwism in Samaria. Haggai attacked these groups, demonstrating on the basis of two examples from ritual law that cultic purity is not transferable whereas cultic impurity is contagious, and concluding that the same was true of "these people," and that the site where they offered sacrifice would become unclean (Hag. 2:10-14). This conclusion probably aimed at excluding from work on the Temple and the cult those whose sacrifices would make the sacred site unclean. Thus the tendency toward exclusiveness that had been inaugurated by Deuteronomic theology was intensified.

At least a portion of those who were excluded, primarily the inhabitants of Samaria, did not accept their exclusion without resistance. They addressed themselves first to the competent Persian satrap, who thereupon came to Jerusalem with the intention of prohibiting work on the Temple. But since Cyrus' edict permitting the rebuilding was discovered in the Persian archives, the attempt failed. The work could be continued, and the Temple was ready to be dedicated in the year 515 B.C., with great celebration. By then, however, Zerubbabel was no longer residing in Jerusalem.

The new Temple was built on the site of the old and to its dimensions.[2] The ark and the two pillars were no longer present; the ten lampstands were replaced by a single one with seven branches. According to II Chron. 3:14, the Holy of holies was separated by a curtain; I Chron. 29:2 suggests mosaics. While people feared at the outset that they would get only a mean structure that could not stand comparison with the Solomonic Temple (Hag. 2:1-9), the Temple appears gradually to have grown so imposing that Ecclus. 49:12 could extol its magnificence. Perhaps the effect was enhanced by the repair and addition of colonnades, mentioned in a decree of Antiochus III about 200 B.C.[3] Later the Temple suffered frequent damage in the wars with the Seleucids.

The Israelites in Palestine and the Diaspora were divided into several intellectual and religious parties. In the Babylonian Diaspora the dominant party adhered strictly and unflinchingly to the law,

[2] See the bibliography for § 10.
[3] Josephus, *Antiquities*, xii. 3. 3.

refusing to make any concessions to other influences or admit liberalizing modifications. In Judea the dominant party, consisting for the most part of returnees from Babylonia, was equally stringent, apparently in association with nationalistic endeavors and, in part, messianic hopes. Alongside this group a priestly and theocratic party gradually consolidated its position, concerned more with expanding the community than with legal rigor. The new Jerusalem upper class, which sought to ally itself with the upper class in Samaria, was even more open or careless.[4] The military colony at Elephantine in Egypt had long departed furthest from genuine Yahwism (see § 11.5).[5] In the temple built there prior to 525 B.C., contrary to the Deuteronomic program of cultic centralization, a popular syncretism was practiced, which the Babylonian Diaspora attacked in at least one instance, with Persian assistance, in the mazzoth decree of Darius II (419 B.C.). The temple was destroyed around 410 B.C. at the instigation of Egyptian priests, presumably rebuilt again before 402 B.C., and probably finally destroyed a few years later. The Jewish colony presumably left Elephantine at that time. In Arabia, too, there seems to have been a Diaspora from the sixth or fifth century on,[6] though nothing is known about its attitude.

Morgenstern has sought to eke out the scanty historical and religious data about the period following the reconstruction of the Temple.[7] From Lamentations and certain Psalms or prophetical texts (above all Trito-Isaiah) he has concluded that there was a nationalistic Judean revolt against the Persians after their defeat at the battle of Marathon (490 B.C.), based on faith in Yahweh's will to establish a world empire and his eternal promise to the Davidic dynasty. A king was installed (Psalm 2) with the throne name Menahem (found in Lam. 1:2, 9, 16-17, 21; Isa. 51:12-13) on New Year's Day in 486, but the revolt soon collapsed. The king fell into the hands of the Edomites (Ps. 89:39 ff. [Eng. 89:38 ff.]), and Jerusalem was destroyed once more. This hypothesis, however, is untenable; some of the texts cited are erroneously dated, others erroneously interpreted.

[4] The love and marriage songs of the Song of Solomon may stem from these circles.
[5] E. König, "Religionsgeschichtliche Hauptmomente in den Elephantinetexten," ZAW, XXXV (1915), 110-19; E. G. Kraeling, "New Light on the Elephantine Colony," BA, XV (1952), 50-67; B. Porten, "The Structure and Orientation of the Jewish Temple at Elephantine—a Revised Plan of the Jewish District," JAOS, LXXXI (1961), 38-42; A. Vincent, La religion des Judéo-Araméens d'Éléphantine, 1937; C. C. Wagenaar, De Joodse kolonie van Jeb-Syene in de 5e eeuw v. Chr., 1928.
[6] See I. Ben-Zvi, "The Origins of the Settlement of Jewish Tribes in Arabia," Eretz-Israel, VI (1960), 130-48.
[7] J. Morgenstern, "Jerusalem—485 B.C.," HUCA, XXVII (1956), 101-78; XXVIII (1957), 15-47; XXXI (1960), 1-19; idem, "Further Light from the Book of Isaiah upon the Catastrophe of 485 B.C.," ibid., XXXVII (1966), 1-28.

2. *Early post-exilic prophecy. a*) Haggai and Zechariah are the only prophets from this period whose names are known.[8] Both were certain that those who had returned from Babylonia after 538 B.C. were the sacred remnant of Israel, which was to be delivered from the judgment (see § 20.1). The promises spoken by the prophets were therefore directed at this remnant, the returnees; they were the people of the eschatological age of salvation. Now that the judgment was a thing of the past, all interest concentrated on a single question: when will that age of salvation finally begin that must follow after the judgment, as was already predicted by Deutero-Isaiah? The eschatological schema (before/after) and expectation of the imminent coming of the eschaton made the "when" of the age of salvation an urgent question.

Haggai looked upon the day Zerubbabel laid the new cornerstone as the beginning of the new area, after which there would be only blessings (Hag. 2:15-19); he expected the completion of the rebuilding to be marked by an earthquake signaling completion of the change and the full beginning of the age of salvation (2:1-9), in which Zerubbabel, the Davidic king, would reign as messianic king of the eschaton (2:20-23). In the description of what the age of salvation would be like, the present economic distress made religious expectations take a back seat to future worldly goods. Haggai hoped that following the earthquake all nations would come to Jerusalem to offer their treasure as tribute owed to Yahweh, the Lord of the world. This would enable the Temple to be outfitted magnificently, so that it would gleam in fabulous radiance (2:6-8). After this we encounter an often gross materialism in descriptions of the age of salvation, a feature that was later to characterize apocalyptic representations as well.

Zechariah likewise dated the beginning of the age of salvation from the laying of the cornerstone (Zech. 8:9-13); he insisted, how-

---

[8] On Haggai, see A. Bentzen, "Quelques remarques sur le mouvement messianique parmi les Juifs aux environs de l'an 520 avant Jésus-Christ," *RHPhR*, X (1930), 493-503; F. Hesse, "Haggai," in *Rudolph Festschrift*, 1961, pp. 109-34; K. Koch, "Haggais unreines Volk," *ZAW*, LXXIX (1967), 52-66; J. W. Rothstein, *Juden und Samaritaner*, 1908; L. Waterman, "The Camouflaged Purge of Three Messianic Conspirators," *JNES*, XIII (1954), 73-78; H. W. Wolff, *Haggai*, 1951. On Zechariah, see K. Galling, *Studien zur Geschichte Israels im persischen Zeitalter*, 1964, pp. 109-26; K. Marti, *Der Prophet Sacharia, der Zeitgenosse Serubbabels*, 1892; idem, "Zwei Studien zu Sacharja," *ThStKr*, LXV (1892), 207-45, 716-34; idem, "Die Zweifel an der prophetischen Sendung Sacharjas," in *Wellhausen Festschrift*, 1914, pp. 279-97; L. G. Rignell, *Die Nachtgesichte des Sacharja*, 1950; J. W. Rothstein, *Die Nachtgesichte des Sacharja*, 1910.

ever, that the full arrival of the age must await not only the rebuilding of the Temple but also the banishment of sin and the inward renewal of the nation. Futhermore he undergirded the expectation of material prosperity with ethical requirements. In view of the imminent convulsion, he was no longer concerned with the observance of solemn lamentations and fast days, but with obedience to the ethical commandments of Yahweh. Finally, he allowed himself to be induced by a delegation from the Babylonian Diaspora to crown Zerubbabel symbolically as messianic king of the eschaton (6:9-15, emended). But he divided the messianic dignity between two representatives by including the high priest as agent for spiritual affairs (4:1-6aα, 10b-14).

b) That the rebuilding of the Temple did not go uncontested is shown by the audacious prophetical discourse in Isa. 66:1-4, which rejects its reconstruction in a rationalistic manner reminiscent of wisdom instruction, together with the whole sacrificial cult, which is labeled idolatry.

The oracles of salvation in Isaiah 60–62 derive from a prophet markedly influenced by Deutero-Isaiah. But he lacked the latter's universalistic perspective and theocentric approach, while emphasizing totally earthly happiness for Jerusalem. This city, not Yahweh, is the focus of attention; salvation is restricted to it, while the other nations can only be servants of the saved community. Therefore this prophet can be considered the descendant of earlier nationalistic prophecy.

From the beginning of the fifth century B.C. derive Isa. 56:1-8, prophetical instruction dealing with the question of whether eunuchs and foreigners can be members of the community, a problem that was important after the rebuilding of the Temple; Isa. 56:9—57:13, which attacks the leaders of the community, accusing them of neglecting their duties, seeking personal gain and pleasure, and deserting Yahweh; and Isaiah 59, in which a prophet solves the problem of why eschatological salvation was delayed after the completion of the Temple by pointing to sin as the cause of the delay.

The major portion of the so-called Isaiah Apocalypse (Isaiah 24–27) probably derives from the fifth century B.C.: the three prophetical liturgies in 24:1-20, depicting the eschatological judgment and the dissolution of urban life; 24:21–25:12, describing the reduction of Yahweh's enemies and the beginning of God's universal sovereignty; and 27:1-6, 12-13, describing the eschatological battle of Yahweh, the preservation of Israel, and the reunification of all Israelites.

There are other prophetical traditions that probably originated in the early post-exilic period, which cannot be dated more precisely. The most important are: the messianic promises in Isa. 9:1-6 (Eng. 9:2-7); 11:1-9; the oracles concerning Moab in Isaiah 15–16 and against Egypt in Isa. 19:1-15; the prophetical liturgies in Isa. 33:1-6; 7-24; the description of the eschatological age in Isaiah 34–35; the eschatological promise in Isa. 57:14-21; the discourse concerning proper fasting in Isa. 58:1-12; the discourse about keeping the Sabbath in Isa. 58:13-14; the description of Yahweh as the eschatological avenger of Israel against the nations in Isa. 63:1-6; the promises in Micah 4–5; the critical, invective, or minatory discourses in Mic. 6:1–7:7; and the promise of Jerusalem's eschatological exaltation in Mic. 7:8-20.

3. *Outcome.* The Temple had been dedicated without Zerubbabel, whom the Persian regime had recalled as being politically unreliable and had not replaced with a new commissar. This was the outward sign of an incipient change in the intellectual situation. The hope gradually vanished that the eschatological age of salvation was about to be inaugurated imminently under the rule of a messianic king in Jerusalem. After the dedication of the Temple all went on as before. Those who continued to cherish the eschatological hope were confronted with the question of why the eschaton was delayed; some responded by citing the sinfulness of the community, others evaded the question with an increase of religious fervor.

At first after the removal of Zerubbabel the high priest gained the upper hand, and with him the priestly and theocratic party, whose interests were primarily cultic and legal. The high priest, as Yahweh's representative, became the real head of the community. Many ancient traditions of the Temple were revived. The door was opened wide to those who wanted to enter the community, even those Haggai had wanted to exclude.

The differences between the two movements—on the one hand the prophetical and eschatological, on the other the priestly and theocratic—were considerable. The former was characterized by separation from all uncleanness, ardent hopes and desires often materialistic in nature, expectation of Yahweh's imminent coming and the inclusion of the nations upon their conversion, but until then harshness and intolerance toward the surrounding world. The latter harbored no eschatological hopes, but rather associated Yahweh's sovereignty with fulfillment of the law, especially its cultic and ritual prescriptions; they therefore opened the community to as many adherents as possible, because everyone who offers sacrifice to Yahweh and fulfills Yahweh's law contributes to the realization of salvation. Under the leadership of this latter party the community enjoyed considerable outward prosperity after the completion of the Temple, but soon confronted an internal crisis.

§ 26 DEVELOPMENT OF ESCHATOLOGY

K. BALTZER, "Das Ende des Staates Juda und die Messias-Frage," in *Von Rad Festschrift*, 1961, pp. 33-43; A. BENTZEN, *King and Messiah*, 1955; G. R. BERRY, "Messianic Predictions," *JBL*, XLV (1926), 232-37; L. E. BROWNE, *The Messianic Hope in Its Historical Setting*, 1951; J. COPPENS, "L'espérance messianique," *ALBO*, IV.9, 1964; L. DÜRR, *Ursprung und Ausbau der israelitisch-jüdischen Heilandserwartung*, 1925; G. FOHRER, *Messiasfrage und Bibelverständnis*, 1957; *idem*, "Die Struktur der alttestamentlichen Eschatologie," in his *Studien zur alttestamentlichen Prophetie (1949-1965)*, 1967, pp. 32-58; H. GRESSMANN, *Der Messias*, 1929; L. HARTMANN, *Prophecy Interpreted*, 1966; J. LINDBLOM, "Gibt es eine Eschatologie bei den alttestamentlichen Propheten?" *StTh*, VI (1952), 79-114; N. MESSEL, *Die Einheitlichkeit der jüdischen Eschatologie*, 1915; S. MOWINCKEL, *He That Cometh*, 2nd ed., 1959; G. PIDOUX, *Le Dieu qui vient*, 1947; O. PLÖGER, *Theokratie und Eschatologie*, 2nd ed., 1962; P. VOLZ, *Die Eschatologie der jüdischen Gemeinde*, 1934.

1. *Eschatological events. a)* In the course of the post-exilic period the eschatological expectations initiated by Deutero-Isaiah developed quickly (see § 24.4), finding adherents at first in extensive circles until, following the disappointment of imminent expectations, they remained limited to smaller groups. Again and again representatives of these expectations appeared; finally they were absorbed by apocalyptic. The following discussion will present post-exilic eschatology as a whole.

The distinction and division between two ages as the basic feature of all eschatological expectation is clearly illustrated by the discourse contained in Hag. 2:15-19, spoken by the prophet in September of 520 B.C., on the day the new cornerstone was laid for the Temple. In it the prophet called upon men to direct their gaze to the future, be alert to it, and compare it with what had gone before, now part of the past. He proclaimed for the Jerusalem community a turning point, which he identified with that very day as the watershed betwteen two eras. Looking back over the past, he described the calamity—consisting in a curse upon all means of sustenance—that had brought the community to the brink of despair. Looking ahead into the future, he saw an age of blessing in prosperity and increase based on the word of Yahweh: "From this day forth I will bless you!" The "today" of this statement Haggai identified with the day of the cornerstone laying as the day of the great upheaval, the boundary between two ages, when the old era comes to an end and the new one begins.

Zechariah made a similar distinction in essentially the same way. In his first discourse, Zech. 1:1-6, the admonition in 1:3 is followed by and based upon a historical analysis (1:4-6), in which the prophet surveys the previous age, now brought to an end by the momentous intervention of Yahweh through his judgment upon Judah and through the Exile. The past could be both understood and evaluated. The observer could see that it was a history in which Yahweh's words and decrees were realized, as proclaimed by the earlier prophets. Therefore the admonition to get on with the building of the Temple must be taken seriously as Yahweh's requirement for the beginning of a new age, in order that the promise of salvation contained in the visions to follow might likewise be realized. Zech. 8:14-15 accordingly distinguished two ages, one characterized by Yahweh's purpose to destroy, the other by his purpose to save.

b) Besides the notion of two sequential ages, which was funda-mental to the structure of eschatological prophecy, this prophecy from the very outset evolved certain features of the eschatological event which often practically follow one upon another like the acts of an eschatological drama. On the basis of the more extensive texts we can distinguish five basic forms of this drama beside that con-tained in Deutero-Isaiah (§ 24.4); they differ most clearly in the various treatments accorded to the other nations.

1) The views of Haggai and Zechariah were similar. For Haggai, the first act was the promise of blessing on the day the cornerstone was laid (Hag. 2:19; cf. 2:9), together with the preservation of the community in all its purity by exclusion of those who were unclean (2:10-14). As the next act he expected convulsions in the natural order (2:6, 21) and among the nations (2:7) in which their power would be destroyed (2:22); Zerubbabel would then be installed as messianic ruler (2:23). In the case of Zechariah the sequence of events appears to have been somewhat different, although the order of his visions does not necessarily imply an identical temporal se-quence in the events envisioned. The first act was probably the destruction of the power of the Gentile world (2:1-4 [Eng. 1:18-21]),

which was actually to blame for Israel's misfortunes (1:15) and would fall prey to their former subjects (2:13). Then would follow the creation of wonderful circumstances for the Jerusalem community (1:17; 2:5-9 [Eng. 2:1-5]; 8:4-5, 12), among whom Yahweh would dwell to protect them by his presence (2:14, 16 [Eng. 2:10, 12]; 8:3), together with the destruction of the sinners in Judea (5:1-4) and the removal of sin from the community (5:5-11), followed by the assembly and return of the Diaspora (6:1-8; 8:7-8). In addition the reign of the Messiah would be inaugurated (3:1-7; 4; 6:9-15) and many men and nations would join Israel (2:15 [Eng. 2:11]; 8:20-22). The new elements not found in Deutero-Isaiah were primarily the extension of destruction from Babylonia to the nations, the purification of the community, and the messianic conception with the mention of specific figures.

2) The so-called Isaiah Apocalypse (Isaiah 24–27) comprises primarily three originally independent prophetical liturgies. Of these, 24:1-20 announced eschatological judgment upon the whole earth and its inhabitants, including the dissolution of urban life, and upon the heavens—because men had sinned against the Noachian laws, which were binding upon all. Isa. 24:21–25:12 expected the enemies of Yahweh to be deprived of their power and to have their capitals destroyed, after which (for those who survived) there would be a universal banquet with Yahweh on Zion to mark the beginning of God's reign. According to 27:1-6, 12-13, however, Israel would be protected after Yahweh's eschatological battle, and its Diaspora would be assembled out of all the world.

3) In the second half of the fourth century B.C., Deutero-Zechariah in Zech. 9:11-17; 10:3-12 shared with the basic forms already discussed the expectation that the prisoners would be released to return home, that the Diaspora would be assembled, and that paradisal fertility would be created. As in Deutero-Isaiah, the empire currently ruling the world would be conquered to make the age of salvation possible, but this would be done by Israel itself, supported in the decisive battle by God, who would appear in a theophany. This concept seems to have included not only the destruction of the power of the empire, but also the destruction of the nation bearing that power. This would be even clearer if Zech. 11:4-16 in the form we now have it should derive from the same author.

4) Joel, who was roughly contemporaneous with Deutero-Zechariah (fourth century B.C.), depicted two phases: (a) Yahweh himself would challenge the nations to an eschatological attack upon himself

and upon Israel before Jerusalem (Joel 4:2, 9-10 [Eng. 3:2, 9-10]);
in fact they were being summoned to a final judgment on account
of their sins against Israel (4:2-3, 12 [Eng. 3:2-3, 12]). The judgment would take place in the form of an annihilating battle near
Jerusalem, depicted in the image of a harvest (4:13-17 [Eng. 3:13-
17]), demonstrating Jerusalem's inviolability (4:16-17 [Eng. 3:16-17]).
Here we find linked the extension to all the nations, undertaken by
Haggai and Zechariah, and the idea of a final battle represented by
Deutero-Zechariah. (b) The final judgment would be followed by
paradisal blessings and peace (4:18-21 [Eng. 3:18-21]). These same
two phases are also found in Zechariah 14, but with two differences
in contrast to Joel: Jerusalem is not inviolable, but is conquered,
plundered, and stripped of its inhabitants until the partial destruction of the nations takes place following the theophany of Yahweh
and his entry into Jerusalem; and the survivors from among the
nations will share in Israel's salvation.

5) The very late oracles Zech. 12:1–13:6; 13:7-9, on the other
hand, appear to presuppose that the age of salvation has already
dawned; this must have taken place peacefully and without any
defeat of the world empire or the nations. At a later date, however,
Jerusalem and the saved community will be threatened by an attack
on the part of the nations, in which Yahweh himself will once again
risk everything. The defeat of the nations and deliverance of
Jerusalem will be followed by the purification of the community;
the sinners will be eliminated, and final salvation will come to pass.

These various forms share the following features: (1) destruction
of the power of the world empire or the nations, or the general
destruction of the nations themselves; (2) deliverance and liberation
of Israel as the eschatological community to enjoy salvation, together
with the purification of the community and the assembly of the
Diaspora in Jerusalem; (3) the creation of wonderful and paradisal
circumstances for the community; (4) inauguration of God's direct
sovereignty or the reign of the Messiah; (5) conversion of the nations
or a remnant of them. In these expectations we see to a large extent
the eschatological transformation of the preaching of the pre-exilic
optimistic prophets.

2. The structure of eschatology. The interpretation and description
of the eschatological event and the hoped-for new and everlasting
age of salvation were marked in eschatological prophecy by a considerable number of structural elements that cannot be isolated from

the whole, but rather define it in detail. Each of these individual elements focuses on two polar motifs that can be linked (*a, e, h*) or between which transitional forms can exist (*b, g*).

a) The judgment upon the present era, drawing to a close, was largely determined by Deutero-Isaiah; it is the era of sin and the punishment that follows sin (Isa. 40:2; 51:17; 57:17). When the punishment came to be identified with a particular historical event (the fall of Judah and the Exile), it was natural to think of it as punishing the sins of the earlier age; on this point the estimate ultimately agreed with the bitter complaint of the deportees in Ezek. 18:2. Isa. 9:1 (Eng. 9:2), on the other hand, depicted the preceding age generally as chaotic activity, with the people walking in the "darkness" of disaster and death, languishing, as it were, in the nether world of the dead shades. These two views are linked together by the explanation that the miserable situation of darkness and disease in which the community stands in need of light and healing is due to sin—not past, but present (Isa. 59:1-8). The present age is characterized by man's perpetual and therefore present sin in the transgression of the Noachian laws (Isa. 24:5, 20; 26:21). In fact this present sinfulness can delay the coming of the age of salvation, whether the sin is refusal to get on with the rebuilding of the Temple (Haggai) or blood-guiltiness and injustice (Isa. 59:1-4).

b) Deutero-Isaiah saw the beginning of the new age as being imminent. This expectation can be heard repeatedly in his discourses (cf. Isa. 43:10-17), especially those concerning Cyrus, whose deeds were meant to help inaugurate the age of salvation. The prophet could even look upon what was to come as though it were already present (48:20) or, in fictitious retrospect, treat it already as a past event (40:9-11; 48:2). In this regard he was following the structure of earlier prophetical preaching, which had always dealt with the present moment and the immediate future. But the two final discourses concerning the servant of Yahweh (Isa. 50:10-11; 52:13–53:12), to the extent that they refer to Deutero-Isaiah himself, reflect the tragic disappointment of these exaggerated hopes. Later, however, the dawn of the age of salvation was once more proclaimed to be imminent (Isa. 56:1-2; 61:2); it was even called the "nearness of God" (Isa. 58:2) or represented as already taking place (Hag. 2:19; Isa. 57:14). Its continued delay, however, led not only to passionate impatience (Isaiah 62), but also to postponement based on present sinfulness (Isaiah 59) or to a refusal to set any date, so that the beginning of the revolution came to appear as a possibility that could take place at any time, for which a man must prepare himself through fulfillment of his cultic and ritual obligations (Malachi). This marked the transition to an indefinite postponement of the new age, the result of repeated disappointments.

c) The eschatological prophets often associated the great upheaval at the change from one era to the next with an earth-shaking convulsion, either limited or universal. For Deutero-Isaiah this convulsion befell the ruling power of Babylon (see also Isaiah 13; 21:1-10; Jeremiah 50–51), which, as the symbol of the old world, was to be demolished when the latter perished. This would be achieved by Yahweh, doing battle as a warrior according to the ancient notion (Isa. 42:13),[1] or by a leader appointed as king by Yahweh and commissioned by him. For Haggai the convulsion was to affect even the natural order and the nations (Hag. 2:6-7, 21-22); for Zechariah, it was to befall all nations (Zech. 1:15; 2:1-4 [Eng. 1:18-21]). Later the expectation came increasingly to refer to the dominant world power (Zech. 9:1 ff.; 11:1 ff.), often referred to symbolically by means of such historical names as Assyria (Isa. 10:24-27a), Babylon (Isa. 14:22 [2]), Moab (Isa. 25:10), or Edom (Isaiah 34). All this continued the line taken by the earlier prophets, and not least the optimistic ones, which saw Yahweh's hand at work in political crises. A totally different tradition was echoed in the motif of the eschatological attack of the nations upon Israel or Jerusalem. This motif represented an eschatological transformation of Ezekiel's discourse against Gog (Ezekiel 38–39), which was itself derived from Jeremiah's threat based on the foe from the north (Jeremiah 4–6; cf. Joel 2:10: "the northern one")[3]; it was also associated with what had originally been mythological ideas and was permeated in part with the notions of the optimistic prophets. These expectations and fears of a violent military upheaval gradually replaced the other motif of a miraculous inauguration of the time of salvation without such outward events. At the very least Yahweh was expected to intervene in the affairs of the eschatological community. For Zech. 5:1-4, this intervention was

---

[1] See the comprehensive treatment by H. Fredriksson, *Jahwe als Krieger*, 1945.

[2] The framework of Isaiah 14 (vss. 1-4a, 22-23) derives from the post-exilic period, as can be seen above all from the author's reliance on exilic and post-exilic texts (Isa. 49:22-23; 56:1-8; 61:4-9; Zech. 2:12-16 [Eng. 2:8-12]; 8:20-23); see G. Quell, "Jesaja 14,1-23" in *Festschrift Friedrich Baumgärtel*, 1959, pp. 131-57.

[3] See B. S. Childs, "The Enemy from the North and the Chaos Tradition," *JBL*, LXXVIII (1958), 187-98; O. Eissfeldt, *Baal Zaphon, Zeus Kasios und der Durchzug der Israeliten durchs Meer*, 1932; G. Fohrer and K. Galling, *Ezechiel*, 1955, pp. 212-16; A. Lauha, *Zaphon, der Norden und die Nordvölker im Alten Testament*, 1943; G. Wanke, *Die Zionstheologie der Korachiten*, 1966.

to involve the destruction of the thievish and perjured local inhabitants in addition to the general upheaval; Isa. 59:17-18; 65:11 ff. appear to think only in terms of removal of the wicked and idolatrous from the community of Israel itself.

d) For Deutero-Isaiah, the eschatological upheaval was founded solely on Yahweh's redemptive will. In his preaching the doctrine of redemption, which can be traced in prophetical theology from Hosea through Jeremiah and Ezekiel, found its culmination. "Repentance" was neither the prerequisite for nor the means of redemption, but its consequence: because Yahweh has forgiven and forgives, man can and must repent (Isa. 44:21-22; 55:6-7). Precisely the reverse obtains for Zech. 1:3: "Return to me, and I will (once more) return to you." In Zechariah's situation, the demand for repentance as the prerequisite and condition for the inauguration of the age of salvation meant an end to the neglect of work on the Temple and an eagerness to get to work. In this cultic association we see the greatest difference between this and earlier prophecy. In Isa. 56:1-8 it is observance of the Sabbath and avoidance of evil (by excluding aliens and eunuchs from the community), in Isaiah 58 active love for one's fellowman, and in Isaiah 59 rejection of sin that is mentioned as the necessary condition for the inauguration of the age of salvation and participation in it: in fact, Isa. 61:8 goes so far as to term "everlasting assurance" the "reward" for steadfast patience. Thus two different views stood in contrast to each other.

e) The realization of the eschatological transformation could be imagined in particularistic and nationalistic terms or in universalistic terms; in the former, which appears especially often, nationalistic prophecy found its most vigorous successor. According to this view, at the time of the world convulsion (see c) Yahweh would execute judgment on Israel's behalf against the world power or the nations, primarily according to the threat they represented against the eschatological community. This judgment, executed by Yahweh or by Israel itself, played an important rôle in all eschatological expectations. Yahweh would even give entire nations as a ransom for the liberation and assembly of the dispersed deportees, or make them servants of the future community of salvation. Apart from the material benefits that were also hoped for (see h), these nationalistic promises also had a universalistic aspect to the extent that some or all other nations were affected by the realization of the future age. As in nationalistic prophecy, which expected salvation primarily for Israel, these nations, however, would meet with judgment and destruction. Only as survivors of the judgment, converted through the eschatological events, would they have a certain share in the salvation to come (see *i*). But we also encounter the notion of a truly universal realization of salvation for the benefit of all men, based on the theology of the great individual prophets. This idea is most clearly expressed in Zeph. 3:9-10: Yahweh will give the nations new, pure lips to call upon him, to serve him with one accord, and to bring offerings from the entire world. Deutero-Isaiah, too, speaks in one passage of direct salvation for the waiting nations (Isa. 51:4-6), salvation which the author of Isa. 52:13–53:12 saw realized through the vicarious suffering of the servant of Yahweh. On the basis of the idea of creation, Isa. 17:7-8 speaks of the eschatological conversion of all men without the intervention of any further events. More frequently we encounter a combined nationalistic and universalistic realization: salvation is promised universally to all the world, but is to be attained at the national and religious center of Israel, in Jerusalem (Isa. 2:2-4; 25:6 ff.; 56:7; Jer. 3:17; Zech. 8:20 ff.; with threatening overtones in Zech. 14:16 ff.).

f) The preceding examples show that eschatological prophecy in general did not think in terms of the end of the world, but saw eschatological events taking place within the framework of the world of nations. For the most part, the salvation expected in the new age was to be realized within this framework. Here eschatological prophecy took account of political or historical circumstances (as in Deutero-Isaiah or Zech. 1:7-15), or else elaborated its theological reflections without such points of contact (see Joel 4 [Eng. Joel 3]; Zechariah 12–14).

By way of contrast, we often find theories that involved the cosmos in the eschatological events or even interpreted eschatology itself in cosmic terms. The point of departure for these theories was Deutero-Isaiah's inclusion of nature by virtue of his belief in creation, an important element in his thought. Hag. 2:6, 21, for example, look forward to a convulsion in the natural realm as well as in the world of nations; Isa. 13:10, 13; 24:1 ff., 18 ff.; Jer. 4:23-26 look for cosmic effects of the final judgment, which can bring about the end of the existing world (Isa. 34:4; 51:6). To the end of the old cosmos corresponds the beginning of a new cosmos (Zech. 14:6), which will be everlasting (Isa. 65:17-18; 66:22) and within which Yahweh will shine as an everlasting light (Isa. 60:19-20).

g) The future age of salvation was frequently expected as a restoration of the earlier age. This restorative eschatology is characterized outwardly in Zech. 10:6; Ps. 85:5 (Eng. 85:4) by the word *šûb* in the hiphil, meaning "restore," but above all through the phrase *šûb šᵉbû/ît*, "restore the fortunes," whose meaning in this sense is clear from Ezek. 16:53 and Job 42:10.[4] The expression is encountered almost exclusively in eschatological theology, where it seems practically to have served as a fixed idiom for eschatological restoration. With equal frequency, however, eschatological prophecy looked forward not to the restoration but to the renovation of the old order. The age of salvation was to mean essentially a renewal of the world. This is especially clear in Deutero-Isaiah's contrast between the "former things" and "new things." Jerusalem also and above all will be made new, as Zech. 2:5-9 (Eng. 2:1-5) and the parallel with creation in Isa. 60:1-2 show. The author of Isaiah 62 went even a step further, speaking of a new name for Jerusalem signifying its new saving nature, as did the author of Isa. 2:2, who used originally mythological concepts to depict the city as the mountain of God and the center of paradise. These expectations culminated in the prediction of a new creation of the cosmos (see *f*).

h) The saving benefits of the new age were understood in terms of abundant blessings and material prosperity (Zech. 1:17). A basic element was the expected rebuilding of Jerusalem, its Temple, and the cities of Judah (Isa. 44:26; 45:13; 54:11-12; 58:12; 60:10, 13; 61:4), whereby Jerusalem was to become the hub of the universe and the center of Yahweh's everlasting kingdom (Isa. 2:2; 24:23; 60:10-11).[5] Immense riches would flow thither to supply the needs of the Temple or the saved community; at the same time a stream of blessings would issue from the city (Joel 4:18 [Eng. 3:18]; Zech. 14:8, drawing on Ezek. 47:1-12). Partially as a consequence of this, partially as a result of the renewal of the world (see *g*), paradisal fertility of the land is mentioned with striking frequency (e.g., Isa. 30:23-25; 51:3; Amos 9:13; Joel 4:18 [Eng. 3:18]; Ps. 144:13-14).[6] The abundance of blessings includes also the increase of Israel

[4] E. L. Dietrich, שבות שוב, *die endzeitliche Wiederherstellung bei den Propheten*, 1925. For a different interpretation (alleviation of guilt), see E. Baumann, "שוב שבות, eine exegetische Untersuchung," *ZAW*, XLVII (1929), 17-44. For a discussion of the form of the phrase, see R. Borger, "Zur שוב שבו/ית" *ZAW*, LXVI (1954), 315-16.

[5] G. Fohrer, "Zion-Jerusalem im Alten Testament," *ThW*, VII, 291-318; H. Gross, *Weltherrschaft als religiöse Idee im Alten Testament*, 1953; N. W. Porteous, "Jerusalem-Zion: The Growth of a Symbol," in *Rudolph Festschrift*, 1961, pp. 235-52.

[6] A. de Guglielmo, "The Fertility of the Land in Messianic Prophecies," *CBQ*, XIX (1957), 306-11.

346 Early Post-Exilic Period

through numerous offspring (Isa. 44:3-4; 49:19-21; 54:1-3; 60:22), the elimination of bodily infirmities (Isa. 29:18; 32:3-4; 33:23; 35:5-6), human longevity corresponding to the Israelite conception of life (Isa. 65:10; Zech. 8:4) until death itself is destroyed (Isa. 25:8), and everlasting peace among men and animals (Isa. 2:4; 9:4 [Eng. 9:5]; 11:6-9; 65:25; Zech. 9:10; Ps. 46:10 [Eng. 46:9]).[7] On the other hand, there were to be religious and spiritual benefits: the removal of uncleanness (Zech. 13:1 ff.); sinlessness (Isa. 60:21; 65:25; Zech. 5:5-11), so that no evil is done (Isa. 11:9) and Israel is termed "holy," i.e., set apart from its previous life and dedicated to Yahweh (Isa. 4:3; 62:12). Israel was accordingly to receive the spirit of prophetical inspiration, which makes possible a direct relationship with Yahweh (Joel 3:1-2 [Eng. 2:28-29]). Here we find an echo—albeit in grosser terms—of the belief in redemption typical of earlier prophecy. In the last analysis, however, the two aspects, outward prosperity and religious salvation, can be separated only artificially; to the mind of that age they belonged together, as their linking in Isa. 11:6-9; 58:11-12; Ps. 85:11-13; 90:13-17 shows. All this will arouse joy and gladness, which are both an echo of the benefits received and themselves a final benefit (Isa. 42:10-22; 44:23; 48:20; 49:13; 51:11; 52:8-9; 61:3; 65:13-14, 18; 66:10).

i) The whole Israelite community would first share in the salvation of the new age in and around Jerusalem, the center of their world; this group was frequently referred to as the "remnant" of Israel. This term, which originally referred to the less important part surviving a catastrophe (see § 20.1), became toward the end of the Exile a term of mixed pride and humility denoting those who had been preserved from destruction, who applied it to themselves not as worthless leftovers but as the elect agents of the saving future. The participation of this "remnant" community in salvation could be interpreted exclusively, in a sense that led to their being set apart and to the exclusion of others (Hag. 2:10-14; Isa. 61:9). On the other hand, the community could be called upon to open itself to absorb others—who would, of course, have to obey the requirements of the cultic law (Isa. 56:1-8; Zech. 9:1-8). Usually participation in salvation was promised to the nations as a second, extended circle. That they might belong to the "people" worshiping Yahweh (Zech.

[7] W. Eichrodt, *Die Hoffnung des ewigen Friedens im alten Israel*, 1920; G. Fohrer, *Glaube und Welt im Alten Testament* 1948, pp. 230-58; H. Gross, *Die Idee des ewigen und allgemeinen Weltfriedens im Alten Orient und im Alten Testament*, 1956.

2:15 [Eng. 2:11]) would be due to their conversion in the light of their experiences (Isa. 2:2-4; 45:3, 5-6, 14-17), their insight based on Yahweh's summons (Isa. 45:20-25), missionary work among them (Isa. 42:1-4, 6; 49:6), or vicarious suffering whose benefits they might appropriate (Isa. 52:13–53:12). The right of the nations to be counted among the worshipers of Yahweh would be revealed by their desire to be instructed concerning the way of life demanded by Yahweh (Isa. 2:3), by their participation in Yahweh's banquet (Isa. 25:6 ff.), or by their eager clinging to a member of the saved community (Zech. 8:23) or to one of the pilgrims going to Jerusalem (Isa. 2:2-3; Zech. 14:16 ff.). Here again we have both particularistic and universalistic motifs (see e). In all cases, however, the participation of Israel and the nations was conceived in collective or corporate terms; the individual was to share in salvation only as a member of the community or of his people.

3. *Messianic expectation. a)* Eschatological prophecy had two different theories as to who would exercise authority over the earth in the age of salvation. Some believed that Yahweh himself would reign as king and thus establish the sovereignty of God (Isa. 24:23; 33:22; 43:15; 44:6; Obad. 21; Mic. 2:13; 4:7; Zeph. 3:15; Zech. 9:1-8; Mal. 3:1; Ps. 47; 96–99; 146:10; 149:2). Others, on the contrary, assumed that not Yahweh himself but a human king appointed by him would reign as his representative and governor. This ruler is usually termed the "Messiah," although the OT never uses this title for the figure so designated today; such use began with post-OT Judaism and the New Testament. In the discussion to follow we will continue to use the title, since it is the familiar term; but one must note that the OT prophecies in question make no mention of the "Messiah." This means that we must be on the lookout against importing the notions of early Judaism and primitive Christianity into the OT texts, which must instead be studied closely in order to determine their particular expectations.

The messianic prophecies include first of all Isa. 9:1-6 (Eng. 9:2-7), a passage which speaks of a "child" and "son" upon the throne of David, with the throne name "Wonderful Counselor, Divine Hero, Possessor of Spoil, Maintainer of Peace." Isa. 11:1-9 speaks of a shoot from the "stump of Jesse," the Davidic dynasty, and his peaceful reign is clearly messianic. In like fashion Isa. 11:10 and 16:5 speak of a shoot from the "root of Jesse," or of a righteous ruler and "judge," associated with David by means of a later addi-

348   Early Post-Exilic Period

tion. Jer. 23:5-6 (33:15-16) also mentions a branch of David, who shall rule in righteousness and justice. Ezek. 17:22-24 uses the metaphor of a sprig from the top of a cedar. Mic. 5:1, 3 (Eng. 5:2, 4), speaking of Beth Ephrathah or Bethlehem, plays verbally on the home of the Davidic dynasty, from which the messianic ruler was to come. Hag. 2:20-23 speaks of Zerubbabel, the Davidic commissar for Jerusalem appointed by the Persians, as the imminent Messiah; Zech. 6:9-15 does the same in the symbolic crowning, which originally referred to Zerubbabel. In Zech. 4:1-6aα, 10b-14, the messianic dignity is divided between a secular ruler and a spiritual ruler: the politician Zerubbabel and the high priest Joshua; the latter is included because there are priestly functions to be performed and a political ruler is therefore not sufficient. Finally, Zech. 9:9-10 describes the royal entrance of the messianic king into Jerusalem.

The figure of "him whom they have pierced" in Zech. 12:9–13:1 is difficult to interpret and cannot be taken into account. A late addition in Mal. 3:23-24 (Eng. 4:4-6) speaks of Elijah as the forerunner of Yahweh when he appears for judgment; but this passage is not messianic in the strict sense, because although the returning Elijah is a messianic figure, Yahweh himself is expected rather than a Messiah (Mal. 3:1).

Other frequently cited texts have been erroneously given a messianic interpretation over the course of time, and in fact have quite different meanings:

1) There is no promise, messianic or otherwise, in Gen. 3:15; Isa. 7:14; and Ps. 22:19 (Eng. 22:18). Gen. 3:15 is a curse upon sinful mankind, and speaks of an eternal enmity between man and serpent that will make each seek to kill the other. In Isa. 7:14, the Hebrew word 'almâ, translated "virgin" by the Septuagint, actually means "young woman." Furthermore, the context and the statements that follow in 7:18-22 show that the sign prophesied by Isaiah was a threat of disaster, according to which the fields would be forsaken and desolate within a few years. Ps. 22:19 (Eng. 22:18) was interpreted messianically because of the misunderstanding of the author of the Gospel of John, who made the parallel members of the Hebrew verse, which deal with the same incident, refer to two different acts, the division of garments and the casting of lots for a cloak. The psalm is in fact the prayer of a sick man that was answered.

2) The discourses concerning the servant of Yahweh cannot be interpreted as messianic prophecies (see § 24.3).

3) Finally, there are many other OT passages that have been interpreted messianically but refer in fact to the reigning or—in some cases—expected king of Judah or Israel. This applies to the royal psalms, as well as the obscure world šîlô in the Judah section of the so-called Blessing of Jacob (Gen. 49:10) and the terms "star out of Jacob" and "scepter out of Israel" in the prophecy of Balaam (Num. 24:17), which probably refer to David.

Equally non-messianic was Ezekiel's expectation that the deported king Jehoiachin would be restored to his rightful place (Ezek. 21:30-32 [Eng. 21:25-27]) or that another descendant of David would reign in the future as "prince" (Ezek. 37:23-25; 34:23-24). Other discourses or statements, all probably dating from the exilic period, that express hopes for the restoration of the state of Judah and the re-establishment of the Davidic dynasty are similar in nature: Isa. 32:1; Jer. 30:9, 21; Hos. 3:5aβ; Amos 9:11-15; Mic. 4:8. These expectations for the future merely constituted a preliminary transitional stage leading to the concept of a Messiah.

All told, the OT contains 11 (12) messianic prophecies. The small number of them itself shows that the notion of a Messiah was not the focal point of eschatology. In addition, only a few of the prophecies derive from the prophets in whose books they are found. Those in Haggai 2; Zechariah 4 and 6 can be ascribed to the two prophets in question; those in Zechariah 9 can be ascribed to Deutero-Zechariah. All the others derive from anonymous prophets of the post-exilic period, and are later than Haggai and Zechariah.

b) The later title "Messiah" was well chosen in that it represents an abbreviated form of the phrase *mᵉšiaḥ yhwh*, "anointed of Yahweh," originally applied to the reigning king (§ 12.2). The title thus characterizes the eschatological figure likewise as a king. It is to be noted, however, that the Persian king Cyrus was also so referred to (Isa 45:1) and that later we read of the anointing of the priest (Lev. 4:3 and *passim*), of all priests (Exod. 28:41), of prophets (I Kings 19:16; Isa. 61:1), and of the patriarchs (Ps. 105:15; I Chron. 16:22). Anointing was accordingly meant to signify that a man entered into a more intimate relationship with Yahweh than was usually the case. Thus the title "Messiah" describes the eschatological figure as one standing in an especially intimate association with Yahweh.

The expectation of such a Messiah arose in the early post-exilic period, after the fall of Judah and the deposition of the Davidic dynasty, after the Exile and liberation, when a new community under Persian sovereignty had come into being in Judea, but eschatological prophecy was promising an everlasting age of salvation as a realization of God's sovereignty, to be exercised primarily within the context of a new Israelite nation and empire on Palestinian soil. But nation and empire as conceived by the age necessitated a ruler. The real ruler would undoubtedly be Yahweh himself. Those who did not share the view that he could appear and reign on earth in bodily form expected that he would appoint an earthly representative to rule on his behalf. This representative is the Messiah: the future king of the eschatological age of salvation, exercising his rule as Yahweh's representative upon earth. He would rule in the coming national and religious empire that Yahweh would one day miraculously establish. Messianic expectations thus sprang up and flourished wherever people thought in eschatological terms and at the same time remained faithful to the Davidic monarchy. That such expectations are met with so rarely and remained in the background is because these circles were few in number and had no enduring influence.

Also deserving of mention is the explanation that the notion of a Messiah was the product of the mythological and cultic background of the ancient Near East. Several scholars formerly espoused this view, which was put forward most vigorously by Gressmann. It looked upon the Messiah as an eschatological figure, derived from the king of paradise—a notion that had supposedly invaded Israel at an early date, coming from Babylonia and Egypt. Throughout the entire ancient Near East, according to this theory, the king was looked upon as Messiah and depicted with the aid of the messianic ideology; the ancient Near Eastern monarchic idea reflected even more ancient messianic conceptions. This view, however, is disproved by the observation that there is no trace of any eschatology anywhere in the ancient Near East outside Israel (except in late Persian religion); it was always the reigning king who was praised and glorified.

S. Mowinckel has a different theory. As he explains it, Yahweh's kingship was at first experienced as a reality in the festival of Yahweh's enthronement; at the same time, the earthly king was celebrated as his anointed, representing the hopes and aspirations of the dynasty and the nation. Sobered by the unfortunate experiences of the late monarchy, the people projected this reality into the future as an ideal. Form and content of the messianic hope thus derived from the Israelite notion of kingship as a preliminary stage in the development of messianic expectations proper; but this Israelite royal ideology was itself intimately associated with the ancient Near Eastern concept of kingship. But the existence of an enthronement festival in Israel is highly dubious (see § 16.3); and in Babylonia, the land of the classical New Year's festival involving the enthronement of Marduk and the king, no eschatology or messianic expectations ever arose, although the disappointments of everyday life were just as great.

Others emphasize even more the connection between ancient Near Eastern kingship and messianic expectations by taking as their point of departure a cultic schema common to the entire ancient Near East, and using the term "messianic" to describe the royal ideology that is supposed to constitute the focus of this schema (see § 12:2). This term does not refer to eschatological messianism but to the fully developed royal ideology. According to this view kingship was a religious and political institution. By the grace of God, the king embodied the deity in his person and played the rôle of the deity in the cult. At the same time he represented the community, the nation as a whole. On him depended victory and prosperity, rain and fertility, the safety of natural and human life and the order of the cosmos, which he asserted in the face of the forces of chaos. All this is supposed to have been comprised in the ideology associated with the figure of the king; since this ideology represented the king as an ideal figure with whom were associated hopes for salvation, the term "messianic" must be applied to it. The arguments against this view have already been presented (§ 12.2). They eliminate any chance of deriving messianic expectations from a supposed ancient Near Eastern royal ideology. These expectations could arise only after the deposition of the Davidic dynasty, within the framework of an eschatological hope.

c) In personal terms, the Messiah is always a mortal descendant of the deposed Davidic dynasty. When the imminent expectations of Haggai and Zechariah led them to designate someone who could assume sovereignty at once, they found him in the figure of Zerubbabel, a grandson of the former king Jehoiachin. After the collapse of the hopes pinned on him, no more mention was made of a specific person; people spoke instead in general terms of a shoot or root springing forth from the stump of Jesse, of a descendant of the ancient lineage of Bethlehem. It is not David in person who returns miraculously, no David resurrected or reincarnate, no David redivivus. That would be an impossible notion for the OT period. Even when the eschatological ruler was simply called "David," this was only an abbreviated way of referring to a descendant of the earlier dynasty.

The Messiah is not a supernatural being coming down to earth but a human being like any other. He is set apart solely by his particularly close relationship with Yahweh as the latter's representative and his descent from the earlier dynasty. There is nothing miraculous about the Messiah; the miracle will be the age of salvation inaugurated by Yahweh and the empire established by him.

At times, of course, we are not dealing with a specific person or even a single individual. An individual Messiah was not expected, but a messianic Davidic dynasty. Even when only a single shoot was mentioned, he appeared as the figure in whom the messianic dynasty would first take on visible form. He merely marks the beginning of the everlasting age of salvation and is the first of an endless series.

d) The task of the Messiah will be to sit upon the throne of David and reign as a righteous king. Apart from the second, priestly Messiah envisioned by Zechariah, from the very beginning the Messiah was assigned a function and significance that was political in the widest sense. He is a political figure of the eschatological world.

Negatively, this means that in the OT the Messiah does not bring salvation and is not a savior. The salvation to come is always the gift of Yahweh; even in Isa. 9:1-6 (Eng. 9:2-7) it is Yahweh who performs everything. The person of the Messiah is secondary to the God who appoints him; his work is only that of an agent and representative of Yahweh, the true king. Positively, it means that the Messiah—filled with spirit of Yahweh as the source of his power—acts as a military leader and champion, defending the people and the land against all attacks, securing perpetual peace, and creating happiness and prosperity, peace and security, order and brotherly love. He does all this as the earthly ruler after the beginning of the age of salvation.

e) Early Judaism on the one hand continued the line of development found in the OT, likewise looking for a national and political Messiah belonging to the earthly order. He differed from the OT figure in that the expectation was much more particularistic, focusing on the Jews alone, and also in that the Messiah henceforth became a bringer of salvation and a savior. On the other hand, there was expected a universalistic Messiah belonging to the supernatural order, a figure already presupposed by the book of Daniel (see § 27.6). This figure was called the Son of Man. Only rarely were attempts made to merge the two conceptions (Esdras and the Apocalypse of Baruch).

4. *Outcome.* The basic distinction between two ages and numerous other details show that eschatological prophecy represented a post-exilic reinterpretation of the message of the great pre-exilic prophets, undergirded by the uniform and inviolable expectation of salvation for Israel that these prophets had long called into question and continuing the message of salvation—primarily found in the preaching of the cult prophets—on a new plane. But this expectation and promise of salvation for Israel oversimplified the concept of God by neglecting other aspects, or debased it by assigning salvation to Israel and destruction to the nations in the sense of nationalistic religion. The contrast between the eschatological prophets and the great individual prophets was heightened by the fact that eschatological prophecy usually did not hope for a basic transformation of man and a new approach to life, but for a new age and a new form of the world in which man lived. According to eschatological prophecy, Yahweh does not transform man and then, through man, transform the world, but rather transforms the world and only thus indirectly transforms man, if indeed man is not thought capable in

his own right of earning a share in salvation. This was a fateful change: with few exceptions, Yahweh no longer was thought to intervene directly in the lives of men, but to affect them indirectly through their outward circumstances. It followed that the expected salvation was to be everlasting; as soon as man found himself to be in a state of salvation, he would be relieved of the necessity of repeating his decision and placed in a state of static enjoyment.

Thus eschatological prophecy was based on a misunderstanding of the message of the great individual prophets and on the optimistic illusion of God's exclusive will to save Israel. At the same time, it was from the very beginning a prophecy of vain hopes and fruitless expectations. It held fast to one basic feature of Yahwism in considering the new age to be imminent. This proclamation of a new age about to be inaugurated was in total harmony with the emphasis that Yahwism placed on man's present situation, and thus also with the claim of all other prophetical activity to deal with the particular present and the immediate future. But these imminent expectations involved an unexpected and unintended consequence: the realization that the promised salvation was not coming to pass. This led to disappointment over the delay and renewed promises of consolation in the immediate future. Even the really eschatological expectations of Deutero-Isaiah, which went beyond the predictable political achievements of Cyrus and their effects, did not come to pass but rather contributed to the prophet's tragic end, in which a disciple tried somehow to find some meaning (Isa. 52:13–53:12). In like fashion the eschatological hopes of Haggai and Zechariah associated with the building of the Temple gave way to reality; their disappointment led to the temporary victory of the competing cultic and ritual piety, which was not eschatological. The insufficiency of this latter form of religion produced the crisis reflected in the book of Malachi, which Ezra sought to alleviate through a strictly legalistic religiosity.

CHAPTER TWO: LATE POST-EXILIC PERIOD

§ 27 Events, Figures, and Religious Attitudes

G. R. BERRY, "The Unrealistic Attitude of Postexilic Judaism," *JBL*, LXIV (1945), 309-17; A.-M. BRUNET, "La théologie du Chroniste," *BEThL*, XII (1959), 384-97; H. CAZELLES, "La mission d'Esdras," *VT*, IV (1954), 113-40; M. DELCOR, "Hinweise auf das samaritanische Schisma im Alten Testament," *ZAW*, LXXIV (1962), 281-91; N. N. GLATZER, *Anfänge des Judentums*, 1966; U. KELLERMANN, *Nehemia*, 1967; J. C. H. LEBRAM, "Nachbiblische Weisheitstraditionen," *VT*, XV (1965), 167-237; *idem*, "Die Theologie der späten Chokma und häretisches Judentum," *ZAW*, LXXVII (1965), 202-11; J. MACDONALD, *The Theology of the Samaritans*, 1964; G. F. MOORE, "The Rise of Normative Judaism," *HThR*, XVII (1924), 307-73; XVIII (1925), 1-38; S. MOWINCKEL, *Studien zu dem Buche Ezra-Nehemia*, 3 vols., 1965-65; J. M. MYERS, "The Kerygma of the Chronicler," *Interpr*, XX (1966), 259-73; R. NORTH, "Theology of the Chronicler," *JBL*, LXXXII (1963), 369-81; J. PAULUS, "Le thème du Juste Souffrant dans la pensée grecque et israélite," *RHR*, CXXI (1940), 18-66; O. PLÖGER, *Theokratie und Eschatologie*, 2nd ed., 1962; H. H. ROWLEY, "Nehemiah's Mission and Its Background," *BJRL*, XXXVII (1954/55), 528-61 (= his *Men of God*, 1963, pp. 211-45); *idem*, "The Samaritan Schism in Legend and History," in *Israel's Prophetic Heritage* (Muilenburg Festschrift), 1962, pp. 208-22; H. H. SCHAEDER, *Esra der Schreiber*, 1930.

1. *The crisis of the Jerusalem community and Malachi.* The internal crisis of the Jerusalem community is revealed by two complaints raised by a prophet around 465 B.C. This prophet is called Malachi (Mal. 1:1) although the word is not a proper name but rather the term "my messenger" taken from 3:1. He castigated the carelessness and dishonesty of the Israelites in their fulfillment of their cultic obligations: the priests were offering inferior sacrifices— blind, lame, and sick animals (1:6–2:9)—and the community were withholding their tithes from the Temple (3:6-12). Observance of the cult was becoming more and more external; while the priests looked upon it primarily as a source of income, the people tried to give as little as possible. The prophet also dealt with the problem of mixed marriages. Since substantially more men than women had returned from the Exile and the discrepancy had not yet been made up, many men had taken wives from among the indigenous inhabitants of the land whether they were Israelites or not. In the period

354

of the prophet attempts seem to have been made to forbid such marriages in the future and dissolve the existing mixed marriages once the women had given birth to the desired children (2:10-16). Malachi also attacked this intolerant measure. The discourses concerning fasting in Isa. 58:1-12 and observing the Sabbath in Isa. 58:13-14 bear witness to further grievances.

In addition, two foreign influences were having their effect on the community: the still surviving religious notions and practices of Canaanite religion, which are attacked in Isa. 56:9–57:13; and Persian religion, with its sharp dualism between good and evil, its rejection of animal sacrifice and emphasis on ethical conduct, its concept of a judgment after death upon the bridge of judgment, and its final apotheosis of the world into the kingdom of God. Canaanite religion entangled the Israelites in sexual cults; Persian religion shattered a purely cultic religiosity like that which predominated in Jerusalem. Thus Yahwism appeared to be in mortal danger in Jerusalem. The necessary reforms were introduced by the Babylonian Diaspora, which was religiously stricter.

2. *The Priestly Document.*[1] The Priestly source stratum of the Hexateuch, which was created in the fifth century B.C., expressed the strict religious attitude of the Babylonian Diaspora. It gives an account of history that diverges markedly from the earlier source strata, completing the concentration on the Mosaic period begun by E, Deuteronomy, and the Holiness Code. In the primal history it tells the story of creation, the deluge, and Noah; for the rest, as in the story of the patriarchs, it restricts itself primarily to mere genealogies or pedigrees linking the individual narratives and remarks. Thus the account leads up as rapidly as possible to Israel's earliest history and the Moses tradition. In fact, the primal history, the story of the patriarchs, and even the account of the exodus from Egypt were reduced to the status of a mere introduction to the revelation at Sinai, with which all the important material is associated. Except for the Sabbath, the dietary laws, circumcision, and Passover,

---

[1] K. Elliger, "Sinn und Ursprung der priesterlichen Geschichtserzählung," *ZThK*, XLIX (1952), 121-43 (= his *Kleine Schriften zum Alten Testament*, 1966, pp. 174-98); S. Grill, "Die religionsgeschichtliche Bedeutung der vormosaischen Bündnisse (Gen 9,9-17; 17,9-14)," *Kairos*, II (1960), 17-22; K. Koch, "Die Eigenart der priesterlichen Sinaigesetzgebung," *ZThK*, LV (1958), 36-51; J. Roth, "Thèmes majeurs de la tradition sacerdotale dans le Pentateuque," *NRTh*, XC (1958), 696-721; W. Zimmerli, "Sinaibund und Abrahambund," *ThZ*, XVI (1960), 268-80 (= his *Gottes Offenbarung*, 1963, pp. 205-16).

P traced all the important ordinances back to the revelation at Sinai or the period immediately following and to Moses as their mediator.

Characteristic is the intimate association of historical narrative and law, which are indissolubly joined. Within the narrative framework Yahweh publishes his particular decrees, to be accounted "everlasting ordinances" applying both to the situation at hand and to the future from generation to generation. The narrative lays the groundwork for the eternal law, and the eternal law necessitates the presentation of the narrative. For this reason the narrative material is unevenly distributed. Where it is not connected with divine ordinances, it rarely goes beyond genealogies and brief remarks intended to tie the whole together. On the other hand, the account becomes quite circumstantial when cultic institutions are to be derived from history (cf. Gen. 1:1–2:4a; 6:9–9:17*; 17).

Besides a chronology, the genealogies, and the formula "These are the generations of . . . ," P organized his history primarily by means of a division into four great periods characterized by various stages in Yahweh's revelation and the obligation of man or Israel. The first stage begins with the creation of the world, at which Yahweh assigned to man a share in his dominion over the world, offered him vegetarian nourishment, and instituted the Sabbath. The second stage begins after the Deluge with the Noachian laws and the rainbows as a sign to remind men of Yahweh. The third stage follows with Abraham and the commandment and sign of circumcision; the fourth and last is the revelation at Sinai with the whole cultic program that is to obtain for all time.

For the story told by P and the ordinances recorded by him not only applied to the past but were intended also and above all for the present and future. Like the Holiness Code that he incorporated, P comprised a program, so that when Ezra undertook his reforms he could rely primarily on the ordinances of P. The retrojection of this program into the past was intended to legitimize it and lend it authority. Because Yahweh had long ago decreed his eternal ordinances, they must be accepted without questioning in the present and for the future.

In P, Yahweh himself became a totally transcendent God. He appears to man neither in real form nor in dreams. Only his *kābôd*, his "glory," is revealed; and even that is veiled, to be seen only by Moses. In contrast to the notion of the deity's dwelling and perpetual presence in the Temple, the Deuteronomic idea of Yahweh's revealed presence is taken up and extended: in the tent sanctuary of the desert period,[2] intended to prefigure the later Temple, Yahweh merely appears occasionally in the cloud with his *kābôd*.

The relationship between this transcendent God and man is also altered, as represented in the camp order in Numbers 2.[3] The priests and Levites are encamped as a kind of protective wall between the sanctuary and the people. The latter no longer have direct access to Yahweh; they must go through the priests as mediators. In similar fashion, Yahweh no longer speaks directly to the people, but through Moses and Aaron.

3. *Nehemiah and Ezra.* The resolution of the crisis within the Jerusalem community is inextricably associated with the names of Nehemiah and Ezra. The tradition presents many problems, mostly literary and chronological. There are many divergent views, not least with respect to the sequence and dating of the two men.

Apart from the theory that Nehemiah alone is a historical figure, and Ezra only a literary substitute adapted to the views of a later period, three basically different views deserve mention. All they have in common is their dating of Nehemiah's ministry in the reign of Artaxerxes I, in the years 445-432 B.C. (or a bit later).

1) Ezra and Nehemiah exercised their ministry during the time of Artaxerxes I, in the sequence indicated by tradition: Ezra beginning in 458, followed by Nehemiah.

2) Ezra and Nehemiah exercised their ministry during the time of Artaxerxes I. First the city wall was repaired under the leadership of Nehemiah, who then departed because he recognized the necessity of internal reform. This was carried out by Ezra, but was interrupted by the disturbances that followed the law against mixed marriages. Nehemiah then returned and succeeded in having Ezra's law observed.

3) Nehemiah exercised his ministry in Jerusalem during the time of Artaxerxes I; Ezra exercised his ministry under Artaxerxes II, beginning in 398. This view, which seems most probable when all the arguments are weighed,[4] provides the basis for the following discussion.

a) Nehemiah, son of an Israelite family in Babylon and cupbearer to the Persian king, was sent by the king at his request to serve as governor in Jerusalem. As a consequence, Jerusalem and its en-

[2] M. Haran, "The Nature of the 'Ōhel Môēdh' in Pentateuchal Sources," *JSS*, V (1960), 50-65.

[3] A. Kuschke, "Die Lagervorstellung der priesterschriftlichen Erzählung," *ZAW*, LXIII (1951), 74-105.

[4] J. A. Emerton, "Did Ezra Go to Jerusalem in 428 B.C.?" *JThSt*, NS XVII (1966), 1-19.

virons, roughly extending from Mizpah in the north to the area north of Hebron in the south, was separated from the province of Samaria and made into an independent province. As its governor, Nehemiah contributed to the external and internal order of the community—to the external order by repairing the city wall, which had partially been destroyed when the Babylonians conquered Jerusalem (Nehemiah 2 ff.), through the resettlement of some of the local population in the city, which was only partially inhabited (11: 1-2), and through a general remission of debts (5:1 ff.); to the internal order by seeing that the Levites received their tithes (12: 44 ff.; 13:10 ff.), that men rested on the Sabbath (13:15 ff.), and through his opposition to mixed marriages (13:23 ff.). In other words, he exercised his ministry primarily in the political arena and introduced no new religious ideas, although politico-messianic expectations may have centered on him without his knowledge or even against his will. It is possible that such expectations led the Persian regime to recall him suddenly (Kellermann). At any rate, he laid the foundations for the peace and relative independence of the new province, making a religious reform possible.

b) The reform is associated with the name of Ezra, who exercised his ministry around 398 B.C. in Jerusalem, after the Persian king had given him far-reaching authority and commissioned him to order the affairs of the community in Judea-Jerusalem on the basis of a law code Ezra had at hand. Once more a caravan returned to Palestine, this time with Ezra, and there reinforced the movement in whose spirit Ezra intended to act.

The first thing he did was to recite before the people the law he had brought with him; its impression was so great and effective that the entire community undertook to obey it. This law refers at least to P, as the connections between Neh. 8:13 ff. and Lev. 23:40, as well as Neh. 8:18 and Lev. 23:36, show. It is possible that we are even dealing with the Pentateuch as a combination of the source strata JNEDP, since some of Ezra's measures are not based on the ordinances of P: Neh. 10:31 (Eng. 10:30); 13:1 ff. are based on Exod. 34:16; Deut. 7:2 ff.; 23:4 ff. (Eng. 23:3 ff.), and Neh. 10:32 (Eng. 10:31) on Deut. 15:2. If so, the Hexateuch must have come into being soon after the composition of P, which was incorporated in Babylonia; the book of Joshua, whose program for the distribution of the land was unacceptable to the Persians, was set apart as an independent entity. This hypothesis is also supported by the fact that during the fourth century B.C. the Samaritans adopted the Pentateuch as the officially recognized foundation of their religion. During the Exile, the earlier source strata had been revised and edited in the Deuteronomistic spirit. Now, around the end of the fifth or the beginning of the fourth century B.C., the Hexateuch as a whole came into being as a revision and expansion of its Deuteronomistic predecessor, with P as the controlling framework. For political reasons it was abbreviated, leaving only the Pentateuch—a work of the Babylonian Diaspora, an account of history and collection of laws from the creation of the world to the death of Moses, which Ezra raised to the status of obligatory foundation for the early Judaism that was coming into being.

The second thing Ezra did was to apply the law rigorously to the most critical problem of his time: mixed marriages. According to the new law those marriages in which one partner was of non-Israelite origin had to be dissolved. Since the majority of the people agreed and only a minority protested, all was soon carried out according to Ezra's principles; special cases were examined and decided by a committee. Thus the segregation of the community introduced by the Deuteromomic law and continued by Haggai was effectively complete. Outside the community, it is true, resentment and unrest were aroused in Palestine. As a consequence the Persian regime, which was especially concerned to have peace and security in its western provinces, summoned Ezra back to court; he never returned to Jerusalem.

His work nevertheless laid the foundations for the period to come, so that he later came to be compared to Moses and glorified as the finisher of Moses' work. In fact he created early Judaism and laid its religious foundations in the Pentateuch. He ascribed equal importance to ethical and ritual conduct; the priestly heirarchy for a considerable period exercised leadership within the community; deliberate segregation involved the danger of arrogance toward others; and the legalistic approach to life led to the danger of a religion based on *do ut des*. Ezra's reform finally set the mainstream of Yahwism on the course that turned its back on the insights and principles that had previously prevailed, above all on the message of the prophets. Here we are dealing with more than a reshaping of Israelite Yahwism—a new religion was in the making.

4. *The period after Ezra's reform. a)* In the decades following Ezra's reform, the life of early Judaism was determined by the law, at least in Judea and in the Babylonian Diaspora. This religion of

the law, which also assigned a central position to cultic ritual, clearly became the dominant trend, having begun to prevail after Deuteronomy and the Exile. Prophetical influence receded apace. Both phenomena went together: the greater the influence of legalistic piety, the weaker became the prophetical faith.

b) That there were also other religious tendencies can be seen from the books of Jonah and Ruth, both of which were composed after Ezra's reform in the fourth century B.C. The former attacked the particularistic notion, embodied in the figure of the prophet Jonah, that salvation was restricted to Israel and that the threats against other nations retained their absolute force, contradicting particularistic intolerance and arrogance. The book of Ruth also breathes a spirit of magnanimity toward those belonging to another nation, in whose destiny can be perceived the benevolent governance of Yahweh and upon whom his blessing is wished.

c) Yet another basic attitude is represented by the Chronicler's History, which was composed no earlier than the second half of the fourth century, and probably in the period around 300 B.C. (I–II Chronicles, Ezra, Nehemiah).[5] Its author omitted almost everything that happened before David (except for the death of Saul) and outside Judah; in the case of the few ideal Judahite kings, he eliminated everything that could place them in an unfavorable light or replaced the account with another version. This procedure, together with the Chronicler's own material, radically altered the account of the monarchy vis-à-vis that given in the books of Samuel and Kings.

Notable is the religious glorification of David, who is intimately linked with the Temple and its cult, for which he is said to have made all the necessary provisions. His time is depicted as the ideal state of affairs, a worthy object of aspiration. Reference is repeatedly made to Yahweh's unshakable promises and pledges to the Davidic dynasty. Thus in the late period there appeared a yearning for the Davidic dynasty; the Chronicler probably cherished hopes for a fu-

---

[5] G. J. Botterweck, "Zur Eigenart der chronistischen Davidgeschichte," *Tübinger ThQ*, CXXXVI (1956), 402-34; A. Caquot, "Peut-on parler de messianisme dans l'œuvre du Chroniste?" *RThPh*, XCIX (1966), 110-20; N. D. Freedman, "The Chronicler's Purpose," *CBQ*, XXIII (1961), 436-42; G. von Rad, *Das Geschichtsbild des chronistischen Werkes*, 1930; *idem*, "Die levitische Predigt in den Büchern der Chronik," in *Procksch Festschrift*, 1934, pp. 113-24 (= his *Gesammelte Studien zum Alten Testament*, 1958, pp. 248-61 [English: *The Problem of the Hexateuch and Other Essays*, 1966, pp. 267-80]); W. F. Stinespring, "Eschatology in Chronicles," *JBL*, LXXX (1961), 209-19; C. C. Torrey, *The Chronicler's History of Israel*, 1954; A. C. Welch, *The Work of the Chronicler, Its Purpose and Date*, 1939.

ture restoration of the Davidic monarchy. The same idea is expressed in the secondary revision and expansion of the ending of the book of Ruth (4:17*b*, 18-22), associated it with David and turning it into an episode in the early history of the Davidic house.

Also typical of the Chronicler's History is the presentation of events according to a schema based on the doctrine of retribution, which the Chronicler applied more to individuals than to the nation as a whole. The disasters of all kinds that befell the kings he explained as punishment for their sins, among the most grievous of which he counted offenses against priests and prophets (see, for example, II Chronicles 33). But direct miraculous intervention by Yahweh also determined the course of history (see, for example, II Chron. 20: 1-30). We thus encounter in heightened form the ancient notions of Yahweh's acting in the destinies of men and nations and of the correlation between Yahweh's actions and human conduct.

Finally, the Chronicler exhibited high esteem for the cult of the Jerusalem Temple, the only legitimate sanctuary, whose significance he defended against the Samaritan community, which had come into being around 350 B.C. (see below under 5.). His interest centered on the actual performance of the cult, so that he described the sacrificial offerings in detail. But access to the sacred areas and ceremonies was reserved to the appropriate cultic personnel, and music to accompany the worship was restricted to the Levites.

d) Many Psalms were composed in the post-exilic period: almost two thirds of the hymns and prayers preserved in the Psalter probably derive from this period. The faith expressed in these Psalms centered accordingly on two focal points: the Temple cult and the law.

Unlike P, the Psalms actively maintained the notion that Yahweh has his dwelling place in the Temple; at any rate, the people associated the notion of Yahweh's perpetual presence with the Temple. He had chosen Zion to be his place of residence. Therefore he would protect it; therefore streams of religious and material blessing would flow from the Temple; therefore all who belonged to Yahweh's people had their citizenship there, wherever they might be dispersed. The presence of the Temple gave Jerusalem such dignity and authority that it seemed to be the very hub of the universe. To be able to live there was reason for praise and thanksgiving. Even to be allowed to enter the Temple, to abide there temporarily as a visitor under the protection of the Temple or permanently as a priest, was a special favor. There was often a great yearning to visit the Temple, there to take part in the cult. Even if one might spend one's entire life there, one day in the sanctuary was better than a thousand elsewhere. The further away one lived, the more desirable appeared its splendor. Eager expectation thrilled through the pilgrim who was about to see with his own eyes what he had known only through hearsay. Already on the dangerous journey to Jerusalem he had experienced Yahweh's protection. Then he gazed in awe at the city and Temple, experienced the cult, and returned home in thanksgiving, ready to tell his children all the wonders he had seen. Of course critical voices also made themselves heard; they will be discussed below (§ 28.4).

The second focal point for the faith of the post-exilic Psalms was the law, which, like the cult, established a connection between Yahweh and man. All life was bound up with the law, because Yahweh judges justly and rewards each according to his deeds. The law was the great distinguisher of spirits; therefore the Psalms repeatedly distinguish the just and upright on the one hand from the evil and wicked on the other. The truth enshrined in this legalistic religion, as the Psalms themselves reveal, lies in the recognition that belief and life, belief and conduct, constitute a unity. A faith that does not lead to conclusions about what a man must do and what a man must not do is dead; Augustine's statement about the *misera necessitas non posse non peccandi* was for the most part not shared by the OT with respect to the believer. The doctrine of retribution in turn makes it easy to understand the insistence on one's own innocence, which the supplicant wanted to see confirmed so as not to appear rejected by Yahweh in the eyes of the multitude. As a result, in several Psalms it came to the point where the supplicant curses his enemies and prays for their destruction, so that he himself will be justified before men. There are of course other attempted solutions (Psalms 49 and 73).

e) Despite the general devaluation of prophecy, individual prophets still appeared. In the first half of the fourth century B.C. Joel exercised his ministry as a cult prophet at the Jerusalem Temple.[6] His message was occasioned by a drought and plagues of locusts, which he interpreted in part as signs of the Day of Yahweh; in addition, he proclaimed Yahweh's eschatological judgment upon the nations. He took as his point of departure the economic distress

---

[6] J. Bourke, "Le jour de Yahvé dans Joël," *RB*, LXVI (1959), 5-31, 191-212; W. Cannon, "'The Day of the Lord' in Joel," *ChQR*, CIII (1927), 32-63; A. S. Kapelrud, *Joel Studies*, 1948; H.-P. Müller, "Prophetie und Apokalyptik bei Joel," *Theologia viatorum*, X (1965/66), 231-52.

of daily life occasioned by natural catastrophes, at the same time keeping in view the day of the eschatological upheaval. In accordance with his mandate he strove to avert the economic disaster and called on men to turn to Yahweh in their hour of need. He called for the summoning of cultic assemblies for penance, with fasting and lamentation, and emphasized the necessity of returning to Yahweh, albeit without presupposing any guilt. He spoke of the Day of Yahweh in universalistic terms, but only in the judgment upon the nations, in contrast to his particularistic restriction of salvation to his own people.

Isaiah 65 contains invectives and threats against those members of the community who turn apostate, and promises for the devout. The message of this unknown prophet from the fourth century centers on the two focal points of salvation and destruction at the eschaton.

Deutero-Zechariah (Zechariah 9–11) [7] comprises two series of discourses: the first, from the last decades of the fourth century B.C., is based on the historical situation, giving a prophetical analysis of events from the siege of Tyre by Alexander the Great (332 B.C.) to the first wars of the Diadochi (9:1-8, 11-17; 10:3-12; 11:4-16); the second comprises a series of isolated discourses by various authors from the same or a later period (9:9-10; 10:1-2; 11:1-3, 17).

Isa. 66:5-24 is a larger unit comprising three prophetical discourses of the third century B.C.; made up primarily of promises intermixed with some threats, these discourses predict an imminent eschatological upheaval with its consequences for the apostate and the faithful.

In Trito-Zechariah (Zechariah 12–14) sayings by several authors from the first half of the third century B.C. have been assembled. With the exception of Zech. 12:9-14, which obviously refers to a judicial murder, they are purely eschatological in orientation and make no reference to concrete historical data. The emphasis is on the destiny and internal development of Jerusalem.

f) In the context of these profound intellectual changes, the concept of wisdom was subjected to thorough theological analysis and employment.[8] Wisdom was understood as a divine appeal to man, as a mediator of revelation, as the great educator of Israel

[7] C. Brouwer, *Wachter en herder*, 1949; B. Heller, "Die letzten Kapitel des Buches Sacharja im Lichte des späteren Judentums," *ZAW*, XLV (1927), 151-55; P. Lamarche, *Zacharie IX-XIV*, 1961; B. Otzen, *Studien über Deuterosacharja*, 1964.

[8] G. Fohrer, "σοφία κτλ," *ThW*, VII, 476-96.

364 Late Post-Exilic Period

and the nations, and even as the divine principle given to the world since creation. Thus all theological reflection could be brought together and unified under the general term "wisdom" in a previously unsuspected fashion. The inclusion of creation and revelation involved the areas that had been ignored by earlier practical wisdom, and led to the creation of a comprehensive theological system. In addition to Proverbs 1–9 [9] and Job 28, we find hints of this mode of thought in the inspired wisdom of Elihu, who senses that he is in the constant possession of wisdom (Job 32–37),[10] but also in God's words in the book of Job, in which the natural world as creation is at least incipiently related to the revelation given to men. Some Psalms, too, bear witness to wisdom theology (Psalms 1; 19:8-15 [Eng. 19:7-14]; 34; 36; 37; 49; 73; 105; 106; 112; 119; 128; 133).

The concept of wisdom in Job 28 and Proverbs 1–9 demands special treatment. Although in Job 28 wisdom is subordinate to Yahweh, incorporated into his creative activity and identified with the mysteries of God's creation of the world, we can still catch glimpses of what had been independent status, in which wisdom was a separate heavenly entity, pre-existent alongside the deity. This theory reflects mythological ideas, most likely a gnostic myth. The same myth, together with other elements, stands in the background of the concept of wisdom found in Proverbs 1–9. This explains why wisdom, which according to Job 28 is inaccessible to man, speaks to him as teacher and revealer, since she seeks a dwelling place among men (which, in the myth, she does not find and therefore returns to heaven). According to Proverbs 1–9, wisdom does not exist from the beginning alongside the deity, but was created at the beginning of his work. Here we see the influence of the myth of the primeval man, created before the world and therefore possessed of special empirical wisdom. In addition the concept of wisdom in Proverbs 1–9 was affected by the image of the prophet proclaiming his message.

Wisdom theology shared with legalistic piety the doctrine of double retribution, according to which Yahweh punishes or rewards every man while still alive according to his conduct. Everyone reaps what he has sown. Therefore the man who is upright and devout does not meet with trouble; only the wicked and impious man is punished with misfortune. Anyone who suffers deserves his mis-

[9] G. Boström, *Proverbiastudien*, 1935; A. Hulsbosch, "Sagesse créatrice et éducatrice," *Augustinianum*, I (1961), 217-35, 433-51; II (1962), 5-39; III (1963), 5-27; P. Humbert, "La 'femme étrangère' du Livre des Proverbes," *RES*, 1937, pp. 49-64; W. A. Irwin, "Where Shall Wisdom Be Found?" *JBL*, LXXX (1961) 133-42.

[10] G. Fohrer, "Die Weisheit des Elihu (Hi 32-37)," *AFO*, XIX (1959/60), 83-94 (= his *Studien zum Buche Hiob*, 1963, pp. 87-107.

fortune. He would do well to search out his open or secret sins. But this also means conversely that one can conclude from the misfortune that strikes a man that he has sinned and that his misfortune represents his punishment. The man to whom life is good is himself good; the man who experiences evil must be evil. Therefore if a man was struck by disaster he was obviously a secret sinner, from whom one would carefully keep one's distance so as not to become involved in his misfortune.

The book of Job was a vigorous protest against this doctrine.[11] The author of the book had also learned that life does not take its course placidly and harmoniously, but he did not ascribe this fact to some dubious retribution. For the Job of his book saw through the theology of his friends. As representatives of the devout community and proper society, they seek to apportion light and darkness rationally, to veil the dark and mysterious ground of existence, and facilely to explain both its bright and its shadowed side. Good and evil, joy and suffering, fortune and misfortune are corresponding terms, and are distributed righteously and equitably. Job sees through the meaninglessness of the rationalistic calculation with which the doctrine of retribution answers the question of the riddle of existence and the meaning of suffering. Because this theory is inadequate, he surrenders all assurances in the face of the suffering whose onset shatters his life. He decides to renounce comfortable tradition and safe calculation, breaking through into new and unexplored territory. He acknowledges his inescapable situation as his true situation and acknowledges the God who is at work in all that happens as his true lord. At the point of despair over the possibility of life based on his own efforts he sees a new life based on the possibility offered by Yahweh. Therefore he casts himself without hesitation or reservation into the arms of this God; in confident surrender to him he finds the answer to his burning question. Here we find the authentic faith of the prophets, applied to the situation and problems of another era.

[11] G. Fohrer, *Studien zum Buche Hiob*, 1963; J. Hempel, "Das theologische Problem des Hiob," *ZSTh*, VI (1929), 621-89 (= his *Apoxysmata*, 1961, pp. 114-73); P. Humbert, "Le modernisme de Job," *VTSuppl*, III (1955), 150-61; A. Jepsen, *Das Buch Hiob und seine Deutung*, 1963; H. Knight, "Job (Considered as a Contribution to Hebrew Theology)," *SJTh*, IX (1956), 63-76; W. Lillie, "The Religious Significance of the Book of Job," *ET*, LXVIII (1956/57), 355-58; H. H. Rowley, "The Book of Job and Its Meaning," *BJRL*, XLI (1958/59), 167-206 (= his *From Moses to Qumran*, 1963, pp. 141-83); A. Weiser, "Das Problem der sittlichen Weltordnung im Buche Hiob," *ThBl*, II (1923), 154-64 (= his *Glaube und Geschichte im Alten Testament*, 1961, pp. 9-19).

In similar fashion the author of Psalms 73 found the solution to the riddle of life in the experience of communion with God, in which he was vouchsafed assurance of God's protection and guidance:

> Nevertheless I was continually with thee,
>> thou dost hold my right hand.
> Thou dost guide me with thy counsel,
>> and leadest me *by the hand after thee.*   (Ps. 73:23-24)

Since this God is always near, even when the outlook is dark and obscure, the solution to all questions is found in him; the solution in fact consists in communion with him and surrender to him. These are the highest goals; nothing in heaven or on earth is equally desirable:

> Whom have I in heaven *alongside thee?*
>> And there is nothing upon earth that I desire besides thee.
> My flesh and my heart may fail,
>> but God is my portion forever.
> For lo, those who are far from thee shall perish;
>> thou dost put an end to those who are false to thee.
> But for me God is my good fortune;
>> in the Lord I have found refuge.   (Ps. 73:25-28)

Qoheleth (Ecclesiastes), too, like the author of Job, had lost his faith in a cardinal tenet of wisdom theology, the doctrine of retribution.[12] It is true that he ascribed a certain relative value to wisdom theology (2:3, 14; 4:13; 10:12). In the last analysis, however, it remains profitless (2:15; 9:11), and is no better than folly (1:16-17; 6:8). Thus Qoheleth attacked the self-assurance with which the system sought to comprehend the world and life in their entirety, pointing out the limits that render all security and thus all profit unattainable: death and woman (2:15-16, 21; 7:26). All in all, man's destiny does not depend on his upright and devout conduct, as the doctrine asserts, but lies impenetrably and indiscernibly in the hands of Yahweh (8:17; 9:1). Since the system propounded by wisdom theology was worthless, there was nothing left but to enjoy to the full the "portion" in life that has been granted man in an active life (9:7-10) instead of striving for ultimate gain. The first portion of Qoheleth's advice to enjoy life has close parallels in the Egyptian

---

[12] K. Galling, *Die Krise der Aufklärung in Israel,* 1952; A. Lauham "Die Krise des religiösen Glaubens bei Kohelet," *VTSuppl,* III (1955), 183-91; O. Loretz, *Qohelet und der Alte Orient,* 1964; J. Pedersen, "Scepticisme israélite," *RHPhR,* X (1930), 317-70; W. Zimmerli, *Die Weisheit des Predigers Salomo,* 1936.

Harper's Song and in the counsel given by the gods' cupbearer in the Gilgamesh Epic, which likewise mentions the negative limit (death). The second portion of Qoheleth's advice—full enjoyment of an active life—finds its counterpart in the comfort Gilgamesh receives from his great project, the city wall of Uruk, except that for Gilgamesh the work is the result of his activity, while Qoheleth has in mind the activity itself. These parallels can hardly be accidental, but are associated with the conservative aspect of Qoheleth. He appropriated an ancient viewpoint and opposed it to the system of wisdom theology. For this system was like Gilgamesh's striving for immortality, because its purpose was to create something unique, enduring, and definitive. In its stead, Qoheleth pointed out man's limited possibilities and sought to recall the earlier pragmatic stage of wisdom instruction. Therefore he was not universally skeptical and resigned, as is usually assumed, but only with respect to the possibilities of a theological system that claimed to be a panacea, and of course also with respect to folly. There still remains the possibility suggested already in the Gilgamesh Epic—but reinterpreted as a possibility granted by Yahweh, which man receives from his hand as the "portion" allotted him (2:24-25; 3:13; 5:17-18 [Eng. 5:18-19]).

g) The Hellenistic Roman world outside Palestine, Egypt especially, was the home of Hellenistic Judaism.[13] It maintained its ethnic and religious individuality and cultivated its ties with Jerusalem, to which pilgrimages were made and the Temple tax paid. Even more exclusively than in Palestine the synagogue was the center of religious life. Hellenistic Judaism had been markedly influenced by the religion of Jerusalem after the reform of Ezra, and in similar fashion kept itself separate from the world about it through observance of the Sabbath, circumcision, and purity regulations.

But knowledge of Hebrew and Aramaic was soon lost; Greek was the general language of colloquial speech. Therefore the Holy Scriptures soon had to be translated into Greek so that they could be understood. Starting in the third century B.C., this need gradually gave rise to the first Greek translation of the nascent Old Testament, the Septuagint (LXX). The translation of the Pentateuch was finished by the middle of the third century, that of Joshua—Kings and the prophets by about 200 B.C., and that of most of the other books during the first century B.C. These translations likewise reflected the spirit of Hellenistic Judaism influenced by the intellec-

13 BHH, II, 690-91; RGG, III, 209-12, 979-86.

tual milieu of Hellenism, forming a part of the more extensive body of Jewish literature that came into being primarily in Egypt.[14]

No more than an episode, albeit of extended duration, was the Jewish temple at Leontopolis, north of Memphis.[15] It was established about 160 B.C. by Onias, a son of the Jerusalem high priest Onias deposed by Antiochus IV Epiphanes at the instigation of Hellenistic circles. The sacrificial cult could be performed there until A.D. 73. This temple had only minor significance, since the Egyptian Jews adhered to the Jerusalem Temple.

5. *The Samaritan community.* In the course of the fourth century B.C. the worshipers of Yahweh in the province of Samaria finally broke off relationships with Jerusalem and constituted their own Samaritan community with a temple on Mount Gerizim.[16] While the separation took place about 350, permission to build a temple may not have been forthcoming until, with the collapse of the Empire, Jerusalem's privileges became a dead letter or could be disputed.

The reason these events took place was not any desire on the part of the Samaritans for a syncretistic religion. They were lenient in questions of mixed marriage and admission to the cult, since they did not share the exclusivistic tendencies of the Jerusalem community. In other respects they were more conservative than the latter. For they based their faith on the Pentateuch alone, not on the additional works that early Judaism increasingly considered sacred.

The real reason for the separation was the old opposition between north and south, which had already led to the breakup of the Davidic and Solomonic state, especially aversion to the Davidic dynasty,

---

[14] *RGG*, V, 1707-9; G. Bertram, "Die religiöse Umdeutung altorientalischer Lebensweisheit in der griechischen Übersetzung des Alten Testaments," *ZAW*, LIV (1936), 153-67; *idem*, "Praeparatio evangelica in der Septuaginta," *VT*, VII (1957), 225-49; G. Gerleman, "The Septuagint Proverbs as a Hellenistic Document," *OTS*, VIII (1950), 15-27; K. Koch, "Der hebräische Wahrheitsbegriff im griechischen Sprachraum," in *Was ist Wahrheit?* 1965, pp. 47-65; L. Prijs, *Jüdische Tradition in der Septuaginta*, 1948.

[15] M. A. Beek, "Relations entre Jérusalem et la diaspora égyptienne au 2e siècle avant J.-C.," *OTS*, II (1943), 119-43; H. Lietzmann, "Jüdisch-griechische Inschriften aus Tell el-Yehudieh," *ZNW*, XXII (1923), 280-86; F. Stähelin, "Elephantine und Leontopolis," *ZAW*, XXVIII (1908), 180-82.

[16] *BHH*, I, 513; *RGG*, II, 1202; *IDB*, II, 384-85; R. J. Bull and G. E. Wright, "Newly Discovered Temples on Mt. Gerizim in Jordan," *HThR*, LVIII (1965), 234-37; E. J. Bull *et al.*, "The Fifth Campaign at Balâṭah (Shechem)," *BASOR*, CLXXX (1965), 7-41; H. H. Rowley, "Sanballat and the Samaritan Temple," *BJRL*, XXXVIII (1955/56), 166-98 (= his *Men of God*, 1963, pp. 246-76).

which had once more acquired high status in Jerusalemite circles, as illustrated above all (though for a somewhat later period) by the Chronicler's History. With the exception of the Pentateuch, the Samaritans rejected all the sacred scriptures because in them they found glorification of Jerusalem and the Davidic line and even expectation of a Messiah belonging to the house of David rather than the tribe of Joseph.

The cause of the schism was therefore not Samaritan opposition to the law or the Jerusalem Temple, but opposition to the south's claim to exercise political and religious leadership and to David as a national and religious hero.

6. *The Maccabean period and apocalypticism. a)* The rule of the Seleucids in the Syrian state that followed the breakup of Alexander's empire[17] produced bitter altercations. Antiochus IV Epiphanes (175-164 B.C.) intended to hellenize the Jews as he hellenized his other subjects. But only a small Jewish upper class in Jerusalem was inclined in this direction; among the masses, rejection of this program was combined with political disaffection toward the Seleucids. In this situation Antiochus decided to adopt stern measures. The Jerusalem Temple was transformed into a sanctuary of Zeus; observance of the Sabbath and festivals, the practice of circumcision, and possession of law scrolls were made punishable by death. Throughout the countryside heathen altars were set up and the Jews were persuaded or compelled to offer sacrifice upon them.

Soon armed rebellion against Antiochus broke out, first on the part of Mattathias, a priest belonging to the Hasmonean family, and his followers, then also on the part of the Hasideans, a group of Jews with extraordinary zeal for the law. They soon became the backbone of the struggle for religious liberty and constituted the opposition to the priestly aristocracy, which supported the Syrian attempts at hellenization. After the death of Mattathias, leadership of the resistance passed to one of his sons, Judas Maccabeus. In the year 164 B.C. he was able to occupy the Jerusalem Temple, cleanse it of its defilement and restore it to the use of the Jewish cult. This marked the victory of the religious struggle. The Hasideans withdrew, but the Maccabeans continued to fight for political liberty, which they achieved temporarily in 142 B.C. and permanently in 129 B.C. There were once again Jewish kings, the Hasmoneans; but they

[17] *BHH,* III, 1764-68; *RGG,* V, 1686; *IDB,* IV, 266-67.

proved failures both politically and religiously. Hatred toward them increased and finally in the year 63 B.C. caused the people to ask the Romans to establish their sovereignty.

b) In this period the apocalyptic approach to life took shape, the last to be recorded in the OT.[18] After the failure of imminent eschatological expectations in the late post-exilic period, because everything remained as it was despite the vain promises of the prophets, and extensive segments of the community had turned their backs on eschatology, the latter developed into apocalypticism, utilizing wisdom theology and foreign influences, above all the cosmic and ethical dualism of Iran. Of the apocalyptic writings only the book of Daniel, which inaugurates the series of apocalypses, was incorporated into the OT. These apocalypses sought to reveal the mysteries of the eschaton and offered disclosures concerning the coming and passing of world epochs, so that one might determine both the date when all history would come to an end and the relative position of the present hour. A contrast was made between world history as a whole and the kingdom of God, which would be inaugurated after a future judgment. This dualism of deity and world was associated with ideas of the dissolution of the existing world by a new creation and the establishment of a theocracy under which those harboring apocalyptic expectations would live, either immediately or after their resurrection. Thus earlier prophecy was finally replaced by new ways of thought and belief.

c) The book of Daniel [19] was composed in the years 167-164 B.C; it was finished by mid-December 164 at the latest, since its author was familiar with the persecution instituted by Antiochus IV Epiphanes, his return from his second campaign in Egypt (169), and the desecration of the Jerusalem Temple (167), but knew

---

[18] G. R. Berry, "The Apocalyptic Literature of the Old Testament," *JBL*, LXII (1943), 9-16; J. Bloch, *On the Apocalyptic in Judaism*, 1953; S. B. Frost, *Old Testament Apocalyptic*, 1952; G. Hölscher, "Problèmes de la littérature apocalyptique juive," *RHPhR*, IX (1929), 111-14; J. Lebram, "Die Weltreiche in der Jüdischen Apokalyptik," *ZAW*, LXXVI (1964), 328-31; M. Noth, *Das Geschichtsverständnis der alttestamentlichen Apokalyptik*, 1953 (= his *Gesammelte Studien zum Alten Testament*, 2nd ed., 1960, pp. 248-73 [English: *The Laws in the Pentateuch and Other Studies*, 1964, pp. 194-214]); B. Reicke, "Official and Pietistic Elements of Jewish Apocalypticism," *JBL*, LXXIX (1960), 137-50; H. H. Rowley, *The Relevance of Apocalyptic*, rev. ed., 1947; D. S. Russell, *The Method and Message of Jewish Apocalyptic*, 1964; R. Smend, Über jüdische Apokalyptik," *ZAW*, V (1885), 222-51; B. Vawter, "Apocalyptic: Its Relation to Prophecy," *CBQ*, XXII (1960), 33-46.

[19] For a detailed discussion, see S-F, § 74.

nothing of Antiochus' death (December 164). The book is an out-growth of the conflicts of this period.

As an apocalypse it sought to determine the date of the end of history and the relative position of the present. In 8:26 the end seems to lie in the distant future, but this is because we are dealing with a retrospective presentation of history as "prophecy" down to the time of the author. What had appeared far off to the purported Daniel of the Babylonian Exile had meanwhile drawn near.

As a further development of eschatology, the apocalyptical under-standing of history contrasted the history of the world as a whole with the sovereignty of God. It looked upon the course of history as a unity that would reach its culmination in a goal determined by Yahweh: the last judgment, which would be followed for the devout by a new age in which there would be no history. Until that time history is divided into the epochs of the successive world empires. The statue of various metals that is destroyed by a stone (Daniel 2) is an image of world history viewed as a whole and at the same time divided into epochs. Until the eschaton this is the stage on which human life takes place, burdened with the heritage of the past, replete with opportunities for decision in the present, responsible toward the future.

In the light of all these considerations, the book sought to strengthen the patience and courage of the devout believers in the midst of persecution, give them new hope, and exhort them to follow the example of Daniel, remaining true to their faith to the point of martyrdom. It sought to assure them that the period of suffering would soon run its course, because the day was near on which Yahweh would put an end to the powers of the world and inaugurate his eternal rule. In this connection, the book dealt with two questions, whether those who had fallen in the struggle on behalf of the faith could share in the eschatological salvation, and whether at the last judgment all men would have to answer for their deeds before the judgment-seat of Yahweh, by proclaiming the resurrection of the dead (see § 28.5).

In addition, 7:13-14 mentions the "Son of Man" (meaning one who is human or like a human being), a figure occurring in other documents of early Judaism and in the NT alongside the Davidic Messiah (§ 26.3), who represents a further development of the figure of the Messiah. Of course Daniel 7 clearly identifies the Son of Man with eschatological Israel; but the author seems to have borrowed an earlier concept of an individual figure and reinterpreted it to apply to the community. Apart from certain improbable considerations, scholars have pointed out the extensive agreement between the expectations associated with this figure and the conceptions of a primal man,[20] suggesting that expectation of the Son of Man was a Jewish modification of myths found throughout the ancient Near East; the reinterpretation in Daniel 7 would mean that such expectation must have been familiar by the beginning of the second century B.C. at the latest. Others, denying the association of the Son of Man with Israel, have pointed out the similarity of the relationship between the "ancient of days" (Dan. 7:9) and the Son of Man to that between El and Baal in the Ugaritic texts; they trace the transfer of rule from the ancient of days to the Son of Man back to the notion of a young god attaining sovereignty in place of an aged god. Such a notion was preserved in at least some of the Canaanite myths; at present the rivalry between Baal and El attested in the Ugaritic texts is the best evidence for it.[21] But the question remains whether the special makeup of the Ugaritic pantheon could have continued to exercise such an influence, and whether the Son of Man in Daniel 7 really represents an individual.

§ 28 Objects and Contents of Faith

A. BERTHOLET, *Die Stellung der Israeliten und Juden zu den Fremden,* 1896; W. BOUSSET and H. GRESSMANN, *Die Religion des Judentums im späthellenistischen Zeitalter,* 3rd ed., 1926; A. CAUSSE, "Judaïsme et syncrétisme oriental à l'époque perse," *RHPhR,* VIII (1928), 301-28; W. EISS, "Der Kalender des nachexilischen Judentums (mit Ausnahme des essenischen Kalenders)," *WdO,* III.1-2 (1964), 44-47; I. ELBOGEN, *Der jüdische Gottesdienst in seiner geschichtlichen Entwicklung,* 4th ed., 1962; H. G. JUDGE, "Aaron, Zadok and Abiathar," *JThST,* NS VII (1956), 70-74; J. KRITZINGER, *Qehal Jahweh: Wat dit is en wie daaraan behoort,* Dissertation, 1957; E. LANGTON, *The Ministries of the Angelic Powers,* 1937; idem, *Essentials of Demonology,* 1949; L. ROST, *Die Vorstufen von Kirche und Synagoge im Alten Testament,* 1939; H. C. M. VOGT, *Studie zur nachexilischen Gemeinde in Esra-Nehemia,* 1966; H. WILLRICH, *Juden und Griechen vor der makkabäischen Erhebung,* 1895.

1. *Yahweh and angels, Satan and demons. a)* For the late period, the uniqueness and transcendence of Yahweh had long been accepted as basic to the concept of God. We find frequent references to

---

[20] S. Mowinckel, *He That Cometh,* 2nd ed., 1959, pp. 427 ff.

[21] C. Colpe, "ὁ υἱὸς τοῦ ἀνθρώπου," *ThW,* VIII, 418-25.

Yahweh's uniqueness, less often in the OT than in the deutero-canonical and noncanonical books of early Judaism. Other expressions and idioms emphasize his exaltedness and transcendence, for instance in the LXX the terms *pantokrátōr* ("almighty") and *hýpsistos* ("most high," translating *'elyón*).[1] This terminology corresponded to a new undersanding of God's kingship (Mal. 1:14; Ps. 103:19; 145:1 ff.), which, like that of Deutero-Isaiah, is universal, but without being inaugurated as an eschatological event; it appears as a present condition, although it is not visible to every eye. This present sovereignty of Yahweh as king is no longer restricted to Israel (§ 14.1), but is expressed in the law that serves to order the world, to which man must submit obediently. This finally led to the notion of a kingship of Yahweh existing from the very beginning and established at the creation of the world (see I Chron. 29:11; Dan. 3:33; 4:31, 34 [Eng. 4:3, 34, 37]).

The claim of this fundamental monotheistic confession was clothed in the words of Deut. 6:4, no longer interpreted as requiring inward unity in the conception of God (see § 22.1), but as saying, "Yahweh is our God, Yahweh is unique." This dogma, which was to be inculcated by daily repetition, elevated the idea of Yahweh's uniqueness to a position of centrality; it gave to the believer his inward superiority to Oriental and Hellenistic polytheism as well as to Persian and gnostic dualism, because it convinced him that there was no other God besides Yahweh.

The notion of Yahweh's transcendence likewise made it easier for extensive circles in early Judaism to be content with political impotence. If Yahweh, who exercised his governance over all the world while remaining invisible and unapproachable, set forth his exalted position only indirectly in the law and the cult, not through direct intervention on behalf of his community, what mattered was no longer political power but the victory within man of the one God over the hostile power.

Corresponding to this conception of God there was increasing reluctance to use the name "Yahweh," out of fear of desecrating it. Within the Holy Scriptures outside the Pentateuch the word *'ădônāy,* "Lord," was frequently used in addition to or instead of the divine name. In the earlier period, following Canaanite example, it had been used as an honorific attribute, primarily as a term of address

---

[1] For a discussion of the term "God of heavens," which probably derives from the diplomatic terminology of the Persian administration, see D. K. Andrews, "Yahweh the God of Heavens," in *Meek Festschrift,* 1964, pp. 45-57.

in prayer; now, however, it referred to Yahweh as Lord of the universe and expressed his absolute sovereignty over the world. The LXX accordingly translated the name "Yahweh" as *kýrios,* "Lord." [2] Other common renderings were "heaven" (Dan. 4:23) and "the name" (in colloquial usage); besides there were nonce words such as "the ancient of days" (Dan. 7:9).

In the context of this emphasis on Yahweh's uniqueness and transcendence the divine powers gradually evolved into hypostases, that is, independent entities able to act on their own. In their actions one could sense the operation of Yahweh himself, without encountering him directly. The word-hypostasis characterized the operation of God from creation on as spiritual determination and permeation; the spirit-hypostasis emphasized the dynamism and vitality of Yahweh, making any kind of deism impossible; the wisdom-hypostasis, as Yahweh's creative idea of the world, combined with acknowledgment of the world's internal fitness, order, and beauty the subordination of the cosmic forces to the one God.

b) The realm between Yahweh and man was far from empty. Because God's transcendence was perceived as distance, this realm was filled with the intermediary world of the angels, who constituted a link between the distant God and man. Thus the earlier conception of Yahweh's heavenly court was gradually transformed into an angelology whose beginnings can already be made out in the OT. One notion was that there were angels of peoples and nations, who were to secure Yahweh's unrestricted sovereignty over all nations (Deut. 32:8-9; Isa. 24:21); in Dan. 4:14 the actual governance of the world appears to be delegated to them under the sovereign authority of the Most High. The nation of Israel also has such an angel assigned to it, whose name is Michael (Dan. 10:13, 21; 12:1). Once, in Elihu's discourses in the book of Job, a mediating angel is mentioned who can intercede with Yahweh for a sick person, whereupon the latter is healed (Job 33:23 ff.).[3] Only in this one instance does the OT assign mediating functions to an angel.

c) Like Israel in the period of the monarchy, Deutero-Isaiah still believed that everything, good and evil, came from Yahweh, who created light and darkness, made weal and woe (Isa. 45:7). Later men gradually became convinced that the one exalted and holy

---

[2] W. W. Graf Baudissin, *Kyrios als Gottesname im Judentum und seine Stelle in der Religionsgeschichte,* 1929.

[3] S. Mowinckel, "Die Vorstellungen des Spätjudentums vom heiligen Geist als Fürsprecher und der johanneische Paraklet," *ZNW,* XXXII (1933), 97-130.

God could only do good, and that evil must therefore have a different origin. This origin was seen as being embodied in Satan, Yahweh's antagonist.

In the early post-exilic period we find the first mentions of Satan, but as part of Yahweh's world, a member of the heavenly court (Zech. 3:1 ff.; Job 1:6 ff.; 2:1 ff.) who appears like others before Yahweh for an audience, reports to him, and receives instructions from him. He is frequently interpreted as a kind of public prosecutor after the pattern of ancient Near Eastern royal courts, bringing men's wickedness to the attention of Yahweh; the name "Satan" is interpreted as a title or function, "adversary." [4] But it is more accurate to understand the term as referring to his conduct: he is called Satan ("enemy," "opponent") because he is the heavenly being who is hostile to man.[5] In the Chronicler's account of how David is induced to take a census, however, "Satan" has become a proper name (I Chron. 21:1, without the article); the figure so designated takes over a function formerly ascribed to Yahweh (compare II Sam. 24:1). Incitement to evil was also linked with this figure. Thus the groundwork was laid for introducing an author and representative of evil into the faith of Yahwism. The later period developed this notion further, but without succumbing to dualism, since Satan was considered a fallen angel cast down from heaven or an evil spirit created by Yahweh.

At the same time there developed a concept of evil spirits, possibly as embodying what had originally been an evil or lying spirit emanating from Yahweh (see I Sam. 16:14; I Kings 22:22). The old demonology also underwent considerable development. Previously only external misfortunes had been blamed on demons; now they also appeared in the guise of tempters inciting men to moral evil, to sin. All these developments gradually led to the notion of an ordered realm of evil hostile to the sovereignty of Yahweh, within which evil beings operate as angels of Satan to entice men away from the dominion of God.

2. *Yahweh, the world, and man.* a) The creation narrative of P in Gen. 1:1–2:4a developed the logical conclusions implicit in the altered concept of God: the creative word of Yahweh plays a crucial

---

[4] See, for example, B. L. Randellini, "Satana nell' Antico Testamento," *Bibbia e Oriente*, V (1963), 127-32.

[5] For a detailed discussion, see G. Fohrer, *Das Buch Hiob*, 1963, pp. 82-83. 481-501.

rôle, and man is said to be created in the image and likeness of God (Gen. 1:26-27).[6] The latter was meant on the one hand to exclude the ancient Near Eastern concept of a direct physical relationship between man and the deity and emphasize the absolute exaltedness and uniqueness of Yahweh, since man is no more than a likeness of God. On the other hand, it was meant to maintain the existing connection between them, since, according to Gen. 5:3, the term suggests the relationship between father and son. Thus the absolute distinction between Yahweh and man was emphasized, while the relationship between them was maintained despite and within the distinction.

Man's likeness to God means that Yahweh entrusts him with dominion over the world, letting him share his own sovereign power. Psalm 8, which brings man somewhat closer to Yahweh than does Genesis 1, emphasizes this sovereign authority:

> Thou hast made him little less than God,
>   and dost crown him with glory and honor.
> Thou hast given him dominion over the works of thy hands;
>   thou hast placed all things under his feet,
> all sheep and oxen,
>   and also the beasts of the field,
> the birds of the air, and the fish of the sea,
>   whatever passes along the paths of the sea.
> (Ps. 8:6-9 [Eng. 8:5-8])

b) Just as the passages dealing with creation give voice to the notion of God's sovereignty and communion with God, so for a long time the idea was retained that Yahweh governs the destinies of men and nations. Of course this idea was later limited by belief in the operation of angels and demonic powers, and finally in apocalypticism by the assumption that the course of history had long been pre-ordained.

---

[6] P. Bachmann, "Der Mensch als Ebenbild Gottes," in *Ihmels Festschrift*, 1928, pp. 273-79; P. G. Duncker, "L'immagine di Dio nell' uomo (Gen 1,26.27)." *Bibl*, XL (1959), 384-92; H. Gross, "Die Gottebenbildlichkeit des Menschen," in *Lex tua veritas* (Junker Festschrift), 1961, pp. 89-100; J. Hehn, "Zum Terminus 'Bild Gottes'," in *Sachau Festschrift*, 1915, pp. 36-52; F. Horst, "Der Mensch als Ebenbild Gottes," in his *Gottes Recht*, 1961, pp. 222-34; P. Humbert, *Études sur le récit du paradis et de la chute dans la Genèse*, 1940, pp. 153-75; L. Köhler, "Die Grundstelle der Imago-Dei-Lehre, Genesis 1,26," *ThZ*, IV (1948), 16-22; J. J. Stamm, *Die Gottebenbildlichkeit des Menschen im Alten Testament*, 1959; T. C. Vriezen, "La création de l'homme d'après l'image de Dieu," *OTS*, II (1943), 87-105; H. Wildberger, "Das Abbild Gottes, Gen. 1,26-30," *ThZ*, XXI (1965), 245-59, 481-501.

According to the dominant theory, Yahweh particularly governs the destinies of individuals in total righteousness according to the principles of the doctrine of retribution, apportioning rewards and punishments according to men's actions. We have already discussed the counterarguments of the author of Job and of Qoheleth (see § 27.4). There was nevertheless an increasing awareness of the sinfulness and wickedness of each individual. No man is just before God (Job 9:2-3); if God remembers sins instead of forgiving them, no man can stand before him (Ps. 130:3). The sinner cannot escape his judgment.[7] But it was likewise the goal of the legalistic and cultic approach to life to overcome the tension between Yahweh's wrath and his mercy through the precise regulation of penance and expiation. People generally operated on the assumption that man is free to obey God's will and thus attain life and salvation.

c) As a consequence of the altered religious and theological situation, the visible world no longer appeared to be the ultimate reality, but was set against a secret background. There came into being a belief in a divine realm beyond this world, which would be revealed at the end of history or in which the believer might share having passed through death. In the present life, however, there was no longer a personal relationship between God and man. Instead, two powers—Yahweh and Satan—contended for man and his soul, each supported by a host of good and evil angels. Man became the battlefield between good and evil.

History was furthermore interpreted as reflecting the struggle between these angels and spirits, indeed as the battlefield between Yahweh and the hostile powers. Since this struggle was to result in the transcendent existence of a supra-mundane kingdom of God, secular history also was given an invisible background and a supernatural goal.

These notions produced a profound and momentous change in Yahwism: what had been a personal relationship between Yahweh and man was transformed into a two-sided struggle for man; a religion of this world was transformed into a religion of the beyond. Fundamental structural elements of Yahwism were surrendered; a new religion was coming into being.

3. *The law.* More than ever before P based the existence of Israel on an eternal divine ordinance, determined unilaterally by

---

[7] K.-H. Bernhardt, "Zur Gottesvorstellung von Psalm 139," in *Holtz Festschrift*, 1965, pp. 20-31.

Yahweh without consulting Israel. In his autonomous plenitude of power Yahweh placed his obligation upon Israel and gave Israel his law, which Israel could only accept humbly and obediently. Thus God's power influences human life totally through the law, while obedience to the law constitutes the formative principle of human existence. The crucial point is obedience to the law. This emphasis on legalism relativized the Temple cult; at the same time, legalistic religion came to replace wisdom. The law took the place of fear of God in wisdom instruction (see Ps. 1; 19:8-15 [Eng. 19:7-14]; 119) and later was even associated with the concept of wisdom itself (Ecclesiasticus 24).

The law meanwhile consisted of a plethora of individual precepts whose number grew steadily; at one point 613 precepts were enumerated: 365 prohibitions and 248 commandments. These were multiplied in order to form a fence about the law; in other words, the requirements of the law strictly interpreted were surrounded by numerous other ordinances. Transgression of one of them left the law itself unimpugned.

Another important task was the application of the law to all the details of everyday life and the cult; it was also necessary to supplement the law to provide for those cases for which there was no specific precept. In the earlier period priestly tradition and instruction had regulated such questions; now such regulations had to be derived from the fixed written form of the law code. This was the task of the scribes. Educated as theologians and jurists, they imparted binding regulations concerning religion and ethics, legal questions and the conduct of everyday life. Later there developed the theory of an oral torah that had been transmitted ever since Yahweh had instructed Moses, as well as various schools of scriptural exegesis, whose views could diverge widely (Pharisees—Sadducees). Jesus Sirach described the ideal scribe in the following terms: [8]

> Whoever devotes his soul to the *fear of God*
> and gives his mind to the law of the most high,
> will seek out the wisdom of all the ancient,
> and be occupied in prophecies.
> He will keep the sayings of renowned men,
> and penetrate the *depths* of parables.
> He will seek out the secrets of grave sentences
> and be conversant in the riddles of parables.

[8] The translation is based on V. Hamp, *Sirach*, 1951.

He will serve in the circle of the great
and appear before princes.
He will travel through strange countries,
he will experience good and evil among men.
He will incline his heart to seek the Lord,
and will pray before the most high.
He will open his mouth in prayer
and make supplication for his sins.
If *God, the most high,* wills it,
he will be filled with the spirit of insight;
he will bring forth words of wisdom
and give thanks to the Lord in prayer.
He *shall understand* counsel and knowledge,
and into secrets he shall inquire.
He will reveal the discipline of his teaching
and glory in the law of the Lord.
Many will commend his insight,
and it shall never pass away;
his memorial shall not cease,
and his name shall live from generation to generation.
(Ecclus. 38:34b–39:9)

4. *Temple cult and synagogue worship. a)* As a consequence of the centrality of the law, the Temple and its cult, despite the enthusiasm recorded in several Psalms (see § 27.4), as a whole became an increasingly peripheral part of religious life. The cult was performed because it was prescribed by the law. Therefore the significance of the Temple was gradually replaced by the synagogue, in which the law was taught.

Within the Temple cult sacrifice still played an important rôle. The sacrificial regulations of the Pentateuch had meanwhile been gone over carefully and precisely to prevent omissions and abuses that could rob the sacrifices of their propitiatory power. For their purpose was primarily to obtain God's mercy; this is also expressed by the fact that the sin offering came to enjoy special esteem. According to the systematic organization of the sacrificial system, this offering was employed only in cases of unpremeditated transgression of a commandment (Lev. 4:2; 5:1 ff.; Num. 15:22 ff.); its purpose was apparently to purify and sanctify the worshiper. The use of the sacrificial blood was correspondingly complex: besides being poured out at the foot of the altar, it was applied to the horns of the altar of burnt offering (Lev. 4:25, 30) or the altar of incense (Lev. 4:7, 18) and sprinkled seven times before the veil of the sanctuary (Lev. 4:6, 17). We read of the "purification" of objects such as the altar and the doorposts of the Temple (Lev. 8:15; 16:14 ff.; Ezek. 43:19-20;

45:18-19) and the use of the offering as a sacrifice of sanctification
(Lev. 8:14 ff.; 14:12 ff.; Num. 6:9 ff.).

Music and singing were also cultivated. The books of Chronicles
make frequent mention of solemn occasions celebrated with music
(I Chron. 15:16 ff.; 29:20; II Chron. 5:12-13; 20:21 ff.; 23:13; 29:27)
and exhibit particular interest in the Temple personnel engaged in
music and song. The choirs of Temple singers sang the hymns, to
which the community responded "Amen" or "Hallelujah" (see Ezra
3:11; Neh. 8:6; I Chron. 16:36).

After the beginning of the post-exilic period, the high priest
stood at the head of the extensive priestly hierarchy.[9] In many respects what had been royal functions and privileges had been transferred to him; several details of his costume may derive from the
raiment of the king. A good impression of his importance and of
some of his functions is provided by the panegyric on the high priest
Simon II (218-192 B.C.): [10]

> How glorious he was when he looked out of the tent,
>   and when he stepped forth through the veil:
> he was like a gleaming star amidst the clouds
>   and like the full moon on feast-days,
> like the sun shining over the palace of the king,
>   and like the rainbow that appears in the clouds,
> like a blossom on the boughs on the feast-days,
>   and like a lily by the waters,
> like the greenery of Lebanon in the days of summer,
>   and like fire and incense upon the food offering,
> like a vessel covered with gold and a cup
>   encrusted with jewels,
> like a sprouting olive tree covered with fruit,
>   and like a (wild) olive with luxuriant branches.
> (How glorious he was) when he put on the robe of honor
>   and was clothed in *all* his magnificence,
> when he went up to the lofty altar
>   and filled the court of the sanctuary with splendor,
> when he took the portions (of sacrificial flesh) from the hands
>   of his brethren,
>   while he himself stood by the pile of wood for the sacrifice,
> encircled by his sons
>   like young cedars on Lebanon;

[9] N. B. Barrow, *The High Priest*, 1947; K. Elliger, "Ephod und Choschen," *VT*, VIII (1958), 19-35; J. Gabriel, *Untersuchungen über das alttestamentliche Hohepriestertum*, 1933; J. Morgenstern, "A Chapter in the History of the High-priesthood," *AJSL*, LV (1938), 360-77; F. Stummer, "Gedanken über die Stellung des Hohenpriesters in der alttestamentlichen Gemeinde," in *Episcopus, Studien über das Bischofsamt*, 1949, pp. 1-30.
[10] The translation is based on V. Hamp, *Sirach*, 1951.

like willows by the brook there surrounded him
  all the sons of Aaron in their glory.
The burnt offerings of Yahweh were in their hands,
  from all the congregation of Israel,
until he had finished the service at the altar,
  and the order of the burnt offerings piled up for the most high.
He stretched forth his hand to the cup
  and offered of the blood of the grape;
he poured it out at the foot of the altar
  as a sweet-smelling savor for the most high, the king of the
    universe.
Then the sons of Aaron sounded
  upon the chased trumpets;
they blew and made a mighty noise resound
  for a memorial of the most high.
All those assembled made haste
  and fell down to the earth upon their faces
to worship before the most high,
  the holy one of Israel.
Then resounded the singing (of psalms),
  and *sweet melody was raised* above the crowd.
The people of the land rejoiced
  in prayer before the merciful one,
until he had completed the *service of Yahweh*
  and offered to him his prescribed sacrifices.
Then he went down, and lifted up his hands
  over the whole congregations of Israel.
The blessing of Yahweh was upon his lips,
  and in (the naming of) his name he could rejoice.
Then they fell down a second time
  to *receive the blessing* from him.   (Ecclus. 50:5-21)

The priesthood was composed primarily of Zadokite priests who had returned with the first group to come back from Babylonia. Some priests also returned with Ezra who traced their lineage back to Ithamar (Ezra 8:2) and therefore were probably descendants of Abiathar (see I Sam. 22:20; I Chron. 24:3). A certain accommodation was achieved between the rival groups by declaring Aaron the ultimate ancestor of both; but the Zadokite priests retained the position of leadership. Later, when the Hasmonean kings claimed the office of high priest for themselves, the Zadokite groups withdrew and formed the Qumran community.

Levites were also among the group returning from Exile, but in smaller numbers. After their degradation through Ezek. 44:4-31 they constituted a lower order of priests. In the course of time, and after apparently violent conflicts, other groups succeeded in being included among the Levites: singers, musicians, and door-keepers.[11]

b) In the synagogue,[12] worship took place on the morning of the Sabbath. The account of Ezra's recitation of the law (Nehemiah 8), which is modeled on synagogue worship, allows us to reconstruct what it was like, at least in the period of the Chronicler. It was worship comprising reading and instruction (8:3), which began with a summons to read the Torah (8:1). The scribe entered the pulpit on which stood a reading desk (8:4), opened the scroll of the Torah (8:5), and praised Yahweh; the congregation responded, "Amen" (8:6). As the Hebrew text was read, it was translated verse by verse into the vernacular (8:8). The reading was followed by a sermon in the form of a free address (8:9 ff.); in the earlier period it was very brief and parenetic in content.

The confession of faith called the Shema, consisting of three texts from the Pentateuch (Deut. 6:4-8; 11:13-21; Num. 15:37-41), appears to be ancient, as do many prayer formulas. In the subsequent period worship was further developed and elaborated.

c) Feasts and festivals continued to include observance of New Moon Sabbath (§ 10.2), the Feast of Passover and Unleavened Bread, the Feast of Weeks, and the Feast of Booths (§ 16.3; 22:2). P attempted to ground the latter two feasts in the history of Israel by associating the events at Sinai with the Feast of Weeks and the obligation laid upon the people by Yahweh with the same festival (cf. Exod. 19:1), and by explaining the Feast of Booths on the basis of the use of booths by the Israelites during the exodus from Egypt (Lev. 23:42-43). Besides the Feast of Booths, ever since the Exile two additional feasts were celebrated in the fall during the seventh month: New Year's Day and the Day of Atonement.

The first day of the seventh month, as the first day of the autumnal year, became New Year's Day in the absolute sense (in addition to years beginning for various purposes on the first day of the first, sixth, and ninth month); it was observed with a "memorial blast of trumpets" (Lev. 23:24-25).

The tenth day of the seventh month marked the great Day of Atonement (Leviticus 16; see also Lev. 23:27-32; 25:9; Deut. 29:7-11 [Eng. 29:8-12]).[13] The first act performed on this day was the re-

---

[11] H. Gese, "Zur Geschichte der Kultsänger am zweiten Tempel," in *Michel Festschrift*, 1963, pp. 222-34.

[12] *BHH*, III, 1906-10; *RGG*, VI, 557-59; *IDB*, IV, 476-91.

[13] S. Adler, "Der Versöhnungstag in der Bibel, sein Ursprung und seine Bedeutung," *ZAW*, III (1883), 178-85, 272; E. Auerbach, "Neujahrs- und Versöhnungs-Fest in den biblischen Quellen," *VT*, VIII (1958), 337-43; T. K. Cheyne,

moval of sins from the priests and the people; this was followed
later by purification of the Temple. For this purpose the sins were
transferred to the "scapegoat" in a special ritual, and the scapegoat was driven forth into the desert, to the demon Azazel who
resided there (§ 14.3). While the origin of the ritual appears to lie
in an apotropaic sacrifice offered annually to a desert demon
(§ 13.3), the date of origin of the Day of Atonement is unknown.
It is unlikely that it replaced an earlier New Year's festival or was
originally a nomadic celebration preceding the change of pasturage from settled territory to the desert. The festival cannot have
been fixed before the Exile, because it presupposes the assignment
of the Feast of Booths to the fifteenth day of the month.

In addition, beginning in the late post-exilic period, the Feast of
Purim was celebrated,[14] a national secular festival on the fourteenth
and fifteenth of Adar (February/March). The book of Esther
contains its festival legend. The historical background is a persecution and deliverance of the Jews in the eastern Diaspora during
the Persian period; further details cannot be made out. The name
is derived from the determination of the day appointed for the
destruction of the Jews by *pûr*, which is equated with Hebrew
gôrāl, "lot." We are dealing with what was originally not a Jewish
festival; it may have been Persian in origin, although this cannot be
determined with any certainty (*farvardīgān*, the Persian feast of the
dead; Sakaia festival; Mithrakana festival). Possibly we should speak
only of isolated features from a festival schema. In any case the
Persian festival first underwent development in Mesopotamia,
whence its name derives (Assyrian *puru'um, pūrum*); it was then
adopted by Judaism and legitimized by means of the festival legend.
It made its way from the Diaspora to Palestine before the middle of
the first century B.C.; it is first mentioned in II Macc. 15:36-37
(about 50 B.C.).

Finally, the most important successes of the Maccabean wars were
celebrated on their anniversaries. The eight-day festival of the dedication of the Temple (Hanukkah) [15] deserves first mention; it com-

---

"The Date and Origin of the 'Scapegoat'," *ZAW*, XV (1895), 153-56; S. Landers-
dorfer, *Studien zum biblischen Versöhnungstag*, 1924; M. Löhr, *Das Ritual von
Lev. 16*, 1925; I. Schur, *Versöhnungstag und Sündenbock*, 1934.

[14] V. Christian, "Zur Herkunft des Purim-Festes," in *Nötscher Festschrift*, 1950,
pp. 33-37; T. H. Gaster, *Purim and Hanukkah in Custom and Tradition*, 1950;
G. Gerleman, *Studien zu Esther*, 1966; P. de Lagarde, *Purim*, 1887; H. Ringgren,
"Esther and Purim," *SEA*, XX (1956), 5-24; H. Zimmern, "Zur Frage nach dem
Ursprung des Purimfestes," *ZAW*, XI (1891), 157-69.

[15] Hochfeld, "Die Entstehung des Hanukkafestes," *ZAW*, XXII (1902), 264-84;

memorates the rededication of the Temple in the year 164 B.C. Other observances included the Day of Nincanor, commemorating Judas' victory over the Seleucid general Nicanor, and the day of Simon's taking of the "acra" or citadel of Jerusalem, which was celebrated for a time.

d) As in the pre-exilic period, voices criticizing the cult often made themselves heard; but they usually differed from the earlier criticism of the prophets. The author of Psalm 40, for example, states:

> Sacrifice and offering thou dost not desire;
> burnt offering and sin offering thou hast not required.
> (Ps. 40:7)

The author proposes instead to observe God's law and praise Yahweh in the synagogue assembly. Thus this form of worship is actually set over against the Temple cult. Qoheleth likewise appears to prefer synagogue worship; to attend it and hear the law explained is worth more than the sacrifice that the fool offers. The caution and restraint of the wise man can be heard in the admonition not to be hasty in prayer and to fulfill an oath quickly (Eccles. 4:17–5:6 [Eng. 5:1-7]). Psalms 69 and 141 also prefer other forms of thanksgiving to sacrifice:

> I will praise the name of God with a song;
> I will magnify him with thanksgiving.
> This will please Yahweh more than an ox
> or a bull with horns and hoofs.
> (Ps. 69:31-32 [Eng. 69:30-31])

> Let my prayer be counted as incense before thee,
> and the lifting up of my hands as an evening sacrifice!
> (Ps. 141:2)

This notion could be associated with a line of argument that is frankly rationalistic, as in Psalm 50, which put the following words into Yahweh's mouth:

> I will accept no bull from your house,
> nor he-goat from your folds.
> For every beast of the forest is mine,
> the cattle on a thousand hills.

J. Morgenstern, "The Chanukkah Festival and the Calendar of Ancient Israel," *HUCA*, XX (1947), 1-136; XXI (1948), 365-496; O. S. Rankin, *The Origins of the Festival of Hanukkah*, 1930.

I know all the birds *of the air,*
and all that moves in the field is mine.
If I were hungry, I would not tell you;
for the world and all that is in it is mine.
Do I eat the flesh of bulls,
or drink the blood of goats?
Offer to God thanksgiving,
and thus pay your vows to the Most High.
Call upon me in the day of trouble;
I will deliver you, and you shall glorify me.
(Ps. 50:9-15).

Another note is struck by Micah 6 and Psalm 51, which follow
in the footsteps of pre-exilic prophecy:

With what shall I come before Yahweh,
and bow myself before God on high?
Shall I come before him with burnt offerings,
with calves a year old?
Will Yahweh be pleased with thousands of rams,
with myriads of rivers of oil?
Shall I give my first-born to atone for me,
the fruit of my body as atonement for my life?
It has been told you, O man, what is good;
and what does Yahweh require of you?
Nothing but to do justice,
to love fidelity,
and to walk humbly with your God. (Mic. 6:6-8)

Thou hast no delight in sacrifice;
were I to give a burnt offering, thou wouldst not be
pleased.
My sacrifice, O God, is a humble spirit;
a broken heart thou wilt not despise.
(Ps. 51:18-19 [Eng. 51:16-17]).

5. *Man's fate after death.*[16] a) The old notion of a cheerless fate

[16] W. Baumgartner, "Der Auferstehungsglaube im Alten Orient," *ZMR*,
XLVIII (1933), 193-214; G. J. Botterweck, "Marginalien zum alttestamentlichen
Auferstehungsglauben," *WZKM*, LIV (1957), 1-8; S. H. Hooke, "Israel and the
After-Life," *ET*, LXXVI (1964/65), 236-39; *idem*, "After Death: The Extra-
Canonical Literature," *ibid.*, 273-76; F. König, *Zarathustras Jenseitsvorstellungen
und das Alte Testament,* 1964; N. A. Logan, "The Old Testament and a Future
Life," *SJTh,* VI (1953), 165-72; R. Martin-Achard, *De la mort à la résurrection
d'après l'Ancien Testament,* 1956; A. Nicolainen, *Der Auferstehungsglaube in der
Bibel und ihrer Umwelt,* 1944; F. Nötscher, *Altorientalischer und alttestament-
licher Auferstehungsglaube,* 1926; O. Schilling, *Der Jenseitsgedanke im Alten
Testament,* 1951; K. Schubert, "Die Entwicklung der Auferstehungslehre von der
nachexilischen bis zur frührabbinischen Zeit," *BZ,* NF VI (1962), 177-214; N. H.

awaiting the shades of the dead in the underworld continued into the late post-exilic period. As before, exceptions are few (see § 17.3).

Psalm 49 may indicate a different hope with respect to the fate of man after death, if the poor believer or devout poor man is being contrasted to the self-confident rich who come to an inescapable end [17]—because for him there is a hope beyond death. It is hard to see, however, wherein this hope consists:

> But God will ransom my soul
> from the power of Sheol, for he will receive me.   (Ps. 49:16 [Eng. 49:15])

This is contrasted to the fate of the rich man, who cannot ransom himself. Neither, of course, can the devout man; but Yahweh can do it. And he does do it—not for the rich man, but for the poor believer. It is he whom Yahweh will ransom from Sheol, i.e., protect or liberate from the underworld. Thus the author promised the believer preservation and deliverance from death, so that he would not see the grave, and would live once again or even forever. Then the situation will be the opposite of what it is in the present: the devout believer, now oppressed, will experience a happier fate than the rich man who has lived in self-confidence and satiety. Of course there is no explanation of how and where compensation will be made and the believer avenged: there is surely no thought of any assumption or resurrection; but the notion of retribution for the suffering believer, which awaits him in the beyond after death, is simply left in the air, as we should expect for this idea, which is unique in the OT. Perhaps we encounter it in more developed form in the parable of the rich man and poor Lazarus (see Luke 16:19-31).

Eschatological prophecy remained more restrained. It was content to predict an increased life span for the Israelites, without any change in the fate awaiting them after death. Death was merely to be delayed as long as possible, so that the number of old men and

---

Snaith, "Justice and Immortality," *SJTh*, XVII (1964), 309-24; E. F. Sutcliffe, *The Old Testament and the Future Life*, 1946; G. Wied, *Der Auferstehungsglaube im späten Israel in seiner Bedeutung für das Verhältnis von Apokalyptik und Weisheit*, Dissertation, Bonn, 1964/65.

[17] For a discussion of the "religion of the poor," which became important in the subsequent period and is occasionally hinted at in the OT, see A. Causse, "La secte juive et la nouvelle piété," *RHPhR*, XV (1935), 385-419; A. Gelin, *Les pauvres de Yahvé*, 1953; A. Kuschke, "Arm und reich im Alten Testament mit besonderer Berücksichtigung der nachexilischen Zeit," *ZAW*, LVII (1939), 31-57; R. Martin-Achard, "Jahwé et les ᵃnāwīm," *ThZ*, XXI (1965), 349-57; J. van der Ploeg, "Les pauvres d'Israël et leur piété," *OTS*, VII (1950), 236-70.

women, who would need to carry a staff because of the burdens of
age, would increase (Zech. 8:4), and a man a hundred years old
would still be considered young:

> No more shall there be in it
> an infant that lives but a few days,
> or an old man who does not fill out his days,
> for the child shall die a hundred years old,
> and he who does not reach a hundred will be accounted
> accursed.   (Isa. 65:20)

The only passage to predict that Yahweh would destroy death forever was the late addition to Isa. 25:8, which misinterpreted the
tears and reproach of men that Yahweh would wipe away at the
beginning of the blessed eschaton as referring to death. Then the
question of man's fate after death would not even arise.

b) Only in the latest period of the OT did a different expectation spring up, which proved to be pregnant for the future and
influenced the subsequent period: hope for a resurrection of the
dead. This hope radically transformed all the ideas of man's fate
after death. In the OT itself, it is true, resurrection plays a very
minor rôle, since there is only one passage referring to it. All the
other texts that have been claimed to mention hope of resurrection
in fact have a different meaning.

Hos. 6:1-2 does not express any hope for a resurrection on the third day,
borrowed from the cult of withering and reviving vegetation gods; neither
does it contain any trace of a resurrection of the dead or even of a train of
thought leading in that direction. The text refers rather to the recovery
of a sick man. Israel is being likened to an injured man, as the expression
"heal" and "bind up" show, as well as the employment of the "clinical
history" familiar from the psalms of lament, with its sequence tear-heal,
strike-bind up, revive-raise up from the sickbed. In other words, the nation
feels wounded and hopes for healing in just two or three days (a phrase
taken from numerical proverbs), that is, within a very short time.
Ezek. 37:1-14 is an account of a vision and audition, with which there
was associated an ecstatic trance on the part of the prophet: Ezekiel experiences the revivification of the dry bones that represent the Israelites. This
image derives from the complaint of the Israelites deported to Babylonia,
who lamented their dashed hope and said that their bones were dried up
and that they were perishing (37:11). Like sickness, the Exile was a weakened form of life, which was gradually perishing. In the eyes of the deportees
the process was already so far advanced that they were actually cut off from
life and resembled the skeletons of the dead. Just as Ezekiel's image derived
from the lamentations of the deportees, so their use of it derived from the
old conception of the relationship between life and death, applied to the

Exile. In both cases death and revival are used metaphorically and symbolically. We are not dealing with the resurrection of Israelite corpses, but with the momentary condition of the deportees, who were a dead people, and with their future condition, in which they would once more be a living people. Ezekiel therefore does not presuppose any belief in resurrection. This can also be seen from his reply to Yahweh's question as to whether the bones can live again: "Thou knowest," that is, I do not know, it is beyond human knowledge (37:3).

Neither is any resurrection of the executed Servant of Yahweh being referred to when Isa. 53:10 says that he will see his offspring, and 53:12 says that Yahweh will give him "the many" for spoil. This simply means that men will appropriate to themselves the redemption accomplished by his vicarious suffering. From the loneliness of his sacrifice will issue the abundance of those who receive life from it and therefore can be called his offspring.

Isa. 26:7-21 contains what is primarily a prayer, resembling a lament, for the longed-for coming of the eschaton (26:7-18a); it concludes with an assurance of divine aid (26:18b-19) and a consequent summons to Israel (26:20-21). The prayer declares the failure of all human efforts to bring about the end; to this failure is contrasted the assurance of divine aid: Yahweh alone can and will destroy the wicked and accompany the nation of the righteous out of their distress into eschatological salvation. Isa. 26:19, addressed to Yahweh, presents this assurance:

> Thy dead shall live!
> My bodies shall rise!
> The dwellers in the dust
> *shall awake* and sing for joy!
> For thy dew is a dew of light,
> and the land will bring forth the shades of the dead.
> (Isa. 26:19)

Like Ezek. 37:1-14, this passage speaks metaphorically and symbolically of the salvation of new life to be expected at the eschaton. Your dead, my bodies will rise up and live—we, your people, will experience under your governance the aid that we cannot bring to ourselves, enjoy the salvation that you bring! In addition, the absolute statement in 26:14 that the dead shall not arise and live, to which 26:19 forms a contrast, suggests the view that this latter verse is meant only symbolically and does not presuppose any belief in resurrection. There is added the second image of the heavenly dew that enables the earth once more to bring forth her dead.

Psalm 16 refers unambiguously to deliverance from deadly peril (16:10-11); Psalm 73 extols life in this world in communion with Yahweh (73:25 ff.). There is not the slightest suggestion of any hope for resurrection. The same is true for Job 19:25-27; it is one of Job's attempts to induce Yahweh to acknowledge his innocence. He beseeches Yahweh to help him as a defence witness and attorney against his friends who are persecuting him and against condemnation by an ignorant future generation. Yahweh is to testify on Job's behalf right here on earth; Job would like to see

Yahweh appear on his behalf in a theophany upon earth while he is still alive in his disfigured, emaciated body.

For an OT hope in a resurrection there remains a single text, from the second century B.C.: Dan. 12:2:

> At that time shall arise
>> Michael, the great guardian angel
>> who has charge of your people.
> There shall be a time of trouble,
>> such as never has been since there was a nation
>> till that time.
> But at that time your people will be delivered,
>> every one whose name shall be found written in the book.
> And many of those who sleep in the dust of the earth shall
>> awake,
>> some to everlasting life,
>> others to everlasting contempt.
> But those who are wise shall shine
>> like the brightness of the firmament;
> and those who have turned many to righteousness,
>> like the stars for ever and ever.
>
> (Dan. 12:1-3)

With the repeated phrase "at that time" the author of the book of Daniel refers to the persecution instigated by Antiochus IV Epiphanes, which he describes briefly as the time of troubles preceding the eschaton—more grievous than any other epoch since the creation of the world—although the appearance of Michael, the heavenly representative of Israel, suggests that a decision in Israel's favor has been reached in heaven. It follows that Israel's true deliverance will take place in that time of trouble; the trouble will come to an end and the eschaton will begin. Then there will take place the double resurrection of the dead, whose fate after death thereby takes a new turn. This resurrection is limited to Israel, and is conceived in total harmony with Israelite ideas: until now the dead have "slept in the dust of the earth"; now they will "awake." The whole man, not just a part of him, returns to life. It is clear that this does not mean a life in the beyond, but a new life in this world; but it will be "everlasting," that is, of endless duration. There is no description of the new fate that awaits the Israelites after death, so that we cannot say what is meant by "everlasting contempt" as opposed to "everlasting life." The exceptional position accorded the "wise" make clear only that those who awake to everlasting life are those to whom the wise have imparted a knowledge that is crowned by justification that leads to life in the form of a resurrection: the wisdom of the eschatological faith. Any Israelite who allows himself to be guided by this wisdom is among those who will share in the resurrection to eternal life.

Within the context of the book of Daniel this means that the faithful portion of Israel will be included under God's everlasting sovereignty. Contrary to the traditional view of the OT, these dead are not removed forever from God's sovereignty, but are incorporated into it through the resurrection; Yahweh's authority also extends to those condemned to everlasting contempt. Thus the author of the book of Daniel closes the ancient gap in the list of those subject to Yahweh's sovereignty: not only the living, but also the dead are included after their awakening at the beginning of the eschaton.

Thus the notion that man was separated from Yahweh after death and finally excluded from God's sovereignty and communion with God gave way to the expectation of being restored to God's sovereignty in consequence of the resurrection at the beginning of the eschaton. This was a significant step forward, albeit not totally in line with what the authors of the book of Job and Psalm 73 considered crucial, and with what can so fulfill man that the question of what is to come becomes immaterial: total experience of God's sovereignty and communion with God in this life (Ps. 73:25-28).

1. INDEX OF PASSAGES

2. INDEX OF HEBREW WORDS

3. GENERAL INDEX

Scribe, 378
Secret experience, 239, 285
Semitic migration. *See* Migration
Separatism, 158, 159, 185, 332, 336, 346, 359, 368
Septuagint, 367
Seraphim, 174-75
Servant of Yahweh, 323, 344, 348
Shechem, 64, 91, 112
Sheol, 219. *See also* Underworld
Shiloh, 91-92, 108, 110 ff., 117
Simeon, 62
Sin, 193-94, 266, 271
Sin offering, 379
Sinai, 73-74, 167-68
Sinai narrative, 69, 80-81
Singers, Temple, 213, 380
Singing, 60, 158, 311, 361, 380
Solidarity formula, 186, 262
Solomon, 128 ff.
Son of God, 145 ff., 149, 187, 248, 262
Son of Man, 352, 371-72
Song, 60, 211, 380
Spirit, 107, 169, 215, 236, 238, 346, 374
Stones, sacred, 41, 47
Suffering, vicarious, 344, 347
Surrogate name. *See* Name, surrogate
Symbolic action, 233, 238, 240 ff., 247, 267, 286-87, 318
Synagogue, 311, 367, 379 ff.
Syncretism, 103, 127, 130 ff., 134 ff., 140-41, 152, 281, 292, 301, 313, 333

Taboo, 34, 99, 217
Tabor, 112
Tammuz, 54, 173
Temple, 47, 57, 112, 126, 129, 135 ff., 140-41, 157, 165, 167, 198 ff., 261, 295, 300-301, 307-8, 310-11, 315, 317, 323, 330 ff., 335, 345, 356, 360 ff., 368, 379-80
Temple dedication festival, 203
Tent, 83, 101, 109
Teraphim, 114
Thank offering, 207

Theocracy, 370
Theogony, 171
Theophany, 107, 167-68, 188, 270, 339
Tithe, 208, 212, 358
Torah, 191-92, 378
Tradition, 201, 274-75, 283, 319
Tradition, historical. *See* Historical tradition
Transcendence of God, 158, 357, 373
Trees, sacred, 41, 47, 300
Tribal league, 89 ff.
Tribal sayings, 32
Trito-Isaiah, 363

Ugarit, 43 ff.
Underworld, 219 ff., 385-86
Unleavened bread, 68, 100-101, 117, 201, 301, 383
Urim and Thummim, 83, 115

Vengeance, blood. *See* Blood vengeance
Vicarious suffering. *See* Suffering, vicarious
Vision, 107, 226-27, 239, 244, 318, 322
Vow, 58, 153, 209

War, 89, 118, 282
War, holy. *See* Holy war
War of Yahweh, 118, 153
Weeks, Feast of, 117, 201-2, 301, 382
Wen-Amon, 226
Wheat harvest festival, 202
Wisdom, 130-31, 138-39, 142, 161 ff., 195, 278, 288-89, 363 ff., 370, 374, 378
Wisdom, academic, 130, 162
Wisdom, practical, 130, 138, 162, 195, 364
Word, 178-79, 231, 238, 242, 374, 375
Worship. *See* Cult

01